Land Tenure in the Ramesside Period

Studies in Egyptology

Edited by: W. V. Davies, Keeper
Department of Egyptian Antiquities
The British Museum

Editor Designate: A. B. Lloyd
Professor of Classics and Ancient History
University College of Swansea

Editorial Adviser: A. F. Shore, Professor of Egyptology,
University of Liverpool.

The Egytian Temple
Patricia Spencer

The Administration of Egypt in the Old Kingdom
Nigel Strudwick

Corpus of Reliefs of the New Kingdom from the Memphite Necropolis and Lower Egypt Volume 1
Geoffrey Thorndike Martin

Problems and Priorities in Egyptian Archaeology
Jan Assmann, Günter Burkard and Vivian Davies

Lost Tombs
Lise Manniche

Decoration in Egyptian Tombs of the Old Kingdom
Yvonne Harpur

Untersuchungen zu den Totenbuchpapyri der 18. Dynastie
Irmtraut Munro

The Monuments of Senenmut
Peter F. Dorman

The Fort Cemetery at Hierakonpolis
Barbara Adams

The Duties of the Vizier
G. P. F. van den Boorn

A Glossary of Ancient Egyptian Nautical Titles and Terms
Dilwyn Jones

Forthcoming:

The Cobra Goddess of Ancient Egypt
Sally B. Johnson

The Private Chapel in Ancient Egypt
Ann H. Bomann

Land Tenure in the Ramesside Period

Sally L. D. Katary

KEGAN PAUL INTERNATIONAL
LONDON & NEW YORK

First published in 1989 by Kegan Paul International Limited
P.O. Box 256, London WC1B 3SW

Distributed by
John Wiley & Sons Ltd,
Southern Cross Trading Estate
1 Oldlands Way, Bognor Regis
W. Sussex PO22 9SA, England

Routledge, Chapman & Hall Inc.
29 West 35th Street
New York, NY 10001, USA

Printed in Great Britain by
Whitstable Litho Printers Ltd., Whitstable, Kent

ISBN 0-7103-0298-3

To

Ronald J. Williams

and

Jac. J. Janssen

Table of Contents

LIST OF TABLES xiii

MAP xiv

PREFACE xv

ACKNOWLEDGMENTS xvii

ABBREVIATIONS xix

AUTHOR'S INTRODUCTION xxi

CHAPTER 1 -- THE WILBOUR PAPYRUS

(1) Plan and Organization of Text A 1
(2) The Places of Measurement in Text A 9
(3) Apportioning and Non-Apportioning Paragraphs 11
(4) The Corresponding Pōsh A and B Entries; Pōsh C Entries 18

CHAPTER 1 -- NOTES 24

CHAPTER 2 -- STATISTICAL MEASURES AND TESTS

(1) The Use of the Statistical Method in the Analysis of the Data of P. Wilbour 29
(2) Measuring Socio-Economic Variables 29
(3) Measures of Central Tendency: Averages 31
(4) Comparison of Averages 32
(5) Measures of Variation or Dispersion 33
(6) The Uses of Standard Deviation 36
(7) The Concept of "Confidence" and the Confidence Interval 37
(8) Measurement of Association 38

CHAPTER 2 -- NOTES 40

CHAPTER 3 -- COMPUTER OPERATIONS

(1) Coding Criteria and Method
  (a) Variables Coded in the Data File 42
  (b) Computed Variables 43
(2) The Capabilities of the Package Program SPSS
  (a) One-way Frequency Distributions, Measures of Central Tendency, and Dispersion 46
  (b) Crosstabulation Analysis 47

CHAPTER 3 -- NOTES 47

CHAPTER 4 -- SUBPROGRAM CONDESCRIPTIVE: DESCRIPTIVE STATISTICS FOR CONTINUOUS VARIABLES

(1) The Continuous Variables 48
(2) Variable 9 Arouras 49
(3) Variable 10 Arouras Special Case 50
(4) Variable 14 Assessed Arouras 52
(5) Variable 46 ⅃¦Figure 52
(6) Variable 11 Land-cubits First Figure and Variable 12 Land-cubits Second Figure 53
(7) Variable 28 Land-cubits Subtotal 11 and 12 55
(8) Variable 13 Land-cubits Single Figure 56
(9) The Grand Total Land Computed Variables 56

CHAPTER 4 -- NOTES 57

CHAPTER 5 -- SUBPROGRAM FREQUENCIES: ONE-WAY FREQUENCY DISTRIBUTIONS WITH DESCRIPTIVE STATISTICS

(1) Table Format 59
(2) The Qualitative Variables
  (a) Variable 1 Section of Text (Geographic Zone) 59
  (b) Variable 2 Format of Entry 61
  (c) Variable 43 Land Measure I Arouras or Land-cubits (Variety I, Sub-variety IA, Variety II) 61
  (d) Variable 44 Land Measure II Arouras or Land-cubits (Variety I, Sub-variety IA, Variety I/II, Variety II, Sub-variety IIA) 62
  (e) Variable 45 Type of Aroura Measured Entry (Variety I or Sub-variety IA) 63
  (f) Variable 18 Institutional Class and Variable 3 Institutional Group 63
  (g) Variable 4 Land-owning Institution 66
  (h) Variable 39 Dynasty of Founding of Land-owning Institution 67
  (i) Variable 5 Deity or King 68
  (j) Variable 19 Type of Religious Institution 70
  (k) Variable 16 Occupational Group and Variable 7 Occupation or Title of Smallholder 70
  (l) Variable 34 Sex of Smallholder 72
  (m) Variable 15 Type of Land 72
  (n) Variable 17 Special Entry 73
  (o) Variable 20 Type of <u>Pōsh</u> Entry 75
  (p) Variable 21 Type of Apportioning Paragraph 75

(q) Variables 22 and 23 Dual Geographic Location A and B 77
(r) Variable 31 Geographic Location (Measurement Area) 77
(3) The Quantitative Variables
(a) Aroura Measured Plots (Variables 9, 1Ø, and 14) 78
(b) Land-cubit Measured Plots (Variables 11, 12, 28, and 13) 8Ø
(c) Variable 33 Percentage of Assessment 1 and Variable 37 Percentage of Assessment 2 83

CHAPTER 5 -- NOTES 84

CHAPTER 6 -- SUBPROGRAM CROSSTABS: CROSSTABULATIONS AND MEASURES OF ASSOCIATION

(1) The Subprogram 88
(2) The Crosstabulations
(a) Variable 1 Section of Text (Geographic Zone) by Variable 31 Geographic Location 9Ø
(b) Variable 1 Section of Text by Variable 3 Institutional Group and Variable 4 Land-owning Institution 91
(c) Variable 1 Section of Text by Variable 5 Deity or King 97
(d) Variable 4 Land-owning Institution and Variable 3 Institutional Group by Variable 31 Geographic Location 1ØØ
(e) Variable 18 Institutional Class, Variable 19 Type of Religious Institution, and Variable 39 Dynasty of Founding of Land-owning Institution by Variable 31 Geographic Location 1Ø2
(f) Variable 5 Deity or King by Variable 31 Geographic Location 1Ø5
(g) Variable 2 Format of Entry by Variable 31 Geographic Location 1Ø5
(h) Variable 43 Land Measure I Arouras or Land-cubits (Variety I, Sub-variety IA, Variety II) by Variable 1 Section of Text and Variable 31 Geographic Location 1Ø9
(i) Variable 44 Land Measure II Arouras or Land-cubits (Variety I, Sub-variety IA, Variety I/II, Variety II, Sub-variety IIA) by Variable 1 Section of Text and Variable 31 Geographic Location 111
(j) Variable 45 Type of Aroura Measured Entry (Variety I or Sub-variety IA) by Variable 31 Geographic Location 112
(k) Variable 45 Type of Aroura Measured Entry (Variety I or Sub-variety IA) by Variable 17 Special Entry 113
(l) Variable 43 Land Measure I Arouras or Land-cubits (Variety I, Sub-variety IA, Variety II) by Variable 4 Land-owning Institution and Variable 5 Deity or King; Variable 44 Land Measure II Arouras or Land-cubits (Variety I, Sub-variety IA, Variety I/II, Variety II, Sub-variety IIA) by Variable 4 Land-owning Institution and Variable 5 Deity or King 115
(m) Variable 1 Section of Text by Variable 17 Special Entry; Variable 17 Special Entry by Variable 31 Geographic Location 117
(n) Variable 17 Special Entry by Variable 4 Land-owning Institution, Variable 5 Deity or King, Variable 3 Institutional Group, and Variable 19 Type of Religious Institution 119
(o) Variable 21 Type of Apportioning Paragraph by Variable

4 Land-owning Institution, Variable 3 Institutional Group, Variable 18 Institutional Class, Variable 19 Type of Religious Institution, and Variable 39 Dynasty of Founding of Land-owning Institution 121
(p) Variable 21 Type of Apportioning Paragraph by Variable 5 Deity or King 128
(q) Variable 21 Type of Apportioning Paragraph by Variable 31 Geographic Location 130
(r) Variable 43 Land Measure I Arouras or Land-cubits (Variety I, Sub-variety IA, Variety II) and Variable 44 Land Measure II Arouras or Land-cubits (Variety I, Sub-variety IA, Variety I/II, Variety II, Sub-variety IIA) by Variable 21 Type of Apportioning Paragraph 132
(s) Variable 7 Occupation or Title of Smallholder by the Quantitative Variables of Size of Plot 133
(t) Variable 7 Occupation or Title of Smallholder by Variable 14 Assessed Arouras 138
(u) Variable 7 Occupation or Title of Smallholder by Variable 20 Type of Pōsh Entry 142
(v) Variable 7 Occupation or Title of Smallholder and Variable 16 Occupational Group by Variable 31 Geographic Location 143
(w) Variable 43 Land Measure I Arouras or Land-cubits (Variety I, Sub-variety IA, Variety II) and Variable 44 Land Measure II Arouras or Land-cubits (Variety I, Sub-variety IA, Variety I/II, Variety II, Sub-variety IIA) by Variable 7 Occupation or Title of Smallholder 149
(x) Variable 43 Land Measure I Arouras or Land-cubits (Variety I, Sub-variety IA, Variety II) and Variable 44 Land Measure II Arouras or Land-cubits (Variety I, Sub-variety IA, Variety I/II, Variety II, Sub-variety IIA) by Variable 15 Type of Land 150
(y) Variable 15 Type of Land by Variable 31 Geographic Location 151
(z) Variable 9 Arouras by Variable 31 Geographic Location 153
(aa) Variable 10 Arouras Special Case by Variable 31 Geographic Location 155
(bb) Variable 14 Assessed Arouras by Variable 31 Geographic Location 157
(cc) Variable 28 Land-cubits Subtotal 11 and 12 by Variable 31 Geographic Location 161
(dd) Variable 13 Land-cubits Single Figure by Variable 31 Geographic Location 163
(ee) Variable 45 Type of Aroura Measured Entry (Variety I or Sub-variety IA) by Variable 7 Occupation or Title of Smallholder 165

CHAPTER 6 -- NOTES 167

CHAPTER 7 -- RELATED RAMESSIDE ECONOMIC TEXTS

(1) The Turin Taxation Papyrus 169
(2) P. Turin 1882, verso (P. Turin A) 0,1-1,4 182
(3) P. Amiens 184
(4) Other Texts Related to the Transport of Grain Revenues 192
(5) The Griffith Fragments 196

(6) The Gurob Fragments 200
(7) The Louvre Leather Fragments 201
(8) Texts in Complaint of Excess Tax or Rent
(a) P. Valençay I 207
(b) P. Bologna 1094, 5,8-7,1 216
(9) Texts Relating to the Acquisition and Allocation of Landholdings
(a) The Inscription of Mose 220
(b) P. British Museum 10412 222
(c) P. Berlin 3047 223

CHAPTER 7 -- NOTES 225

CHAPTER 8 -- MAJOR FINDINGS AND RESEARCH AGENDA

(1) Sub-variety IA Entries: An Evaluation of Menu's Interpretation 236
(2) Zones of Plot Location and Institutional Groups 245
(3) The Unit of Land Measure and the Classification of Unassessed Plots 247
(4) The Headings of the Apportioning Paragraphs: A Preliminary Appraisal 250
(5) ỉdb and pʿt-land: Location and Unit of Measure 254
(6) Two Significant Determinants of Size of Plot and Assessment Value
(a) The Variables of Size of Plot 259
(b) Assessment Value (Variable 14 Assessed Arouras) 263
(7) Directions of Future Research
(a) Detailed Analysis of the Crosstabulations 266
(b) Crosstabulation Analysis of the Percentage of Assessment Variables 267
(c) Analysis of the Abbreviated Expressions in the Sub-variety IIA Entries 267
(d) Variable 40 Individual Smallholder 268
(e) Three-Way Crosstabulation Analysis 269
(f) Subprogram BREAKDOWN 270
(g) Analysis of the Non-Apportioning Paragraphs; Analysis of Text B 270
(h) A Study of Proper Names in P. Wilbour 271

CHAPTER 8 -- NOTES 271

BIBLIOGRAPHY 273

APPENDICES

A Labels for Variable 4 Land-owning Institution 284

B Labels for Variable 22 Dual Geographic Location A 287
Labels for Variable 23 Dual Geographic Location B

C Labels for Variable 31 Geographic Location 288

D List of Occupations and Occupational Groups 292

E Data of Subprogram CONDESCRIPTIVE 294

F Tables of Subprogram FREQUENCIES 297

G Examples of Tables of Subprogram CROSSTABS 314

INDICES

Index of Egyptian Words and Phrases in P. Wilbour 317

Index of Measurement Areas in P. Wilbour 319

Index of Persons in P. Wilbour 321

ADDITIONS 322

List of Tables

Table 1	Landholdings of the Theban, Heliopolitan, and Memphite Groups According to Section of Text (Geographic Zone)	after p. 246
Table 2	Cramer's V Values of Crosstabulations with Variable 43 Land Measure I and Variable 44 Land Measure II	after p. 249

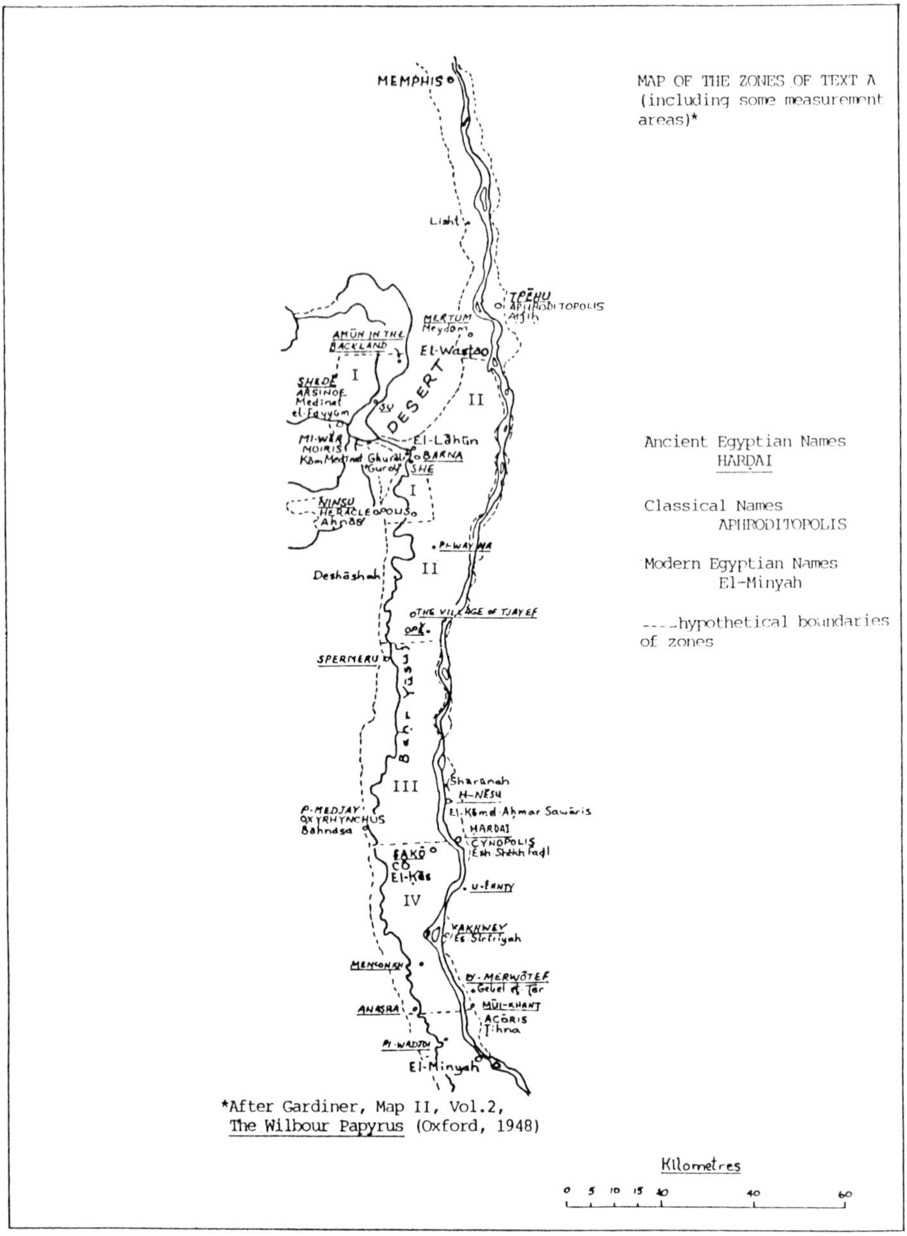

MAP OF THE ZONES OF TEXT A

Preface

The impact of the computer upon scientific Egyptological studies, coupled with the application of statistical techniques, has as yet been fairly limited, and almost entirely restricted to the fields of archaeology and linguistics. Of course, large amounts of sufficiently homogeneous material allowing for data analysis and the construction of sets of relationships between variables are rare, although by no means lacking. The Wilbour Papyrus, however, is the only extant text which, by virtue of the large quantities of both qualitative and quantitative data it contains, lends itself to the kinds of statistical analysis available in social science computer software in order to discover underlying patterns and trends. Earlier studies, particularly that of its editor, Alan H. Gardiner, and, subsequently, those of Bernadette Menu and I.A. Stuchevsky, have already provided us with a basic insight into the general structure of the text, as well as several details; but the bulk of the low level data such as the numerous figures and the many occupations and titles have as yet largely resisted convincing explanation. It is the merit of the present book that the author has made a first step in that direction.

Clearly, one cannot expect immediately the final solution of all problems. The author herself speaks, in this connection, of "a sound basis for further investigation" (p. 250). Since the material is so extensive and the difficulties are so intricate, she has wisely restricted her analysis to the apportioning paragraphs of Text A. The major value of the present study, therefore, is the demonstration that her method leads to reliable results. This does not mean, however, that it does not contain numerous valuable observations concerning all kinds of minor points, as anyone studying the economic and administrative aspects of New Kingdom Egypt will quickly discover in turning the pages of this book. Moreover, the statistical approach is certainly not the only one used. The extensive chapter 7, for instance, in which the author compares her results from the preceding chapters with the contents of all other relevant New Kingdom papyri, is mainly based on traditional Egyptological methods. Section (1) of chapter 8, again, presents a fine example of what can be achieved by a combination of both the statistical and traditional methods, particularly since the author also applies here her knowledge of accountancy. By these means she is able to demonstrate convincingly that Mme. Menu's at first view so plausible interpretation of the Sub-variety IA is highly unlikely to be correct.

A moot point in discussions about the Wilbour Papyrus is the question to what extent it can be considered to be a valid sample of the fields in Middle Egypt during the Twentieth Dynasty. The text deals almost exclusively with temple land and the landed properties of some specialized institutions, such as the Treasury of Pharaoh and the Landing-Places of Pharaoh. Hardly any royal domains are included, and private landed property--if it existed--is entirely absent. The obvious answer to the question is that we have to work with whatever data we happen to possess. Lack of evidence concerning other types of fields, here and in other relevant papyri that have been preserved, at best suggests that temple domains were preponderant in Middle Egypt during the pertinent period.

It requires a careful study of each separate section, with an open mind for the possibilities of the applications of the statistical method to our material, fully to realize to what extent Dr. Katary has advanced our knowledge of the Wilbour Papyrus. Once, Gardiner wrote (<u>The Wilbour Papyrus</u>, vol. II, p. 201): "This lengthy book is drawing to a close, yet its main problem remains intact, unsolved, barely even formulated. That problem concerns the administrative purposes to be served by the figures ascertained or decided upon by the officials responsible for the two texts [i.e., Texts A and B]. Could those purposes be revealed in full, doubtless we should find ourselves in possession of a fairly comprehensive picture of Late Ramesside agricultural finance. Unhappily so desirable a revelation has not been vouchsafed to me." With the present study in hand, I venture to state that we are now a large stretch advanced on the path from this desperate confession to that happy state: fully to fathom what the Wilbour Papyrus can teach us about the agriculture and economy of the New Kingdom.

Jac. J. Janssen

Acknowledgments

The present study evolved out of my doctoral thesis completed in the Department of Near Eastern Studies of the University of Toronto in 1977 under the supervision of Professor Ronald J. Williams. Over the intervening years, he has steadfastly read and reread the manuscript in its various stages of evolution and provided many useful suggestions. His continued support of my efforts to integrate traditional methods of study in Egyptology with the kinds of statistical analysis utilized by social scientists is deeply appreciated.

In 1982, an unpublished study of mine relating to P. Wilbour found its way into the capable hands of Professor Dr. Jac. J. Janssen, Emeritus Professor of Egyptology, Rijksuniversiteit, Leiden, The Netherlands. Over the past five years, he has given most generously of his time and energy in reading and critically evaluating my work. This volume has greatly benefited from his rigorous criticism and the exchange of often differing ideas and perspectives. It is in large part due to his persistent encouragement of my research that this work has finally seen the light of day.

I would also like to thank Mr. James P. Hughes of Systemhouse, Toronto for enabling me to revise and rerun the original program and for designing new programs for future analysis at the computer facilities of the Regional Municipality of Sudbury in 1980.

My deep appreciation also goes to Professor Cynthia M. Whissell, Professor of Psychology at Laurentian University in Sudbury, Ontario who helped me to understand and utilize the concepts and techniques of applied statistics. I am also most grateful to Professor Whissell for kindly permitting me to revise both my data file and SPSS program under her direction at the computer facilities of Laurentian University in 1985. Since then, she has patiently answered a multiplicity of technical questions arising from the new tables generated by the revised SPSS program.

My thanks are also due to Mr. Tin-Chee Wu, Senior Planner with the Regional Municipality of Sudbury, for his advice on various questions in statistics.

I should also like to express my appreciation to Ms. Helen Sandys-Wunsch who not merely typed the manuscript, but also assisted me in editing it. Her patience and scrupulous attention to detail have much improved the readability of a complex and difficult manuscript.

My thanks are also due to Ms. Nellie Maria Lanteigne, LL.B. who spent countless hours helping me to proofread and edit the manuscript. Her many insightful comments and questions from the perspective of a lawyer specializing in real estate have proved invaluable. My thanks go also to Ms. Laurie Siscoe who assisted in proofreading parts of the manuscript.

I wish to express my gratitude to Mr. David Hughes, Chief Cartographer of the Regional Municipality of Sudbury, for his assistance in producing the photostat for the hieroglyphs which appear in the manuscript.

I would like to express my appreciation to Mrs. Kathleen Simpson for her invaluable assistance in printing the final copy of the manuscript.

My thanks also go to the Rev. Dr. John Sandys-Wunsch, Provost of the College of Thorneloe University federated with Laurentian University in Sudbury, for his advice and many suggestions over the past year.

I would also like to acknowledge Mr. W. V. Davies, Deputy Keeper of the Department of Egyptian Antiquities at the British Museum, for his recommendation of my manuscript for publication by Routledge and Kegan Paul Ltd. (Kegan Paul International). I am also grateful to Mr. Peter Hopkins, Chairman and Managing Director of Routledge and Kegan Paul Ltd., for the publication of this work.

I would also like to acknowledge the financial support of the American Philosophical Society, Philadelphia which allowed me to continue the work begun in my doctoral thesis.

Last of all, I would like to thank my husband Narasim Katary, Director of Long-Range Planning, the Regional Municipality of Sudbury who has patiently and tirelessly contributed his criticisms of the manuscript, from the point of view of a planner-economist, from the very beginning of my research. Special appreciation goes to my daughter Shannon for her patience and understanding of her mother's long hours and need for peace and quiet over the past year.

Abbreviations

AEO	Alan H. Gardiner, Ancient Egyptian Onomastica, 3 vols. (Oxford, 1947).
ASAE	Annales du Service des Antiquités de l'Égypte (Cairo, 1900-).
BAR	James H. Breasted, Ancient Records of Egypt: Historical Documents, 5 vols. (Chicago, 1906-7).
BIFAO	Bulletin de l'Institut français d'archéologie orientale (Cairo, 1901-).
BiOr	Bibliotheca Orientalis (Leiden, 1943-).
Bull. MMA	Bulletin of the Metropolitan Museum of Art, New York (New York, 1905-).
CAH	The Cambridge Ancient History, 3rd ed. (Cambridge, 1970-75).
CCG	Catalogue général des antiquités égyptiennes du Musée du Caire (Cairo and other places, 1901-).
CdE	Chronique d'Égypte (Brussels, 1925-).
DFIFAO	Documents de fouilles de l'Institut français d'archéologie orientale (Cairo, 1934-).
FIFAO	Fouilles de l'Institut français d'archéologie orientale (Cairo, 1924-).
Gardiner, Commentary	Alan H. Gardiner, The Wilbour Papyrus, 3 vols. (Oxford, 1941-48), vol. 2, Commentary (1948).

Gardiner, Synopsis or Syn.	Alan H. Gardiner, The Wilbour Papyrus, 3 vols. (Oxford, 1941-48), vol. 2, Commentary (1948), pp. 124-157.
Gardiner, Translation	Alan H. Gardiner, The Wilbour Papyrus, 3 vols. (Oxford, 1941-48), vol. 3, Translation (1948).
JAOS	Journal of the American Oriental Society (New Haven, 1843-).
JARCE	Journal of the American Research Center in Egypt (Glückstadt and other places, 1963-).
JEA	Journal of Egyptian Archaeology (London, 1914-).
JNES	Journal of Near Eastern Studies (Chicago, 1942-).
JRAS	Journal of the Royal Asiatic Society (London, 1834-).
LEM	Alan H. Gardiner, Late-Egyptian Miscellanies [Bibliotheca Aegyptiaca VII] (Brussels, 1937).
L.Eg.	Late Egyptian.
LRL	Jaroslav Černý, Late Ramesside Letters [Bibliotheca Aegyptiaca IX] (Brussels, 1939).
MÄS	Münchner Ägyptologische Studien (Berlin, 1962-).
PSBA	Proceedings of the Society of Biblical Archaeology (London, 1879-1918).
RAD	Alan H. Gardiner, Ramesside Administrative Documents (Oxford, 1948).
Rec. trav.	Recueil de travaux relatifs à la philologie et à l'archéologie égyptiennes et assyriennes (Paris, 1870-1923).
RdE	Revue d'égyptologie (Paris, 1933; Cairo, 1936-51; Paris, 1950-).
SAOC	Studies in Ancient Oriental Civilization, Oriental Institute, University of Chicago (Chicago, 1931-).
WB., Beleg.	Adolf Erman and Hermann Grapow, Wörterbuch der aegyptischen Sprache, 5 vols., Belegstellen, 5 vols. in 6 vols. (Berlin, 1971).
ZÄS	Zeitschrift für ägyptische Sprache und Altertumskunde (Leipzig, 1863-1943; Berlin and Leipzig, 1956-).

Author's Introduction

Text A of P. Wilbour is an enumeration of what appears to have been the assessment of some 2800 plots of agricultural land located in Middle Egypt during year 4 of Ramesses V (1142 B.C.). The entries of Text B of P. Wilbour, a later addition to Text A, pertain only to "khato-lands of Pharaoh" and comprise a separate but related document. The fields described in P. Wilbour Text A extended somewhere to the north of Crocodilopolis (Medīnet el-Fayyūm) and southwards almost to Ṭihna just short of el-Minyah. The fact that P. Wilbour records data for plots located as far to the north as Medīnet el-Fayyūm is very fortunate indeed, since most pharaonic administrative documents of any length pertain to the area of Thebes in Upper Egypt.

This great treasure of the Brooklyn Museum, surpassed in length only by the Great Harris Papyrus and P. Ebers, has the potential to shed light upon many facets of economic life in Ramesside Egypt. The enormity of the data provided by this document is at once awesome and overwhelming. Moreover, while it seems likely that the subject of the document is the revenue accruing to various institutions from plots located in Middle Egypt, it is not as yet known for what purpose the list was compiled, or why these particular landholdings were enumerated (altogether comprising only a minute fraction of the cultivable land in the area). Thus, P. Wilbour poses some difficult and intriguing questions which must be kept in mind at all times.

P. Wilbour provides great challenges not only to the philologist in the transcription and translation of the greatly abbreviated hieratic text, but to the student of social and economic history who desires to make use of its detail to enlarge the understanding of the structure and operations of the ancient Egyptian agricultural economy and the principal players, i.e., the temples and secular institutions, the Crown (State), and the smallholders and farm-labourers (iḥwtyw) who actually cultivated the land.

Since the publication of Sir Alan H. Gardiner's groundbreaking three volume study of P. Wilbour over the years 1941-48, The Wilbour Papyrus, 3 vols. (Oxford, 1941-48), Index by Raymond O. Faulkner (vol. IV) (Oxford, 1952), students of economic history and Egyptologists alike have expressed great interest in the document. The study of Bernadette Menu, Le régime juridique des terres et du personnel attaché à la terre dans le Papyrus Wilbour (Lille, 1970), is an extremely useful and original contribution to the study of ancient Egyptian economic history which provides an interpretation of the data which is both novel and thought-provoking. An English summary by Jac. J. Janssen of I.A. Stuchevsky's major study of P. Wilbour, Zemledel'tsy gosudarstvennogo khozyaistva drevnego Egipta epokhi Ramessidov (The Cultivators of the State Economy in Ancient Egypt During the Ramesside Period), published in Moscow in 1982, will shortly appear in Bibliotheca Orientalis. We look forward to the publication of this summary which, at long last, will make the work of Stuchevsky readily available to Western scholars. No study known to the present author, however, attempts to analyze the various socio-economic factors both explicit and implicit in P. Wilbour as variables which may be subjected to a wide variety of statistical analyses such as those included in the present study. The decision was made, therefore, to subject the data of P. Wilbour to an exploratory statistical analysis using SPSS (Statistical Package for the Social Sciences), an integrated system of computer programs designed for the analysis of social science data. The enormity of the undertaking was soon realized and a humbler objective defined which limited the analysis to the data of the Text A apportioning paragraphs.

The aim of the present study is to establish a framework within which the socio-economic data of P. Wilbour may be retrieved, analyzed, and evaluated. The study also endeavours to relate the data of P. Wilbour to contemporary and near-contemporary Egyptian economic and administrative documents in order to give the data a historical context.

Certain priorities have been established in the analysis. First, the emphasis has been placed upon the rigorous definition of the variables and their respective categories. Second, priority has been given to the description of the data of P. Wilbour by means of two SPSS subprograms. Third, relationships between variables have been explored by means of an SPSS crosstabulation subprogram and a total of more than 300 crosstabulations executed.

The great utility of the tables generated by this study is not merely their concise organization of the massive P. Wilbour apportioning data into a format which can be made directly accessible to scholars of various interests, but also their identification of data which are worthy of intensive study. By subjecting the apportioning data of P. Wilbour to statistical analysis, it is possible to distinguish between data which are statistically significant and data which are statistically trivial. It is possible, therefore, to avoid time-consuming searches in directions which are not likely to yield meaningful results, and to concentrate instead upon more productive avenues of inquiry identified by the application of the laws of probability expressed in terms of various statistics such as chi-square and

Cramer's V. Once important areas worthy of detailed investigation have been identified, it is possible to apply more specialized techniques of statistical analysis to further examine specific points of interest. Provided we are willing to tentatively accept the data of P. Wilbour as a sample of apportioning data reflecting a sector of the Ramesside economy of Middle Egypt during the mid-Twentieth Dynasty, it is possible to make cautious inferences concerning the structure of the economy of Middle Egypt at this point in history. It is the author's contention that allowing ourselves to be governed by excessive caution and conservatism in approaching data which do not conform perfectly to the ideal of a random sample is as mistaken an approach as the failure to exercise reasonable caution in drawing inferences from the statistical analysis of such data. If we are not willing to take some risk in accepting the data of P. Wilbour as an availability sample worthy of detailed, cautious evaluation, we gain nothing only to forfeit a golden opportunity to enlarge our understanding of the operations of the Late Ramesside economy. Should further study confirm the author's view of the document as one in a regular series of records compiled for the express purpose of bringing earlier records up to date, there is even greater justification for studying the data of P. Wilbour by means of rigorous statistical analysis.

Despite the restriction of the scope of the present study to the basic description of the Text A apportioning data and the execution of crosstabulation analysis, the data generated by the subprograms utilized are so massive as to warrant a lifetime of work in order to exhaustively analyze and evaluate them. It is therefore impossible to do justice to this vast wealth of data in the course of a single volume. While the present study makes no claim to be definitive, it is indicative of the kinds of things a statistical analysis of the P. Wilbour data can reveal about the system of land tenure operative in Middle Egypt during the mid-Twentieth Dynasty. The attempt has been made, therefore, to convey the general content of only a limited number of tables and to discuss in detail only a limited amount of data of particular interest. No amount of discussion, however, is an adequate substitute for a leisurely consideration of the tables themselves. Unfortunately, it has not been possible to include all of the tables described in this study. While tables produced by subprograms CONDESCRIPTIVE and FREQUENCIES have been included in their entirety, tables generated by subprogram CROSSTABS are far too lengthy for inclusion in this volume. Those tables selected for inclusion in the Appendix are among the shorter crosstabulations and are intended to serve primarily as examples of crosstabulation analysis. Crosstabulation tables which are not included in this volume are available from the author upon request.

The final chapter of this study concludes with the delineation of future avenues of research and appropriate methodology for such studies. It is hoped that the not too distant future will see the completion of another volume which will not only expand upon the points raised here, but hopefully integrate and evaluate data generated by additional SPSS subprograms as well.

1 The Wilbour Papyrus

(1) Plan and Organization of Text A

Text A of P. Wilbour records what appears to be the assessment of approximately 2800 plots of agricultural land in Middle Egypt during year 4 of Ramesses V.(1) The fields therein described extended somewhere to the north of Crocodilopolis (Medīnet el-Fayyūm) and southwards almost to Ṭihna just short of El-Minyah. Thus, the fields extended over a distance of about 140 kilometers and were owned (or virtually owned) and administered by a wide variety of secular and religious institutions.(2)

Text A of P. Wilbour is a unique register of institutionally owned landholdings consisting of no less than 4500 lines in 102 columns. The register is divided into 279 stereotyped paragraphs organized into four sections corresponding to four consecutive periods of assessment--roughly from July 2 to 24 (Gregorian).(3) Each paragraph begins with the identification of what is apparently the land-owning institution, religious or secular, under which are ordered a series of assessment lines enumerating plots of varying sizes measured in either land-cubits (mḥ-t3) or arouras (sṯ3t). Each paragraph specifies the geographic location of each plot, two or more plots usually enumerated under the same location. Measurement lines begin with the rubricized phrase: "MEASUREMENT made in ...," or "MEASUREMENT made to the north (south, etc.) of..." The assessment lines which follow provide details concerning each plot in question, listing the name and occupation of the responsible party, the size of the plot, and the assessment (if any) levied on the land calculated as a share in the harvest.

The 279 paragraphs are divided among the four sections of the text, corresponding not only to consecutive periods of assessment, but also to distinct geographic zones which seem to reflect a north to south orientation in the original field records. A large number of institutions are duplicated from one zone to the next such that the total number of individual land-owning institutions in Text A is found to be only 96. The temple of Medīnet Habu, for example, occurs in §§64-68 of Section II, §§127-36 of Section III,

(4), and §§220-30 of Section IV. The paragraphs devoted to each institution are differentiated according to the official in charge of the various "administrative districts"  (rmnyt).

Only two of the four sections of the text are complete. A large portion of Section I is lost as is the very end of Section IV.(5) The four sections correspond to four consecutive periods of assessment totalling about 23 days inclusive of the unknown number of days represented by Section I. The introductory lines of Sections II through IV indicate that the data were recorded over the period from year 4, second month of 3ḫt, day 15 to year 4, third month of 3ḫt, day 1. The document as we have it today clearly represents a later draft of the original field data, since the data of each of the four sections have been organized under the headings of the various institutions in a nearly identical sequence repeated from section to section. The work was compiled by two scribes, the first of whom was a competent scribe who was responsible for most of the document (up to A68,20 and continuing A69,1-72,30 and again A75,1 to within the last two lines of col. 95). The second and far less competent scribe wrote the remainder of Text A in his more cursive and abbreviated style.

Each section of the text, with the exception of Section I, the first half of which appears to be lost, is comprised of five subsections, the first three of which correspond to the three major temple groups, Theban, Heliopolitan, and Memphite, well-known from P. Harris I.(6) A fourth temple category which may be compared with the Kleine Tempel section in P. Harris I we will call "Other Religious." The fifth subsection consists of secular institutions. The Theban Group, for example, extends over many paragraphs: Section II (§§51ff.), Section III (§§117ff.), and Section IV (§§208ff.), commencing with the House of Amun-Rēʿ, King of the Gods at Karnak and including several other Theban chapels and temples. These temples were evidently separate administrative entities which undoubtedly functioned under the aegis of the Karnak temple of Amūn. Following the Theban Group come six or possibly seven temples which are associated with Heliopolis and belong to the Heliopolitan Group. These temples are followed by seven temples associated with Memphis and belong to the Memphite Group, the oldest and most esteemed of which was that of "Ptaḥ, the Great, South of His Wall, Lord of ʿAnkhtowĕ" (§80). The last temple group includes all other temples generally smaller in size and importance appropriately labelled "Other Religious." The sequence Theban-Heliopolitan-Memphite-Other Religious is occasionally upset by intercalations of extraneous religious and secular institutions. In Section III, four paragraphs are misplaced (§§140-43), while in Section IV, two paragraphs are incorrectly placed (§§234-35). While not systematically rigid, the general scheme of the text is clear and cannot be mistaken.

The order of paragraphs is reminiscent of the order of temples in P. Harris I where the temples also divide into the same four major groups, the sequence of which is identical to that of P. Wilbour. The group devoted to smaller temples in P. Harris I reveals a distinct geographic orientation from south to north as is also the case with temples of the group Other Religious in P. Wilbour. The south to north sequence of temples of the group

Other Religious in P. Wilbour, however, is broken intermittently by the intercalation of several small sanctuaries, the exact locations of which are not at all certain. Since the same temples do not necessarily occur in all sections of P. Wilbour, the south to north orientation of the temples of the group Other Religious is not as readily apparent in P. Wilbour as it is in P. Harris I.

The first temple which heads the Theban Group is the great House of Amun-Rēʿ, King of the Gods at Karnak (§§ 51ff.). This establishment is followed by the chapel of Tiʿo, consort of Amenophis II (§57) and the temple of Mūt, the Great, Lady of Ishru (§213), both situated in the Karnak complex. The Theban temples which follow are arranged in chronological order going backward in time, beginning with the "Mansion" 𓉗 (ḥwt) of Ramesses V (§58, the first occurrence, so too with the institutions which follow), that of Ramesses IV (§60), that of Ramesses III (Medīnet Habu) (§64), that of Ramesses II (the Ramesseum) (§69), the "House" 𓉐 (pr) of Ḥaremḥab (§70), and an institution which may have been the funerary foundation of Tuthmosis II (§75).(7) The exact locations of the foundations of Ramesses IV and Ramesses V are uncertain as is the location of the temple of Ḥaremḥab.(8) The sequence of the Theban temples in reverse chronological order is reminiscent of the contemporary P. Amiens, a document which details the transportation of grain revenue of the "House of Amūn" (pr ʾImn) (see chapter 7(3)).(9)

The Heliopolitan temples include the "metropolitan" temples located in Heliopolis itself as well as temples located at a greater or smaller distance from Heliopolis. Of the metropolitan temples, the most significant was that of Re-Ḥarakhte (§144). P. Harris I 37b,2, among other sources, is clear testimony to the supreme importance of this establishment.(10) Other metropolitan temples include those built by Ramesses II (§76) and Merenptaḥ (§79), the former known from other sources, the latter attested only in P. Wilbour.(11) The Heliopolitan temples in the outlying areas include three of the largest establishments enumerated in P. Wilbour, the most important of which was a cult centre known as "Those of the Mansion of Ramesses-ḥeḳ-Ōn in the House of Rēʿ north of Ōn" (§77). This temple was a foundation of Ramesses III which may be identified with the remains of a temple at Tell el-Yahūdīyah. Also significant was the House of Ḥaʿpy, Father of the Gods (§238) which is confirmed by P. Harris I (29,7) as belonging to the Heliopolitan Group.

The Memphite temples are headed by the "House of Ptaḥ, the Great, South of His Wall, Lord of ʿAnkhtowĕ" (§80) followed by the "Great Seat of Ramesses-meriamūn in the House of Ptaḥ" (§3A) and two closely associated establishments related to the Sed-festival called the "House of [Ra]messes-meriamūn, [Repeater of Sed]-festivals in the House of Rēʿ (?) (§83) and the "Mansions of Festival" (§189) respectively. Two other temples of Ramesses II are numbered among the Memphite Group, one temple with the epithet "Beloved Like Ptaḥ" (§82) and the other simply described as being "in the House of Ptaḥ" (§149). In addition, there are two foundations of Merenptaḥ known as the "House of Ptaḥ of Merenptaḥ and of Ramesses-meriamūn" (§232) and the "Mansion of Merenptaḥ-ḥotp(ḥi)māʿĕ in the House of Ptaḥ" (§240) respectively.(12)

The group of relatively small temples is composed of various temples each designated the "House" (pr) of a particular deity. There are temples associated with the gods ʿAnti (§265), Ḥeryshef (§§4, 8, 9), Bata (§§91, 160, 268), the Divine Ennead (§25), Ḥatḥōr (§§264, 267), Ḥar-Min and Isis (§157), Isis alone (§§19, 34), Mont (§§62, 249), Nephthys as consort of Seth (§§28, 94, 168), Osiris (§§11, 87, 250), Sobek (§§12, 20, 21, 261), Sobek-Rēʿ (§§159, 254), Thoth (§§89, 90, 140, 252), Tawēret (§102), and the deified king Sesostris III (§36). Also belonging to the group of relatively small temples are shrines of the various forms of the god Amūn with their respective epithets (e.g., §96 Amūn, Founder of the Earth; §97 Amūn Tjayef; §98 Amūn of the Island). There is also the temple of Onūris (§186) which occurs outside the geographically arranged series. Interspersed among the entries of smaller temples are sanctuaries in Menʿonkh (§263), Sakō (§§162, 272), Spermeru (§169), Heracleopolis (§7), She (§26), Shatina (§35), Su (§29), and the Keep of ʿOnayna (§101), each identified as a "Sunshade of Re-Ḥarakhte" (šwt-Rʿ-Ḥr-3ḫty). Virtually unknown before the Amarna period, these establishments appear to have been small peripteral temples located outside the precincts of the main local temple.(13) Also mentioned are various "Tabernacles" (sšm-ḫw) which appear to have been a type of cult-object (literally "protected image") (§§78, 141-43, 235, and possibly also 71-74).(14)

The secular institutions include "Landing-Places of Pharaoh" (mniw(t) Pr-ʿ3) (§§37, 84-85, 154-55, 241), various "Fields of Pharaoh" (3ḫw(t) Pr-ʿ3) (§§86, 156, 242), the Treasury of Pharaoh (§§192, 196-97), the Royal harems of Memphis and Mi-wēr (pr ḫnr) (§§38-39, 110-12, 277-79), and the establishments of queens (§§109, 153, 172, 193, 276). Also belonging to the secular category are the royal minĕ-lands (§§40-43, 198-200) and khato-lands (§§44-50, 113-16, 201-7) which always occur together at the end of each section of the text (with the exception of Section IV where these paragraphs are lost). Although these two categories of Royal lands appear to have been located at least in part upon fields ascribed to temples, their administration would appear to have often devolved upon various officials acting on behalf of the Crown.

After the identification of the institution in a main heading, paragraphs often contain sub-headings which identify the administrative units of the institution and the officials in charge of these units. These subordinate headings commence with the word rmnyt, a term which applies to the various fields in various localities managed as a single administrative unit under the charge of a senior administrator. Gardiner translates the word rmnyt as "(administrative) domain," while Menu renders it "département."(15) In subsequent paragraphs dealing with the same institution, the full heading with the name of the institution is omitted so that the paragraphs begin with the identification of the individual domain and its chief administrative officer.

The name of the chief administrative officer is always introduced by the compound preposition ((r-)ḫt) "under the authority of." Sometimes this line, referred to by Gardiner as the "sub-heading," is followed by another line or "sub-sub-heading" which introduces yet another official whose name is preceded by the compound preposition  (m-ḏrt) "by the hand of" (e.g., §§ 58, 64, 127). The sub-heading would appear to introduce an official of the highest authority who exercised general supervision over the lands encompassed by the domain; whereas the sub-sub-heading would appear to introduce an official of lower rank probably more directly involved in the actual day-to-day work in the fields of the domain.

In the most complex paragraph headings, the sub-heading with the name of the senior administrator governs subsequent sub-sub-headings in the same way the heading with the name of the institution governs subsequent sub-headings. Occasionally, the sub-heading begins with the word rmnywt, that is, "domains" (e.g., §§52, 60, 127), but the singular may also occur (e.g., §§ 64, 215) and still have the force of governing subsequent sub-sub-headings. In paragraphs where the heading with the name of the institution is omitted, the sub-heading moves up to the first place by appending the words "pr pn" as the identification of the institution, while the sub-sub-heading moves up to second place (so §§ 52, 66). Similarly, an original sub-heading may tacitly govern the next paragraph, in which case a line which by form and meaning is a sub-sub-heading, moves up to the position of sole heading (e.g., §§ 53, 61, 65).(16) Gardiner calls these headings "virtual sub-headings" since they are headings of paragraphs which are subordinate in thought to a real heading, but are not presented as subordinate. Paragraphs 60-63 which pertain to the funerary temple of Ramesses IV are a good example of this practice.

There are also paragraphs where the heading with the name of the institution and what would have been the sub-heading with the name of the chief administrative officer are subsumed in the same line. In A38,40-41 (§92), for example, it is written: "THE HOUSE of Seth, Lord of Spermeru, under the authority of ((r-) ẖt) the prophet Ḥuy." Then the scribe adds a completely superfluous line: "DOMAIN of this house under his authority." There is also the example of §117 where the sub-heading and sub-sub-heading are combined in a single entry (A44,4-5) so as to read: "DOMAIN of the House of Ramesses-meriamūn in the House of Amūn under the authority of the Steward of Amūn, '(administered) by the hand of the controller Amenḥotpe."

The administrators of the various domains include a wide variety of lay officials as well as temple officials. Among the temple officials are a number of prophets (ḥm-nṯr) at Heracleopolis (§4), Sakō (§91), and Spermeru (§92) who occur as chief administrators ((r-) ẖt). Although some of these prophets were probably first prophets, the only prophet actually identified as such is the high priest of Amūn (Ramessenakhte). The high priest of Heliopolis is referred to by his title wr m3w "Greatest of Seers." A large number of ordinary priests (wʿb) occur as smallholders in the apportioning paragraphs and sometimes looking after (m-ḏrt) temple lands on behalf of a prophet (e.g., Pōsh B entry A88,32), but never occur in the headings or sub-headings. The same may be said to apply to several god's fathers (ỉt-nṯr) who also occur as smallholders in Text A. In connection with the estate of the Karnak temple of Amūn (§§52, 117, 152, 208) and the funerary temple of Ramesses III at Medīnet Habu (§§131, 223, and perhaps also §129), we find the "Steward of Amūn" (ỉmy-r pr ʾImn) and, alternately, the "Steward Usimaʿrenakhte" who also occurs in Text B as the principal administrator of khato-land of Pharaoh. A second steward of Amūn (Pēl) occurs in §226 pertaining to the temple of Medīnet Habu and may have been the predecessor of Usimaʿrenakhte. The title ỉdnw "deputy" also occurs in the sub-headings where it is not always certain of what official the ỉdnw was the deputy. While there is no doubt that the ỉdnw were individuals who substituted for various and sundry officials, it is very rare that information is forthcoming giving the rank or title of the official the ỉdnw replaced. Some ỉdnw were military officers as the title ỉdnw n mšʿ "adjutant of the army" clearly indicates, while other ỉdnw appear to have been replacements for temple staff. There is, for example, the ỉdnw Ptaḥemḥab who in §215 is connected with the funerary temple of Ramesses V.(17) The "controllers" (rwḏw) who occur in the actual or virtual sub-headings of Text A (as in the Theban paragraphs 51, 53, 58, 61, 64-67) were apparently individuals who performed a managerial role at some distance from their administrative centres. This may be the reason why they do not occur attached to smaller temples the fields of which usually were located nearby. These rwḏw apparently worked under the authority of ((r-) ḥt) senior administrators some of whom were probably purely honorary appointees. In light of these considerations, Menu describes the controller as an "employé subalterne" tied to the domain entrusted to his management.(18)

The evidence of the paragraph headings of P. Wilbour is strong indication that members of the civil (State) administration participated in the management of temple holdings. In Section II, fields of the temple of Medīnet Habu are recorded as administered by the "Dispatch-writer of Pharaoh" (sš šʿt n Pr-ʿ3) assisted by two controllers (§§64-65); while fields of the funerary establishment of Ramesses IV (§60) are described as being under the administrative authority of a certain Neferʿabĕ "who is dead" (nty mt), probably to be equated with the mayor of Ḥardai of that name (A56,46-47 and B17,13). A domain of the funerary temple of Ramesses V (§124), moreover, is indicated as administered by a "scribe of the Granary of Pharaoh." Other lay officials include a former "overseer of the Treasury" in connection with the funerary temple of Ramesses IV in §126 and a "chief of the record-keepers" (ḥry s3w sšw) in connection with the funerary temple of Ramesses V in §§125 and 217. Unexpected certainly are the occurrences of a "stablemaster of the Residence" in §121 (House of Amun-Rēʿ, King of the Gods) and two simple soldiers (wʿw) in §§274 and 275 pertaining to foundations of Ramesses V and Merenptaḥ respectively. Gardiner was cautious, however, in remarking that although lay officials were often called upon to administer distant provincial estates, this does not necessarily mean that they had any decision-making authority in the temple administration generally.(19)

Occasionally the word srw () "officials" is encountered in P. Wilbour as a sort of comprehensive designation for the officials responsible for the administration of the fields of various temples. There are five cases in P. Wilbour (§§56, 124, 135, 212, 215) and several cases in P. Harris I (10,3.4.5; 12a,2; 32a,9; 51a,3) where temple domains are indicated as having been under the authority of ((r-)ḫt) srw. In the case of P. Wilbour, the lines which follow the phrase (r-) ḫt srw each identify a specific functionary. This led Gardiner to the conclusion that the word srw must have had the more narrow meaning "State officials" rather than "temple officials" which he judged superfluous in the context. (20)

The organization of paragraphs pertaining to the estate of any institution was apparently guided by the general principle that fields belonging to the same institution should be differentiated on the basis of the officials responsible for their cultivation. This is not the only principle, however, which influenced the order and organization of the temple (and secular) estates in Text A. The second principle identified by Gardiner has to do with what might be called the "type of service" the individual domains were called upon to render. Gardiner cites the paragraphs relating to the feeding of temple-herds as an example of one type of service. (21) P. Harris I indicates that herds of cattle were among the specific gifts of Ramesses III to temples in Thebes (10,7-11) and Memphis (51a,4). These herds appear to have been parallel to and on an equal footing with the different temple buildings founded by Ramesses III in both these cities. P. Harris I suggests, moreover, that the herds and the subordinate temples each had their own separate staff and personnel. The impression of the autonomy of the temple-herds is strengthened by the existence of paragraphs in P. Wilbour devoted to the domains responsible for the supply of fodder for the herds. These "herbage" paragraphs commence with the word 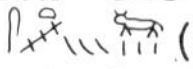 (smw) in the phrase "Herbage of such and such an institution." The herbage paragraphs are not included among the ordinary paragraphs pertaining to the various institutions, but rather are entered in a separate series of their own near the conclusion of each section of the text (§§31-33, 104-7, 174-86, 243-46). Each series observes the internal chronological and geographical order the individual temples themselves follow in each section.

Another series of paragraphs pertaining to services rendered by temple domains are the "white goat" paragraphs 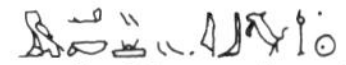 (mk ỉb ḥd) (§§187-195 and §247) which appear to be similar in intent and format to the herbage paragraphs. White goat paragraphs evidently specify land set aside for the feeding of herds, the administration of which was apparently the responsibility of certain institutions. Like the herbage paragraphs, white goat paragraphs come near the end of each of the four sections of the text. There are also four paragraphs which specify a domain the fields of which provided "provender (for) asses of (i.e., 'from') the Northern Oasis" (Treasury of Pharaoh (§§196-97); the House of Amun-Rēʿ, King of the Gods (§209); and the temple of Medīnet Habu (§222)) which also appear to designate a type of "service function." While such paragraphs belonging to the House of Amun-Rēʿ, King of the Gods and the temple of Medīnet Habu are found in the main sequence of the paragraphs belonging to these two temples, those of the Treasury of Pharaoh follow the white goat paragraphs of Section III, but precede the paragraphs which enumerate *minĕ* and *khato*-land at the end of the section.

There is yet another type of paragraph which is similar to the herbage and white goat paragraphs and undoubtedly related to them. This variety of paragraph has the heading "domain of this house (*rmnyt pr pn*) under the authority of the overseer of cattle PN (*(r-)ḫt ỉmy-r ỉḥw* PN)." These paragraphs occur frequently with the smaller temples for which there are no herbage paragraphs (§§5, 18, 165), but also with larger better known temples which do have herbage paragraphs as, for example, the temple of Medīnet Habu (§§135-36 cf. §175) and the temple of Ramesses II at Memphis (§149 cf. §184). It is unlikely, therefore, that these paragraphs should be interpreted as simply an alternate expression of the ordinary herbage paragraph. In the case of the House of Amun-Rēᶜ, King of the Gods, there is both a herbage paragraph (§174) and a special paragraph within the same section of the text (§12Ø) which ascribes to the fields in question the same purpose presupposed for the herbage paragraphs. Thus, §174 begins: "Herbage of the House of Amun-Rēᶜ, King of the Gods," while §12Ø commences: "Domain of the divine offerings [of Amun]-Rēᶜ, King of the Gods: 'Domain which makes provender for cattle under the authority of the overseer of cattle Ramessenakhte.'" It is possible, of course, that §12Ø is to be interpreted not as a duplication of the herbage paragraph, but as a special case which is similar but not identical.

Paragraphs beginning with the word *šmw* 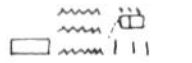 (WB. IV, 481, 1ff.) are in large supply (§§6, 17, 22, 27, 63, 93, 95, 1ØØ, 166, 171, 251, 26Ø, 266, 269, 271, 273). The word *šmw* in these paragraph headings is followed by the word *pš* 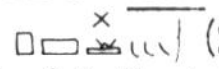 (§17) with variant 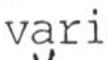 which means "to apportion" or "to divide" (*pšš*, L.Eg. *pš* WB. I, 553, I, 6ff.). The *šmw pš* paragraphs are spaced out over the entirety of the text, occurring most frequently in the subsections devoted to the smaller temples. *Šmw pš* paragraphs are found only in conjunction with those temples which appear to have been of only small or moderate size with only two possible exceptions, §63 which pertains to the funerary temple of Ramesses IV at Thebes and §251 which pertains to the temple of Osiris at Abydus. The larger temples have instead paragraphs commencing with the words *rmnyt pš* (*n pr pn*) translated to mean the "apportioning (apportioned) domain (of this house)." These paragraphs are placed at or near the end of the series of paragraphs devoted to a single institution. Because those institutions with *šmw pš* paragraphs tend to be the smaller institutions, the *šmw pš* paragraphs are often the last of only two or three paragraphs pertaining to such institutions. The tendency of both types of paragraphs to occur at or near the end of a series of paragraphs devoted to a single institution, together with the apparent mutual exclusivity of the terms, leads to the possible understanding that *šmw pš* paragraphs fulfill for small to medium size institutions the same function as do *rmnyt pš* paragraphs for relatively large institutions. This is an understanding which can be evaluated by means of statistical analysis.

(2) The Places of Measurement in Text A

Most of the place names in the measurement lines of Text A are completely unknown; only a very few are attested elsewhere. Many of the institutions which owned and administered the fields in Text A are known from other sources. Their locations are found to range over a very great part of Egypt. The approximation of the location of the otherwise unknown measurement locations begins with the differentiation of the various institutions on the basis of relative size and prominence on the reasonable assumption made by Gardiner that the geographic range of the estate of a land-owning institution is likely to have been roughly proportionate to the institution's size and prominence.(22) A second assumption, also suggested by Gardiner, holds that a temple or other institution of relatively small size is unlikely to have owned land outside its immediate vicinity. The problem arises with the grouping of temples which do not belong to one of the three major groups (Theban, Heliopolitan, and Memphite) into a single category identified by Gardiner with the Kleine Tempel group of P. Harris I. Needless to say, merely because a temple was not affiliated with one of the three major temple groups does not mean that it should be regarded as "small," as certainly must be the case with the temple of Osiris at Abydus (§§87 and 250). Nor should the fact that a temple is relatively or even completely unknown be considered proof positive that we are dealing with a "small" or "unimportant" temple.

The northernmost institution in Text A is the foundation of Ramesses III bearing the name "Those of the Mansion of Ramesses-ḥeḳ-Ōn in the House of Reʿ north of Ōn" (§77), abbreviated in P. Wilbour as "Those of the Mansion" (Na-t-ḥō), situated at Tell el-Yahūdīyah. The southernmost institution is that of the House of Mont, Lord of Hermonthis (§249). Land-owning institutions appear to have been sparsely situated from Hermonthis in the south to Hermopolis in Middle Egypt. Northwards from Hermopolis to just beyond Crocodilopolis, however, institutions become increasingly more densely situated. Relatively few institutions were situated north of the Fayyūm, the majority of these institutions having been located in the vicinity of Memphis or Heliopolis.

It is sometimes possible to combine the information provided in the paragraph headings which give the name of the institution with data of the measurement lines which provide geographic place names in order to arrive at conclusions concerning the location of unknown or little known temples. A good case in point is §30 in Section I in which the locality the "New Land of Swo" is given as the locale of fields belonging to the House of Amūn, Lord of Thrones of the Two Lands in the Backland. This temple is numbered among the temples of the group Other Religious in Section I and is also mentioned in P. Harris I 61b,16 where indication is that it may have been located just south of Aṭfīḥ (P. Harris I 61b,17). Because the House of Amūn, Lord of Thrones of the Two Lands was probably a relatively small temple, it is likely that the fields to which it claimed title were located within a relatively small radius of it. Thus, the otherwise unknown locality, the "New Land of Swo," may perhaps have been situated just south of Aṭfīḥ.

In his study of P. Wilbour, Gardiner constructed a useful table (Table I) which distributes the temple-sites as they occur over the four sections of Text A.(23) The table reveals an internal order of temple-sites which reflects a north to south geographic orientation. Section I, for example, includes many sites which were located in the northern part of the Heracleopolitan nome in the vicinity of Ḥardai (Cynopolis). Gardiner also constructed a second table (Table II) to test the hypothesis that the geographical areas of the four sections of the text which correspond to the four consecutive periods of survey were, in fact, mutually exclusive.(24) Of the 142 places of measurement ("measurement areas") in this table, 129 are restricted to one section of the text. Of the 13 exceptions, there are 4 which are found to skip an entire section (i.e., I to III; II to IV), occurring in sections that are not even consecutive. It is possible, of course, that at least some of these cases are examples of homonymity, since it is self-evident that the more common the place name, the more likely it is that there was more than one locality with the same name (e.g., Opĕ in Sections II and III, No. 21 in Table II and the House of Ptaḥmosĕ in Sections I and II, No. 36 in Table II). This principle also pertains to localities in P. Wilbour which are also attested in other sources. There is the case of the Mound of Naḥiḥu (Table II, No. 6), for example, a place name that occurs many times in P. Wilbour. It seems improbable that the Naḥiḥu of P. Wilbour could be the same as that of P. British Museum 10447, since the Naḥiḥu of P. British Museum 10447 appears to have been located near Nefrusi in the Hermopolitan nome (XVth nome of Upper Egypt) which cannot have been the location of the Naḥiḥu of P. Wilbour.(25) Since Naḥiḥu was a very common personal name during the Ramesside Period, it would be quite reasonable to suppose that there may have been more than one locality with that name.

The mutual exclusivity of the four sections of Text A with their north to south geographic orientation, together with the south to north geographic orientation of the so-called "smaller" temples of the group Other Religious, provides at best a relative geography of place names for Text A. With so small an amount of the total available agricultural land of Middle Egypt accounted for in Text A of P. Wilbour (2.5% according to Fairman, see p. 23), numerous geographic locations have undoubtedly been passed over such that the distances between otherwise unknown localities are all but impossible to estimate. Within the paragraphs belonging to individual domains, a relative geography probably does apply, each subsequent measurement area probably being somewhat south of (or at least on a parallel with) the one which precedes. We can say very little, however, about the relative location of the individual plots enumerated within the series of entries headed by a single measurement line because of our ignorance of the surveying methods which underlie the sequence of the individual plots. The precise location of successive measurement areas, and within them of individual plots, is and will continue to be a tantalizing but unsolvable problem without more precise knowledge of the most elementary principles of surveying and recording utilized by the Ramesside assessors.(26)

(3) Apportioning and Non-Apportioning Paragraphs

The paragraphs of Text A are of two varieties distinguished from each other by differences both in form and content. The "non-apportioning" paragraph is easily identified by the consistent occurrence of three figures written in red in each assessment line. The entries of the "apportioning" paragraphs, on the other hand, take several formats with combinations of red and black figures predominating such that there is no possible confusion with non-apportioning entries. Non-apportioning paragraphs appear to deal solely with land cultivated collectively on behalf of a land-owning institution by unidentified field-labourers under the direction of a special class of ỉḥwtyw individually identified in these paragraphs and held responsible for the cultivation of the plots assigned to them. The apportioning paragraphs appear to deal solely with land leased (?) by the institution to individual smallholders who paid over to the institution so small a "rent" as to be relatively independent. Menu in her study of P. Wilbour uses the terminology "paragraphes normaux" and "paragraphes de répartition" to distinguish the two types of paragraphs.(27)

Apportioning paragraphs are often immediately identifiable by the occurrence of the word pš in the paragraph heading in the phrase šmw pš or rmnyt pš. The land-owning institution is generally identified by name in a previous (non-apportioning) paragraph heading. In the case of the temples of the group Other Religious, however, the paragraph heading consists solely of the name of the institution. It is the format of the quantitative data which follow in the subsequent assessment lines which identifies these paragraphs as apportioning paragraphs. Gardiner translates the phrase rmnyt pš (n pr pn) as "apportioning domain (of this house)," while Menu translates the phrase "district de répartition (de cette maison)." Gardiner's translation of the alternate phrase "šmw pš (n pr pn)" as "apportioned harvest-taxes (of this house)" is paralleled by Menu's translation of the phrase as "district de répartition soumis à la taxe de moisson."

The heading of the paragraph is followed by one or more "measurement lines" which provide the locality with reference to which one or more plots were situated. The measurement line is in turn followed by a single line or series of assessment lines identifying the individual smallholder(s) by name and occupation together with specifications of the plot(s) he or she cultivated.

The quantitative data of the apportioning entries take several formats: (1) three figures, the first black and the second and third red (Gardiner's Variety I); (2) four figures, the first black, the second also black, and preceded by what is apparently an explanatory sign ⌋ in black, and followed by two figures in red as above in (1) (Sub-variety IA); (3) two black figures separated by a ditto dot (Variety II); (4) one black figure followed by an explanatory phrase (Sub-variety IIA); and (5) one black figure followed by an explanatory phrase but measured in a different unit from that of (4) (not formally categorized by Gardiner).

Variety I is the most common format of assessment in the P. Wilbour apportioning paragraphs, there being 1193 entries of this format. Variety I entries consist of three figures, the first in black ink and the remaining two in red ink (here denoted by underline):

A66,35 .5.$\frac{1}{2}$ mc. $1\frac{2}{4}$
A32,24 .3 ar..$\frac{1}{4}$, mc. $1\frac{2}{4}$
A17,38 arouras 3 ar..$\frac{1}{2}$, mc. $1\frac{2}{4}$

The figure in black represents the size of the plot measured in arouras (1 aroura = 2/3 acre). The second figure in red ink is also a value in arouras, although consistently very much smaller than the first figure, while the third figure, also in red ink, is a measure of grain which is invariably written (i.e., $1\frac{2}{4}$ per aroura). The red aroura figure is likely to be the assessed part of the plot to which the rate $1\frac{2}{4}$ mc. applies. Although the measure signified by the sign is undoubtedly to be understood as khar (ḫ3r) rather than oipĕ (ỉpt), Gardiner renders it simply "measure of capacity" (abbreviation "mc.") in order to remain neutral as to which interpretation of the sign is correct. This practice is retained in the present study because of its familiarity, even though it is now evident that the unit of measure is the khar. The black aroura figure is occasionally preceded by the word "aroura" (st3t), but more often than not, a little black "ditto dot" is entered serving to repeat the measure of the preceding line. The black aroura figure ranges between 1 and 110 arouras, plots of 3 or 5 arouras being the most frequent. The red aroura figure has most often the values ¼, ½, or 1 aroura, although figures of 2 arouras or more will occur if the black figure is 10 arouras or more. In Variety I entries (so too Sub-variety IA below), the hieratic numerals for "1" (sometimes), "2," "3," and "4" (always) are supplied with a hook at the top left (so for "4") wherever the unit aroura is intended.(28) Gardiner's translation employs the abbreviation "ar." wherever the word "aroura" is indicated by the hook. The word "aroura" is written out in full, however, wherever the hieratic employs the full writing of the word ().

Sub-variety IA is a variant of Variety I of which there are 247 examples. The first black figure in these entries is separated from the first red figure by the appearance of a second black figure preceded by the sign. This sign is most often written by the first scribe very much like a right angle with a shorter vertical member, but sometimes with an angle very much less than a right angle, e.g., in A31,18. The second scribe, however, writes this sign quite differently (). This sign is followed by values ranging from 1 to 20, 5 being the most common value, e.g.:

A17,12 20 5.$\frac{1}{4}$, mc. $1\frac{2}{4}$
A54,9 .20 10.$\frac{1}{2}$, mc. $1\frac{2}{4}$
A60,23 40 arouras 10.$\frac{1}{4}$, mc. $1\frac{2}{4}$

The hieratic numerals "1" and "2" following this peculiar sign have the same hook with which figures meant to be understood as arouras are furnished in Variety I and Sub-variety IA entries.

Of the several possible interpretations of the sign which Gardiner suggests, only one merits consideration in view of his belated realization that the hook which is attached to the values following the sign ⅃ signifies a value in arouras. The only plausible interpretation Gardiner suggests is that the sign ⅃ is a precursor of the Greek sign for subtraction which is customarily written as a precise right angle.(29) If Gardiner's interpretation is correct, the sign ⅃ might signify a portion of the plot to be excluded in the calculation of expected revenue, or an amount of land which is no longer part of the parcel the original size of which is indicated by the black aroura figure. Menu's radically different interpretation of the sign ⅃ , however, views the sign as signifying the actual size of plot of two or more equal size Variety I plots located in the same measurement area, having the same assessment (red (aroura) figure), and cultivated by the same smallholder condensed in a single assessment line as a sort of shorthand in which the initial black aroura figure totals the combined area of the shorthanded entries.(30) The relative merits of these and other possible interpretations will be assessed in the concluding chapter of this study.

The 217 examples of Variety II entries consist of two black figures, the first preceded by either the word "land-cubit" (mḥ-t3) or the familiar black ditto dot which recalls the previously mentioned land measure; while the second figure is always preceded by the black ditto dot:

A23,19	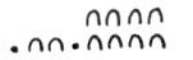	.20.80
A86,20		.4.20
A86,6		land-cubits 4.20

Variety II entries differ from Variety I and Sub-variety IA entries in that there is no figure in red to indicate an assessment value or an assessment rate. Yet the division of the plot into two very unequal parts reflects some fiscal purpose even though there is no indication of any revenue to be paid on these plots. The implication seems to be that were these plots to be taxed, this is the division on the basis of which revenue owing would be calculated. The fact that there is no red ink in these entries strongly suggests that Variety II entries were not subject to the fiscal operation applicable to the aroura measured plots. If anything, they appear to be almost incidental to the enumeration of the aroura measured plots with which Text A is evidently primarily concerned.

A variant of Variety II referred to by Gardiner as Sub-variety IIA consists of a single black figure followed by one of the following four explanations:

(1) 	m šwt	"being dry"
(2) 	wšr (??)	"waterless??"
(3) 	wsf	"resting," "idle," "fallow"
(4) 	bw ptrỉ.f (?)	"not seen," "it was not seen" after two examples (A89,37; 90,34) where the penultimate sign is not, as usual, written in ligature with its neighbours.(31)

Some of these plots are identified as measured in land-cubits by the occurrence of the word mḥ-t3 as is also the case with some Variety II entries. Most of these plots, however, evidence the black ditto dot recalling the previously mentioned land measure. Sub-variety IIA plots, moreover, are generally of a size that can be easily divided into two components as in the case of Variety II plots. Thus, in A6,22 ".50 wsf," the plot could be divided as "land-cubits 10.40" as in the preceding Variety II entry A6,21. Similarly, in A6,x+8.9, the plots identified as ".100 wsf" could be easily divided as ".20.80" as in the preceding Variety II entry A6,x+7. The ease with which these divisions may be executed is further evidence of the likelihood of the correct classification of such plots as land-cubit measured. If the plots of the Variety II entries are correctly interpreted as assessed (but not taxed) land-cubit measured plots, plots of Sub-variety IIA are probably correctly identified as unassessed land-cubit measured plots.

There are also entries which resemble the entries of land-cubit measured Sub-variety IIA where the value "3" is written with the hook which elsewhere signifies a plot measured in arouras (either Variety I or Sub-variety IA) as in A75,45-47. It would seem, therefore, that these entries do not belong to land-cubit measured Sub-variety IIA, but to a separate category altogether. Gardiner suggests that the values "5" and "10" which occur in supposed Sub-variety IIA entries in close proximity to the hooked hieratic "3's" should also perhaps be interpreted in terms of arouras, although he refrains from identifying them as such in his translation.(32) He also suggests that the isolated cases of unassessed plots with the value "5" and multiples of 5 short of 100, which are interspersed among long runs of aroura measured Variety I and Sub-variety IA entries, may also be aroura measured. In the present study, all entries which resemble land-cubit measured Sub-variety IIA entries, but could conceivably be aroura measured, are relegated to a separate category designated Variety I/II to which there is no equivalent in Gardiner's typology. These entries number 277, while entries which can be more or less unequivocably categorized as Sub-variety IIA number 210.

There are also some entries which consist solely of a single black figure without comment or explanation. It is probable that such entries should be interpreted as incomplete entries. In A28,13-16, for example, one entry of 200 land-cubits is followed by another entry of ".200" and two entries of ".500," the accompanying ditto dots indicating that they should be interpreted in terms of land-cubits (the preceding unit of measure):

A28,13-16	The controller Pḥenu land-cubits	200
	Another measurement (made) [for him]	.200
	Another measurement (made) for him	.500
	Another measurement (made) for him, m šwt	.500

Since these figures are relatively large, they are unlikely to be incomplete writings of either Variety I or Variety II. Their relative size in combination with the occurrence of the words m šwt in A28,16 suggests that these are unusual examples of land-cubit measured Sub-variety IIA.

Gardiner points out in his Commentary that the use of the terms sṯ3t (aroura) and mḥ-t3 (land-cubit) throughout Text A is sparse and erratic. He notes, however, that "prior to col. 96 sṯ3t is never attached to any type of assessment except I - including pōsh-entries of Type B- and IA, and that from beginning to end of Text A mḥ-t3 is never attached to any type of assessment except II and IIA" (referring only to lines in which these words are actually written). Moreover, he continues, "if the dots presumed to be equivalent to 'ditto' were interpreted quite strictly in every case, it would be easy to prove that both varieties and both sub-varieties of assessment could be calculated either in arouras or in land-cubits, but the result of such an inference would be devastating, and would destroy any hope we may have of finding any intelligible motive at all for the assessments."(33) Thus, it is certainly unwise to rely entirely upon the scribes' use of the dots to make sound judgments concerning their application. It would appear, therefore, as Gardiner himself points out that as a rule it is the form of the assessment, rather than the entry's position with respect to the last-named unit of area that should guide the reader with respect to the unit intended.

Of the two scribes, the first is certainly the more reliable. While sparing in his use of both units of measure, the first scribe inserts them, for the most part, with discernible forethought. It is evident, however, that he tends to insert the word sṯ3t much less frequently than the word mḥ-t3. On the basis of the work of the first scribe, Gardiner compiled a useful list of motives for the insertion of a unit of measure:

(1) Because the preceding assessment was, or must be presumed to have been, in terms of the other unit.
(2) Because a line of measurement has immediately preceded and broken the sequence of assessments.
(3) Because the entry in question consists of two lines, so that the assessment itself falls beneath a word not part of an assessment.
(4) Because the entry stands at the top of a column.
(5) Where no reason can be assigned.(34)

In the case of the second scribe, however, the insertion of the words for both land-cubit and aroura is much less reliable. This scribe shows a strong predilection for the word sṯ3t, inserting it in long sequences of Variety I and Sub-variety IA entries where the unit of measure is never in doubt (col. 68, l. 20 onward and cols. 96-97). On the other hand, he avoids the insertion of the word mḥ-t3. Simple error probably is the explanation for two occurrences of the word sṯ3t (A97,10.23) where the data consist of two black figures separated by a black dot as in Variety II entries. The first scribe, on the other hand, never inserts the word sṯ3t in Variety II entries. The combinations of values which occur in these two entries ("4" and "8"; "10" and "40") are found to occur in the work of the first scribe with the word mḥ-t3 actually inserted (A18,1; 38,22; 17,46). The value "4" in A97,10, moreover, lacks the hook which signifies a value in arouras. It is probable, therefore, that simple error is the logical explanation for the occurrence of the word sṯ3t in these two cases.

A key characteristic of the apportioning paragraphs is the enumeration of a large number of smallholders who appear to have cultivated their allotted plots in the manner of virtual owners (Stuchevsky's "private possessors"). The names of these individuals are preceded by their respective occupations of which there are 54. Clerical occupations include (ordinary) priest (wʿb), god's father (ỉt-nṯr), and prophet (ḥm-nṯr) with specific mention of the high priest of Amūn and the high priest of Heliopolis (wr m3w "Greatest of Seers"). There are many stablemasters (ḥry ỉḥ) attested, many of whom were probably connected with the Royal Residence (n ḫny sometimes appended) and employed by the military in times of war. Among the military occupations attested are those of soldier or infantryman (wʿw), charioteer (kṯ), adjutant of chariotry (ỉdnw n tnt-ḥtr), quartermaster (?) (3tw), shieldbearer (ḳrʿ), swordbearer (?) (ḫpšy), and Sherden (Šrdn). Few skilled craftsmen are represented, there being only one example each of builder (or potter) (ỉḳd), carpenter (ḥmww), coppersmith (ḥmty), weaver (sḫty), alabaster worker (?) (šsy), and three occurrences of embalmer (wtw). While there are many occurrences of individuals identified simply as ỉḥwty with several possible connotations (see below), there are considerably fewer occupations of a pastoral nature, the most frequently occurring of which is herdsman (mnỉw). Also relating to the raising of livestock, but occurring only infrequently are the occupations fattener of cattle (wš3 ỉḥw), head of the cow-stable (ḥry mḏwt), and shepherd (mnỉw sỉw). Among the professional occupations represented are those of physician (swnw), scribe (sš) (of the army, temple, Treasury, etc.), and controller (rwḏw). There are also numerous women smallholders (e.g., A47,34; 57,20ff.) as the term ʿnḫ(t) n nỉwt 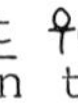 "lady" or "citizeness" indicates. These women may have been the widows or daughters of deceased smallholders as Menu suggests, but there is also the very real possibility that some of these women may have been smallholders in their own right rather than simply by title of inheritance.(35) The role of women in the Nineteenth Dynasty Inscription of Mose is persuasive evidence that women played a significant active role in the ownership of landed property (see chapter 7 (9)(a)).

Occasionally, deceased individuals are recorded as smallholders in Text A (e.g., A25,9; 34,51). In some of these entries, the occurrence of the phrase m-ḏrt msw.f suggests the inheritance of a plot by unidentified siblings as in A52,54; 53,4; and 56,42. Other entries are accompanied by the phrase 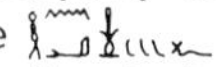 ḥnʿ snw.f(s) which Gardiner renders "together with his (her) brethren" (e.g., A32,41; 42,33; 44,19.32 and feminine ending A36,23.24). This phrase also suggests the division of an estate among siblings after the death of the parents. Sometimes a plot is indicated as having been registered formerly in the name of (wn (m) rn n) an individual other than the present smallholder as in A46,40-41; 47,29-30; 57,3. This notation probably reflects the transfer of the rights and obligations of tenancy from one individual to another where the two parties probably were not related. Very frequently, a plot is recorded in the name of one individual but cultivated by another party, possibly a sublessee, the preposition m-ḏrt "by the hand of" preceding the name and occupation of the second party. This type of entry is most common with persons of high rank or prestige such as the first prophet of Amūn (ḥm-nṯr tpy) in A32,51, the high priest of Heliopolis ("Greatest of Seers") in A34,49, the vizier (ṯ3ty) in A92,27, and a Royal prince (s3 nsw) in A37,14-15. Other such instances of the delegation of responsibility occur in association with individuals whose status or wealth is not so easily ascertained as, for example, with charioteers and scribes. Very often Sherden occur as the surrogate cultivators (A42,27; 44,24; 48,45-46; etc.). Occasionally, however, no second party is identified, the preposition m-ḏrt having the suffix f, i.e., "by his (own?) hand" referring back to either the individual just named (i.e., "for his (own?) benefit") or the preceding smallholder.

Non-apportioning paragraphs commence with a heading which identifies the land-owning institution as in §7 "[THE SUNSHADE of Re]-Ḥarakhte which is in Ninsu." This line is followed by a measurement line which in turn governs subsequent assessment lines so as to read: "[MEASURE]MENT made in the Pond of Iia's Tomb: [Plot (cultiva]ted by) the ỉḥwty Raʿmosĕ 10, mc. 5, mc. 50." There is often only one plot of land entered under each measurement area. Moreover, the ỉḥwty identified in one measurement line was probably held responsible for the cultivation of the plots enumerated in one or more subsequent assessment lines as is indicated by the presence of the pronomial suffix f in the word ỉḥt.f. The ỉḥwtyw identified by name were evidently the individuals held responsible for producing the grain revenue of these plots. They are certainly to be distinguished from the chief administrators whose names are preceded by the preposition r-ḫt "under the authority of" in the headings of the non-apportioning paragraphs. These ỉḥwtyw are also to be distinguished from the ỉḥwtyw who are relatively independent smallholders of plots enumerated in the apportioning paragraphs, but probably were on the same footing as the individuals (mostly ỉḥwtyw) who cultivated the plots which are the subject of the corresponding Pōsh A and B entries (see below).

Of the 279 paragraphs in Text A, 156 are non-apportioning paragraphs, while 116 are apportioning paragraphs. Another 7 paragraphs make up a third category and are referred to by Gardiner as "harem" paragraphs because they concern landholdings of the Royal harems.(36) Non-apportioning paragraphs are found in association with a wide variety of institutions. All but one (§162) of the paragraphs devoted to the "Sunshades of Re-Ḥarakhte" (šwt Rʿ-Ḥr-3ḫty) and those devoted to "Tabernacles" (sšm-ḫw) are non-apportioning paragraphs as are paragraphs headed "The god of Usimaʿrēʿ-meriamūn" (§§71-74). Also non-apportioning are the paragraphs pertaining to Royal landholdings described as the minĕ-land and khato-land of Pharaoh. Two paragraphs pertaining to the Treasury of Pharaoh (§§196-97) and one devoted to the Royal harems (§39) are also non-apportioning as are paragraphs pertaining to the Houses of the King's (Great) Wife (§§109, 172, 276 with the exception of §153 which is apportioning). Apportioning paragraphs, on the other hand, include those pertaining to the Fields of

Pharaoh (§§86, 156, 242) and Landing-Places of Pharaoh (§§84, 85, 154, 155, 241 with the exception of §37). The 10 "white goat" paragraphs and the 24 "herbage" paragraphs are also numbered among the apportioning paragraphs.

(4) The Corresponding Pōsh A and B Entries; Pōsh C Entries

There are among the paragraphs of Text A three special applications of the word pš which are relevant to this discussion. These usages are called "Pōsh entries" by Gardiner and are of three types: Pōsh A, Pōsh B, and Pōsh C.(37) Pōsh entries are to be distinguished from the Pōsh headings which govern paragraphs and read "Apportioning domain (ṛmnyt) (of)," or "Apportioned šmw (of)." Pōsh A entries, of which there are 151 in Text A, occur only in non-apportioning paragraphs and are generally the concluding lines of a non-apportioning paragraph. For each Pōsh A entry there is a corresponding Pōsh B entry. Some Pōsh A and B entries, however, are incomplete or lacking altogether in the document as we have it today.

The corresponding Pōsh A and B entries record a transaction between two institutions which, according to Menu's novel interpretation of these entries, recognizes the indebtedness of one institution to another with the sum of that indebtedness actually stipulated in each of the corresponding entries, albeit expressed differently.(38) The "debtor" institution, the name of which occurs in the heading of the non-apportioning paragraph to which the Pōsh A entry belongs, is the owner or virtual owner of a plot the data of which (size, rate, estimated yield) are given in red in the Pōsh A entry. The debtor institution owes to the "creditor" institution an amount of grain measured in sacks which is specified in the second line of the Pōsh A entry together with the name of the creditor recipient. The creditor institution, the name of which occurs in the heading of the paragraph to which the corresponding Pōsh B entry belongs, receives an amount of grain from the debtor institution of the Pōsh A entry which is implied in the second line of the Pōsh B entry. The amount of grain received is identical with that of the Pōsh A entry, but is not expressed in sacks per se and needs to be extrapolated from the Pōsh B data by process of multiplication:

Pōsh A (A29,33-34)

Plot (ỉḥt) (cultivated by) the ỉḥwty Benenka 10, mc. 5, mc. 50
Apportioned for the House of Osiris, Lord of Abydus, sacks 3¾

Pōsh B (A37,32-33)

The ỉḥwty Benenka in apportionment of land (cultivated for) (m pš n ỉḥt) The Mansion in the House of Amūn, ' (in the) domain (under the authority of) the controller Merymāʿě .10.2½ AR., mc. $1\frac{2}{4}$

In this example, cited by both Gardiner and Menu, the temple of Medīnet Habu (Menu's "temple débiteur") owns a plot of 10 arouras the yield of which is estimated at the rate of 5 mc. per aroura for a total of 50 mc. This temple, however, owes 7.5% of this amount (apparently a fixed rate) or $3\frac{3}{4}$ sacks to the House of Osiris at Abydus ("temple créancier"). This amount of $3\frac{3}{4}$ sacks is recorded in the second line of the Pōsh A entry so that, according to Menu, it may be deducted from the taxable income of the debtor institution, the temple of Medīnet Habu, at the time of the collection of tax due on net taxable income from the various institutions. The Pōsh B entry records the payment of the 7.5% debt ($3\frac{3}{4}$ sacks) so that it may be added to the net taxable income of the temple of Osiris, but since the data of the Pōsh B entry are made to conform to the format of the ordinary apportioning entries, the figure of $3\frac{3}{4}$ sacks as such does not appear in the Pōsh B entry. The amount of $3\frac{3}{4}$ sacks must be obtained from the data of the Pōsh B entry by multiplying the red (aroura) figure by the rate $1\frac{2}{4}$ mc. The two entries have in common the identical size of plot and location of plot (the latter according to the measurement lines governing each of the corresponding entries). The size of plot differs in the Pōsh A and B entries only in that it is written in red in the Pōsh A entry, but in black in the Pōsh B entry. Thus, the corresponding Pōsh entries appear indeed to constitute a type of double-entry bookkeeping as Gardiner himself suggested.(39)

How exactly are the data of the corresponding Pōsh entries related to each other? In all but 8 of the 118 Pōsh B entries with Pōsh A counterparts, the red rate of the Pōsh A entry is 5 mc. per aroura as in the above example. Where the rate of the Pōsh A entry is 5 mc., the area in arouras given as the red aroura figure in the Pōsh B entry when multiplied by the rate $1\frac{2}{4}$ mc., the invariable rate of the apportioning entries, yields the number of sacks in the corresponding Pōsh A entry. Furthermore, the red aroura figure of the Pōsh B entry is exactly one-quarter the value of the initial black aroura figure of the Pōsh B entry. The relationship between the Pōsh A and B entries in these cases may be expressed in the form of Gardiner's equation:

$$5n \times \frac{3}{40} = n/4 \times 1\frac{2}{4}$$

where n equals the basic number of arouras and $\frac{3}{40}$ (7.5%) equals the fraction which the sack figure (A) constitutes of the value of the third red (mc.) figure of the Pōsh A entry.(40)

The rates $7\frac{2}{4}$ and 10 mc. per aroura rarely occur in the non-apportioning entries, there being just 25 cases of the rate $7\frac{2}{4}$ mc. and 16 cases of the rate 10 mc. with fewer yet examples of combination rates. Only a very few of these cases occur in Pōsh A entries, two of which (A17,6 and 18,36) have no corresponding Pōsh B entries. Nevertheless, on the basis of only 8 cases, Gardiner was able to make the following generalizations.(41) First, where the Pōsh A rate is 10 mc., the red aroura figure of the Pōsh B entry equals one-quarter (¼) the value of the preceding black aroura figure, but unlike in the case of the Pōsh A rate 5 mc., this red figure when multiplied by $1\frac{2}{4}$ mc. does not yield the value of the sack figure in the corresponding Pōsh A entry. When the rate is $7\frac{2}{4}$ mc. or a combination of rates, the red aroura figure of the Pōsh B entry is neither one-quarter the value of the preceding black aroura figure, nor does it yield the amount of sacks in the Pōsh A entry when multiplied by $1\frac{2}{4}$ mc.

While Gardiner's detailed examination of the eight cases of corresponding Pōsh A and B entries does not resolve the anomalies he describes, it does suggest some possible explanations of these anomalies one of which Menu believes is the probable solution to the curious arithmetic. Menu gives serious weight to the unique occurrence of the Pōsh B rate 3 mc. in A76,5, the importance of which Gardiner himself only half realized. She expresses the view that the assessors whose records (papyri, potsherds) were utilized by the scribes of P. Wilbour thought it advisable in the case of Pōsh B entries where the rate underlying the Pōsh A percentage was higher than 5 mc. to call attention to both the source of this income and the rate underlying the Pōsh A percentage ($7\frac{2}{4}$ mc. or 10 mc.) by adjusting the invariable Pōsh B rate $1\frac{2}{4}$ mc. in the Pōsh B entry. In order to do so, they divided the number of sacks in the Pōsh A entry by 3 rather than $1\frac{1}{2}$ to obtain the red aroura figure of the Pōsh B entry, and multiplied the red aroura figure of the Pōsh B entry by 3 rather than $1\frac{1}{2}$ to obtain the number of sacks in the Pōsh A entry. The scribes of P. Wilbour, she continues, having been far less well-versed in the peculiarities of the fiscal system to which these records belonged, erroneously corrected the rate 3 mc. per aroura to the usual rate $1\frac{2}{4}$ mc. which they were so accustomed to writing. Fortunately for us, however, they overlooked one entry--that of A76,5--and left it intact. She concludes that these eight cases aside, "on peut affirmer que les entrées 'pš' de Type A et les entrées 'pš' de Type B sont deux expressions distinctes d'une seule et même obligation."(42) The amount of grain paid by the temple débiteur of the Pōsh A entry to the temple créancier of the corresponding Pōsh B entry had to be simultaneously recorded as both an item of income for the temple créancier and a deduction for the temple débiteur in the calculation of net taxable income by the authorities responsible for the assessment detailed in P. Wilbour.

Menu also concludes that the cause for the indebtedness of the one institution to the other in the corresponding Pōsh entries which gave rise to the payment recorded so curiously in these entries as a sort of double-entry bookkeeping was probably the hiring out of the services of staff of the creditor institution in order to improve the productivity of the plot owned by the debtor institution rather than the rental of the plot per se. The latter possibility is improbable as it necessitates the identification of the institution named in the heading of the corresponding apportioning paragraph as the land-owning institution, since that temple is the recipient of the grain specified in the non-apportioning paragraph. Such a view does not accord with the understanding of the plots detailed in the non-apportioning paragraphs as "terres détenues en toute propriété par les temples." Moreover, she adds, temples and secular institutions did not exercise true ownership rights over the apportioning domains, but rather a sort of "suzerainty" over their inhabitants.(43)

Fairman's comments upon the so-called anomalous cases should also be taken into consideration since they bring to bear data of Text B which are relevant, at the very least, to the Pōsh A and B entries involving khato-land.(44) Fairman's contention is that the red aroura figure of the Pōsh B entry is the assessment on the plot as a whole expressed in terms of "newly cultivated land" (nḫb-land) regardless of the actual quality of the soil of the plot. When the actual plot consisted of "ordinary arable land" (ḳ3yt-land) or "newly cultivated land," the first red figure of Pōsh B invariably constitutes one-quarter of the total plot size. When "tired-land" (tnỉ-land) or a combination of varieties of land were at issue (the "mixed" plots), however, the red aroura figure of the Pōsh B entry does not equal one-quarter of the total area unless the size of plot has been converted into the equivalent of nḫb-land. Fairman supports this view with evidence from Text B.

In recent years, Stuchevsky has reconsidered the problem of the corresponding Pōsh A and B entries.(45) He offers a new formula to express the relationship between the Pōsh A and B entries to replace Gardiner's formula 5n x 3/40 = n/4 x 1½ which holds true only in those corresponding entries where the land in question was ḳ3yt-land, the "standard average grain harvest" (yield) of which was calculated as 5 sacks per aroura. Stuchevsky's formula applies to plots assessed at 7½ sacks per aroura (tnỉ-land) as well as plots assessed at 10 sacks per aroura (nḫb-land). In this formula, the value n/4 is replaced by (1k + 1.5t + 2n)/4 where k = ḳ3yt-land, t = tnỉ-land, and n = nḫb-land. Stuchevsky's complete formula for expressing the relationship between Pōsh A and B entries is therefore:

7.5% (5k + 7½t + 10n) = (1k + 1.5t + 2n)/4 x 1½.

In this formula, the invariable Pōsh B rate 1½ "mc." must be interpreted in terms of the sack (ẖ3r) as also the rate and expected yield of the plot in the Pōsh A entry. Stuchevsky goes on to explain the anomalous cases of corresponding Pōsh entries which so troubled Gardiner. Stuchevsky asserts that the plots in question were not reduced to the rate of ḳ3yt-land, but rather to that of nḫb-land such that it is necessary to multiply the usual rate 1½ sacks of the Pōsh B entry by 2 in order to obtain the rate of 3 sacks per aroura which when multiplied by the red aroura figure of the Pōsh B entry equals the number of sacks in the second line of the Pōsh A entry (7.5% of the expected yield). The formula obtained for these special entries therefore would be

(0.5k + 0.75t + 1n)/4 x 1½ x 2.

Stuchevsky understands the plots of the non-apportioning entries as collectively cultivated plots which were fully taxable. He uses the relationship between the corresponding Pōsh A and B entries to infer that the general rate of assessment was actually 30% of the standard average grain harvest. In the case of plots of ḳ3yt-land in the corresponding Pōsh A and B entries, the area of the plot subject to taxation (the red aroura figure) was only one-quarter (¼) of the total area of the plot (the black aroura figure). When the red aroura figure is multiplied by the Pōsh B rate $1\frac{2}{4}$ sacks per aroura, the product equals 7.5% of the standard average grain harvest specified in the third red figure of the Pōsh A entry. This percentage is expressed in sacks in the second line of the Pōsh A entry where it is said to be "apportioned for (pš n)" the institution of the corresponding Pōsh B entry. Were the plot fully taxable, the tax would be four times as great as the sack figure stipulated in the corresponding Pōsh A entry and would amount to 30% of the standard average grain harvest. Thus, (p/k) x $1\frac{2}{4}$ = (100/5) x $1\frac{2}{4}$ where p = the taxable portion of the plot and k = the rate of assessment of ḳ3yt-land. Stuchevsky uses data of the P. Wilbour harem paragraphs (e.g., A43,11), where it can be established that the harems paid to the State one-third ($\frac{1}{3}$) of their harvest, to prove that a general tax rate of 30% is valid. The actual cultivators, therefore, had to pay 30% of the yield of their plots to the State. The number of sacks specified in the second line of the Pōsh A entry is understood by Stuchevsky as an administrative fee which was transferred to the service personnel of the institution that actually administered the plot by an "agent of the fisc" or "pseudo-cultivator" as he understands ỉḥwty in this context. Stuchevsky carefully distinguishes such ỉḥwtyw from both ordinary unidentified field-labourers (also called ỉḥwtyw) and those ỉḥwtyw who occur as smallholders or "private possessors" in the apportioning entries (exclusive of Pōsh B entries).

Stuchevsky's interpretation of the data of the corresponding Pōsh A and B entries opens the door to a considerably different interpretation of the economic structure underlying the data of not only P. Wilbour, but also various contemporary and near-contemporary economic texts. We look forward to the forthcoming article by Janssen for a detailed presentation of Stuchevsky's ideas.(46)

We now come to the last of the special Pōsh entries--the relatively rare Pōsh C entries of which there are 37 interspersed among the apportioning entries of Text A. Sixteen of these entries occur in association with Theban temples, while eight occur in association with secular institutions. Pōsh C entries appear to have no connection with adjacent lines. They are very often found to follow immediately upon an indication of the place of measurement (A17,9; 37,23; 45,18) or even fall between two such lines (A23,30; 95,31.33). An example of a Pōsh C entry is:

A36,36 Apportioned for Amūn of the City, (cultivated) by the hand of (m-ḏrt) the slave Tjatj, 10 ⌋ 5.$\frac{1}{2}$, mc. $1\frac{2}{4}$

The initial pš in these entries is almost always followed by the preposition n introducing the name of a local deity. Only rarely is it followed by the name of a private individual--a vizier in A90,13 and A76,13-14 and an unidentified dispatch-writer of Pharaoh (sš šʿt n Pr-ʿ3) in A36,41.

Gardiner suggested that the sole function of the formula pš n in these 37 cases may have been to stress the difference in the status of the local deities and officials of high rank vis-à-vis the ordinary smallholders of the apportioning entries.(47) This explanation does not, of course, explain why a vizier and a dispatch-writer of Pharaoh should be so honoured while high status individuals such as the first prophet of Amūn, the high priest of Heliopolis, and a Royal prince should be relegated to the "ordinary" apportioning entries. This approach presumes that the plot rather than the grain produced by the plot was apportioned for the various cults and two high-ranking officials. Menu's assessment of these entries is similar to Gardiner's.(48) She concludes that these entries record small parcels of land cultivated probably in large part by priests and prophets on behalf of local forms of the major Egyptian deities such as Amūn of the New Land (A17,9), Ḥatḥōr of (Pen-)Shōs (A61,9), and Seth of the Dyke (A37,23), the sanctuaries of which not only did not possess fields in their own right as did the temples of the non-apportioning paragraphs, but also did not always merit permanent clerical staff. Stuchevsky, on the other hand, views the initial pš n as signifying that an amount of grain rather than an amount of land has been apportioned for a local sanctuary or high official by a "private possessor" whose name is introduced by the preposition m-ḏrt "by the hand of."(49) This is not the place to discuss the relative merits of these conflicting interpretations, but rather to identify interpretations which have substance and should be kept in mind in evaluating data of chapters 4-6.

A final point which requires mention in this brief synopsis of Text A concerns the amount of land involved in the 279 paragraphs of Text A. A calculation of the number of arouras involved in the enumeration of plots in Text A, such as that undertaken by Fairman, establishes the fact that Text A is concerned with only a very small percentage of the available agricultural land.(50) The figure of 2.5% derived from Fairman's calculations of the total amount of land under assessment in Text A of the total cultivable land as represented by the northern half of Minia Province and all of Beni Suef Province (the Fayyūm excluded for lack of reliable statistics), is such a very small percentage of the whole that, even allowing for a considerable margin of error in the figures, the amount of land recorded in Text A is still a very small percentage of the total available agricultural land in Middle Egypt during the Ramesside Period. Adding to this figure the land with which Text B is concerned, barely 4.6% of the total agricultural land is accounted for.

Assuming that the land detailed in Text A was owned by or entrusted to temples and other institutions, with the exception of a relatively small amount of khato and minĕ-land, we have yet to account for a staggering percentage of the agricultural land of Middle Egypt. It has long been generally accepted that private ownership of land, or at least something very close to the private ownership of land as we know it, existed during the New Kingdom.(51) It is highly unlikely, however, that all the agricultural land of Middle Egypt unaccounted for in P. Wilbour is to be summarily assigned to the private sector. For that matter, it could be said on the basis of present knowledge that it is highly unlikely that even 50% of the cultivable land in Middle Egypt was at this time in private hands. The amount of Crown-land in Text A as represented by khato and minĕ-land, on the other hand, is so negligible as to be outright suspicious. It is likely, therefore, that we should be prepared to raise the Crown component of agricultural lands substantially. Stuchevsky's very different conception of P. Wilbour as a document which records nothing but State-owned property (temple land viewed as a variety of State property which also included so-called "Crown-land") is one way of dealing with such questions, but does not explain why so little of the cultivable land in Middle Egypt at this time shows up in the records of P. Wilbour.(52)

Many years ago, Fairman suggested as a solution to these difficulties the idea that the cultivable land assessed in Text A was sharāḳi-land under summer cultivation. Fairman argued that the date of the assessment is incompatible with present day knowledge of the schedule and procedures of land-survey and assessment, and concluded that P. Wilbour is concerned with fields under summer cultivation which would normally be harvested in August. According to Fairman, such lands would have been largely berm-lands, lands on the sloping banks of the Nile, and possibly also some land along canal-banks, i.e., what today is known as sharāḳi-land. This hypothesis is based upon evidence from P. Sallier IV, vs. 10,1-13b,7 concerning threshing activities carried out on "the great threshing-floor of the high-land (ḳ3yt)" between the 26th day of the second month of 3ḫt and the 12th day of the fourth month of 3ḫt in year 3 of Merenptaḥ (ca. July 18 to September 3).(53) Baer's doubt concerning the relevance of the practice of summer cultivation to the context of P. Wilbour is based in part on his rejection of Fairman's other two supports for his hypothesis, the Ḥeḳanakhte Papers and the Inscription of Rekhmirēʿ, but is also based upon his belief that the addition of privately owned land "would substantially increase the amount of land under cultivation at the time that P. Wilbour was assessed and raise the proportion substantially over that listed by Fairman as normal for summer cultivation."(54)

An alternate approach to this problem in P. Wilbour is, of course, to view the document as an enumeration of cultivated land of a particular legal or administrative status such as required a separate listing. This line of thought gives rise to a number of possible explanations for the inclusion of these particular plots in the P. Wilbour assessment records which will be explored in the present study.

NOTES

[1]P. Wilbour is dated to year 4 of Ramesses V by an allusion to the "Mansion of Millions of Years of Ramesses-Amenḫikhopshef-meriamūn" as the "Mansion of Pharaoh" in corresponding Pōsh entries (see in §58 (A25,21) the corresponding entries A25,26 = 38,38; 26,4-5 = 34,20; in §214 (A76,27) see A76,34 = 83,22; 76,37 = 85,42-43). In the Ramesside Period, it was already customary to refer to the reigning king as "Pharaoh." See Gardiner, Commentary, p. 10 and nn. 1-2.

[2]The question of whether or not the institutions, religious and secular, to which the plots of Text A are ascribed technically "owned" these plots outright with full ownership rights, or merely administered them, is addressed by I.A. Stuchevsky in his study of P. Wilbour (see below n. 46). Stuchevsky's premise is that the plots enumerated in P. Wilbour were owned by the State such that "temple land" was merely a variety of State land and "private ownership," as we know it, did not exist. While this is a very important issue, its resolution is not prerequisite to a statistical analysis of the data of the Text A apportioning paragraphs. The validity of Stuchevsky's interpretation does, of course, make considerable difference in the general understanding of P. Wilbour and land tenure in general in ancient Egypt, and must be considered a very real alternative to the understanding of the ancient Egyptian economic system prevalent to date among Egyptologists in the West. While the present study retains the term "land-owning institution" in both variable labels and general discussion, the author acknowledges that it is certainly conceivable that the institutions of P. Wilbour were not "absolute" land-owners, but rather "virtual land-owners." As such, they may have exercised considerable authority over the landed property entrusted to them by the State. The familiar term "Crown-land" is also retained in the present study, but understood as denoting a specific variety of State land, which was under the aegis of Pharaoh as the titular head of the State, and administered by various civil and religious officials.

[3]Gardiner in his Commentary, pp. 9-10, calculated the date of P. Wilbour as roughly July 17 to August 8 (Julian), a period of 23 days, on the basis of the dating of year 4 of Ramesses V to 1158 B.C. Now there is reason to think that year 4 of Ramesses V corresponds to 1142 B.C., the date of P. Wilbour therefore recalculated as July 2-24 (Gregorian). Jac. J. Janssen provides this information in his forthcoming article in JNES.

[4]Gardiner, Synopsis, §§137-38, pp. 144-45 and §69, p. 135. Although the name of the temple in §137 reads: "The Mansion of the King of Upper and Lower Egypt Usimaʿrēʿ-meriamūn in the House of Amūn," the royal name should be emended to read "Usimaʿrēʿ-setpenrēʿ" (Ramesses II), the paragraphs thus pertaining to the Ramesseum rather than the funerary temple of Ramesses III at Medīnet Habu.

[5]Gardiner, Commentary, pp. 4, 9, 11. Since the first column of which fragments have been preserved also appears to have been the first column when the document was complete, as suggested by the occurrence of a free space of 5 cm. before that column, it is possible that the first half of Section I was contained in a separate roll.

[6]W. Erichsen, Papyrus Harris I: Hieroglyphische Transkription [Bibliotheca Aegyptiaca V], (Brussels, 1933). See also Herbert D. Schädel, Die Listen des grossen Papyrus Harris: Ihre wirtschaftliche und politische Ausdeutung [Leipziger

Ägyptologische Studien 6], (Glückstadt-Hamburg-New York, 1936).

[7]§75 The Mansion of the King ʿAkheperen(?)rēʿ in the House of Amūn. This may have been a funerary foundation of Tuthmosis II (or Amenophis II if the royal name is to be emended). See Gardiner, Synopsis, §75, p. 136.

[8]Gardiner, Synopsis, §§58, 60, and 70, pp. 132-33, 135. Note that the temple (pr) of Ḥaremḥab which is the subject of §70 is probably to be identified with the temple remains located near the IXth Pylon at Karnak.

[9]Gardiner, RAD, pp. vi-vii, 1-13; idem, "Ramesside Texts Relating to the Taxation and Transport of Corn," JEA 27 (1941), pp. 37-56, pl. 7.

[10]Gardiner, Commentary, p. 12 and Synopsis, §144, p. 145.

[11]Gardiner, Synopsis, §§76, 79, pp. 136-37. Note that the Mansion of Merenptaḥ-ḥotp(ḥi)māʿĕ in the House of Rēʿ occurs only in a non-apportioning paragraph (§79) in P. Wilbour.

[12]Gardiner, Synopsis, §232, p. 153 and also §240, p. 154.

[13]Gardiner, Commentary, p. 16.

[14]Ibid., pp. 16-17 with n. 3, p. 16. Note the case of §262 pertaining to the "Image of Usikhaʿaʿrēʿ-setpenrēʿ-meriamūn which is in Menʿonkh."

[15]Bernadette Menu, Le régime juridique des terres et du personnel attaché à la terre dans le Papyrus Wilbour (Lille, 1970), pp. VIII, VIII n. 4, 19, 26-30, 31, 33, 34, 36, 38, 43, 45, 46, 47, 52, 53, 54, 55, 96, 97, 98, 157, and passim in her translations.

[16]Gardiner, Commentary, pp. 18-19.

[17]Ibid., p. 20.

[18]Menu, Le régime juridique, p. 52.

[19]Gardiner, Commentary, p. 22.

[20]The "scribe of the granary of Pharaoh" who appears in §124 would support the interpretation of srw as "State officials" rather than "temple officials." The cases of ạn overseer of the granary, a (former) overseer of cattle, and a ỉdnw (twice) in §§56, 135, 212, and §215 are less certain in interpretation. See Gardiner, Commentary, p. 22.

[21]Ibid., pp. 22-23.

[22]Ibid., pp. 36-37.

[23]Ibid., Table I, p. 15 and Map I after p. 54.

[24]Ibid., Table II, after p. 36.

[25]Gardiner, JEA 27, p. 59, n. 5; idem, RAD, pp. 59, 5.9.

[26]Wolfgang Helck, Materialien zur Wirtschaftsgeschichte des Neuen Reiches II, Akademie der Wissenschaften und der Literatur in Mainz [Abhandlungen der Geistes- und Sozialwissenschaftlichen Klasse Jahrgang 1960, Nr. 11] (Mainz, 1961), pp. 298-329. Here Helck attempts an ingenious (and, of course, hypothetical) reconstruction of the geography of the text.

[27]Menu, Le régime juridique, p. VIII n. 4.

[28]Gardiner, Commentary, p. 212. The exceptional treatment of the numeral for "1" probably results from the fact that when the hook was added, confusion with the hieratic form of the numeral "5" was very likely and possibly inevitable. See p. 212 for examples of questionable readings.

[29]Ibid., p. 92.

[30]Menu, Le régime juridique, pp. 103-7.

[31]Gardiner, Commentary, pp. 94-95.

[32]Ibid., pp. 214-15.

[33]Ibid., pp. 96-97.

[34]Ibid., p. 97.

[35]Menu, Le régime juridique, p. 112, and also pp. 76, 130.

[36]Gardiner, Commentary, pp. 18, 55-56; Synopsis, §§38, 110, 277 (Memphis); §§39, 111-12, 278-79 (Mi-wĕr). Paragraph 39, however, is a non-apportioning paragraph unlike the other harem paragraphs.

[37]Ibid., pp. 57-59, 72-74, 87-90.

[38]Menu, Le régime juridique, pp. 83-91.

[39]But see William F. Edgerton, Review of Alan H. Gardiner, The Wilbour Papyrus, 3 vols. (Oxford, 1941-48) in JAOS 70 (1950), pp. 301-3.

[40]Gardiner, Commentary, p. 101.

[41]Ibid., pp. 101-2.

[42]Menu, Le régime juridique, p. 89.

[43]Ibid., pp. 89-91. See too Wolfgang Helck, Zur Verwaltung des

Mittleren und Neuen Reiches [Probleme der Ägyptologie ed. Hermann Kees, III] (Leiden-Cologne, 1958), p. 129.

44 H.W. Fairman, Review of Alan H. Gardiner, The Wilbour Papyrus, 3 vols. (Oxford, 1941-48) in JEA 39 (1953), pp. 120-23.

45 I.A. Stuchevsky, "Data from the Wilbour Papyrus and Other Administrative Documents Relating to the Taxes Levied on the State ('Royal') Land-Cultivators in Egypt of the Ramesside Era," Vestnik drevnei historii (1974), pp. 3-21 with English summary, pp. 20-21. This summary has been supplemented with material from the forthcoming article by Jac. J. Janssen in BiOr. See below n. 46.

46 Jac. J. Janssen, "Agrarian Administration in Egypt During the Twentieth Dynasty," review and summary of I.A. Stuchevsky, Zemledel'tsy gosudarstvennogo khozyaistva drevnego Egipta epokhi Ramessidov (The Cultivators of the State Economy in Ancient Egypt During the Ramesside Period) (Moscow, 1982) forthcoming in BiOr.

47 Gardiner, Commentary, p. 59.

48 Menu, Le régime juridique, p. 149.

49 Janssen, forthcoming in BiOr.

50 Fairman, JEA 39, pp. 118-20.

51 Klaus Baer, "The Low Price of Land in Ancient Egypt," JARCE 1 (1962), pp. 25-45.

52 It is possible that Stuchevsky has addressed this question in material not presently available to the author.

53 Fairman, JEA 39, pp. 119-20. Since year 3 of Merenptaḥ is now thought to be 1209 B.C., the dates would be August 5 to September 20 (Gregorian). These new dates actually strengthen Fairman's argument (so Jac. J. Janssen, private correspondence, March 1986). Note that the day by day calendar itself ends at the third month of 3ḫt, day 29 (vs. 13b,7). The date, fourth month of 3ḫt, day 12, occurs in vs. 10,5 of P. Sallier IV.

54 Baer, JARCE 1, p. 40, n. 98.

2 Statistical Measures and Tests

(1) The Use of the Statistical Method in the Analysis of the Data of P. Wilbour

As the preceding chapter has indicated, a vast amount of socio-economic data can be extracted from the data of P. Wilbour concerning occupations; the social composition of neighbourhoods; plots of cultivable land, their varieties, locations, sizes, crops, and assessment; the administration of cultivable land; the interrelations between and among religious and secular institutions; cults of major and minor deities as well as the funerary cults of kings; and so on. When properly analyzed and cautiously interpreted, these data will add greatly to our understanding of the ancient Egyptian economy.

Statistical analysis allows the social scientist to take up vast quantities of raw data, such as those of P. Wilbour, not only for purposes of describing coherently the underlying trends, patterns, and relationships which are discernible, but also to express the results in terms of probabilities. When coping with a vast quantity of data not merely insufficiently analyzed,(1) but also virtually unique within the field,(2) a tool is required which is capable of disentangling the complexity of the mass, separating out interwoven strands and determining, as far as possible, how each relates to the other and to the whole. Only when this sort of tedious and exacting exercise is completed can we hope to apply the special knowledge of our discipline to interpret and expand upon the bare outlines provided by the statistical method.

(2) Measuring Socio-Economic Variables

There are two types of variables encountered in the study of any socio-economic data: quantitative variables and qualitative variables. Both types of variables may be defined as any object or event which can vary in successive observations either in quantity or in quality.

Quantitative variables are those variables which can take on various magnitudes, i.e., variables which exist in greater or smaller amounts. The size of plot or the size of assessment are examples of quantitative variables which may be identified among the data of P. Wilbour. A quantitative variable may be measured in terms of any of a large number of possible units, each resulting magnitude of which is called a variate. In the case of P. Wilbour, we encounter quantitative variables measured in arouras and land-cubits. The series of variates of each quantitative variable may be arranged in order of magnitude from lowest to highest, smallest to largest or vice versa.

Qualitative variables, on the other hand, do not vary in magnitude, but rather in quality or kind. These "qualities" are called attributes. Thus, variable 3 Institutional Group, for example, includes the attributes "Theban," "Heliopolitan," "Memphite," "Other Religious," and "Secular," while variable 15 Type of Land includes the attributes "pʿt," "ỉdb," and "Neither." Since these attributes cannot be arranged in order of magnitude, they may be considered in whatever sequence is most useful and convenient to the researcher.

It is important to bear in mind that some variables seem to belong to both categories of variables as, for example, variable 7 Occupation or Title of Smallholder. On the one hand, this variable is clearly a qualitative variable with attributes which are not intrinsically measurable in units in the way size of plot, for example, can be measured in terms of arouras or land-cubits. On the other hand, it is possible to rank the attributes of this variable on the basis of external criteria, perhaps social prestige. Since such a ranking is not intrinsic to the attributes to which it is applied, it merely reflects the separable social values that often adhere to them.

Quantitative variables are of two varieties, continuous and discrete. A continuous (quantitative) variable is a variable which can take on any value on its range. That is to say, in the measurement of a continuous variable, the range over which the characteristic extends may be imagined as divisible into smaller and smaller intervals theoretically without end ("theoretical indivisibility"). The size of a plot is an example of a continuous variable which may be identified among the data of P. Wilbour. Discrete (quantitative) variables, on the other hand, are restricted to isolated values on their ranges as, for example, the population of smallholders in Text A which is expressed in the form of integers obtained by "counting heads." It should be noted, however, that a discrete count is exact only when it is on a sufficiently limited scale of human observation and not subject to rapid change. In the case of a variable such as Individual Smallholder, as in most social research, what appear to be "exact counts" are really only approximations because of the mutability of human life and the technical impossibility of obtaining "exact counts." Thus, the terms "discrete" and "exact" are not at all interchangeable. The difference between discrete and continuous in a statistical context lies in the nature of the data rather than in the degree of accuracy, the latter subject at all times to human error.(3)

There are two types of data grouping in statistical analysis which correspond to the two types of variables, quantitative and qualitative. In quantitative grouping, variates are grouped into ordered class intervals, while in qualitative grouping, attributes are distributed among classes which are exhaustive and mutually exclusive. Thus, the sizes of aroura measured plots may be grouped into any convenient number of graduated intervals as, for example: .01 aroura to 5.0 arouras; 5.01 to 10.0 arouras; 10.01 to 15.0 arouras, if the grouping of such data proves useful. The classification of plots according to the type of institution, religious or secular, however, is by definition two-fold such that the sequence of the categories is of no consequence.

(3) Measures of Central Tendency: Averages

In dealing with quantitative data, it is necessary first to organize the material into a frequency distribution, and then to summarize the data in a single value which is representative of the values in the distribution. If such a value is to be representative of the set of observations, it must be a value at which the data have a tendency to concentrate, i.e., the value must be a central value which is most representative of the aggregate. Such a central value resulting from the efficient condensation of quantitative data is referred to as a measure of central tendency.

The average is a central value around which the values of the distribution cluster. It is the most common locational value after the extremes, the minimum and the maximum. There are several differently defined averages which express different aspects of central tendency. The most commonly used average is the arithmetic mean (or simply mean $\bar{X}$). The mean is the sum of the observed values divided by the number of observations summed. The concept of mean revolves around the idea of variates in a distribution as deviations from a central norm which is considered the true value. The deviations on both sides of the central value constitute departures or errors from that norm. From this point of view, the mean is considered the true value. The true value emerges when the deviations cancel each other out (i.e., when their net value is zero). If there were no errors in the distribution, we would observe the true value. Thus, the mean is defined as the value which would occur if all the values in any given aggregate were equal.

The arithmetic mean, however, is not a universally applicable average. It reflects the magnitude of every observation and is therefore said to be sensitive to extreme values. This sensitivity to extreme values makes it of doubtful value in some situations. If a distribution contains extreme values, the mean will be "pulled" toward these values and so lose its typicality as a measure of central tendency. The greatest advantage of the mean, however, is that it can be used as a basis for a number of valuable computations such as variance and standard deviation which will be examined later in this chapter.

The median is another average which is useful in describing and understanding distributions of quantitative data. It is the value that divides a set of observations ordered with respect to the magnitude of values so that the number of items above it is equal to the number of items below it. The median is therefore called the "position average." The great utility of the median in contrast to the mean lies in the fact that it is the most representative average of any distribution. This is because the aggregate distance between the median and each of the values in the distribution is less than from any other point.

The mode of a distribution is that value obtained most frequently in a series of observations, i.e., the value at which the concentration of items is most dense. The mode is also called the probability average because it is the most probable value in any given distribution. While the mode provides the most probable value in the distribution, it does not reveal the degree of probability of that value. A second limitation lies in the fact that the mode is not easily manipulated (i.e., does not lend itself to algebraic manipulation) and cannot be used as a basis for further computation as the mean can be. Since it is influenced by the interval width employed, the mode may also be said to lack stability. The usefulness of the mode, however, in many ways outweighs its disadvantages provided that it is used in conjunction with other measures of central tendency. The modal value is appropriate where it is important to know the predominate class, size, or quantity. The mode is also significant as the only average applicable to qualitative variables.

(4) Comparison of the Averages

The choice among mean, mode, and median as an appropriate measure of central tendency must be made on the basis of three criteria:

(1) the purpose for which the data are assembled;
(2) the pattern of the data distribution; and
(3) various technical considerations (arithmetical) which restrict the choice of average.

The first criterion is self-explanatory. The second, however, requires some comment. If a distribution is symmetrical, i.e., has values distributed identically on either side of the mean, the mean, mode, and median are identical:

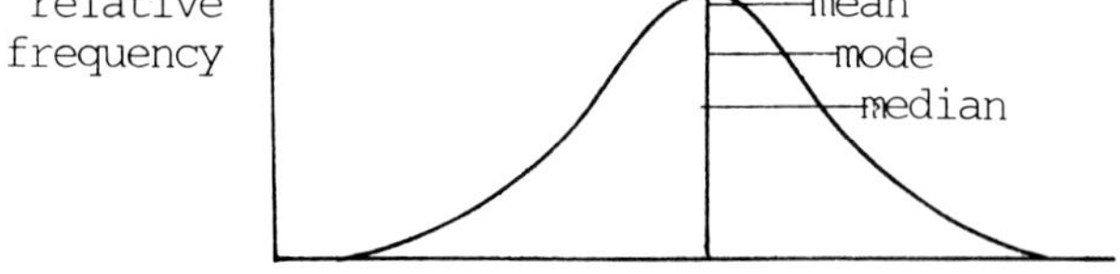

As the distribution becomes more and more skewed (i.e., lacking in symmetry), the three averages continue to diverge more and more until the mean loses its typicality altogether. At such a point, the mode and the median are more meaningful measures of central tendency. A skew to the right or "positive skew" would result in divergent values with the longer tail to the right:

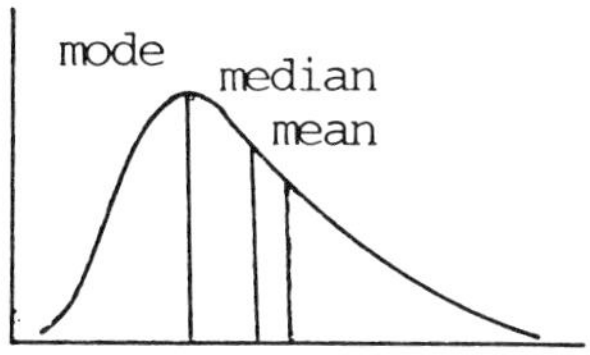

A skew to the left or "negative skew" would result in precisely the opposite order of averages:

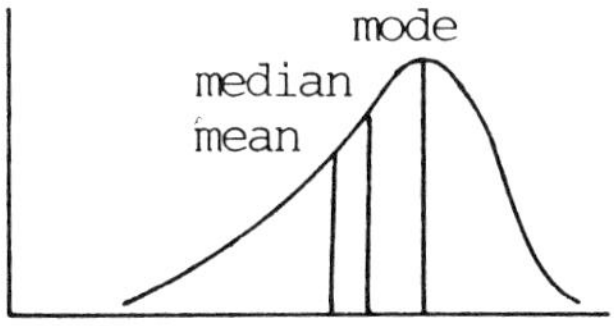

In a skewed distribution, the mode is not influenced by the flanks of the distribution. The mean, however, being sensitive to each individual value, is pulled in the direction of the extreme values. The median, in turn, is pulled toward the tail of the distribution by the relative frequency of the values in that tail, although the attraction is limited by the relative sparsity of items in the tail. While it does not matter which average is used in the case of a perfectly symmetrical distribution, since all averages have the identical value, most distributions we encounter are somewhat positively or negatively skewed. Thus, it is important to keep in mind what each measure of central tendency reveals about the distribution. In dealing with a distribution which is not perfectly symmetrical, it may be more useful to use the mode or median, since the arithmetic mean becomes less and less representative of central tendency as the degree of skewedness increases. Where a measure of the highest frequency (i.e., typicality) is desired, the mode is the most appropriate measure of central tendency; where a measure of the middle position (relative position) of the range of the variable is desired, the median is the most appropriate measure of central tendency; and where the "true value" of a distribution is required, the mean is the most appropriate measure of central tendency.

The last two measures of location or central tendency used in this study are the measures of the extreme values, the maximum and the minimum. The maximum as a measure of location or central tendency is that value below which lies the remainder of the values in the distribution. Similarly, the minimum is that value above which lies the remainder of the values in the distribution. Neither the maximum nor the minimum are complicated values to compute or to interpret.

(5) Measures of Variation or Dispersion

Once the averages have been determined, it is necessary to

consider the degree of variation among the observed values in the distribution. If there is a relatively low degree of variation among the observed values, a high degree of uniformity among the items in the distribution is indicated such that the values are considered to be homogeneous. If, on the other hand, there is a relatively high degree of variation, a low degree of uniformity among the values in the distribution is indicated such that the data are considered to be heterogeneous. No dispersion whatever would indicate perfect uniformity, all items in the distribution having the same value (i.e., the "ideal condition").

There are two ways of measuring the degree of variation among values in any distribution. These measures are called the parameters of the distribution:

(1) measures of range including all or a specific percentage of the items; and
(2) measures based upon deviations of variates from a central value.

The simplest and crudest measure of variation is the total range (or simply range). The range of a distribution is that interval which encompasses all the values in the distribution, i.e., range is the difference between the highest and lowest values of the distribution. This parameter is most useful in situations where the purpose of investigation is to determine the extent of the extreme variations. What, for example, is the range of plot size in the case of Variety II plots? What is the range of plot size in the case of Sub-variety IA plots? The disadvantages of range, however, are considerable. Since range depends solely upon the highest and lowest values, it is by definition sensitive to unusual values in the series which are by nature infrequent, erratic, and unstable. Therefore, range by itself gives an inadequate impression of the volume of variation. What is required is a parameter which is less likely to be upset by extreme values. Moreover, range does not provide measurement of the variation of values and gives no indication of the pattern of variation.

One way to measure the degree of variation among observed values is to take variation as measured by deviations from a norm. In the case of a perfectly symmetrical (normal) distribution, it does not matter which measure of central tendency is used: mode, mean, and median all will have the identical value. In a distribution which is not perfectly symmetrical, however, where the three measures of central tendency are not identical, it becomes necessary to select the most representative value. The value most appropriate to normal or relatively normal distributions is, of course, the (arithmetic) mean. The resulting measure of deviation, the arithmetic deviation, is straightforward and easily calculated. Variation, however, is more commonly measured by squared deviations which are universally taken from the mean of the distribution. Squared deviations have a practical utility which is incomparably greater than that of simple (arithmetic) deviations. They may be expressed in three ways: as the sum of squares, as variance, and as standard deviation. Of these, the most useful are variance and standard deviation as they eliminate the variable factor of frequency which is a disadvantage of the sum of squares.

The variance of a set of measurements is the average of the squared deviations of the measurements from their mean. A small variance will indicate the relative homogeneity of data, values clustering closely about the mean; while a large variance will indicate the relative heterogeneity of data, values located far away from the mean. Standard deviation is the positive square root of the variance. Standard deviation is more convenient to use as a measure of variation than the variance because it is based upon the same units as the original variable and has therefore a more "intuitive" interpretation. A standard deviation of 10 years, for example, has more intuitive meaning than a variance of 100 "square years."

Both variance and standard deviation may be used to determine the relative variability of any two distributions. Thus, it is possible to determine whether, for example, Variety II plots (variable 28 Land-cubits Subtotal 11 and 12) vary more in size than Sub-variety IIA plots (variable 13 Land-cubits Single Figure); or whether the first component of Variety II plots (variable 11 Land-cubits First Figure) varies more in size than the second component of Variety II plots (variable 12 Land-cubits Second Figure). To answer such questions two statistical tests are available: Snedecor's F-test (Variance Ratio Test) and the Coefficient of Relative Variation (CRV or CV).

Snedecor's F-test compares the variance of one distribution with that of another in order to determine the statistical significance of the larger variance. If the statistical significance of the larger variance is upheld, the distribution with the larger variance is considered to be the more heterogeneous. The variance of one distribution may be compared with that of another distribution using the F-test provided two conditions are fulfilled:

(1) the observed measures have an absolute zero; and
(2) the observed means are of the same unit of measure.

Thus, the F-test can be used to compare the variability of the distribution of unassessed aroura measured plots (variable 10 Arouras Special Case) with that of assessed aroura measured plots (variable 9 Arouras), since both variable 9 and variable 10 are measured in arouras on a scale from zero to infinity. If, however, we wish to compare the variability of the distribution of an aroura measured variable with that of a land-cubit measured variable, the F-test of variance is not appropriate. Instead, we must use the Coefficient of Relative Variation. The CRV is a measure of relative variability obtained by norming the standard deviation on its origin, the mean. Thus:

$$CRV = (100s)/\bar{X} \quad \text{where } \underline{s} = \text{standard deviation}, \ \bar{X} = \text{mean of sample}$$

When the standard deviation of a distribution is small in comparison with a large mean and the resultant CRV value is relatively small, it can be said that there is great homogeneity of data such that the mean may be considered typical of the array of values. A theoretical CRV value of zero (0) would indicate complete homogeneity of data such that there is no variation and consequent complete typicality of the mean. A large CRV, on the other hand, indicates that there is great heterogeneity of data such that the mean is not at all typical of the array. CRV values in excess of 100 percent are indicative of increasingly skewed or abnormal distributions; the higher the CRV value, the more pronounced the skew. As the combination of a relatively small mean and a relatively large standard deviation in a distribution will tend to inflate the CRV, the CRV as a measure of relative variability should be abandoned in favour of Snedecor's F-test provided that the distributions we are comparing are measured in the same unit.

(6) The Uses of Standard Deviation

Standard deviation has been used for over 100 years as a means of measuring the dispersion or variation of values within a distribution. Using the standard deviation and the mean of a distribution, we may describe the distribution of any continuous variable in terms of what is called the Empirical Rule, provided that the distribution is a normal distribution, or sufficiently approaches a normal distribution to be identified as such:

(1) the interval $\bar{X} - s$ to $\bar{X} + s$ will contain approximately 68% of the measurements;
(2) the interval $\bar{X} - 2s$ to $\bar{X} + 2s$ will contain approximately 95% percent of the measurements;
(3) the interval $\bar{X} - 3s$ to $\bar{X} + 3s$ will contain approximately 99.7% of the measurements.

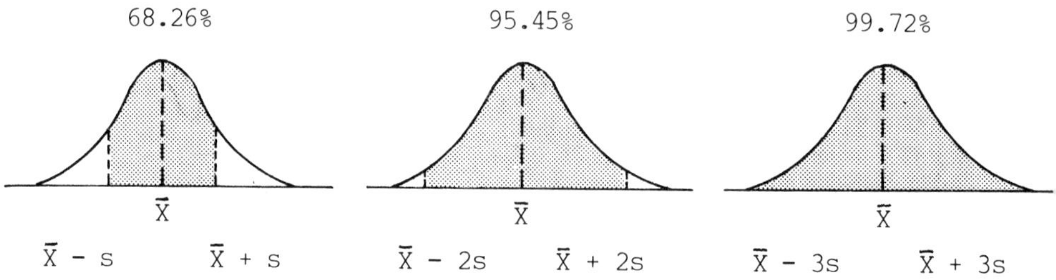

Thus, for every possible s distance from the mean, there is a corresponding percentage of area or "frequency." At one s distance from the mean, we leave behind 34% of the items; at 2s distances, we leave behind 48% of the items; and at 3s distances from the mean, we leave behind 49.8% of the items.

To determine whether a distribution is a normal distribution or sufficiently approaches a normal distribution to warrant description in terms of the Empirical Rule, the median or mode of the distribution is compared with the mean. One measure is enough, provided that the measure is used consistently. If the median or mode differs from the mean by less than the standard deviation, the distribution may be considered "normal."

(7) The Concept of "Confidence" and the Confidence Interval

In speaking of a measure of central tendency such as the mean, or a measure of variation such as standard deviation, or in using proportions to describe data, it is important to be aware that such figures are all estimates and, as such, must be viewed in perspective. The reliability of means, standard deviations, and proportions is closely related to the size of the sample under consideration and its typicality of the population it represents. In using such parameters of population, it is not a matter of an absolute value, but rather a range of values over which the estimate extends. This range of values is the range within which we have confidence that the particular parameter is actually located.

To convey the feeling of confidence with respect to a given range, we speak of an associated probability. This probability tells us to what extent it is believed that the parameter actually lies within the range computed. In a large sample, confidence in parameters such as the various averages, standard (and arithmetic) deviations, and proportions will be maximal. In a small sample, however, the reliability of these parameters will be questionable, not only because of the possibility of bias, but also because the average standard deviation or proportion in the sample may differ greatly from the true population parameters these measures estimate.

The case of P. Wilbour is certainly most unusual. This document constitutes the only sample of data from land registers long enough and complete enough to discuss and analyze with a reasonable degree of confidence in the results. It is, however, a sparse sample in that some of the variables analyzed are mutually exclusive, while others pertain to only a limited number of cases. It is also important to note that since the data of P. Wilbour are all that we have, they do not conform to the desirable procedure of random sampling. In random sampling, data are selected in such a way that every different sample of n elements in the population has an equal probability of being chosen. We are also not at all certain just what the data of P. Wilbour represent and what factors determined the inclusion of these particular plots in this document. For these reasons, it is necessary to approach the analysis with a degree of caution and reservation required by the limitations of availability sampling.(4) Because of the limitations of the sample, it is wise to subject the various parameters of the distributions to the process of estimation of confidence intervals. The estimation of confidence intervals for these parameters allows us to determine what degree of confidence we may have in their validity. Although confidence intervals can be constructed for both measures of central tendency and variation, the present study is restricted to the calculation of confidence intervals for the (sample) means.

The confidence interval of the mean consists of two figures called points of estimation, the higher of which is called the upper confidence limit and the lower of which is called the lower confidence limit. The computation of the upper and lower confidence limits based upon the mean of the sample (the apportioning data of Text A) allows us to state with confidence that in 95 times out of 100, the mean of the population (all apportioning data for the area of which P. Wilbour is the available sample) will lie between the points of estimation. The construction of confidence intervals enables us to use sample means to speak with considerable confidence about unknown population means.

(8) Measurement of Association

The concept of association in statistics is grounded in the principle of contingency. The principle of contingency holds that any event or happening in nature is the product of the joint operation of two or more elements, each of which contributes to some degree to the resultant observation. Factors of contingency promote the occurrence of events to varying degrees such that every outcome is modified either in character or kind as in the case of qualitative variables, or in magnitude as in the case of quantitative variables.

It is possible to make judgments concerning association by means of intuitive association, i.e., we observe the occurrence of an event, make note of what factors seem to play a role in the event, and then note with the successive repetition of the event how accurate we can be in forecasting the outcome by observing causal or linking factors. We note, for example, the frequency with which the occupation w῾w "soldier" occurs in joint association with zone 3 or with Variety I plots of 3 arouras. We cannot determine how strong the association is, nor can we tell which way the association goes, i.e., whether the occupation determines the zone or the zone determines the occupation. What we can establish, however, is whether the relationship between one variable and another is likely to be causal, one variable determining the value of the other, or the product of joint association with a third factor.

Precision is impossible to achieve solely on the basis of intuitive reasoning. Patterns of relationship can be so extraordinarily complex that a considerably more exacting and reliable test of association is required. Such a test must take into account the following points:

(1) every event is the outcome of multiple factors;
(2) the force of these respective factors varies in intensity;
(3) the effect of an increase or change in any given factor may be either to promote or to inhibit the event in question;
(4) the separate factors may reinforce, counteract, or cancel one another;
(5) the effect of one factor may be to serve as a "catalyst" or inhibitor of the effects of another;
(6) the event may feed back on the factors that produced it; and
(7) one may assume that an event is affected by a given factor

when, in fact, it is the other way around.(5)

There are two indications of the association of variables which should be noted:

(1) the relative frequency with which certain attributes happen together (the principle of joint occurrence); and
(2) parallel changes in two or more series of quantitative observations (the principle of covariance).

The first of these indications of association is clear enough, "statistical variables, like human beings, usually are judged 'by the company they keep.'"(6) The second pertains only to quantitative variables where a unit change in one variable is paralleled with some degree of regularity by a comparable unit change in the other variable.

The first step in discussing association between variables is to ask the question: is the alleged association between two variables a real association, or is it merely an illusory association due to chance? In other words, are the values displayed statistically significant? First, it is necessary to establish the reality of the association and then, and only then, attempt to measure the degree of association and derive conclusions from that measurement.

In order to test the statistical probability of association between variables, the test statistic chi-square (χ^2) is employed. This application of the versatile chi-square statistic is known as the Test for Independence or the Pearson Test for Association after Karl Pearson, the mathematician who first described the distribution of chi-square at the turn of the century.(7) This test allows us to confirm or deny the test or "null hypothesis" that the two variables are independent of each other. If we reject this null hypothesis, we tacitly accept the alternate hypothesis that association is indeed present, the observed frequencies highly unlikely under the null hypothesis.

In order to test the null hypothesis that the two variables are independent of each other, we decide upon the level of risk we are willing to accept that we are falsely rejecting the null hypothesis that the two variables are independent of each other. We call this level of risk the significance level of the relationship. It is customary in social science research to accept a significance level of .01 or .05. A significance level of .01 means that we take the risk of 1% that we are falsely rejecting a true null hypothesis of statistical independence. In other words, there is a 1% risk that the relationship we observe occurred simply by chance as opposed to a 99% probability that the observed relationship is indicative of a systematic, statistically significant relationship between the variables. The smaller the level of significance, the smaller the chance of falsely rejecting a true null hypothesis. But, by decreasing the risk of rejecting a true null hypothesis, we increase the risk of failing to reject the null hypothesis when it is false. In order to resolve this problem, it is necessary to consider the probable consequences of being wrong in either direction. Generally speaking, if in rejecting the null hypothesis and therewith confirming the alternate (substantive) hypothesis, a new series of more intensive studies will be undertaken to clarify and extend the line of reasoning on which the study was originally based, the researcher is probably justified in taking a high risk of erroneous rejection. Subsequent study will bear out his mistake in rejecting the null hypothesis. But, if the false rejection of the null hypothesis will lead to action that will not in itself establish his error, the researcher is justified in requiring that the null hypothesis be rejected only if there is a very small chance of doing so erroneously. The convention of setting the level of significance at .05 or .01 is considered appropriate in those instances where the null hypothesis opposes the alternate (substantive) hypothesis. It should be set aside, however, when there are clear justifications for taking a greater or lesser risk.(8)

Although chi-square can be used to determine whether or not the relationship between two variables is statistically significant with specific probabilities attached, it is not in itself a direct measure of the degree of association. The significance level indicates only the percentage of probability that direct association is operative between two variables. For a measure of the actual degree of association present, we use the bivariate statistic Cramer's V.

Cramer's V is a bivariate statistic which is a slightly modified version of the older statistic phi (ϕ) applicable only to two by two (2 x 2) crosstabulations. Cramer's V adjusts phi for either the number of rows or the number of columns in the table, depending upon which of the two is smaller. Cramer's V takes on the value of zero where there is no relationship between the variables. Its upper limit is +1 when there is a perfect association between two variables; i.e., when it is possible to predict the category of the one variable with prior knowledge of the category of the other variable with no possibility of error. The higher the Cramer's V value, the higher the degree of association between the variables. Cramer's V, moreover, is the only measure of association which is applicable to qualitative variables of which the P. Wilbour variable list is largely comprised. It is important to keep in mind, however, that while Cramer's V is a valuable measure of the degree of association between variables, it does not reveal the manner in which the variables are associated. Thus, it cannot tell us whether the variables are interdependent or which variable determines the values of the other variable.

NOTES

[1]Up until now, no thorough statistical analysis of P. Wilbour has ever been undertaken. Gardiner's publication of the text is mostly a descriptive study in the course of which many interesting points have come to light which bear further detailed examination. The

more recent study of Menu, Le régime juridique des terres et du personnel attaché à la terre dans le Papyrus Wilbour, (Lille, 1970), explores the juridical aspects of the text. An English summary of I.A. Stuchevsky's recent study of P. Wilbour, Zemledel'tsy gosudarstvennogo khozyaistva drevnego Egipta epokhi Ramessidov (The Cultivators of the State Economy in Ancient Egypt During the Ramesside Period) (Moscow, 1982), by Jac. J. Janssen is shortly to appear in BiOr.

[2]P. Wilbour is the only Ramesside text of its kind with the possible exception of the Louvre Leather Fragments. These fragments are of limited use for comparative study because of both sheer brevity and the poor state of preservation. A post-Ramesside text, P. Prachov, published with a photograph by Turaev (Papyrus Prachov [Zapiski Vostočnogo Otdeleniya Russkogo Arkheologičeskogo Obščestva 12] (Leningrad, 1927)), appears to be a government document similar to P. Wilbour and must be studied in detail before any meaningful comparisons can be made. The photographs in Turaev's publication, however, are very poor and cannot be used to any worthwhile results. P. Reinhardt (P. Berlin 3063), also a post-Ramesside hieratic text with similarities to P. Wilbour, has been studied by Malinine and Parker, whose preliminary remarks appear in Akten des 24. Internationalen Orientalisten-Kongresses, 1957, pp. 78-80.

[3]J. Mueller, K. Schuessler, and H. Costner, Statistical Reasoning in Sociology, 2nd. ed. (Boston, 1970), pp. 11-12.

[4]Ibid., pp. 350-51. "Availability sampling" is often the only alternative to abandoning an inquiry altogether. It is widely used in sociological studies and considered "quite legitimate, so long as the inferences drawn from (it) are accompanied by reservations which are made necessary by the ill-defined relation between universe and sample."

[5]Ibid., p. 240.

[6]Ibid., p. 241.

[7]Ibid., pp. 432-37.

[8]Ibid., pp. 400-1.

3 Computer Operations

(1) Coding Criteria and Method

The 2245 apportioning entries analyzed in this study have been considered with an eye to identifying variables which can be compared and evaluated.(1) The aim of the study is to make responsible and statistically significant generalizations concerning the data of the P. Wilbour apportioning paragraphs and to speculate with reasonable certainty on the ramifications of the analysis. The consideration of these massive data begins with a clear definition of the variables as they occur in P. Wilbour either explicit or implicit in the data of the apportioning paragraphs. Although the variables number 1 through 46, there are only 36 variables in the present variable list. Three variables have been deleted from the original list because of unresolved difficulties in the classification of data, while two others were deleted when it become evident that the subtotals and grand totals they provided were unlikely to have any meaning in the context of the document.(2)

All 36 variables do not apply to each and every apportioning entry. Some variables apply to only a small number of entries, while other variables, especially quantitative variables, are mutually exclusive. Not all of the variables in the variable list, however, will be analyzed in the present study. Variable 32 Name of Smallholder and variable 4Ø Individual Smallholder will be considered in a separate study after due consideration is given to the tables generated by the present study.

The following is a list of the variables as defined in the present study in the sequence of their coding for computer input:

(a) Variables Coded in the Data File

(1) Section of Text (Geographic Zone)
(2) Format of Entry (Variety I, Sub-variety IA, Variety I/II, Variety II, Sub-variety IIA)
(3) Institutional Group (Theban, Heliopolitan, Memphite, Other Religious, and Secular)

(4) Land-owning Institution
(5) Deity or King
(6) Geographic Location (Measurement Area)--see recoded variable 31
(7) Occupation or Title of Smallholder
(8) Name of Smallholder--see recoded variable 32
(9) Arouras (initial black aroura figure in Variety I and Sub-variety IA entries--data of the two formats separately computed in some analyses)
(10) Arouras Special Case (single black aroura figure in Variety I/II entries)
(11) Land-cubits First Figure (Variety II entries)
(12) Land-cubits Second Figure (Variety II entries)
(13) Land-cubits Single Figure (Sub-variety IIA entries)
(14) Assessed Arouras (red aroura figure in entries of Variety I and Sub-variety IA)
(15) Type of Land (p‛t, ỉdb, Neither)
(16) Occupational Group (Crafts, Military, Agriculture, Animal Husbandry, Administration, Religious, Domestic, Other)
(17) Special Entry (ḥnk, 3ḥt n ḥtrỉ, mḥt, and w3ḏ)
(20) Type of Pōsh Entry (Pōsh B, Pōsh C, Neither)
(21) Type of Apportioning Paragraph (Herbage, White Goat, šmw pš, rmnyt pš, None of These)
(22) Dual Geographic Location A (the first of two measurement areas)
(23) Dual Geographic Location B (the second of two measurement areas)
(31) Geographic Location (Measurement Area)--recoded variable 6
(32) Name of Smallholder--recoded variable 8
(46) ⌟ Figure

(b) Computed Variables (variables derived from coded data)

(18) Institutional Class (Secular or Religious)
(19) Type of Religious Institution (Funerary or Ordinary Cult)
(27) Grand Total Arouras 9 and 10
(28) Land-cubits Subtotal 11 and 12
(29) Grand Total Land-cubits 11, 12, and 13
(33) Percentage of Assessment 1 (V14/V46 x 100--Sub-variety IA only)
(34) Sex of Smallholder
(37) Percentage of Assessment 2 (V14/V9 x 100--Variety I only)
(38) Grand Total Land 27 and 29/100
(39) Dynasty of Founding of Land-owning Institution (Eighteenth Dynasty, Nineteenth Dynasty, Twentieth Dynasty, Undated)
(40) Individual Smallholder
(43) Land Measure I Arouras or Land-cubits (Variety I, Sub-variety IA, Variety II)
(44) Land Measure II Arouras or Land-cubits (Variety I, Sub-variety IA, Variety I/II, Variety II, Sub-variety IIA)
(45) Type of Aroura Measured Entry (Variety I or Sub-variety IA)

The sequence of the above variables was originally designed to move from the general to the specific, related variables occurring in adjacent columns as, for example, variable 3 Institutional Group and variable 4 Land-owning Institution. Over the course of the long and tedious coding procedure, however, new variables were added and existing variables refined such that the logic of the original sequence of coding was disrupted.

A brief perusal of the variable list discloses the fact that most of the variables are qualitative variables, while relatively few variables are quantitative variables. Some qualitative variables such as variable 18 Institutional Class and variable 19 Type of Religious Institution were added to the variable list after the coding of the data had been completed by extrapolating data from variables with more specific categories (variable 3 Institutional Group and variable 4 Land-owning Institution). Variable 6 Geographic Location (Measurement Area) and variable 8 Name of Smallholder were coded with the first eight letters of their respective categories. These eight character codes were discontinued, however, when the analysis was transferred to the more flexible and widely used package program SPSS (see below). The eight letter codes were then transformed into numeric codes of up to three digits to meet the technical requirements of SPSS. Variable 31 Geographic Location and variable 32 Name of Smallholder, therefore, are not additional variables, but rather recoded variables which utilize numeric codes for the actual geographic locations and names of smallholders of which they are comprised.

Only seven quantitative variables were actually coded in the data file: aroura measured variables 9, 1Ø, 14, and 46 and land-cubit measured variables 11, 12, and 13. The remaining quantitative variables were obtained by a combination of, or computation upon two or more of the original seven variables as, for example, variable 28 Land-cubits Subtotal 11 and 12 which represents the sum of the values of land-cubit measured variables 11 and 12. Of the seven coded quantitative variables, a maximum of three will occur in any one entry: variable 9 Arouras, variable 46 ⌋Figure, and variable 14 Assessed Arouras. No one entry will contain values for both aroura measured variables 9 and 1Ø, or all three land-cubit measured variables (11, 12, and 13); nor will a single entry contain values for one or more aroura measured variables in combination with one or more land-cubit measured variables.

Each and every entry will be lacking data of a number of variables, both quantitative and qualitative. This is due in large part to the mutual exclusivity of some quantitative variables. There are also instances where the data of one or more qualitative variables are lacking without signifying an accidental omission or loss of data. Such data may be lacking simply because they do not pertain to each and every entry as, for example, variable 17 Special Entry; or because these data were either not known to, or considered necessary by the two scribes who recorded the entries in the version of the document we have today. Missing data may also be the result of a break in the text or the illegibility of signs. Fortunately, since the document has been relatively well-preserved, these difficulties are largely limited to the beginning of Section I of Text A. Lost too are the paragraphs pertaining to Crown-land at the very end of Section IV.

Most qualitative variables have codes of only one or two characters (numeric, alphabetic, or a combination of both). Only in the case of variables 6 and 8 are there codes in excess of two characters. The codes for these two variables preserve the initial eight letters of the personal name or geographic location. Codes of this length were used initially in order to eliminate the high potential for the duplication of proper names had shorter alphabetic codes been used. Since several personal names and geographic locations begin with the same first several letters, e.g., Amenmosĕ, Amennakhte; Setmosĕ, Setnakhte, eight letter codes were found to be the shortest alphabetic codes by means of which all proper names could be distinguished one from the other. In the case of variable 8 Name of Smallholder, wherever the name of the smallholder is followed by an indication of filiation, that filiation has been incorporated into the eight letter code by inserting a -S(on) or -D(aughter) as the last two characters of the code. This procedure was adopted on the assumption that filiation was used to distinguish like-named smallholders of the same occupation who occur in proximate entries. Thus, it is possible to distinguish the scribe Amenmosĕ, son of Setnakhte from the scribe Amenmosĕ for whom there is no information of filiation provided. The somewhat cumbersome eight letter codes for variables 6 and 8 were later transformed into numeric codes of up to three digits and entered directly into the data file as the new variables 31 and 32.

Variable 8 Name of Smallholder recoded as variable 32 Name of Smallholder records approximately 600 personal names which identify individual smallholders. Even when filiation is taken into account, there is the potential for two or more different identities to be subsumed under the same name and occupation. To deal with this problem, an additional means of distinguishing like-named smallholders of the same occupation was employed which takes into account any epithet or other descriptive information in the individual entry which more precisely defines the occupational responsibilities of the individual smallholder. The temple-scribe (sš ḥwt-nṯr) Khaemtīr, for example, may be distinguished from the ordinary scribe (no additional information) Khaemtīr; the scribe of the army (sš mšʿ) Pkhōre may be distinguished from the ordinary scribe Pkhōre by means of data of a new variable Occupational Group. This variable assigns the temple-scribe Khaemtīr to the occupational group "Religious," the scribe of the army Pkhōre to the group "Military," and the undifferentiated scribes (simple sš) to the occupational group "Administration." It is most unfortunate that there are so few apportioning entries where the occupation of the smallholder is augmented by an epithet or other description which facilitates the identification of individual smallholders.

Despite the relative paucity of information which permits the distinguishing of like-named smallholders of the same occupation, an attempt has been made to marshal the evidence of personal name, filiation, occupation (or title and sometimes rank), and occupational group in order to provide an admittedly tentative estimate of the number of individual smallholders in the geographic area to which the apportioning data of P. Wilbour apply. Each of the individual "identities" so derived has been provided with a unique serial number and entered directly into the data file as variable 40 Individual Smallholder. Once created, however, this variable was set aside temporarily and will be used in future statistical operations outlined in the concluding chapter of this preliminary study. Variable 8 Name of Smallholder has also been set aside temporarily for use in a projected study of personal names in P. Wilbour.

(2) The Capabilities of the Package Program SPSS

SPSS (Statistical Package for the Social Sciences) is an integrated system of computer programs designed for the analysis of social science data.(3) It is of use to social scientists, computer scientists, and statisticians alike and attempts to satisfy the following four criteria:

(1) That the statistical procedures be mathematically and statistically correct;
(2) That the program design and code be computationally efficient;
(3) That the logic and syntax of the system parallel the way in which social scientists approach data analysis; and
(4) That the system provide statistical procedures and data-management facilities tailored to the particular needs of empirical social researchers.(4)

SPSS provides a unified comprehensive package that enables the social scientist to carry out a wide variety of data analyses simply and conveniently. It provides the usual range of "descriptive statistics" such as minimum, maximum, range, median, mode, mean, sum, etc., in the description of the sample distribution and permits crosstabulation analysis. SPSS also permits many types of more specialized analysis the applicability of which will be determined, to a large degree, by the results of the simpler procedures.

(a) One-Way Frequency Distributions, Measures of Central Tendency, and Dispersion

There are in SPSS two subprograms which have been utilized in the present study in order to examine the distributional characteristics of each variable. Subprogram CONDESCRIPTIVE, which pertains to quantitative data only, provides common measures of central tendency and variation as well as other descriptive statistics relevant to continuous quantitative variables. Subprogram FREQUENCIES, on the other hand, pertains to qualitative as well as quantitative variables and provides tables of absolute (raw) and relative frequencies for each variable as well as descriptive statistics such as are available in subprogram CONDESCRIPTIVE. In the case of the qualitative variables, the only relevant statistic is the mode which can be identified at a glance in the frequency table produced by subprogram FREQUENCIES.

(b) Crosstabulation Analysis

The SPSS subprogram CROSSTABS has been utilized in order to produce two-way crosstabulation tables and to compute bivariate statistics based upon these tables. The tables compute frequency counts expressed as percentage of row total, column total, and table total. Various bivariate statistics are available to determine the statistical significance of the relationship between any two variables (chi-square) and to measure the degree of association between the variables (Cramer's V).

NOTES

[1]A recent review of the data file with both minor corrections to the file and major reclassifications of data of variable 2 Format of Entry, variable 1Ø Arouras Special Case, and variable 13 Land-cubits Single Figure resulted in some major changes to some of the original tables of subprograms CONDESCRIPTIVE and FREQUENCIES. The recent revision also removed three duplicate entries from the file and added ten entries with very incomplete data. The tables of both subprograms CONDESCRIPTIVE and FREQUENCIES reflect these changes. Most of the tables of subprogram CROSSTABS have also been recomputed. Some tables have not been recomputed because the impact of the revision was either nil or negligible.

[2]There were originally 44 variables in the variable list of the SPSS program written for this study. Some variables, such as variable 24 Type of Geographic Orientation of Plot, were eventually deleted because of unresolved difficulties in the classification of data. Five quantitative variables were eventually deleted as it became evident that the subtotals and grand totals of arouras and land-cubits they reflected were unlikely to be meaningful.

[3]N.H. Nie, C.H. Hull, J.G. Jenkins, K. Steinbrenner, and D.H. Brent, SPSS: Statistical Package for the Social Sciences, 2nd ed. (New York, 1975).

[4]Ibid., p. xxi.

4 Subprogram CONDESCRIPTIVE: Descriptive Statistics for Continuous Variables

(1) The Continuous Variables

The continuous quantitative variables identified in the present study have been analyzed by means of the SPSS subprogram CONDESCRIPTIVE which computes descriptive statistics for continuous quantitative variables. The following six descriptive statistics available in the subprogram are of relevance to the present study: mean, range, sum, minimum, maximum, and standard deviation.(1) These statistics may be used directly as measures in their own right, as in the case of the mean, range, minimum, and maximum; or indirectly, as in the case of both the mean and the standard deviation, in equations such as those used to produce the confidence intervals for the mean.

The continuous variables which are the subject of this chapter include the seven variables which have been coded directly from the document itself: (1) variable 9 Arouras; (2) variable 10 Arouras Special Case; (3) variable 11 Land-cubits First Figure; (4) variable 12 Land-cubits Second Figure; (5) variable 13 Land-cubits Single Figure; (6) variable 14 Assessed Arouras; and (7) variable 46 ⌋ Figure. The remaining continuous variables were computed by summing the values of two or more of these seven variables. The computed variables provide both subtotals and grand totals of both arouras and land-cubits as, for example, variable 28 Land-cubits Subtotal 11 and 12 which is the likely size of plot for land-cubit measured Variety II entries and variable 27 Grand Total Arouras 9 and 10 which sums up the aroura values of size of plot of Variety I, Sub-variety IA, and Variety I/II entries. Variable 38 Grand Total Land 27 and 29/100 sums up the values of all aroura measured plots and all land-cubit measured plots, the latter divided by 100 in order that the sum be expressed conveniently in arouras. Some subtotal and grand total land variables created at the beginning of this study were eventually dropped from the analysis as it became increasingly evident that they were unlikely to be meaningful. An example would be variable 35 Arouras Subtotal 9 and 14 which sums the values of variable 9 (initial black aroura figure) and variable 14 (red aroura figure) on the hypothesis that the size of plot for entries of Variety I and Sub-variety IA is equal to the sum of the initial black aroura figure and the red aroura figure. This variable no longer exists in the variable list.

Of the 2245 apportioning entries in Text A of P. Wilbour analyzed in this study, 2141 contain continuous quantitative data which can be statistically analyzed. The remaining 104 entries are lacking such data as a result of a break in the text, the illegibility of the scribal hand, or accidental omission on the part of the scribe.

(2) Variable 9 Arouras

Variable 9 Arouras analyzes the values of the initial black aroura figure of entries of Variety I and Sub-variety IA. An example would be: (A35,37) ".5.$\frac{1}{2}$, mc. $1\frac{2}{4}$" where the value of variable 9 Arouras is 5 arouras. It is found that 1451 entries (84.1%) of the 1726 aroura measured entries may be assigned to Variety I and Sub-variety IA. There are only 275 entries (15.9%) which may be assigned to Variety I/II which is characterized by the presence of a single black (aroura) figure followed by an explanatory word or phrase (see too below variable 10 Arouras Special Case). The mean of variable 9 is 7.23 arouras with a confidence interval calculated as 6.79 to 7.67 arouras. The computation of the 95% confidence interval for the mean permits us to state with only a 5% risk of error that the mean size of plot for the population of which P. Wilbour is the available sample lies within the interval computed. The values of variable 9 vary over a range of 109 arouras from a minimum of 1 aroura to a maximum of 110 arouras with a median of 5 arouras and a mode of 5 arouras. The sum total for variable 9 is 10,493 arouras.

It is also possible and extremely useful to compute the descriptive statistics for variable 9 Arouras as pertain to Variety I plots as compared with Sub-variety IA plots. The 1193 entries of Variety I plots are found to have a mean of 5.64 arouras with a confidence interval of 5.32 to 5.96 arouras. This mean is substantially smaller than that which results when we analyze data of both Variety I and Sub-variety IA plots (7.23 arouras). The values of entries of Variety I plots vary over a range of 109 arouras from a minimum of 1 aroura to a maximum of 110 arouras with a median of 5 arouras and a mode of 5 arouras. These two averages are identical to those computed for variable 9 inclusive of data of both Variety I and Sub-variety IA plots. The sum total of variable 9 computed for entries of Variety I is 6724 arouras, a value substantially smaller than that computed for variable 9 inclusive of data of both Variety I and Sub-variety IA plots.

The 245 entries of Sub-variety IA have a mean of 14.14 arouras with a confidence interval of 12.43 to 15.84 arouras. There are two Sub-variety IA entries where the values of variable 9 are lacking. The mean of 14.14 arouras is twice that computed for variable 9 inclusive of data of both Variety I and Sub-variety IA plots (7.23 arouras) and two and one half times greater than the mean computed from data of Variety I plots only (5.64 arouras).

The values of variable 9 computed from data of Sub-variety IA plots vary over a range of 98 arouras from a minimum of 2 arouras to a maximum of 1ØØ arouras with a median and mode both of 1Ø arouras. Thus, while the range of variable 9 values computed from data of Sub-variety IA plots is only slightly smaller than that computed from data inclusive of both Variety I and Sub-variety IA plots, the median and mode are twice as great. These data suggest that Sub-variety IA entries denote a type of plot which is substantively different from that denoted by Variety I entries. The difference between Variety I entries and Sub-variety IA entries will be further explored by means of crosstabulation analysis in chapter 6.

(3) Variable 1Ø Arouras Special Case

Variable 1Ø Arouras Special Case was created in order to analyze the quantitative data of entries apparently to be understood in terms of arouras, but resembling the format of land-cubit measured Sub-variety IIA: (A37,46) ".3 ar. it was not seen?" as compared with (A38,23) ".(i.e., land-cubits) 5Ø resting." In the present study, these aroura measured entries are identified as Variety I/II, a class of entry which does not exist in Gardiner's typology.

The existence of Variety I/II as a legitimate class of entry to be compared with land-cubit measured Sub-variety IIA was suggested by Gardiner's belated but crucial discovery that the hieratic numerals for "1" (sometimes), "2," "3," and "4" (always) when referring to arouras are supplied with a hook at the top on the left.(2) Entries such as the above ".3 ar. it was not seen?" are clearly to be distinguished from those Sub-variety IIA entries where there is no doubt that the land-cubit is the correct unit of measure. Gardiner's discovery opened up the possibility that entries other than the relatively rare occurrences of "3 ar." also belong to a separate aroura measured category, and that some of the entries which Gardiner identified as land-cubit measured Sub-variety IIA are not land-cubit measured after all. Gardiner also noted that Sub-variety IIA entries with the word "land-cubits" prefixed have the values "6," "12," and "24." He suggested that since entries of Variety I and Sub-variety IA are very frequently of a size of 5 arouras and multiples thereof, "all the multiples of 5 short of 1ØØ refer to arouras, while all the multiples of 6 refer to land-cubits."(3) All cases of "1ØØ" (m šwt, wšr??, wsf, bw ptrỉ.f?) can be confidently assigned to land-cubit measured Sub-variety IIA, and therefore pose no problem in classification.

The general principle conceived by Gardiner for distinguishing between aroura measured and land-cubit measured entries is certainly intriguing and worthy of serious consideration. In the present study, therefore, entries categorized as Variety I/II, the quantitative data of which are analyzed under variable 1Ø Arouras Special Case, consist not only of all cases of "3 ar.," but also all cases of "5" and multiples of 5 ("1Ø," "2Ø," "4Ø," "5Ø," and "8Ø") which do not belong to Variety I, Sub-variety IA, or Variety II. Gardiner's further observation that many cases of "5" and "1Ø" occur in close proximity to entries of "3 ar.," and that in many cases entries of "5" and "10" interrupt long sequences of Variety I and Sub-variety IA entries both of which categories are aroura measured, is persuasive evidence of the probable overall validity of his hypothesis. Gardiner's hypothesis can be evaluated statistically by means of crosstabulation analysis. The starting point for such an evaluation is the assignment of all such entries to a separate category, Variety I/II, and the creation of a separate quantitative variable, variable 10 Arouras Special Case, in order to analyze the quantitative data of these entries.

There are only 275 possible examples of Variety I/II which constitute 15.8% of the aroura measured entries where quantitative data are available. The mean of these plots is 9.07 arouras with a confidence interval of 7.29 to 10.85 arouras. The mean, therefore, is about 2 arouras greater than that of variable 9 Arouras inclusive of data of both Variety I and Sub-variety IA plots. The minimum and maximum values are 3 and 200 arouras respectively. The maximum value of 200 arouras has a frequency of just one entry (A18,21) and is located in a series of entries (A18,6-32) the classification of which as unassessed aroura measured plots is probable but not absolutely certain. Should this plot of "200" be in fact land-cubit measured, which is a distinct possibility, the maximum size of plot for Variety I/II entries would drop to 80 arouras (A42,7-8 ḥnk entry), a figure considerably more in line with the data of aroura measured variable 9. Both from the position of this entry in a series of entries which are probably to be interpreted as aroura measured, and the fact that plots of land donated (ḥnk) to the "god(s) of Pharaoh" are unlikely to have been relatively small land-cubit measured plots, it is very likely that the value "80" is correctly interpreted as aroura measured. The range of 197 arouras is considerably greater than that of variable 9 (inclusive of data of both Variety I and Sub-variety IA entries), but the median is the same as that of variable 9 (5 arouras). The modal size of plot for variable 10 is also 5 arouras, indicating that most smallholders of Variety I/II plots cultivated plots of the same size as those cultivated by the majority of the smallholders of plots of Variety I and Sub-variety IA. The sum total for variable 10 is 2494 arouras as compared with 10,493 arouras for variable 9 inclusive of data of both Variety I and Sub-variety IA plots.

Comparing the variabilities of the distributions of variables 9 and 10 using Snedecor's F-test (of variance) for distributions measured in the same unit, we find that the larger variance of the distribution of variable 10 is statistically significant, the data of variable 10 therefore the more heterogeneous. Removal of the single case of "200" from the distribution of variable 10, however, has the effect of significantly reducing the variance of variable 10 (from 217.86 to 84.64) and bringing it much closer to that of variable 9 (71.20). The range of the distribution of variable 10 also reduces dramatically from 197 arouras to 77 arouras as does the mean of the distribution (from 9.07 arouras to 8.37 arouras as compared with 7.23 arouras for variable 9). For data of variable 10 to be correctly classified as aroura measured, there should not be too great a difference in the variabilities of the distributions of variables 9 and 10. The removal of the single value "2ØØ" from the distribution of variable 1Ø and subsequent reassignment of this value to the distribution of variable 13 Land-cubits Single Figure (land-cubit measured Sub-variety IIA) brings about a much closer correspondence between the distributions of variables 9 and 1Ø.

(4) Variable 14 Assessed Arouras

Variable 14 Assessed Arouras analyzes data of the first red (aroura) figure in entries of Variety I and Sub-variety IA. An example would be: (A35,37) ".5.$\frac{1}{2}$, mc. $1\frac{2}{4}$" where the value of variable 14 Assessed Arouras is $\frac{1}{2}$ aroura. This value, probably to be understood as the portion of the plot assessed at [illegible] per aroura, has a mean of Ø.77 aroura. The 95% confidence interval for the mean of variable 14 is calculated as between Ø.71 and Ø.83 aroura. The minimum and maximum values of variable 14 are Ø.25 aroura and 2Ø.75 arouras respectively. The range for variable 14 is therefore 2Ø.5Ø arouras in which the median is Ø.5Ø aroura. While the modal value for variable 14 is Ø.5Ø aroura with a frequency of 536 occurrences, the value Ø.25 aroura has a frequency of 499 occurrences. These frequencies indicate that the distribution of variable 14 approaches "bimodality," which means that there are two values in the distribution of equal or nearly equal frequency which are the most frequently occurring values in the distribution.

It is possible to compare the variability of the distribution of variable 14 with that of variable 9 Arouras in order to understand the relative variability of assessment and size of plot for entries of Variety I where we know for certain that the value of variable 9 is the size of the plot. We find that the variability of the distribution of size of plot is very much greater than that of the assessment, the data of size of plot being far more heterogeneous. This means that whereas the size of plot of Variety I entries could vary widely, the corresponding assessment in arouras varied very much less, the same assessment value occurring in association with several sizes of plots. It is evident, therefore, that we must look to the various socio-economic factors identified as variables among the apportioning data of Text A as the explanation for the differences we observe in the variabilities of the distributions of these two variables.

The sum total for variable 14 is found to be 1115.25 arouras as compared with 1Ø,493 arouras for variable 9 inclusive of plots of Variety I and Sub-variety IA.

(5) Variable 46 ⌟ Figure

Variable 46 ⌟ Figure pertains to only 247 apportioning entries, all of which belong to Sub-variety IA. Only 4 of the 247 Sub-variety IA entries are lacking data for this variable. The ⌟ figure is the black figure which follows the sign ⌟ known only from P. Wilbour. Gardiner's comment that the sign may be a precursor of the Greek sign for subtraction which is customarily written as a precise right angle is rejected by Menu who interprets the sign as signifying the size of plot of two or more identical consecutive Variety I entries (same size, same assessment value, same smallholder, same location) condensed in a single assessment line as a sort of "shorthand" in which the initial black aroura figure gives the total area of the plots (see pp. 12-13). We know that the numeral following the sign ⌋ is intended to be interpreted as an amount of land measured in arouras because of the presence of a hook at the top left of the hieratic numerals "1" and "2" which follow this sign. This same hook occurs with the hieratic numerals "1" (sometimes), "2," "3," and "4" (always) which signify the size of plot in Variety I entries where we know for certain that the numeral is an amount of land measured in arouras.

There are only five values for variable 46: 1, 2, 5, 10, and 20 arouras. The modal value is 5 arouras which accounts for 168 of the 243 occurrences of this variable or 69.1%. The value of the ⌋ figure with the second highest frequency is 1 aroura of which there are 64 occurrences (26.3%). There are only 9 occurrences of the value 10 arouras and one occurrence each of the values 2 and 20 arouras. The mean for variable 46 is 4.18 arouras. The median is 5 arouras in a range of 19 arouras with a sum of 1016 arouras. Although the mean of the distribution of variable 46 is considerably smaller than that of variable 9 Arouras (7.23 arouras inclusive of data of both Variety I and Sub-variety IA), as is the range (19 arouras as compared with 109 arouras for variable 9); the mode and the median are identical (5 arouras). The mean of variable 46 is considerably more in line with that of variable 9 (5.64 arouras) when data of the Sub-variety IA entries are excluded from the calculation. It is likely, therefore, that the ⌋ figure represents the size of an aroura measured plot in consonance with the data of Variety I entries. This also suggests that the initial black aroura figure in entries of Sub-variety IA represents a parcel or block of two or more plots of which the ⌋ figure denotes a smaller unit. It would not be correct on the basis of these data, however, to conclude that Sub-variety IA entries denote two or more identical consecutive Variety I entries condensed in a single line as Menu has concluded.(4)

(6) Variable 11 Land-cubits First Figure and Variable 12 Land-cubits Second Figure

Variables 11 and 12, Land-cubits First Figure and Land-cubits Second Figure respectively, are a pair of variables which always occur side by side in entries of land-cubit measured Variety II. These variables denote a plot measured in land-cubits such as A37,16: "land-cubits 4.20" where the plot appears to be divided into two unequal parts probably representing the taxable (?) and non-taxable (?) portions of the plot. This pair of variables is to be compared with variable 13 Land-cubits Single Figure which also denotes a land-cubit measured plot. In the case of the Sub-variety IIA entries, the plots are not divided into two components, evidently because the plots could not be assessed at the time of the scribe's visit. In the case of the Variety II entries, it is not known which of the two variables, 11 or 12, represents the taxable (?) portion of the plot and which represents the non-taxable (?) portion. One thing is clear, however: the sum total of variables 11 and 12 is very important as it probably represents the total plot size for entries of Variety II. This is suggested by the values of variable 13 Land-cubits Single Figure which in many cases equal the sum of the values of variables 11 and 12 (see below variable 28 Land-cubits Subtotal 11 and 12).

Of the 415 land-cubit measured plots in the Text A apportioning paragraphs which have sufficient quantitative data to analyze, 216 are Variety II plots, while 199 are Sub-variety IIA plots. There is one plot assigned to Variety I/II which could, however, just as easily be assigned to Sub-variety IIA (A18,21). It is immediately evident that plots measured in land-cubits are far less common in the P. Wilbour apportioning paragraphs than plots measured in arouras, constituting only 19.4% of the 2141 entries for which quantitative data are available. Moreover, assuming that the undivided (unassessed) plots are correctly categorized as to whether they are aroura measured (Variety I/II) or land-cubit measured (Sub-variety IIA), the number of unassessed aroura measured plots as compared with unassessed land-cubit measured plots is very close indeed. This suggests that land-cubit measured plots were considerably more susceptible to the conditions or circumstances (_m šwt_, _wšr_??, _wsf_, _bw ptri͗.f_?) which prevented their division into taxable (?) and non-taxable (?) components than were aroura measured plots.

The mean for variable 11 Land-cubits First Figure is 7.04 land-cubits, while the mean for variable 12 Land-cubits Second Figure is a substantially greater 42.91 land-cubits. The 95% confidence interval for the mean of variable 11 is computed as 6.01 to 8.07 land-cubits, while the 95% confidence interval for variable 12 is computed as 37.85 to 47.97 land-cubits. The minimum and maximum values for variable 11 are 1 land-cubit and 60 land-cubits respectively with a range of 59 land-cubits the median of which is 4 land-cubits. The minimum and maximum values for variable 12 are 4 land-cubits and 195 land-cubits respectively with a range of 191 land-cubits the median of which is 30 land-cubits. Thus, the values of variable 11 are found to vary over a much smaller range, the minimum and maximum values of which are less than one-third those of variable 12. The modal values for variables 11 and 12 are 2 land-cubits and 20 land-cubits respectively, while the sum totals for variables 11 and 12 are 1521 land-cubits and 9268 land-cubits respectively. Variable 11 actually displays what approaches "trimodality," since there are 49 occurrences of the value 4 land-cubits and 49 occurrences of the value 10 land-cubits in addition to the 50 occurrences of the value 2 land-cubits. We should also note in the case of variable 12 that while there are 33 occurrences of the value 20 land-cubits, there are 30 occurrences of the value 40 land-cubits.

The useful tables of the corresponding values of variables 11 and 12 constructed by Gardiner illustrate the curious relationship between the values of the two variables.(5) Even the briefest examination of these tables leads to the inevitable conclusion that the variables do not vary proportionately. In his tables, Gardiner gives the various combinations of the values of variables 11 and 12 together with their absolute (raw) frequencies. For many values of variable 11, several values of variable 12 are possible. The variable 11 value 1 land-cubit, for example, occurs in association with the variable 12 values 11 land-cubits (6 plots), 14 land-cubits (2? plots), 23 land-cubits (3 plots), 49 land-cubits (1 plot), and 99 land-cubits (4 plots). The variable 11 value 2 land-cubits occurs in association with the variable 12 values 4 land-cubits (1 plot), 8 land-cubits (1 plot), 10 land-cubits (20 plots), 22 land-cubits (14 plots), 34 land-cubits (1 plot), 48 land-cubits (5 plots), 73 land-cubits (1 plot), and 98 land-cubits (5 plots). Only two of the variable 11 values, 3 and 60 land-cubits, occur in association with only a single value of variable 12, 8 and 140 land-cubits respectively (thus, ".3.8" and ".60.140" (land-cubits)). It is also possible for a single value of variable 12 to occur in association with more than one value of variable 11 as, for example, the variable 12 value 8 land-cubits which occurs in association with the variable 11 values 2, 3, and 4 land-cubits.

Snedecor's F-test applied to the distributions of variables 11 and 12 indicates that the difference in the relative variability of these two distributions is statistically significant with the data of variable 12 the more heterogeneous. This means that not only do the data of variable 12 have a greater range of values than those of variable 11 as indicated by the statistics range, maximum, and minimum, they also vary more within their range. This suggests that there are one or more linking factors which play a decisive role in determining each individual division of plot. Factors such as occupation of smallholder, land-owning institution, geographic location, and type of land come immediately to mind as potential linking factors and point up the need for two-way and greater crosstabulation analysis.

(7) Variable 28 Land-cubits Subtotal 11 and 12

Variable 28 Land-cubits Subtotal 11 and 12 represents the combined value of variable 11 Land-cubits First Figure and variable 12 Land-cubits Second Figure. Variable 28 was created in order to compute descriptive statistics for plots of Variety II on the hypothesis that the total plot size for plots of Variety II is equal to the sum of the values of the first and second land-cubit figures. The mean value for variable 28 is 49.95 land-cubits (0.50 aroura) with a 95% confidence interval for the mean calculated as 44.28 to 55.62 land-cubits. The minimum value for variable 28 is 6 land-cubits (0.06 aroura) and the maximum value is 200 land-cubits (2 arouras) with a range of 194 land-cubits (1.94 arouras) in which the median is 36 land-cubits (0.36 aroura). The modal value is 24 land-cubits (0.24 aroura). Thus, although plots of Variety II display a very great range in size, more smallholders cultivated plots of 24 land-cubits than any other size. The relatively large mean of the distribution reflects the pull of the higher values in the distribution (i.e., the larger size plots). The median of 36 land-cubits reflects the point in the distribution at which 50% of the smallholders cultivated smaller size plots and 50% cultivated larger size plots. The sum total for variable 28 is 10,789 land-cubits, a figure 16.4% greater than the sum of variable 12.

(8) Variable 13 Land-cubits Single Figure

Entries of variable 13 Land-cubits Single Figure stand in contrast to both assessed land-cubit measured entries (Variety II) and entries in which the unit of measure is the aroura (Variety I, Sub-variety IA, Variety I/II). These Sub-variety IIA entries are to be compared with entries of Variety I/II the quantitative data of which are analyzed under variable 10 Arouras Special Case where the unit of measure is the aroura but no division of the plot has occurred. The mean of variable 13 is 58.26 land-cubits (0.58 aroura) with a 95% confidence interval for the mean calculated as 47.83 to 68.69 land-cubits, while the minimum and maximum values are 4 and 500 land-cubits respectively. The modal value for variable 13 is 12 land-cubits (0.12 aroura) in a range of 496 land-cubits with a median of 50 land-cubits. The sum total of variable 13 is 11,593 land-cubits as compared with 10,789 land-cubits for variable 28 Land-cubits Subtotal 11 and 12, and 9,268 land-cubits for variable 12 Land-cubits Second Figure.(6)

The descriptive statistics of variable 13 suggest the need for a measure of the relative variability of the variable 13 distribution as compared with the distributions of the other land-cubit measured variables identified in the Text A apportioning data. An evaluation of F-test results finds the distribution of variable 13 to have an even greater variability than that of variable 12 Land-cubits Second Figure. The data of variable 13 therefore can be said to be more heterogeneous than those of variable 12. Assuming that the correct size of plot for Variety II entries is the sum of the first and second land-cubit figures (variables 11 and 12), it would be appropriate to compare the relative variability of variable 13 with that of variable 28 Land-cubits Subtotal 11 and 12. The distribution of variable 13 is found to be much more heterogeneous than that of variable 28. While it is possible that the greater variability of the distribution of variable 13 as compared with that of variable 28 is the result of the inclusion in the distribution of variable 13 of data incorrectly identified as land-cubit measured, such an explanation is far less likely than in the case of the also very heterogeneous data of aroura measured variable 10 Arouras Special Case where some data may be incorrectly identified as aroura measured. There is a greater possibility that data identified as aroura measured in the distribution of variable 10 Arouras Special Case are actually land-cubit measured than there is that data identified as land-cubit measured in the distribution of variable 13 Land-cubits Single Figure are actually aroura measured. The classification of the quantitative data of Sub-variety IIA entries is less subject to dispute than is the classification of data of Variety I/II entries.

(9) The Grand Total Land Computed Variables

There are three grand total land computed variables which we will consider in this section: variable 27 Grand Total Arouras 9 and 10 which sums the number of arouras recorded in the apportioning entries of Text A (Variety I, Sub-variety IA, Variety I/II); variable 29 Grand Total Land-cubits 11, 12, and 13 which sums the number of land-cubits recorded in the apportioning entries of Text A (Variety II and Sub-variety IIA); and variable 38 Grand Total Land 27 and 29/100 which sums the total land recorded in the apportioning entries expressed in arouras. Other grand total land computed variables are theoretically possible, depending upon the way in which the size of plot is calculated for entries of Variety I, Sub-variety IA, and Variety II; the above variables, however, have been judged the most likely to be correct.(7)

Variable 27 Grand Total Arouras 9 and 10 is computed from a total of 1726 entries of Variety I, Sub-variety IA, and Variety I/II. Altogether, there is a total of 12,987 arouras including those few entries where there is a value in black undoubtedly to be interpreted as aroura measured which cannot be assigned to any of the three aroura measured categories for lack of adequate evidence. If the value "200" in A18,21 is land-cubit measured rather than aroura measured, this total would drop to 12,787 arouras.

Variable 29 Grand Total Land-cubits 11, 12, and 13 is computed from a total of 415 entries of Variety II and Sub-variety IIA. Altogether, there is a total of 22,382 land-cubits. This total is predicated upon the assumption that the sum of the values of variable 11 Land-cubits First Figure and variable 12 Land-cubits Second Figure is the correct size of plot for entries of Variety II. If the value "200" in A18,21 is land-cubit measured rather than aroura measured, this total increases to 22,582 land-cubits.

Variable 38 Grand Total Land 27 and 29/100 is computed from 2141 entries. The sum total computed for variable 38 is 13,210.82 arouras, the land-cubit total from variable 29 divided by 100 in order that the grand total be expressed in terms of arouras. If the value "200" in A18,21 is land-cubit measured rather than aroura measured, it is necessary to subtract 198 arouras from the above total. The adjusted sum total would then be 13,012.82 arouras.

NOTES

[1]Two measures of central tendency, the mode and the median, are not available in subprogram CONDESCRIPTIVE. To obtain these values, we utilize subprogram FREQUENCIES in which the mode and median may be requested.

[2]Gardiner, Commentary, pp. 211-12; 213-15.

[3]Ibid., p. 215.

[4]Bernadette Menu, Le régime juridique des terres et du personnel attaché à la terre dans le Papyrus Wilbour (Lille, 1970), pp. 103-7.

[5]Gardiner, <u>Commentary</u>, pp. 93-94, figs. (i), (ii), and (iii).

[6]If the case of "200" in A18,21 is correctly interpreted as land-cubit measured rather than aroura measured, the sum total for variable 13 Land-cubits Single Figure should be raised to 11,793 land-cubits and other statistics adjusted accordingly.

[7]If the value of the black ⌋ figure in Sub-variety IA entries is the actual size of plot for the entry, the initial black aroura figure being the parcel or block to which the plot belonged, the sum total arouras cultivated would be smaller than that calculated under either variable 27 Grand Total Arouras 9 and 10 or variable 38 Grand Total Land 27 and 29/100 as presently defined.

5 Subprogram FREQUENCIES: One-way Frequency Distributions with Descriptive Statistics

(1) Table Format

Subprogram FREQUENCIES is designed to provide frequency distributions for both qualitative and discrete quantitative variables. The tables produced by the subprogram provide the absolute or raw frequency, the relative frequency, and the adjusted (relative) frequency for each category of the variables requested. The absolute or raw frequency is the actual number of cases in the data file ("sample") ascribed to each category of a variable. The relative frequency is the absolute frequency of each category of a variable divided by the number of cases in the data file. The adjusted (relative) frequency is the relative frequency adjusted to exclude missing values (cases in the data file where there is no value for a particular variable). In addition, the subprogram provides the cumulative (adjusted) frequency which is the total frequency of all values up to and including a particular category or class interval in the case of discrete quantitative variables (missing values excluded). For the majority of the qualitative variables which occur in the present study, the relative frequency is appropriate only where it is desirable to include the missing values as a legitimate category of the variable. Thus, in the case of variable 15 Type of Land where missing values constitute a legitimate category of the variable (the category Neither as opposed to *pʿt* or *ʾidb*), the relative frequency is appropriate. In the case of variable 2 Format of Entry, however, where missing values reflect lost data, missing values do not constitute a legitimate category and must be excluded from the percentage base. For variable 2 Format of Entry, therefore, the adjusted (relative) frequency is the appropriate frequency.

(2) The Qualitative Variables

(a) Variable 1 Section of Text (Geographic Zone)

It is very difficult to assess the data of variable 1 Section of

Text (Geographic Zone), since both the beginning of Section (Zone) I and the very end of Section (Zone) IV are lacking. The lost beginning of Section I evidently comprised the Theban and Heliopolitan subsections of Text A as well as the beginning of the Memphite subsection, while the lost portion of Section IV is not so easy to reconstruct. Section IV breaks off in a paragraph devoted to the Harem of Mi-wēr (§279). We know from comparison with the data of the other sections of Text A that we are missing the listing of mině and khato-lands which terminates each of the other sections. Comparing the second half of Section IV with the second half of Sections I, II, and III (i.e., from the beginning of the subsection Other Religious (the smaller temples) to the end of the section), it appears that we may be missing little more than the roster of mině and khato-lands. While neither the list of land-owning institutions nor their precise order is exactly the same from section to section, there is sufficient correspondence between the subsection Other Religious of Section IV and the corresponding subsections of Sections I, II, and III to suggest that most, if not all, of the apportioning data in Section IV have been preserved. It is the loss of data of Section I of Text A which poses the really serious problem in any analysis of the data of P. Wilbour.

Section III has the highest concentration of apportioning entries. There are 780 apportioning entries in Section III which constitute 34.7% of the 2245 apportioning entries in Text A analyzed in this study. As there are no entries in Text A which cannot be assigned to one of the four sections of the text, we are able to use the relative frequency rather than the adjusted relative frequency of each section. Had Section IV been complete, it may have exceeded its absolute frequency of 621 entries and relative frequency of 27.7%. The complete Section II, on the other hand, is found to account for 575 apportioning entries constituting 25.6% of the 2245 apportioning entries. Section I accounts for only 269 entries and has therefore a much lower relative frequency of 12.0%. It is possible, however, to suggest a rough estimate of the number of apportioning entries Section I may have originally contained by adding up the number of entries which occur in Sections II, III, and IV from the beginning of the section to the first mention of the Great Seat of Ramesses-meriamūn in the House of Ptaḥ which is the first land-owning institution with apportioning entries to occur in Section I. There are 356 entries in Section II from the beginning of the section to the first apportioning entry of the Great Seat of Ramesses-meriamūn as compared with 381 entries in Section III and 370 entries in Section IV. Since the number of apportioning entries from the beginning of the section to the first apportioning entry of the Great Seat of Ramesses-meriamūn varies within a relatively small range from section to section of the text, it is possible to suggest the mean of 369 entries as a rough estimate of the number of apportioning entries which are missing in Section I. Adding 369 entries to the 269 entries actually preserved in Section I gives a total of 638 apportioning entries for Section I. This figure most closely approaches the absolute frequency of Section IV of 621 apportioning entries or 27.7% of the 2245 apportioning entries.

Although the label of this variable is Section of Text, it is possible to interchange this label with that of Geographic Zone, or possibly Administrative Zone, since the four sections of Text A roughly correspond to four geographic zones which are, for the most part, mutually exclusive. These geographic zones may, in turn, correspond to administrative zones supervised by major administrative centres which may have included the nome capitals of Ḥardai (Upper Egyptian nome 17), Ninsu (Upper Egyptian nome 2Ø), and Tpēḥu (Upper Egyptian nome 22).(1) Ḥardai (Cynopolis) and Ninsu (Heracleopolis) occur frequently in Text A as the locations of apportioning domains; whereas Tpēḥu (Aphroditopolis) occurs mostly in Text B.

(b) Variable 2 Format of Entry

Each apportioning entry is categorized according to the manner in which its data are entered. Only 1Ø1 entries or 4.5% of a total of 2245 apportioning entries have insufficient data to enable us to assign them to one of the five categories of data organization or "format":

Variety I	(A66,35)	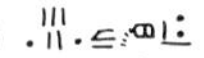	.5.$\frac{1}{2}$, mc. $1\frac{2}{7}$
Sub-variety IA	(A17,12)	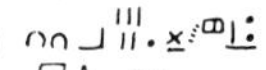	2Ø⌋5.$\frac{1}{4}$, mc. $1\frac{2}{4}$
Variety I/II	(A75,45)	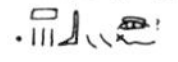	.3 ar. "it was not seen?"
Variety II	(A23,19)	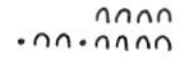	.2Ø.8Ø
Sub-variety IIA	(A75,4Ø)		.6 "waterless??"

Variety I is the modal (most frequently occurring) category of format, accounting for 1193 entries with an adjusted frequency of 55.6% (excluding the 1Ø1 unclassifiable entries). Sub-variety IA is the third most frequently occurring format, accounting for 247 entries with an adjusted frequency of 11.5%. Variety I and Sub-variety IA entries together have a cumulative adjusted frequency of 67.2% (144Ø entries). Aroura measured Variety I/II entries have an absolute frequency of 277 entries with an adjusted frequency of 12.9%. Thus, unassessed aroura measured plots are more numerous than the aroura measured plots denoted by Sub-variety IA. If some Variety I/II plots are erroneously categorized as aroura measured, however, the frequencies for Sub-variety IA and Variety I/II may be even closer. When all aroura measured entries are totalled, there are 1717 entries with a combined frequency of 8Ø.1%. Land-cubit measured Variety II has an absolute frequency of 217 entries with an adjusted frequency of 1Ø.1%; whereas land-cubit measured Sub-variety IIA has an absolute frequency of 21Ø entries and an adjusted frequency of 9.8%. The land-cubit measured formats altogether account for 427 entries with a combined frequency of 19.9%.

(c) Variable 43 Land Measure I Arouras or Land-cubits (Variety I, Sub-variety IA, Variety II)

Variable 43 Land Measure I Arouras or Land-cubits (Variety I, Sub-variety IA, Variety II) was derived from variable 2 Format of Entry in order to tabulate the frequencies of aroura measured plots as compared with land-cubit measured plots. Only aroura measured entries of Variety I and Sub-variety IA are tabulated as the category Arouras, since their classification as aroura measured is beyond dispute. Entries of Variety I/II are not included in the category Arouras because some of these entries are of doubtful classification. Only Variety II entries are tabulated as the category Land-cubits. Sub-variety IIA entries are excluded from the tabulation because of the uncertainty attached to the classification of some of these entries as land-cubit measured.

The category Arouras accounts for 1440 entries or 86.9% of the 1657 entries tabulated. The 588 entries excluded from the table include 277 Variety I/II entries, 210 Sub-variety IIA entries, as well as the 101 entries which cannot be classified for lack of sufficient quantitative data. The category Land-cubits which consists solely of Variety II entries accounts for 217 entries or 13.1% of the 1657 entries tabulated. Variable 43 is intended to serve as a "control variable" to variable 44 Land Measure II Arouras or Land-cubits in order to test the validity of the classification of Variety I/II entries as aroura measured and Sub-variety IIA entries as land-cubit measured as these categories have been defined in the present study.

(d) Variable 44 Land Measure II Arouras or Land-cubits (Variety I, Sub-variety IA, Variety I/II, Variety II, Sub-variety IIA)

Variable 44 Land Measure II Arouras or Land-cubits (Variety I, Sub-variety IA, Variety I/II, Variety II, Sub-variety IIA) was derived from variable 2 Format of Entry in order to tabulate the frequencies of aroura measured entries as compared with land-cubit measured entries with Variety I/II entries assigned to the category Arouras and Sub-variety IIA entries assigned to the category Land-cubits. Variable 44, in effect, enables us to determine whether or not entries classified as Variety I/II and Sub-variety IIA are correctly classified by comparing the bivariate statistics computed for each pair of crosstabulation tables (e.g., variable 1 Section of Text by variable 43 and variable 44; variable 4 Land-owning Institution by variable 43 and variable 44). The closer the values of the bivariate statistics chi-square and Cramer's V, the more likely it is that the classification of entries as either Variety I/II or Sub-variety IIA is indeed correct.

We find that the frequency for the variable 44 category Arouras (Variety I, Sub-variety IA, Variety I/II) is 1717 entries or 80.1% of the 2144 apportioning entries analyzed in the table; whereas the frequency for the variable 44 category Land-cubits (Variety II, Sub-variety IIA) is 427 entries or 19.9% of the 2144 apportioning entries. Entries which cannot be classified under any of the five categories of format because of missing data, number 101 or 4.5% of the 2245 apportioning entries. The addition of the less securely classified entries of Variety I/II and Sub-variety IIA raises the percentage of land-cubit measured entries above that of variable 43 by 6.8% with a corresponding decrease in the percentage of aroura measured entries. Despite the increase in both absolute and adjusted frequencies, land-cubit measured plots remain a small minority of the plots under consideration in the Text A apportioning paragraphs--strongly suggesting that it was the aroura measured plots which were the focal point of P. Wilbour, the relatively few land-cubit measured plots (Variety II and Sub-variety IIA) enumerated for reasons which are not readily apparent.

(e) Variable 45 Type of Aroura Measured Entry (Variety I or Sub-variety IA)

Variable 45 Type of Aroura Measured Entry (Variety I or Sub-variety IA) was derived from variable 2 Format of Entry in order to test the validity of Menu's interpretation of Sub-variety IA entries as one line condensations of the identical data of two or more consecutive Variety I entries in the same measurement area. By crosstabulating this variable with various socio-economic factors represented by such variables as variable 4 Land-owning Institution, variable 7 Occupation or Title of Smallholder, and variable 31 Geographic Location, etc., it is possible to determine whether or not there are any statistically significant and substantively important differences between Variety I entries and Sub-variety IA entries which cast doubt upon Menu's hypothesis.

Variety I has an absolute frequency of 1193 entries with an adjusted frequency of 82.8%. Sub-variety IA, on the other hand, has an absolute frequency of 247 entries with an adjusted frequency of 17.2%. There are altogether 1440 aroura measured entries in the table, the number of entries excluded from the table being 805 or 35.9% of the 2245 apportioning entries analyzed in Text A.

(f) Variable 18 Institutional Class and Variable 3 Institutional Group

There are 50 institutions identified as land-owners in the headings of the Text A apportioning paragraphs. These 50 institutions consist of two major classes: Religious and Secular. Variable 18 Institutional Class is a variable extrapolated from data of the more specific variable 4 Land-owning Institution in order to permit the generalization concerning and juxtaposition of the two major classes of institutions. Temples are found to have the highest frequencies: 2062 entries with a relative frequency of 91.8%. Only 183 entries are ascribed to secular institutions. These 183 entries constitute only 8.2% of the 2245 apportioning entries.

Thus, insofar as the absolute number of plots is concerned, temples, consisting of both funerary temples and ordinary cult temples, overwhelmingly predominate the Text A apportioning paragraphs; whereas secular institutions constitute only a small minority of the institutions identified in the headings of the apportioning paragraphs. If the data of P. Wilbour are at all indicative of the land-owning patterns for the area of Middle Egypt with which P. Wilbour is concerned, the implications of such a situation for the social and economic structure of Middle Egypt would be considerable to say the least.

The data which constitute the class Religious are examined in their components under the heading of variable 3 Institutional Group. Four institutional groups belonging to the class Religious have been identified: the Theban Group, the Heliopolitan Group, the Memphite Group, and the group "Other Religious." These four groups are found to occur in the above sequence in each of the four sections of Text A, although the sequence is occasionally interrupted by misplaced paragraphs and intercalations. The institutional class Secular appears under variable 3 Institutional Group as the Secular Group in juxtaposition to the four temple groups. Variable 3 Institutional Group is subclassified into its 50 component institutions under variable 4 Land-owning Institution.

The Theban Group consists of all temples which occur in the headings of the apportioning paragraphs affiliated with the House of Amūn. This affiliation is expressed in the phrase "in the House of Amūn" which qualifies the names of the temples of the Theban Group. The first member of this group listed in Sections II, III, and IV is the House of Amun-Rēᶜ, King of the Gods at Karnak (§§51, 117, 208). Immediately following this temple in Section II is the hitherto unknown chapel of Tiᶜo, consort of Amenophis II (§57), which may have been located within the Karnak complex. Also numbering among the Theban Group is a series of funerary temples (ḫwt) which follow one another in chronological order backwards, commencing with the Mansion of Millions of Years of the King of Upper and Lower Egypt Usimaᶜrēᶜ-skheperenrēᶜ (Ramesses V) (§58)(2) down to the Mansion of King ᶜAkheperen(?)rēᶜ which may have been a foundation of Tuthmosis II or possibly that of Amenophis II (§75) with the royal name emended. Also numbering among the temples of the Theban Group is the House (pr) of Ḥaremḥab (§70), the remains of which may be those preserved at Karnak near the IX Pylon rather than the funerary temple on the west bank discovered by Hölscher.(3) There is also the House of Ramesses-meriamūn (Ramesses II) in the House of Amūn (§152) to which the Hall of Columns at Karnak evidently belonged.(4) The last Theban temple to occur in the heading of an apportioning paragraph (§213 in Section IV) is the House of Mūt, the Great, Lady of Ishru which is located to the south of the temple of Amun-Rēᶜ at Karnak.

The temples of the Heliopolitan Group which occur as land-owners in the apportioning paragraphs are four in number. Two of the Heliopolitan temples appear to have been situated in Heliopolis proper. The most outstanding of these city temples was the House of Re-Ḥarakhte (§144) also mentioned in P. Harris I (37b,2) as a Heliopolitan temple. Presiding over this establishment was the high priest of Heliopolis (wr m3w) who occurs among the smallholders of Text A. The Mansion of Ramesses-meriamūn in the House of Rēᶜ (§76), a foundation of Ramesses II, is also likely to have been situated in Heliopolis, although there is no conclusive evidence to this effect. The House of Ḥaᶜpy, Father of the Gods (§238) was also a Heliopolitan temple judging from both its position in P. Wilbour and its inclusion among the Heliopolitan temples in P. Harris I (29,7). Its site was evidently at Atar en-Naby, on the east bank 2 kilometers south of Old Cairo. Also belonging to the Heliopolitan Group and located some distance from Heliopolis proper was the Mansion of Ramesses-meriamūn, Beloved Like Rēᶜ (§237) which Gardiner believed to have been situated in the vicinity of Kōm Medīnet Ghurāb at the entrance to the Fayyūm. All these temples appear to have been affiliated with the cult of Rēᶜ, linked by fiscal as well as religious ties. As a group, they appear to have been geographically more widely dispersed than either the Theban temples or the Memphite temples.

The Memphite Group is headed by the House of Ptaḥ, the Great, South of His Wall, Lord of ʿAnkhtowĕ (§80) followed in both Sections II and III of Text A by the Great Seat of Ramesses-meriamūn in the House of Ptaḥ (§3A). Also apparently a Memphite sanctuary was the curiously named House of Ramesses-meriamūn, Repeater of Sed-festivals in the House of Rēʿ (sic) (§83). Although the sign for "Rēʿ" in the full title of this temple is imperfectly preserved, a reading of "Ptaḥ" is impossible.(5) Evidently associated with this temple was the "Mansions of Festival" (§189) which occurs only in a white goat paragraph. The proper classification of the House of Ramesses-meriamūn, Repeater of Sed-festivals among the Memphite temples is indicated by both the stela of a high priest of Memphis dated to the reign of Ptolemy Auletes and P. Harris I (49,12).(6) Other temples belonging to the Memphite Group are two temples of Ramesses II, the Mansion of Ramesses-meriamūn, Beloved Like Ptaḥ (§82) and the Mansion of Ramesses-meriamūn in the House of Ptaḥ (§149). The House of Ptaḥ of Merenptaḥ and of Ramesses-meriamūn (§232) also numbers among the Memphite Group temples and perhaps should be equated with the well-known temple of Merenptaḥ at Memphis. If so, however, it is wrongly placed in P. Wilbour as it interrupts a series of exclusively Theban temples. Another possibility, although an unlikely one, is that this temple should be identified with the Karnak temple of Ptaḥ.(7) Another Memphite temple of Merenptaḥ, the Mansion of Merenptaḥ-ḥotp(ḥi)māʿĕ in the House of Ptaḥ, which was probably a funerary temple of Merenptaḥ at Memphis, occurs only in a non-apportioning paragraph (§240).

The catch-all group Other Religious appears to consist of "local" temples which vary greatly in size and importance. As has already been noted, there is a strong similarity between the group Other Religious in P. Wilbour and the Kleine Tempel section of P. Harris I. In both of these documents, these temples are enumerated in what appears to be a south to north geographical sequence.

The frequency table for variable 3 Institutional Group indicates that the Theban Group has by far the highest frequency of the four institutional groups. The Theban Group accounts for 1085 entries or 48.3% of the apportioning entries. Second to the Theban Group is the conglomerate group Other Religious which accounts for 457 entries with a relative frequency of 20.4%. The Heliopolitan Group has an absolute frequency of 352 entries and a relative frequency of 15.7%, while the Memphite Group has an absolute frequency of 168 entries and a relative frequency of 7.5%. It is noteworthy that some entries of temples of the Memphite Group are preserved in Section I, the first entries of which are ascribed to the Great Seat of Ramesses-meriamūn in the House of Ptaḥ. Despite the fact that the Theban subsection of Section I is missing, the frequency of the Theban Group is more than twice that of the group Other Religious which has the second highest frequency among institutional groups. Were all the data of Section I available, the Theban Group would doubtless command a substantially higher percentage of apportioning entries. The Heliopolitan Group would also increase in both absolute and relative frequencies, but by how much we cannot say. When the data of the Heliopolitan Group in Sections II, III, and IV are considered, the number of Heliopolitan entries is found to vary too widely from section to section to permit an estimate of the number of Heliopolitan entries Section I may have originally contained.

(g) Variable 4 Land-owning Institution

The frequencies of each of the 50 land-owning institutions which occurs or is implied in the headings of the apportioning paragraphs are tabulated individually under variable 4 Land-owning Institution.

The highest frequency occurs with the funerary temple of Ramesses V (Usimaʿrēʿ-skheperenrēʿ) which accounts for 359 entries or 16.0% of the 2245 apportioning entries. The funerary temple of Ramesses III (Usimaʿrēʿ-meriamūn) at Medīnet Habu has the second highest frequency among the 50 institutions, accounting for 266 entries with a relative frequency of 11.8%. Also accounting for more than 10% of the apportioning entries is the House of Amun-Rēʿ, King of the Gods which has an absolute frequency of 255 entries and a relative frequency of 11.4%. Only one Heliopolitan temple, the Mansion of Ramesses-meriamūn in the House of Rēʿ, has a comparatively high frequency. This temple accounts for 240 entries or 10.7% of the apportioning entries. The Great Seat of Ramesses-meriamūn in the House of Ptaḥ, has the highest absolute and relative frequencies among the Memphite temples. This temple accounts for 69 of the apportioning entries or 3.1%. Among the temples of the group Other Religious, the House of Sobek-Rēʿ, Lord of Anasha and the House of Ḥeryshef, King of the Two Lands, have the highest absolute and relative frequencies. These temples each account for 111 entries with a relative frequency of 4.9%. Secular institutions are relatively low in their absolute and relative frequencies. The highest frequency among these institutions is that of the Landing-Place of Pharaoh in Ḥardai. This institution accounts for 85 apportioning entries which constitute 3.8% of the 2245 apportioning entries.

Although the lowest frequencies occur predominantly with temples belonging to the group Other Religious, three temples of the Theban Group, the House of Mūt, the Great, Lady of Ishru; the funerary temple of Ramesses IV (Ḥeḳmaʿrēʿ-setpenamūn); and the House of Ramesses-meriamūn in the House of Amūn each account for 3 entries or fewer, or less than 0.1% each of the 2245 apportioning entries. The House of Tiʿo is another Theban temple with a very low absolute frequency. Four entries with a relative frequency of 0.2% are ascribed to this temple at Karnak. The fact that four of the ten Theban temples have such low frequencies suggests that simply because a temple was affiliated with the House of Amūn did not guarantee that it would command a sizable estate, at least insofar as landholdings set aside for smallholders are concerned. The predominance of the Theban Group in the ownership of such plots is established by just three temples, the funerary temples of Ramesses III and Ramesses V, and the House of Amun-Rēʿ, King of the Gods.

The predominance of the funerary temple of Ramesses V among land-owning institutions in the Text A apportioning paragraphs requires some consideration. The high absolute and relative frequencies of the funerary temple of Ramesses V, which exceed those of so great a funerary foundation as that of Ramesses III at Medīnet Habu, suggest that Ramesses V probably appropriated plots belonging to the funerary estates of earlier kings for his own funerary temple. If the data of P. Wilbour are at all indicative, the funerary estate of Ramesses IV (probably located in the vicinity of Medīnet Habu), is a likely source of these extensive landholdings since, at the time P. Wilbour was compiled, the funerary estate of Ramesses IV appears to have been largely depleted of plots cultivated by smallholders.(8) Despite the enormity of the size of Ramesses V's funerary estate as compared with that of Ramesses IV, documentation from Ramesses V's brief reign does not support a view of him as any more outstanding or enterprising a ruler than Ramesses IV.(9) If anything, the building projects initiated by Ramesses IV are the more impressive as also the inscriptional evidence from his reign from as far north as Serābīt el-Khādim in the Sinai and as far south as Buhen in the Sudan.(10) The relative wealth in apportioned landholdings of the funerary temple of Ramesses V as compared with the impoverished condition of that of Ramesses IV would appear to be the result of the simple usurpation of the temple landholdings of one unremarkable king by another, supplemented no doubt by landholdings usurped from other funerary estates. It is also possible that Ramesses V transferred to his own funerary estate landholdings of the Ramesseum, following the example of Ramesses III who, according to the evidence of P. Harris I (11,7; 10,3), very likely enriched his own funerary estate at Medīnet Habu at the expense of that of his great predecessor Ramesses II.(11) The Ramesseum is found to rank fifth in absolute and relative frequencies after the funerary temples of Ramesses V; Ramesses III; the House of Amun-Rēᶜ, King of the Gods; and the Mansion of Ramesses-meriamūn in the House of Rēᶜ.

(h) Variable 39 Dynasty of Founding of Land-owning Institution

Variable 39 Dynasty of Founding of Land-owning Institution is a variable which has been extrapolated from data of variable 4 Land-owning Institution. Variable 39 serves to classify the land-owning institutions, both secular and religious, on the basis of the dynasty during which they were established wherever that information can be ascertained. This variable has four categories: Eighteenth Dynasty, Nineteenth Dynasty, Twentieth Dynasty, and "Undated." In this last category are grouped all institutions which cannot be assigned to one of the dynasties of the New Kingdom with reasonable certainty or which predate the New Kingdom. Variable 39 is designed to evaluate Gardiner's speculation that the data of P. Wilbour constitute certain evidence of the continued existence--if not flourishing--of the funerary foundations of at least some of the predecessors of Ramesses V.(12) Gardiner's discussion makes reference to the thesis based upon evidence of P. Harris I (11,7; 10,3) that despite the high regard in which Ramesses III held his great namesake Ramesses II, he annexed landholdings of the Ramesseum which he presented to Amūn and appropriated personnel of that great temple for his own funerary temple at Medīnet Habu. While Gardiner's evaluation of the P. Wilbour data takes this view seriously into account, noting internal evidence in support of this thesis (§137), it is favourable to the view of the Ramesseum, and other earlier Theban temples as well, as living institutions at the time of the compilation of P. Wilbour. Gardiner notes that the same can be said of earlier Heliopolitan and Memphite foundations, although to a lesser extent. He further speculates that the paucity of landholdings ascribed to the Ramesseum may have been the result of Ramesses III's transfer to his own funerary foundation of the main administration of the Ramesseum and the lands under its administration such that only plots set aside for smallholders remained under the jurisdiction of the Ramesseum itself. We may legitimately, however, question the fate of the foundations of renowned kings of earlier periods as, for example, Tuthmosis III or Amenophis III which are not even mentioned in the paragraphs of P. Wilbour.

By classifying each institution which appears in the headings of the apportioning paragraphs according to the dynasty of founding, it is possible to evaluate the relationship between the dynasty of founding of land-owning institution and the various socio-economic variables identified among the apportioning data of P. Wilbour. Relationships found to be both statistically significant and substantively important will indicate differences between and among institutions differentiated on the basis of the dynasty during which they were established. If we are interested in comparing the frequencies of institutions established during different reigns as, for example, the reigns of Ramesses II, Ramesses III, Ramesses IV, and Ramesses V for which we have so much data, it is best to consult variable 4 Land-owning Institution where the royal names incorporated into the names of the temples founded by these kings conveniently identify the reign to which they belong.

Secular institutions with but one exception, the House of the King's (Great) Wife (Ḥenwʿōte or Twertenro), fall into the category Undated for lack of definite evidence which would assign them to a particular dynasty of founding. As a result, the categories Eighteenth, Nineteenth, and Twentieth Dynasties are almost entirely comprised of religious institutions.

Institutions dating to the Eighteenth Dynasty account for only 48 entries and constitute just 2.1% of the 2245 apportioning entries. Nineteenth Dynasty institutions account for 656 entries with a relative frequency of 29.2%, while Twentieth Dynasty institutions account for 647 entries with a relative frequency of 28.8%. Institutions which cannot be assigned to one of these three dynasties account for 894 entries or 39.8% of the apportioning entries.

(i) Variable 5 Deity or King

Variable 5 Deity or King identifies the figure to whom religious services were principally directed in the case of each temple, funerary or (ordinary) cult. There are therefore two distinct groups into which the categories of this variable divide: that of "Deity" which is comprised of the spectrum of the Egyptian pantheon: solar deities, chthonic deities, anthropomorphic deities, theriomorphic deities, and so on; and that of "King" which is comprised of the five pharaohs who were the focal point of the funerary cults of the five funerary foundations which are recorded in the headings of the apportioning paragraphs as land-owning institutions. Altogether, there are 26 categories for variable 5 Deity or King of which 21 are (ordinary) deities and 5 are kings.

Listed first in all tables involving this variable are the deities Amūn and Amun-Rēʿ, the distinction maintained in order to facilitate convenient comparison of frequencies for the god Amūn simply as Amūn and in other less well-known aspects, and merged with Rēʿ as the composite deity Amun-Rēʿ.(13) Following Amūn and Amun-Rēʿ are the five kings whose funerary foundations are named as land-owning institutions in the Text A apportioning paragraphs. They are listed by their prenomens as they appear in the formal names of the funerary foundations. Since funerary foundations from the Eighteenth Dynasty through the Twentieth Dynasty were essentially temples dedicated to the god Amūn in which funerary services were performed and rites observed for the deceased pharaoh, it is useful to have the names of the kings arranged sequentially after Amūn and Amun-Rēʿ.

The god Amūn together with Amun-Rēʿ accounts for 307 entries or 14.9% of the 2062 entries ascribed to temples. The kings who follow immediately in the table account for 792 entries with a combined adjusted frequency of 38.4%. When these 792 entries are added to the 307 ascribed to the cult of Amūn (including Amun-Rēʿ), the cumulative adjusted frequency reaches 53.3%. Of these five kings, the funerary cult of Ramesses V (Usimaʿrēʿ-skheperenrēʿ) has the highest frequency (359 entries, 17.4%) followed by that of Ramesses III (Usimaʿrēʿ-meriamūn) (266 entries, 12.9%). The funerary cult of Ramesses IV (Ḥeḳmaʿrēʿ-setpenamūn) has the lowest frequency (3 entries, 0.1%), one-quarter that of the funerary cult of Tuthmosis II (or possibly Amenophis II?) (12 entries, 0.6%). The funerary cult of Ramesses II (Usimaʿrēʿ-setpenrēʿ) has less than half the frequency of that of Ramesses V (152 entries, 7.4% as compared with 359 entries, 17.4%).

These frequencies for the funerary cults of Ramesses V and several of his predecessors invite the same general comments as those occasioned by the data of variable 4 Land-owning Institution. The reigning Ramesses V probably appropriated landholdings belonging to the funerary estates of earlier kings including that of his immediate predecessor (and father?) Ramesses IV which has such a small number of plots ascribed to it in the apportioning paragraphs of P. Wilbour. If such were the case, it is also quite possible that Ramesses V did not hesitate to appropriate landholdings of (his grandfather?) Ramesses III at Medīnet Habu, not to mention those of the funerary temple of Ramesses II (the Ramesseum). Nevertheless, these data do not disprove in any way Gardiner's speculation that the data of P. Wilbour reflect a view of the Ramesseum and other Theban temples established prior to the reign of Ramesses V as living, if not flourishing, institutions at the time of the compilation of P. Wilbour.

Of the remaining cults, that of Rēʿ, as distinguished from Re-Ḥarakhte, has the highest frequency: 318 entries or 15.4% of the apportioning entries ascribed to temples. The cult of Rēʿ is therefore second in absolute and adjusted relative frequencies to the funerary cult of Ramesses V. The cult of Ptaḥ is third in rank, accounting for 168 apportioning entries with an adjusted frequency of 8.1%. These frequencies confirm the evidence of P. Harris I where the temple groups Theban, Heliopolitan, and Memphite reflect the relative wealth of the gods Amūn, Rēᶜ, and Ptaḥ in declining order of magnitude.

Among the cults represented by temples of the group Other Religious, that of Sobek-Rēᶜ, Lord of Anasha has the highest frequency: 111 entries which constitute 5.4% of the 2062 apportioning entries in the table. Equal in frequency is the cult of Ḥeryshef, King of the Two Lands which also accounts for 111 entries with an adjusted frequency of 5.4%. Next in frequency is the cult of Sobek, including Sobek, the Shedtite and Sobek, Lord of..., which accounts for 50 entries with an adjusted frequency of 2.4%. All of these frequencies are well below those of the god Ptaḥ.

The category "Osiris-Sety" records the primary cult association of the temple of Sety I at Abydus. Like the temple of Ramesses II at Abydus, that of Sety I was chiefly dedicated to the cult of Osiris and that of the deceased pharaoh. Interestingly enough, it is the cult of "Osiris-Sety" rather than that of Osiris, Lord of Abydus which accounts for the greater number of entries: 39 entries or 1.9% of the 2062 apportioning entries in comparison with only 17 entries or 0.8% for the cult of Osiris, Lord of Abydus.

(j) Variable 19 Type of Religious Institution

Variable 19 Type of Religious Institution was derived from variable 4 Land-owning Institution to enable us to make the distinction between funerary and (ordinary) cult temples in all types of analysis. Funerary temples account for 792 entries with an adjusted relative frequency of 38.4%. Ordinary cult temples account for 1270 entries or 61.6% of the 2062 entries tabulated.

(k) Variable 16 Occupational Group and Variable 7 Occupation or Title of Smallholder

The 54 occupations of smallholders which occur in the Text A apportioning entries may be classified into eight occupational groups: Crafts (Skilled Labour), Military, Administration, Religious, Domestic, Agriculture, Animal Husbandry, and a catch-all group "Other." Subprogram FREQUENCIES provides the computations of absolute, relative, and adjusted relative frequencies for each of these groups.

While many occupations may be classified very easily as, for example, wᶜw "soldier" or "infantryman" as Military and wᶜb "(ordinary) priest" as Religious, other occupations are not so easily classified. The occupation ḥry iḥ "stablemaster," for example, most frequently occurs in the literature of the period associated with military personnel, although it is, by definition, an occupation of animal husbandry. Moreover, it is not at all certain whether the stablemasters we encounter frequently in lists of rank were really military officers, since the duties and activities of stablemasters suggest that they had no military role.(14) The responsibilities of some stablemasters clearly involved interaction with civil authorities and (grain) storage facilities. Such stablemasters as are encountered in protocols and military lists of rank may therefore have acted as civil rather than military officials. While in the present study, the occupation stablemaster has been classified under Animal Husbandry in consonance with its basic meaning, some of the stablemasters enumerated as smallholders in the P. Wilbour apportioning entries were undoubtedly military personnel.

Also difficult to classify accurately are the designations ỉdnw "deputy" and šmsw "retainer" or "follower" which are only rarely augmented by an epithet or other descriptive information which specifies for whom or under whose authority such an individual was employed. Also problematic is the term ꜥnḫ(t) n nỉwt "lady" or "citizeness" which is hardly an "occupation" per se, but rather a designation prefixed to the names of women smallholders perhaps having a special connotation in connection with land tenure. Thus, ꜥnḫ(t) n nỉwt must be relegated to the catch-all category "Other" until further clarification is forthcoming. In view of the above difficulties, there remains a certain subjectivity and arbitrariness in classification which cannot be altogether eliminated.

Of the 2245 apportioning entries, 135 cannot be classified according to the categories of variable 16 Occupational Group because the occupation of the smallholder has not been preserved in the document as we have it today. The remaining 2110 entries are distributed very unevenly among the eight categories of occupational group. The occupational group with the highest absolute and adjusted frequencies is that of Animal Husbandry which accounts for 691 entries with an adjusted frequency of 32.7%. It is important to keep in mind, however, that the smallholders of 471 of these entries are stablemasters, some, if not many of whom, were undoubtedly attached to the military. The group with the second highest frequency is that of the Military which accounts for 451 entries with an adjusted frequency of 21.4%. If slightly more than half of the stablemasters of the apportioning entries were indeed military personnel, the occupational group Military would have a higher frequency than the group Animal Husbandry. The relative importance of the military among the smallholders of Text A is thus easily established. The group Agriculture which consists of 204 ỉḥwtyw and a single scribe of the granary has an absolute frequency of 205 entries and an adjusted frequency of 9.7%, figures which are certainly much lower than might be anticipated. Occupations of the group Religious account for 345 entries with an adjusted frequency of 16.4%. The occupational group Administration accounts for 123 entries with an adjusted frequency of 5.8%. The groups Crafts (Skilled Labour) and Domestic both have relatively low frequencies: 8 and 18 entries respectively with adjusted frequencies of 0.4 and 0.9% respectively. The catch-all group "Other" accounts for 269 entries and has an adjusted frequency of 12.7%. The relatively high frequency of the group "Other" is largely due to the inclusion in this group of the title or designation ꜥnḫ(t) n nỉwt which accounts for 228 entries.

The eight categories of occupational group are subclassified in variable 7 Occupation or Title of Smallholder which consists of 54 occupations or titles. The occupation with the highest frequency is that of stablemaster which accounts for 471 entries with an adjusted frequency of 22.3%. Substantially lower frequencies occur with the occupations soldier (253 entries, 12.0%); (ordinary) priest (249 entries, 11.8%), ʿnḫ(t) n nỉwt (228 entries, 10.8%); and ỉḥwty (204 entries, 9.7%). The occupations which occur only once in the apportioning entries are as follows: alabaster worker (?) (šsy), brander (of cattle?) (ṯ3y 3bw), bearer of divine offerings (?) (f3y (ḥtpw?) nṯr), builder (or potter) (ỉḳd), carpenter (ḥmww), coppersmith (ḥmty), captain of shieldbearers of Pharaoh (ḥry ḳn Pr-ʿ3), fattener of cattle (wš3 ỉḥw), fisherman (wḥʿ), head of the cow stable (ḥry mḏwt), King's Son (s3 nsw), physician (swnw), shepherd (mnỉw sỉw), vizier (ṯ3ty), and weaver (sḫty).

It is striking that as many as 15 of the 54 occupations (or titles) of smallholder occur only once in the apportioning entries. This suggests that these occupations were at best only marginally associated with the kind of land tenure with which the data of the apportioning entries are concerned. The fact that only 5 occupations (stablemaster, soldier, priest, ʿnḫ(t) n nỉwt, and ỉḥwty) account for more than 65% of these apportioning entries suggests that the cultivation of such plots was an activity in which large numbers of individuals from relatively few walks of life engaged. These few occupations, moreover, would seem to have had very little else in common on present evidence. Only the occupations soldier and stablemaster can be said to have been related in view of the frequency with which these occupations occur together in protocols and military lists of rank.

(l) Variable 34 Sex of Smallholder

Variable 34 Sex of Smallholder is derived from variable 7 Occupation or Title of Smallholder in order to provide ready comparison of frequencies according to the sex of the smallholder. This type of variable is known as a "dichotomy" because there are only two mutually exclusive categories, Male and Female. Like variable 18 Institutional Class, variable 19 Type of Religious Institution, and variable 16 Occupational Group, variable 34 Sex of Smallholder is a variable which permits us to make generalizations about data which have been subclassified in other variables.

The modal class for this variable is that of Male which accounts for 1882 entries or 89.2% of the 2110 apportioning entries where the name of the smallholder is preserved. The class Female accounts for only 228 entries or 10.8% of these entries. All women smallholders are identified as ʿnḫ(t) n nỉwt.

(m) Variable 15 Type of Land

The plots in the apportioning paragraphs are rarely identified as to the type or quality of the land. Only in the case of 242 plots (10.8%) do we know the type of land involved. Specification of the type of land occurs not in the individual entry, however, but in the preceding measurement line which gives the location of the plots which follow. There are 58 plots (2.6%) identified as pʿt-land as compared with 184 plots (8.2%) identified as ỉdb-land. Although the term ḳ3yt-land occurs in some of the Text A measurement lines, it appears to be solely an indication of the relative position of the land, i.e., land standing higher than the surrounding land.(15)

The terms ỉdb (WB. I, 153, 2ff.) and pꜥt (WB. I, 504, 2) are known from the Golénischeff Onomasticon (I,12) where they appear side by side following the words šꜥy "sand" and m3wt "new land" and are perhaps to be understood antithetically.(16) The word ỉdb is best known from the expression ỉdbwy Ḥr "the two river-banks of Horus" as a synonym for "Egypt" which leads to the WB. translation "Ufer," "Uferland." An intriguing occurrence of the term ỉdb is in the text of a donation stela of the Twenty-fourth Dynasty where the word is determined with the water sign. On this stela, Tefnakhte presents the goddess Neith with "10 arouras of land in the ỉdb-land, field added by the Inundation god (Ḥaꜥpy) to be called 'the New Land of the House of Neith.'"(17) This reference suggests that ỉdb-land is a term which has to do with the possibilities of irrigation, although in what technical sense we cannot as yet ascertain. An occurrence of the word roughly contemporary with P. Wilbour is in P. Leiden I 370 vs. 8 (No. 5 LRL), a letter concerning "three ỉdb-lands" which are to be cleared of trees (šnw), presumably in preparation for the cultivation of the land.(18) The use of the term ỉdb in one of the problems of the Moscow Mathematical Papyrus suggested to Gardiner that plots described as ỉdb-land probably had the shape and proportions of the sign which is the determinative of the word.(19) Upon the strength of the above evidence, Gardiner translated ỉdb as "riparian land" and understood the term to refer to plots consisting of a long strip of land abutting at one end upon the river or a canal. References to pꜥt-land are few and far from illuminating such that it is not possible to gauge the relative worth or quality of pꜥt-land as compared with ỉdb-land. We cannot even be certain that it is correct to view these terms antithetically in either the Golénischeff Onomasticon or in P. Wilbour.

The occurrence of the two terms in P. Wilbour, however, provides a golden opportunity to compare and contrast them in the context of the many variables which may be identified in the apportioning entries. Variable 15 Type of Land has been created in order to provide a means for evaluating these terms using two-way crosstabulation analysis. The value of the analysis is enhanced by the creation of a third category "Neither" which allows the comparison of ỉdb and pꜥt plots with the vast majority of plots for which no type of land is specified in the measurement line.

(n) Variable 17 Special Entry

There are four types of "special entry" among entries of the apportioning paragraphs which are analyzed under variable 17 Special Entry. Since the four categories: (1) ḥnk "donated land"; (2) 3ḥt n ḥtrỉ "field for horses"; (3) mḥt "flax"; and (4) w3ḏ "vegetables" or "herbs" are related to each other ostensibly only insomuch as they denote special circumstances which distinguish their respective entries from all other apportioning entries, comparisons of their respective data must be made with this fact in mind. It is possible, however, that we may find links between and among these categories.

There are 37 plots among the apportioning entries identified as "Land donated (ḥnk) to the god(s) of Pharaoh." They first occur in Section I (A17,11) and are last encountered in Section IV (A90,27). These plots are specified as being "under the authority of (r-ḫt)" a particular individual identified as a military officer, civil administrator, scribe, or priest. Ḥnk entries have a connection with four non-apportioning paragraphs in Text A (§§71-74) devoted to "the god of Usimaʿrēʿ-meriamūn" (Ramesses III) which have been intercalated into the end of the Theban series of Section II. Two entries in these paragraphs (A33,10-11 (§73) and 33,14-15 (§74)) are Pōsh A entries the corresponding apportioning entries of which (A31,8 and 30,25) take the form of ḥnk entries rather than the usual Pōsh B entries. This leads to the conclusion that we would be correct in identifying the word "Pharaoh" in these entries with Ramesses III rather than the reigning pharaoh Ramesses V. The god(s) of Pharaoh of most of the ḥnk entries may possibly have been wayside statues surrounded by fields donated to them perhaps by the high officials or prophets in charge of them.(20) As such these "gods" may possibly be compared with the sšm-ḥw, twt, and ỉb-ỉbw mentioned in P. Harris I 11,1-3 "to which the officials, standardbearers, controllers, and people of the land contributed, and which Pharaoh (L.P.H.) placed upon the foundation (sdf) of the House of Amun-Rēʿ, King of the Gods in order to protect them and defend them to all eternity: 2,756 gods, making 5,164 persons." The ḥnk entries may also have connection with Text B as is suggested by the occurrence of the red annotation m ḥnk... several times in Text B (B6,29; 15,1.3.28). In B15,1, the reading "in donated land of the mayor Dḥutmosĕ" suggests that although the king is traditionally depicted as the donor of all landed property, private donors may in fact have been the real donors as was the case with numerous donation stelae.(21)

The second type of special entry is that of plots apparently set aside for the maintenance of horse-teams of Pharaoh the expanded formula for which is 3ḥt n ḥtrỉ ḍd.n ḥry ỉḥ PN. There are 49 examples of these entries which have the following four variants: (a) A10,6; 44,49; 46,16; 47,11; (b) A44,41; 45,14.15.16.26; etc., and always from col. 48 onwards; (c) A40,14; 42,4.30; and (d) A36,39.42 and probably also A35,24. Gardiner's understanding of this phrase as "Field for horses which the stablemaster X named (lit. 'spoke of')" is reasonable in light of P. Sallier I 9,1-9,9 (LEM, pp. 87-88) which supports such an understanding and, happily enough, expands upon it.(22) P. Bologna 1094,2,7-3,5 (LEM, p. 3) may also be mentioned in relation to these peculiar apportioning entries as it seems to imply that the stablemasters who claimed title to such plots could be extremely overbearing and cause endless difficulties for their administrators.

The third type of special entry is that in which the crop is specified as flax (mḥt). There are only four examples of this type of entry (A6,x+17; 7,43.48; 8,4) all occurring within the first several paragraphs of Section I. It is possible, however, that the occurrence of the word mḥt in A6,x+17 also applies to four of the following seven plots.

The final category of special entry is that in which plots are indicated as "(cultivated) in vegetables (or herbs)" ( m w3ḏ). This is a rare category with only three occurrences, one each in Section I (A6,x+15), Section II (A40,10), and Section III (A44,33).

(o) Variable 20 Type of Pōsh Entry

The two types of special Pōsh entries, Type B and Type C, which occur in the apportioning paragraphs are tabulated under the heading of variable 20 Type of Pōsh Entry. Of the 2245 apportioning entries analyzed in Text A, only 165 are Pōsh entries of Type B or C. There are 128 Pōsh B entries which constitute only 5.7% of the 2245 apportioning entries and only 37 Pōsh C entries which constitute only 1.6% of the apportioning entries. Since 92.7% of the apportioning entries are neither Pōsh B nor Pōsh C entries, it is evident that the 165 Pōsh B and C entries represent a departure from the standard format, either in the sense of being fundamentally different from, or in the sense of being longer writings of the format which occurs in the vast majority of apportioning entries. In the case of the far more numerous Pōsh B entries, their peculiar relationship to the non-apportioning Pōsh A entries argues in favour of their interpretation as a fundamentally different type of entry from the vast majority of apportioning entries. In the case of the Pōsh C entries, it is possible to argue their interpretation as a fuller writing of the usual apportioning entry, the difference being that Pōsh C entries, which pertain largely to plots ascribed to local deities cultivated by (m-ḏrt) a variety of individuals usually identified as priest or ỉḥwty, are introduced by the words pš n. It is possible that the words pš n serve to stress the status of the deity or high-ranking official responsible for the plot as Gardiner surmised.(23) A comparison of the Pōsh B and C entries with the ordinary apportioning entries in crosstabulation analysis serves to test this idea as well as the alleged unique status of Pōsh B entries.

(p) Variable 21 Type of Apportioning Paragraph

Variable 21 Type of Apportioning Paragraph tabulates apportioning entries according to the type of paragraph to which the entries belong. There are five varieties of apportioning paragraphs: (1) those which commence with the words smw n pr Name of Institution ("Herbage of the House of Name of Institution"); (2) those which commence with the words mk ỉb ḥḏ ("Food for White Goats"); (3) those which commence with the words šmw pš n pr pn ("Apportioned šmw (harvest-taxes?) of this House"); (4) those which commence with the words rmnyt pš n pr pn ("Apportioning Domain of this House"); and (5) those which consist solely of the name of the land-owning institution (tabulated under the category "None of These").

Variable 21 Type of Apportioning Paragraph was created in part to test the hypothesis of Gardiner that "another principle which influenced the organization of the temple estates was the type of service which the separate domains were called upon to render."(24)

It was Gardiner's speculation that the headings of the apportioning paragraphs serve to identify the purpose for which the revenue of the various plots enumerated under these headings was ultimately intended.

The first of these alleged domain services which Gardiner identified is that of supplying fodder for such great temple-herds as are enumerated in P. Harris I (Theban Section 10,7-11; Memphite Section 51a,4) as the specific gifts of Ramesses III. The format of P. Harris I could lead to the conclusion that the herds of cattle were autonomous entities which stood very much on the same footing as the temple buildings in Thebes and Memphis founded by Ramesses III. According to Gardiner, the impression of the autonomy of the temple-herds in P. Wilbour is enhanced by the fact that whole paragraphs are devoted to the domains which appear to have produced their food or herbage (smw), although the herds themselves are not specifically mentioned. The special status of these herbage paragraphs is clearly indicated by the fact that they are not ordered among the paragraphs devoted to the domains of the individual institution to which they belong, but instead are grouped together in a series of their own either in close proximity to the secular institutions as in Section I (§§31-33) and Section II (§§104-7) or immediately preceding the white goat paragraphs as in Section III (§§174-86). In Section IV (§§243-46), they are intercalated along with a single white goat paragraph (§247) and paragraphs of two secular institutions (§§241 and 242) into the main sequence of Memphite institutions. The herbage paragraphs in each section follow the same chronological and geographical sequence followed by the institutions themselves within each section. Herbage paragraphs account for 381 entries or 17.0% of the 2245 apportioning entries in Text A.

The second type of apportioning paragraph identified by Gardiner as signifying a "service function" is that of the white goat paragraph, the peculiar headings of which read: "Food for White Goats" (§§187-88, 190-93, 247) mk ỉb ḥḏ and alternately, "Domain of White Goats" (§§189, 194-95) rmnyt ỉb ḥḏ. These paragraphs are ordered similarly to the herbage paragraphs. White goats are also mentioned in Text B of P. Wilbour where some khato-lands are said to be located "(on) fields of Food for White Goats of T-ḥō (Medīnet Habu) in the House of Amūn" (B17,32; 18,19; 20,18; 22,14; and 24,31).(25) White goat paragraphs account for only 79 entries or 3.5% of the apportioning entries.

Another 16 paragraphs (§§6, 17, 22, 27, 63, 93, 95, 100, 166, 171, 251, 260, 266, 269, 271, 273) commence with the words šmw pš and account for 312 entries or 13.9% of the apportioning entries. Although Gardiner speculated that these 16 paragraphs pertain to fields set aside for the production of grain for the sustenance of priests and other staff of the temples in parallel with the herbage and white goat paragraphs, he concluded that they were more likely to pertain to fields set aside for the production of grain for the "harvest-tax."(26) These paragraphs occur in association with temples thought to have been of small to medium size, and also include §63 which pertains to the funerary temple of Ramesses IV and §251 which pertains to the temple of Osiris at Abydus.

The apportioning paragraphs of relatively large temples in the major metropolitan areas (Thebes, Heliopolis, and Memphis) introduced by the words rmnyt pš account for 113Ø entries or 5Ø.3% of the 2245 apportioning entries. In all, there are 24 rmnyt pš paragraphs (§§3, 54, 55, 59, 68, 69, 76, 8Ø, 118, 119, 123, 134, 138, 144, 145, 147, 15Ø, 158, 211, 218, 228, 231, 236, 237). Unlike herbage and white goat paragraphs, rmnyt pš paragraphs are located in the main sequence of paragraphs belonging to what appear to have been relatively large temples. Gardiner concluded that "apportioning domain paragraphs perform for the larger and more distant temples the same function that the harvest-tax paragraphs perform for the smaller temples, that in fact the two kinds of paragraph are merely different forms of one and the same kind."(27) In the following chapter, we will attempt to evaluate the validity of Gardiner's conclusion.

The fifth type of apportioning paragraph has a heading consisting of only the name of the institution. Paragraphs designated "None of These" account for 343 entries or 15.3% of the apportioning entries. This type of paragraph occurs only with temples belonging to the group Other Religious.

(q) Variables 22 and 23 Dual Geographic Location A and B

Variables 22 and 23 Dual Geographic Location A and B always occur together and therefore may be said to comprise a pair of geographic location variables. They have been created in order to take into account apportioning entries where plots are described with respect to two geographic points of reference. The first point of reference in these cases is as valid an orientation as the second point of reference. It is incorrect, therefore, to fix the location of such a plot without giving both points of reference. As an example we may cite the measurement line A28,3: "MEASUREMENT made to the east of Opĕ (and to) the east of Maire-woodĕ." For such entries, there will be no data entered under variable 31 Geographic Location.

It is clear from the frequencies table that it was most unusual to fix the location of a plot in this manner. The locations of only 6Ø of the 2245 plots enumerated in the apportioning paragraphs or 2.7% are described with reference to two localities. In the case of variable 22, which records the first of the two localities, the Mound of Karoti accounts for just over one-third of these entries or Ø.9% of the apportioning entries, while in the case of variable 23, which records the second of the two localities, N-ʿawĕ has the very same frequencies.

(r) Variable 31 Geographic Location (Measurement Area)

Of the 185 measurement areas which serve to identify the location of the plots of the apportioning entries, 28 account for 1.Ø% or more of the plots. The 1Ø measurement areas with the highest absolute and adjusted frequencies are as follows: (1) Sakō (no. 149) 91 plots, 4.2%; (2) Menʿonkh (no. 155) 83 plots, 3.8%; (3) Sharopĕ (no. 94) 76 plots, 3.5%; (4) Ḥuiniuti (no. 88) 59 plots, 2.7%; (5) the Village of Inroyshes (no. 32) 57 plots, 2.6%; (6) Mi-ēḫu (no. 56) 52 plots, 2.4%; (7) Irkak (no. 182) 5Ø plots, 2.3%; (8) the Granary of Reeds (no. 96) 46 plots, 2.1%; (9) the New Land of... (no. 12) 39 plots, 1.8%; and (10) the Village of Djasasati (no. 39) 36 plots, 1.7%.(28)

Of these 28 measurement areas, only Spermeru is among the major towns identified by O'Connor as relatively important towns in the region that appear to have been administrative centres.(29) Sakō, however, does occur in O'Connor's fig. 3(a) where it is indicated as having been somewhat smaller than Spermeru in the amount of land it owned or controlled. Whereas the location of Sakō is clearly to be sought in zone 4, Spermeru was probably located at or near the border between zones 3 and 4. The Shelter (<u>ỉsbt</u>) of Sakō (no. 151), probably located near Sakō, accounts for another 16 plots with an adjusted frequency of 0.7%. Similarly, the measurement area, the Dyke (<u>dnỉt</u>) of Spermeru (no. 84), which accounts for only 3 plots with an adjusted frequency of 0.1%, was probably located in the vicinity of Spermeru.

It is also to be noted that there are 26 measurement areas with a frequency of 1 plot only and an adjusted relative frequency of less than 0.1%.

(3) The Quantitative Variables

(a) Aroura Measured Plots (Variables 9, 10, and 14)

The data of variable 9 (initial black aroura figure in entries of Variety I and Sub-variety IA), variable 10 Arouras Special Case (single black figure in entries of Variety I/II), and variable 14 Assessed Arouras (red aroura figure in entries of Variety I and Sub-variety IA) are analyzed by means of subprogram FREQUENCIES in order to obtain absolute and adjusted relative frequencies for each value in their respective distributions. As the frequencies for variable 46 ⌋ Figure have already been given in chapter 4 (5), they will not be repeated here.

The values of variable 9 Arouras inclusive of data of both Variety I and Sub-variety IA have a range of 109 arouras from a minimum of 1 aroura (4 cases) to a maximum of 110 arouras (1 case). The 1451 occurrences of the initial black aroura figure are inclusive of the three values of what is presumably the initial black aroura figure where there are insufficient data preserved in the entry to enable us to assign the entry to either Variety I or Sub-variety IA (A27,44; 85,15; 33,30). Of the twenty-three values of variable 9 tabulated, the value 5 arouras is the modal value. In the case of Variety I entries, we know that the value 5 arouras is the modal size of plot. Such may also be the case with Sub-variety IA entries if the initial black aroura figure is indeed the size of plot. Plots of 5 arouras account for 752 entries with an adjusted frequency of 51.8% of the 1451 entries tabulated. Plots of 3 arouras have the second highest frequency among values of variable 9 and account for 339 entries or 23.4% of the entries tabulated. Plots of 3 and 5 arouras together account for 1091 entries or 75.2% of the 1451 entries tabulated. Plots of 10 arouras account for 175 entries or 12.1% of the total entries; whereas plots of 20 arouras account for 100 entries or 6.9%. Plots of 2 arouras account for 23 entries or 1.6%. The remaining eighteen values in the distribution of variable 9 account for 62 entries or 4.3% of the 1451 occurrences of variable 9 among the 2245 apportioning entries.

When the analysis of the values of the black aroura figure is limited to the 1193 Variety I entries where we know for certain that the black aroura figure is correctly interpreted as the size of plot, a slightly different frequency distribution emerges.(30) There are altogether twenty values for entries of Variety I, the minimum of which is 1 aroura (4 cases) and the maximum of which is 110 arouras (1 case). The modal value (size of plot) is 5 arouras as was the case with the previous distribution. Plots of 5 arouras account for 711 entries and have a relative adjusted frequency of 59.6% of the 1193 entries tabulated. Plots of 3 arouras have the second highest frequency and account for 325 entries or 27.2% of the entries tabulated. Plots of 3 and 5 arouras together account for 1036 entries or 86.8% of the 1193 Variety I entries. Plots of 10 arouras have the third highest frequency (55 entries, 4.6%) as was the case with the previous distribution inclusive of values of both Variety I and Sub-variety IA entries. In the distribution of values of Variety I, however, there are considerably fewer values of 10 arouras, since 118 of the 175 cases of the value 10 arouras belong to the distribution of Sub-variety IA entries. Plots of 20 arouras account for 40 entries with an adjusted frequency of 3.4%. The remaining sixteen values of the black aroura figure in the 1193 Variety I entries account for 62 entries or 5.2% of the entries tabulated.

When the analysis of variable 9 Arouras is limited to the 245 Sub-variety IA entries where it is uncertain how the initial black aroura figure should be interpreted, the result is a frequency distribution very different from the two discussed above as a result of the relatively high frequencies of the higher values of the initial black aroura figure. There are eleven values in this distribution, the minimum of which is 2 arouras (1 case) and the maximum of which is 100 arouras (2 cases). The modal value of the initial black aroura figure in Sub-variety IA entries is 10 arouras accounting for 118 entries with an adjusted frequency of 48.2% of the 245 entries tabulated. The value 20 arouras has the second highest frequency and accounts for 60 entries or 24.5% of the entries tabulated. The values 10 and 20 arouras together account for 178 entries or 72.7% of the 245 Sub-variety IA entries. The value 5 arouras accounts for 40 entries or 16.3% of the 245 entries. The remaining eight values of the initial black aroura figure in the Sub-variety IA entries account for 27 entries or 11.0% of these entries.

Variable 14 Assessed Arouras, the companion variable to variable 9 Arouras, which records the values of the red aroura figure in entries of Variety I and Sub-variety IA, has a markedly smaller range of values: ¼ aroura (499 cases, 34.5%) to 20½¼ arouras (1 case, 0.1%) inclusive of the data of Pōsh B entries. The modal assessment value for variable 14 is ½ aroura which accounts for 536 entries with an adjusted frequency of 37.1%. The assessment value with the second highest frequency is ¼ aroura which accounts for 499 entries with an adjusted frequency of 34.5%. The assessment value with the third highest frequency is 1 aroura which has an absolute frequency of 276 entries with an adjusted frequency of 19.1%. There are relatively few entries in which the assessment value exceeds 1 aroura. Excluding the 38 entries (2.6%) with an assessment value of 2½ arouras and the 28 entries (1.9%) with an assessment value of 5 arouras (mostly Pōsh B entries), there are only 64 entries or 4.4% in which the assessment value exceeds 1 aroura. Assessment values in excess of 5 arouras account for only 12 entries and constitute only 0.9% of the 1445 entries tabulated. It should be noted that while there are 1451 entries tabulated for variable 9 Arouras, there are only 1445 entries tabulated for variable 14 Assessed Arouras. The difference of 6 entries is explained by the fact that there are 6 fewer entries in which data of variable 14 Assessed Arouras are preserved than there are of variable 9 Arouras.

Variable 10 Arouras Special Case pertains to what were evidently unassessed aroura measured plots. There are only eight values for variable 10, the highest of which ("200") is of doubtful validity as aroura measured. These values are undoubtedly correctly identified as sizes of plots for Variety I/II entries. The most frequently occurring size of plot is 5 arouras of which there are 149 cases constituting 54.2% of the 275 entries tabulated. The size of plot with the second highest frequency is 10 arouras which accounts for 50 entries or 18.2% of the 275 entries. The size of plot with the third highest frequency is 3 arouras which accounts for 43 entries or 15.6% of the total entries. The size of plot with the fourth highest frequency is 20 arouras of which there are 22 occurrences constituting 8.0% of the 275 entries. Since in the case of variable 10 Arouras Special Case, we are tabulating data of plots which have not, as a rule, been understood as aroura measured, but because of their proximity to aroura measured entries are also likely to be aroura measured, we must exercise caution in any interpretation of the data. The only plots which are unquestionable examples of Variety I/II aroura measured plots are those entries where the value "3" has a hook on the top left of the numeral which indicates that the numeral is to be interpreted in terms of the aroura. In creating this variable, we are testing the possibility that unassessed plots with the value "5," and multiples of 5 short of 100 which often occur in close proximity to Variety I/II plots of "3 ar.," or interspersed among Variety I and Sub-variety IA entries, are also aroura measured. The single plot of "200" in A18,21 which occurs as the highest value of the distribution of variable 10 remains a highly questionable case which very likely belongs to the distribution of variable 13 Land-cubits Single Figure.

(b) Land-cubit Measured Plots (Variables 11, 12, 28, and 13)

Variable 11 Land-cubits First Figure and variable 12 Land-cubits Second Figure pertain to land-cubit measured plots of Variety II only. Each of these variables should be considered singly as well as in sum, since variable 28 Land-cubits Subtotal 11 and 12 may well represent the size of plot in entries of Variety II.

Variable 11 Land-cubits First Figure, the first of the land-cubit measured values for plots of Variety II (e.g., the "2" in ".2.48"), is consistently the smaller of the two values. There are eight values in the variable 11 distribution, the minimum of which is 1 land-cubit (14 cases) and the maximum of which is 60 land-cubits (2 cases). The modal value in the distribution of variable 11 is 2 land-cubits of which there are 50 occurrences with an adjusted frequency of 23.1% of the 216 entries of Variety II in which the quantitative data have been preserved. The values 4 and 10 land-cubits each account for 49 entries or 22.7% of the 216 entries tabulated. The distribution of variable 11 is therefore an example of "multi-modality," a situation in which there are two or more "humps" or concentrations of data in a single distribution. In the case of variable 11, there are three nearly equal concentrations of data such that the values 2, 4, and 10 land-cubits are the most frequently occurring values for the smaller land-cubit figure in Variety II entries. If variable 11 is the assessed value of Variety II plots, the values 2, 4, and 10 land-cubits are the most common assessment values of assessed land-cubit measured plots. There are 27 Variety II entries in which the first land-cubit value is 5 land-cubits (12.5%) and 23 entries in which the first land-cubit value is 20 land-cubits (10.6%). There are 14 entries in which the first land-cubit value is only 1 land-cubit. These 14 entries constitute 6.5% of the 216 entries tabulated. There are only 2 occurrences each of the values 3 and 60 land-cubits, each constituting only 0.9% of the 216 entries.

Variable 12 Land-cubits Second Figure, the second of the two land-cubit measured values in Variety II entries (e.g., the "48" in ".2.48"), is consistently larger--very often much larger--than the first land-cubit value. The range of values of variable 12 is 191 land-cubits as compared with 59 land-cubits for variable 11 with a minimum of 4 land-cubits (1 case) and a maximum of 195 land-cubits (1 case). While the modal value for variable 12 is 20 land-cubits of which there are 33 occurrences constituting 15.3% of the 216 Variety II entries, there are 30 occurrences of the value 40 land-cubits (13.9%). There are 20 occurrences of the value 10 land-cubits (9.3%) and 21 occurrences of the value 80 land-cubits (9.7%). The value 8 land-cubits accounts for 20 Variety II entries (9.3%), while the value 45 land-cubits accounts for 15 entries (6.9%), and the value 22 land-cubits accounts for 14 entries (6.5%). The remainder of the variable 12 values account for fewer than 10 entries each.

Variable 28 Land-cubits Subtotal 11 and 12 is the sum total of the values of variable 11 Land-cubits First Figure and variable 12 Land-cubits Second Figure and is very likely to represent the size of plot for entries of land-cubit measured Variety II. There are altogether eleven values for variable 28 which extend over the range 6 land-cubits (1 case) to 200 land-cubits (6 cases). The modal value for variable 28 is 24 land-cubits which has an absolute frequency of 60 entries and an adjusted frequency of 27.8% of the 216 Variety II entries tabulated. Second highest in frequency is the value 50 land-cubits which accounts for 52 entries with an adjusted frequency of 24.1%. The value with the third highest frequency is 100 land-cubits. Plots of 100 land-cubits account for 47 entries with an adjusted frequency of 21.8%. Fourth highest in frequency is the value 12 land-cubits, a relatively small size of plot, which accounts for 42 Variety II entries or 19.4% of the entries tabulated. The remaining seven values of the variable 28 distribution (6, 1Ø, 11, 36, 75, 15Ø, and 2ØØ land-cubits) have substantially lower absolute and adjusted frequencies. The value with the highest frequency among these seven values is 2ØØ land-cubits which accounts for 6 Variety II entries and has an adjusted frequency of 2.8%. The remaining six values each account for only 1 or 2 entries.

If variable 28 is correctly interpreted as signifying the size of plot of apportioned (but not taxed) land-cubit measured plots, it would appear that land-cubit measured plots were allocated according to more or less strictly regulated sizes: 12, 24, 5Ø, and 1ØØ land-cubits being the usual sizes of plots. Plots of sizes other than these high frequency sizes appear to represent deviations from the norm.

The distribution of variable 13 Land-cubits Single Figure reveals the predominance of the values 12, 24, 5Ø, and 1ØØ land-cubits as the most frequently occurring sizes of plots for the 199 entries of Sub-variety IIA which have quantitative data for analysis. The modal value of variable 13 is 12 land-cubits which has an absolute frequency of 66 and an adjusted frequency of 33.2% of the 199 entries tabulated. The values 5Ø and 1ØØ land-cubits have absolute frequencies of 42 and 41 entries respectively and account for 21.1% and 2Ø.6% respectively of the 199 entries. The value 24 land-cubits has an absolute frequency of 21 entries with an adjusted frequency of 1Ø.6%. As these high frequency values in the distribution of variable 13 also occur as high frequency values in the distribution of variable 28 Land-cubits Subtotal 11 and 12, there is a strong correspondence between the two distributions. This correspondence is enhanced by the fact that other values in the distribution of variable 13 Land-cubits Single Figure correspond to values in the distribution of variable 28: 6, 36, 75, and 2ØØ land-cubits. Since in the case of variable 13 Land-cubits Single Figure we can be relatively certain that we are dealing with actual sizes of plots, it is probable that we would be correct in identifying the size of plot for entries of Variety II as the sum total of the first and second land-cubit figures (variable 28 Land-cubits Subtotal 11 and 12).

The correspondence between the distributions of variable 13 Land-cubits Single Figure and variable 28 Land-cubits Subtotal 11 and 12 is highest when the value "5" and multiples of 5 short of 1ØØ of doubtful classification are removed from the distribution of variable 13 and reclassified as belonging to the distribution of aroura measured variable 1Ø Arouras Special Case in accordance with Gardiner's astute conjecture to this effect (see chapter 4 (3)).

We should also consider the value 2ØØ land-cubits in the distribution of variable 13 which has an absolute frequency of 11 entries and an adjusted frequency of 5.5%. These data suggest that the single plot of "2ØØ" (A18,21), which occurs in a series of entries (A18,6-32) probably to be interpreted as aroura measured Variety I/II entries (variable 1Ø Arouras Special Case), is likely to be interpreted as land-cubit rather than aroura measured as is also suggested by the significant reduction in the relatively high variability of the distribution of variable 1Ø Arouras Special Case when this value is eliminated from the distribution. Another value of 2ØØ land-cubits in the distribution of variable 13 Land-cubits

Single Figure would be consistent with the frequency of 11 plots of 200 land-cubits already tabulated for this distribution.

(c) Variable 33 Percentage of Assessment 1 and Variable 37 Percentage of Assessment 2

Variable 33 Percentage of Assessment 1 pertains to Sub-variety IA entries only and computes the percentage the value of variable 14 Assessed Arouras (red aroura figure) constitutes of the corresponding value of variable 46⅃ Figure (the black aroura figure following the sign ⅃) on the hypothesis that the size of plot for apportioning entries of Sub-variety IA is the aroura figure which follows the sign ⅃. In the case of an entry such as (A35,35) ".20⅃5.$\frac{1}{2}$, mc.1$\frac{2}{4}$," the value 5 arouras is interpreted as the size of plot, the assessed aroura value being $\frac{1}{2}$ aroura or 10% of the plot size.

Variable 37 Percentage of Assessment 2, on the other hand, pertains to Variety I entries only and computes the percentage the value of variable 14 Assessed Arouras (red aroura figure) constitutes of the corresponding value of variable 9 Arouras (initial black aroura figure) which is undoubtedly to be interpreted as the size of the plot. In the case of such an entry as (A66,35) ".5.$\frac{1}{2}$, mc.1$\frac{2}{4}$," the value 5 arouras is the size of plot, the assessed aroura value being $\frac{1}{2}$ aroura or 10% of the plot size.

Taking variable 33 Percentage of Assessment 1 first, we find that there are 59 entries of a total of 232 Sub-variety IA entries or 25.4% for which quantitative data are preserved where the red aroura figure constitutes 10% of the alleged plot size. In the case of 56 of the 232 entries or 24.1%, the red aroura figure constitutes 25% of the plot size, while in the case of another 50 entries or 21.6%, the red aroura figure constitutes 5% of the plot size. There are also 49 entries or 21.1% where the red aroura figure constitutes 20% of the plot size.

In the case of variable 37 Percentage of Assessment 2, we find that 318 entries or 31.0% of the 1027 Variety I entries for which quantitative data are preserved (excluding Pōsh B entries) are such that the red aroura figure constitutes 10% of the plot size as represented by the black aroura figure. There are 193 entries or 18.8% where the red aroura figure constitutes 5% of the plot size and 169 entries or 16.5% where the red aroura figure constitutes 20% of the plot size. In the case of 153 entries or 14.9%, the red aroura figure constitutes just 8.3% of the plot size.

The minimum and maximum percentages of assessment for variable 33 Percentage of Assessment 1 which tallies Sub-variety IA entries are 2.5% (2 entries, 0.9%) and 50% (6 entries, 2.6%) respectively with a range of 47.5% in which the median percentage of assessment is 20%. The mean of the distribution of variable 33 is calculated as 16.7%. It is evident from a scan of the frequency distribution of variable 33 that the percentage of assessment is in no way proportionate to the size of plot interpreted as the black aroura figure following the sign ⅃.

The minimum and maximum percentages of assessment for variable 37 Percentage of Assessment 2 which tallies Variety I entries are 0.8% (1 entry, 0.1%) and 66.7% (1 entry, 0.1%) respectively with a range of 65.9% in which the median is 10% as compared with 20% for variable 33. The mean of the distribution of variable 37 is calculated as 12.2% as compared with 16.7% for the distribution of variable 33. Once again, we see that the percentage of assessment is not proportionate to the size of plot.

It is clear from the various parameters calculated for the distributions of variable 33 and variable 37 that the distributions are indeed very different. If the distributions of the two variables are very different, it is unlikely that we are correct in supposing that there is no essential difference between entries of Variety I and those of Sub-variety IA. This assumption of no essential difference underlies Menu's interpretation of the Sub-variety IA entries as instances of scribal shorthand in which two or more identical consecutive Variety I entries enumerated in the same measurement area are condensed in a single line.(31)

In order to statistically verify the observed differences in the distributions of the two variables reflected in their parameters (mean, mode, median, minimum, and maximum percentages of assessment), we use a chi-square test of statistical significance. This test will tell us whether or not the observed frequencies of the two distributions match the frequencies we would expect to find were the two distributions of percentage of assessment essentially the same. The chi-square test executed on the data of both distributions indicates that the distributions of the two variables are not homogeneous. The Cramer's V value of the relationship between the two variables is 0.45000.

Thus, any interpretation of Sub-variety IA entries which is based upon the assumption that there is no essential difference between plots of Variety I and plots the data of which are expressed in the format of Sub-variety IA entries should be rejected as statistically untenable. The differences we observe in a comparison of the distributions of the data of Variety I and Sub-variety IA entries indicate that we should look for one or more linking factors among the variables we have identified in Text A as the explanation for these differences.(32)

NOTES

[1]David O'Connor, "The Geography of Settlement in Ancient Egypt," in *Man, Settlement and Urbanism*, Peter J. Ucko, Ruth Tringham, and G.W. Dimbleby, eds. (London, 1972), pp. 690-96.

[2]Hereafter, in introducing the name of an institution, only the paragraph number of the first occurrence of the institution in Text A is given.

[3]Gardiner, *Synopsis*, §70, p. 135; Bertha Porter and Rosalind L.B. Moss, *Topographical Bibliography of Ancient Egyptian Hieroglyphic Texts, Reliefs and Paintings*, vol. II, 2nd ed., rev. and enl. (Oxford, 1972), pp. 180-81; Uvo Hölscher, *Excavations at Ancient Thebes 1930-1* [*Oriental Institute Communication* 15] (Chicago, 1932), pp. 47-53.

[4]Gardiner, Synopsis, §§117, 152, pp. 142, 146. The subsumption of this temple under the heading of the House of Amun-Rēᶜ, King of the Gods in Section III (§117) is unique in P. Wilbour. See too §152 also in Section III where the fields are administered by the Steward of Amūn. It is possible that the reference to a "House of Ramesses-meriamūn" in B8,25 (and possibly also B3,2Ø and 5,4) also pertains to this temple.

[5]The reading of the deity's name is discussed briefly in Gardiner, Commentary, p. 13, n. 2; Synopsis, §83, p. 138.

[6]Kurt Sethe, Untersuchungen zur Geschichte und Altertumskunde Aegyptens, vol. III (Leipzig, 1896), p. 135. See too Gardiner, Commentary, p. 13, nn. 3.4.

[7]Gardiner, Commentary, p. 13 and Synopsis, §232, p. 153; Porter and Moss, Topographical Bibliography, vol. III (Oxford, 1931), p. 223.

[8]C. Robichon and A. Varille, "Fouilles des temples funéraires thébains (1937)," RdE 3 (1938), pp. 99-1Ø2.

[9]W. Pleyte and F. Rossi, Papyrus de Turin, 2 vols. (Leiden, 1869-76), pls. 51-6Ø; Gardiner, RAD, pp. 73-82; T. Eric Peet, "A Historical Document of Ramesside Age," JEA 1Ø (1924), pp. 116-127; for Ramesses V's stela at Gebel es-Silsila see Porter and Moss, Topographical Bibliography, vol. V (Oxford, 1937), p. 213.

[1Ø]L. Christophe, "Ramsès IV et le musée du Caire," Cahiers d'histoire égyptienne, series III, fasc. I (Cairo, 195Ø), pp. 47-67; idem, "Quatre enquêtes ramessides," Bulletin de l'Institut d'Égypte 37 (1956), pp. 5-37.

[11]W. Erichsen, Papyrus Harris I: Hieroglyphische Transkription [Bibliotheca Aegyptiaca V] (Brussels, 1933), p. 14 (11,7) and p. 12 (1Ø,3).

[12]Gardiner, Commentary, pp. 11-12 and n. 6 to p. 11; Synopsis, §69, p. 135.

[13]The other aspects of Amūn in the headings of the apportioning paragraphs are as follows: Amūn of the Beautiful Foreland, in Memphis; Amūn Tjayef; Amūn, Foreteller of Victory; and Amūn, Lord of Sharopě.

[14]Alan R. Schulman, Military Rank, Title, and Organization in the Egyptian New Kingdom [MÄS 6] (Berlin, 1964), pp. 51-53.

[15]Gardiner, Commentary, pp. 27-29. Ḳ3yt-land in Text B, however, appears to have a very specific connotation which may underlie the red rate figure "5 mc." in the non-apportioning paragraphs of Text A. In Text B, ḳ3yt-land is contrasted with both nḫb-land and tnỉ-land and likely refers to ordinary arable land. See H.W. Fairman, Review of Alan H. Gardiner, The Wilbour Papyrus, 3 vols. (Oxford,

1941-48) in JEA 39 (1953), pp. 120-23.

16 Gardiner, Commentary, p. 26.

17 Jean Capart, Recueil de monuments égyptiens, vol. 2 (Brussels, 1902-5), p. 92. See too Wilhelm Spiegelberg, "Die Tefnachthosstele des Museums von Athen," Rec. trav. 25 (1903), pp. 190-98.

18 Edward F. Wente, Late Ramesside Letters [SAOC 33] (Chicago, 1967), p. 31, note ae (11,2) suggests the translation "brush" for šnw "tree," provided that the clearing was achieved through burning, and in light of the fact that wood was so costly in Egypt.

19 Battiscombe Gunn and T. Eric Peet, "Four Geometrical Problems from the Moscow Mathematical Papyrus," JEA 15 (1929), pp. 167-85.

20 Gardiner, Commentary, p. 17.

21 Ibid., pp. 17, 112 with n. 4. See too pp. 86-87.

22 Ibid., p. 78.

23 Ibid., p. 59.

24 Ibid., p. 22.

25 Non-apportioning paragraphs which may be related to the herbage and white goat appportioning paragraphs include §§5, 18, 149, and 165: "Domain of this house under the authority of the overseer of cattle PN" and the sub-heading of §120: "Domain which makes fodder (wnmt) for cattle under the authority of the overseer of cattle, Ramessenakhte." Four other non-apportioning paragraphs of interest (§§196-97 belonging to the Treasury of Pharaoh; §209 belonging to the House of Amun-Rēᶜ, King of the Gods; and §222 belonging to the funerary temple of Ramesses III at Medīnet Habu) have sub-headings which read: "Domain of this house which makes fodder (for) Northern Oasis asses." See Commentary, p. 23.

26 Gardiner, Commentary, p. 24, nn. 2-7.

27 Ibid., p. 25.

28 The numbers for the measurement areas used in the present study do not correspond to the numbers assigned by Gardiner to the measurement areas which occur in his Table II. These numbers are the three digit codes assigned by the SPSS program to the original eight letter codes used to identify individual measurement areas in the data file. They are provided here to enable the reader to locate the individual measurement areas in the frequency table of variable 31 Geographic Location.

29 O'Connor, Man, Settlement and Urbanism, pp. 690-91 with fig. 3(a).

[30]It is important to note that in addition to the 245 Sub-variety IA entries which have dropped out of the previous table (1451 cases) inclusive of Variety I and Sub-variety IA entries, an additional 13 entries have also been eliminated. In these 13 entries, data of the black aroura figure have been preserved, but the entries cannot be assigned to either Variety I or Sub-variety IA because they are incomplete.

[31]Bernadette Menu, Le régime juridique des terres et du personnel attaché à la terre dans le Papyrus Wilbour (Lille, 1970), pp. 103-7.

[32]There is no SPSS table for this chi-square test of statistical significance as the result of technical problems with the program which could not be resolved in the short-term. Therefore, the computation was completed by hand. The same pertains to frequency tables for both of these quantitative variables which have no computer print-outs.

6 Subprogram CROSSTABS: Crosstabulations and Measures of Association

(1) The Subprogram

Subprogram CROSSTABS is an SPSS procedure for contingency table analysis which computes and displays two-way to n-way crosstabulation tables. Various statistical tests as well as a variety of measures of association are available in this procedure of which the chi-square test of statistical independence and the Cramer's V measure of association have been selected as appropriate for the present study.

The test statistic chi-square (χ^2) may be used to establish the probability of association between two variables; that is, whether or not a systematic relationship exists between two variables the data of which are displayed in the format of a contingency table. The chi-square statistic is computed upon actual table frequencies. It measures the differences between the actual or "observed" frequencies and those "expected" under the "null hypothesis" that the two variables are statistically independent of each other, the sample outcome possible but highly improbable. As the differences between the observed and expected frequencies increase, the value of chi-square also increases. As the value of chi-square increases, the null hypothesis of non-association becomes progressively less and less tenable and more likely to be rejected. A relatively large chi-square value thus tends to cast doubt upon the null hypothesis that the two variables are statistically independent; whereas a relatively small chi-square value tends to support it. In rejecting the null hypothesis that no association is present and operative, we tacitly accept the alternate hypothesis that some degree of association is present and the variables are not independent of each other.

In order to test the null hypothesis that the two variables are independent of each other, it is necessary to decide upon an appropriate level of significance; that is, the level of risk we are willing to accept of falsely rejecting the null hypothesis that the variables are independent of each other. It is customary in social science research to accept a significance level of .Ø1 or .Ø5. A significance level of .Ø1 means that we take the risk of only 1% that we are falsely rejecting a true null hypothesis of statistical independence. In other words, there is a 1% chance that the observed relationship between the variables occurred purely by chance as opposed to a 99% probability that the observed relationship is indicative of a systematic, statistically significant relationship between the variables. The smaller the level of significance, the smaller the risk of falsely rejecting a true null hypothesis. But by decreasing the risk of falsely rejecting a true null hypothesis, we correspondingly increase the risk of failing to reject the null hypothesis when it is false. In the case of the data of the P. Wilbour apportioning paragraphs, the decision was made to accept a significance level of .Ø1, since further studies are planned which will hopefully clarify and extend the line of reasoning on which the study was originally based.

Although the chi-square test permits us to determine the probability that association is present in the relationship between two variables, chi-square is not in itself a measure of the degree of that association. There are several measures of association which may be requested in the subprogram. Of these, Cramer's V has been selected as the most appropriate to the present study. The Cramer's V statistic varies from zero (Ø) to unity (+1). The higher the Cramer's V value, the stronger the degree of association between the variables. A Cramer's V value of Ø.75ØØØ, for example, is indicative of a very high degree of association between the variables. Given the large size of the P. Wilbour data file, even the smallest of trends are indicated as statistically significant. Since it is not feasible to discuss all these trends, as a rule only tables with Cramer's V values of Ø.4ØØØØ or higher have been selected for discussion. This is a more or less arbitrary cut-off point which should not be misinterpreted as implying that tables with lower Cramer's V values are not also worthy of consideration. A few tables with Cramer's V values less than Ø.4ØØØØ are discussed in relation to tables with higher Cramer's V values to which they may be meaningfully compared. Other tables with lower Cramer's V values are discussed because certain cells in the table reflect an anomaly worthy of special consideration even though the table as a whole does not reflect a particularly high degree of association.

One note of caution is necessary before consideration of the individual crosstabulations. The occurrence of relatively high frequencies of zero and low frequency cells in many of the crosstabulations discussed below has the net effect of artificially lowering the chi-square significance level and thus introducing some degree of distortion into the resultant Cramer's V value. This situation arises in any crosstabulation where one or both of the variables has a relatively large number of categories as, for example, in the case of variable 7 Occupation or Title of Smallholder where the number of categories (occupations) is 54. An even more extreme example is variable 31 Geographic Location where there are 185 measurement areas. This distortion effect does not detract from the overall validity of the bivariate statistics, however, but indicates that the degree of association between the variables should be understood as "relative" rather than "absolute" as would be the case with smaller crosstabulations. The Cramer's V values of such large tables, nevertheless, remain indicative of the degree of association between the variables and may be compared without hesitation. In the case of a variable such as variable 5 Deity or King where there are 26 categories, it is possible to remove the effect of distortion relatively easily by deleting single occurrence and low frequency cults. This can be done without sacrificing the inherent meaningfulness of the crosstabulation (i.e., its "ecological validity"). In the case of variable 31 Geographic Location, on the other hand, although it is possible to reduce the number of locations considerably by deleting single occurrence and low frequency measurement areas, the lower limit to which the categories may be reduced (28) without sacrificing the meaningfulness of the crosstabulation will also result in a crosstabulation with a relatively large number of zero and low frequency cells. In such a situation, absolute precision in both the chi-square significance level and the resultant Cramer's V value is neither necessary nor particularly desirable.

It should also be stated at the outset of the crosstabulation analysis that the attempt has been made to keep the technical language to a minimum. As a result, the discussions which follow, by and large, are lacking in the precise technical formulations that social scientists normally use and expect to read in statistical studies. In a field such as Egyptology, where the vast majority of scholars are not accustomed to crosstabulation analysis and hypothesis testing, the lack of precise technical language is a small price to pay if it facilitates understanding among a greater proportion of interested scholars. In describing data of variable 31 Geographic Location, for example, analyzed by means of subprogram CROSSTABS, the usual formulation "(X occurs) in association with (Y)" has been replaced, in the vast majority of cases, by the simple phrase "occurs in." Instead of saying "4 plots of ỉdb-land occur in association with Sharopě," we say "4 plots of ỉdb-land occur in Sharopě." Our comprehension of this statement derives from our understanding of the term "measurement area" as a geographic reference point used to identify the location of a plot. It is hoped that this preliminary crosstabulation analysis of Text A apportioning data is both sufficiently intelligible and thought-provoking to encourage other Egyptologists to utilize such analysis in studying data which, like those of P. Wilbour, are well-suited to such a methodology.

(2) The Crosstabulations

(a) Variable 1 Section of Text (Geographic Zone) by Variable 31 Geographic Location

In his analysis of P. Wilbour (Table II), Gardiner demonstrated that the four sections of Text A probably are to be viewed as denoting four geographic zones which are, for the most part, mutually exclusive. The crosstabulation of variable 1 Section of Text by variable 31 Geographic Location represents the overwhelming statistical confirmation of this hypothesis. The relationship between variable 1 Section of Text and variable 31 Geographic Location is found to be statistically significant with a Cramer's V value of Ø.99548. This means that with prior knowledge of the measurement area of a plot (i.e., a geographic reference point used to identify the location of a plot), it is possible to predict the geographic zone of plot location with virtually no chance of error. It is also true that with prior knowledge of the zone of plot location, it is possible to predict the measurement areas with virtually no chance of error. There are only 6 measurement areas of a total of 185 which occur in more than one section of the text: "the Stable" in Sections I and III; the House of Ptaḥmosĕ in Sections I and II; Opĕ, Sōshen, and Iy-idḥu in Sections II and III; and Mi-emsaḥ in Sections III and IV. Only "the Stable" occurs in sections of the text which are not consecutive. The data of these exceptions suggest that we are dealing with plots located in zones which were contiguous. In the case of "the Stable," the vagueness of the name suggests that we are dealing with two different locations the names of which are simple homonyms.

(b) Variable 1 Section of Text by Variable 3 Institutional Group and Variable 4 Land-owning Institution

The relationship between variable 1 Section of Text and variable 4 Land-owning Institution is found to be statistically significant with a Cramer's V value of Ø.63474 indicative of a relatively high correlation between the two variables. The table indicates that 4 of the 5Ø institutions (8.Ø%) occur in association with four zones; 9 institutions (18.Ø%) occur in association with three zones; 1Ø institutions (2Ø.Ø%) occur in association with two zones; while 27 institutions (54.Ø%) occur in association with only one of the four geographic zones. Thus, the majority of the 5Ø institutions owned (or virtually owned) land within a very limited geographic area. It appears to have been relatively rare for an institution to hold title to land dispersed over all four of the zones. The House of Amun-Rēʿ, King of the Gods at Karnak is one of the 4 institutions ascribed properties dispersed over all four zones. The geographic distribution of its landholdings is such that 116 plots of its 255 plots (45.5%) occur in zone 2, 91 plots (35.7%) occur in zone 3, and 39 plots (15.3%) occur in zone 4. Only 9 plots (3.5%) occur in zone 1 because of the loss of the Theban subsection. These 9 plots are herbage entries which come toward the end of Section I. The other 3 institutions which have landholdings dispersed over all four zones are the funerary temple of Ramesses II (Usimaʿrēʿ-setpenrēʿ); the Mansion of Ramesses-meriamūn, Beloved Like Rēʿ; and the Great Seat of Ramesses-meriamūn in the House of Ptaḥ. The last of these temples, the Great Seat of Ramesses-meriamūn in the House of Ptaḥ, which accounts for 69 apportioning entries, is the first institution to occur in Section I after the loss of an unknown number of lines. Two secular institutions, the Landing-Place of Pharaoh in Ḥardai and the Fields of Pharaoh, have moderately high frequencies of apportioning entries (85 and 48 respectively) which occur dispersed over zones 2, 3, and 4. The only temple of the group Other Religious to have plots in as many as three zones (2, 3, and 4) is the Mansion of King Menmaʿrēʿ in Abydus which has a frequency of 39 apportioning entries, 84.6% of which occur in association with zone 3.

When we view the table from the perspective of the institutions represented in each zone, we find that zone 1 landholdings came under the ownership--or virtual ownership--of only 9 institutions: the House of Ḥeryshef, King of the Two Lands (111 plots, 41.3%); the funerary temple of Ramesses II (Usimaʿrēʿ-setpenrēʿ) (50 plots, 18.6%); the House of Sobek, the Shedtite (48 plots, 17.8%); the Great Seat of Ramesses-meriamūn in the House of Ptaḥ (19 plots, 7.1%); the Sunshade of Re-Ḥarakhte in She (15 plots, 5.6%); the House of Osiris Khant-ʿAru (11 plots, 4.1%); the House of Amun-Rēʿ, King of the Gods (9 plots, 3.3%); the Mansion of Ramesses-meriamūn, Beloved Like Rēʿ (4 plots, 1.5%); and the House of Sobek, Lord of (?) ... (2 plots, 0.7%). Thus, the most frequently occurring institution by far in zone 1 is the House of Ḥeryshef, King of the Two Lands. The 111 plots ascribed to this temple constitute 100% of the temple's total landholdings in the apportioning paragraphs. The same is true of the House of Sobek, the Shedtite; the House of Sobek, Lord of (?)...; the Sunshade of Re-Ḥarakhte; and the House of Osiris Khant-ʿAru. The lack of data at the beginning of Section I, however, seriously handicaps the evaluation of data of zone 1, since the main sequences of paragraphs for Theban and Heliopolitan institutions are completely lacking. What frequencies we have for these institutions are derived from three herbage paragraphs (§§31-33) near the end of Section I. Some data of the Memphite subsection are also lacking as Section I commences with the Great Seat of Ramesses-meriamūn in the House of Ptaḥ rather than the House of Ptaḥ, the Great, South of His Wall, Lord of ʿAnkhtowĕ which is the first Memphite temple in Sections II and III.

In the case of zone 2, most of the plots are ascribed to just 3 institutions, the funerary temple of Ramesses V (Usimaʿrēʿ-skheperenrēʿ) accounting for the largest number of plots (138 plots, 24.0% of the 575 plots in zone 2). Second highest in frequency is the House of Amun-Rēʿ, King of the Gods which accounts for 116 plots or 20.2% of the plots in zone 2; while the third highest in frequency in zone 2 is the funerary temple of Ramesses III (Usimaʿrēʿ-meriamūn) at Medīnet Habu which accounts for 100 plots or 17.4% of the plots in zone 2. The institution with the fourth highest frequency is the funerary temple of Ramesses II (Usimaʿrēʿ-setpenrēʿ) (the Ramesseum) which accounts for 39 plots or 6.8% of the plots in zone 2. Accounting for nearly the same number of plots as the Ramesseum are 2 secular institutions, the Landing-Place of Pharaoh at Ḥardai (35 plots, 6.1%) and the Fields of Pharaoh (in the Keep of ʿOnayna) (31 plots, 5.4%). The rest of the institutions each account for less than 5.0% of the plots in zone 2. Many institutions, especially the temples of the group Other Religious, are ascribed no plots whatever in zone 2.

Of the temples of the group Other Religious which are found to have landholdings in zone 2, only the House of Seth, Lord of Pi-

Wayna (Syn. §99) appears to have actually been situated in zone 2; the remaining temples having been situated in such places as Sakō (Syn. §91 El-Ḳēs in the north of zone 4); Spermeru (Syn. §92 between Oxyrhynchus and Heracleopolis in the north of zone 3); Pi-Wadjoi (Syn. §90 some 5 kilometers south of the southern boundary of zone 4); Memphis (Syn. §103 far north of zone 1); Na-Usimaʿrēʿ-meriamūn (Syn. §89 Esh-Shēkh ʿIbādah); and Abydus (Syn. §§87-88). These data suggest that temples of the group Other Religious, like the relatively large temples of the three major temple groups, were also very often absentee landlords of plots sometimes located at a considerable distance from the temples themselves. The importance of temples of the group Other Religious in zone 2, however, appears to have been not very great, temples of this group accounting for only 59 plots or 10.3% of the 575 plots located in this zone.

The above data make it abundantly clear that funerary temples were the predominant land-owners in zone 2 with the funerary temple of Ramesses V, in whose fourth year of reign the document was written, accounting for the largest number of plots. It should be noted as well that zone 2 is the only zone in which plots of the funerary temple of Ramesses IV (Ḥeḳmaʿrēʿ-setpenamūn) were located. The occurrence of plots of the Fields of Pharaoh (in the Keep of ʿOnayna) in zone 2 is perhaps to some degree explained by the fact that the Keep of ʿOnayna was probably located between the zone 2 measurement areas Pi-Wayna and Temĕ (Syn. §§85, 101). The presence of plots belonging to the Landing-Place of Pharaoh in Ḥardai (Cynopolis) is less easily explained, however, since Ḥardai was located at or near the border between zones 3 and 4. It is possible, however, that since Ramesses V undoubtedly appropriated for his own funerary estate a relatively large number of landholdings in zone 2, as reflected in the data of P. Wilbour, he also may have enriched the landholdings of the "secular" establishments of which he was the obvious principal beneficiary (Landing-Place of Pharaoh, Fields of Pharaoh).

The distribution of landholdings of the various institutions over zone 3 shows that the predominant institution is the funerary temple of Ramesses V with 137 plots or 17.6% of the 780 plots of zone 3. The funerary temples of Ramesses II and Ramesses III account for 47 and 77 plots respectively or 6.0% and 9.9% respectively of the plots in zone 3. Once again, the House of Amun-Rēʿ, King of the Gods is a major landholder, accounting for 91 plots or 11.7% of the plots in zone 3. Very close in frequency to the great Karnak temple is the Mansion of Ramesses-meriamūn in the House of Rēʿ with 84 plots or 10.8% of the plots in zone 3; while the Mansion of Ramesses-meriamūn in the House of Ptaḥ accounts for 63 plots or 8.1% of the plots in zone 3. The remaining 25 institutions to which plots located in zone 3 are ascribed each account for less than 5.0% of the plots in zone 3. Twelve of these institutions belong to the group Other Religious of which the Mansion of King Menmaʿrēʿ in Abydus has the highest absolute and relative frequencies (33 plots, 4.2%).

It would appear that the Theban funerary temples are once again the predominant land-owners with the House of Amun-Rēʿ, King of the Gods also high in absolute and relative frequencies. There are also numerous temples of the group Other Religious represented in zone 3. Temples of this group are found to have been located not merely in zone 3 as is the case with the House of Seth, Lord of Spermeru and probably the House of Amūn, Lord of Sharopě, but also in zone 2 (the House of Seth, Lord of Pi-Wayna; the House of Amūn Tjayef), and zone 4 (the House of Bata, Lord of Sakō; the House of Sobek-Rēᶜ, Lord of Anasha; the Sunshade of Re-Ḥarakhte in Sakō; and the House of Amūn, Foreteller of Victory which is in Sakō). Some temples of the group Other Religious which are land-owners in zone 3 were situated quite far to the south of the P. Wilbour area as, for example, the House of Thoth of Na-Usimaʿrēᶜ-meriamūn (Syn. §89 Esh-Shēkh ʿIbādah); the House of Onūris, Lord of This (in herbage paragraph 186); the Mansion of King Menmaʿrēᶜ in Abydus; and the House of Ḥar-Min and Isis (Syn. §157) probably located at Coptus. The fact that so many temples of the group Other Religious are ascribed landholdings in zone 3, an area far removed from the temples themselves, indicates a situation in which absentee landlords played a significant role in the agricultural economy (as also in zone 2), and suggests that some of these institutions were not so "small" or "unimportant" as might be imagined from their lack of mention or prominence in other documents. We know this to have been the case with the House of Osiris, Lord of Abydus which numbers among the group Other Religious. Certainly there is reason to think that other temples of the group Other Religious may have been more significant in economic terms than we have hitherto supposed.

Whether the temples of the group Other Religious which occur so frequently as absentee land-owners in zones 2 and 3 administered these far-flung plots themselves or whether the plots were administered by officials of civil administrative districts which corresponded to the four geographic zones identified with the four sections of Text A, it is not possible to say for certain. Administrators (r-ḫt) are not specified for many of the temples of the group Other Religious. Where these officials are identified, they are found to be prophets (ḥm-nṯr). Prophets are also frequently found to be administrators of khato-land (concluding paragraphs of Sections I, II, and III) in company with such civil administrators as the mayors of various towns (§§45, 46, 115, 202) and the chief taxing-master (§§200-1). These facts suggest that prophets were accustomed to working in consort with civil authorities in order to manage agricultural land of particular concern to Pharaoh as head of State.

The distribution of the landholdings of the various land-owning institutions over zone 4 reveals the predominant institution to be the Mansion of Ramesses-meriamūn in the House of Rēᶜ. This temple of Ramesses II, situated perhaps in Heliopolis (Syn. §76), accounts for 141 of the 621 plots in zone 4 or 22.7%. The institution with the second highest frequency of plots in zone 4 is the House of Sobek-Rēᶜ, Lord of Anasha with 92 plots or 14.8% of the plots in zone 4. The funerary temple of Ramesses III accounts for the third highest number of plots in zone 4: 89 plots or 14.3% of the total. The institution with the fourth highest frequency is the funerary temple of Ramesses V which accounts for 84 plots or 13.5% of the plots in zone 4. The institution with the fifth highest frequency is the Heliopolitan temple, the Mansion of Ramesses-meriamūn, Beloved Like Rēʿ to which 44 plots in zone 4 are ascribed (7.1%). The House of Amun-Rēʿ, King of the Gods has a slightly lower frequency of 39 plots or 6.3% of the plots in zone 4, a much smaller percentage than is the case with this great temple in the case of zones 2 and 3 where it accounts for 20.2 and 11.7% of the plots in zones 2 and 3 respectively. It is noteworthy that the funerary temple of Ramesses II has a relatively low frequency in zone 4 (16 plots, 2.6%) as compared with the funerary temples of Ramesses III and Ramesses V.

The Great Seat of Ramesses-meriamūn in the House of Ptaḥ which has the highest absolute and relative frequencies of the Memphite temples accounts for only 21 plots or 3.4% of the plots in zone 4. Secular institutions are represented by only 2 institutions, the Landing-Place of Pharaoh at Ḥardai (32 plots, 5.2%) and the Fields of Pharaoh (7 plots, 1.1%). As is the case with zone 2, many of the temples of the group Other Religious do not occur as land-owners in zone 4. There are only 10 temples of the group Other Religious which have any landholdings enumerated in zone 4. Of these 10 temples, the House of Sobek-Rēʿ, Lord of Anasha is the predominant land-owner as indicated above. This fact is consistent with the location of Anasha in the far south of zone 4. The high frequency of the holdings of this temple in this zone may reflect the success of a local temple in establishing a substantial estate within its immediate vicinity, zone 4 accounting for 82.9% of this temple's 111 plots (19 plots, 17.1% in zone 3). The remaining 9 institutions each account for 1.0% or less of the plots in zone 4. Of these 9 institutions, the House of Thoth, Lord of Hermopolis has the highest absolute and relative frequencies, accounting for 6 plots or 1.0% of the plots in zone 4. The location of these 6 plots in zone 4 (100% of the temple's total plots in the apportioning paragraphs) is consistent with the location of Hermopolis south of zone 4 and qualifies the temple as yet another absentee landlord to appear in the records of P. Wilbour.

The crosstabulation of variable 3 Institutional Group and variable 1 Section of Text has a lower Cramer's V value (0.33749) than that of the above crosstabulation with variable 4 Land-owning Institution. We find that plots ascribed to Theban temples account for a decreasing number and percentage of the plots as we progress southward from zone 2 to zone 4 (disregarding data of Section I where only herbage entries of the Theban Group occur). This is curious, since the location of the city of Thebes far to the south of the P. Wilbour area would suggest that landholdings of temples of the Theban Group logically ought to increase in number and percentage as we go south from zone 2 to zone 4. Disregarding for the present, data of zone 1, we find that 409 of the 575 plots in zone 2 or 71.1% were ascribed to temples of the Theban Group; whereas 372 of the 780 plots in zone 3 or 47.7% were ascribed to temples of the Theban Group. Temples of the Theban Group account for 245 of the 621 plots in zone 4 or 39.5%. Thus, the absolute number and relative frequency of Theban landholdings actually decrease as we go southward. The situation of Heliopolitan landholdings is precisely the opposite from that of Theban landholdings: the absolute number and corresponding percentage of landholdings ascribed to Heliopolitan temples increase as we progress southward from zone 2 to zone 4 (once again disregarding the incomplete data of Section I). We find that 18 of the 575 plots in zone 2 or 3.1% were ascribed to temples of the Heliopolitan Group; whereas 141 of the 780 plots in zone 3 or 18.1% were ascribed to temples of the Heliopolitan Group. As for zone 4, 189 of the 621 plots in zone 4 or 30.4% belonged to Heliopolitan temples. These findings are curious in view of the location of the city of Heliopolis far to the north of zone 1. Plots of temples of the Memphite Group reveal no such clear pattern in their distribution over the four geographic zones.

Returning to the Theban Group, it is interesting to find that disregarding zone 1, the 1085 plots of the Theban Group have a nearly even distribution over zones 2 and 3 (409 plots, 37.7% in zone 2 and 372 plots, 34.3% in zone 3) with a lower frequency of 245 plots, 22.6% in zone 4; whereas 93.8% of the 352 plots of the Heliopolitan Group are located in zones 3 (141 plots, 40.1%) and 4 (189 plots, 53.7%). Thus, of the two temple groups, the Heliopolitan is the most strongly associated with the southernmost landholdings of Text A. The landholdings of the Memphite Group are curious insofar as 104 plots or 61.9% of the 168 plots ascribed to the Memphite Group are located in zone 3 and constitute 13.3% of the 780 plots in this zone. Temples affiliated with a city located relatively far north, therefore, are ascribed landholdings located relatively far in the south of the area of Middle Egypt to which the data of P. Wilbour pertain. The data of landholdings of the Theban and Heliopolitan groups, and to some extent the Memphite Group, suggest that the geographic location of the cult centres (Thebes, Heliopolis, and Memphis) played relatively little role in determining the geographic distribution of the landholdings of the constituent temples.

The group Other Religious is the one institutional group which permits an analysis of plot location over all four geographic zones, since landholdings of this group are preserved in their entirety in zone 1. The plots of the group Other Religious number 187 in zone 1 where these plots comprise 69.5% of the 269 zone 1 plots. These statistics are, of course, due in part to the loss of the main sequences of the Theban and Heliopolitan groups in the beginning of Section I. What is most curious, however, is the fact that the 187 plots of the group Other Religious in zone 1 constitute as much as 40.9% of the 457 plots ascribed to temples of this group in the apportioning paragraphs. The zone with the second highest number of plots ascribed to temples of the group Other Religious is zone 4 which accounts for 123 plots or 26.9% of the group's landholdings in the apportioning paragraphs. The data indicate, therefore, that plots of the group Other Religious occur in relatively large numbers both in the extreme north and extreme south of the P. Wilbour area with substantially lower concentrations of plots in the central zones 2 and 3 (59 plots, 12.9% and 88 plots, 19.3% respectively).

Secular institutions do not occur among the land-owners in zone 1 according to the Text A apportioning data, nor do they account for a substantial number of plots in zones 2, 3, or 4. The highest concentration of plots belonging to secular institutions occurs in zone 3 where 75 of the 183 secular ascribed plots (41.Ø%) were located. Zone 2 accounts for 69 plots (37.7%), while zone 4 accounts for 39 plots (21.3%). Plots of secular institutions constitute 12.Ø% of the plots in zone 2, 9.6% of the plots in zone 3, and 6.3% of the plots in zone 4.

The results of the crosstabulations of both variable 3 Institutional Group and variable 4 Land-owning Institution by variable 1 Section of Text are especially revealing and, certainly to some extent, surprising. Since the data of P. Wilbour pertain only to Middle Egypt, we are unable to comment about Heliopolitan landholdings north of Heliopolis or Theban landholdings south of Thebes so as to confirm or deny the data of P. Wilbour as regards the location of Theban and Heliopolitan landholdings. The tendency of Theban temples to account for a decreasing number and percentage of plots as we progress zone by zone from the north to the south, as well as the tendency of Heliopolitan temples to account for an increasing number and percentage of plots as we progress zone by zone from the north to the south, are findings which suggest that preconceived ideas about the logical distribution of plots zone by zone based upon the factor of distance from the major cult centres may well be premature. Given these findings, it would be most interesting to examine the locations of plots granted to temples by royal gift in order to determine whether or not there was any geographic pattern which might reflect government policy in awarding land grants to temples affiliated with different cult centres. Since the crosstabulation of variable 1 Section of Text (Geographic Zone) and variable 4 Land-owning Institution has established that individual temples did not necessarily possess land in their immediate neighbourhood, we must consider the individual temples as well as the temple groups in this regard.

(c) Variable 1 Section of Text by Variable 5 Deity or King

The relationship between variable 1 Section of Text and variable 5 Deity or King is statistically significant with a relatively high Cramer's V value of Ø.5791Ø indicative of a relatively high correlation between the variables.

The plots of 11 cults are located in only one of the four geographic zones of P. Wilbour. These cults and the zones in which 1ØØ% of their respective plots were located are as follows: Ḥatḥōr (1 plot in zone 4); Ḥeryshef (111 plots in zone 1); Ḥaʿpy (4 plots in zone 4); Ḥar-Min and Isis (1 plot in zone 3); Mont (2 plots in zone 4); Mūt (3 plots in zone 4); Nephthys (1 plot in zone 2); Onūris (9 plots in zone 3); Sobek (5Ø plots in zone 1); and ʿAnti (5 plots in zone 4). The funerary cult of Ramesses IV (Ḥeḳmaʿrēʿ-setpenamūn), which accounts for 3 plots in zone 2, also numbers among these cults.

The restriction of plots of the cults of Ḥeryshef and Sobek to zone 1 (Section I) (111 plots and 5Ø plots respectively) is consistent with the fact that Ḥeryshef was the tutelary god of Heracleopolis Magna and Sobek the tutelary god of Crocodilopolis, the former situated just south of the Fayyūm, the latter located in the Fayyūm. Low frequency Theban cults such as those of Mont and Mūt not surprisingly are located in zone 4, the southernmost of the four zones of Text A. Plots of the cults of Onūris (Lord of This) and Ḥar-Min and Isis (probably at Coptus), however, are not located in zone 4 where we might expect them to be located because of the southern location of both of these temples, but rather in zone 3 just to the north. With so few plots as evidence, however, it is premature to make any judgment on the possible implications of this situation.

While the low frequencies of the cults of Onūris and Ḥar-Min and Isis can be explained to some extent by the fact that these were probably local cults of limited wealth and popularity, the single plot of the cult of Ḥatḥōr in zone 4 is surprising. It would be expected that the cult of so popular a national deity as Ḥatḥōr would be well-represented among the apportioning data of Text A. We find major cults such as those of Amun-Rēʿ, Rēʿ, and Ptaḥ, on the other hand, represented by relatively large numbers of plots relatively well-distributed over zones 2, 3, and 4. The plots of the cult of Amun-Rēʿ, King of the Gods, show a marked decrease both in number and percentage over zones 2, 3, and 4, 116 plots or 45.5% of a total of 255 plots recorded for this cult occurring in zone 2, 91 plots or 35.7% occurring in zone 3, and 39 plots or 15.3% occurring in zone 4. The zone 2 plots ascribed to the cult of Amun-Rēʿ constitute 22.9% of the 506 plots of zone 2. The plots of the cult of Amūn, as distinguished from Amun-Rēʿ, have a similar distributional pattern in zones 2 and 3 (20 and 13 plots respectively), but increase in zone 4 (19 plots). The plots of the cult of Rēʿ show a marked increase over zones 2 to 4: 18 plots or 5.7% of the 318 plots of this cult occur in zone 2, 111 or 34.9% occur in zone 3, and 185 plots or 58.2% occur in zone 4. This cult accounts for an increasing percentage of the plots in each zone from zone 2 to zone 4 (3.6% in zone 2; 15.7% in zone 3; 31.8% in zone 4). The plots of the cult of the Memphite god Ptaḥ reveal no such easily identifiable pattern. Their highest concentration is in zone 3 (61.9%) where they account for 14.8% of the plots in that zone.

Progressing to cults with lower frequencies, we find that whereas all 50 of the plots of the cult of Sobek are located in zone 1 and constitute 18.6% of the plots in zone 1, 19 plots or 17.1% of the 111 plots of the cult of Sobek-Rēʿ are located in zone 3 as compared with 92 plots or 82.9% in zone 4. These plots belong solely to the House of Sobek-Rēʿ, Lord of Anasha located probably in the vicinity of Ṭihna at the southern boundary of zone 4. Thus, the location of these plots of the cult of Sobek-Rēʿ, which constitute 2.7% of the plots in zone 3 and 15.8% of the plots in zone 4, is not at all surprising. The cult of Osiris is not at all well-represented in these data. Eleven of the 17 plots (64.7%) of the House of Osiris, Lord of Abydus occur in zone 1. Only 4 plots (23.5%) are found to occur in zone 4 where we might well expect the majority of the plots to occur, while only 2 plots (11.8%) occur in zone 2. Plots of the cult of Osiris-Sety pertaining to the temple founded by Sety I at Abydus (Mansion of King Menmaʿrēʿ at Abydus), however, are concentrated in zone 3 where 33 plots or 84.6% of the 39 plots are located. There are only 5 plots of this cult located in zone 2, 1 in zone 4, and none at all in zone 1. We would perhaps expect the concentration of plots for an institution located so far to the south to occur in zone 4. The cult of Re-Ḥarakhte is another popular cult with a fairly low frequency (51 plots) in the Text A apportioning data. Plots of the cult of Re-Ḥarakhte are concentrated in zone 3 (32 plots, 62.7%). Fifteen plots (29.4%) occur in zone 1, 4 plots (7.8%) in zone 4, while no plots whatever occur in zone 2.

The funerary cults are clearly the preeminent cults to occur in the Text A apportioning paragraphs. The funerary cult of Ramesses V (Usimaʿrēʿ-skheperenrēʿ) alone accounts for 359 plots or 17.4% of the 2062 plots ascribed to temples. There is a nearly even distribution of these 359 plots between zones 2 and 3: 138 plots located in zone 2 and 137 plots located in zone 3 comprising 38.4 and 38.2% of the 359 plots respectively. There are no plots ascribed to this funerary cult in zone 1 and only 84 (23.4%) in zone 4. These plots comprise 27.3, 19.4, and 14.4% of the plots in zones 2, 3, and 4 respectively. The funerary cult of Ramesses III (Usimaʿrēʿ-meriamūn) is second highest in absolute and adjusted frequencies accounting for 266 plots or 12.9% of the 2062 plots in the table. These plots are concentrated in zone 2 where 100 plots or 37.6% of the 266 plots occur. The remainder of the plots occur in zone 3 (77 plots, 28.9%) and zone 4 (89 plots, 33.5%). These plots comprise 19.8, 10.9, and 15.3% of the plots in zones 2, 3, and 4 respectively. As in the case of the funerary cult of Ramesses V, there are no plots whatever in zone 1. It is with the funerary cult of Ramesses II (Usimaʿrēʿ-setpenrēʿ) that there is what at first appears to be a markedly different distribution. There are substantially fewer plots for this important Nineteenth Dynasty funerary cult: 152 plots or 7.4% of the total plots ascribed to temples in the Text A apportioning paragraphs. The highest frequency occurs in zone 1 where 50 plots or 32.9% of the 152 plots occur. These 50 plots occur in a herbage paragraph (§32) of the Ramesseum which happens to be the only herbage paragraph in Section I belonging to a funerary temple. Thus, the funerary temples of Ramesses III, Ramesses IV, and Ramesses V which we might expect to have their own herbage paragraphs in Section I are not represented at all by such paragraphs. This fact, in conjunction with the loss of the beginning of Section I, explains the absence of the funerary cults of Ramesses III, Ramesses IV, and Ramesses V in zone 1. The absence of herbage paragraphs is not necessarily a negative judgment upon the influence, wealth, or popularity of a cult, however, since Section II contains herbage paragraphs only for the funerary cults of Ramesses II (§106) and Ramesses V (§105); Section III only for the cults of Ramesses II (§176) and Ramesses III (§175); and Section IV only for the cult of Ramesses II (§243). This evidence, together with evidence of data of the ordinary non-funerary cults to which plots located in two or more geographic zones are ascribed, suggests that we ought not to expect herbage domains to exist for each and every funerary cult in each and every zone of plot location. The funerary cult of Ramesses V is the prime example, since this funerary cult is ascribed only one herbage paragraph (§105 in Section II) and is, nevertheless, the predominant cult represented in the Text A apportioning paragraphs.

(d) Variable 4 Land-owning Institution and Variable 3 Institutional Group by Variable 31 Geographic Location

The relationship between variable 4 Land-owning Institution and variable 31 Geographic Location is found to be statistically significant with a relatively high Cramer's V value of 0.69173. The great number of cells which occur in this massive table with zero and low frequencies, however, has the net effect of artificially lowering the chi-square value and distorting the Cramer's V value to some degree. For the present, however, it is enough to say that the variables are highly correlated. With so high a Cramer's V value, we can predict the land-owning institution on the basis of prior knowledge of the measurement area of plot location and vice versa with a relatively high degree of accuracy. While we can measure the degree of association in a given relationship as reflected in the Cramer's V value, we cannot determine the direction of the association, i.e., which variable determines the values of the other variable. We must rely upon our knowledge of the subject matter to identify the direction of the association in a given relationship. Given the factors of institution and geographic location of plot, it is likely that it was the institution which determined the geographic location of a plot and not the other way around. The fact that the correlation between the two variables is considerably less than perfect (i.e., Cramer's V value of 1.00000) reflects the effects of other variables upon the relationship observed such that we can say that there were probably two or more co-determinants of the geographic location of a plot.

Such a massive crosstabulation as this requires a detailed examination such as is beyond the scope of the present preliminary study. At the very least, we can say that the relationship between institution and geographic location of plot is one of the most fruitful and worthwhile areas for detailed examination. It will be valuable in the future to eliminate low frequency categories of both variables and rerun the crosstabulation in order to determine what effect, if any, the reduction of the number of zero and low frequency cells has upon the resultant Cramer's V measure of association.

The relationship between variable 3 Institutional Group and variable 31 Geographic Location is found to be statistically significant with a very high Cramer's V value of 0.77231 which indicates that the variables are very highly correlated. Thus, it is possible to be highly accurate in predicting the institutional group with prior knowledge of the geographic location of a plot and vice versa.

Of the 185 measurement areas of the Text A apportioning paragraphs, 117 or 63.2% occur in association with only one institutional group. Of these 117 measurement areas, 26 have frequencies of 1 plot only and are therefore of limited value in assessing the relationship between the two variables. In the case of 25 of the 117 measurement areas where 100% of the plots are ascribed to institutions of a single group, the frequencies are 10 plots or more to a maximum of 50 plots in the case of Irkak in zone 4. These 25 high frequency measurement areas are examples of localities where there was mixed ownership (or virtual ownership) of plots differentiated on the basis of institutional group affiliation reflecting, no doubt, the economic wealth and influence of the five groups of institutional land-owners.

In 41 of the 97 measurement areas (42.3%) where plots of the Theban Group occur, there are no plots of any other institutional group. In 16 of the 45 measurement areas (35.6%) where plots of the Heliopolitan Group occur, there are no plots of any other institutional group. The Memphite Group accounts for only 10 measurement areas with perfect association. These 10 measurement areas constitute 26.3% of the 38 measurement areas where plots ascribed to Memphite temples occur. In 37 of the 75 measurement areas (49.3%) where plots of the group Other Religious occur, there are no plots ascribed to any other institutional group. All of the plots in 13 of the 38 measurement areas (34.2%) where plots of the Secular Group occur are ascribed to secular institutions.

There are 38 measurement areas where the plots belong to institutions of two institutional groups. This number includes 14 measurement areas with frequencies of fewer than 10 plots. The most common combinations of ownership are Theban and Other Religious; Theban and Heliopolitan; and Theban and Memphite. There are 22 measurement areas where the plots enumerated belong to institutions of three institutional groups. This number includes 6 measurement areas with frequencies of fewer than 10 plots. The most common combinations of ownership are those of Theban, Other Religious, and Secular, on the one hand, and Theban, Memphite, and Secular, on the other hand.

There are only 6 measurement areas where the plots belong to institutions of four of the five institutional groups: Tent-ḥemy in zone 2 (21 plots); Pi-Medjwe in zone 2 (13 plots); the Granary of Reeds in zone 3 (46 plots); Spermeru in zone 3 (35 plots); Sakō in zone 4 (91 plots); and ʿawen-grove in zone 4 (24 plots). The Secular Group is absent in the case of Tent-ḥemy, Spermeru, and ʿawen-grove. The group Other Religious is absent in the case of Pi-Medjwe; the Heliopolitan Group in the case of the Granary of Reeds; and the Memphite Group in the case of Sakō. The Theban Group is represented in all of these measurement areas.

All five institutional groups are represented in the zone 3 measurement areas Ḥuiniuti and Sharopě. In the case of Ḥuiniuti, the Theban Group accounts for 24 of the 59 plots or 40.7%; whereas in the case of Sharopě, the Theban Group accounts for 51 of the 76 plots or 67.1%.

Thus, plots ascribed to the Theban Group occur in more measurement areas than plots ascribed to any other institutional group and also account for 100% of the plots in more measurement areas than any other institutional group. The prominence of the Theban temples is also established in the 38 measurement areas where the plots were owned by institutions of two institutional groups; the 22 measurement areas where the plots were owned by institutions of three institutional groups; the 6 measurement areas where the plots were owned by institutions of four institutional groups; not to mention the two zone 3 measurement areas where all five institutional groups are represented.

(e) Variable 18 Institutional Class, Variable 19 Type of Religious Institution, and Variable 39 Dynasty of Founding of Land-owning Institution by Variable 31 Geographic Location

The relationship between variable 18 Institutional Class and variable 31 Geographic Location is statistically significant with a high Cramer's V value of Ø.74582. Of the 185 measurement areas, only 25 measurement areas or 13.5% occur as the locations of plots ascribed to both religious and secular institutions. While none of these measurement areas are single occurrence measurement areas, 9 have frequencies of fewer than 1Ø plots. A total of 147 measurement areas or 79.4% occur as the locations of plots ascribed to temples exclusively; whereas only 13 measurement areas or 7.Ø% occur as the locations of plots ascribed to secular institutions exclusively. Of the 147 measurement areas which have perfect correlations (1ØØ%) with religious institutions, 22 are single occurrence measurement areas (84.6% of the 26 single occurrence measurement areas). Of the remaining 125 measurement areas, 55 have frequencies of 1Ø or more plots. Of the 13 measurement areas which have perfect correlations with secular institutions, 4 are single occurrence measurement areas. The fact that only 2 of the remaining 9 measurement areas have frequencies of 1Ø or more plots is suggestive of the relatively minor role played by secular institutions as land-owning institutions according to the data of P. Wilbour. These findings suggest that the local agricultural economies of the majority of measurement areas (67.6% excluding single occurrence measurement areas) may have been dominated by the fiscal priorities of temples in the absence or virtual absence of secular institutions. The local agricultural economies of only a small number of measurement areas were evidently dominated by the interactions of the fiscal priorities and policies of various combinations of religious and secular institutions which we cannot assume to have been identical or even necessarily in consonance with each other. An even smaller number of measurement areas came under the influence of secular institutions possibly in the absence of temples as land-owners. Since the only secular institutions which occur in the headings of the apportioning paragraphs appear without exception to have been Crown (State) institutions (Treasury of Pharaoh, Fields of Pharaoh, Landing-Place of Pharaoh, etc.), there may not have been any apportioned landholdings ascribed to towns per se as might be expected of Ḥardai (Cynopolis), Ninsu (Heracleopolis), and Tpēḥu (Aphroditopolis) which were important administrative centres according to the evidence of both Text A and Text B of P. Wilbour.

The relationship between variable 19 Type of Religious Institution and variable 31 is also statistically significant with a slightly higher Cramer's V value (Ø.78994) than that of the previous relationship. Of the 172 measurement areas where plots ascribed to temples occur, 42 or 24.4% are comprised of plots belonging to both funerary and ordinary cult temples. Of these 42 measurement areas, only 7 have frequencies of fewer than 1Ø plots. None of these measurement areas are single occurrence measurement areas. There are 1Ø1 measurement areas or 58.7% comprised of plots belonging to ordinary cult temples exclusively. Of these 1Ø1 measurement areas, 2Ø are single occurrence measurement areas; whereas 27 have frequencies of 1Ø or more plots. There are 29 measurement areas or 16.9% comprised of plots belonging to funerary temples only. Of these 29 measurement areas, 6 are single occurrence measurement areas; whereas 7 have frequencies of 1Ø or more plots.

Comparing data of this crosstabulation with data of the previous crosstabulation, we find that 13 measurement areas (7.Ø%) are such that the plots ascribed to them belonged to both funerary and ordinary cult temples as well as secular institutions. These measurement areas include localities with relatively low frequencies such as the Lake of Dīme in zone 3 and Ḥ-saḥto in zone 2 as well as high frequency measurement areas such as the Village of Inroyshes in zone 2, Ḥuiniuti in zone 3, and Sakō in zone 4. None of the 13 measurement areas are located in zone 1. In the case of 1Ø of these measurement areas, the distribution of plots among the three categories of land-owning institutions is very uneven. A good example is Sharopě in zone 3 where 51 plots are ascribed to funerary temples, 21 plots are ascribed to ordinary cult temples, and 4 plots are ascribed to secular institutions. Pen-Shōs in zone 3 and the Lake of Dīme also in zone 3 are the two cases of relatively even distributions. In the case of Pen-Shōs, 5 plots are ascribed to funerary temples, 7 plots are ascribed to ordinary cult temples, while 5 plots are ascribed to secular institutions. In the case of the Lake of Dīme, 4 plots are ascribed to funerary temples, 3 plots are ascribed to ordinary cult temples, while 2 plots are ascribed to secular institutions. Ḥuiniuti in zone 3 is a locality where one type of institution predominates by a wide margin: 5Ø plots are ascribed to ordinary cult temples, while 4 plots are ascribed to funerary temples and 5 plots to secular institutions. Sakō in zone 4 is a most unusual measurement area in that funerary temples account for 52 plots, ordinary cult temples account for 18 plots, and secular institutions account for 2Ø plots. These 2Ø plots ascribed to secular institutions account for 22.2% of the 9Ø plots in Sakō and 1Ø.9% of the 183 plots ascribed to secular institutions. Twenty plots is the highest frequency of plots ascribed to secular institutions to occur in a single measurement area. Pi-Wayna in zone 2 is also noteworthy in that funerary temples account for a large number of the plots (23 of a total of 31 or 74.2%) as compared with ordinary cult temples (1 plot only). Secular institutions account for the remaining 7 plots in Pi-Wayna.

The above described patterns of ownership, characteristic of only 7.Ø% of the 185 measurement areas, lead to the impression that the local economies of the large majority of measurement areas were influenced predominantly by only a single type of institution. There is no question but that the fiscal priorities and policies of ordinary cult temples dominated the local economies of a much greater proportion of measurement areas than those of either funerary temples or secular institutions.

The relationship between variable 39 Dynasty of Founding of Land-owning Institution and variable 31 Geographic Location is found to be statistically significant with a relatively high Cramer's V value of Ø.7Ø448. This crosstabulation is intended to be studied in conjunction with the crosstabulations of variable 4 Land-owning Institution and variable 5 Deity or King with variable 31 Geographic Location where data of individual reigns within the Nineteenth and Twentieth Dynasties may be compared. Variable 39 Dynasty of Founding of Land-owning Institution organizes the data of land-owning institution according to the broader categories of dynasty of founding chiefly for purposes of comparing the data of Nineteenth and Twentieth Dynasty institutions.

Of the 2157 entries analyzed in the table, 644 or 29.9% are ascribed to institutions of the Nineteenth Dynasty; whereas 592 entries or 27.4% are ascribed to institutions of the Twentieth Dynasty. Only 48 entries or 2.2% are ascribed to institutions of the Eighteenth Dynasty; whereas a substantial 873 entries or 40.5% are ascribed to institutions the dynasty of founding of which either predates the Eighteenth Dynasty, or cannot be fixed to any particular dynasty of founding. Comparison of the frequencies of institutions which can be securely dated to the Nineteenth and Twentieth Dynasties reveals no radical disproportion in the absolute number or relative frequency of their landholdings as they are distributed among the measurement areas of the Text A apportioning paragraphs.

Of the 185 measurement areas of variable 31 Geographic Location, only 32 or 17.3% are locations in which 100% of the plots are ascribed to institutions established during the Nineteenth Dynasty as compared with 19 measurement areas or 10.3% in which 100% of the plots are ascribed to institutions established during the Twentieth Dynasty. In the case of both institutions established during the Nineteenth Dynasty and institutions established during the Twentieth Dynasty, however, 5 of the measurement areas with perfect correlation have frequencies of 10 or more plots. Moreover, 9 measurement areas are single occurrence measurement areas in the case of Nineteenth Dynasty institutions as compared with 4 measurement areas in the case of the Twentieth Dynasty institutions. Thus, there are some marked similarities indeed in the distributions of plots of both Nineteenth Dynasty and Twentieth Dynasty institutions among the 185 measurement areas of the Text A apportioning paragraphs. Twenty-three measurement areas or 12.4% occur as the locations of plots ascribed to institutions of both the Nineteenth and Twentieth Dynasties. There is only a single measurement area (Pen-Shete in zone 4) in which all of the plots are ascribed to an Eighteenth Dynasty institution. Only 3 measurement areas, Ḥuiniuti, Sakō, and the Shelter of Sakō, are ascribed plots which may be assigned to all four of the categories of variable 39.

Although the funerary temple of Ramesses II (the Ramesseum) has a much lower frequency of apportioning entries in Text A than the funerary temples of either Ramesses III (Medīnet Habu) or Ramesses V, the frequency of Nineteenth Dynasty institutions in this crosstabulation is increased by the inclusion of data of other temples founded by Ramesses II as, for example, the Mansion of Ramesses-meriamūn, Beloved Like Rēʿ and the Mansion of Ramesses-meriamūn in the House of Ptaḥ. The data of this crosstabulation strongly suggest, therefore, that Nineteenth Dynasty institutions were very much alive and flourishing at the time of the compilation of P. Wilbour in year 4 of Ramesses V, despite the much lower frequency of apportioning entries ascribed to the funerary temple of Ramesses II as compared with those of both Ramesses III and Ramesses V. Gardiner's speculation concerning the status of temples established prior to the reign of Ramesses V, whether Theban, Heliopolitan, or Memphite, is thus convincingly validated from at least one avenue of approach.

(f) Variable 5 Deity or King by Variable 31 Geographic Location

The crosstabulation of variable 5 Deity or King by variable 31 Geographic Location makes it possible to consider plot location from the perspective of the 26 individual cults represented by one or more of the 45 temples of the apportioning paragraphs. The geographic distribution of the landholdings of an institution is likely to reflect the relative success of an individual institution as a corporate entity in the acquisition and utilization of agricultural land. The geographic distribution of the landholdings of a cult, on the other hand, reflects not only the relative success of affiliated temples in the acquisition and utilization of agricultural land, but also, to some degree, the contemporary popularity of the individual cult.

The relationship between variable 5 Deity or King and variable 31 Geographic Location is found to be statistically significant and substantively important as reflected in the chi-square and Cramer's V values. The Cramer's V value of Ø.6887Ø reflects virtually the same degree of association as in the previous crosstabulation of variable 4 Land-owning Institution by variable 31 Geographic Location. This high correlation suggests that the plots of individual cults can be expected to occur in certain predictable measurement areas. So too the plots of individual measurement areas can be expected to be the property of temples of certain predictable cults. The fact that the correlation between variable 5 Deity or King and variable 31 Geographic Location is no greater than that between variable 4 Land-owning Institution and variable 31 Geographic Location suggests that there was no overall strategy on the part of the individual priesthoods which either governed or guided affiliated temples in the acquisition of their landholdings over the geographic area to which the data of P. Wilbour pertain. It will be possible to make a more precise evaluation of the relationships between variables 4 and 5 and variable 31 Geographic Location when low frequency institutions, cults, and measurement areas are excluded from the analysis. While guaranteeing greater precision in the values of the bivariate statistics calculated for these relationships, this procedure requires the elimination of data which, while statistically trivial, are nevertheless of considerable interest to the Egyptologist. Reduction of the number of cults to those with relatively high frequencies is, therefore, not an ideal solution to the problem, but merely another approach to it.

(g) Variable 2 Format of Entry by Variable 31 Geographic Location

The relationship between variable 2 Format of Entry and variable

31 Geographic Location is found to be statistically significant with a relatively high Cramer's V value of 0.62055. There are 3 measurement areas among the 185 measurement areas which occur in the measurement lines of the Text A apportioning paragraphs where the plots recorded have insufficient data preserved to permit categorization as Variety I, Sub-variety IA, Variety I/II, Variety II, or Sub-variety IIA. These measurement areas therefore do not appear in the crosstabulation.

There are 74 measurement areas among the 182 measurement areas (40.7%) analyzed in the table where all of the plots belong to only one variety of data format. Only 7 of these measurement areas have frequencies of 10 or more plots. The plots of 50 of the 74 measurement areas are, without exception, aroura measured plots of Variety I. Variety I, it will be recalled, has the highest frequency among the five varieties of data format, pertaining to 55.6% of the apportioning entries. Fourteen of these 50 measurement areas are single occurrence measurement areas. The plots of 9 of the 74 measurement areas which have perfect association with one variety of format are, without exception, aroura measured plots of Sub-variety IA, i.e., aroura measured plots differing from Variety I aroura measured plots in the presence of the sign ⌋ which apparently elucidates how the data of size of plot are to be interpreted. None of these measurement areas have frequencies of 10 or more plots. The plots of 14 of the 74 measurement areas are classified as belonging to aroura measured Variety I/II, one of two varieties of unassessed plots. The highest frequency among these 14 measurement areas is 9 plots. There is only 1 measurement area among the 74 where all of the plots belong to a land-cubit measured format. This is P-mi-Sobk in zone 1 to which 2 Sub-variety IIA plots (unassessed land-cubit measured plots) are ascribed.

There are 55 measurement areas (30.2%) where the plots fall into two categories of data format, the most common combination being that of aroura measured Variety I and aroura measured Sub-variety IA (33 measurement areas). Sub-variety IA plots predominate in only 3 of the 182 measurement areas, 2 of which have frequencies in excess of 20 plots (the Temple of Sobek and ʿawen-grove in zone 4). The combination of aroura measured categories Variety I and Variety I/II is characteristic of 8 measurement areas only, while the combination of land-cubit measured categories Variety II (assessed) and Sub-variety IIA (unassessed) is characteristic of 9 measurement areas. The combinations of Sub-variety IA and Variety I/II; Variety I and Variety II; and Sub-variety IA and Sub-variety IIA are unusual combinations of plots among the 55 measurement areas.

There are 27 measurement areas among the 182 measurement areas (14.8%) where there are three varieties of plots, the most frequent combinations being those of Variety I, Sub-variety IA, and Variety I/II, on the one hand, and Variety I, Variety II, and Sub-variety IIA, on the other hand. The frequencies for these 27 measurement areas vary from 4 to 75 plots. The plots of 18 measurement areas (9.9%) consist of four of the five varieties, the most commonly absent of which is aroura measured Variety I/II. All but 3 of these 18 measurement areas have frequencies of 10 or more plots. There are only 8 measurement areas where all five varieties of plots occur: the Village of Inroyshes, Tent-ḥemy, the Village of Djasasati, and Smaʿa in zone 2; Tayʿankhe, Sakō, Menʿonkh, and Irkak in zone 4. Of these 8 measurement areas, Tayʿankhe has the lowest frequency (13 plots); whereas Sakō has the highest frequency (89 plots). It is quite possible that the occurrence of all five varieties of plots in a single measurement area is one useful index of relative size among measurement areas.

Looking at the 2Ø measurement areas to which 25 or more plots are ascribed, we see a complex mosaic of patterns in the distribution of the five varieties of plots. Of these 2Ø measurement areas, 7 have frequencies of 5Ø or more plots and are therefore most worthwhile discussing individually. These 7 measurement areas are the following: the Village of Inroyshes, 52 plots; Mi-ēḥu, 52 plots; Ḥuiniuti, 56 plots; Sharopě, 75 plots; Sakō, 89 plots; Menʿonkh, 79 plots; and Irkak, 5Ø plots. Four of these 7 high frequency measurement areas (the Village of Inroyshes, Sakō, Menʿonkh, and Irkak) also number among the measurement areas to which all five varieties of plots are ascribed. Thus, these measurement areas appear to have been both relatively large in terms of the absolute number of plots ascribed to them and sufficiently large in geographical area to have encompassed both aroura and land-cubit measured plots which may denote entirely different types of cultivation. Variety I plots are far in excess of any other variety in the Village of Inroyshes, Sakō, and Irkak. Mi-ēḥu and Sharopě are examples of measurement areas in which Variety I plots predominate in association with aroura measured plots of Sub-variety IA and Variety I/II. Ḥuiniuti, on the other hand, is comprised of 55 Variety I plots and a single plot of Sub-variety IA. Only in Menʿonkh are there more land-cubit measured Variety II plots (2Ø) than aroura measured Variety I plots (14). When we include data of the unassessed Variety I/II and Sub-variety IIA plots, land-cubit measured plots in Menʿonkh still outnumber aroura measured plots. Irkak has both a high concentration of Variety I plots and a high concentration of Sub-variety IIA plots. The plots of this measurement area are distributed such that there is an equal number of aroura measured and land-cubit measured plots (25 plots of each land measure).

There are 11 measurement areas which have frequencies of 26 to 49 plots each. In each measurement area, there are anywhere from one to five varieties of plots represented. Where there are two varieties of plots, the combinations are Variety I and Sub-variety IA; and Variety I and Variety I/II. There are 3 measurement areas where three varieties of plots occur, the combinations of which are Variety I, Variety II, and Sub-variety IIA; Variety I, Sub-variety IA, and Variety I/II; and Variety II, Variety I/II, and Sub-variety IIA. In another 3 measurement areas there are four varieties of plots represented. The Village of Djasasati in zone 2 is ascribed plots of all five varieties, while the Sycomores of Irkak in zone 4 is ascribed plots of Variety I only. The predominance of the two land-cubit measured formats is evident only in the zone 1 measurement areas T(?)-miē-ḥi-tjayef and the Great Byre.

These data suggest that the cultivation of the relatively small land-cubit measured plots is not likely to have been a significant component of the agricultural economies of many towns and villages in the area of Middle Egypt to which the data of P. Wilbour pertain. The fact that there is a very limited number of measurement areas where unassessed land-cubit measured Sub-variety IIA and aroura measured Variety I/II plots predominate suggests that the lack of assessment for these plots was an important concern (problem?) for relatively few localities. Assuming that the terms m šwt and wšr (??) have been correctly understood by Gardiner as relating to the irrigation of the land,(1) these difficulties appear to have been limited to a relatively small number of localities. In the case of measurement areas where Sub-variety IA plots predominate, there is no hint or suggestion that these plots reflect the constraints of the physical environment. Since the only immediately distinguishable difference between Variety I and Sub-variety IA entries turns upon the interpretation of the data of size of plot in Sub-variety IA entries, the curious Sub-variety IA entries may denote plots the size of which underwent some alteration since the time of the previous assessment. In view of the fact that 49 plots or 20.7% of the Sub-variety IA plots occur in only 3 measurement areas, all of which are located in zone 4, it is possible that local economic considerations favoured the splitting off of a portion of a larger parcel of land, or the consolidation of 2 or more plots under a single smallholder. The initial black aroura figure may represent the total parcel size or the size of a newly consolidated plot.

It is very difficult to generalize about the location of the five varieties of plots on the basis of this complex crosstabulation. Our difficulty in drawing conclusions from this table, beyond noting the fact of the statistical significance and substantive importance of the relationship between the variables, is explained in part by the fact that the table reflects several different but related trends which need to be distinguished. It is evident that land-cubit measured plots differ from aroura measured plots in their distribution over the 182 measurement areas analyzed in the table. It is also evident that some measurement areas tend to have substantially more unassessed plots than other measurement areas. Finally, while it is evident that the peculiar Sub-variety IA plots tend to occur in association with "ordinary" Variety I plots which are also aroura measured, it is also clear that Sub-variety IA plots predominate in certain measurement areas where they may comprise as much as 100% of the plots.

Moreover, difficulty in generalizing about the data of the present table is certainly due in considerable part to the occurrence of unassessed plots in many measurement areas which obscures the patterns of distribution of assessed plots of Variety I, Sub-variety IA, and Variety II. Since we cannot be certain that we have correctly classified all unassessed plots as either aroura measured (Variety I/II) or land-cubit measured (Sub-variety IIA), the distribution of plots we observe in this crosstabulation may be to some degree deceptive. The inferences we derive from these data stand a greater chance of being correct if we remove the data of unassessed plots from the crosstabulation.

Thus, the simultaneous occurrence of several trends among the data compounded by the occurrence of numerous unassessed plots of uncertain land measure necessitates the creation of new variables to distinguish the various trends and remove the effect of the unassessed plots upon the distribution of assessed plots. The resultant tables will also provide the individual chi-square and Cramer's V values for each dominant trend and thereby measure both the statistical significance and substantive importance of each trend.

(h) Variable 43 Land Measure I Arouras or Land-cubits (Variety I, Sub-variety IA, Variety II) by Variable 1 Section of Text and Variable 31 Geographic Location

Variable 43 Land Measure I Arouras or Land-cubits (Variety I, Sub-variety IA, Variety II) was derived from data of variable 2 Format of Entry in order to permit the crosstabulation analysis of data of format of entry (type of plot) and geographic location where plots are distinguished according to the land measure of the plot, aroura or land-cubit. Variable 43 Land Measure I excludes data of all unassessed plots in order that the inferences drawn from the table have the highest potential of being correct.

Crosstabulation of variable 43 Land Measure I and variable 1 Section of Text (Geographic Zone) reveals that the relationship is statistically significant and substantively important as reflected in the moderately high Cramer's V value of 0.47242. Discounting, for the present, data of Section I (zone 1) where an unknown number of entries are lost, we see that aroura measured plots (Variety I and Sub-variety IA) occur predominantly in zone 3 where 719 plots or 49.9% of the 1440 aroura measured plots of Variety I and Sub-variety IA occur. The remainder of the aroura measured plots are nearly equally divided between zone 2 and zone 4: 345 plots or 24.0% of the 1440 plots occur in zone 2; whereas 340 plots or 23.6% of these plots occur in zone 4. The 345 aroura measured plots in zone 2 constitute 89.6% of the 385 plots in zone 2; whereas the 340 aroura measured plots in zone 4 constitute 82.3% of the 413 plots in zone 4.

Land-cubit measured plots (Variety II) are distributed very differently. Their highest concentration is in zone 1 where 77 land-cubit measured plots occur, constituting 35.5% of the 217 land-cubit measured plots of Variety II. Thus, zone 1 is the zone with the highest absolute frequency of land-cubit measured plots of Variety II, despite the incomplete condition of Section I. These 77 plots constitute 68.1% of the 113 plots in zone 1. Were Section I complete, this high percentage would very likely decrease. As the text stands, there are only 36 aroura measured plots of Variety I and Sub-variety IA in zone 1 which constitute only 2.5% of the 1440 aroura measured plots in the table. While the 77 land-cubit measured plots comprise 68.1% of the 113 plots in zone 1, the 36 aroura measured plots comprise only 31.9% of these 113 plots. The correlation between zone 1 and land-cubit measured plots is so strong that it is probable that zone 1 was an area particularly well-suited to the small-scale cultivation denoted by land-cubit measured plots. Zone 4 accounts for 73 land-cubit measured plots which comprise 33.6% of the 217 land-cubit measured plots and 17.7% of the 413 plots in zone 4. Zones 2 and 3 have the lowest frequencies of Variety II land-cubit measured plots, accounting for 40 plots (18.4%) and 27 plots (12.4%) respectively (10.4% and 3.6% of the plots in these two zones).

The markedly different distribution of aroura measured plots (Variety I and Sub-variety IA) as compared with land-cubit measured plots (Variety II only) over the four geographic zones of Text A suggests that there is a substantive difference between aroura measured and land-cubit measured plots which hinges upon the location of the plot. We can pursue this possibility by crosstabulating variable 43 Land Measure I with variable 31 Geographic Location.

When variable 43 Land Measure I is crosstabulated with variable 31 Geographic Location, the significantly higher Cramer's V value of 0.75261 suggests a much higher degree of correlation between the variables than was the case with the previous crosstabulation. There are 117 measurement areas among the 167 measurement areas which occur in the table where 100% of the plots are aroura measured. Of the 117 measurement areas, 33 have frequencies of 10 or more aroura measured plots. Plots in only 10 measurement areas are, without exception, land-cubit measured. Of these 10 measurement areas, the highest frequency is 9 plots occurring in 2 measurement areas. Plots in 40 measurement areas are both aroura and land-cubit measured, the ratio varying from locality to locality. Only 10 measurement areas have an even or nearly even distribution of aroura measured and land-cubit measured plots. These data suggest that land-cubit measured plots tended to be restricted to a limited number of towns and villages, and that the type of cultivation which characterized land-cubit measured plots was an important feature of the agricultural economy of relatively few towns and villages in the part of Middle Egypt to which the data of P. Wilbour pertain. It is possible that the location of land-cubit measured plots was determined by the individual institution which permitted the cultivation of the relatively small plots only in certain of the localities where it owned or administered land. These data also suggest the possibility that one significant difference between aroura measured and land-cubit measured plots may have been the crop(s) with which they were planted. The occasional notation of land-cubit measured plots as plots cultivated with flax (mḥt) (A6,x+17; 7,43.48; 8,4) and "in vegetables" (m w3ḏ) (A6,x+15; 40,10; 44,33) suggests that a difference in the crop cultivated may have set the land-cubit measured plots apart from the often considerably larger aroura measured plots. The very fact that there is no mention of any rate of assessment or produce forthcoming from the assessed land-cubit measured plots (Variety II) is in itself strongly suggestive of a substantive difference between aroura and land-cubit measured plots beyond size per se.

(i) Variable 44 Land Measure II Arouras or Land-cubits (Variety I, Sub-variety IA, Variety I/II, Variety II, Sub-variety IIA) by Variable 1 Section of Text and Variable 31 Geographic Location

Variable 44 Land Measure II Arouras or Land-cubits (Variety I, Sub-variety IA, Variety I/II, Variety II, Sub-variety IIA) is also derived from data of variable 2 Format of Entry and differs from variable 43 Land Measure I in the inclusion of data of the unassessed plots (Variety I/II and Sub-variety IIA). The new variable is a "test variable" designed to test the validity of the classification of the unassessed plots as either aroura or land-cubit measured (Variety I/II and Sub-variety IIA respectively). The closer the correspondence between the distributional patterns of the crosstabulations involving these two variables, the higher the probability that the present classification is correct (see pp. 14, 5Ø-52). Variable 43 Land Measure I serves as a "control variable" as it excludes data of the unassessed plots from the analysis and focusses instead upon plots the land measure of which is not at issue.

The distribution of aroura measured as compared with land-cubit measured plots in the crosstabulation of variable 44 Land Measure II by variable 1 Section of Text is very similar to that of the crosstabulation of variable 43 Land Measure I by variable 1 Section of Text. The close correspondence of the two crosstabulations is reflected in the Cramer's V values of the two crosstabulations which are Ø.47242 in the case of variable 43 Land Measure I and Ø.43137 in the case of variable 44 Land Measure II. These crosstabulations are sufficiently small in size (having no zero or low frequency cells) as to preclude any distortion in the values of their bivariate statistics.

In the crosstabulation with variable 44, zone 3 also has the highest frequency of aroura measured plots, 736 plots or 42.9% of the 1717 aroura measured plots. There is also a nearly even distribution of aroura measured plots between zones 2 and 4, there being 44Ø aroura measured plots (25.6%) in zone 2 and 458 plots (26.7%) in zone 4. Zone 1 continues to have a very low frequency of aroura measured plots. There are only 83 aroura measured plots in zone 1 which comprise only 4.8% of the 1717 aroura measured plots and 36.2% of the 229 plots in zone 1. As in the previous crosstabulation, zones 1 and 4 have a nearly even distribution of land-cubit measured plots: 146 plots in zone 1 comprising 34.2% of the 427 land-cubit measured plots as compared with 154 plots in zone 4 comprising 36.1% of these plots. The 146 land-cubit measured plots in zone 1 comprise a substantial 63.8% of the 229 plots in zone 1. The 154 land-cubit measured plots in zone 4, however, comprise only 25.2% of the 612 plots in zone 4. Zone 3 continues to have the lowest frequency of land-cubit measured plots among the four zones: 38 plots or 8.9% of the 427 land-cubit measured plots. The frequency for zone 2 of 89 land-cubit measured plots (2Ø.8%) is more than twice that of zone 3. Thus, the addition of data of the unassessed plots to the analysis results in a relationship between the variables which is very similar to that of the previous crosstabulation. These data suggest that unassessed plots have, for the most part, been correctly identified as aroura or land-cubit measured.

The crosstabulation of variable 44 Land Measure II and variable 31 Geographic Location is also substantially similar to the previous crosstabulation in which variable 43 Land Measure I was crosstabulated with variable 31 Geographic Location. The Cramer's V value for the relationship between variable 44 Land Measure II and variable 31 Geographic Location is a slightly higher Ø.77519 as compared with Ø.75261 for the relationship between variable 43 Land Measure I and variable 31 Geographic Location. A total of 182 measurement areas occur in the table, 127 of which consist entirely of aroura measured plots. Of these 127 measurement areas, 35 have frequencies of 1Ø or more aroura measured plots. In only 1Ø measurement areas, on the other hand, are all the plots land-cubit measured. Of these 1Ø measurement areas, 4 have frequencies of 1Ø or more land-cubit measured plots. Of these 4 measurement areas, the New Land of... in zone 1 has the highest frequency (23 such plots). This leaves 45 measurement areas as the locations of plots of both land measures. These 45 measurement areas include 8 measurement areas where the distribution of aroura and land-cubit measured plots is even or nearly even. Two measurement areas, Menʿonkh and Irkak in zone 4, are high frequency measurement areas. The figure of 45 measurement areas where plots of both land measures occur is comparable to the 4Ø measurement areas where plots of both land measures occur in the crosstabulation of variable 43 Land Measure I and variable 31 Geographic Location. The addition of data of unassessed plots to the analysis does not substantially alter the distribution of aroura and land-cubit measured plots among the measurement areas of the Text A apportioning paragraphs. The tables are sufficiently similar to lend substantial credibility to the present criteria for the classification of unassessed plots. It is highly probable that unassessed plots with the value "5" and multiples of 5 short of 1ØØ are to be classified as aroura measured.

(j) Variable 45 Type of Aroura Measured Entry (Variety I or Sub-variety IA) by Variable 31 Geographic Location

Variable 45 Type of Aroura Measured Entry (Variety I or Sub-variety IA) is derived from data of variable 2 Format of Entry and takes into account only the assessed aroura measured plots the data of which correspond to Variety I and Sub-variety IA. This crosstabulation provides a means of testing Menu's hypothesis that Sub-variety IA entries denote a type of shorthand in which identical consecutive Variety I entries are condensed in a single one line entry. Crosstabulation analysis will identify any statistically significant trends among the data which suggest that the two formats of data denote distinct categories of plots which are intrinsically different from each other in one or more regards.

Crosstabulation of this variable with variable 1 Section of Text indicates only a low degree of correlation between the variables as revealed by the Cramer's V value of Ø.17728. The crosstabulation of variable 45 Type of Aroura Measured Entry with variable 31 Geographic Location, however, reveals both statistically significant and substantive differences in the distribution of plots of these two formats over the 157 measurement areas in which Variety I and Sub-variety IA plots occur. The Cramer's V value measuring the substantive importance of the relationship is a relatively high Ø.59368.

There are 72 measurement areas among the 157 measurement areas analyzed in the table (45.9%) where Variety I plots occur to the exclusion of Sub-variety IA plots. Nine of these 72 measurement areas have frequencies of 1Ø or more plots. The highest frequency (34 plots) is that of Pen-Roḥu in zone 3. There are 12 measurement areas (7.6%) where Sub-variety IA plots occur to the exclusion of Variety I plots. The highest frequency among these 12 measurement areas is 6 plots (Pen-Ḥedj in zone 4). In 73 measurement areas (46.5%), however, both Variety I and Sub-variety IA plots occur. There are 7 measurement areas among the 73 where the percentage of Sub-variety IA plots exceeds that of Variety I plots even though there are just greater than five times as many Variety I entries as Sub-variety IA entries among the apportioning entries. In the case of Imy-tay-m-t-nē, the Temple of Sobek, and ʿawen-grove, there are substantially more Sub-variety IA plots than Variety I plots. Altogether, these three concentrations of Sub-variety IA plots in zone 4 account for 49 Sub-variety IA plots or 2Ø.7% of the 237 Sub-variety IA plots analyzed in the table. The remaining 4 measurement areas account for only 2 Sub-variety IA plots each with the exception of the Keep of Wadjmosě in zone 2 which accounts for 3 Sub-variety IA plots.

This crosstabulation, with its relatively high Cramer's V value, is evidence of a statistically significant and substantively important difference between Variety I plots and Sub-variety IA plots. It is one significant indication that the ingenious hypothesis put forward by Menu to explain the curious Sub-variety IA entries is unlikely to be correct.

(k) Variable 45 Type of Aroura Measured Entry (Variety I or Sub-variety IA) by Variable 17 Special Entry

The relationship between variable 45 Type of Aroura Measured Entry (Variety I or Sub-variety IA) and variable 17 Special Entry is found to be statistically significant and substantively important as reflected in the phi value of Ø.74866. The bivariate statistic phi has been calculated as the measure of the degree of association instead of Cramer's V as the crosstabulation reduces to a two by two table with the dropping out of two categories of special entry (mḥt and w3ḏ) which pertain to land-cubit measured entries only.

The table indicates that 23 of the 3Ø complete ḥnk entries or 76.7% take the form of Sub-variety IA entries, while only 7 ḥnk entries or 23.3% take the form of Variety I entries. This distribution, indicative of a very high correlation between Sub-variety IA and plots identified as donated land, is in itself a strong indicator that Sub-variety IA entries denote plots which are in some way(s) substantively different from those denoted by ordinary Variety I entries. Of the 7 ḥnk entries which do not occur in the table, 4 are examples of aroura measured Variety I/II entries and 3 are incomplete entries which are probably also aroura measured. The evidence of the initial black aroura figure in entries of Sub-variety IA, moreover, suggests that these plots may have been relatively large in size as would not be inconsistent with the character of plots consecrated to the cult of a god(s) of Pharaoh, none of which are land-cubit measured. A relatively large size of plot would also be consistent with the possible interpretation of the initial black aroura figure in the Sub-variety IA entries as indicating a parcel or block of plots newly consolidated, the component size of which is indicated by the black ⌟ figure (see chapter 8 (1)).

It is not surprising that the initial black aroura figure of 15 of the 23 Sub-variety IA entries is found to be 20 arouras, multiples of 20 arouras up to a maximum of 100 arouras accounting for 6 more of these entries. Only 2 of the 23 Sub-variety IA ḥnk entries (A46,4 and 81,22) attest a value of less than 20 arouras. Moreover, the incomplete ḥnk entries, which cannot be assigned to any format of entry for lack of adequate data, have the relatively high values ".50" (A27,44 and 85,15) and ".60" (A33,30) which are very probably to be interpreted as aroura measured Sub-variety IA entries because they both occur in a series of Variety I and Sub-variety IA entries. The values ".50" and ".60" are far more typical of the array of values for the initial black aroura figure of Sub-variety IA entries than they are of the black aroura figure of Variety I entries.

The table indicates that in contrast to the ḥnk entries, 42 of the 44 3ḥt n ḥtrỉ entries which occur in the table or 95.5% take the form of Variety I entries; whereas only 2 entries or 4.5% take the form of Sub-variety IA entries. These data indicate that the ratio of Variety I 3ḥt n ḥtrỉ entries to Sub-variety IA 3ḥt n ḥtrỉ entries is far greater than that of the apportioning entries as a whole where the ratio of Variety I entries to Sub-variety IA entries is just greater than 5 to 1. This indicates that we are looking at a distribution with an extremely high correlation with Variety I. In all but 2 of these 3ḥt n ḥtrỉ entries (A36,39 and 62,35), the value of the black aroura figure is 5 arouras, the modal size of plot for Variety I entries. The two exceptions are the 2 Sub-variety IA entries with an initial black aroura figure of 10 arouras and a ⌟ figure of 5 arouras. These data suggest that the black ⌟ figure should indeed be understood as a size of plot as Menu interprets it in her explanation of the Sub-variety IA entries.(2) This does not mean, however, that it is necessarily correct to interpret Sub-variety IA entries as a means of condensing the data of two or more identical consecutive Variety I entries, as the relationship between the ⌟ figure and the initial black aroura figure remains open to interpretation. The data of this crosstabulation actually cast considerable doubt upon Menu's interpretation of the Sub-variety IA entries as scribal shorthand, since the distribution of both the ḥnk and 3ḥt n ḥtrỉ entries between Variety I and Sub-variety IA is not what we would expect were there no essential difference between Variety I and Sub-variety IA.

(1) Variable 43 Land Measure I Arouras or Land-cubits (Variety I, Sub-variety IA, Variety II) by Variable 4 Land-owning Institution and Variable 5 Deity or King; Variable 44 Land Measure II Arouras or Land-cubits (Variety I, Sub-variety IA, Variety I/II, Variety II, Sub-variety IIA) by Variable 4 Land-owning Institution and Variable 5 Deity or King

The relationship between variable 43 Land Measure I Arouras or Land-cubits (Variety I, Sub-variety IA, Variety II) and variable 4 Land-owning Institution is statistically significant with a Cramer's V value of 0.57338. The data of this crosstabulation reflect a relatively high degree of correlation between the variables which indicates that there is a substantive difference in the distribution of assessed land-cubit as compared with assessed aroura measured plots as they are ascribed to the 50 institutions identified in variable 4 Land-owning Institution. The aroura measured plots of Variety I and Sub-variety IA analyzed in this table are 1440 in number and constitute 86.9% of the 1657 plots analyzed in the table. The land-cubit measured plots of Variety II number 217 and constitute 13.1% of the total plots.

Of the 49 institutions which occur in the table, 23 are such that 100% of their assessed landholdings are aroura measured. These 23 institutions include many low frequency institutions such as the House of Mūt, the Great, Lady of Ishru (3 plots); the House of Ramesses-meriamūn in the House of Amūn (2 plots); and the House of Amūn Tjayef (1 plot). On the other hand, there are some institutions among the 23 with very high frequencies as, for example, the Mansion of Ramesses-meriamūn in the House of Ptaḥ (63 plots); the Landing-Place of Pharaoh in Ḥardai (76 plots); and the House of Re-Ḥarakhte (30 plots). The House of Sobek, the Shedtite is the only institution of which 100% of the plots (a total of 17) are land-cubit measured--a situation which is curious indeed. All of these plots are located in zone 1.

The landholdings of the remaining 25 institutions consist of both aroura and land-cubit measured plots. These 25 institutions include both high frequency and low frequency institutions, some with even distributions of aroura and land-cubit measured plots, others with very uneven distributions of aroura and land-cubit measured plots. Even or nearly even distributions of aroura and land-cubit measured plots tend to occur in association with low frequency institutions such as the House of Ḥaʿpy, Father of the Gods; the House of Amūn, Foreteller of Victory; and the House of Osiris Khant-ʿAru.

Most of the high frequency institutions have very uneven distributions of aroura and land-cubit measured plots. In the case of the funerary temple of Ramesses V, 283 plots or 99.3% are aroura measured and only 2 plots or 0.7% are land-cubit measured. In the case of the funerary temple of Ramesses III, 221 plots or 98.7% are aroura measured and only 3 plots or 1.3% are land-cubit measured. The Heliopolitan temple, the Mansion of Ramesses-meriamūn, Beloved Like Rēʿ, has a frequency of 58 aroura measured plots or 98.3% and only a single land-cubit measured plot (1.7%). In the case of the House of Amun-Rēʿ, King of the Gods, there are 120 aroura measured plots (75.5%) and 39 land-cubit measured plots

(24.5%). The landholdings of another high frequency institution, the funerary temple of Ramesses II, are distributed such that 80 plots or 85.1% are aroura measured and 14 plots or 14.9% are land-cubit measured. The Mansion of Ramesses-meriamūn in the House of Rēʿ has a slightly higher proportion of land-cubit measured plots: the 134 aroura measured plots constitute 72.8% of the total plots ascribed to this institution; whereas the 50 land-cubit measured plots constitute 27.2% of these plots. The House of Ḥeryshef, King of the Two Lands is the only high frequency institution to evidence a higher ratio of land-cubit measured plots to aroura measured plots. There are only 6 aroura measured plots ascribed to this temple which constitute only 14.0% of its landholdings in the apportioning paragraphs as compared with 37 land-cubit measured plots or 86.0%. The much lower frequency institution, the Sunshade of Re-Ḥarakhte in She (a total of 10 plots), is ascribed only 3 aroura measured plots as compared with 7 land-cubit measured plots.

The Cramer's V value for this table enables us to judge whether or not there is a substantive difference in the distribution of aroura measured plots as compared with land-cubit measured plots among the 50 institutions identified in variable 4. The Cramer's V value of 0.57338 suggests that there is indeed a substantive difference which may reflect different policies among the various institutions in the utilization of agricultural land. Since land-cubit measured plots often follow Pōsh B entries in the apportioning paragraphs, the table may also reflect the tendency of some institutions, such as the House of Amun-Rēʿ, King of the Gods, to enter into proportionately more interinstitutional transactions, such as those reflected in the corresponding Pōsh A and B entries, than other institutions. Thus, if Menu's interpretation of these entries is correct, institutions seeking assistance in raising the productivity of their grain producing aroura measured plots would enter into such transactions with a select group of institutions which perhaps specialized in these services. We may also be observing a reflection of the suitability of the land of some institutions for the small-scale cultivation of certain crops such as flax, as suggested by the data of the House of Ḥeryshef, King of the Two Lands, a fairly large temple at Heracleopolis, to which plots cultivated in flax are ascribed in Section I of Text A.

The relationship between variable 44 Land Measure II and variable 4 Land-owning Institution is also found to be statistically significant. This relationship has a Cramer's V value of 0.58227 which is nearly identical to that of the previous crosstabulation. The nearly identical Cramer's V values for these two crosstabulations suggest that the quantitative data of variable 10 Arouras Special Case (Variety I/II) and variable 13 Land-cubits Single Figure (Sub-variety IIA) have been, for the most part, correctly classified.

A look at the crosstabulation of variable 43 Land Measure I by variable 5 Deity or King reveals a statistically significant relationship with a Cramer's V value of 0.52105 which is only slightly lower than that of the relationship between variable 43 Land Measure I and variable 4 Land-owning Institution. This slightly lower degree of association could be interpreted as evidence that the decision of how much land to allocate for cultivation as relatively small land-cubit measured plots, and how much to allocate for cultivation as the larger grain producing aroura measured plots, was a policy decision more likely made at the institutional level than a policy decision made at a higher level and adhered to by all temples in which a particular deity was worshipped. The Cramer's V value for the crosstabulation of variable 44 Land Measure II and variable 5 Deity or King is Ø.51788. This Cramer's V value indicates the same degree of association as in the previous crosstabulation and suggests that the quantitative data of variable 1Ø Arouras Special Case and variable 13 Land-cubits Single Figure have been, for the most part, correctly classified.

(m) Variable 1 Section of Text by Variable 17 Special Entry; Variable 17 Special Entry by Variable 31 Geographic Location

The relationship between variable 1 Section of Text and variable 17 Special Entry is found to be statistically significant with a Cramer's V value of Ø.5Ø195. This Cramer's V value is indicative of a moderately high degree of association between the variables. With the exception of the low frequency w3d entries, each category of special entry occurs predominantly in only one or two zones of plot location.

Ḫnk plots occur predominantly in zone 3 as indicated by a frequency of 16 of the 37 ḫnk plots or 43.2%. Ten ḫnk plots (27.Ø%) occur in zone 2; whereas 9 ḫnk plots (24.3%) occur in zone 4. Two ḫnk plots or 5.4% occur in zone 1. Of the 16 ḫnk plots that occur in zone 3, 7 occur in the measurement area of Sharopě. Five of these entries occur in paragraphs of the funerary temple of Ramesses V. Since the beginning of Section I is lost, the relatively low frequency of ḫnk plots in zone 1 (2 cases) should be viewed with caution--especially in view of the fact that ḫnk entries are found to be highly correlated with the funerary cults of Ramesses II, Ramesses III, and Ramesses V in other sections of the text.

The 3ḥt n ḥtri͗ plots apportioned for various stablemasters are found to occur mostly in zone 3, as 42 of the 49 3ḥt n ḥtri͗ entries or 85.7% occur in Section III of Text A. Only one 3ḥt n ḥtri͗ plot occurs in zone 1; whereas 6 plots or 12.2% occur in zone 2.

Plots expressly designated for the cultivation of flax (mḥt) are limited to zone 1 where all 4 of the flax entries occur. Three of these entries (A7,43.48; 8,4) occur just a few lines apart in the zone 1 measurement area the New Land of ... in a paragraph belonging to the House of Ḥeryshef, King of the Two Lands. There are quantitative data preserved for only one of these plots (A7,48 "Flax...1ØØ resting"). The data of A7,43 are only partially preserved; whereas those of A8,4 are completely lacking. The fourth plot occurs in A6,x+17 and is a Variety II entry (.1Ø.4Ø). It is one of 1Ø plots ascribed to the overseer of cattle ʿAshaemḥab(sed?). This series of 1Ø plots is the longest series of apportioning entries ascribed to a single smallholder in Text A.

Plots expressly designated for the cultivation of herbs or vegetables (w3ḏ) occur once each in zones 1 (A6,x+15), 2 (A40,10), and 3 (A44,33). The plot in A6,x+15 is the first entry of the series of 10 entries ascribed to the overseer of cattle ʿAshaemḥab(sed?). The land-cubit measured Variety II plot in A40,10 follows a Pōsh B entry naming the prophet Wennofreʿ and belongs to a šmw pš paragraph of the House of Seth, Lord of Pi-Wayna. The Variety II plot in A44,33 ascribed to the retainer (šmsw) of the Sherden Pḳaha (?) follows an aroura measured Sub-variety IA entry ascribed to the same individual.

The relationship between variable 17 Special Entry and variable 31 Geographic Location is statistically significant with an even higher Cramer's V value of 0.89738 indicative of a very high degree of correlation between the two variables. The four categories of variable 17 Special Entry occur in association with only 49 of the 185 measurement areas which comprise variable 31 Geographic Location. The 3 plots specified as cultivated "m w3ḏ" occur in 3 measurement areas: Ninsu in zone 1, the Temple of Seth in zone 2, and Pen-Shōs in zone 3; whereas the 4 plots specified as cultivated in flax occur in 2 measurement areas, Ninsu (1 plot) and the New Land of... (3 plots) both in zone 1.

Ḥnk plots occur in 27 measurement areas, 7 plots located in Sharopĕ (zone 3) alone. These plots constitute 19.4% of the 36 ḥnk entries where the measurement area is known. The remaining measurement areas where ḥnk plots occur account for only 1 or 2 ḥnk entries each.

Nine 3ḥt n ḥtrỉ plots occur in the Castle of Iōt in zone 3 and constitute 19.1% of the 47 3ḥt n ḥtrỉ plots where the measurement area is known. Four 3ḥt n ḥtrỉ plots occur in both Sharopĕ and the Granary of Reeds, both measurement areas located in zone 3, while 3 3ḥt n ḥtrỉ plots occur in both Ḥuiniuti and the Mound of Naḥiḥu, also located in zone 3. The remaining 20 measurement areas where 3ḥt n ḥtrỉ plots occur have frequencies of only 1 or 2 plots each.

These findings indicate that both plots of donated (ḥnk) land and plots intended to provide sustenance for the horse-teams of Pharaoh are highly correlated with zone 3. The occupation ḥry ỉḥ which occurs in the standardized formula for the 3ḥt n ḥtrỉ entries (3ḥt n ḥtrỉ ḏd.n ḥry ỉḥ PN) is found to be very highly correlated with zone 3. The 42 3ḥt n ḥtrỉ plots which occur in zone 3 constitute 19.3% of the 218 occurrences of the occupation stablemaster in zone 3. Zone 3 is also highly correlated with military occupations (soldier, charioteer, shieldbearer, standardbearer, etc.). Stablemasters often occur in association with military personnel in both protocols and lists of rank as has previously been remarked (see pp. 70-71). The probability is high, therefore, that at least some of the zone 3 stablemasters numbered among military personnel. Since the 3ḥt n ḥtrỉ entries constitute so large a percentage (19.3%) of the zone 3 occurrences of the occupation stablemaster, the possibility is enhanced that these fields were under military administration. The single case of an 3ḥt n ḥtrỉ entry where the occupation stablemaster does not occur in the introductory formula is that of a zone 3 (Spermeru) plot ascribed to a charioteer (Sub-variety IA entry, 10⌋5 arouras). The occurrence of the charioteer as the party responsible for the cultivation of a plot expressly identified as 3ḥt n ḥtrỉ is one more point in favour of an interpretation of these landholdings as serving the needs of the chariotry of the Egyptian military forces.

The high correlation between ḥnk entries and zone 3 is also curious. Whereas 15 of the 37 ḥnk plots are indicated as having been under the authority of (r-ḫt) various scribes, 12 ḥnk plots were under the authority of various military personnel. This establishes a connection between the military and landholdings dedicated to the god(s) of Pharaoh which were of particular concern to the king, and suggests that military personnel were at the disposal of the king in administering the finances of estates belonging to cults of special royal favour.

(n) Variable 17 Special Entry by Variable 4 Land-owning Institution, Variable 5 Deity or King, Variable 3 Institutional Group, and Variable 19 Type of Religious Institution

The relationship between variable 17 Special Entry and variable 4 Land-owning Institution is found to be statistically significant with a relatively high Cramer's V value of 0.69041. This means that special entries of the categories ḥnk, 3ḥt n ḥtrỉ, mḥt, and w3ḏ tend to occur in association with certain land-owning institutions to the exclusion of most other land-owning institutions. Thus, given prior knowledge of the category of special entry, we can be reasonably confident of accurately predicting the land-owning institutions and vice versa.

Ḥnk entries occur most frequently in paragraphs belonging to the funerary temple of Ramesses V. Eleven ḥnk entries are ascribed to this funerary temple and constitute 29.7% of the 37 ḥnk entries analyzed in the table. The second highest frequency of ḥnk entries occurs in association with the funerary temple of Ramesses III at Medīnet Habu. This funerary temple accounts for 10 of the ḥnk entries or 27.0%. Also accounting for a relatively high frequency of ḥnk entries is the Mansion of Ramesses-meriamūn in the House of Rēᶜ (5 entries, 13.5%). The funerary temple of Ramesses II accounts for just 3 ḥnk entries or 8.1%. The remainder of the institutions to which ḥnk entries are ascribed have frequencies of only 1 or 2 ḥnk entries each. There are 40 institutions to which no ḥnk entries at all are ascribed. Ḥnk entries, therefore, are not only unusual in Text A, but also tend to occur in association with relatively few institutions, the highest concentrations occurring in association with funerary temples.

3ḥt n ḥtrỉ entries occur in paragraphs belonging to the funerary temple of Ramesses V (9 entries, 18.4%), the House of Amun-Rēᶜ, King of the Gods (7 entries, 14.3%), the Mansion of Ramesses-meriamūn in the House of Rēᶜ, (7 entries, 14.3%), the Mansion of Ramesses-meriamūn in the House of Ptaḥ (7 entries, 14.3%), and the funerary temple of Ramesses II (the Ramesseum) (6 entries, 12.2%). The remainder of the institutions to which 3ḥt n ḥtrỉ entries are ascribed each account for only 1 or 2 of these entries. There are 34 institutions to which no 3ḥt n ḥtrỉ entries whatever are ascribed.

The 4 plots specifically identified as cultivated in flax (mḥt) occur only in §6 belonging to the House of Ḥeryshef, King of the Two Lands (A6,x+17; 7,43.48; 8,4). The 3 plots specifically identified as cultivated "in vegetables" (m w3ḏ), on the other hand, occur once each in paragraphs belonging to the House of Ḥeryshef, King of the Two Lands; the House of Seth, Lord of Pi-Wayna; and the House of Amun-Rēʿ, King of the Gods (A6,x+15; 40,10; 44,33).

The relationship between variable 17 Special Entry and variable 5 Deity or King, a variable derived from data of variable 4 Land-owning Institution, is found to be negligibly different from the relationship described above. The Cramer's V value for the relationship between variable 17 Special Entry and variable 5 Deity or King is 0.68870 as compared with 0.69041 for the previous crosstabulation. This means that the reorganization of the data of land-owning institution according to the gods worshipped in the individual temples, funerary and ordinary cult, has a negligible impact upon the degree of association with the four categories of special entry.

The table indicates that ḥnk entries are strongly associated with the funerary cults of Ramesses V and Ramesses III (11 entries, 33.3% and 10 entries, 30.3% respectively). The funerary cult of Ramesses II has a much lower frequency of 3 ḥnk entries (9.1%). The cult of Rēʿ has a higher frequency of 5 entries (15.2%); whereas the cult of Osiris-Sety (temple of Sety I at Abydus) accounts for 2 entries (6.1%) and the cults of Amun-Rēʿ and Mūt 1 entry each. 3ḥt n ḥtrỉ entries are strongly associated with the funerary cults of Ramesses V and Ramesses II accounting for 9 entries (19.6%) and 6 entries (13.0%) respectively. These entries also occur frequently in association with the cults of Rēʿ (9 entries, 19.6%), Ptaḥ (8 entries, 17.4%), and Amun-Rēʿ (7 entries, 15.2%). The cult of Amūn accounts for 2 entries (4.3%), while the cults of Osiris, Re-Ḥarakhte, Seth, and Thoth each account for a single 3ḥt n ḥtrỉ entry. One 3ḥt n ḥtrỉ entry is ascribed to the funerary cult of Ramesses III. Flax entries occur only in association with the cult of Ḥeryshef; whereas entries of plots cultivated m w3ḏ occur once each in association with the cults of Ḥeryshef, Seth, and Amun-Rēʿ.

In view of the relatively high Cramer's V values of the above two crosstabulations, it is worthwhile to look at the relationship between variable 17 Special Entry and variable 3 Institutional Group in order to determine whether or not this degree of association persists when institutions are grouped according to the broader categories Theban, Heliopolitan, Memphite, Other Religious, and Secular. We find that the relationship between these variables is also statistically significant, but not as substantively important as reflected in the lower Cramer's V value of 0.39611.

The crosstabulation of variable 17 Special Entry by variable 19 Type of Religious Institution (Funerary or Ordinary Cult) is also statistically significant with a Cramer's V value of 0.45427. Twenty-four of the 33 ḥnk entries (72.7%) analyzed in the table occur in paragraphs belonging to funerary temples; whereas 9 of the ḥnk entries (27.3%) occur in paragraphs belonging to ordinary cult temples. Thirty of the 46 3ḫt n ḥtrỉ entries (65.2%) analyzed in the table occur in paragraphs belonging to ordinary cult temples; whereas 16 of these entries (34.8%) occur in paragraphs belonging to funerary temples. Plots specifically identified as cultivated in either flax or vegetables occur without exception in paragraphs belonging to ordinary cult temples.

In sum, we can say that both ḫnk and 3ḫt n ḥtrỉ entries appear to denote special types of plots which are highly correlated with specific institutions which are relatively few in number. The ḫnk entries are most highly correlated with the funerary temples of Ramesses III (Medīnet Habu) and Ramesses V. With the exception of the 5 ḫnk entries which are ascribed to the Mansion of Ramesses-meriamūn in the House of Rēʿ and the 2 ḫnk entries ascribed to the Mansion of King Menmaʿrēʿ in Abydus, ḫnk entries are ascribed to temples of the Theban Group only. The remaining 4 ḫnk entries are ascribed to secular institutions: the Landing-Place of Pharaoh in Ḥardai, the Fields of Pharaoh in Ḥardai, and the House of the King's Great Wife. It is immediately evident that ḫnk entries are directly associated with the Crown, an association made explicit in the formula of these entries: "Land donated to the god(s) of Pharaoh under the authority of (PN)."

3ḫt n ḥtrỉ entries are also strongly associated with the Theban temples, especially the funerary temples of Ramesses II and Ramesses V and the House of Amun-Rēʿ, King of the Gods. There is, however, no high correlation of these entries with the funerary temple of Ramesses III as there is with ḫnk entries. If 3ḫt n ḥtrỉ entries represent plots specially allocated to serve the needs of the military as well they might, the high correlation with Theban temples may reflect a government policy to utilize land of the Theban temples in particular to serve the needs of the horse-teams used by the military. The location of these temples in and around a major city such as Thebes, the southern capital, would perhaps have facilitated the administration of these special parcels and the utilization of any revenues derived from them. The choice of parcels located on the land of royal funerary temples may possibly reflect a preference for dealing with institutions which were perhaps more immediately accessible to the Crown.(3)

(o) Variable 21 Type of Apportioning Paragraph by Variable 4 Land-owning Institution, Variable 3 Institutional Group, Variable 18 Institutional Class, Variable 19 Type of Religious Institution, and Variable 39 Dynasty of Founding of Land-owning Institution

The relationship between variable 21 Type of Apportioning Paragraph and variable 4 Land-owning Institution is statistically significant with a high Cramer's V value of Ø.64992. Since each entry in the data file has been identified according to the type of apportioning paragraph to which it belongs (Herbage, šmw pš, rmnyt pš, White Goat, None of These), it is appropriate to refer to herbage entries, šmw pš entries, rmnyt pš entries, white goat entries, and entries of the category None of These (no special heading) in describing data of each crosstabulation.

Herbage entries belong predominantly to the funerary temple of

Ramesses II (Usimaʿrēʿ-setpenrēʿ). A total of 97 herbage entries or 25.5% of the 381 herbage entries in Text A are ascribed to the funerary temple of Ramesses II and constitute 63.8% of the 152 plots ascribed to this temple. The second highest frequency of herbage entries is that of the Mansion of Ramesses-meriamūn, Beloved Like Rēʿ. A total of 75 herbage entries or 19.7% of the herbage entries in Text A are ascribed to this Heliopolitan temple and constitute 96.2% of its 78 apportioning entries. To the House of Amun-Rēʿ, King of the Gods are ascribed 63 herbage entries or 16.5% of the 381 herbage entries in Text A. These 63 entries constitute only 24.7% of the 255 apportioning entries ascribed to this major land-owning institution. Considerably lower frequencies of herbage entries are ascribed to the funerary temple of Ramesses III (Usimaʿrēʿ-meriamūn) and the funerary temple of Ramesses V (Usimaʿrēʿ-skheperenrēʿ) which account for 10 herbage entries (2.6%) and 20 herbage entries (5.2%) respectively. Another relatively large institution according to the evidence of P. Wilbour, the Mansion of Ramesses-meriamūn in the House of Rēʿ, is conspicuously low in herbage entries (4 entries, 1.0%), while 2 other major institutions, the House of Sobek-Rēʿ, Lord of Anasha and the House of Ḥeryshef, King of the Two Lands are ascribed no herbage entries at all. We note, moreover, that there are 3 low frequency institutions to which relatively high frequencies of herbage entries are ascribed. Altogether, the House of Ḥaremḥab in the House of Amūn; the Mansion of King Menmaʿrēʿ in Abydus; and the House of Onūris, Lord of This account for 54 herbage entries or 14.2% of the total herbage entries. The 9 herbage entries ascribed to the House of Onūris, Lord of This comprise 100% of its apportioning entries. These data suggest that the provision of fodder for temple-herds, if indeed this was the function of herbage domains, was not restricted solely to the relatively large institutions which might be expected to be the preeminent owners of such herds on the basis of P. Harris I (10,7-11 and 51a,4).

White goat entries, which occur in special paragraphs of their own near the end of each section of Text A as do the herbage entries, occur in association with relatively few institutions. There are only 79 white goat entries which occur most frequently in association with the funerary temple of Ramesses II (30 entries, 38.0%). Thirteen white goat entries (16.5%) are ascribed to the funerary temple of Ramesses V, while 17 entries (21.5%) are ascribed to the Treasury of Pharaoh. The remaining 19 white goat entries are ascribed to 6 institutions each of which has a frequency of 5 or fewer of these entries. Thus, the provision of fodder for special herds of white goats also appears to have been limited to relatively few institutions. Unlike herbage entries, however, white goat entries are ascribed to secular institutions (the House of the King's Great Wife and the above-mentioned Treasury of Pharaoh).

<u>Šmw pš</u> entries belong predominantly to the House of Ḥeryshef, King of the Two Lands. A total of 111 of the 312 <u>šmw pš</u> entries in Text A or 35.6% are ascribed to the House of Ḥeryshef, King of the Two Lands and constitute 100% of the apportioning entries ascribed to this temple. This is not an unusual situation. There are 8 institutions among the 15 institutions to which <u>šmw pš</u> entries are

ascribed where the šmw pš entries constitute 100% of the apportioning entries. Of these 8 institutions, the House of Amūn Tjayef and the House of Nephthys of Ramesses-meriamūn each have an absolute frequency of only 1 apportioning entry. A total of 92 šmw pš entries comprising 29.5% of the 312 šmw pš entries are ascribed to the House of Sobek-Rēʿ, Lord of Anasha. These 92 šmw pš entries constitute 82.9% of the 111 apportioning entries ascribed to this temple. The remaining 19 apportioning entries ascribed to this temple occur in a paragraph with no special heading other than the name of the institution. Another 48 šmw pš entries (15.4%) are ascribed to the House of Sobek, the Shedtite and constitute 100% of the apportioning entries ascribed to this temple. The above 3 institutions account for 251 šmw pš entries or 80.4% of the 312 šmw pš entries in Text A. The remaining 12 institutions account for 61 šmw pš entries. None of these 12 institutions are secular institutions. With the exception of the funerary temple of Ramesses IV (Ḥeḳmaʿrēʿ-setpenamūn), which accounts for 3 šmw pš entries, all of these temples belong to the group Other Religious. Gardiner's observation that šmw pš paragraphs are restricted to small to medium size land-owning institutions is reasonable in light of these data.

Two temples to which šmw pš entries are ascribed are also ascribed white goat entries. These temples are the House of Seth, Lord of Spermeru (4 white goat entries) and the House of Seth, Lord of Pi-Wayna (5 white goat entries). Five temples with šmw pš entries are also ascribed apportioning entries in paragraphs with no special heading other than the name of the land-owning institution. With the exception of the House of Sobek-Rēʿ, Lord of Anasha referred to above, these temples are low frequency temples of the group Other Religious. The House of Osiris, Lord of Abydus is one of these temples.

Rmnyt pš entries are found to occur predominantly in association with funerary temples. The funerary temple of Ramesses V has the highest frequency of rmnyt pš entries in Text A. There are 325 rmnyt pš entries ascribed to this temple which constitute a substantial 28.8% of the 1128 rmnyt pš entries in Text A analyzed in the table.(4) The funerary temple of Ramesses III is second highest in frequency of rmnyt pš entries, the 256 rmnyt pš entries ascribed to this temple constitute 22.7% of the 1128 rmnyt pš entries. The Mansion of Ramesses-meriamūn in the House of Rēʿ has the third highest frequency of rmnyt pš entries, the 235 rmnyt pš entries constituting 20.8% of the 1128 rmnyt pš entries analyzed in the table. Also accounting for a relatively high frequency of rmnyt pš entries is the House of Amun-Rēʿ, King of the Gods to which 192 rmnyt pš entries or 17.0% of the 1128 rmnyt pš entries are ascribed. These four temples, three of which are Theban, thus account for 1008 of the 1128 rmnyt pš entries or 89.4%. The remaining 7 institutions, all of which are temples, account for the remaining 120 rmnyt pš entries. The Mansion of King Menmaʿrēʿ in Abydus is the only temple of the group Other Religious to which rmnyt pš entries are ascribed (6 entries, 0.5%).

There are 342 apportioning entries analyzed in the table which occur in paragraphs the headings of which consist solely of the name of the institution.(5) There are a total of 29 institutions to which such paragraphs are ascribed. These institutions tend to have relatively low frequencies. Eighteen of these institutions are such that these entries comprise 100% of their apportioning entries. Two secular institutions, the Landing-Place of Pharaoh in Ḥardai and the Landing-Place of Pharaoh in the Keep of ʿOnayna, are among these 18 institutions. Two secular institutions, the Landing-Place of Pharaoh in Ḥardai and the Fields of Pharaoh, are noteworthy as institutions with relatively high frequencies: 85 entries or 24.9% of the 342 entries of these paragraphs in the case of the Landing-Place of Pharaoh in Ḥardai and 47 entries or 13.7% in the case of the Fields of Pharaoh. The Landing-Place of Pharaoh in the Keep of ʿOnayna, on the other hand, accounts for 14 such entries (4.1%), while the House of the King's Great Wife accounts for 17 of these entries (5.0%).

The 25 temples, which are ascribed paragraphs with no special heading other than the name of the institution, belong to all four temple groups: Theban, Heliopolitan, Memphite, and Other Religious. The House of Mūt, the Great, Lady of Ishru; the House of Tiʿo in the House of Amūn; the Mansion of King ʿAkheperen(?)rēʿ in the House of Amūn; the House of Ramesses-meriamūn in the House of Amūn; and the House of Ḥaremḥab in the House of Amūn are the Theban temples included in this group. The House of Ḥaʿpy, Father of the Gods is the only Heliopolitan temple in the group, while the Great Seat of Ramesses-meriamūn in the House of Ptaḥ; the Mansion of Ramesses-meriamūn, Beloved of Ptaḥ; the House of Ramesses-meriamūn, Repeater of <u>Sed</u>-festivals; and the House of Ptaḥ of Merenptaḥ and of Ramesses-meriamūn are the Memphite temples in the group. The temples of the group Other Religious are 15 in number and account for relatively few apportioning entries in Text A in the vast majority of cases.

Thus, the 29 institutions to which paragraphs with no special heading are ascribed are a motley group indeed. With the exception of a few high frequency institutions such as the House of Sobek-Rēʿ, Lord of Anasha; the Great Seat of Ramesses-meriamūn in the House of Ptaḥ; and the Landing-Place of Pharaoh in Ḥardai, the predominant characteristic of this group is a relatively low frequency of apportioning entries. Barring these few relatively high frequency institutions, the institutions which occur in the headings of paragraphs with no special heading appear to be among the "smallest" institutions of the Text A apportioning paragraphs.(6)

By and large, the crosstabulation of variable 21 Type of Apportioning Paragraph by variable 4 Land-owning Institution confirms Gardiner's contention that we can distinguish between "relatively large" institutions to which <u>rmnyt pš</u> paragraphs are ascribed and "small to medium size" institutions to which <u>šmw pš</u> paragraphs are ascribed. No institution which has a <u>rmnyt pš</u> paragraph also has a <u>šmw pš</u> paragraph. It is not unusual, however, for temples with <u>rmnyt pš</u> paragraphs to also have an herbage paragraph or a white goat paragraph ascribed to them. There are 11 temples with <u>rmnyt pš</u> paragraphs which are also ascribed herbage paragraphs, although the ratio of <u>rmnyt pš</u> entries to herbage entries is very uneven and varies widely from institution to institution. Only 2 of these 11 institutions, the Great Seat of Ramesses-meriamūn in the House of Ptaḥ and the Mansion of King Menmaʿrēʿ in Abydus, are ascribed paragraphs with no heading other than the name of the institution. Thus, it could be argued that the ascription of herbage paragraphs and white goat paragraphs to institutions which have rmnyt pš paragraphs constitutes evidence for the relatively large size of these institutions. The distribution of herbage entries, as we have seen above, however, gives rise to some doubt that the relative size of the institution determined whether or not its landholdings might be utilized for the provision of fodder for temple-herds.

The relationship between variable 21 Type of Apportioning Paragraph and variable 3 Institutional Group is statistically significant with a Cramer's V value of 0.54086 as compared with 0.64992 for the relationship between variable 21 Type of Apportioning Paragraph and variable 4 Land-owning Institution. The difference between these two Cramer's V values is relatively small compared with the differences we usually encounter when variable 3 Institutional Group and variable 4 Land-owning Institution are each crosstabulated with another variable. The values obtained in the above two crosstabulations indicate that both relationships are characterized by a similar moderately high degree of association.

We find that 208 of the 381 herbage entries or 54.6% are ascribed to Theban temples; whereas 94 of these entries or 24.7% are ascribed to Heliopolitan temples. Memphite temples account for 43 herbage entries or 11.3%, while temples of the group Other Religious account for 36 herbage entries or 9.4%. There are no herbage entries whatever ascribed to institutions of the Secular Group.

Šmw pš entries, of which there are 312, are ascribed only to temples of the Theban Group and the group Other Religious. We find that 309 šmw pš entries or 99.0% are ascribed to temples of the group Other Religious; whereas only 3 entries or 1.0% are ascribed to temples of the Theban group. The 309 šmw pš entries constitute 67.6% of the 457 plots ascribed to the group Other Religious; whereas the 3 šmw pš entries constitute just 0.3% of the 1085 entries ascribed to the Theban Group.

Rmnyt pš entries belong predominantly to Theban temples. There are 798 rmnyt pš entries ascribed to temples of the Theban Group which constitute 70.7% of the 1128 rmnyt pš entries analyzed in this table. These 798 entries constitute 73.5% of the 1085 entries ascribed to the Theban Group. Temples of the Heliopolitan Group account for 253 rmnyt pš entries or 22.4% of the 1128 rmnyt pš entries. These 253 entries account for 71.9% of the plots ascribed to the Heliopolitan Group. There is a substantially lower frequency of rmnyt pš entries for the Memphite Group. The 71 rmnyt pš entries ascribed to temples of the Memphite Group constitute just 6.3% of the 1128 rmnyt pš entries, but 42.3% of the 168 entries ascribed to temples of the Memphite Group. Only 6 rmnyt pš entries (0.5%) occur in association with temples of the group Other Religious. These 6 plots constitute only 1.3% of the 457 plots ascribed to temples of the group Other Religious. No rmnyt pš entries are ascribed to secular institutions.

White goat entries occur predominantly in association with temples of the Theban Group. Forty-three of the 79 white goat entries or 54.4% are ascribed to Theban temples. These 43 white goat entries constitute just 4.0% of the 1085 plots ascribed to the Theban Group. There are 19 white goat entries or 24.1% which are ascribed to secular institutions. These 19 plots account for 10.4% of the 183 plots ascribed to secular institutions. Temples of the Memphite and Other Religious groups are ascribed 8 and 9 white goat entries respectively. These entries account for 10.1 and 11.4% of the white goat entries respectively. The 8 white goat entries account for 4.8% of the 168 Memphite entries, while the 9 white goat entries account for 2.0% of the 457 entries of the group Other Religious. No white goat entries occur in association with temples of the Heliopolitan Group. It is interesting to note that the herds of cattle granted as the specific gifts of Ramesses III to temples in P. Harris I occur only in the Theban and Memphite sections of the document (10,7-11 and 51a,4 respectively). No such herds are mentioned as granted to Heliopolitan temples. Data of P. Wilbour suggest that plots set aside for the production of food for herds of white goats are indicative of a specialized agricultural use in which Theban temples played the leading role.

The relationship between variable 21 Type of Apportioning Paragraph and variable 18 Institutional Class (Religious or Secular) is statistically significant with a Cramer's V value of 0.63764. The degree of association in this relationship is relatively high because herbage entries, *šmw pš* entries, and *rmnyt pš* entries occur only in association with temples. White goat entries, on the other hand, are distributed such that 60 entries or 75.9% occur in association with temples; whereas 19 entries or 24.1% occur in association with secular institutions. A total of 179 entries (52.3%), which occur in paragraphs with no heading other than the name of the institution, are ascribed to temples; whereas 163 entries (47.7%) are ascribed to secular institutions.

The relationship between variable 21 Type of Apportioning Paragraph and variable 19 Type of Religious Institution (Funerary or Ordinary Cult) is statistically significant with a Cramer's V value of 0.44327 which indicates that the relationship is not as strong as that of variable 21 Type of Apportioning Paragraph and variable 18 Institutional Class. A total of 606 *rmnyt pš* entries or 53.7% of the 1128 *rmnyt pš* entries analyzed in the table are ascribed to funerary temples; whereas 522 such entries or 46.3% are ascribed to ordinary cult temples. Whereas 127 herbage entries or 33.3% are ascribed to funerary temples; 254 entries or 66.7% are ascribed to ordinary cult temples. Forty-three white goat entries or 71.7% of the 60 white goat entries are ascribed to funerary temples. Only 17 white goat entries or 28.3% are ascribed to ordinary cult temples. *Šmw pš* entries are nearly perfectly correlated with ordinary cult temples: 309 *šmw pš* entries or 99.0% of the 312 *šmw pš* entries in Text A occur in *šmw pš* paragraphs belonging to ordinary cult temples. The funerary temple of Ramesses IV is the only funerary temple to which *šmw pš* entries are ascribed (3 entries, 1.0%). Entries in paragraphs with no special heading (None of These) are also highly correlated with ordinary cult temples. Only 12 entries of a total of 179 such entries or 6.7% are ascribed to funerary temples. The remaining 167 entries or 93.3% are ascribed to ordinary cult temples.

The relationship between variable 21 Type of Apportioning Paragraph and variable 39 Dynasty of Founding of Land-owning Institution is also statistically significant with a Cramer's V value of 0.43497. Since there are few institutions which can be dated with certainty to the Eighteenth Dynasty, as well as a great many institutions the establishment of which either predates the Eighteenth Dynasty or cannot be fixed to any particular dynasty of founding, we are best advised to limit our comments to institutions established during the Nineteenth and Twentieth Dynasties. It should be kept in mind that if we wish to compare the institutions established in particular reigns of the Nineteenth or Twentieth Dynasties, that can be best achieved by reference to tables in which variable 4 Land-owning Institution and variable 5 Deity or King are crosstabulated with variable 21.

A glance at the distribution of apportioning entries according to the type of paragraph to which they belong reveals some interesting points. First, the 381 herbage entries are distributed such that 233 entries or 61.2% are ascribed to Nineteenth Dynasty institutions; whereas only 30 such entries or 7.9% are ascribed to Twentieth Dynasty institutions. We encounter a similar situation with regard to white goat entries. Of the 79 white goat entries in Text A, 38 entries or 48.1% are ascribed to Nineteenth Dynasty institutions; whereas only 15 entries or 19.0% are ascribed to Twentieth Dynasty institutions. These figures reflect the frequencies of not only the funerary temple of Ramesses II as compared with those of Ramesses III, Ramesses IV, and Ramesses V, but also those of the many temples established by Ramesses II to which herbage and white goat entries are ascribed. The Mansion of King Menmaʿrēʿ in Abydus (Sety I) also increases the frequencies of Nineteenth Dynasty institutions as it accounts for 27 entries or 7.1% of the herbage entries. Notwithstanding the megalomania of Ramesses II in erecting temples to his own glory, it is possible that additional herbage domains and domains intended for the cultivation of food for white goats were created as and when the need arose such that older institutions might be expected to account for a larger proportion of both herbage and white goat entries than more recently established institutions. Another possible explanation for the high proportion of herbage and white goat entries in association with Nineteenth Dynasty temples could be that herbage and white goat plots were of lower agricultural value than the plots enumerated in the šmw pš and rmnyt pš paragraphs such that later kings did not bother to appropriate them for their own funerary estates.

A second point worth noting is the fact that 308 of the 312 šmw pš entries or 98.7% are relegated to the category Undated. This happens because šmw pš entries are highly correlated with so-called "small to medium size" institutions which belong largely to the institutional group Other Religious. Most of these temples cannot be ascribed to a particular dynasty of founding. The category Twentieth Dynasty is ascribed 3 of the remaining 4 šmw pš entries, all of which belong to the funerary temple of Ramesses IV.

One šmw pš entry is ascribed to the category Nineteenth Dynasty (the House of Nephthys of Ramesses-meriamūn).

A third point of interest concerns the distribution of rmnyt pš entries. A total of 581 rmnyt pš entries or 51.5% occur in rmnyt pš paragraphs ascribed to Twentieth Dynasty institutions; whereas only 329 such entries or 29.2% occur in rmnyt pš paragraphs ascribed to Nineteenth Dynasty institutions. There are 218 such entries or 19.3% which occur in paragraphs ascribed to institutions which are undated. The figures reflect, to a considerable degree, the fact that later dating institutions, in particular the funerary temples of Ramesses III and Ramesses V, have high frequencies of apportioning entries. The lands ascribed to them were in part no doubt appropriated from earlier such institutions--perhaps indeed from the funerary estate of Ramesses II which has a much lower frequency of apportioning entries than either the funerary estate of Ramesses III or that of the reigning king, Ramesses V.

(p) Variable 21 Type of Apportioning Paragraph by Variable 5 Deity or King

The relationship between variable 21 Type of Apportioning Paragraph and variable 5 Deity or King is statistically significant with a Cramer's V value of 0.60003 indicative of a relatively high degree of correlation between the variables.

Cults to which herbage, white goat, and rmnyt pš entries are ascribed include the funerary cults of Ramesses II and Ramesses V and the cult of the Memphite god Ptaḥ. The funerary cult of Ramesses III is ascribed both herbage and rmnyt pš entries as are the cults of Amun-Reʿ, Reʿ, Re-Ḥarakhte, and Osiris-Sety (the Mansion of King Menmaʿreʿ at Abydus). Although the funerary cults of Ramesses II and Ramesses V are both ascribed herbage, white goat, and rmnyt pš entries, the distributions of the three types of entries are very uneven. In the case of the funerary cult of Ramesses V, there are 325 rmnyt pš entries which constitute 90.5% of the 359 entries ascribed to this cult. The 20 herbage entries constitute only 5.6% of the total entries, while the 13 white goat entries constitute only 3.6% of the total entries. In the case of the funerary cult of Ramesses II, on the other hand, the 25 rmnyt pš entries constitute only 16.4% of the 152 apportioning entries. Herbage entries, of which there are 97, constitute 63.8% of the total entries; whereas the 30 white goat entries constitute 19.7% of the total entries. Although the funerary cult of Ramesses III is ascribed no white goat entries, the distribution of rmnyt pš and herbage entries approaches that of the cult of Ramesses V: the 256 rmnyt pš entries constitute 96.2% of the 266 entries; whereas the 10 herbage entries constitute only 3.8% of the total entries. All 3 entries of the funerary cult of Ramesses IV occur in a šmw pš paragraph; whereas all 12 entries of the funerary cult of ʿAkheperen(?)reʿ (Tuthmosis II or Amenophis II?) occur in a paragraph with no special heading. The distributions of apportioning entries of the Theban funerary cults are thus markedly different.

The distribution of apportioning entries of the cult of

"Osiris-Sety" pertaining to the Mansion of King Menmaʿrēʿ in Abydus is most similar to that of the funerary cult of Ramesses II in that 27 entries or 69.2% of the 39 entries are herbage entries; whereas 6 entries or 15.4% of the total entries are rmnyt pš entries. There are, however, no white goat entries ascribed to this cult. Another 6 entries or 15.4% of the entries ascribed to the cult of Osiris-Sety occur in a paragraph with no special heading. Comparing these figures with those of the cult of Osiris (House of Osiris, Lord of Abydus), we find that 13 of the 17 entries or 76.5% occur in a paragraph with no special heading; whereas the remaining 4 entries or 23.5% occur in a šmw pš paragraph. The relatively low frequency of apportioning entries ascribed to the cult of Osiris in Text A is rather surprising, as is the fact that entries of this cult occur in a šmw pš paragraph, a type of paragraph most often associated with temples likely to have been of only small to medium size.

Comparing the frequencies of the cults of Amun-Rēʿ, Rēʿ, and Ptaḥ, we find that two of these cults are almost identical in the distribution of their apportioning entries among the five types of apportioning paragraphs. In the case of the cult of Amun-Rēʿ, which reflects only the entries ascribed to the House of Amun-Rēʿ, King of the Gods at Karnak, 192 of the 255 entries or 75.3% are rmnyt pš entries; whereas 63 entries or 24.7% are herbage entries. There are no white goat entries ascribed to the cult of Amun-Rēʿ. In the case of the cult of Rēʿ, which includes two temples of the House of Rēʿ, 238 entries or 74.8% of the 318 entries are rmnyt pš entries; whereas 79 entries or 24.8% are herbage entries. No white goat entries are ascribed to the cult of Rēʿ. Entries of the cult of Ptaḥ, which includes six temples of the House of Ptaḥ, are very differently distributed. The 71 rmnyt pš entries constitute only 42.3% of the 168 apportioning entries; whereas the 43 herbage entries constitute 25.6% of the total entries. The 8 white goat entries constitute 4.8% of the 168 entries. A total of 46 entries or 27.4% occur in paragraphs with no special heading. Entries ascribed to the cult of Amūn, which includes temples dedicated to local forms of the god Amūn as well as temples of the House of Amūn which are not funerary temples, include 6 šmw pš entries which constitute 11.5% of the 52 entries, but no rmnyt pš entries. The 28 entries occurring in paragraphs with no special heading account for 53.8% of the total entries; whereas the 18 herbage entries account for 34.6% of the 52 entries. Entries ascribed to the cult of Re-Ḥarakhte are the most evenly distributed. The 51 apportioning entries are distributed such that 15 entries or 29.4% occur in one rmnyt pš paragraph, another 15 entries or 29.4% occur in one herbage paragraph, and 19 entries or 37.3% occur in several šmw pš paragraphs. Only 2 entries or 3.9% occur in a paragraph with no special heading. There are no white goat entries ascribed to the cult of Re-Ḥarakhte.

The entries of the cults of Ḥathōr, Mont, Ḥar-Min and Isis, Mūt, Ḥaʿpy, and Thoth occur exclusively in paragraphs with no special heading; whereas entries of the cults of Ḥeryshef, Nephthys, Sobek, and ʿAnti occur exclusively in šmw pš paragraphs. The entries of the cults of Bata and Sobek-Rēʿ are divided between šmw pš paragraphs and paragraphs with no special heading. The majority of entries in the case of the cult of Bata (62.5%) occur in a paragraph with no special heading; whereas the majority of entries in the case of the cult of Sobek-Rēᶜ (82.9%) occur in a šmw pš paragraph.

(q) Variable 21 Type of Apportioning Paragraph by Variable 31 Geographic Location

The relationship between variable 21 Type of Apportioning Paragraph and variable 31 Geographic Location is statistically significant with a relatively high Cramer's V value of Ø.67193. This relatively high Cramer's V value indicates that there is a relatively high correlation between the type of apportioning paragraph and the geographic location of the plot.

Of the 185 measurement areas of the Text A apportioning paragraphs, only 13 of these measurement areas are ascribed plots in both šmw pš and rmnyt pš paragraphs. The 13 measurement areas are distributed over all four of the geographic zones with the highest frequencies occurring in zones 2 and 4. In all but 3 of these measurement areas (Sekh-(en)-Wᶜab-yeb in zone 2, Pen-Kenroy and Sapa both in zone 3), the distribution of šmw pš and rmnyt pš plots is very uneven. In 6 measurement areas, there are at least twice as many rmnyt pš plots as šmw pš plots. In 4 measurement areas, on the other hand, there is a predominance of šmw pš plots. Of the 13 measurement areas where both šmw pš and rmnyt pš plots occur, only Sakō in zone 4 and the Village of Inroyshes in zone 2 have relatively high frequencies. The remaining measurement areas have considerably lower frequencies. Other measurement areas among the 185 measurement areas with relatively high frequencies such as Mi-ēḥu in zone 2; Ḥuiniuti, Sharopě, and Spermeru in zone 3; and Menᶜonkh in zone 4 are largely comprised of rmnyt pš plots in combination with herbage or white goat plots and plots enumerated in paragraphs with no special heading.

Šmw pš plots occur in 49 measurement areas located in all four zones of Text A. In more than half of these measurement areas (27), šmw pš plots constitute 1ØØ% of the total plots enumerated. Only 4 of the 27 measurement areas are ascribed only a single plot. Rmnyt pš plots, on the other hand, occur in 95 measurement areas located in all four zones of Text A with the lowest frequency occurring in zone 1. In just less than half of these measurement areas (45), rmnyt pš plots constitute 1ØØ% of the plots enumerated. Only 8 of these 45 measurement areas are ascribed only a single plot. Since temples belonging to the Theban, Heliopolitan, and Memphite groups tend to have rmnyt pš rather than šmw pš paragraphs ascribed to them, it is not surprising that rmnyt pš plots have a relatively low frequency in zone 1. The loss of the Theban and Heliopolitan subsections, as well as part of the Memphite subsection in Section I of Text A, has resulted in a very limited number of rmnyt pš paragraphs and their respective entries for zone 1. We also note that although there are nearly four times as many rmnyt pš entries in Text A as šmw pš entries (113Ø as compared with 312), rmnyt pš entries occur in association with proportionately fewer measurement areas than do šmw pš entries.

Herbage plots are ascribed to a total of 50 measurement areas occurring in all four geographic zones. The highest concentration of herbage plots is in zone 3. In 18 of these measurement areas, herbage plots constitute 100% of the plots enumerated. Four of these measurement areas are single occurrence measurement areas. Only 2 measurement areas (the Mound of Yēbes in zone 2 and the Great Byre in zone 1) have frequencies of 10 or more herbage plots.

White goat plots occur in 16 measurement areas, all but one of which (the Houses of Irkak in zone 4) are located in zone 3 (Mi-ēmsaḥ occurs in both zones 3 and 4). Seven of these measurement areas have perfect correlations with white goat plots. While none of these perfect correlation measurement areas are single occurrence measurement areas, only the House of Psiūr in zone 3 has a frequency of 10 or more white goat plots.

Entries of paragraphs the headings of which consist solely of the name of the institution occur in 69 measurement areas, only 3 of which are located in zone 1. Of these 69 measurement areas, 24 are such that these entries constitute 100% of the apportioning entries ascribed to them. Of these 24 measurement areas, 10 are ascribed only a single plot; whereas 2 have frequencies of 10 or more plots (P-ma in zone 2 and Imy-tay-m-t-nē in zone 4). These data indicate that paragraphs with no heading other than the name of the land-owning institution are characterized by proportionately more single occurrence measurement areas than any other type of apportioning paragraph. This finding could be interpreted as evidence that most of the institutions (all temples) which occur in the headings of apportioning paragraphs with no heading other than the name of the institution were relatively small in size.

We must also examine the percentage of entries of each type of paragraph which occurs in association with measurement areas where there is perfect association. A total of 217 šmw pš plots or 71.1% of the 305 šmw pš plots analyzed in the table occur in localities where they constitute 100% of the plots enumerated. A total of 401 rmnyt pš plots or 38.2% of the 1051 rmnyt pš plots analyzed in the table occur in localities where they constitute 100% of the plots enumerated. A total of 104 herbage plots or 27.3% of the 381 herbage plots analyzed in the table occur in localities where they constitute 100% of the plots enumerated, while 51 white goat plots or 64.6% of the 79 white goat plots analyzed in the table occur in localities where they constitute 100% of the enumerated plots. A total of 82 of the 342 entries in paragraphs with no special heading or 24.0% occur in localities where they constitute 100% of the plots enumerated. Thus, although 65.4% of the 185 measurement areas have perfect association with plots enumerated in only one type of apportioning paragraph, the majority of the plots of only šmw pš paragraphs and white goat paragraphs occur in measurement areas where there is perfect association (100% of the plots are either šmw pš plots or white goat plots). The majority of the plots enumerated in rmnyt pš paragraphs, herbage paragraphs, and paragraphs with no special heading occur in measurement areas where the plots enumerated belong to two or more types of apportioning paragraphs.

To sum up, there is a tendency for individual measurement areas to be characterized by plots enumerated under the heading of only a single type of apportioning paragraph. Since paragraph headings appear to identify separate and individual domains of institutions which may have had distinct (service?) functions, it would appear that the tendency was for the local economies to be dominated by the interests of a single type of domain. This conclusion suggests that there was some degree of specialization among measurement areas as to the purpose for which their produce was intended (fodder for cattle, fodder for white goats, grain for the harvest-tax (?), etc.).

(r) Variable 43 Land Measure I Arouras or Land-cubits (Variety I, Sub-variety IA, Variety II) and Variable 44 Land Measure II Arouras or Land-cubits (Variety I, Sub-variety IA, Variety I/II, Variety II, Sub-variety IIA) by Variable 21 Type of Apportioning Paragraph

The relationship between variable 43 Land Measure I Arouras or Land-cubits (Variety I, Sub-variety IA, Variety II) and variable 21 Type of Apportioning Paragraph is statistically significant with a Cramer's V value of 0.41275. This crosstabulation takes into account only assessed plots, i.e., aroura measured plots of Variety I and Sub-variety IA and land-cubit measured plots of Variety II. Unassessed plots of aroura measured Variety I/II and land-cubit measured Sub-variety IIA are excluded from the analysis.

The table indicates that herbage entries in the vast majority of cases are aroura measured plots (Variety I or Sub-variety IA). There are 271 aroura measured herbage entries or 92.8% of a total of 292 herbage entries analyzed in the table. Only 21 herbage entries or 7.2% are land-cubit measured. All 75 white goat entries in the table are aroura measured. Rmnyt pš entries are predominantly aroura measured. There are 769 aroura measured rmnyt pš entries or 89.3% of a total of 861 rmnyt pš entries analyzed in the table. Only 92 rmnyt pš entries or 10.7% are land-cubit measured. Similarly, entries in paragraphs with no special heading (None of These) are also predominantly aroura measured. Of the 275 such entries, 257 or 93.5% are aroura measured and only 18 entries or 6.5% are land-cubit measured. There is a great difference, however, in the distribution of šmw pš entries. The 154 šmw pš entries are distributed such that 68 entries or 44.2% are aroura measured and 86 entries or 55.8% are land-cubit measured. This means that although šmw pš and rmnyt pš entries are mutually exclusive vis-à-vis the individual institutions identified in the headings of the apportioning paragraphs, these two types of paragraphs and their respective entries are very different indeed when the entries are distinguished on the basis of the unit of land measure. Since plots measured in land-cubits may conceivably differ from plots measured in arouras in respect to both the crop(s) cultivated and the proportion of the harvest which the smallholder himself might retain for his own needs, this difference between šmw pš and rmnyt pš entries has considerable importance. Moreover, the distribution of šmw pš and rmnyt pš entries we observe in this table is sufficiently unexpected to cast doubt upon Gardiner's conclusion that rmnyt pš paragraphs perform for the larger and more distant land-owning institutions the same function that šmw pš paragraphs perform for smaller land-owning institutions.(7)

A look at the crosstabulation of variable 44 Land Measure II Arouras or Land-cubits (Variety I, Sub-variety IA, Variety I/II, Variety II, Sub-variety IIA) and variable 21 Type of Apportioning Paragraph (Cramer's V value of 0.40520) reveals a similar anomaly in the distribution of šmw pš and rmnyt pš entries. The addition of unassessed aroura measured plots of Variety I/II and unassessed land-cubit measured plots of Sub-variety IIA to the analysis raises the ratio of land-cubit measured šmw pš entries to aroura measured šmw pš entries. The 169 land-cubit measured šmw pš entries constitute 60.1% of the 281 šmw pš entries; whereas the 112 aroura measured šmw pš entries constitute only 39.9% of the šmw pš entries. There is also a corresponding increase in the frequency of land-cubit measured rmnyt pš entries. The 187 land-cubit measured rmnyt pš entries constitute 17.3% of the 1082 rmnyt pš entries in the table; whereas the 895 aroura measured rmnyt pš entries constitute 82.7% of the rmnyt pš entries. As in the case of the previous crosstabulation, these unexpected frequencies in the distribution of šmw pš and rmnyt pš entries between the two units of land measure raise doubt as to whether šmw pš and rmnyt pš paragraphs can possibly be on the same footing.

The nearly identical Cramer's V values of the two crosstabulations are also very significant in that they provide yet another indication that the unassessed plots in the apportioning paragraphs are, for the most part, correctly classified as either aroura or land-cubit measured (Variety I/II and Sub-variety IIA respectively).

(s) Variable 7 Occupation or Title of Smallholder by the Quantitative Variables of Size of Plot

It is possible to evaluate the relationship between variable 7 Occupation or Title of Smallholder and variable 9 Arouras by reducing what would be an extremely long and cumbersome table to a much smaller, more manageable size. This is accomplished by removing low frequency sizes of plots from the analysis. The table obtained is both statistically significant and substantively important as indicated by the Cramer's V value of 0.47453. Further reduction in the size of the table to obtain an even more precise Cramer's V value may be accomplished by eliminating low frequency occupations. Variable 9 Arouras includes data of both Variety I and Sub-variety IA entries.

We find that plots of a size of 3 arouras occur predominantly in association with the occupation soldier which accounts for 195 plots of this size. These 195 plots constitute 58.6% of the 333 plots of 3 arouras analyzed in this table and 90.3% of the aroura measured plots ascribed to soldiers in this table. The occupation with the second highest frequency of plots 3 arouras in size is that of ʿnḫ(t) n nỉwt which accounts for 39 such plots or 11.7% of the 333 plots of 3 arouras. These 39 plots constitute only 26.4% of the 148 plots ascribed to women smallholders in this table. This is indeed a small percentage compared with the 90.3% in the case of the occupation soldier. Priests account for 23 plots of 3 arouras or 6.9% of the 333 plots of 3 arouras. These 23 plots constitute 21.7% of the 106 plots ascribed to priests in this table, a percentage in line with that of ʿnḫ(t) n nỉwt. The remaining 22 occupations to which plots of 3 arouras are ascribed each account for less than 5.0% of the 333 plots of 3 arouras among the 1322 plots of Variety I and Sub-variety IA analyzed. Needless to say, among the higher frequency occupations, none is so strongly associated with 3 aroura plots as that of soldier. This high correlation does indeed suggest the existence of a general policy in the allocation of plots among the various occupations of smallholders as Menu suggests.(8)

Plots of 5 arouras occur predominantly in association with the occupation stablemaster which accounts for 337 such plots or 45.9% of a total of 734 plots of 5 arouras. These 337 plots constitute 90.3% of the 373 plots ascribed to stablemasters. The occupation herdsman accounts for 86 such plots or 11.7%. These 86 plots constitute 72.3% of the 119 plots ascribed to herdsmen. Women smallholders account for 84 plots or 11.4% of the 734 plots of 5 arouras. These 84 plots, however, constitute only 56.8% of the 148 plots ascribed to women smallholders. Priests account for 56 plots of 5 arouras or 7.6%. The 56 plots constitute 52.8% of the 106 plots ascribed to priests in this table, a frequency comparable to that of ʿnḫ(t) n nỉwt. The remaining 37 occupations to which plots of 5 arouras are ascribed each account for less than 3.0% of the 734 plots of 5 arouras. The high correlation between high frequency occupations such as stablemaster and herdsman and plots of 5 arouras suggests the existence of a general policy of land allocation which determined the size or sizes of plots allocated to individuals of certain occupations as is also the case with plots of 3 arouras in size. It should be noted that the 734 plots of 5 arouras analyzed in this table constitute 55.5% of the total entries in the table, making 5 aroura plots the modal size of plot by a wide margin over plots of 3 arouras. The 333 plots of 3 arouras in size constitute only 25.2% of the 1322 plots of Variety I and Sub-variety IA analyzed in this table.

Plots of 10 arouras in size are 158 in number and constitute 12.0% of the 1322 plots of Variety I and Sub-variety IA. Individuals identified as ỉḥwtyw account for the largest number of plots of 10 arouras: 21 plots or 13.3% of the 158 plots. These 21 plots comprise 27.3% of the 77 plots ascribed to ỉḥwtyw. ʾIḥwty is the one occupation where the assessed aroura measured plots are fairly evenly distributed over all five sizes of plots. There are 21 plots each of both 5 and 10 arouras, 16 plots of 20 arouras, 13 plots of 3 arouras, but only 6 plots of 2 arouras. The occupations scribe, priest, and stablemaster each account for 18 plots of 10 arouras or 11.4% of the 10 aroura plots. Whereas the 18 plots of 10 arouras of the occupation scribe constitute 40.0% of the 45 plots ascribed to this profession, the 18 plots of 10 arouras of the occupation priest constitute 17.0% of the total frequency of 106 plots ascribed to this profession. The 18 plots of 10 arouras ascribed to the occupation stablemaster, however, account for only 4.8% of its total frequency of 373 plots. The occupation herdsman accounts for 16 plots of 10 arouras or 10.1% of the 158 plots of 10 arouras. These 16 plots constitute 13.4% of the total frequency of 119 plots ascribed to this pastoral occupation. The remaining 18 occupations which occur in association with plots of 10 arouras each account for less than 10.0% of the 10 aroura plots.

Plots of 20 arouras in size also occur predominantly in association with <u>ỉḥwtyw</u>. The 16 plots of 20 arouras ascribed to this occupation constitute 21.3% of the 75 plots of 20 arouras and 20.8% of the total frequency of 77 plots ascribed to <u>ỉḥwtyw</u>. Another 10 plots of 20 arouras or 13.3% occur in association with the military rank of charioteer (<u>kṯ</u>) and constitute one-third of the plots ascribed to charioteers. Seven plots of 20 arouras or 9.3% occur in association with both the occupations herdsman and <u>ʿnḫ(t) n nỉwt</u> and comprise 5.9% and 4.7% respectively of the plots ascribed to these occupations. The occupation scribe accounts for 6 plots of 20 arouras or 8.0%. These 6 plots constitute 13.3% of the 45 plots ascribed to this occupation. The remaining 15 occupations each account for less than 7.0% of the 75 plots of 20 arouras. Plots of 20 arouras in size account for only 5.7% of the 1322 plots analyzed in this table.

It is evident that as the plots increase in size, their distribution becomes more even among the occupations to which they are ascribed. The high frequency occupations have a strong tendency to occur predominantly in association with one size of plot which varies from occupation to occupation. This tendency is most dramatically exemplified in the distributions of aroura measured plots of the occupation stablemaster where 90.3% of the plots are 5 arouras in size, soldier where 90.3% of the plots are 3 arouras in size, and herdsman where 72.3% of the plots are 5 arouras in size.

The relationship between variable 7 Occupation or Title of Smallholder and variable 10 Arouras Special Case is also statistically significant with a Cramer's V value of 0.62163 indicative of a relatively high degree of correlation between the variables. There are 242 plots analyzed in this crosstabulation, 143 of which (59.1%) are 5 arouras in size. Five arouras is found to be the modal size of plot in accord with data of the previous crosstabulation where 5 aroura plots constitute 55.5% of the total plots. There are only 46 plots in this table which are 10 arouras in size (19.0%), 37 plots which are 3 arouras in size (15.3%), and a mere 16 plots (6.6%) which are 20 arouras in size. The greatest disparity between the distribution of Variety I/II plots in the present table and that of Variety I and Sub-variety IA plots in the previous crosstabulation comes with plots of 3 arouras in size which constitute only 15.3% of the 242 plots of Variety I/II plots as compared with 25.2% of the 1322 plots of Variety I and Sub-variety IA. It should be kept in mind that we are absolutely certain of the correct unit of measure only in the case of plots of Variety I/II which have the value "3," because only these entries have the hook at the top left of the numeral which ensures that the plot is to be interpreted as aroura measured.

The occupation with the highest frequency of unassessed aroura measured plots is that of stablemaster to which 55 plots of Variety I/II (22.7%) are ascribed. Fifty of these 55 plots or 90.9% are 5 arouras in size. These 55 plots constitute 35.0% of the 143 plots of this size. Women smallholders have the second highest frequency in the table accounting for 48 plots or 19.8% of the Variety I/II plots. A total of 33 of these plots or 68.8% are 5 arouras in size. These 33 plots constitute 23.1% of the 143 plots of 5 arouras. The 30 plots of the occupation priest are distributed such that 19 plots or 63.3% are 5 arouras in size and 10 plots or 33.3% are 10 arouras in size. The 28 plots of the occupation soldier are distributed such that 24 plots or 85.7% are 3 arouras in size and constitute 64.9% of the 37 plots of 3 arouras. Another 3 plots or 10.7% are 10 arouras in size. The relatively high frequency of Variety I/II plots of 5 arouras ascribed to stablemasters, women smallholders, and priests together with the relatively high frequency of plots 3 arouras in size ascribed to soldiers are in accord with the data of the previous crosstabulation with variable 9 Arouras. This suggests that plots classified as aroura measured Variety I/II are correctly classified.

The relationship between variable 7 Occupation or Title of Smallholder and variable 28 Land-cubits Subtotal 11 and 12 is found to be statistically significant with a moderately high Cramer's V value of 0.49474. Variable 28 Land-cubits Subtotal 11 and 12 represents the size of plot of Variety II plots where the sum of the first and second land-cubit figures (variables 11 and 12) is considered the actual size of plot.

The highest frequency occupation in this table by far is that of ỉḥwty to which are ascribed 55 plots or 28.1% of the 196 land-cubit measured Variety II plots analyzed in this table. Second highest in frequency is the occupation priest to which are ascribed 38 plots or 19.4% of the 196 Variety II plots. The occupations scribe and stablemaster each have frequencies of 17 plots or 8.7% of the 196 plots analyzed in the table. There are 26 Variety II plots ascribed to the occupation ỉḥwty which are 24 land-cubits in size. These 26 plots constitute 47.3% of the total frequency of 55 plots ascribed to this occupation and 44.8% of the 58 plots of this size. There are 13 plots of 12 land-cubits (23.6%) and 15 plots of 50 land-cubits (27.3%) ascribed to the occupation ỉḥwty. Only 1 plot of 100 land-cubits is ascribed to a ỉḥwty. The distribution of Variety II plots over the five sizes of plots which occur in the table is most even in the case of the occupation priest. Eleven of the 38 plots (28.9%) ascribed to this occupation are 24 land-cubits in size, 10 plots (26.3%) are 12 land-cubits in size, 9 plots (23.7%) are 100 land-cubits in size, and 8 plots (21.1%) are 50 land-cubits in size. The 17 plots ascribed to the occupation scribe are most often of the relatively large size of 100 land-cubits. The 6 plots of 100 land-cubits account for 35.3% of the 17 plots ascribed to scribes. One plot ascribed to a scribe is 200 land-cubits in size. The 17 plots of the occupation stablemaster are the least evenly distributed plots of the high frequency occupations. There are 9 plots of 12 land-cubits which constitute 52.9% of the 17 plots; whereas 4 plots or 23.5% are 24 land-cubits in size. There are also 2 plots of 50 land-cubits and 2 plots of 100 land-cubits ascribed to the occupation stablemaster. The occupation most highly correlated with the largest size of plot is that of overseer of cattle to which 4 plots of 200 land-cubits are ascribed. These plots constitute 66.7% of the 6 plots of 200 land-cubits.

There is clearly a trend here for land-cubit measured Variety II plots where the size of plot is calculated as the sum of the first and second land-cubit figures (variable 11 Land-cubits First Figure and variable 12 Land-cubits Second Figure) to be strongly associated with certain occupations: ỉḥwty, priest, scribe, and stablemaster. The 23 occupations to which plots of Variety II are ascribed are diverse and indeed represent all the occupational groups identified in variable 16 Occupational Group. Only a very few occupations, however, can be expected to be highly correlated with land-cubit measured Variety II plots. Thus, we can expect to find ỉḥwty and priest as the most frequently occurring occupations of smallholder for these relatively small land-cubit measured plots with scribes and stablemasters also accounting for a significant proportion of the smallholders. The apparent restriction of high frequencies of Variety II plots to a very few occupations of smallholders, of which ỉḥwty has the highest frequency, could be interpreted as support for Menu's interpretation of the Variety II plots. In this interpretation, she asserts that cultivators (mostly ỉḥwtyw, but also scribes, priests, and stablemasters) were granted land-cubit measured plots by various institutions for their own use rent-free in return for their services in the cultivation of the aroura measured plots belonging to these institutions enumerated in the non-apportioning paragraphs.(9)

The relationship between variable 7 Occupation or Title of Smallholder and variable 13 Land-cubits Single Figure is found to be statistically significant with a moderately high Cramer's V value of 0.48651. Variable 13 Land-cubits Single Figure consists of all land-cubit measured plots which belong to unassessed Sub-variety IIA. There are 174 of these entries analyzed in the present crosstabulation. Of these 174 Sub-variety IIA entries, 63 pertain to plots 12 land-cubits in size. These 63 plots constitute 36.2% of the 174 plots analyzed in the table. The second highest in frequency are plots of 50 land-cubits of which there are 41 or 23.6%. The 38 plots which are 100 land-cubits in size comprise 21.8% of the 174 plots; whereas the 21 plots which are 24 land-cubits in size comprise 12.1% of the total plots. There are only 11 plots of 200 land-cubits which constitute 6.3% of the 174 plots.

Of the 21 occupations to which Sub-variety IIA plots are ascribed, that of priest has the highest frequency. A total of 39 Sub-variety IIA plots are ascribed to this occupation, 16 of which or 41.0% are 12 land-cubits in size. Ten plots of 50 land-cubits (25.6%) and 9 plots of 24 land-cubits (23.1%) are also ascribed to the occupation priest. The occupation ỉḥwty has the next highest frequency of Sub-variety IIA entries. There are 28 such plots ascribed to the occupation ỉḥwty of which 18 or 64.3% are 12 land-cubits in size. Half of the remaining 10 plots are 24 land-cubits in size and half are 50 land-cubits in size. The third highest frequency occupation is that of scribe. The 23 plots of this occupation are distributed among all five sizes of plots of variable 13. Eight plots (34.8%) are 12 land-cubits in size; whereas another 8 plots are 50 land-cubits in size. Plots of 100 land-cubits account for 5 plots or 21.7%. There is only one plot of 24 land-cubits and one plot of 200 land-cubits ascribed to the occupation scribe. Prophet is the occupation with the fourth highest frequency. The 15 plots ascribed to this occupation are such that 10 plots or 66.7% are 100 land-cubits in size, while 3 plots or 20.0% are 50 land-cubits in size. Of the remaining 2 plots, one is 24 land-cubits in size, while the other is 200 land-cubits in size.

With the exception of the occupation stablemaster which has a frequency of 11 Sub-variety IIA plots, all other occupations have a total frequency of fewer than 10 such plots. As was the case with variable 28 Land-cubits Subtotal 11 and 12, the occupations which occur in the table are extremely diverse representing all of the occupational groups of variable 16 Occupational Group. There is a high degree of correspondence between the occupations which occur in the two crosstabulations. While the distributions of plots ascribed to the occupations which occur in the two tables may differ, they are sufficiently similar to suggest that plots classified as Sub-variety IIA in the present study have been, by and large, correctly classified as land-cubit rather than aroura measured.

(t) Variable 7 Occupation or Title of Smallholder by Variable 14 Assessed Arouras

The relationship between variable 7 Occupation or Title of Smallholder and variable 14 Assessed Arouras is found to be statistically significant with a Cramer's V value of 0.36271. Although this relationship has a comparatively low degree of association among the relationships discussed at length in the present study, it is sufficiently high to indicate that the occupation or title of smallholder was a factor of some significance in determining the assessment value (the red aroura figure) in entries of aroura measured Variety I and Sub-variety IA. The Cramer's V value for this relationship is lower than that of the relationship between occupation or title of smallholder and the size of plot represented by variable 9 Arouras. This indicates that the occupation or title of smallholder was probably a more significant determinant of the size of a Variety I or Sub-variety IA plot, as specified by the initial black aroura figure, than it was of the assessment placed upon the plot.

The relationship between variable 14 Assessed Arouras and variable 7 Occupation or Title of Smallholder has been evaluated by reducing the twenty assessment values of the variable 14 distribution to the five highest frequency assessment values: $\underline{\frac{1}{4}}$ aroura, $\underline{\frac{1}{2}}$ aroura, $\underline{1}$ aroura, $\underline{2\frac{1}{2}}$ arouras, and $\underline{5}$ arouras. There are 466 aroura measured plots with an assessment value of $\underline{\frac{1}{4}}$ aroura which constitute 35.7% of the 1304 entries analyzed in the table. The 520 plots with an assessment value of $\underline{\frac{1}{2}}$ aroura constitute 39.9% of the 1304 total entries. The assessment value $\underline{1}$ aroura accounts for only 255 entries or 19.6% of the entries analyzed in the table. Plots with assessment values of $2\frac{1}{2}$ and 5 arouras have substantially lower frequencies: 36 entries (2.8%) and 27 entries (2.1%) respectively. Thus, there is a nearly even distribution of plots with the most frequently occurring assessment values, $\frac{1}{4}$ and $\frac{1}{2}$ aroura, the remaining three assessment values in the table accounting for less than 25.0% of the remaining Variety I and Sub-variety IA entries.

The occupation with the highest frequency of $\frac{1}{4}$ aroura assessment values is that of soldier which accounts for 122 of the 466 occurrences of this assessment value or 26.2%. The 122 occurrences constitute 57.3% of the 213 occurrences of the occupation soldier analyzed in the table. The occupation with the second highest frequency of the assessment value $\frac{1}{4}$ aroura is that of stablemaster which accounts for 117 occurrences of this assessment value or 25.1%. These 117 occurrences constitute just 31.0% of the 377 occurrences of the occupation stablemaster analyzed in the table. The occupation with the third highest frequency of the assessment value $\frac{1}{4}$ aroura is that of ʿnḫ(t) n nỉwt which accounts for 55 of the 466 occurrences of this assessment value or 11.8%. These 55 occurrences constitute less than half the frequency of the occupation stablemaster and account for 35.9% of the 153 occurrences of ʿnḫ(t) n nỉwt in the table. The occupation priest accounts for 37 of the 466 occurrences of the assessment value $\frac{1}{4}$ aroura or 7.9%. These 37 occurrences account for a substantial 34.6% of the 107 occurrences of this occupation. The occupation herdsman accounts for 33 occurrences of the assessment value $\frac{1}{4}$ aroura or 7.1%. These 33 occurrences constitute 29.2% of the 113 occurrences of this occupation in the table. The frequencies for the occupations priest and herdsman are thus very similar. Scribes account for 14 of the 466 occurrences of the assessment value $\frac{1}{4}$ aroura or 3.0%. These 14 occurrences account for 35.9% of the 39 occurrences of the occupation scribe analyzed in the table. The occupation ỉḥwty accounts for 13 occurrences of the assessment value $\frac{1}{4}$ aroura or 2.8%. These 13 occurrences constitute 19.4% of the 67 occurrences of this occupation analyzed in the table. It is indeed evident, therefore, that the occupations soldier and stablemaster are very highly correlated with the assessment value $\frac{1}{4}$ aroura and that the occupations ʿnḫ(t) n nỉwt, priest, herdsman, scribe, and ỉḥwty are considerably less highly correlated with this assessment value. The remaining 28 occupations which occur in association with the assessment value $\frac{1}{4}$ aroura have frequencies of fewer than 10 cases and constitute less than 2.0% of the 466 occurrences of this assessment value among the 1304 Variety I and Sub-variety IA entries analyzed in this table.

The occupation with the highest frequency of assessment values of $\frac{1}{2}$ aroura is that of stablemaster which accounts for 164 of the 520 occurrences of this assessment value in the table or 31.5%. These 164 occurrences constitute 43.5% of the 377 occurrences of the occupation stablemaster in the table. Assessment values of $\frac{1}{4}$ and $\frac{1}{2}$ aroura together account for 74.5% of the 377 occurrences of the occupation stablemaster. The occupation soldier has the second highest frequency of assessment values of $\frac{1}{2}$ aroura. The occupation soldier accounts for just 82 of the 520 occurrences (15.8%) of this common assessment value. The occupation with the second highest frequency of assessment values of $\frac{1}{2}$ aroura has, therefore, exactly one-half the frequency of the modal occupation, stablemaster. The occupation *ʿnḫ(t) n nỉwt* accounts for 68 occurrences of the assessment value $\frac{1}{2}$ aroura or 13.1%, while the occupation herdsman accounts for 58 occurrences of this assessment value or 11.2%. The 68 occurrences of this assessment value in association with the occupation *ʿnḫ(t) n nỉwt* constitute a substantial 44.4% of the occurrences of this occupation; whereas the 58 occurrences of the assessment value $\frac{1}{2}$ aroura in association with the occupation herdsman constitute an even more substantial 51.3% of the occurrences of this occupation. Priests have the next highest frequency of the assessment value $\frac{1}{2}$ aroura: 33 occurrences or 6.3%. These 33 occurrences account for 30.8% of the 107 occurrences of this occupation in the table. The assessment values $\frac{1}{4}$ and $\frac{1}{2}$ aroura together account for 65.4% of the occurrences of this occupation. The remaining 29 occupations which occur in association with the assessment value $\frac{1}{2}$ aroura account for fewer than 20 cases or less than 5.0% of the 520 occurrences of this assessment value among the 1304 Variety I and Sub-variety IA entries analyzed in the table. Among this group are the occupations *ỉḥwty* which accounts for 12 of the occurrences of the assessment value $\frac{1}{2}$ aroura or 2.3%, and scribe which accounts for 16 occurrences of this assessment value or 3.1%. In the case of *ỉḥwty*, however, there is a fairly even distribution over four of the five assessment values in the table.

The occupation with the highest frequency of assessment values of 1 aroura is also that of stablemaster which accounts for 95 of the 255 occurrences of this assessment value or 37.3%. These 95 occurrences constitute 25.2% of the 377 occurrences of this occupation in the table. Altogether, the assessment values $\frac{1}{4}$, $\frac{1}{2}$, and 1 aroura account for 99.7% of the 377 occurrences of the occupation stablemaster analyzed in the table. Thirty occurrences of the assessment value 1 aroura or 11.8% are ascribed to the occupation priest and account for 28.0% of the 107 occurrences of this occupation analyzed in the table. The occupation with the third highest frequency of the assessment value 1 aroura is that of *ʿnḫ(t) n nỉwt* which accounts for 29 occurrences of this assessment value or 11.4%. The 29 occurrences of this value constitute 19.0% of the 153 occurrences of *ʿnḫ(t) n nỉwt* analyzed in the table. The occupation herdsman accounts for 22 occurrences of the assessment value 1 aroura or 8.6%. These 22 occurrences constitute 19.5% of the 113 occurrences of this occupation analyzed in the table. The assessment value 1 aroura accounts for only 5 occurrences of the occupation *ỉḥwty* or 7.5% and is therefore the assessment value with which this occupation has the weakest association. These 5 entries account for only 2.0% of the 255 occurrences of this assessment value analyzed in this table. The occupation retainer (*šmsw*) accounts for 13 occurrences of the assessment value 1 aroura or 5.1%. These 13 occurrences account for a substantial 50.0% of the 26 occurrences of the occupation retainer analyzed in the table. The occupation Sherden has a frequency of 12 occurrences of the assessment value 1 aroura or

4.7%. These 12 occurrences account for 31.6% of the 38 occurrences of this occupation analyzed in the table. The occupation charioteer also accounts for 12 occurrences of this assessment value or 4.7%. In the case of charioteer, these 12 occurrences of the assessment value 1 aroura account for a somewhat higher percentage of the occurrences of this occupation analyzed in the table (41.4% of the 29 occurrences). The remaining 20 occupations which occur in association with the assessment value 1 aroura each account for less than 3.0% of the 255 occurrences of this assessment value.

The assessment value 2½ arouras occurs in association with only 9 of the 48 occupations, the highest frequency of which is that of ỉḥwty which accounts for 22 of the 36 occurrences of this assessment value or 61.1%. These 22 occurrences constitute 32.8% of the 67 occurrences of ỉḥwtyw analyzed in this table. The occupations with the second and third highest frequencies of the assessment value 2½ arouras are those of scribe (4 entries, 11.1%) and priest (3 entries, 8.3%). The remaining 6 occupations which occur in association with the assessment value 2½ arouras (controller (rwḏw), deputy (ỉdnw), ʿnḫ(t) n nỉwt, servant (sḏmw), stablemaster, and soldier) each account for only 1 or 2 occurrences of this assessment value.

The assessment value 5 arouras occurs in association with only 8 occupations. The occupation with the highest frequency is also that of ỉḥwty which accounts for 15 of the 27 occurrences of this assessment value or 55.6%. These 15 occurrences constitute 22.4% of the 67 occurrences of ỉḥwty analyzed in the table. The occupation with the second highest frequency of the assessment value 5 arouras is that of priest which accounts for only 4 occurrences or 14.8% of the 27 occurrences of this assessment value. The remaining 6 occupations which occur in association with the assessment value 5 arouras (controller, prophet, scribe, Sherden, soldier, and chief of thr-warriors) each account for only 1 or 2 occurrences of this high assessment value.

It is clear that while the lower assessment values ¼ and ½ aroura tend to occur in association with a large number of the occupations of smallholders (35 and 34 of the 54 occupations respectively), both values tend to occur predominantly in association with soldiers and stablemasters with herdsmen and women smallholders also accounting for a substantial number of occurrences of these assessment values. All other occupations have relatively low correlations with these assessment values. The assessment value 1 aroura differs from the lower assessment values with respect to the frequencies of the occupation soldier. Whereas the occupation soldier has relatively high frequencies in association with the assessment values ¼ and ½ aroura, it has a relatively low frequency in association with the assessment value 1 aroura. Once again, stablemasters, herdsmen, and women smallholders each account for a substantial number of the occurrences of this assessment value. The higher assessment values which have substantially lower frequencies than the lower three assessment values are very differently distributed. The assessment values 2½ and 5 arouras are both highly correlated with the occupation ỉḥwty with relatively low frequencies ascribed to the other occupations. Thus, the lower assessment values are found to be largely distributed among 4 occupations (stablemaster, soldier, herdsman, and ꜥ*nḫ(t) n nỉwt*); whereas the higher assessment values are very strongly associated with a single occupation, *ỉḥwty*, which accounts for relatively few occurrences of the lower assessment values $\frac{1}{4}$, $\frac{1}{2}$, and 1 aroura. The table takes into account the 128 *Pōsh* B entries which are highly correlated with such *ỉḥwtyw* (see below (u)) as appear to have constituted a special class of *ỉḥwtyw* to be distinguished from the *ỉḥwtyw* of the ordinary aroura measured apportioning entries. Therefore, the high correlation of the assessment values $2\frac{1}{2}$ and 5 arouras with the occupation *ỉḥwty* reflects to a considerable degree the higher assessments of the *Pōsh* B plots.

The Cramer's V value for this crosstabulation of 0.36271 suggests that the occupation of smallholder was an important, but certainly not the primary determinant of the assessment value placed upon plots of Variety I and Sub-variety IA. The primary determinant of assessment value is probably to be found in a variable which has both a higher Cramer's V value in crosstabulation with variable 14 than that of the relationship we have just explored, and which is, at the same time, highly correlated with the occupation or title of smallholder. The identity of this variable must be sought in further crosstabulations with both variable 7 Occupation or Title of Smallholder and variable 14 Assessed Arouras.

(u) Variable 7 Occupation or Title of Smallholder by Variable 20 Type of *Pōsh* Entry

The relationship between variable 7 Occupation or Title of Smallholder and variable 20 Type of *Pōsh* Entry is statistically significant with a moderately high Cramer's V value of 0.50250. *Pōsh* C entries are found to drop out of the table altogether because the beneficiary of the plot was apparently a chapel of some minor cult, the plot having been cultivated by (*m-ḏrt*) the agency of a *ỉḥwty* or a scribe in most cases. The crosstabulation serves to determine whether or not there was any substantive difference between the occupations of the cultivators of the *Pōsh* B plots and the smallholders of the ordinary apportioning entries.

The occupation with the highest frequency of *Pōsh* B entries is that of *ỉḥwty* which accounts for 79 of the 124 *Pōsh* B entries analyzed in the table or 63.7%. The 79 *Pōsh* B entries ascribed to the occupation *ỉḥwty* constitute 38.7% of the 204 occurrences of this occupation in the apportioning entries. Since *Pōsh* B entries are without exception Variety I entries, and there are 97 Variety I entries ascribed to *ỉḥwtyw*, the 79 *Pōsh* B entries constitute 81.4% of the Variety I entries ascribed to *ỉḥwtyw*. The occupation scribe has the second highest frequency of *Pōsh* B entries: 13 *Pōsh* B entries or 10.5% of the 124 *Pōsh* B entries analyzed in the table. These 13 *Pōsh* B entries constitute 12.0% of the 108 occurrences of this occupation. Controllers (*rwḏw*) account for 10 *Pōsh* B entries or 8.1%. These 10 entries constitute 35.7% of the 28 apportioning entries ascribed to controllers. The occupation with the fourth highest frequency of *Pōsh* B entries is that of priest which accounts for just 9 Pōsh B entries or 7.3%. The 9 Pōsh B entries account for just 3.6% of the 249 occurrences of this occupation among the apportioning entries. The occupations ỉdnw, Sherden, soldier, and prophet each account for 2 Pōsh B entries; whereas the occupations standardbearer, servant (sḏmw), stablemaster, chief of thr-warriors, and ꜥnḫ(t) n nỉwt each account for only 1 Pōsh B entry.

It is especially interesting to note that while ỉḥwtyw occur in association with 63.7% of the Pōsh B entries, these 79 entries constitute only 38.7% of the 204 occurrences of this occupation in the apportioning paragraphs. The remaining 125 entries ascribed to ỉḥwtyw include 91 land-cubit measured entries (57 Variety II entries and 34 Sub-variety IIA entries), 18 Variety I entries, 1 Sub-variety IA entry, and 3 Variety I/II entries. The plots of 12 apportioning entries in which ỉḥwtyw occur as smallholders are lacking data which enable us to classify the entries in accordance with the five categories of variable 2 Format of Entry. Excluding the 79 Pōsh B plots and the 91 land-cubit measured plots, there are, therefore, a minimum of 22 aroura measured plots which are not the subject of corresponding Pōsh A and B entries. Thus, while the vast majority of ỉḥwtyw occurring in aroura measured apportioning entries were involved in the special Pōsh A and B interinstitutional transactions, some ỉḥwtyw (at least 22) were undoubtedly on a par with the smallholders of the ordinary (non-Pōsh) apportioning entries. These data establish the validity of Menu's hypothesis that the term ỉḥwty embraces several classes of ỉḥwtyw.(10) Her interpretation of the corresponding Pōsh A and B entries in which the services of a "spécialiste de la terre" were contracted for the purpose of improving the productivity of a plot of land as part of a transaction between two institutions distinguishes "cultivateurs-fonctionnaires" from "cultivateurs de métier" who were obliged to serve as field-labourers. Stuchevsky's more recent hypothesis that there existed three distinct classes of ỉḥwtyw recognizes the validity of a third category of ỉḥwtyw to be identified with the ordinary smallholders of the apportioning paragraphs (Stuchevsky's "private possessors").(11)

(v) Variable 7 Occupation or Title of Smallholder and Variable 16 Occupational Group by Variable 31 Geographic Location

The relationship between variable 7 Occupation or Title of Smallholder and variable 31 Geographic Location is statistically significant with a Cramer's V value of 0.40665. While this Cramer's V value is not particularly high, it is possible that it could increase were single occurrence and low frequency measurement areas as well as occupations eliminated from the analysis. Nevertheless, it is evident that the relationship between variable 7 Occupation or Title of Smallholder and variable 31 Geographic Location is a very important relationship which is certainly worthy of an in-depth analysis.

The relationship between variable 16 Occupational Group and variable 31 Geographic Location is also found to be statistically significant with a Cramer's V value of 0.42979. This Cramer's V value is sufficiently high to warrant the conclusion that the occupational group of a smallholder was a significant determinant of the location of the plot(s) ascribed to him.

In this crosstabulation, 183 of the 185 measurement areas of the Text A apportioning paragraphs occur in association with one or more of the eight occupational groups: Crafts (Skilled Labour), Military, Agriculture, Animal Husbandry, Administration, Religious, Domestic, and Other. Two measurement areas do not occur in the table because data of occupation or title of smallholder are lacking. There are a total of 2031 entries analyzed in this table.

Of the eight occupational groups, that of Animal Husbandry has not merely the highest frequencies, but also occurs in association with the greatest number of measurement areas. This occupational group accounts for 660 plots or 32.5% of the 2031 plots distributed among 118 measurement areas. Fifteen of these measurement areas are instances of perfect association (100%). Five of these measurement areas are single occurrence measurement areas (1 plot, 100%). There are 6 measurement areas with frequencies of greater than 20 plots ascribed to smallholders of the group Animal Husbandry. Of these 6 measurement areas, 4 are located in zone 3 (Ḥuiniuti, Sharopě, the Granary of Reeds, and Pen-Roḥu). Mi-ēḥu is located in zone 2; whereas Irkak is located in zone 4. The highest frequencies (36 plots, 5.4%) are shared by Mi-ēḥu and Ḥuiniuti. Sharopě accounts for 28 plots or 4.2%, while Irkak accounts for 26 plots or 3.9%. The Granary of Reeds accounts for 23 plots of smallholders of the group Animal Husbandry or 3.5%, while Pen-Roḥu accounts for 22 plots or 3.3%. The remaining 112 measurement areas each account for fewer than 20 of these plots. One hundred of these 112 measurement areas each account for fewer than 10 plots. It is important to keep in mind that the occupation stablemaster (ḥry ỉḥ) is assigned to this occupational group in keeping with its basic definition and has a frequency of 471 entries or 21.0% (relative frequency) of the 2245 apportioning entries. Many of these 471 stablemasters may have been attached to the military and therefore could be justifiably classified as belonging to the group Military.

The occupational group Military, to which 442 plots or 21.8% of the 2031 plots analyzed in the table are ascribed, excludes the data of the occupation stablemaster. Were even half of these data removed from the occupational group Animal Husbandry and reclassified as Military, the frequencies of the group Military would far exceed those of the group Animal Husbandry. The 442 plots ascribed to smallholders of the group Military are distributed among 91 of the 183 measurement areas analyzed in the table. These 91 measurement areas include 5 where there is perfect association, each measurement area ascribed a single plot. The measurement area with the highest frequency of plots ascribed to individuals with military rank or title is Sharopě in zone 3 which accounts for 21 plots or 4.8% of the 442 plots. Sakō in zone 4 has a frequency of 20 such plots or 4.5%, while Na-Amūn, also located in zone 4, has a frequency of 19 plots or 4.3%. The Village of Inroyshes in zone 2, as well as Spermeru in zone 3, accounts for 15 of these plots or 3.4%. There are 75 measurement areas each of which accounts for fewer than 10 plots ascribed to smallholders of the group Military.

The occupational group with the third highest frequency of plots is the group Religious which accounts for 334 plots or 16.4% of the 2031 plots analyzed in the table. The 334 plots are distributed among 94 of the 183 measurement areas. Eleven of the measurement areas have perfect association with the group Religious. Of these 11 measurement areas, 6 are single occurrence measurement areas (1 plot, 100%). The measurement area with the highest frequency of plots ascribed to smallholders of the group Religious is Sakō in zone 4 which accounts for 22 such plots or 6.6%. T(?)-miē-ḥi-tjayef in zone 1 accounts for 20 of these plots or 6.0%. The measurement area the New Land of... in zone 1 has a frequency of 17 plots or 5.1%. The measurement area ...nukhesh, also in zone 1, accounts for 11 of these plots or 3.3%. There are 3 measurement areas which have frequencies of 10 plots or 3.0%: the Tomb of Pernūte in zone 1, Menʿonkh in zone 4, and Tent-meriteḥu also in zone 4. The remaining 87 measurement areas have frequencies of 9 plots or fewer.

The occupational group Other has the fourth highest frequency among the eight occupational groups represented in the table. There is a total of 251 plots or 12.4% of the 2031 plots analyzed in the table which are ascribed to individuals who must be assigned to this wide-ranging category. The group Other includes the 228 women smallholders (<u>ʿnḫ(t) n nỉwt</u>) as well as the occupations <u>ỉdnw</u>, physician, and Royal prince (<u>s3 nsw</u>). There are 73 measurement areas which occur in association with the group Other, 4 of which are single occurrence measurement areas. There are no measurement areas which have perfect association with this occupational group where the total frequency is greater than 1 plot. The highest frequency measurement area by far is Sakō in zone 4 which accounts for 24 such plots or 9.6%. Second highest in frequency is Menʿonkh, also in zone 4, which has a frequency of 17 plots or 6.8%. The Village of Inroyshes in zone 2 accounts for 12 plots ascribed to the occupational group Other or 4.8%. Pi-Wayna, also in zone 2, accounts for 10 more plots or 4.0%. The remaining 69 measurement areas each account for fewer than 10 such plots.

The occupational group Agriculture accounts for 201 plots or 9.9% of the 2031 entries analyzed in the table. All but one of these plots are ascribed to <u>ỉḥwtyw</u>. One plot is ascribed to a scribe of the granary of Pharaoh. The <u>ỉḥwtyw</u> represented in the table include both the ordinary smallholders of the apportioning entries (Stuchevsky's "private possessors") and those of the <u>Pōsh</u> B entries (Stuchevsky's "agents of the fisc" or "pseudo-cultivators") (see section (u) above). (See too ADDITIONS, p. 322)

The occupational group Administration which has a frequency of 118 plots or 5.8% of the 2031 plots analyzed in the table is composed largely of scribes, but also includes controllers (<u>rwḏw</u>) an overseer of the Treasury, and a vizier. The 118 plots ascribed to smallholders of the group Administration are distributed among 44 measurement areas. The House of Erenūfe in zone 3 is the only case of perfect association (1 plot, 100%). The highest frequency measurement area by far is Menʿonkh in zone 4 to which 15 of the 118 plots or 12.7% are ascribed. Second highest in frequency is the Island of Amūn Manifold-of-Brave-Deeds in zone 2 to which 8 such plots or 6.8% are ascribed. Third highest in frequency is the zone 2 measurement area Pi-p-ma to which 7 of these plots or 5.9% are ascribed. The zone 4 measurement area U-ʿAnti accounts for 6 plots ascribed to smallholders of the group Administration or 5.1%. The remaining 40 measurement areas account for 5 plots or fewer. It is possible that the relatively even distribution of plots ascribed to smallholders of the group Administration was the result of a policy decision on the part of the government (Stuchevsky's "State") to allocate plots to scribes in such a way as to make available to the general populace the services of those skilled in reading and writing. Such individuals would have been essential to the operation of village and town councils and judicial bodies (ḳnbt). Needless to say, we would expect some concentrations of individuals of administrative occupations to occur in larger towns as is certainly the case here with Menʿonkh.

The 17 occurrences of the occupational group Domestic, which includes the occupations servant (sḏmw) and slave (ḥm), constitute only 0.8% of the 2031 entries analyzed in the table. The 17 plots are distributed over 12 measurement areas, only one of which is a single occurrence measurement area (P-Kharuru in zone 4). The highest frequency occurs in the zone 4 measurement area Irkak which accounts for 3 of these plots or 17.6%. The remaining 11 measurement areas each account for only 1 or 2 plots.

The 8 occurrences of the occupational group Crafts (Skilled Labour) constitute only 0.4% of the 2031 entries analyzed in the table. They are distributed over 6 measurement areas, 4 of which are located in zone 4 (Imy-tay-m-t-nē, Sakō, Menʿonkh, and U-ʿAnti). Four of the measurement areas have frequencies of only a single plot each (the Island of Amūn Overrunning-<His>-Boundary in zone 2, Sharopě in zone 3, Menʿonkh and U-ʿAnti both in zone 4). Only Imy-tay-m-t-nē and Sakō have frequencies of 2 plots each.

It is very much worthwhile at this point to consider the distribution of occupational groups with respect to the individual measurement areas. Needless to say, high frequency measurement areas are the most useful and instructive to consider. There are 21 measurement areas with frequencies of 25 plots or more (1.2% or more of the 2031 entries analyzed). Of these 25 measurement areas, there are only 5 to which 50 or more plots (2.5% or more) are ascribed. These measurement areas are the following: Mi-ēḥu in zone 2 (50 plots, 2.5%); Ḥuiniuti (58 plots, 2.9%) and Sharopě (67 plots, 3.3%) in zone 3; and Sakō (89 plots, 4.4%) and Menʿonkh (81 plots, 4.0%) in zone 4.

The 89 plots ascribed to Sakō in this table are fairly evenly distributed among the occupational groups Military (20 plots, 22.5%), Religious (22 plots, 24.7%), and Other (24 plots, 27.0%). The group Animal Husbandry (including stablemaster) has a frequency of 17 plots or 19.1%. The occupational group Crafts (Skilled Labour) accounts for only 2 plots (2.2%) in Sakō, while the group Agriculture accounts for 4 plots (4.5%). Clearly, Sakō was a settlement of some size with a concentration of military personnel as suggested by the frequencies of both the groups Military and Animal Husbandry, the latter of which includes stablemasters, many of whom may have been assigned to the military. Another indication of Sakō's character as a relatively large military-based settlement is the very low frequency of ỉḥwtyw (4 plots, 4.5%). Since the term ỉḥwty includes both "ordinary" smallholders (Stuchevsky's "private possessors"), who appear to have been first and foremost cultivators per se, as well as those ỉḥwtyw responsible for the cultivation of plots detailed in the Pōsh B entries, their absence is especially interesting. No interinstitutional transactions such as those indicated by the corresponding Pōsh A and B entries are in evidence with respect to plots situated in or near Sakō. Military personnel may have taken first priority in the allocation of plots, 33.8% of which were 3 arouras in size (the size of plot ascribed to 90.3% of the soldiers in the apportioning entries). We also note that although there is a high frequency of stablemasters in or near Sakō, herbage entries account for only 11 plots or 12.1% of the 91 plots in Sakō analyzed in the crosstabulation of variable 31 Geographic Location by variable 21 Type of Apportioning Paragraph. Rmnyt pš entries comprise the vast majority of these cases (55 plots, 60.4%). There are no scribes or controllers attested for Sakō. The two scribes of the army in the apportioning paragraphs (A84,7; 65,23) occur in Irkak in zone 4 and the Granary of Reeds in zone 3. The relatively high frequencies of the group Religious, on the other hand, may well be explained by the relatively large size of Sakō among the measurement areas of the apportioning paragraphs indicated by its frequency of 91 plots or 4.2% of the 2161 apportioning entries where data of geographic location are available.(12) A relatively large population in or near Sakō would probably have required a larger number of priests to attend to the needs of the local population (funerary, educational, medical, etc.,).

The 81 plots ascribed to the zone 4 measurement area Menʿonkh are more evenly distributed over the eight categories of occupational group as compared with Sakō, also located in zone 4. The occupational group Agriculture has the highest frequency among the eight groups. The group Agriculture accounts for 21 plots or 25.9% of the 81 plots ascribed to Menʿonkh in this table. Women smallholders (the group Other), as well as smallholders of the group Administration, which consists largely of scribes, also have relatively high frequencies. The 17 plots of the group Other (13 of which are ascribed to women) account for 21.0% of the 81 plots, while the 15 plots of the group Administration account for 18.5% of these plots. Occupations of the group Animal Husbandry account for 10 plots or 12.3% as do occupations of the group Religious. There are only 5 plots or 6.2% ascribed to the group Military, figures which would increase considerably if some of the stablemasters were reassigned to this group. Occupations of the group Domestic (servant and slave) account for only 2 plots or 2.5%. There is only a single plot which is ascribed to an artisan (a carpenter (ḥmww)). The relatively large population of Menʿonkh, as suggested by the number of plots ascribed to smallholder heads of households, appears to have been more heterogeneous in its occupational composition than that of Sakō.

Sharopě in zone 3 has a frequency of 67 plots or 3.3% of the 2031 plots analyzed in this table. There is no doubt whatever that Sharopě was primarily a military settlement. Twenty-one of its 67 plots or 31.3% were allocated to individuals of military rank or title. Moreover, 28 of the 67 plots, or 41.8% are assigned to individuals of the occupational group Animal Husbandry which includes stablemasters. Only 8 plots or 11.9% are ascribed to the group Other. All 8 of these plots are ascribed to women. The low frequencies of women smallholders are in accord with what might be expected of a predominantly military settlement. The frequencies of the group Agriculture are also very low (5 plots, 7.5%). Four of the 5 plots assigned to this occupational group are ascribed to ỉḥwtyw. One plot is ascribed to a scribe of the granary of Pharaoh (A53,9). Three of the four ỉḥwtyw occur in Pōsh B entries and therefore number among Stuchevsky's "agents of the fisc" or "pseudo-cultivators." These ỉḥwtyw, therefore, would have been officials responsible for the cultivation of plots which were the subject of the corresponding Pōsh A and B entries rather than ordinary smallholders who usually cultivated their own plots (Stuchevsky's "private possessors"). These ỉḥwtyw may also be contrasted with the "field-hands" or "farm-labourers," also referred to as ỉḥwtyw, who cultivated the fields of the non-apportioning entries. The remaining three occupational groups (Crafts (Skilled Labour), Administration, and Domestic) each account for only a single plot in or near Sharopě. The group Religious is ascribed only 2 plots or 3.0%.

Ḥuiniuti in zone 3 was also perhaps a predominantly military settlement. The 58 plots ascribed to Ḥuiniuti in this table (2.9% of the 2031 plots analyzed) are distributed among the five occupational groups represented (Animal Husbandry, Military, Religious, Other, and Administration) such that the vast majority of plots (36 plots, 62.1%) are ascribed to the group Animal Husbandry. These 36 plots include 34 plots assigned to stablemasters. Eight plots each (13.8%) are ascribed to smallholders of the groups Military and Religious. Only 4 plots or 6.9% are ascribed to women smallholders. Two plots (3.4%) are ascribed to individuals of the group Administration. The high frequency of stablemasters ascribed to Ḥuiniuti is undoubtedly related to the moderately high correlation between this zone 3 measurement area and herbage paragraphs. The 15 herbage plots ascribed to Ḥuiniuti constitute 25.4% of the 59 plots ascribed to this measurement area in the crosstabulation of variable 21 Type of Apportioning Paragraph by variable 31 Geographic Location (see section (q)). If the majority of the 34 stablemasters of the group Animal Husbandry were attached to the military, Ḥuiniuti would indeed qualify as a predominantly military settlement. The absence of occupations of the group Crafts (Skilled Labour), Agriculture, and Domestic, as well as the comparatively low frequencies of women smallholders, also suggests that Ḥuiniuti was a military settlement with a relatively homogeneous population.

These four examples of the occupational distribution of high frequency measurement areas are illustrative of the variety of patterns in the occupational composition of towns and villages which occur among the Text A measurement areas. The data of this table are also useful in providing a gauge of the relative population density of the towns and villages in Middle Egypt based upon a count of the individual heads of households who occur as smallholders in Text A. To that end, this table can be used in conjunction with variable 40 Individual Smallholder which attempts to identify individual smallholders among the measurement areas of Text A. This table and the preceding crosstabulation with variable 7 Occupation or Title of Smallholder should be studied in detail in order to derive a system of classification for the towns and villages of Middle Egypt in which both occupational composition and relative population density are taken into account.

(w) Variable 43 Land Measure I Arouras or Land-cubits (Variety I, Sub-variety IA, Variety II) and Variable 44 Land Measure II Arouras or Land-cubits (Variety I, Sub-variety IA, Variety I/II, Variety II, Sub-variety IIA) by Variable 7 Occupation or Title of Smallholder

We have already established statistically significant and substantively important relationships between variable 7 Occupation or Title of Smallholder and several important variables identified in the data of the Text A apportioning paragraphs. It is appropriate, therefore, that we now observe how the unit of measure of plots recorded in the apportioning paragraphs relates to the occupation or title of the smallholder. The relationship between variable 43 Land Measure I Arouras or Land-cubits (Variety I, Sub-variety IA, Variety II) and variable 7 Occupation or Title of Smallholder is statistically significant with a Cramer's V value of 0.43375 which indicates that we can infer the probable unit of measure of a plot with prior knowledge of the occupation or title of smallholder and vice versa with a moderately high probability of being correct.

Most low frequency occupations such as brander (of cattle?), builder (or potter), captain of retainers, Medjay, oxherd, and weaver occur exclusively in association with aroura measured plots of Variety I and Sub-variety IA. High frequency occupations, on the other hand, often have very uneven distributions of aroura measured and land-cubit measured plots, aroura measured plots having the much higher frequency. The occupation stablemaster, for example, is ascribed 376 aroura measured plots of Variety I and Sub-variety IA which constitute 95.7% of the 393 plots ascribed to this occupation in this table. Women smallholders (ʿnḫ(t) n nỉwt) are ascribed 150 aroura measured plots which constitute 94.9% of the 158 plots ascribed to them. The occupation herdsman is ascribed 120 aroura measured plots which constitute 96.8% of the 124 plots ascribed to this occupation in this table. Some occupations, however, have a much more even distribution of land-cubit measured and aroura measured plots. The plots of the occupation ỉḥwty are distributed such that 98 plots or 63.2% of the 155 plots are aroura measured and 57 plots or 36.8% are land-cubit measured. The plots of the occupation priest are distributed such that 109 plots or 72.2% of the 151 plots are aroura measured and 42 plots or 27.8% are land-cubit measured. Looking at occupations with lower frequencies, we see that the 19 plots ascribed to the occupation controller are distributed such that 13 plots or 68.4% are aroura measured and 6 plots or 31.6% are land-cubit measured. The 23 plots ascribed to the occupation prophet are distributed such that 11 plots or 47.8% are aroura measured and 12 plots or 52.2% are land-cubit measured. These examples suffice to demonstrate that the occupation of smallholder played a significant role in determining whether the plot(s) ascribed to an individual smallholder would be aroura measured or land-cubit measured. Since aroura measured plots differ in size from land-cubit measured plots by a factor of 1ØØ, and are likely to denote different types of cultivation, this finding is especially noteworthy.

The Cramer's V value for the relationship between variable 44 Land Measure II Arouras or Land-cubits (Variety I, Sub-variety IA, Variety I/II, Variety II, Sub-variety IIA) and variable 7 Occupation or Title of Smallholder is somewhat higher than that of the previous crosstabulation (Cramer's V value of Ø.48655 as compared with Ø.43375). Comparison of the distributions of the two tables suggests that the data of unassessed Variety I/II and Sub-variety IIA are, for the most part, correctly classified.

(x) Variable 43 Land Measure I Arouras or Land-cubits (Variety I, Sub-variety IA, Variety II) and Variable 44 Land Measure II Arouras or Land-cubits (Variety I, Sub-variety IA, Variety I/II, Variety II, Sub-variety IIA) by Variable 15 Type of Land

The relationship between variable 43 Land Measure I Arouras or Land-cubits (Variety I, Sub-variety IA, Variety II) and variable 15 Type of Plot is statistically significant with a Cramer's V value of Ø.395Ø5. Although this Cramer's V value is not as high as the Cramer's V values of most of the tables chosen for discussion in the present study, the table is very much worth consideration. Only assessed aroura measured plots (Variety I and Sub-variety IA) and land-cubit measured plots of Variety II are included in the analysis.

The table indicates that 8 of the 29 entries of plots identified as p‘t-land in the measurement lines of the Text A apportioning paragraphs or 27.6% denote aroura measured plots of Variety I or Sub-variety IA; whereas 21 of these entries or 72.4% denote land-cubit measured plots of Variety II. Plots identified as ỉdb-land in the measurement lines of Text A are distributed such that 45 plots or 45.5% of the 99 plots are aroura measured plots of Variety I or Sub-variety IA; whereas 54 plots or 54.5% are land-cubit measured plots of Variety II. Thus, there is a nearly equal proportion of aroura and land-cubit measured plots of ỉdb-land in contrast to plots of p‘t-land where the overwhelming majority of the plots (72.4%) are land-cubit measured. The remaining 1529 plots analyzed in the table are comprised of neither p‘t nor ỉdb-land. They are distributed such that 1387 plots or 9Ø.7% are aroura measured, while only 142 plots or 9.3% are land-cubit measured. Thus, the distributions of plots of both p‘t-land and ỉdb-land in this crosstabulation are very different from the distribution of the overwhelming majority of plots which consist of neither p‘t nor ỉdb-land. This suggests that there is a substantive link between both p‘t-land and ỉdb-land and the small-scale cultivation denoted by the Variety II data format. The frequencies of this table suggest that p‘t-land was probably especially well-suited to small-scale cultivation; whereas ỉdb-land may have been equally well-suited to the demands of small and large-scale cultivation.

The relationship between variable 44 Land Measure II Arouras or Land-cubits (Variety I, Sub-variety IA, Variety I/II, Variety II, Sub-variety IIA) and variable 15 Type of Plot is also statistically significant with a somewhat higher Cramer's V value than that of the previous crosstabulation (0.44896 as compared with 0.39505). This table reflects the addition of data of the unassessed aroura and land-cubit measured plots to the analysis.

In this table, both pꜥt and ỉdb-land are more highly correlated with land-cubit measured data formats (Variety II and Sub-variety IIA). Plots comprised of neither pꜥt nor ỉdb-land are slightly less highly correlated with aroura measured formats (Variety I, Sub-variety IA, Variety I/II) than in the previous crosstabulation. Plots identified as pꜥt-land in the Text A measurement lines are distributed such that 8 plots or 16.0% are aroura measured (Variety I, Sub-variety IA, Variety I/II) and 42 plots or 84.0% are land-cubit measured (Variety II and Sub-variety IIA). Plots identified as ỉdb-land are distributed such that 54 plots or 31.2% are aroura measured and 119 plots or 68.8% are land-cubit measured. Plots which are comprised of neither pꜥt nor ỉdb-land are distributed such that 1655 plots or 86.2% of a total of 1921 such plots are aroura measured and only 266 plots or 13.8% are land-cubit measured. Thus, the addition of unassessed aroura and land-cubit measured plots to the analysis increases the correlation between pꜥt-land and ỉdb-land and land-cubit measured formats.

The data of these crosstabulations give us a new perspective on the terms pꜥt and ỉdb which enlarges our understanding of these terms to a small degree. The correlations of these tables are also important in that they suggest that there is indeed a substantive difference between the type of cultivation denoted by aroura measured formats (Variety I, Sub-variety IA, Variety I/II) and that denoted by land-cubit measured formats (Variety II and Sub-variety IIA) in which the type of land played some role. Moreover, since the Cramer's V values of these crosstabulations are very close, there is additional evidence that the unassessed plots in the apportioning paragraphs are, for the most part, correctly classified as either aroura measured (Variety I/II) or land-cubit measured (Sub-variety IIA).

(y) Variable 15 Type of Land by Variable 31 Geographic Location

The relationship between variable 15 Type of Land and variable 31 Geographic Location is found to be statistically significant with a relatively high Cramer's V value of 0.72785. It is immediately evident that specification of the plot in terms of the variety of land, pꜥt or ỉdb, was most unusual. Of a total of 2157 entries analyzed in the table, 183 entries or 8.5% are identified as ỉdb-land; whereas only 58 entries or 2.7% are identified as pꜥt-land. There is a single plot (A7,40) among the 184 plots of ỉdb-land for which the name of the measurement area is lacking. This plot, therefore, does not occur in the crosstabulation.

The 58 plots of p‘t-land occur in 11 measurement areas; whereas the 183 plots of ỉdb-land occur in 31 measurement areas. Plots identified as consisting of p‘t-land and plots identified as consisting of ỉdb-land occur together in only 4 measurement areas: the New Land of... in zone 1, the Tomb of Pernūte also in zone 1, the Village of Djasasati in zone 2, and Sharopě in zone 3. The distribution of p‘t plots and ỉdb plots is found to be very uneven in all of these locations. The 10 plots identified as p‘t-land constitute 27.0% of the 37 plots ascribed to the New Land of ...; whereas the 3 plots identified as ỉdb-land constitute only 8.1% of the plots in this locality. The 3 plots identified as p‘t-land constitute 17.6% of the 17 plots ascribed to the Tomb of Pernūte; whereas the 10 plots identified as ỉdb-land constitute 58.8% of these plots. The 17 plots of the Village of Djasasati identified as p‘t-land constitute 47.2% of the 36 plots ascribed to this locality; whereas the single plot identified as ỉdb-land constitutes only 2.8% of the plots ascribed to the Village of Djasasati. Sharopě is the only locality among the four where neither p‘t-land nor ỉdb-land constitutes a significant proportion of the total plots. There is only a single plot of p‘t-land ascribed to the high frequency measurement area Sharopě. The 4 plots of ỉdb-land ascribed to Sharopě constitute only 5.3% of the 76 plots in this zone 3 measurement area. The remaining 71 plots or 93.4% consist of neither p‘t-land nor ỉdb-land.

A major difference between plots of p‘t-land and plots of ỉdb-land is their distribution over the 185 measurement areas of the Text A apportioning paragraphs. The 58 plots of p‘t-land are distributed over 11 measurement areas such that 45 plots or 77.6% occur in only 4 measurement areas, 2 of which, ...nukhesh and the New Land of..., are located in zone 1. The other 2 measurement areas are Tent-ḥemy and the Village of Djasasati, both located in zone 2. The 12 plots of p‘t-land ascribed to ...nukhesh comprise 100% of the plots in this measurement area; whereas the 10 plots of p‘t-land ascribed to the New Land of ... comprise only 27.0% of the 37 plots attested for this measurement area. The 6 plots of p‘t-land ascribed to Tent-ḥemy comprise 28.6% of the 21 plots ascribed to this measurement area; whereas the 17 plots of p‘t-land ascribed to the Village of Djasasati comprise 47.2% of the 36 plots attested. Plots of ỉdb-land, however, are distributed such that their highest concentration is in a single measurement area, Men‘onkh in zone 4 where 46 of the 183 plots of ỉdb-land or 25.1% occur. These 46 plots account for 56.1% of the 82 plots ascribed to Men‘onkh. No p‘t plots whatever are ascribed to Men‘onkh. The remaining 137 ỉdb plots are distributed such that no more than 13 plots occur in any one measurement area (13 ỉdb plots being the total frequency of the New Land of Bunero in zone 1).

Thus, we know that plots of both p‘t-land and ỉdb-land tend to occur in association with relatively few measurement areas, there being only 4 measurement areas where plots of both varieties of land occur. We also know that although plots of p‘t-land occur in 11 measurement areas, 77.6% of the 58 plots of p‘t-land occur in only 4 of these measurement areas. Plots of ỉdb-land differ from plots of p‘t-land in that they are more evenly distributed over the 31 measurement areas to which they are ascribed, notwithstanding the fact that 25.1% of the 183 *ỉdb* plots occur in a single measurement area. These data enable us to make some distinctions between plots identified as consisting of *pʿt*-land and plots identified as consisting of *ỉdb*-land which contribute in a small way to a better understanding of these imperfectly understood topographical terms.

(z) Variable 9 Arouras by Variable 31 Geographic Location

The relationship between variable 9 Arouras (initial black aroura figure in entries of Variety I and Sub-variety IA) and variable 31 Geographic Location is statistically significant with a Cramer's V value of 0.49777. The Cramer's V value indicates that there is a moderately high degree of correlation between the size of aroura measured Variety I and Sub-variety IA plots and the geographic location of these plots. Altogether, there are twenty-three sizes of plots for entries of Variety I and Sub-variety IA ranging from 1 aroura (4 plots) to 110 arouras (1 plot). Values of variable 9 Arouras with frequencies of fewer than 10 occurrences have been eliminated from the table in order to reduce the number of zero and low frequency cells which tend to distort the Cramer's V value. Only the five highest frequency sizes of plots occur in the table. The modal size of plot is 5 arouras which accounts for 729 plots or 54.2% of the 1344 entries analyzed. The size of plot with the second highest frequency is 3 arouras. Plots of 3 arouras account for 330 plots in the table or 24.6%. Plots of 10 arouras (169 plots, 12.6%), 20 arouras (95 plots, 7.1%), and 2 arouras (21 plots, 1.6%) will also be discussed below.

The 729 Variety I and Sub-variety IA plots of 5 arouras occur in 114 measurement areas, the highest frequencies occurring in Sakō in zone 4 (45 plots, 6.2%); Ḥuiniuti in zone 3 (44 plots, 6.0%); Mi-ēḥu in zone 2 (34 plots, 4.7%); Pen-Roḥu in zone 3 (31 plots, 4.3%); Sharopě in zone 3 (29 plots, 4.0%); the Granary of Reeds also in zone 3 (28 plots, 3.8%); and the Sycomores of Irkak (21 plots, 2.9%) in zone 4. Altogether, these 7 measurement areas account for 232 plots or 31.8% of the 729 Variety I and Sub-variety IA plots of 5 arouras. There are 107 measurement areas which account for 20 plots of 5 arouras or fewer, 17 of which have frequencies of between 10 and 20 plots. There are 90 measurement areas where fewer than 10 plots of 5 arouras occur. The highest concentrations of these 5 aroura plots occur in measurement areas of zone 3.

The 330 Variety I and Sub-variety IA plots of 3 arouras occur in 66 measurement areas, the highest frequencies occurring in Sharopě in zone 3 (27 plots, 8.2%) and Sakō in zone 4 (25 plots, 7.6%). Sharopě and Sakō together account for only 52 plots or 15.8% of the 330 Variety I and Sub-variety IA plots of 3 arouras. There are another 8 measurement areas which account for 10 or more of these plots: Ḥuiniuti (10 plots, 3.0%); Spermeru (12 plots, 3.6%); Pen-Shōs (13 plots, 3.9%); Pen-Iḳarya (15 plots, 4.5%); and Yaya (16 plots, 4.8%), all located in zone 3. The Village of Inroyshes in zone 2 accounts for 15 plots of 3 arouras or 4.5%, while *ʿawen*-grove and the Shelter of Sakō, both in zone 4, account for 10 plots (3.0%) and 12 plots (3.6%) respectively. The remaining 56 measurement areas in the table each have frequencies of fewer than 1Ø plots (3.Ø%). The highest concentrations of these 3 aroura plots occur in measurement areas of zone 3 as is the case with plots of 5 arouras, the modal size of plot. A major difference between the distributions of 5 aroura plots and 3 aroura plots, however, is the density of their distribution. Whereas high frequency measurement areas (more than 2Ø plots) account for 31.8% of the 5 aroura plots, high frequency measurement areas account for only 15.8% of the 3 aroura plots.

The 169 Variety I and Sub-variety IA plots of 1Ø arouras occur in 83 measurement areas, the highest frequencies occurring in the Temple of Sobek in zone 4 (9 plots, 5.3%); Spermeru in zone 3 (8 plots, 4.7%); and Yaya also in zone 3 (7 plots, 4.1%). The remaining 8Ø measurement areas have frequencies of 5 or fewer Variety I and Sub-variety IA plots where the initial black aroura figure is 1Ø arouras. The highest concentrations of these 1Ø aroura plots occur in measurement areas of zone 3.

The 95 Variety I and Sub-variety IA plots of 2Ø arouras occur in 59 measurement areas, the highest frequencies occurring in Sharopĕ in zone 3 (6 plots, 6.3%) and the Temple of Sobek in zone 4 (6 plots, 6.3%). The House of Ptaḥmosĕ in zone 1 accounts for 4 plots of 2Ø arouras or 4.2%. The remaining 56 measurement areas each account for 1, 2, or 3 of these plots. There is a nearly equal distribution of Variety I and Sub-variety IA plots of 2Ø arouras in zones 3 and 4.

The 21 Variety I and Sub-variety IA plots of 2 arouras occur in just 12 measurement areas, the highest frequencies occurring in the zone 4 measurement areas Menʿonkh (5 plots, 23.8%) and Irkak (3 plots, 14.3%). The remaining 1Ø measurement areas each account for only 1 or 2 plots. The highest concentrations of these 2 aroura plots occur in measurement areas of zone 4. It is thus evident that low frequency sizes of plots (2 and 2Ø arouras) tend to have higher correlations with zone 4 measurement areas; whereas high frequency sizes of plots are most highly correlated with measurement areas of zone 3.

The patterns in the distribution of the five highest frequency sizes of plots in individual measurement areas is another aspect of this crosstabulation which is well worth consideration. It is perhaps most worthwhile to consider the high frequency measurement areas in this regard. Sharopĕ in zone 3 is such that 29 of the 66 plots analyzed or 43.9% are 5 arouras in size, while 27 plots or 4Ø.9% are 3 arouras in size--a nearly even distribution of 3 and 5 aroura plots. There are 6 plots of 2Ø arouras (9.1%), 3 plots of 1Ø arouras (4.5%), and only 1 plot of 2 arouras (1.5%). In the case of Ḥuiniuti, also in zone 3, on the other hand, the 44 plots of 5 arouras constitute 78.6% of the 56 plots; whereas the 1Ø plots of 3 arouras constitute only 17.9% of these plots. There is only 1 plot of 1Ø arouras and 1 plot of 2Ø arouras ascribed to Ḥuiniuti. A similar distribution occurs in the case of the zone 2 measurement area Mi-ēḥu which has a total frequency of 46 plots analyzed in this table. Pen-Roḥu in zone 3, however, has an even more skewed distribution of the values of variable 9 Arouras. In this case, the 34 plots are distributed such that 31 plots or 91.2% are 5 arouras in size; whereas only 3 plots or 8.8% are 3 arouras in size. Spermeru in zone 3 has a very different distribution of its 34 plots analyzed in the table. Twelve plots or 35.3% are 3 arouras in size and another 12 plots or 35.3% are 5 arouras in size. There are 8 plots of 10 arouras which constitute 23.5% of the 34 plots ascribed to Spermeru. The 23 plots ascribed to the Temple of Sobek in zone 4 are just as evenly distributed. Eight plots or 34.8% are 5 arouras in size, 9 plots or 39.1% are 10 arouras in size, and 6 plots or 26.1% are 20 arouras in size. Numerous other measurement areas could be cited, but it suffices to say that there is a wide variety of distributional patterns among the 151 measurement areas which occur in joint association with values of variable 9 Arouras. These distributions may be usefully studied with an eye to identifying patterns in the distribution of the various sizes of plots among the measurement areas of the Text A apportioning paragraphs.

On the basis of the above data, we can say without a doubt that there is a fairly strong correlation between the size of Variety I and Sub-variety IA plots and their geographic distribution which should be explored in detail.

It will be valuable in the future to eliminate the single occurrence and low frequency measurement areas from the analysis in order to further reduce the distortion, if any, in the Cramer's V value. It will also be most useful to crosstabulate the values of variable 9 Arouras eliminating the Sub-variety IA entries where the size of plot is not altogether certain. Such a table could be compared with one in which the values of the black ⌋ figure of the Sub-variety IA entries are crosstabulated with variable 31 Geographic Location. Both tables could then be compared with the present table to observe differences and similarities.

(aa) Variable 10 Arouras Special Case by Variable 31 Geographic Location

The relationship between variable 10 Arouras Special Case and variable 31 Geographic Location is statistically significant with a relatively high Cramer's V value of 0.75404 indicating that there is a relatively high correlation between the size of unassessed aroura measured plots and their geographic location. Only 47 of the 185 measurement areas of the Text A apportioning paragraphs occur in the table. These are the only measurement areas which occur in association with unassessed aroura measured plots (Variety I/II). There are altogether only seven sizes of plots ranging from 3 arouras (43 plots) to 80 arouras (1 plot) excluding the single occurrence of the value "200" which probably belongs to the distribution of variable 13 Land-cubits Single Figure which denotes unassessed land-cubit measured plots (A18,21 in Section I). The modal size of plot for variable 10 is 5 arouras (129 plots, 53.5%). The size of plot with the second highest frequency is 10 arouras (48 plots, 19.9%), while the size of plot with the third highest frequency is 3 arouras (42 plots, 17.4%). One plot of 3 arouras has dropped out of the table because the measurement area is unknown. The size of plot with the fourth highest frequency is 20 arouras (22 plots, 9.1%). As was the case with variable 9 Arouras, values of variable 10 with frequencies of fewer than 10 cases have been eliminated from the table in order to reduce the number of zero and low frequency cells which tend to distort the Cramer's V value.

The 129 Variety I/II plots of 5 arouras occur in 31 measurement areas, the highest frequencies occurring in Pi-Wayna (20 plots, 15.5%); the Village of Djasasati (11 plots, 8.5%); and Ḥ-saḥto (10 plots, 7.8%) in zone 2, as well as Menʿonkh (12 plots, 9.3%) in zone 4. Also having relatively high frequencies are Smaʿa (8 plots, 6.2%) in zone 2 and Sakō (8 plots, 6.2%) in zone 4. The remaining 25 measurement areas have frequencies of anywhere from 1 to 7 plots each. The highest concentrations of these 5 aroura plots of Variety I/II occur in measurement areas of zone 2.

The 48 Variety I/II plots of 10 arouras occur in 17 measurement areas, the highest frequencies occurring in the Mounds of Roma in zone 4 (10 plots, 20.8%); the Pond of the House of Baʿalit (9 plots, 18.8%); and Gerg (7 plots, 14.6%) both in zone 1. The remaining 14 measurement areas have frequencies of only 1, 2, or 3 plots each. There is a nearly even distribution of Variety I/II plots of 10 arouras between zones 1 and 4.

The 42 Variety I/II plots of 3 arouras occur in 13 measurement areas, the highest frequencies by far occurring in the zone 4 measurement area Na-Amūn (18 plots, 42.9%). The Village of Inroyshes in zone 2 has the second highest frequencies of unassessed plots of 3 arouras (8 plots, 19.0%), while the Pond of the House of Baʿalit has the third highest frequencies of these 3 aroura plots (4 plots, 9.5%). The remaining 10 measurement areas each account for only 1, 2, or 3 plots of 3 arouras. The highest concentrations of these 3 aroura plots by far occur in measurement areas of zone 4.

The 22 Variety I/II plots of 20 arouras also occur in 13 measurement areas, the highest frequencies occurring in the Lake of ʿAnbu in zone 1 (4 plots, 18.2%) and the Castle of Merysēt in zone 2 (3 plots, 13.6%). The remaining 11 measurement areas each account for only 1 or 2 such plots. These plots of 20 arouras have their highest concentrations in measurement areas of zone 1. This is most intriguing as Section I of Text A is incomplete. Were all the data of Section I available, it is possible that zone 1 would account for an even greater proportion of unassessed aroura measured plots.

The distribution of the four highest frequency sizes of Variety I/II plots can be usefully considered in the case of 4 measurement areas which have relatively high frequencies (15 plots or more) among the 47 measurement areas which occur in this table. Pi-Wayna in zone 2 has the highest frequencies among the 47 measurement areas. The 25 plots are distributed such that 20 plots are 5 arouras in size (80.0%), 3 plots are 3 arouras in size (12.0%), and 2 plots are 10 arouras in size (8.0%). There are no plots of 20 arouras. In the case of Na-Amūn in zone 4, there are only two sizes of plots attested. Plots of 3 arouras account for 18 of the 24 plots or 75.0%; whereas plots of 5 arouras account for only 6 plots or 25.0%. Landholdings of the zone 4 measurement area Menʿonkh, which has a total frequency of 16 plots analyzed in this table, are distributed over all four sizes as is not unexpected in the case of a high frequency measurement area. Not surprisingly, the distribution of these 16 plots is very uneven. Twelve plots or 75.0% are 5 arouras in size; whereas 2 plots or 12.5% are 10 arouras in size. There is only 1 plot of 3 arouras (6.3%) and only 1 plot of 20 arouras (6.3%). The Pond of the House of Baʿalit in zone 1 accounts for a total of 15 plots. Their distribution is also very uneven. There are 9 plots of 10 arouras or 60.0%, 4 plots of 3 arouras or 26.7%, and 2 plots of 20 arouras or 13.3%.

The data of this crosstabulation indicate that the size of unassessed aroura measured plots very definitely varies with the geographic location of the plot. It is likely, therefore, that the geographic location of a plot played a significant role in determining its size. Unlike assessed aroura measured plots (variable 9 Arouras), however, Variety I/II plots are not located predominantly in zone 3. Zone 3 is the zone with the lowest concentration of Variety I/II plots. The fact that Variety I/II plots have their highest frequencies in association with measurement areas with relatively low frequencies of assessed aroura measured plots of Variety I and Sub-variety IA suggests that the location of the plot was, in large part, the explanation for the lack of assessment. Plots in certain predictable measurement areas were subject to circumstances or conditions which made their assessment impossible (problems having to do with irrigation, soil conditions requiring the land to lie fallow that season, smallholders being absent during the growing season, etc.). The only notable exception is the high frequency measurement area Menʿonkh in zone 4 to which a total of 83 apportioning entries are ascribed in Text A. Nineteen of these plots are assessed aroura measured plots (Variety I and Sub-variety IA); whereas 16 are unassessed aroura measured plots (Variety I/II) according to the crosstabulation of variable 2 Format of Entry by variable 31 Geographic Location (see above (g)).

In the future, this table will be further reduced in size by eliminating single occurrence and low frequency measurement areas to further reduce distortion in the Cramer's V value.

(bb) Variable 14 Assessed Arouras by Variable 31 Geographic Location

The relationship between variable 14 Assessed Arouras and variable 31 Geographic Location is statistically significant with a Cramer's V value of 0.64682 which indicates that there is a relatively high correlation between the assessment placed upon a plot (red aroura figure in entries of Variety I and Sub-variety IA) and the location of the plot. Values of variable 14 with frequencies of fewer than 20 cases have been eliminated from the table in order to reduce the number of zero and low frequency cells. There are twenty assessment values in the case of variable 14 ranging from $\frac{1}{4}$ aroura (499 plots) to $20\frac{1}{2}\frac{1}{4}$ arouras (1 plot only). Only the five highest frequency assessment values occur in the table. The modal assessment value is $\frac{1}{2}$ aroura (519 plots, 38.9%), while the assessment value with the second highest frequency is $\frac{1}{4}$ aroura (491 plots, 36.8%). The assessment value with the third highest frequency is 1 aroura (259 plots, 19.4%).

The assessment values 2½ and 5 arouras have substantially lower frequencies. There are 37 plots with the assessment value 2½ arouras (2.8%) and only 28 plots with the assessment value 5 arouras (2.1%).

Of the 148 measurement areas analyzed in this table, 64 measurement areas or 43.2% occur exclusively in association with a single assessment value. Thirty of these measurement areas have frequencies of only a single plot. Fifteen of the 64 measurement areas with perfect association are ascribed aroura measured plots with an assessment value of ¼ aroura. The highest frequency of the assessment value ¼ aroura among these 15 measurement areas is that of the Mound of Yēbes in zone 2 to which 15 such plots or 3.1% are ascribed. Twenty-five of the 64 measurement areas are ascribed aroura measured plots with the assessment value ½ aroura. The highest frequency among these 25 measurement areas is that of the House of Psiūr in zone 3 where 18 such plots or 3.5% occur. Thirteen of the 64 measurement areas with perfect association have an assessment value of 1 aroura. Of these 13 measurement areas, the highest frequency is that of Pen-Ity in zone 3 to which 8 plots with an assessment value of 1 aroura (3.1%) are ascribed. Six of the 64 measurement areas with perfect association occur only in association with the assessment value 2½ arouras, while only 5 measurement areas occur only in association with the assessment value 5 arouras.

The lowest assessment value ¼ aroura occurs in association with a total of 68 measurement areas. Eleven of these measurement areas account for 15 or more plots with an assessment value of ¼ aroura. The highest frequency of the 491 occurrences of the assessment value ¼ aroura by far occurs in association with the zone 4 measurement area Sakō. The 62 plots comprise 12.6% of the 491 occurrences of this assessment value. The measurement area with the second highest frequency of the assessment value ¼ aroura is the Sycomores of Irkak also in zone 4. There are 25 plots with this assessment value or 5.1% ascribed to this measurement area. Irkak, also in zone 4, accounts for 22 plots with an assessment value of ¼ aroura or 4.5%, while Sharopě in zone 3 accounts for 21 such plots or 4.3%. The Temple of Sobek in zone 4 and the Village of Inroyshes in zone 2 each account for 20 plots with an assessment value of ¼ aroura or 4.1%. The remaining 62 measurement areas account for fewer than 20 of the 491 occurrences of this assessment value. There are 49 measurement areas among the 62 which account for fewer than 10 of these values.

It is interesting to note that in the case of 4 of the 6 measurement areas with the highest frequencies of the assessment value ¼ aroura (Sakō, the Sycomores of Irkak, Irkak, and the Temple of Sobek), this assessment value constitutes more than 80.0% of the total number of plots ascribed to each measurement area. In the case of Irkak in zone 4, the 22 occurrences of the assessment value ¼ aroura account for 91.7% of the 24 occurrences of this measurement area analyzed in the table; whereas in the case of Sakō, also in zone 4, the 62 occurrences of this assessment value account for 82.7% of the 75 occurrences of this measurement area. Sharopě in zone 3 is the measurement area with the lowest percentage of plots with an assessment value of ¼ aroura among the 6 high frequency measurement areas. The 21 plots with an assessment value of $\frac{1}{4}$ aroura constitute just 32.3% of the 65 plots ascribed to this measurement area. The highest frequencies of the assessment value $\frac{1}{4}$ aroura occur in association with measurement areas of zone 4.

The assessment value $\frac{1}{2}$ aroura which occurs in a total of 90 measurement areas is somewhat differently distributed among the 148 measurement areas analyzed in this table. The highest frequency of assessment values of $\frac{1}{2}$ aroura occurs in Ḥuiniuti in zone 3. The 44 plots with an assessment value of $\frac{1}{2}$ aroura account for 8.5% of the 519 plots with this assessment value. These figures are to be compared with those of Sakō in zone 4 which has the highest frequency of plots with an assessment value of $\frac{1}{4}$ aroura (62 plots, 12.6%). There are 37 plots with the assessment value $\frac{1}{2}$ aroura ascribed to the zone 2 measurement area Mi-ēḥu which comprise 7.1% of the 519 plots with an assessment value of $\frac{1}{2}$ aroura. The zone 3 measurement area the Granary of Reeds accounts for 32 of the 519 plots with an assessment value of $\frac{1}{2}$ aroura or 6.2%. The 29 plots with an assessment value of $\frac{1}{2}$ aroura ascribed to Sharopĕ in zone 3 comprise 5.6% of the 519 plots. Nineteen plots with an assessment value of $\frac{1}{2}$ aroura or 3.7% are ascribed to the zone 3 measurement area Pen-Roḥu. There are 76 measurement areas with frequencies of fewer than 10 plots with an assessment value of $\frac{1}{2}$ aroura as compared with 49 measurement areas with frequencies of fewer than 10 plots with an assessment value of $\frac{1}{4}$ aroura. Whereas the assessment value $\frac{1}{4}$ aroura has the highest frequencies in association with measurement areas of zone 4, the assessment value $\frac{1}{2}$ aroura has the highest frequencies in association with measurement areas of zone 3.

The plots in Ḥuiniuti, which has the highest frequency of plots with the assessment value $\frac{1}{2}$ aroura, are distributed such that 44 plots or 77.2% of the 57 plots have an assessment value of $\frac{1}{2}$ aroura; whereas only 13 plots or 22.8% have an assessment value of 1 aroura. No other assessment value occurs in association with this zone 3 measurement area. The 47 plots ascribed to Mi-ēḥu in zone 2 are such that 37 plots or 78.7% have an assessment value of $\frac{1}{2}$ aroura, 8 plots or 17.0% have an assessment value of $\frac{1}{4}$ aroura, and only 2 plots or 4.3% have an assessment value of 1 aroura. In the case of the Granary of Reeds, the 40 plots are also distributed over the three lowest assessment values. Thirty-two plots or 80.0% have an assessment value of $\frac{1}{2}$ aroura, 7 plots or 17.5% have an assessment value of 1 aroura, and 1 plot or 2.5% has an assessment value of $\frac{1}{4}$ aroura. The zone 3 measurement area Sharopĕ has plots distributed among four of the five assessment values in the table. Only the assessment value $2\frac{1}{2}$ arouras does not occur in association with Sharopĕ. A total of 21 of the 65 plots ascribed to Sharopĕ in this table have an assessment value of $\frac{1}{4}$ aroura (32.3%) as compared with 29 plots or 44.6% with an assessment value of $\frac{1}{2}$ aroura. There are 14 plots or 21.5% with an assessment value of 1 aroura, but only 1 plot (1.5%) with an assessment value of 5 arouras.

The 259 plots with an assessment value of 1 aroura occur in association with 63 measurement areas. The highest concentration of these plots occurs in the zone 3 measurement area, the Castle of Iōt. These 21 plots with an assessment value of 1 aroura account for 8.1% of the 259 plots with this assessment value. The next highest frequencies are those of Sharopě in zone 3 and the Byre of Horus in zone 2. The 14 occurrences of the assessment value 1 aroura in these measurement areas each comprise 5.4% of the 259 plots with an assessment value of 1 aroura. Ḥuiniuti and Spermeru, both in zone 3, each have a frequency of 13 plots with an assessment value of 1 aroura or 5.0% of the 259 plots. Pi-Kasha in zone 4 also accounts for 13 plots with an assessment value of 1 aroura or 5.0%. The zone 3 measurement area Pen-n-Nḥasy accounts for 11 plots with an assessment value of 1 aroura or 4.2%. The Houses of Irkak in zone 4 accounts for 10 of these plots or 3.9%. The remaining 55 measurement areas each account for fewer than 10 plots with an assessment value of 1 aroura. Like the assessment value ½ aroura, the assessment value 1 aroura has the highest frequencies in association with measurement areas of zone 3.

Plots with an assessment value of 1 aroura account for widely diverging percentages of the total frequencies of the measurement areas with which they have the highest correlation. In the case of the Castle of Iōt in zone 3, 21 of the 31 plots or 67.7% have an assessment value of 1 aroura as compared with 10 plots or 32.3% with an assessment value of ½ aroura. As noted above, Sharopě occurs in association with four of the five assessment values, the assessment value 1 aroura accounting for 14 of the 65 plots or 21.5%. In the case of Ḥuiniuti, the 13 plots with an assessment value of 1 aroura account for only 22.8% of the 57 plots ascribed to Ḥuiniuti as compared with 44 plots with an assessment value of ½ aroura which account for 77.2% of the 57 plots. Spermeru in zone 3 is one of three measurement areas to occur in association with all five assessment values. The two highest assessment values, 2½ and 5 arouras, however, have very low frequencies in association with Spermeru. The assessment value 1 aroura accounts for 13 plots or 38.2% of the 34 plots ascribed to this zone 3 measurement area. In the case of the zone 3 measurement area, Pen-n-Nḥasy, however, the 11 plots with an assessment value of 1 aroura account for a substantial 61.1% of the 18 plots as compared with 3 plots with an assessment value of ¼ aroura or 16.7% and 4 plots with an assessment value of ½ aroura or 22.2%. These few examples suffice to indicate the variety of distributional patterns of assessment values among the measurement areas of the Text A apportioning paragraphs.

The 37 cases of the assessment value 2½ arouras occur in association with 33 measurement areas. These 33 measurement areas each have a frequency of only 1 or 2 occurrences of the assessment value 2½ arouras with the exception of Opě in zone 2 which accounts for 3 plots with an assessment value of 2½ arouras or 8.1%. These 33 measurement areas are fairly evenly distributed over all four zones of Text A. The 28 cases of the assessment value 5 arouras occur in association with 25 measurement areas. These 28 occurrences are distributed over all four zones of Text A. No one measurement area has a frequency of more than 2 occurrences of this assessment value. Thus, the highest assessment values, 2½ and 5 arouras, are much more evenly distributed over the four zones of Text A than are the lower assessment values, ¼,

$\frac{1}{2}$, and 1 aroura.

The higher Cramer's V value of the relationship between variable 14 Assessed Arouras and variable 31 Geographic Location (Ø.64682) compared with that of the relationship between variable 9 Arouras and variable 31 Geographic Location (Ø.49777) suggests that the assessment value of a plot was more highly correlated with the geographic location of the plot than was the size of the plot. Moreover, variable 31 Geographic Location appears to be the variable which is both highly correlated with variable 7 Occupation or Title of Smallholder and more highly correlated with variable 14 Assessed Arouras than is variable 7 Occupation or Title of Smallholder. It is possible, therefore, that variable 31 Geographic Location was the primary determinant of the assessment value placed upon an aroura measured plot of Variety I or Sub-variety IA. The fact that the correlation between variable 14 Assessed Arouras and variable 31 Geographic Location is much higher than the correlation between variable 14 Assessed Arouras and variable 7 Occupation or Title of Smallholder, suggests that there was a system of land assessment operative at this point in time, in which the assessment value of a plot was determined largely by the location of the plot and, only secondarily, by the occupation or title of the smallholder.

(cc) Variable 28 Land-cubits Subtotal 11 and 12 by Variable 31 Geographic Location

The relationship between variable 28 Land-cubits Subtotal 11 and 12 and variable 31 Geographic Location is statistically significant with a relatively high Cramer's V value of Ø.63283 indicating that there is a relatively high correlation between the size of land-cubit measured plots of Variety II and the geographic location of these plots. Only 49 of the 185 measurement areas occur in the table. The remaining 136 measurement areas drop out of the table because they occur in association with either aroura measured plots or unassessed land-cubit measured plots (Sub-variety IIA). There are only eleven sizes of plots for variable 28 calculated as the sum of variable 11 Land-cubits First Figure and variable 12 Land-cubits Second Figure. These values range from 6 land-cubits (1 plot) to 2ØØ land-cubits (6 plots). The modal size of plot is 24 land-cubits (6Ø plots, 29.Ø%), while the size of plot with the second highest frequency is 5Ø land-cubits (52 plots, 25.1%). There are 47 plots or 22.7% which are 1ØØ land-cubits in size and 42 plots or 2Ø.3% which are 12 land-cubits in size. The 6 plots of 2ØØ land-cubits constitute 2.9% of the 2Ø7 Variety II plots analyzed in the table. The remaining six sizes of plots of variable 28 have been dropped from the table in order to reduce the number of zero and low frequency cells.

The 6Ø Variety II plots of 24 land-cubits occur in 32 measurement areas, the highest frequencies occurring in Menʿonkh (9 plots, 15.Ø%) and Irkak (7 plots, 11.7%), both located in zone 4. The remaining 3Ø measurement areas account for 1, 2, or 3 Variety II plots of 24 land-cubits.

The 52 Variety II plots of 5Ø land-cubits occur in 26 measurement areas, the highest frequencies occurring in the Great

Byre in zone 1 and the Village of Djasasati in zone 2, each of which accounts for 7 plots of 50 land-cubits or 13.5%. T(?)-miē-ḥi-tjayef in zone 1 accounts for 5 Variety II plots of 50 land-cubits or 9.6%. The remaining 23 measurement areas each account for 1, 2, or 3 of these plots.

The 47 Variety II plots of 100 land-cubits occur in 21 measurement areas, the highest frequencies occurring in T(?)-miē-ḥi-tjayef in zone 1, the Island of Amūn Manifold-of-Brave-Deeds in zone 2, and Menʿonkh in zone 4, each of which has a frequency of 7 plots or 14.9%. The Tomb of Pernūte in zone 1 accounts for 4 of these plots of 100 land-cubits or 8.5%. The remaining 17 measurement areas each account for 1, 2, or 3 of these plots.

The 42 Variety II plots of 12 land-cubits occur in 18 measurement areas, the highest frequency occurring in Tent-mer-iteḥu in zone 4 (7 plots, 16.7%). Five Variety II plots of 12 land-cubits occur in both the Houses of the Grooms in zone 3 and the Village of Kasha in zone 4, each locality accounting for 11.9% of the 42 plots of 12 land-cubits. The Great Byre in zone 1 accounts for 4 Variety II plots of 12 land-cubits or 9.5%. The remaining 14 measurement areas account for 1, 2, or 3 Variety II plots of 12 land-cubits.

The 6 Variety II plots of 200 land-cubits occur in only 4 measurement areas. Of these 4 measurement areas, Ninsu, ...ershati, and the New Land of Bunero are located in zone 1. Three of the 6 plots are ascribed to Ninsu alone. The fourth measurement area is the Island of Amūn Uniting-Himself-with-Eternity in zone 2.

It is also useful to consider the distribution of the various sizes of Variety II plots with respect to the individual measurement areas which occur in this table. The measurement area with the highest frequency is Menʿonkh which accounts for 20 plots of Variety II. The Variety II plots in this zone 4 measurement area are distributed among four of the five sizes of plots analyzed in the table. The 9 plots of 24 land-cubits account for 45.0% of the 20 plots; whereas the 7 Variety II plots of 100 land-cubits account for 35.0% of these plots. There are 2 plots of 12 land-cubits and 2 plots of 50 land-cubits ascribed to Menʿonkh. Altogether, these 4 plots constitute 20.0% of the 20 plots ascribed to Menʿonkh. No plots of 200 land-cubits are ascribed to Menʿonkh. The zone 1 measurement area T(?)-miē-ḥi-tjayef accounts for 15 plots of Variety II. As is the case with Menʿonkh, there are no plots of 200 land-cubits ascribed to T(?)-miē-ḥi-tjayef. There are 7 plots of 100 land-cubits ascribed to T(?)-miē-ḥi-tjayef which account for 46.7% of the 15 plots of Variety II. The 5 plots of 50 land-cubits account for 33.3% of the 15 plots. There are 2 plots of 24 land-cubits (13.3%) and 1 plot of 12 land-cubits (6.7%) ascribed to this zone 1 measurement area. The Great Byre, also in zone 1, accounts for 12 plots of Variety II. Seven of these plots are 50 land-cubits in size and constitute 58.3% of the 12 plots ascribed to this measurement area. There are 4 plots of 12 land-cubits (33.3%) and 1 plot of 100 land-cubits (8.3%). No plots of either 24 land-cubits or 200 land-cubits are ascribed to the Great Byre. Irkak in zone 4 has the fourth highest frequency of Variety II plots. Seven of a total of 11 plots or 63.6% are 24 land-cubits in size as compared with 3 plots or 27.3% which are 12 land-cubits in size. Only 1 plot (9.1%) is 50 land-cubits in size. There are no Variety II plots of either 100 land-cubits or 200 land-cubits ascribed to Irkak. These 4 measurement areas are indicative of the variation in the distribution of various sizes of Variety II plots within individual measurement areas.

The data of this crosstabulation indicate that the size of plot of land-cubit measured plots of Variety II tends to vary with the geographic location of the plot. As many as 17 of the 49 measurement areas are found to occur in association with only one size of plot which varies from location to location. These 17 measurement areas, however, have relatively low frequencies of assessed land-cubit measured plots and include 11 single occurrence measurement areas. Measurement areas with higher frequencies of these plots tend to be characterized by a variety of sizes of land-cubit measured plots, three or four sizes of plots not being uncommon.

(dd) Variable 13 Land-cubits Single Figure by Variable 31 Geographic Location

The relationship between variable 13 Land-cubits Single Figure and variable 31 Geographic Location is statistically significant with a Cramer's V value of 0.58682 indicative of a moderately high degree of association between unassessed land-cubit measured plots (Sub-variety IIA) and the geographic location of these plots. Only 45 measurement areas occur as the locations of Sub-variety IIA plots. There are altogether eleven sizes of Sub-variety IIA plots ranging in size from 4 land-cubits (1 plot) to 500 land-cubits (3 plots). The modal size of plot is 12 land-cubits (66 plots, 36.5%). The size of plot with the second highest frequency is 50 land-cubits (42 plots, 23.2%). Sub-variety IIA plots of 100 land-cubits have the third highest frequency (41 plots, 22.7%). Plots of 24 land-cubits have the fourth highest frequency (21 plots, 11.6%). There are 12 plots of 200 land-cubits if we include the case of "200" in A18,21 as land-cubit rather than aroura measured. Values of variable 13 with frequencies of fewer than 10 cases have been eliminated from the table in order to reduce the number of zero and low frequency cells.

The 66 Sub-variety IIA plots of 12 land-cubits occur in 27 measurement areas, the highest frequencies occurring in Menᶜonkh (11 plots, 16.7%) and Irkak (8 plots, 12.1%) both in zone 4. Tent-mer-iteḥu, also located in zone 4, accounts for 6 of these plots or 9.1%. The New Land of... and Great Byre both in zone 1 each account for 4 plots of 12 land-cubits or 6.1%. The remaining 22 measurement areas each account for 1, 2, or 3 plots of 12 land-cubits. The highest frequencies of Sub-variety IIA plots of 12 land-cubits occur in measurement areas of zone 4.

The 42 Sub-variety IIA plots of 50 land-cubits occur in 24 measurement areas, no more than 4 plots occurring in any one locality (...nukhesh in zone 1 and the Village of Djasasati in zone 2). These plots are fairly evenly distributed over zones 1, 2, and 4, the highest frequencies occurring in zone 1 measurement areas (14 plots).

The 41 Sub-variety IIA plots of 100 land-cubits occur in 21 measurement areas, the highest frequency occurring in Menʿonkh in zone 4 (7 plots, 17.1%). Four such plots or 9.8% are ascribed to the zone 1 measurement area T(?)-miē-ḥi-tjayef. The remaining 19 measurement areas each account for 1, 2, or 3 plots of 100 land-cubits. The highest concentrations of these plots of 100 land-cubits by far occur in measurement areas of zone 4.

The 21 Sub-variety IIA plots of 24 land-cubits occur in 11 measurement areas, no more than 3 plots occurring in any one locality. The highest concentrations of these plots occur in measurement areas of zones 1 and 4.

The 11 Sub-variety IIA plots of 200 land-cubits occur in 7 measurement areas, the highest frequency occurring in Pi-p-ma in zone 2 to which 3 such plots or 27.3% are ascribed. The highest concentrations of these 200 land-cubit plots occur in measurement areas of zones 1 and 2 which account for 4 and 5 such plots respectively. One more plot of 200 land-cubits (A18,21), the land measure of which is not absolutely certain, is probably to be added to these 11 plots of Sub-variety IIA 200 land-cubits in size.

It is useful at this point to consider the distribution of the various sizes of unassessed land-cubit measured plots ascribed to individual high frequency measurement areas. Menʿonkh in zone 4 has by far the highest frequency of unassessed land-cubit measured plots. The 22 plots ascribed to Menʿonkh in this table are distributed such that the 11 plots of 12 land-cubits account for 50.0% of the plots. Sub-variety IIA plots of 100 land-cubits account for 7 plots or 31.8% of the 22 plots ascribed to Menʿonkh. In addition, there are 2 plots of 24 land-cubits (9.1%) and 2 plots of 50 land-cubits (also 9.1%). There are no plots of 200 land-cubits ascribed to Menʿonkh. Irkak, also in zone 4, accounts for 14 unassessed land-cubit measured plots. Plots of 12 land-cubits have the highest frequencies: 8 plots or 57.1% of the 14 plots ascribed to Irkak. There are 3 plots of 24 land-cubits (21.4%), 2 plots of 50 land-cubits (14.3%), and 1 plot of 100 land-cubits (7.1%). There are no plots of 200 land-cubits. The next highest frequencies of unassessed land-cubit measured plots occur in the zone 1 measurement areas, the New Land of ... and T(?)-miē-ḥi-tjayef. Both measurement areas occur in association with four of the five sizes of Sub-variety IIA plots. No plots of 200 land-cubits are ascribed to either locality. The distribution of the remaining four sizes of plots is quite similar in both localities. The difference is that 4 plots of 12 land-cubits or 40.0% are ascribed to the New Land of ...; whereas only 1 plot of 12 land-cubits or 10.0% is ascribed to T(?)-miē-ḥi-tjayef. On the other hand, 4 plots of 100 land-cubits or 40.0% are ascribed to T(?)-miē-ḥi-tjayef; whereas only 1 plot of 100 land-cubits or 10.0% is ascribed to the New Land of ... The remaining 41 measurement areas have frequencies of fewer than 10 unassessed land-cubit measured plots. Twelve of these measurement areas are single occurrence measurement areas which have perfect association with a single size of Sub-variety IIA plot. The sizes of plots which have perfect association with these 12 measurement areas vary considerably from measurement area to measurement area.

When we compare the Cramer's V values of the relationships between assessed and unassessed aroura measured plots (variable 9 Arouras and variable 10 Arouras Special Case) and geographic location with the Cramer's V values of the relationships between assessed and unassessed land-cubit measured plots (variable 28 Land-cubits Subtotal 11 and 12 and variable 13 Land-cubits Single Figure) and geographic location, we find that the two pairs of Cramer's V values are markedly different. While the Cramer's V values for the relationships between assessed and unassessed land-cubit measured plots and geographic location are not significantly different (0.63283 and 0.58682 respectively), the Cramer's V values for the relationships between assessed and unassessed aroura measured plots and geographic location are considerably different (0.49777 and 0.75404 respectively). The disparity we observe certainly requires some explanation. It is certainly possible that the Cramer's V value of the crosstabulation of variable 9 Arouras by variable 31 Geographic Location might be higher if we understand the value of the black ⌋ figure in Sub-variety IA entries rather than the initial black aroura figure to be the size of the plot(s). It is questionable, however, whether the divergence in the Cramer's V values of the crosstabulations with variables 9 and 10 can be entirely accounted for by such an explanation. It is entirely possible that the divergence between the two pairs of crosstabulations as reflected in their Cramer's V values is evidence of a substantive difference between aroura measured and land-cubit measured plots. This divergence is in line with the substantive differences which have come to light in the crosstabulations of variable 43 Land Measure I Arouras or Land-cubits and variable 44 Land Measure II Arouras or Land-cubits by a number of variables discussed above (see above (h), (i), (l), (r), (w), (x)). The merits of this interpretation of the disparity in the pairs of Cramer's V values of the crosstabulations of the variables of size of plot by variable 31 Geographic Location will be pursued in chapter 8 (6).

(ee) Variable 45 Type of Aroura Measured Entry (Variety I or Sub-variety IA) by Variable 7 Occupation or Title of Smallholder

The crosstabulation of variable 45 Type of Aroura Measured Entry (Variety I or Sub-variety IA) by variable 7 Occupation or Title of Smallholder is statistically significant with a Cramer's V value of 0.42994. The Cramer's V value for this relationship is sufficiently high to indicate that there exists a systematic relationship of substantive importance between the variables.

There are 2 occupations among the 48 occupations in the table which occur predominantly in association with the format of entry we designate Sub-variety IA. The occupation charioteer has the highest correlation with Sub-variety IA entries: 21 entries or 67.7% of the 31 occurrences of this occupation among the apportioning entries. These 21 entries constitute 10.2% of the 206 Sub-variety IA entries analyzed in the table. The occupation prophet also has a relatively high correlation with Sub-variety IA entries. The 8 Sub-variety IA entries constitute 72.7% of the 11 occurrences of this occupation. These 8 Sub-variety IA entries, however, account for only 3.9% of the 206 Sub-variety IA entries.

Six occupations among the 48 occupations analyzed in the table have relatively high frequencies. These occupations include stablemaster (376 entries), soldier (214 entries), *ʿnḫ(t) n nỉwt* (150 entries), herdsman (120 entries), priest (109 entries), and *ỉḥwty* (98 entries). Of these 6 occupations, that of priest has the highest correlation with Sub-variety IA: 28 entries or 25.7% of the 109 occurrences of this occupation as compared with 81 entries of Variety I or 74.3%. These 28 entries constitute 13.6% of the 206 Sub-variety IA entries. Herdsman has the second highest frequency of Sub-variety IA entries among these high frequency occupations: 23 entries or 19.2% of the 120 entries ascribed to herdsmen as compared with 97 Variety I entries or 80.8%. The occupation herdsman accounts for 11.2% of the 206 Sub-variety IA entries. *ʿnḫ(t) n nỉwt* has the third highest frequency of Sub-variety IA entries: 22 entries or 14.7% of the 150 entries ascribed to women smallholders as compared with 128 Variety I entries or 85.3%. These 22 entries constitute 10.7% of the 206 Sub-variety IA entries. The highest frequency occupations, stablemaster and soldier, on the other hand, have relatively low frequencies of Sub-variety IA entries as compared with Variety I entries. The 29 Sub-variety IA entries ascribed to the occupation stablemaster account for only 7.7% of the occupation's total frequency of 376 apportioning entries. Variety I entries, on the other hand, account for 347 of the 376 entries or 92.3%. The 29 Sub-variety IA entries constitute 14.1% of the 206 Sub-variety IA entries. The 12 Sub-variety IA entries ascribed to the occupation soldier account for 5.6% of this occupation's 214 apportioning entries. Variety I entries, on the other hand, account for 202 of the 214 entries or 94.4%. The occupation soldier accounts for only 5.8% of the 206 Sub-variety IA entries. The relatively high frequency occupation *ỉḥwty* has a frequency of only 1 Sub-variety IA entry (1.0%) as compared with 97 Variety I entries (99.0%). Thus, although the occupation *ỉḥwty* has a relatively high frequency among the 48 occupations analyzed in the table, there is only the minimal degree of association with the type of plot denoted by the Sub-variety IA entry. The data of the occupation *ỉḥwty* are unexpected as they deviate considerably from the frequencies expected under the null hypothesis of statistical independence. While other high frequency occupations (most notably soldier) have observed frequencies which also differ considerably from the expected frequencies, none deviates as much from the expected frequencies as that of *ỉḥwty*. If single occurrence and low frequency occupations were deleted from the table in order to reduce the number of zero and low frequency cells which tend to distort the Cramer's V value, it is possible that the degree of association between the two variables would be even greater. These data support the view that Sub-variety IA entries denote plots which are substantively different from plots denoted by Sub-variety IA entries.

Also bearing mention are the occupations scribe and Sherden which have only moderately high frequencies. While in both instances, Variety I entries still comprise the overwhelming majority of the entries, the ratio of Variety I entries to Sub-variety IA entries (3 to 1 for scribe; 4 to 1 for Sherden) is lower than that of the apportioning data as a whole (just greater than 5 to 1). The 48 entries of the occupation scribe are distributed such that 35 entries or 72.9% are Variety I entries and 13 entries or 27.1% are Sub-variety IA entries. The 38 entries ascribed to the occupation Sherden are distributed such that 31 entries or 81.6% are Variety I entries and 7 entries or 18.4% are Sub-variety IA entries. Scribes account for 6.3% of the 206 Sub-variety IA entries, while Sherden account for 3.4% of these entries. Just as the occupation ỉḥwty deviates from the expected frequencies in having an especially low frequency of Sub-variety IA entries, the occupations scribe and Sherden differ from the expected frequencies in having especially high frequencies of Sub-variety IA entries.

It is immediately apparent that the occupations which have relatively high frequencies of Sub-variety IA entries neither share a common occupational group nor stand in marked contrast in any discernible way to occupations with zero or low frequencies of Sub-variety IA entries. Despite our difficulty in perceiving a connecting thread among the occupations with relatively high frequencies of Sub-variety IA entries, the relationship between the variables is both statistically significant and substantively important. The degree of association indicated by the Cramer's V value suggests that the relationship is not a direct causal relationship, but rather the result of the effect of one or more "linking factors" which are highly correlated with both variable 7 Occupation or Title of Smallholder and variable 45 Type of Aroura Measured Entry.

NOTES

[1]Gardiner, Commentary, pp. 94-95.

[2]Bernadette Menu, Le régime juridique des terres et du personnel attaché à la terre dans le Papyrus Wilbour (Lille, 1970), pp. 103-7.

[3]Jac. J. Janssen has made note of a stela of the officer Paḥemnetjer from Sedment which mentions the Ramesseum (private correspondence, February 1985). It is possible that such a reference reflects a link between the military and the royal funerary temples. It is quite possible that it would have been easier and more convenient for the Crown to deal with the administrators of the royal funerary temples than it would have been to deal with those of more independent temples which undoubtedly had a greater autonomy. It would certainly have been to the Crown's advantage to assign any military functions to institutions over which it had maximal control.

[4]Two rmnyt pš entries were inadvertently deleted from the crosstabulation tables involving variable 21 Type of Apportioning Paragraph. The loss of these two entries has a negligible impact

upon the table frequencies.

[5]One entry of the category None of These (paragraphs with no special heading) was inadvertently deleted from the crosstabulation tables involving variable 21 Type of Apportioning Paragraph. The loss of this single entry has a negligible impact upon the table frequencies.

[6]Another way of determining the relative size of land-owning institutions is, of course, to compute the total area of the landholdings enumerated in the Text A apportioning paragraphs. Using the computed quantitative variables 27 Grand Total Arouras 9 and 1Ø; 29 Grand Total Land-cubits 11, 12, and 13; and 38 Grand Total Land 27 and 29/1ØØ, we can easily compute the total land in arouras, land-cubits, or both expressed in arouras for each institution. It is also possible to study the size of plot for variables 9 Arouras, 1Ø Arouras Special Case, 28 Land-cubits Subtotal 11 and 12, and 13 Land-cubits Single Figure using the statistic eta-squared (see chapter 8 (7)(f)) to measure the degree to which the factor of land-owning institution determined the sizes of plots we encounter in the apportioning entries.

[7]Gardiner, Commentary, p. 25.

[8]Menu, Le régime juridique, pp. 1Ø7-15. This system of land allocation may indeed have its origins in a sweeping land reform applicable to all social classes which had been in effect for some time. With the passage of time, however, the rigorous regulations originally enacted were not necessarily consistently applied, as Menu plausibly suggests.

[9]Ibid., pp. 1Ø3, 113-14, 135-39.

[1Ø]Ibid., pp. 139-47.

[11]I.A. Stuchevsky abstracted in Jac. J. Janssen, "Agrarian Administration in Egypt During the Twentieth Dynasty," review and summary of I.A. Stuchevsky, Zemledel'tsy gosudarstvennogo khozyaistva drevnego Egipta epokhi Ramessidov (The Cultivators of the State Economy in Ancient Egypt During the Ramesside Period) forthcoming in BiOr.

[12]Crosstabulations involving the supplementary geographic location variables 22 Dual Geographic Location A and 23 Dual Geographic Location B were intentionally omitted from chapter 6 for lack of time and space. These variables serve to identify the geographic location of a plot in such cases where two equally valid geographic points of reference are provided. It was judged more important to concentrate upon crosstabulations of variable 31 Geographic Location which applies to the vast majority of plots enumerated in the apportioning paragraphs.

7 Related Ramesside Economic Texts

(1) The Turin Taxation Papyrus

Among the most useful of the New Kingdom economic documents to supplement the socio-economic data derived from P. Wilbour is P. Turin 1895 + 2006, a lengthy neatly transcribed document also known as the Turin Taxation Papyrus.(1) The first page of the recto line 1 dates the manuscript to year 12 of the reign of Ramesses XI. The text then proceeds to detail the collection of grain revenues in several towns south of Thebes, the conveyance of this grain by boat (kr) to Thebes, and the ultimate deposition of the same in appointed storage facilities in the city. The collection of the grain at various points of origin (Imiotru, ʿAgni, Npiimu, Esna) was carried out by the "Scribe of the Great and Noble Necropolis of Millions [of Years of Phar]aoh" (rt. 1,6) Dḥutmosĕ upon the orders of no less a personage than the great Viceroy of Kush Penḥasi, undoubtedly acting in his capacity as Overseer of Granaries of Pharaoh.

The text is described as a "DOCUMENT of receipts of grain of khato-land of Pharaoh from the hand of the prophets [of the temples of Upper Egypt which?]' the Fan-bearer on the right of the King (etc.) Penḥasi [ordered to be delivered?]" (rt. 1,3-1,5).(2) Thus, the revenues which are enumerated over the next five pages would appear to have been those derived from the cultivation of a type of Crown-land called "khato-land of Pharaoh" comparable perhaps to the revenues produced by the khato-lands of the Text A non-apportioning paragraphs and the khato-lands with which Text B is exclusively concerned.

Although the title page of the Turin Taxation Papyrus explicitly describes the grain as "grain of khato-land of Pharaoh" (rt. 1,3.7), some of these revenues are referred to elsewhere in the text (rt. 2,3-2,4) as "grain of the harvest" (ỉt šmw ) in connection with three temples: the House of Mont, Lord of Thebes; the House of Khnūm and Nebu; and the Portable Shrine of King Usimaʿrēʿ-meriamūn. Such a description of these revenues is not surprising, however, in view of the fact that in Text B of P. Wilbour, khato-land of Pharaoh is often described as situated "on fields of" various institutions.

It is possible, on the basis of rather limited evidence, that khato-land of Pharaoh consisted of fields the cultivation and administration of which were assigned to various institutions which carried out these activities as the virtual owners of such land. Stuchevsky argues that khato-land of Pharaoh was merely entrusted to temples and State organizations rather than handed over to them in deed and title. He maintains that such lands were cultivated and administered by these institutions either as large domains tilled by State cultivators (iḥwtyw), or in smaller parcels by "private possessors" (nmḥw), some plots going over from one system of cultivation to the other from time to time.(3) The opinion expressed long ago by Gardiner, on the basis of evidence of P. Valençay I (see section 8(a) below), was that these lands consisted of the untenanted fields of various land-owning institutions, appropriated by the Crown, and subsequently cultivated in the manner of the estates detailed in the non-apportioning paragraphs of Text A until suitable tenants could be found. Whether these fields were technically owned by the Crown or by the individual temples, Gardiner believed that the Crown undoubtedly had a claim upon their harvest. Thus, we recognize in Stuchevsky's new interpretation, a radically different conception of Ramesside political and economic organization from that which has prevailed to date.

Many of the plots of khato-land which occur in non-apportioning paragraphs of their own at the end of each of the sections of Text A (except Section IV which is incomplete) are the subject of corresponding Pōsh A and B entries. The non-apportioning entries of these khato-lands are typical Pōsh A entries which identify an institution for which 7.5% of the expected yield is apportioned ("temple créancier"). The corresponding Pōsh B entry is found in an apportioning paragraph of this same institution. In numerous instances, unfortunately, the corresponding Pōsh B entries have not been preserved. Some of the plots of khato-land which have corresponding Pōsh A and B entries also occur in Text B in paragraphs organized according to the chief administrative officer. The plots are described in most cases as situated "on fields of" the institution which is named in the corresponding Pōsh A and B entries. Not all plots of khato-land with corresponding Pōsh A and B entries also occur in Text B, nor do all plots of khato-land with corresponding Pōsh A and B entries match up precisely with entries in Text B which appear to refer to the same piece of land. Minor inconsistencies between Text A and Text B references to what evidently was the same plot of land could be satisfactorily explained by the fact that Text A and Text B are not exactly contemporary, Text B being a later addition, appended after Text A was complete.(4) Other differences may reflect scribal error. Sixteen plots of khato-land which occur in Text A, but do not have corresponding Pōsh A and B entries, appear to correspond to plots mentioned in Text B. Three of these plots are described in Text B as situated "on fields of Pharaoh" rather than any particular institution, religious or secular (B15,10; 16,6; 17,14). The examples of B15,8 and 17,11 may also be cited as they describe the plots as situated "on fields of" the Landing-

Place of Pharaoh (in Mi-wēr and the Keep of ʿOnayna). The phrase "on fields of Pharaoh" also occurs in three Text B references to plots which have corresponding Pōsh A and B entries in Text A.(5) Two of these examples refer to the funerary temple of Ramesses V in which case the description "on fields of Pharaoh" makes eminent sense. It is possible that the phrase "on fields of Pharaoh" was intended to apply to plots of khato-land which were directly administered by representatives of Pharaoh without the medium of a temple or secular institution. It is evident that in the case of fields situated "on fields of Pharaoh," the absence of a temple or other institution in the role of cultivator-administrator would have meant a greater share in the harvest for the Crown. Stuchevsky, on the other hand, maintains that "khato-land of Pharaoh on fields of Pharaoh" was not royal land handed over to temples, but only placed under the administrative control of a neighbouring institution. Such fields may have been the immediate responsibility of the chief administrative officer, the most frequently occurring of whom in Text B is the Royal scribe and steward (of Amūn) Usimaʿrenakhte. Comparing data of Text A and Text B, it would appear that the chief administrator of khato-land Usimaʿrenakhte also occupied the office of chief taxing-master. He occurs in that capacity as chief administrator of both minĕ and khato-land in two non-apportioning paragraphs of Text A (§§200-1).

The evidence of several special notations in Text B leads us to believe that some of the holdings in that document had been previously cultivated by the relatively independent smallholders enumerated in the apportioning paragraphs of Text A. The notation wnw pš n "formerly apportioned for" which occurs several times in the course of Text B strongly suggests this possibility (B11,24-27; 20,18). The individuals so identified include the scribe of the Granary Ḥaremḥab, the scribe Sebknakhte, son of Raʿmosĕ and the scribe Khaʿemtīr who appear to have been ordinary smallholders, unremarkable in any way. That these individuals were no longer smallholders in the area of the P. Wilbour assessment is suggested by the fact that they do not occur as apportionees in any of the apportioning paragraphs.

Relatively little khato-land is enumerated in Text A as compared with Text B which deals with approximately the same geographic area. Undoubtedly, the khato-lands enumerated in Text A were incorporated into the body of that document because of some special attribute they possessed, or some special status they held which distinguished them from the khato-lands enumerated in Text B. It is possible that the khato-lands enumerated in Text A were parcels of land the legal status of which was in the process of reclassification. The inclusion of non-apportioning paragraphs pertaining to these landholdings at the very end of each of the sections of Text A (except for Section IV which is incomplete) is in itself a recognition of a substantive difference between these lands and those which occur in the ordinary non-apportioning paragraphs. The focus of Text B appears to have been the comprehensive enumeration of khato-land revenues within a limited geographic area; whereas the focus of Text A appears to have been both the determination of the amount of grain which the government could expect to realize from the plots enumerated, and the identification of the individuals responsible for the realization of these revenues (Stuchevsky's "agents of the fisc").

Unlike P. Wilbour, the Turin Taxation Papyrus appears to have had as its primary objective the documentation of the registration and conveyance of grain revenues from their point of origin in the countryside to their deposition in the granaries of Thebes, along with the specification of transportation costs incurred along the way. Line 7 of the title page of the Turin Taxation Papyrus implies that the grain collected by the scribe of the Necropolis was intended for the daily sustenance of the workmen of the Theban Necropolis. The fact that khato-lands of Pharaoh contributed toward the upkeep of the community of Necropolis workmen, the support of which was a major Crown priority, suggests that the grain payments received and registered by Dḥutmosĕ are perhaps better described as "revenue reallocations" rather than "taxes," although the latter term has given the document the name by which it is most commonly known. Whether we choose to label such intragovernmental transactions as "taxation" depends both upon how much control the individual institutions exerted over these landholdings (i.e., to what degree the institutions "owned" them) and how wide a definition of the term "tax" or "taxation" we are willing to accept.

The collection and registration of the grain revenues which are the subject of the Turin Taxation Papyrus were apparently authorized by the Viceroy of Kush Penḥasi who is also described as "the General, the Overseer of Granaries of Pharaoh," making him the first Nubian viceroy to lay claim to these titles. It is interesting to note that there is no mention of either the chief taxing-master or the Royal scribe and steward of Amūn in conjunction with these proceedings. This omission would appear significant, since the chief administrator of khato-land in P. Wilbour is the chief taxing-master (Text A) and Royal scribe and steward of Amūn (Text B), both titles held by the same individual, Usimaʿrenakhte. The fact that the operations described in the Turin Taxation Papyrus were authorized by Penḥasi, rather than the chief taxing-master or the Royal scribe and steward of Amūn, suggests that the "Suppression" of the High Priest Amenḥotpe had already taken place.

By year 12 of Ramesses XI, Penḥasi had certainly already taken control of the city of Thebes, establishing a de facto government which placed him in a position to control financial matters which previously would have been in the jurisdiction of the chief taxing-master. This view is compatible with Wente's view of the "Suppression" of Amenḥotpe which posits that Penḥasi's intervention in Upper Egypt occurred with the sanction of the king (Ramesses XI) on behalf of a beleaguered Amenḥotpe hard-pressed by insurrection in his own domain.(6) With the unseating and subsequent flight of the high priest probably also came the unseating of Theban officials both dependent upon him and loyal to him. This may help to explain the departure from anticipated protocol in the contemporary administrative affairs of the House of Amūn. Since both senior government posts and high ecclesiastical offices tended to be monopolized by a few especially wealthy and influential families during the Ramesside Period, it is quite likely that interference in the affairs of the one sphere seriously affected the other.(7) Such might be the explanation for the curious situation in which the Viceroy of Kush under the title the Overseer of Granaries of Pharaoh authorized activities which normally may have been in the jurisdiction of the chief taxing-master or other civil authority.

The major personages encountered in the Turin Taxation Papyrus are well-known from contemporary sources. The scribes of the Necropolis Dḥutmosĕ and Nesamenopĕ are surely to be equated with the scribes (of the Necropolis) Dḥutmosĕ and Nesamenopĕ of the Late Ramesside Letters.(8) The chantress (*šmʿyt*) of Amūn Ḥenttowĕ is also most probably the same chantress Ḥenttowĕ of the Late Ramesside Letters and the wife of Nesamenopĕ.(9) The mayor Pwerʿo of the Turin Taxation Papyrus is surely the infamous bureaucrat against whom the mayor Psiūr laid charges of neglect of duty in the court proceedings documented in the papyri of the royal tomb-robberies beginning in year 16 of Ramesses IX.(10) He is certainly the same individual mentioned in P. Bibliothèque Nationale 199, II (No. 33 *LRL*), a fragment of a letter (?) composed during the *Wḥm Mswt* in which Pwerʿo appears to have already acceded to the office of chief taxing-master.(11)

While many scribes occur as smallholders or administrators in P. Wilbour, no scribe in that document bears the full title "Scribe of the Necropolis." The omission of any mention of these individuals may be indicative, since a number of scribes in P. Wilbour are identified with titles appropriate to their particular posts (e.g., "the treasury-scribe" (Treasury of Pharaoh) in A47,3; "the army scribe" in A84,7; 65,23; "the scribe of the Dispatch Office of Pharaoh" in A16,18; and "the scribe of the Granary of Pharaoh" in A53,9). This is not to say that scribes of the Necropolis could not have been smallholders or administrators of plots of cultivable land in the area of Thebes. The *ỉryw-ʿ3* "doorkeepers," "apparitors," who accompanied Dḥutmosĕ on his rounds, undoubtedly to lend the threat of physical force to his authority if ever there was need, also do not occur in P. Wilbour in any capacity whatever. Mayors, on the other hand, play a significant role in P. Wilbour in the capacity of administrators of *khato*-land in both Text A and Text B. Thus, there is some overlap in the cast of major players identified in P. Wilbour and the Turin Taxation Papyrus.

The cast of lesser players in the Turin document including temple-scribes, prophets, Medjay, and *ỉḥwtyw*, has strong affinities with that of P. Wilbour. Individuals identified as *ỉḥwtyw* occur in rt. 3,12-3,14 as the parties responsible for the payment of relatively large amounts of grain described as "grain of the House of Khnūm and Nebu." A total of 120 sacks are indicated as having been the *šmw* of the *ỉḥwty* Saḥtnūfe, while another 80 sacks are indicated as forthcoming from three *ỉḥwtyw* (Butehamūn, <Nakht?>amūn, and the above-mentioned Saḥtnūfe). Two smaller quantities of grain ($6\frac{2}{4}$ and $13\frac{2}{4}$ sacks) are recorded separately and ascribed to the same three *ỉḥwtyw*. The grand total of 220 sacks put on the boat of the skipper Dḥutweshbi accounts for 55% of the 402 sacks forthcoming from the House of Khnūm and

Nebu (rt. 3,10). The three *ỉḥwtyw* are perhaps to be equated with those *ỉḥwtyw* of Text A of P. Wilbour whom Stuchevsky identifies as "agents of the fisc" responsible for the realization of grain revenue payable to the State from land cultivated by field-labourers who were also called *ỉḥwtyw*.

In contrast to the three *ỉḥwtyw* of rt. 3,12-3,14, are a number of individuals of a wide variety of occupations who hand over to Dḥutmosĕ relatively small amounts of grain anywhere from ¼ sack (the *ỉḥwty* Khensmosĕ in rt. 4,7) to 12 sacks (the *3ʿʿ* Iunē in rt. 4,11). These individuals represent such diverse occupations as herdsman, Medjay, builder (*ḳd*), brander (of cattle?) (*ṯ3y 3bw*), *ỉḥwty*, and *3ʿʿ*. With the exception of *3ʿʿ*, all of these occupations also occur in P. Wilbour in the role of smallholder in the apportioning paragraphs of Text A. The term *3ʿʿ*, which Gardiner understood as denoting a person who speaks a foreign language (hence his translation "foreigner"), may refer to aliens who permanently settled in Egypt to become small-scale cultivators, much like the Sherden of P. Wilbour who occur in the role of smallholder in the Text A apportioning paragraphs.(12)

The events recorded in the recto of the Turin Taxation Papyrus took place over a seven month period from the second month of *3ḫt* day 16 (rt. 2,1) through the first month of *šmw* day 9 (rt. 5,1). The document may be conveniently divided into five sections corresponding to the successive intervals of work. The first section of the text (rt. 2,1-2,15) takes up the entirety of page 2 and records the receipt of grain revenues by the scribe of the Necropolis Dḥutmosĕ from *khato*-land of Pharaoh in the provincial towns of Imiotru and ʿAgni. Also detailed is the delivery of these revenues to Thebes where the bulk of the grain was received by the chantress of Amūn Ḥenttowĕ and the scribe (of the Necropolis) Nesamenopĕ. The arithmetic of these lines is substantially correct and leaves the distinct impression that this is a straightforward record of accounts with no discernible attempts at deception or misrepresentation.

Section 2 of the document (rt. 3,1-3,8) is substantially similar to section 1, but is concerned with the receipt by Dḥutmosĕ and his *ỉryw-ʿ3* of the grain payments of two temples, that of Mont, Lord of Thebes as well as that of the Portable Shrine of King Usimaʿrēʿ-meriamūn (Ramesses III), and the delivery of this grain to the chantress of Amūn Ḥenttowĕ and the scribe (of the Necropolis) Nesamenopĕ for deposit in the granaries at Thebes. Evident in this section are the first indications of omission and oversight on the part of the scribe. There is no indication, however, of any real wrongdoing or deliberate falsification of the figures.

In section 3 of the text (rt. 3,9-4,5), however, there is a significant departure from the relative accuracy and consistency of detail which characterize the first two sections of the text. Section 3 is clearly a separate section unto itself, separated from section 2 by considerable empty space, and from section 4 by a large gap as well. This section commences with the embarkation from Thebes of the scribe of the Necropolis with two boats (*kr*) headed for points south. The section goes on to detail the receipt in Esna of grain of the House of Khnūm and Nebu by Dḥutmosĕ and his ỉryw-ʿ3, and the delivery of the same to the mayor Pwerʿo in Thebes West. It is with this section of the text that the accounts become suddenly wildly inaccurate with more than a suggestion of falsification. The figures have been entered almost cavalierly with numerous arithmetical errors, misplaced lines, and misspellings. As Gardiner has amply detailed the errors and alleged falsifications in the text at this point, it would be tedious and repetitious to repeat them here.(13) It suffices to say that something had happened at this point in the proceedings to play havoc with the previously orderly and regular recording of accounts.

While the precise date of the "Suppression" of Amenḥotpe cannot be established on present evidence, it certainly took place some time prior to year 12 of Ramesses XI because of the appearance of the Viceroy of Kush Penḥasi in the Turin Taxation Papyrus. There it is expressly stated that he commissioned the collection of grain revenues by Dḥutmosĕ. It is even possible that the "Suppression" took place prior to year 9 of Ramesses XI, if the evidence of the trial which is the subject of P. British Museum 10053 verso is correctly linked to the "Suppression" of Amenḥotpe.(14) Wente has commented that the conditions in Thebes at the time of the "Suppression" were probably so grave as to have required armed intervention by Penḥasi and his troops, taking as evidence the fact that it was evidently several months after Penḥasi's seizure of Medīnet Habu that law and order were restored.(15) It is a well-known corollary of war that economic distress usually outlasts the actual termination of hostilities, and that the road to economic recovery is often strewn with obstacles. The liberators themselves often unwittingly contribute to the economic malaise when their troops take advantage of often anarchic conditions to further their own pecuniary gain. In all fairness to Dḥutmosĕ, it seems necessary to admit the possibility, however remote, that local conditions in the wake of the "Suppression" of Amenḥotpe may have precluded the efficient accomplishment of his task.

Section 4 of the text (rt. 4,6-5,4) is a continuation of the haphazard record-keeping which characterizes section 3. Like section 3, the record of section 4 is rife with inaccurate arithmetic, possibly tautologous entries, and outright mistakes. What is certainly different, however, is the fact that the irregularities we encounter go beyond what we might expect by way of deliberate attempts at covering up misappropriations or falsifications of figures. Rather than encountering figures which simply fail to add up properly, or amounts which are unaccounted for in the breakdown of expenses, we find irregularities in form and content such as characterize the final section of the text (rt. 5,5-5,11) as well. Such irregularities are certainly not the hallmark of a scribe intent upon the discrete embezzlement of his employer's accounts. Dḥutmosĕ, for example, foregoes his usual practice of supplying complete dates for his entries (year, month, day), once omitting reference to the date altogether (rt. 4,11). A date does occur, however, in the following line rt. 5,1 (a repeat evidently of rt. 4,11). He also fails to consistently identify the place of origin of the revenues he has collected (rt. 4,6-4,7), and has certainly erred in ascribing the deposition of the very same 18¾ sacks of grain to what were evidently two separate storerooms: "<'The Garner> (šmyt) Overflows'" and "The Storeroom (šꜥyt) which is on Top of 'the Pure Land'" (both in rt. 5,4). It is also curious that the scribe of the counting of the House of Amun-Rēꜥ, King of the Gods, Nesamūn, who was responsible for delivering grain of the House of Mont, Lord of Thebes earlier in the text (rt. 3,1-3,3), should reappear in rt. 4,11 delivering grain in Imiotru without any mention of the House of Mont to which he was attached (r-ḥt the prophet of Mont Amenemōnĕ). There is also the case of the town(s) called Npiimu in rt. 4,9 and Nimu in rt. 5,2 which evidently were the same location, since both entries have in common the same individuals making precisely the same payments (the herdsman Penḥasi, 4 sacks and the chief of Medjay Nesamūn, 1 sack). It is so easy to explain away the irregularities in this document as just one more example of the sloppy bookkeeping of lazy bureaucrats who often engaged in petty theft. We are so well-accustomed to inaccurate record-keeping on the part of Ramesside scribes that, in our cynicism, we might fail to recognize unusual circumstances. Rather than interpret these various irregularities as the work of an incompetent petty embezzler, we might consider such irregularities as the mistakes of an individual whose work had suffered numerous interruptions over which he may not have had any control.

There is yet another difference between the first two sections of the text and the remainder of the accounts which suggest the turbulent historical backdrop of the proceedings as the probable explanation for the irregularities in the form and content of the accounts. Whereas in previous sections it appears that the scribe Dḥutmosĕ and his ỉryw-ꜥ3 were themselves physically present on their rounds of the provincial towns to collect and register the grain, it would appear from section 4 that Dḥutmosĕ was no longer doing the rounds himself. In rt. 5,1-5,2, we encounter the phrase ỉnyt m "brought from" with which Dḥutmosĕ describes the collection of the revenue of the town of Imiotru. If Dḥutmosĕ describes the revenues as "brought from" Imiotru, it can only be because he himself was no longer present to register the revenues at their point of origin, as he evidently had been in the case of revenues of the provincial towns recorded in the previous sections of the text. The question which comes immediately to mind in light of these findings is whether the collection of grain revenues in the provincial towns was part of the usual duties of Dḥutmosĕ as scribe of the Necropolis, or whether the Turin Taxation Papyrus reflects an unusual set of circumstances.

A tentative answer to these questions is perhaps to be derived from a consideration of the correspondence of the Late Ramesside Letters. This collection of fifty-one letters, dating from ca. year 12 (?) of Ramesses XI through year 12 (?) of the Wḥm Mswt, was authored by several individuals, the most frequently occurring of whom is the scribe of the Necropolis Dḥutmosĕ. Dḥutmosĕ was the author of perhaps sixteen of the letters and the recipient of at least seventeen of them according to Wente.(16) These letters yield considerable detail concerning the activities of several scribes of the Necropolis. Several of the letters were written while Ḏḥutmosĕ was north of Thebes on a trip to Middle Egypt. One of the letters, P. Leiden I 370 (No. 5 LRL), provides a wealth of detail concerning the transportation and registration of the grain and its deposition in the Theban granaries, as Ḏḥutmosĕ carefully instructs his son Butehamūn and the chantress Shedemdua how they should handle various situations in his absence. Most of the letters are heavily interwoven with personal concerns as is quite natural with correspondence among relations. A number of the letters are related to Ḏḥutmosĕ's participation in a Nubian campaign dating to ca. year 10 of the Wḥm Mswt. Several letters were written to Ḏḥutmosĕ while he was resident in Thebes by the general Paiankh. Other letters were written by Ḏḥutmosĕ while he was in Nubia on the campaign, and concern business matters at home in Thebes which Butehamūn was instructed to attend to in his father's absence.

Although this large corpus of correspondence provides a wealth of small detail, the difficulty in dating the letters absolutely makes it extremely difficult to generalize about the itinerary of the scribe of the Necropolis in the execution of his day-to-day responsibilities. In the earliest of these letters, P. Bibliothèque Nationale 198, III (No. 47 LRL), written by Ḏḥutmosĕ to his colleague Nes(amenopĕ) in Thebes West, Ḏḥutmosĕ complains about Nesamenopĕ's apparent failure to successfully manage the business of the Theban Necropolis in his absence.(17) He orders his unfortunate colleague to fetch grain due to the workmen "so that the men do not starve and become idle (wsf?) in the commission of Pharaoh, L.P.H."(18) He alludes darkly to "men who are living there confined (ḏdḥ)," to the lack of work for the workmen, and to complaints of fishermen who threaten to involve the vizier.

When Ḏḥutmosĕ orders that grain be fetched for the workmen, he stipulates that the ỉryw-ʿ3 Ḏḥutmosĕ and Khensmosĕ be sent for the task. These appear to be the very same men who accompanied Ḏḥutmosĕ on his rounds of the countryside in the Turin Taxation Papyrus, collecting and registering grain bound for the Theban granaries. While the Turin Taxation Papyrus has as its locale such towns as Esna and Imiotru just south of Thebes, P. Bibliothèque Nationale 198, III may have as its locale the vicinity of Ombos, if the mention of the Ombite (Seth) in the salutation is taken as evidence of the letter's provenance.(19) It is conceivable, therefore, that the events of both the Turin Taxation Papyrus and P. Bibliothèque Nationale 198, III transpired in the same year as Wente suggests.(20) If Wente is correct, P. Bibliothèque Nationale 198, II (No. 46 LRL) may also date to year 12 of Ramesses XI. This letter, of which neither the salutation nor the address is preserved (the address containing only the words "...⌜of the Necropolis⌝"), is thought by Wente to be contemporary with P. Bibliothèque Nationale 198, III and the Turin Taxation Papyrus because of the probable identification of several of the individuals to whom allusion is made. This letter is of little use historically, however, because its content is largely personal and concerns matters with which we have no familiarity at all.

Passing from these letters, there is a gap of quite a few years before we encounter another letter which indicates that Ḏḥutmosĕ was again absent from Thebes. Wente dates four letters to year 6 of the *Wḥm Mswt* or later.(21) Two of them, P. British Museum 10417 (No. 14 *LRL*) and P. Bournemouth (No. 44 *LRL*), were written to Dḥutmosĕ while he was somewhere in Middle Egypt, the former by Amenḥotpe, prophet of Amenophis and the latter by a chantress of Amūn (Shedemdua?). Two other letters, P. Leiden I 369 (No. 1 *LRL*) and P. Leiden I 370 (No. 5 *LRL*), were authored by Dḥutmosĕ while he was in Middle Egypt. P. Leiden I 369 was addressed to his son Butehamūn; whereas P. Leiden I 370 was addressed to both Butehamūn and the chantress Shedemdua. Not very long thereafter (year 7 of the *Wḥm Mswt* or later according to Wente), Dḥutmosĕ was once again resident in Thebes as suggests the evidence of letters written to him from the second prophet of Amun-Rēʿ, Ḥeḳanūfe from a location somewhere in Middle Egypt.

Year 10 of the *Wḥm Mswt* finds Dḥutmosĕ acting as a sort of intermediary or courier for Ḥeriḥor's successor, the general Paiankh.(22) Paiankh himself wrote to Dḥutmosĕ both from somewhere in Nubia, and from a locale south of Thebes, while Dḥutmosĕ was resident in Thebes. Taken together, these letters are evidence of the troubled state of affairs in Upper Egypt over the transition to the Tanite rule of the Twenty-first Dynasty.

The travels of Dḥutmosĕ as reflected in the correspondence of the Late Ramesside Letters apparently allowed him sufficient time to indulge in lengthy criticism and complaint in writing to his subordinates at home in Thebes. His instructions to his staff complain of incompetence, laxity, wrong decisions, and unending procrastination. But running throughout this characteristically Egyptian epistolary style is a vein of gravity which suggests that the Thebaid was not experiencing the best and most settled of times. Since two of the letters, P. Bibliothèque Nationale 198, III and P. Bibliothèque Nationale 198, II, are perhaps to be considered contemporary with the Turin Taxation Papyrus, they too may reflect the same historical backdrop.

If the poor condition of Dḥutmosĕ's bookkeeping is susceptible to interpretation along the lines suggested above, it is probable that he was engaged in the collection and registration of grain revenues only because the usual course of events had been disrupted. Dḥutmosĕ's journey was perhaps a necessity he was obliged to undertake "so that the men do not starve and become idle in the commission of Pharaoh, L.P.H." (P. Bibliothèque Nationale 198, III, vs. 6-7). While he undoubtedly exaggerated the seriousness of the situation to impress others with his own importance, there is certainly some element of truth in his own words.

Dḥutmosĕ's journeys to collect and register the grain intended for the community of Necropolis workmen, as reflected in both the Turin Taxation Papyrus and P. Bibliothèque Nationale 198, III, may possibly have come to a halt with the restoration of order in the Thebaid in the years following the "Suppression" of Amenḥotpe. There are no letters in the corpus of Late Ramesside Letters that can be dated to the period between year 12 of Ramesses XI and year 2 of the *Wḥm Mswt* (year 20 of Ramesses XI). When the correspondence takes up again in year 2 of the *Wḥm Mswt*, there is no suggestion that anything other than business as usual had transpired during the interim.

When next we encounter Dḥutmosĕ writing to his home base in Thebes, it is ca. year 6 or 7 of the Wḥm Mswt according to Wente--several years prior to his involvement with the general Paiankh which evidently occupied a great deal of his time in year 10. The most revealing letter of this period is P. Leiden I 369 (No. 1 LRL), Dḥutmosĕ's open letter to the Necropolis staff (including all workmen!) under the charge of his son, the scribe of the Necropolis Butehamūn. This letter, written in all likelihood from somewhere in Middle Egypt,(23) is especially querulous with perhaps what could be interpreted as an overtone of urgency. Dḥutmosĕ complains that several letters which he had written to his staff at Thebes had gone unanswered; indeed, that he had had no communication with his staff at all. It is evident from this letter that Dḥutmosĕ was concerned that things might not be going well at home. The tone of the letter is certainly more emotional than usual and may have been to some degree the result of the illness from which he claims to have been suffering ("Indeed, I was ill when I arrived north (n ḫd), and I am not at all in my (usual) condition" (vs. 3-4)). The occurrence of the expression "Yar of Namekhay," from which he prays deliverance, suggests perhaps that all was not well with his own mission.(24)

It is just conceivable, therefore, that P. Leiden I 369 should be interpreted as a reflection of trying times, both for Dḥutmosĕ in his unfamiliar post in the field, and for his staff at home in Thebes. Just how trying the times may have been is answered in part by P. British Museum 10417 (No. 14 LRL), a letter from a certain Amenḥotpe, prophet of Amenophis to Dḥutmosĕ, which is perhaps the answer to P. Leiden I 369. This letter mentions "the General, your Lord" who is evidently to be identified with Paiankh, successor of Ḥeriḥor. The serious tone of this letter is unmistakable. The prophet writes that he hopes that Amūn will deliver Dḥutmosĕ safely, bringing him back prospering "danger (ḥty) stn or sḫn (?), Amūn of the Thrones of the Two Lands having rescued (šdỉ) <you>" (vs. 2).(25)

P. Leiden I 370 (No. 5 LRL), a detailed letter from Dḥutmosĕ in Middle Egypt addressed to Butehamūn and Shedemdua in Thebes West, stands in marked contrast to P. Leiden I 369. In this letter, Dḥutmosĕ appears to have his worries under control. His language is tempered with no trace of his former anxiety; his instructions are lucid and concisely stated, the language of a man of authority in control of his affairs. P. Bournemouth (No. 44 LRL), the incomplete letter to which P. Leiden I 370 may have been the direct reply because of subject matter common to both, is also businesslike and precise. It is entirely possible that P. Leiden I 369 and P. British Museum 10417 are to be viewed as the earlier correspondence, dating to the beginning of Dḥutmosĕ's mission when he was still familiarizing himself with the task of collecting and registering the grain revenues. P. Leiden I 370 and P. Bournemouth, on the other hand, may represent a later point in the correspondence when conditions had more or less stabilized and channels of communications improved.

The two letters addressed to Dḥutmosĕ in Thebes West in year 7 of the Wḥm Mswt or later, written by the second prophet of Amun-

Reꜥ, Ḥeḳanūfe from somewhere in Middle Egypt, also appear to reflect a period of calm and normality. The language is crisp and businesslike in both P. British Museum 10300 (No. 23 LRL) and Papyri Turin 1974 + 1945 (No. 24 LRL). The contents of these letters are such as to arouse no great concern in the heart of their recipient. These are letters written purely out of formality, the necessary and appropriate exchange of colleagues who must keep informed of each other's activities, even when these activities are far from momentous.

As scribe of the Necropolis, Dḥutmosĕ's job was to keep the records of the work and wages of the Necropolis workmen. His also was the job of corresponding with both higher authorities to whom he himself was responsible, and with colleagues in other branches of the government. This was an important role which required a conscientious individual of integrity and responsibility. To such an individual would rightly have fallen the task of correcting malfunctions in the administration of the workmen's community which would have jeopardized the day-to-day activities and productivity of the Necropolis workmen. Dḥutmosĕ's traversing of the southern Thebaid would perhaps have been the most expeditious (although time-consuming) means of resolving the immediate supply problems, since he was not only the person most conversant with the records involved, but would also have had the necessary personal contacts to expedite matters with officials of the various institutions. Thus, Dḥutmosĕ's commission to secure the necessary revenues, as described in the Turin Taxation Papyrus, would have been undeniably fitting and appropriate, especially in a period of economic distress such as undoubtedly followed the "Suppression" of Amenḥotpe. The travels of Dḥutmosĕ beginning again in years 6 and 7 (?) of the Wḥm Mswt and again in year 10 of the Wḥm Mswt possibly also reflect troubled conditions in the Thebaid which necessitated Dḥutmosĕ's expeditions.

The likelihood of this view of the Dḥutmosĕ correspondence is more than suggested by the tone of the letters which passed between Dḥutmosĕ and his correspondents in Thebes West. When in P. Bibliothèque 198, III, Dḥutmosĕ instructs his correspondent to send his scribe together with the scribe of the Necropolis Efnamūn and his ỉry-ꜥ3 to fetch the grain for the workmen's rations, the inference is that this was not the usual procedure by means of which grain intended for the workmen's rations was collected and registered for deposition in the Theban granaries. Some failure in the communications network had obviously resulted in a situation requiring swift and decisive intervention. The aggravation conveyed in Dḥutmosĕ's letter would be understandable enough had Dḥutmosĕ been called away from Thebes to correct one malfunction in the system only to have another link in the chain of communications break elsewhere at the same time. If the dispatch of one or more scribes together with ỉryw-ꜥ3 was not the usual procedure for filling the Theban granaries with grain requisitioned for the rations of the Necropolis workmen, the events recorded in the Turin Taxation Papyrus were also likely to have been outside of the usual routine of the scribe of the Necropolis.

Before leaving the recto of the Turin Taxation Papyrus, we

would do well to consider the amount of grain actually delivered to Thebes by Ḏḥutmosĕ, and how this might relate to the background against which the activities of the Turin Taxation Papyrus unfold. The total amount of grain delivered to the Theban granaries by Ḏḥutmosĕ over the course of this document, up to but not including the final section of the recto which is incomplete (rt. 5,5-5,11), is less than 600 sacks. Of this amount, 183¾ sacks were derived from the towns of Imiotru and ʿAgni (rt. 2,13); whereas 337 sacks were derived from the Esna area (rt. 4,1-4,2). The amount of 600 sacks (mostly of emmer) is not a great deal of grain when it is considered that the rations for an ordinary workman consisted of 4 sacks of emmer (bdt) per month plus 1½ sacks of barley (ỉt). The 337 sacks of emmer from Esna, for example, would have been sufficient to sustain 84 families, consisting of 10 persons, including some small children, for one month during the Twentieth Dynasty. Since the number of workmen varied over time, usually numbering about 60 in this period, and since some workmen (chiefs and possibly scribes, ỉryw-ʿ3, and physicians) received in excess of 4 sacks of emmer, it is probable that the total amount of grain received by the mayor Pwerʿo at Thebes was intended exclusively for the payment of the workmen's rations.(26)

The size of the payments delivered to Thebes suggests that Ḏḥutmosĕ's mission to collect the revenues was an act of necessity arising out of unusual circumstances. Depending upon the actual number of workmen employed in the Theban Necropolis at the time, the total of grain payments collected on this mission would have paid the workmen's rations for anywhere from one to two months. This time-frame is in line with the usual delays experienced in the payment of rations to Necropolis workmen according to the evidence gathered by Janssen from year 64 of Ramesses II to year 2 of Ramesses IV.(27) Had the total of grain delivered to Thebes been appreciably larger, it might be argued that Ḏḥutmosĕ's mission was less urgent and more routine; that is, that the collection of grain revenues was one of Ḏḥutmosĕ's responsibilities. Had the figure been appreciably smaller, it is unlikely that a special commission would have been authorized. The impression we receive on the basis of this document is that Ḏḥutmosĕ may have collected exactly the amount he needed to meet the immediate need, and that this mission was undertaken only after more readily available supplies had been exhausted.

The verso of the Turin Taxation Papyrus is dated to year 14, the first month of 3ḫt and consists of a list of payments forthcoming from a number of 3ʿʿw "foreigners," together with that of an unidentified prophet (vs. 2,10), received from the hand of (m-ḏrt) the prophet of Ḥatḥōr Nesamūn. With the exception of vs. 2,10 (?) and 3,9 (following the numbering of the lines in RAD), the payments are in emmer and average 3 sacks per person. These payments range from as little as ¾ sack (vs. 2,6) to as much as 10 sacks (vs. 3,3).

Whereas the first series of entries, those of vs. 2,1-2,11, mentions no locality, the second series, vs. 3,1-3,6, specifies the town of Smen (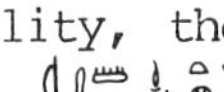), possibly located at or near Gebelein. The third series, vs. 3,7-3,15, identifies Imiotru. The last part of the verso, vs. 4,1-4,4, is completely different. Line 4,1 is dated to the first month of 3ḫt, day 25; whereas lines 4,3-4,4 are dated to the second month of 3ḫt, day 7 and day... respectively. After the date in vs. 4,1, the first entry records the receipt of 80 sacks of emmer (in) the House of Khnūm and Nebu at Esna by the hand of (m-ḏrt) the temple-scribe Penḥasi. The second and third entries omit the place of receipt, but mention the individuals who transferred the grain. These individuals are identified as the temple-scribe Penḥasi and the prophet of Amūn P‘ankha‘ respectively.

It is difficult to draw any meaningful conclusions from such a brief enumeration of revenues. The list may have been written by Dḥutmosĕ, although the hand is certainly larger than that of the recto of the text. The fact that the list dates more than a year later than the recto of the text, and has much less detail to relate, may help to explain what difference there is in the hand.

The appearance of 3‘‘w handing over payments in grain in both the recto and the verso of the Turin Taxation Papyrus certainly suggests the aftermath of the "Suppression" of Amenḥotpe as the historical backdrop for these records. These 3‘‘w are likely to have included Nubian soldiers whom Penḥasi rewarded with land grants in the Thebaid after peaceful conditions had been restored. The receipt of payments from these individuals suggests their permanent settlement in the area. The occurrence of 3‘‘w in the tomb-robberies papyri, as both plaintiffs and defendants, also suggests that they were not averse to permanent settlement in the Thebaid during the Late Ramesside Period.(28)

(2) P. Turin 1882, verso (P. Turin A) 0,1-1,4

Among the Late Egyptian Miscellanies are a number of fragments which belong to a model letter known both as P. Turin 1882, verso and P. Turin A. The recto of this composition, written in a legible literary hand, was dated by Gardiner to the late Nineteenth Dynasty.(29) Whereas the major part of the verso is written in the same cursive hand (so vs. 1,1-3,5 and 4,9-4,10), the thirteen lines which intervene are written in an uncial hand which may be identical with that of the Hymn to Amūn on the recto of the text.

The first nine lines of the verso, 0,1-0,9, were discovered by Capart among fragments in the Geneva Museum.(30) Although these lines are extremely fragmentary, they provide some clues to the identities of the author and recipient. Gardiner, in his notes to the transcription in RAD (82a, n. 15a-b), comments that it is unlikely that lines 0,1-0,6 or 0,7 of the verso belong to the same letter as what follows in 0,8-1,4, but made no attempt to locate the beginning of a new letter. Caminos, on the other hand, translates lines 0,1-1,4 of the verso as a continuous whole which constitutes a single letter.(31)

The opening lines of the letter concern the registration of grain revenues (šmw) of the House of Amun-Rē‘, King of the Gods, and the transport of the grain in ships of the House of Amun-Rē‘, King of the Gods under the supervision of a stablemaster of the Residence. Although the salutation of the letter is lost, together with the names of author and recipient, it is possible to make out the words "House of Amūn" and "[Amun-Rēʿ], King of the Gods" in lines Ø,1-Ø,2. These words suggest that either the author or recipient of the letter belonged to the staff of the great temple of Amūn at Karnak. The only words which remain in verso Ø,3 are r sphr "(in order) to register." In verso Ø,4, it is possible to read only the word ḥm-nṯr "prophet." Verso Ø,5 mentions the names "...Mūt Usimaʿrenakhte," while lines Ø,6-Ø,7 of the verso refer to the god Amūn as "yo[ur good lord]..."

The writer instructs the addressee to (Ø,9) "[...encourage the workmen to carry out? the] business (1,1) of the Place of Truth which Pharaoh said was to be done" and to provide rations (dỉw) for the workmen of the Place of Truth "out of the balance (ḏ3t) of my grain which is in your possession."(32) The unidentified recipient of the letter is then instructed to take note of the tasks carried out by the Necropolis workmen from what was evidently the preceding pay-day and to "register (sphr) the harvest (n3 šmw) of the House of Amun-Rēʿ, King of the Gods, which is in the Southern Province (ʿ rsy), and load it <into> the ships of the House of Amun-Rēʿ, King of the Gods, which are under the command of the stablemaster of the Residence, Paywehem..." (1,2-1,4).

Although this is a model letter and therefore not in itself a genuine item of correspondence, it was very likely based upon fact and reflects actual events of the day. It was customary during the Nineteenth Dynasty for the office of the vizier to supervise the workmen's village at Deir el-Medīna through its own staff, and to take ultimate responsibility for both the payment of wages to the workmen and the supervision of their work schedule. The office of the vizier appointed an official scribe of the Necropolis (two official scribes were recognized early in the Twentieth Dynasty) who carried out these activities within the workmen's village and reported back to the vizier. There was also an official called "the scribe of the vizier" who was the representative of the vizier in his contacts with the workmen according to ostraca from the middle of the Twentieth Dynasty.(33) It is possible that the addressee of this model letter was some such official rather than the scribe of the Necropolis. As for the author of the letter, only an individual of relatively high office would have been entitled to refer to temple revenues as "my grain which is in your possession." The command to register the harvest grain of the House of Amun-Rēʿ, King of the Gods, and to have it transported, is sufficiently peremptory in tone to suggest that the official who dispatched the letter was a man of very high rank and authority in the Karnak temple of Amūn. It is therefore conceivable that a letter of this kind with its air of authority and easy confidence was authorized by no less a dignitary than the Royal scribe and steward of Amūn.

The fact that ships of the House of Amun-Rēʿ, King of the Gods were under the supervision of such a Crown employee as a stablemaster of the Residence is certainly evidence of the essential unity of Temple and Crown. It was the interactions of the two which defined the contours of the Late Ramesside economy.(34) Such a conception of Ramesside government is not really all that far removed from Stuchevsky's conception of the

Egyptian State of which Pharaoh was the titular head.

(3) P. Amiens

P. Amiens is the longest and most detailed document relating exclusively to the transport of grain revenues.(35) Although the text never explicitly stipulates the purpose for which the grain was to be shipped, it does identify the ships as belonging to the "House of Amūn," and the grain as that of various Theban foundations belonging to or affiliated with the "House of Amūn" under the authority of (r-ḫt) the Steward of Amūn Ramessenakhte. The question remains to be answered whether the grain under shipment was revenue accruing to the House of Amūn in the form of rent or revenue owed to the government as a form of "tax." Such a question would never arise following Stuchevsky's line of reasoning, however, as such a distinction between temple revenue (rent) and government (State) revenue (tax) would have no meaning.

The text postdates the reign of Ramesses III because of several occurrences of his nomen and prenomen together with references to the reigning king as "Pharaoh" (compare rt. 5,3.4.6 with rt. 5,2). Moreover, since the date of the accession of the pharaoh of P. Amiens falls between the third month of prt day 29 and the first month of šmw day 7, according to the evidence of vs. 2,x+8.9, we can eliminate the reigns of Ramesses IV, Ramesses V, Ramesses VI, and Ramesses IX from consideration. The date of the accession of Ramesses VII, however, can be established as the fourth month of prt. Thus, it is likely that P. Amiens should be dated to the reign of Ramesses VII.(36)

The first page(s) of the recto of P. Amiens is lost. The text begins with the mention of a ship of a captain ʿAshafēyew, son of Bekenkhons of the House of Amūn, and lists various amounts of grain of various domains "given to him" (rdỉw n.f) in various places in the following format:

rt. 1,1 SHIP of ʿAshafēyew, <son of> Bekenkhons, of the House of Amūn, under his authority (r-ḫt.f):

rt. 1,2 What was given to him in the Island of Amūn Every-Land-Comes-for-the-Love-[of-Him, on] the threshing-floor (ḏnw) of the chief workman (ʿ3 n ỉst) Pḫamnūte, being grain of domain (rmnyt) of the House of Amūn ʿAshafē, 100 sacks (ḫ3r).

The text continues recording amounts of grain of various domains given to ʿAshafēyew on various threshing-floors in various places until rt. 1,8 where a total is given for the cargo of his ship and rations (dỉw) of the crew are recorded. In rt. 1,9, a second ship and its captain are identified. Grain received by the second captain is recorded up until rt. 2,3 where another total is recorded which is followed in rt. 2,4 with the account of yet another ship. So continues the recto with three major breaks intervening up until rt. 5,1 where the format changes abruptly.(37) The lines from rt. 5,1 down to the break in the text after rt. 5,11 provide a summary of the total cargoes of the twenty-one ship flotilla and the foundations from which they were forthcoming:

rt. 5,1 TOTAL (dmḏ), this expedition (wḏyt), 21 barges (wsḫt) making,

rt. 5,2 Grain of domain of the House of Amun-Rēʿ, King of the Gods, which Pharaoh newly established, under the authority of the Steward Ramessenakhte 100$\frac{1}{4}$ 2170$\frac{3}{4}\frac{1}{8}$ sacks. TOTAL, 2271$\frac{1}{8}$. BALANCE (mn), 100$\frac{1}{4}$ 1870$\frac{3}{4}\frac{1}{8}$ (and so forth to the end of the recto).

Although the destination of the twenty-one ship flotilla is never actually stated, it is likely to have been Thebes, since the grain shipments enumerated originated from temple domains in the immediate vicinity of Thebes with but one possible exception.(38) The destination of the ships was probably given in the now missing opening protocol which probably also gave the date, reign, and other particulars.

Although Gardiner's publication of P. Amiens is an invaluable study which examines many points of historical and philological interest, there are several points which require further examination in light of the data of P. Wilbour. One of the most curious problems posed by P. Amiens concerns the interpretation of two pairs of entries: rt. 4,5 and 4,10; rt. 5,3 and 5,4. According to Gardiner, these lines reveal the purpose for which two revenue producing domains were established by Ramesses III. According to Gardiner's translation of rt. 4,5, a domain of the House of Amūn was "(founded) for (?) ((w3ḥ) m) the people who were brought on account of their crimes"; whereas according to rt. 4,10, a domain of the House of Ramesses-meriamūn was "(founded) for (?) the people of the Sherden":

rt. 4,5 What was given to him...being (m) grain of domain of the House of Amūn (founded) for (?) the (m n3) people who were brought on account of their crimes, 95$\frac{1}{4}$ sacks.

rt. 4,10 What was given to him...being (m) grain of domain of the House of Ramesses-meriamūn (founded) for (?) the (m n3) people of the Sherden, 200 sacks. Domain which Pharaoh founded, 52 sacks.

The omitted verbal element in both rt. 4,5 and 4,10 is supplied in the subsequent pair of entries, rt. 5,3 and 5,4, which Gardiner translates: (rt. 5,3) "Corn of domain of the House of Amen-Rēʿ, King of the Gods, which King Usimaʿrēʿ-miamūn founded (w3ḥ) for (?) the people who were brought on account of their crimes..." and (rt. 5,4) "...founded (w3ḥ) for (?) the people of the Sherden and for the Royal scribes of the army..."(39)

Since the transcription of the hieratic group which Gardiner reproduces in RAD as "m n3" seems unquestionable in each of the four instances of its occurrence, scribal error is unlikely to be the explanation. Moreover, in the case of rt. 4,5 and 4,1Ø, the groups occur in different relative positions within their respective lines. While the suggestion of Peet that the troublesome hieratic group be read as "m ỉt n" is an ingenious solution to the problem, it lacks plausibility upon comparison with actual writings of the phrase "m ỉt n" in the same document.(4Ø)

Gardiner's understanding of these lines opens up a whole avenue of questions only to leave them sadly unexplored. His translation of the verb w3ḥ followed by the preposition m is unparalleled. He suggests that the domain cited in rt. 4,5 and 5,3 may have been established to give employment to convicted criminals. He also suggests that the domain cited in rt. 4,1Ø and 5,4 may have been established to give employment to both Sherden and Royal scribes of the army. Unfortunately, Gardiner did not elaborate upon his translations and their ramifications other than to note that the Sherden mercenaries are "very incongruously coupled with 'the Royal scribes of the army.'"(41)

The domain allegedly "established for (?)" convicted criminals may have been related to the practice of having convicted criminals serve their sentences as agricultural labourers (dỉ r ỉḥwty), a practice which is alluded to in contemporary Late Egyptian texts. While the phrase dỉ r ỉḥwty was often used as a threat of rebuke against lazy students of the scribal profession, it was also used to describe the status of a Syrian slave in P. Bologna 1Ø86, 9ff., and as a punishment in the Nauri Decree of Sety I (73.118). Menu, in her study of P. Wilbour, recognizes a class of ỉḥwtyw composed of "(les) condamnés, corvéables et captifs de guerre."(42) The establishment of a foundation utilizing the labour of convicted criminals would certainly have been a financially profitable means of dealing with an age-old social problem. The pool of agricultural labourers was no doubt augmented by those prisoners of war judged unsuitable for domestic service.

As for the foundation established by Ramesses III ostensibly for purposes of giving employment to both Sherden and Royal scribes of the army, the combination of Sherden and military scribes is certainly not as incongruous as Gardiner seems to imply. It can be established on the basis of the evidence of Text A of P. Wilbour that it was not at all unusual for people of the military to live and work in relatively close proximity. Military occupations occur most frequently in Section III of P. Wilbour which corresponds to geographical zone 3. Of the fifty-four occupations of smallholders which occur in the Text A apportioning paragraphs, no fewer than fifteen may be classified as military. The occupation stablemaster is probably also to be considered a military occupation. The occupations scribe and retainer may also be classified as military as and when an appropriate epithet is attached.

Of the fifteen military classified occupations, most find their heaviest concentration in zone 3 as, for example, that of soldier of which there are 3 occurrences in zone 1, 41 in zone 2, 135 in zone 3, and 74 in zone 4; that of standardbearer of which there are 7 occurrences in zone 2, 13 in zone 3, and 4 in zone 4; and that of Sherden of which there are 9 occurrences in zone 1, 16 in zone 2, 26 in zone 3, and 8 in zone 4. The occupation stablemaster which often occurs in a military context in contemporary and near contemporary texts has 11 occurrences in zone 1, 133 in zone 2, 218 in zone 3, and 109 in zone 4. Thus, it is possible to say that military and military related occupations have a tendency to occur predominantly in zone 3. Depending upon the occupation, the second highest frequencies occur in either zone 2 or zone 4.

Of the three military scribes who occur as smallholders in Text A, one is described as a charioteer's scribe and two are described with the epithet "...of the army." In the case of the two scribes of the army, a review of the measurement areas in which their plots occur, reveals the fact that Sherden cultivated neighbouring plots (e.g., the Granary of Reeds in zone 3 and Irkak in zone 4). The charioteer's scribe Ḥori cultivated a plot (A31,48) near the Village of Webkhe (on) the east-side of Tmy in zone 2 where stablemasters and soldiers frequently occur as smallholders along with women smallholders (ʿnḫ(t) n nỉwt). The measurement areas both immediately preceding and following the Village of Webkhe in A31,25; 32,6 (those of Mi-ēḥu and the Village of Inroyshes) were similarly populated, including a military retainer (šmsw n msʿ) (A31,28), and a chief charioteer of His Majesty (A31,39-40) in Mi-ēḥu. Thus, there is some evidence external to P. Amiens for the association of Sherden and (Royal) scribes of the army.

The grain consignments recorded in the recto of P. Amiens provide examples of itemization which illustrate inter-institutional bookkeeping. These lines bring to mind the corresponding Pōsh A and B entries of P. Wilbour. In rt. 2,5-2,6 of P. Amiens, for example, it is recorded:

rt. 2,5	What was given to him in the Island of Amūn Overrunning-His-Boundary, on the threshing-floor (dnw) of the priest Keson, being grain of domain of the House of Ramesses-meriamūn of Ḥe-e-pwoid, under his authority, 600 sacks. Balance (mn) 335. Domain of Tjebu $37\frac{1}{4}\frac{1}{8}$ sacks.
rt. 2,6	What was given to him in this place on this threshing-floor, being grain of domain of the House of Seti-merenptaḥ in the House of Amūn, under his authority, $227\frac{2}{4}\frac{1}{8}$ sacks.

In this example, the 600 sacks of emmer dispatched from fields in Ḥe-e-pwoid belonging to the House of Ramesses-meriamūn (the temple of Ramesses II at Karnak) are itemized as derived from three sources, the third taking up the whole of rt. 2,6. Of the 600 sacks, $227\frac{2}{4}\frac{1}{8}$ sacks were derived from fields evidently in the vicinity of Ḥe-e-pwoid ascribed to the House of Seti-merenptaḥ in the House of Amūn, a Theban temple. The amount of $37\frac{1}{4}\frac{1}{8}$ sacks (rt. 2,5) was derived from a foundation with the abbreviated name, the "Domain of Tjebu," a locality possibly to be identified with Ḳāw el-Kebīr. The "balance" (mn) of 335 sacks was forthcoming from the domain of the House of Ramesses-meriamūn in the House of Amūn. The term "balance" is similarly utilized in rt. 2,11 where an amount of 600 sacks is itemized as derived from two sources: 460 sacks contributed by fields of the House of [Sety](Seti-merenptaḥ) and the "balance" of 140 sacks contributed by the domain of the House of Ramesses-meri[amūn], undoubtedly "of Ḥe-e-pwoid," although there is insufficient room for this restoration.

That a part of the consignment of one institution should have been derived from another institution is not surprising in light of the evidence of P. Wilbour. On the basis of data of Sections II through IV of Text A, the House of Amun-Rēʿ, King of the Gods is found to have been involved in financial transactions with eight other temples, two of which were royal funerary foundations which occur in apportioning paragraphs of their own. Of the two funerary foundations, that of Ramesses III occurs in additional Pōsh B entries signifying financial transactions with another five temples. One of these temples, the House of Sobek-Rēʿ, Lord of Anasha, occurs in an apportioning paragraph of its own with a Pōsh B entry signifying a link with yet another institution (the House of Nephthys in A62,23).

In the examples from P. Amiens, the Theban House of Seti-merenptaḥ appears to have incurred a financial obligation to the temple of Ramesses II also located at Thebes. The cause of this indebtedness is unfortunately not disclosed. This obligation may be analogous to the situation of the corresponding Pōsh A and B entries of P. Wilbour in which one institution administers and cultivates a plot on behalf of another institution, whether for purposes of improving the productivity of the plot as Menu suggests, or to bring in additional revenue equal to 7.5% of the "standard average grain harvest" as Stuchevsky suggests.(43)

The several occurrences of the phrase "...being grain of the House of Amūn, Domain of Khen-Min" in rt. 2,1.8; 3,10 (simply "Domain of Khen-Min" in rt. 1,11; 3,7 establishes the claim of the great Karnak temple to the fields which constitute this domain located in the vicinity of Akhmīm (Panapolis). Unfortunately, the Domain of Tjebu (Antaeopolis) occurs only in rt. 2,5. There is no fuller writing of its name in the text. It is possible that these abbreviated names identify khato-lands situated "on fields of" the House of Amūn. These fields would have been administered from the provincial nome capital where a civil authority, such as the mayor, had the ultimate responsibility for their administration, as suggested by data of Text B (§§11-16). Such a situation would be in accord with the long established role of mayors in administering fields in rural districts adjacent to their administrative seats and their role as khato-land administrators in both Text A and Text B of P. Wilbour.(44) Gardiner himself suggested that the use of the genitive with the names of towns may be indicative of the role of nome capitals in both the administration of temple estates and in the collection of grain revenues derived from them.(45)

The type of bookkeeping encountered in the entries of P. Amiens not merely confirms the existence of fiscal interrelationships between and among institutions, but also establishes the fact that relatively large amounts of grain were the subject of inter-institutional revenue transfers as compared with the relatively small amounts of grain which are the subject of the corresponding

Pōsh A and B entries of P. Wilbour. While the transactions of P. Wilbour occur among a wide variety of institutions, which may or may not have been administratively linked, the transactions of P. Amiens appear to concern only temples of the House of Amūn. The revenues of their domains were probably combined for shipment to a common destination for purposes of expediency and efficiency.(46)

Data of the House of Ramesses-meriamūn in the House of Amūn in rt. 2,5-2,6 indicate that fully 38% of the grain of this foundation, delivered to the ship's captain Minsʿankh, at the Island of Amūn Overrunning-His-Boundary, on the threshing-floor of the priest Keson, was derived from the House of Seti-merenptaḥ in the House of Amūn (227¾⅛ sacks). These data imply a significantly greater degree of financial interdependency of land-owning institutions than can be inferred from P. Wilbour where insufficient data preclude comparable gauges of financial interdependency. The grain revenues of P. Amiens may have constituted income of the House of Amūn stored in the granary of Amun-Rēʿ at Karnak to await distribution among the various sanctuaries having claim to them as Gardiner himself suggested.(47) As such, P. Amiens may have been a strictly internal document of the House of Amūn, unlike P. Wilbour which enumerates the revenue of a great variety of temples and secular institutions.

The consignments of grain recorded over pages 1-4 of the recto of P. Amiens are said to have been given to the particular ship's captain in such and such a location "on the threshing-floor (ḏnw)" of the individual whose name and occupation follow. Of the fifteen so-called threshing-floor "owners," as Gardiner refers to them in his commentary on the text, as many as six are controllers (rwḏw). Four are identified as iḥwtyw. The remaining five individuals are of such diverse occupations as those of priest, scribe, and retainer. This finding suggests that these individuals were not "owners" at all, but rather managers or administrators with considerable responsibilities. This possibility is enhanced by the evidence of both Text A and Text B of P. Wilbour in which such individuals, especially iḥwtyw and controllers, play an important role as administrators of landholdings ascribed to temples.(48)

A study of the headings of both the apportioning and non-apportioning paragraphs in Text A of P. Wilbour reveals the fact that in nearly every case where the compound preposition m-ḏrt is used to express the idea "administered by," the holder of the position is a controller. In Text B, khato-land of Pharaoh appears to have been under the authority of (r-ḫt) controllers in 7 of the 65 cases, a total nearly equalled by the frequent occurrence of the steward of Amūn (6 occurrences) and mayors (also 6 occurrences), exceeded only by the occurrence of prophets in nearly half (32) of the 65 cases.

Menu has suggested that the controllers in P. Wilbour whose names are preceded by the preposition m-ḏrt performed a managerial function and were subordinate to those individuals whose names and titles are preceded by the preposition r-ḫt (thus her designation "employé subalterne").(49) Controllers appear to have worked in cooperation with senior administrators on behalf of numerous institutions to enhance the productivity of various properties and oversee the field-labourers (iḥwtyw) who carried out the actual cultivation of the plots enumerated in both the non-apportioning entries and the corresponding Pōsh A and B entries. These two categories of administrators appear to have had precisely defined roles and functions which, according to Menu, justified the use of the two prepositions to distinguish them. In many cases, controllers probably bore the burden of the responsibility for the cultivation and administration of the fields concerned, since many of the senior administrators probably were more or less honorary appointees. Thus, it is likely that the controllers who occur in P. Amiens in association with threshing-floors were probably not "owners" at all as Gardiner suggested, but rather administrators with precisely defined responsibilities. Stuchevsky's recent reconsideration of the data of P. Wilbour is in accord with this line of thought.(50) According to Stuchevsky, the occurrence of ỉḥwtyw and rwḏw in P. Amiens in connection with threshing-floors is evidence in support of his hypothesis that there existed a category of low-level agricultural administrators who supervised the activities of unidentified field-labourers (also ỉḥwtyw) and played a role in the distribution of the harvest among State organizations and the actual cultivators. These agricultural administrators occur in both the non-apportioning entries and the Pōsh B entries where they are identified by name. Some of these ỉḥwtyw were apparently also rwḏw, hence the occasional alternation of the titles ỉḥwty and rwḏw in the corresponding Pōsh A and B entries.

The important role of controllers in Ramesside times is underscored in the agricultural texts of the verso of P. Sallier IV which include a brief letter written by "the Royal Scribe and Steward of the Mansion of Millions of Years of King Binerēʿ-meriamūn in the House of Amūn, Ḥarnakhte" to the deputy-superintendent (ỉdnw) Menthikhopshef which, after breaking off in mid-sentence, gives way to a series of brief notes concerning winnowing and threshing-floors dated in journal style.(51) In this letter, Ḥarnakhte chides the deputy-superintendent for failing to maintain order and to carry out his responsibilities with regard to the grain intended for the Granary of Pharaoh:

> (vs. 9,2) ...Furthermore, the overseers of the granary have been quarrelling with me (9,3) concerning the grain which you put as cargo upon the transport ship (ḳr) of the Granary of Pharaoh, L.P.H., under the authority of the Royal Scribe and Overseer of the Granary Neferronpĕ who is the superior (nty r ḥ3t) of the adjutant of the army (ỉdnw n p3 mšʿ) Menteḥētef, (9,4) saying: "It is bad and unworthy of the work of Pharaoh, L.P.H.," so they said, and I went to see it and found it was really not good at all. (9,5) Why do you act like this? You must act according to the wish of the controllers. What is this t[heir] ([p3y.]w) causing your heart to grieve (ḫw3)? For you know their way, that...

This letter suggests that more often than not, controllers were disagreeable bureaucrats known to badger and harass the everyday citizen with their overzealous execution of duty. Such perhaps was the opinion of the writer whose closing words suggest first-hand experience in dealing with them. Perhaps too there is a trace of resignation to a life in which petty bureaucrats dictated and enforced the letter of the law with little room for discretion.

P. Turin 1887, also known as the Turin Indictment Papyrus, is another Ramesside text which contributes to our knowledge of the role and character of the controller in the Ramesside Period.(52) In vs. 1,4 of this document from the reign of Ramesses V, it is said that the granary (šmmt) of the House of Khnūm at Elephantine was "under the seal of the controllers of the granary who do the 'controlling' on behalf of the House of Khnūm (?)."(53) This implies that the controllers played a supervisory role in maintaining the security of the grain in storage. It is therefore not at all surprising to encounter controllers in the capacity of threshing-floor managers in P. Amiens, a position which undoubtedly made them responsible for the security of the grain as it awaited shipment to the granaries at Thebes.

The lamentable condition of the verso of P. Amiens, marked by numerous cancellations, displaced margins, superlinear additions, diacritical marks, and inexplicable blanks, suggests that it was one of no doubt numerous preliminary lists utilized by the scribe in compiling such a final document as is represented by the recto of the text. Page 2 of the verso, for example, appears to detail the cargo of a single ship, much like the recto. Page 4 of the verso provides the details of the cargo of another two ships. Whereas the locale of the recto of P. Amiens is the area of the Panopolite and Antaeopolite nomes of Upper Egypt, the locale of the verso of P. Amiens is the Hermopolite nome farther north. Nothing but a few figures remain from verso pages 1 and 3 of the document. The top half of verso p. 2 as well as that of verso p. 4 is lost. Verso p. 2,x+1-13 and verso p. 4,x+1-4 are the sparse remains of what appears to have been a registry of payments in grain forthcoming from fields cultivated by individual smallholders. These individuals are possibly to be equated with the smallholders of the P. Wilbour apportioning paragraphs. The wide range of occupations of the individuals listed in these two pages is reminiscent of that of the smallholders of P. Wilbour. These occupations include three scribes, a prophet (?), a Sherden, a ỉḥwty, and a woman (ʿnḫ(t) n nỉwt). Although no sandal-maker (ṯbw) occurs as a smallholder in Text A of P. Wilbour, other craftspersons do occur. Verso p. 4,x+7ff. and pages 5 and 6 deal with revenue derived from various domains (rmnyt) of the House of Amun-Rēʿ, King of the Gods; the House of Mūt, the Great, Lady of Ishru; and the Portable Shrine of Muterĕ (?) also at Karnak.

Controllers are mentioned in the verso of P. Amiens both as the administrators of domains (vs. 2,x+2) and as agents of the transfer of the grain revenues after the preposition m-ḏrt (vs. 2,x+11.12). They occur in company with scribes in both vs. p. 2 and vs. p. 4. Controllers also occur in the last two pages of the verso in lines which are reminiscent of the headings of the non-apportioning paragraphs of Text A of P. Wilbour, so vs. p. 5,x+4:

> Grain of the regular domain (rmnyt mt) of the House of Amun-Rēʿ, King of the Gods, under the authority of (r-ḫt)

> the steward (of Amūn), by the hand of (m-ḏrt) the controller Setekhmosĕ, 6 sacks.

Thus, the verso of P. Amiens suggests the existence of an administrative hierarchy analogous to that of the domains enumerated in the P. Wilbour non-apportioning paragraphs. The occurrence of "private tenants," as Gardiner referred to the various private persons in P. Amiens who paid over grain as a type of "rent" or "tax," suggests that some of the domains mentioned in the verso of P. Amiens were apportioning domains. Such affinities with P. Wilbour suggest that P. Amiens is concerned with such grain revenues as are enumerated in Text A as derived from temple land listed in both the non-apportioning and apportioning paragraphs. The temples mentioned in P. Amiens appear to have been administratively linked in both their common situation in Thebes and their mutual affiliation with the House of Amūn. The jurisdiction of the steward (of Amūn) Ramessenakhte would have arisen from his capacity as chief administrative officer of the House of Amūn.

(4) Other Texts Related to the Transport of Grain Revenues

It has been established by evidence of both P. Turin 1882, verso 0,1-1,4 and P. Amiens that the House of Amūn possessed ships for the transport of grain revenues. To this should be added the evidence of P. Harris I 4,12-5,1 and 11,8 which records ships belonging to the House of Amūn used to transport grain. Needless to say, the House of Amūn was not the only institution to own and operate ships of its own for the transport of grain revenues.

In P. Harris I, it is said that Ramesses III gave transport vessels (ḳrr) and barges (mnš) to both the House of Rēʿ (29,1; 32a,5) and the House of Ptaḥ (48,6; 51a,13).(54) The section devoted to smaller temples, on the other hand, makes no mention of ships in the enumeration of the wealth of the gods' estates, nor are ships included in the section which pertains to the gods' incomes. This omission is confirmed in the concluding summary of the text (67,10), where the figure of 88 transport vessels (ḳrr and mnš) accounts for the 83 vessels of the House of Amūn, the 3 of the House of Rēʿ, and the 2 of the House of Ptaḥ.(55)

The omission of the mention of ships belonging to the smaller temples does not by any means preclude the possibility of these temples having had the means to transport their own revenue. The evidence of P. Turin 1887 is particularly relevant to this point. P. Turin 1887 is a detailed account of a scandal at the House of Khnūm at Elephantine in the reign of Ramesses V in which a ship's captain, in collusion with scribes, controllers, and ỉḥwtyw of the House of Khnūm, embezzled large amounts of temple revenue on an annual basis. According to the text, grain in part derived from fields in the Delta (vs. 1,10) were customarily conveyed by river to Elephantine and delivered to the granary of Khnūm (vs. 1,7-1,8). In vs. 1,9, it is said that the ship's captain [fell ill?] and died. In his place, the prophet of the House of Khnūm appointed "the merchant and 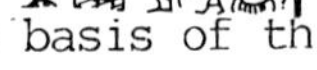 (f3y nbw) Khnemnakhte" [ship's captain].(56) On the basis of this statement, we can perhaps infer a useful piece of information concerning the shipping activities of the temple. Had the ships used in the transport of the grain been under the control of an institution other than the House of Khnūm, it is unlikely that the prophet of the House of Khnūm would have been the one to appoint a new ship's captain. There is a strong likelihood that the ships used to convey the temple revenues were under the direct control of the House of Khnūm. Moreover, considering the fact that the shipping distances involved were considerable, the ships would certainly have had to have been first class vessels of considerable financial value. It is certainly realistic to surmise that the owner institution of such vessels could not have been of insignificant wealth or prestige.

Another text which is relevant to the subject of the collection and transportation of temple grain is P. Louvre 3171, a poorly preserved Eighteenth Dynasty analogon to P. Amiens.(57) P. Louvre 3171 concerns the shipment of the šmw of three ỉḥwtyw by river to the granary of Memphis from localities almost certainly within the vicinity of Memphis. No institution is identified as the owner of the fields for which the three ỉḥwtyw were held responsible. This is not surprising, however, in light of the poor state of preservation of the document.

Baer has interpreted the document as an accounting of the crop or rent of ỉḥwtyw labouring on a State domain. He understands the term spyt "remainder," which describes 600 sacks of grain remaining after the bulk of the grain had been allocated to ships, as either the individual ỉḥwty's own share of the harvest or an amount of grain to be collected at a later date.(58) The occurrence in 3,8 of an amount of 80 sacks set aside for seed on the account of the ỉḥwty Amenmosĕ indicates that the ỉḥwty was not a tenant, but rather an employee of the unidentified institution. As such, he was held responsible for the payment of what was evidently the ṯs prt or "sowing-order," although the term does not occur in the document. According to Stuchevsky, the three ỉḥwtyw were low-level agricultural administrators ("agents of the fisc") responsible for the payment of the grain of three settlements. The likelihood that the three ỉḥwtyw were "agents of the fisc" is indicated by the sheer size of the quantities of grain for which they were responsible. These quantities of grain far exceed the amount of grain any single cultivator could ever hope to produce by himself. Although the area of land for which the three ỉḥwtyw were held responsible is not specified in the text, it is possible to obtain a rough estimate of the possible sizes of plots required to produce such large amounts of grain. Such a calculation makes it possible to compare the area of agricultural land for which each of the ỉḥwtyw was responsible in P. Louvre 3171 with the areas of land for which the ỉḥwtyw identified in the non-apportioning paragraphs of P. Wilbour were held responsible.

Entries for each of the three ỉḥwtyw specify the number of sacks described as the šmw "harvest" of each ỉḥwty delivered to the various ship's captains. These amounts total 1000 sacks in the case of the ỉḥwty Maḥu in 2,1; 50 606¾ (total 656¾) sacks in the case of the ỉḥwty Nebnūfe in 2,8; and 1421 sacks in the case of the ỉḥwty Amenmosĕ in 3,1. If these fields consisted of ḳ3yt-land which, according to the non-apportioning paragraphs of Text A of P. Wilbour, could be expected to yield 5 sacks per aroura (the "standard average grain harvest" according to Stuchevsky), the areas in arouras required to produce yields as large as 1000 sacks, 656¾ sacks, and 1421 sacks would have been very large: approximately 200 arouras for a yield of 1000 sacks; 131 arouras for a yield of 656¾ sacks; and 284 arouras for a yield of 1421 sacks.(59)

When these estimates of agriculturally productive land are compared with data of P. Wilbour, they far exceed the average size of plot cultivated by the relatively independent smallholders in the apportioning paragraphs. They are, however, in line with data of the non-apportioning paragraphs. Thus, it is suggested that P. Louvre 3171 pertains to temple land cultivated collectively by numerous ỉḥwtyw under the supervision of lower-echelon staff also called ỉḥwtyw and sometimes rwḏw. These low-level agricultural administrators were held responsible for the collection and registration of grain revenues owed to the State, here represented by the granary of Memphis.

The evidence of P. Turin 1882 (P. Turin A) vs. 2,2-2,9, in which the negligent student is enjoined to attend to his studies lest he be made a ỉḥwty (dỉ r ỉḥwty) "...appointed to (pay) 300 sacks of grain and set in charge of too many fields...," is also relevant.(60) Although P. Turin 1882 is a miscellany with a didactic purpose, the figure of 300 sacks may be meaningful. This figure is in accord with the yields of grain expected from fields in the charge of the ỉḥwtyw identified by name in the non-apportioning paragraphs of P. Wilbour. It is evident from the data of the non-apportioning paragraphs that a single ỉḥwty was often held responsible for the harvest of relatively large tracts of land situated with reference to more than one measurement area in contrast to the smallholders of the apportioning entries, some of whom are also identified as ỉḥwtyw. The figure of 300 sacks is also in line with the data of P. Bologna 1086, 20-28, a letter dating to the late (?) Nineteenth Dynasty.(61) In this letter, a prophet of the temple of Thoth Pleased-of-Heart-in-Memphis was apparently held responsible for a total of 700 sacks calculated as the produce of three men and a youth. This amount of grain is specifically identified as the ṯs prt "sowing-order" for which the prophet Raʿmosĕ was held accountable. Each adult cultivator was, therefore, responsible for 200 sacks, the youth for half that amount. It is noteworthy that the temple of Thoth Pleased-of-Heart-in-Memphis is mentioned in Text B of P. Wilbour (B7,9) which deals with khato-lands of Pharaoh under the authority of various administrators. In B7,9, the chief administrator is none other than the steward Usimaʿrenakhte. While Gardiner interprets the ṯs prt as that of the prophet Raʿmosĕ, Stuchevsky views it as the responsibility of the four cultivators whom he identifies as "agents of the fisc."

Mention must also be made of P. British Museum 10447, a brief administrative document dating to year 55 of Ramesses II.(62) This document concerns the payment of 800 sacks of emmer from estates near Nefrusi in the Hermopolite nome for the maintenance of the "Great Statue of Ramesses-meriamūn, Beloved-of-Atūm," located in a small temple or shrine near Nefrusi or in a temple at Heliopolis. Line 2 records the payment of 400 sacks described as "the remainder of (outstanding from) (spyt n) year 54 (delivered) by the hand of (m-ḏrt) the scribe of this House Amenemōnĕ," the source of which is indicated to have been two ỉḥwtyw identified by name and filiation. Line 3 records the delivery of another 400 sacks in year 55 by the scribe of this House Ḥarmin. The payments are attributed once again to the two ỉḥwtyw. Each ỉḥwty, therefore, appears to have been responsible for the payment of 200 sacks as was evidently the case in P. Bologna 1086, 20-28. These ỉḥwtyw would also be viewed by Stuchevsky as "agents of the fisc."

It is evident from all these examples that the amounts of grain specified in P. Louvre 3171 are rather high. This suggests that there may have been different levels or grades among ỉḥwtyw who served as "agents of the fisc." The highest echelon may have been those ỉḥwtyw responsible for larger tracts of cultivable land tilled by sufficiently large numbers of field-labourers whose labour produced larger quantities of grain revenue payable to the State.

The grain of all three ỉḥwtyw detailed in P. Louvre 3171 is said to have been conveyed by river to the granary of Memphis. Gardiner interpreted the granary of Memphis as belonging to the secular administration in parallel with the granaries located at Thebes over which the mayor of the West of the City Pwerʿo had authority according to the evidence of the Turin Taxation Papyrus. In P. Louvre 3171, a scribe is said to have accompanied the grain to Memphis, just as Dḥutmosĕ is said to have accompanied the grain he personally collected to Thebes where it was received by the mayor Pwerʿo and the chantress of Amūn and deposited in the Theban granaries. The explanation of such a situation may well lie in the nature of the Egyptian administration as it developed during the Eighteenth Dynasty and was inherited by the Ramesside bureaucracy.

During the Eighteenth Dynasty, the dual character of the Egyptian State was reflected most dramatically in the institution of a dual vizierate: one vizier for Lower Egypt resident at Memphis (or Heliopolis?) and one vizier for Upper Egypt resident at Thebes.(63) Also reflecting the duality of Egyptian politico-economic conditions was the office of the Treasury (of Pharaoh) administered by two overseers of the Treasury corresponding to the two viziers with whom they conferred regularly.(64) The granary (of Pharaoh) was centrally administered by an official whose title, the Overseer of the Granaries of Upper and Lower Egypt, not only reflects the duality of the Egyptian State, but also clearly establishes the fact that there were at least two State granaries, one to serve Upper Egypt and one to serve Lower Egypt.(65)

The organization of the Egyptian civil administration underwent some modifications over the course of the Nineteenth and Twentieth Dynasties but, by and large, the old system prevailed. The dual vizierate was not always operative as generations passed, but the vizier, or viziers when there were two, remained the highest ranking civil servant in the whole of the country.

Since the office of the Lower Egyptian vizier appears to have been located in Memphis (or Heliopolis?), it would not be unreasonable to expect there to have been a State granary in

Memphis or in the vicinity of Memphis. It is possible that the granary of Memphis referred to in P. Louvre 3171 was a State granary serving Lower Egypt, on a parallel with the granary (or granaries) at Thebes serving Upper Egypt, to which Dḥutmosĕ delivered his grain according to the evidence of the Turin Taxation Papyrus. Moreover, it is certainly evident that there was more than one State granary at Thebes. Very possibly there were three, as is suggested by the occurrence of three virtually synonymous words for granary in the Turin document as the storage facilities for the grain collected and registered by Dḥutmosĕ.(66) That these granaries may have belonged to, or been components of, a larger granary complex is also very possible. Thus, it is certainly possible to interpret the granary of Memphis in P. Louvre 3171 as a State granary which was a component of a larger granary complex serving Lower Egypt.

(5) The Griffith Fragments

Another Ramesside economic document which bears mention in relation to P. Wilbour is the recto of a group of papyrus fragments known as the Griffith Fragments. These fragments are all that remain of a single papyrus written in a very small but competent cursive hand which displays characteristics which date it at the earliest to the end of the Twentieth Dynasty.(67) The presence of the nomen Ramesses-meri[amūn] in the cartouche on one isolated fragment complicates the dating of text, however, since it does not belong to any of the last three Ramesside kings.

The only portion of the text complete enough to analyze is the end of the recto containing the remains of three columns consisting of short paragraphs reminiscent of the paragraphs of Text B of P. Wilbour in both form and content. Moreover, as in Text B of P. Wilbour, the fields enumerated were apparently restricted to a limited geographical area. Whereas P. Wilbour pertains to Middle Egypt just south of the Fayyūm, the Griffith Fragments pertain to the Antaeopolite nome farther south. Unlike Text B of P. Wilbour, however, none of the entries are identified as khato-land of Pharaoh. The paragraph headings of the Griffith Fragments identify the administrative units of the temples to which the various fields enumerated were ascribed. Single line entries, introduced by the words sw n ("region of"), identify the exact location and precise area of the individual parcels of land. These entries distinguish between ḳ3yt-land and nḫb-land in each area. If the one complete paragraph of column III can be considered indicative of the original document as a whole, each page ended with the amounts of grain received from both types of land. It is possible, however, that the amount of land detailed in each locality represents only the amount of land liable to taxation rather than the total area cultivated. The quantities of grain specified appear to represent a proportion of the harvest owed to the State by the various institutions enumerated.

In the summation of column I of the Griffith Fragments, under the heading "Domain of the House of Khons '(large gap) g3bw-ỉb,'" occurs the phrase "t3 št Ṯbw" preceding an amount of grain expressed in sacks (ḫ3r). The word št in this phrase is undoubtedly the key to the understanding of the figures in the text and, moreover, serves to link the data to those of P. Wilbour.

Gardiner's understanding of the term št in the Griffith Fragments was that of a feminine collective noun meaning "tax-payers," hence his reading of the phrase as "the tax-payers of Tjebu."(68) Malinine concurred in interpreting the phrase as referring to private persons who cultivated the land for their own benefit, hence his translation "les imposés (št) de Tjebou."(69) Baer, however, disagreed with this understanding of "t3 št Ṯbw," and has convincingly refuted Gardiner's arguments for the existence of a feminine collective noun št "tax-payers" both upon grammatical grounds and simple logic.(70) He remarks that it is not certain that there was a feminine word št meaning "tax-payers" and that the determinative in the Griffith Fragments does not contain the seated man (this latter point admittedly not a strong piece of evidence). He also notes that there is no indication in the Griffith Fragments that assessments were made on any basis other than that of institutional property taken as a whole, while it is evident from the size of the lots that these records did not pertain to the entire body of the tax-payers of Tjebu, nor even to the majority of them. He notes, moreover, that it would be more likely for the word "assessment" to precede quantities of grain than it would the word "tax-payers." There is a masculine št which occurs in the phrase ỉṯ3 p3 št "to take the assessment" in P. Anastasi VI, 26. This usage of št, however, is clear enough in meaning. Baer's understanding of the word št is carried over to the title ʿ3 n št, generally translated "Chief Taxing-Master" (literally "Great One of Assessments"), but probably better translated "Chief Assessing-Master." This title occurs in both P. Wilbour (§200 and implied in §201) and P. Valençay I.(71) Baer interprets the word št similarly as it occurs in P. Anastasi V 27,6 and P. Chester Beatty V rt. 7,12-8,1.

The phrase "t3 št Ṯbw" recalls the entry in P. Amiens (rt. 2,5) which pertains to grain shipments of the domain of the House of Ramesses-meriamūn in the House of Amūn of Ḥe-e-pwoid of which 37¼⅛ sacks of a total of 600 sacks were forwarded by the "Domain of Tjebu" for delivery to the ship's captain Minsʿankh at the Island of Amūn Overrunning-His-Boundary. The phrase "t3 št Ṯbw" in the Griffith Fragments, however, under the paragraph heading "Domain of the House of Khons '(large gap) g3bw-ỉb'" may pertain to the great Theban temple of Khons to the southwest of the Karnak complex.(72) It is possible that "the Assessment of Tjebu" applies not only to the Domain of the House of Khons "(large gap) g3bw-ỉb," but also to revenue of other domains the data of which have been lost. The destination of "the Assessment of Tjebu" as well as grain revenues of two other domains occurring in column I was the granary of the House of Amūn, the probable destination of the grain under shipment in P. Amiens.

When compared with the total revenue of 5653⅛ sacks accruing from the fields of the domain of the House of Ramesses-meriamūn in the House of Amūn in Ḥe-e-pwoid in rt. 5,5 of P. Amiens, the amount of [609¾] sacks restored by Gardiner as "the Assessment of Tjebu" is a relatively small amount. This suggests that "the Assessment of Tjebu" may have been an amount of tax (or rent) revenue in grain accruing from temple lands located in the same geographical area cultivated by private smallholders on their own behalf rather than field-labourers (iḥwtyw) on behalf of the State. While it could be argued that the disparity in the amounts of grain forthcoming from the two Karnak temples is merely the reflection of the relative size of their respective landholdings in the same geographical area, the presence of the word št in the phrase "t3 št Ṯbw" strongly suggests that the Griffith Fragments are concerned only with grain actually owing to the State as determined by an outside agent or agency, quite possibly the nome administration situated at the nome capital. If so, the occurrence of the name of the nome capital Tjebu in this paragraph probably reflects the role of provincial nome capitals in the collection of taxes in grain from fields in their outlying districts. The expression "grain of the Tract (ḳʿḥ) 4 $1066\frac{3}{4}$ sacks," which follows "t3 št Ṯbw" in column I, is further evidence of the validity of this interpretation, as the word ḳʿḥ in Ramesside times was practically synonymous with "nome." (73) Ḳʿḥ also occurs in P. Wilbour in the expression "the Tract of Ḥardai" (A22,11) as the location of an apportioning domain ascribed to the House of Amun-Reʿ, King of the Gods (§§51ff.).

The last paragraph of column III of the Griffith Fragments is also of relevance to P. Wilbour. It is written in the exceptionally large hand of both the unplaced fragments and the headings of columns I to III. The first line reads: "THE SECOND. The Temples," following which are three lines each identifying a temple. The first is that of Osiris, Lord of Abydus; the second is that of Onūris Shu, [son of Reʿ]; while the third is that of Min, Horus, and [Isi]s, the Gods, Lords of Ipu. Each of these brief lines ends with the words "inspected by" (sỉp n) such and such a scribe (one name lacking). Gardiner speculated that this peculiar paragraph may have been a listing of various temples in the provinces under a heading to be understood as "THE SECOND (List-(dnỉt)?). The (subsidiary) Temples" or "THE SECOND (List?) of the Temples," only the first three of which survive. (74) Gardiner noted that the three temples were situated in Abydus, Thinis, and Akhmīm respectively. This geographical sequence prompted him to suggest that the complete document may have been a list of temples with a south to north geographical sequence. If so, the list may have resembled the list of provincial temples in P. Harris I 61a,3ff. Also of note is P. British Museum 10401, an unpublished text in which temple sites follow the south to north sequence: Elephantine, Kōm Ombo, Edfu, Hierakonpolis, El-Kāb, and Esna. (75) Such lists, of course, have affinities with the sub-sections devoted to the smaller temples in Text A of P. Wilbour which also follow a south to north geographical sequence.

The situation in which grain of what appears to have been the "harvest-tax" was stored in what was titled "the granary of the House of Amūn" is a reflection of the essential unity of the temple and Crown components of the Ramesside State. We are probably closest to the reality if we envision two highly interrelated and interdependent spheres of activities: one revolving around the temples and their immediate interests and priorities; the other revolving around the Crown and its immediate interests and priorities. While these spheres of activity overlapped to a considerable degree in day-to-day life, their complete integration was probably achieved only in the theological realm, i.e., in the nationally accepted dogma which made Pharaoh both the supreme high priest of a nation of believers, and the absolute monarch of a tangible political entity.(76) Day-to-day reality, however, was probably not so clear cut a matter. Both the temples and the Crown had their own separate administrations, a situation which inevitably led to confusion because of the inevitable duplication of administrative functions and jurisdictions. Certainly in the Ramesside Period, and undoubtedly earlier as well, the different administrations sometimes found themselves working at cross-purposes as several of the Miscellanies suggest in the numerous attempts of administrators to clarify questions of protocol and jurisdiction.(77) The interrelatedness of the temple and Crown components of the contemporary economy is certainly most dramatically exemplified in the office of the Royal scribe and steward of Amūn. This very high and influential lay office was both closely associated with the Crown and, at the same time, belonged to the administration of the House of Amūn. Usimaʿrenakhte, who held this office in the reign of Ramesses V, was also the chief taxing-master, an office which is likely to have belonged to the civil administration. The wide range of influence and authority his titles convey are more likely evidence of cooperation at the highest level of government than they are of the unfettered growth of the temples at the expense of the Crown. The revenues described in the Griffith Fragments as "t3 št Ṯbw" reflect the essential unity of temple and Crown in carrying out activities which were necessary and beneficial to both. In this case, grain collected as tax revenue on behalf of the State was routinely conveyed to the granary of the House of Amūn. Thus, the House of Amūn played a role in the routine procedure of revenue collection on behalf of the State of which it was a vital and integral part.

In sum, it probably can be said that the Griffith Fragments constitute a very small fragment of what were probably the exhaustive records of the Antaeopolite nome kept by provincial officials under the auspices of the mayor of the nome capital. The Griffith Fragments and Text B of P. Wilbour approach the matter of land assessment from the same perspective, that is, the quantity of grain that land of different qualities (k3yt and nḫb) could be expected to produce. Whereas the plots enumerated in Text B of P. Wilbour are specified as khato-land of Pharaoh situated "on fields of" Pharaoh or, more frequently, various institutions; those detailed in the Griffith Fragments have no such identification. Whether the plots recorded in the Griffith Fragments were cultivated collectively by anonymous iḥwtyw coordinated by rwḏw and iḥwtyw ("agents of the fisc"), or by relatively independent smallholders, as are enumerated in the Text A apportioning paragraphs, the "general assessment rate" of 30%, derived by Stuchevsky from data of the corresponding Pōsh A and B entries, is probably also relevant. A great deal depends upon the understanding of the phrase "t3 št Ṯbw." If "t3 št Ṯbw" is correctly interpreted as meaning "the Assessment of Tjebu," the quantities of grain specified in the Griffith Fragments may well represent the 30% of the expected yield payable to the State on the taxable portion of fields ascribed to various temples with landholdings in the Antaeopolite nome.

(6) The Gurob Fragments

Among the sparse collection of fragments discovered in the area of Kōm Medīnet Ghurāb are two which are relevant to P. Wilbour, P. Amiens, and the Turin Taxation Papyrus.(78) Whereas Fragment L, the largest of the fragments, consists of the remains of three pages or columns referring to the collection of grain revenues after the manner of the Turin Taxation Papyrus, the smaller Fragment M concerns the harvest grain in connection with a series of individual smallholders (?). Fragment L establishes the date of the text in line 1,8 with its reference to the "*šmw* (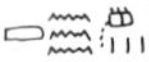) of Year 67, which was reported to him in Year 1" which can only refer to the reigns of Ramesses II and Merenptaḥ respectively. Lines 2,1-2,2 provide the date "Year 67, first month of *3ḫt*, day 18" with reference to the receipt of the "*šmw* of t[he]..." by an unidentified party in the granary of Amenemopě, the mayor of Southern She. Lines 2,3-2,4 give brief mention of "interest-grain" *ỉt n ms* () (literally "grain of the *ms*") exacted (*šdỉ*) by a scribe and received by a "[chief] of doorkeepers" (*ḥry ỉryw-ʿ3*) and a "measurer" (*ḫ3y*).(79) The cast of characters is thus reminiscent of that of the Turin Taxation Papyrus. The mention of a "measurer" brings to mind P. Geneva D 191 (No. 37 *LRL*) in which a "measurer" is responsible for measuring out grain received by the scribe of the Necropolis. Lines 2,5ff. are also very badly damaged, but contain intriguing references to the consignment of the grain for transport by river and the giving of the *ms*-grain (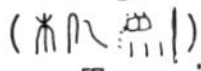) in 3,6 and probably 2,7.

Two individuals are mentioned in connection with the transport of the grain: the mayor of Southern She, an official who occurs as an administrator of *khato*-land in both Text A (§46) and Text B (§13) of P. Wilbour and the overseer of the King's Apartments, an official who also occurs as an administrator of *khato*-land in both Text A (§48) and Text B (§21) of P. Wilbour where the description "of the Harem of Mi-wēr" is appended (B19,8). The latter official also occurs in §41 of Text A as an administrator of *minĕ*-land of Pharaoh and in a *Pōsh* B entry in Text A (A16,16-17) again as an administrator of *minĕ*-land.

Fragment M also concerns the harvest grain (*šmw*) which was apparently the responsibility of several *ỉḥwtyw* and quite possibly a herdsman and a woman (*ʿnḫ(t) n nỉwt*).(80) A controller is also mentioned after the familiar preposition *m-ḏrt*, but nothing further can be deduced about his role in these proceedings because of the extremely poor condition of the text. The situation to which these lines refer, of which we have only the barest of outline, certainly strikes a note of accord with rt. 3,12-3,13 of the Turin Taxation Papyrus where revenue of the House of Khnūm and Nebu in the amount of *220* sacks is disaggregated as the *šmw* of three *ỉḥwtyw*. All of these individuals, *ỉḥwtyw* and *rwḏw*, may have been "agents of the fisc," although the total of *220* sacks in the

Turin Taxation Papyrus seems rather small for three ỉḥwtyw. The mention of the granary of the mayor Amenemopĕ brings to mind the Theban granaries where the mayor Pwerʿo and the chantress of Amūn Ḥenttowĕ received revenue in grain derived from khato-land of Pharaoh consisting of various temple estates as well as fields ascribed to some secular institutions.

It is very likely that the Theban granaries of the Turin Taxation Papyrus and that of Amenemopĕ, the mayor of Southern She were State repositories of grain harvested from fields of various institutions. These revenues had been assessed and allocated for whatever use the State saw fit to designate--including donation to various institutions. The fact that the mayors of Egyptian towns were customarily responsible for the collection and transportation of grain and other types of revenue over the course of the New Kingdom increases the likelihood that the granary of Amenemopĕ was a component of a State network of regional granaries. Moreover, the involvement of such a Crown administrator as the overseer of the King's Apartments in the proceedings to which the Gurob Fragments relate is further indication that "the granary of Amenemopĕ, Mayor of Southern She" was a State operation for purposes of storing incoming revenue from various sources.

It is very possible that the operations detailed in the meagre remains of the document were related to the upkeep of the Harem of Mi-wēr (probably at the site of Kōm Medīnet Ghurāb) which occurs in special "harem paragraphs" in Text A of P. Wilbour (§§39, 111-12, 278-79). According to the Golénischeff Onomasticon (5,7), Mi-wēr and She were neighbouring towns. They occur together in the town-list in the sequence "She, Robana (Barna?), Mi-wēr" immediately following Heracleopolis. While it is curious that there is no mention in P. Wilbour of any temple at Mi-wēr which might be identified with any of those founded by Ramesses II or Tuthmosis III at Kōm Medīnet Ghurāb,(81) it is probable that the Landing-Place of Pharaoh in Mi-wēr (§37) was a port from which were shipped various revenues from the Fayyūm. As such, this "landing-place" of Pharaoh may be identified with the Greek "Ptolemais Harbour" (Πτολεμαίς Ὅρμος) as Gardiner himself suggested.(82)

(7) The Louvre Leather Fragments

Among the scraps of leather known collectively as the Louvre Leather Fragments are some which provide an important supplement to the apportioning paragraphs of Text A of P. Wilbour.(83) The fragments are unfortunately in very poor condition, the leather blackened and the writing obscured in the aging of the material. These scraps are but scanty remnants of what apparently had been a land register of some length and detail similar to P. Wilbour. This fairly well-written and legible text is appreciably earlier in date than P. Wilbour, probably dating to the Nineteenth Dynasty.(84) The occasional notation of dates on fragments among the lot indicate that the register must have been organized in a journal format. The date on one fragment (A) reads: "Regnal year 2, third month of šmw, ..." which probably refers to the reign of either Ramesses II or Merenptaḥ.

Following the date, there is a sizable lacuna. After the lacuna there are traces too fragmentary to be of much help in understanding what follows.(85) Line a,2 gives the names of three scribes and a,3 refers to some "measurement in the...upon (?)/through (?) (ḥr) the House of Amūn." Line a,4 makes reference to some "farmland (iḥt) of the iḥwty(w) (?) Khonsu  12 (or 13?) arouras" (). Line a,5 commences with the verb ini and reads according to Gardiner's transcription: "Brought (acquired?), 1Ø arouras at (the rate of?) 2 sacks (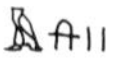) (per aroura) making 15Ø sacks."(86) What follows this troublesome line with its curious arithmetic is a series of entries (a,6-1Ø) recording the name, occupation, and filiation of a number of individuals together with an amount of land in arouras and the group . The list continues in the same manner from b,1 where Fragment A is supplemented by Fragment B (b,1-14). Fragments C through G continue with entries in the same format.

Taken at face value, the aroura measured plots of the Louvre Leather Fragments appear to be very small indeed as compared with those of the apportioning paragraphs of P. Wilbour. The entries of the Louvre Leather Fragments vary from a minimum of ⅛ aroura (b,7.9.1Ø.13, etc.) to a maximum of 3 arouras (b,12; d,1.3.6; e,3.9). The range in the size of plot among apportioning entries of P. Wilbour is considerably greater with aroura measured plots ranging anywhere from 1 (one) aroura (4 cases) to 11Ø arouras (1 case) with a mean of 7.2 arouras. There are no instances in P. Wilbour where the initial black aroura figure which gives the size of plot is composed of a fraction either less than or greater than 1 (one) aroura. Gardiner, and later Malinine, interpreted the Louvre Leather Fragments as a register of very small plots, cultivated by private smallholders, in which the purchase price or amount of rent was calculated at the invariable rate 1¾ sacks (ẖ3r) per aroura.(87)

The occupations of the Louvre Leather Fragments include soldier, charioteer (ktn), and coppersmith (ḥmty). The occupation wʿw has an absolute frequency of 253 cases and an adjusted relative frequency of 12.Ø% in the P. Wilbour apportioning entries. The occupation "coppersmith" occurs only once in P. Wilbour (A92,3). Other occupations of smallholders which occur in the Louvre Leather Fragments are not attested anywhere in P. Wilbour. These diverse occupations include: "distributers" (šd) (?) of rations (diw); "bringers of wood" (inw ḫt); and "inlayers of faience" (nšdy). Unfortunately, the extremely poor condition of the fragments frustrates any further attempt to fruitfully compare their data with those of the P. Wilbour apportioning entries.

Line a,5 is certainly the key to the understanding of this fragmentary document with the occurrence of what is probably a rate of assessment expressed in sacks in a curious arithmetic operation together with the crucial verb ini which appears to define the nature of this transaction, and presumably, of all the subsequent entries. The group 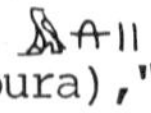, presumably interpreted to mean: "at (?) 2 sacks (per aroura)," might possibly have been a scribal error for 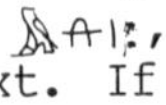, the invariable rate of all subsequent entries in the text. If we emend the rate 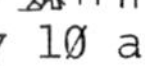 to read 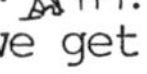 (1¾ sacks) for each aroura, and multiply it by 1Ø arouras, we get the answer 15 sacks ($1\frac{1}{2} \times 10 = 15$) as compared with 20 sacks ($2 \times 10 = 20$) if we do not emend the rate. Neither rate makes very much sense in conjunction with the amount of 150 sacks (or vice versa), but it is just possible that the figure of 15 sacks has been inflated by the power of 10 to read 150 sacks rather than 15 sacks. The entry f,2 "15...ỉr.n [glyph] 300" unfortunately renders this solution highly unlikely. Stuchevsky's interpretation of these lines, however, accounts for the arithmetic problems in a novel manner.(88) According to this new interpretation, the 13 (?) arouras in a,4 when multiplied by the rate of 10 sacks per aroura (the rate of expected yield of nḫb-land) gives 130 sacks to which are added 20 sacks resulting from the multiplication of the 10 arouras in a,5 by the rate 2 sacks per aroura (applicable to an apportioned plot taxed at 2 sacks per aroura) for a grand total of 150 sacks. This solution requires some bold assumptions which, while plausible, are not by any means indisputable. The extent of the lacuna in the document makes it impossible to more than guess the remainder of a,4 ("12 (or 13?) arouras..."), while the rate of 2 sacks per aroura in a,5 looks very suspiciously like an error for $1\frac{2}{7}$ sacks per aroura, which is the both invariable rate of assessment of the apportioning entries of P. Wilbour, and the entries which follow in the body of the Louvre Leather Fragments. In order to make any meaningful comparisons between the Louvre Leather Fragments and P. Wilbour, however, it is essential to establish that the sign [glyph] in the P. Wilbour assessments does indeed signify the same measure.

The problem of interpretation in P. Wilbour lies in the understanding of such writings as [glyph], [glyph], and [glyph]. When the cardinal numbers are taken to represent amounts of oipĕ, the half-oipĕ must be represented by the presence of two dots which elsewhere in Text A represent 2 oipĕ or $\frac{1}{2}$ khar. The question naturally arises why "eye"-notation was not used to represent the half-oipĕ in lieu of two dots.(89) Gardiner suggested that a writing such as [glyph] might signify 1 (khar) and 2 oipĕ (i.e., 6 oipĕ), despite the presence of the initial sign for oipĕ. Similarly, [glyph] might signify 7 khar and 2 oipĕ (i.e., 30 oipĕ). On the basis of examples in Middle Egyptian where the ordinary cardinals come to possess a value different from the apparent value, Gardiner reasoned that "when, in the Wilbour, we find the ordinary signs for the hundreds, tens and units following [glyph] we might have either to interpret the number in question in terms of the sack [glyph], or else, what comes to the same thing, to multiply it by four in order to understand it in terms of the oipĕ."(90)

Černý, however, made note of the fact that although masculine, the sign [glyph] was sometimes preceded by the feminine article: [glyph]. He identified that feminine with ỉpt and concluded that "as soon as a fraction entered into the indication, [glyph], though written, was replaced by ỉpt in reading."(91) Taking Černý's comments into consideration, Gardiner concluded that it was possible that the interpretation of the signs [glyph] and [glyph] was determined by the actual form of the numerals themselves and that "...the prefixed [glyph] or [glyph] merely showed the unit that was uppermost in the scribe's mind, however he may have expressed himself in giving oral utterance to what he had written." Thus, he continued, "written integers would always refer to sacks, dots to oipĕ, and the 'eye'-notation to fractions of the oipĕ." As a possible explanation for the curious usage of these signs, Gardiner suggested that in the case of assessments, the scribe perhaps would have kept in mind the grain measure signified by which would have been used in the registration of the grain. In the case of the sack figure in the P. Wilbour Pōsh A examples, on the other hand, the scribe perhaps would have kept in mind the grain as it would have appeared in sacks ready for transport.

Early on, Gardiner realized that the invariable rate of assessment in the apportioning entries of P. Wilbour was relevant to the interpretation of the transactions enumerated in the Louvre Leather Fragments. He realized that if the group in the Louvre Leather Fragments also signifies a rate of assessment which defines a smallholder's obligations in terms of a lease, it would certainly be valid and appropriate to compare this group to the recurrent group in the Text A apportioning entries.

It becomes immediately apparent in comparing the two rates that an understanding of the sign in Text A of P. Wilbour as khar rather than oipĕ is preliminary to an equating of the two rates. Stuchevsky's recent study of the corresponding Pōsh A and B entries, which resolves the arithmetic of these entries, provides convincing proof that the sign in both the non-apportioning and the apportioning entries does indeed signify the khar rather than the oipĕ such that we are justified in equating the rate $1\frac{2}{4}$ sacks in the Louvre Leather Fragments with the rate $1\frac{2}{4}$ in P. Wilbour.

Assuming that the invariable rates of both the Louvre Leather Fragments and the apportioning entries of P. Wilbour are identical, it remains to be determined exactly to what the rate of the Louvre Leather Fragments was intended to apply. Unlike in the case of the P. Wilbour apportioning entries, there is only one figure in arouras in each of the entries of the Louvre Leather Fragments to which the rate could conceivably apply. The opinions expressed to date interpret the aroura figure in the Louvre Leather Fragments as the actual size of the plot either "purchased" (în͗î) "at the rate of (m)" (?) $1\frac{2}{4}$ sacks per aroura or "acquired" by way of lease "at a rate (rent) of (m)" (?) $1\frac{2}{4}$ sacks per aroura.(92) While both of these interpretations are logical interpretations of the transactions detailed, there is another equally cogent possibility which would also explain the relatively small aroura figures. This is the possibility that the aroura figure in each entry of the Louvre Leather Fragments represents only the assessed portion of the plot rather than the actual size of the plot, and is comparable, therefore, to the red (aroura) figure of the P. Wilbour apportioning entries. This is a conclusion with which Stuchevsky evidently agrees.(93) The complete absence of aroura measured plots in P. Wilbour of a size smaller than 1 (one) aroura suggests such an interpretation. The paucity of complete entries in the Louvre Leather Fragments, however, makes it extremely difficult to compare the data of both texts. The two complete entries in the Louvre Leather Fragments pertain to the plots of two soldiers (wʿw) with the values $\frac{1}{2}\frac{1}{4}$ ($\frac{3}{4}$) aroura and 1 aroura in lines a,6 and a,7. While the value $\frac{3}{4}$ aroura occurs only four times in the P. Wilbour apportioning paragraphs (A26,9;

86,45-46; 93,15-16.18-19) as the assessment value of a plot, there are many cases of the value 1 (one) aroura. Moreover, soldiers are found to occur in association with an assessed aroura value of 1 (one) aroura on plots of both 3 and 5 arouras in size (A37,26; 45,3.6; 46,5; 56,21?).

The Louvre Leather Fragments and the apportioning entries of P. Wilbour also have in common the verb ỉnỉ in contexts which are similar enough to invite comparisons. There are three occurrences of the verb ỉnỉ in the Louvre document: a,5; b,3; and g2,1 according to the numbering of the lines in RAD. A fourth case would have been line f,2 where although the verb is lost, the rest of the line is intact. Each of these lines appears to be a heading governing a series of entries which immediately follows.

The first occurrence of the verb ỉnỉ in a,5 follows a reference to the House of Amūn in a,3. Although little sense can be made of the opening lines, the occurrence of the name of the House of Amūn in a,3 suggests that the entries which follow constitute an enumeration of plots leased to various smallholders perhaps to be compared with the apportioning entries of P. Wilbour. These plots may have been located upon a domain (rmnyt pš?) of the House of Amūn as indeed were many of the apportioned plots of P. Wilbour. The "measurement" referred to in a,3 was evidently connected with the House of Amūn as is suggested by the use of the preposition ḥr ("through," "by means of"). Whether the involvement of the House of Amūn was the result of its title to the plots which follow, or the result of a role as "agent" in the measurement to which a,3 refers, it is not possible to ascertain on the basis of the evidence supplied by the text in its present condition.

The three (four) occurrences of the verb ỉnỉ in the headings of the Louvre Leather Fragments led Gardiner to speculate that the verb ỉnỉ is to be restored in thought before each of the subsequent entries.(94) Although the verb which occurs consistently in the headings of the P. Wilbour apportioning entries is pš rather than ỉnỉ, the verb ỉnỉ occurs in five entries which occur in two apportioning paragraphs (§§54, 70) in Section II of Text A. A sixth example (A37,42 in §88) is actually a marginal notation which was added in a different hand sometime after the completion of the document. The first of these entries reads in the translation of Gardiner: (A23,14) "The scribe Dḥutnūfe, which the scribe Amenḥotpe acquired for himself (?) .100 wsf." The grammatical construction in all five of the P. Wilbour examples is exactly the same. Moreover, while four of the five examples (A23,14.17.18; 24,12) occur in close proximity to each other according to the evidence of the measurement lines, the fifth example (A32,47) occurs sufficiently far removed to preclude the likelihood of a copyist error. There is little possible doubt, therefore, that these five entries were intended to be read exactly as written. This possibility is enhanced by the fact that corrections were made to the data of size of plot in the case of two of the entries (A23,17.18) without any change in the remainder of the entry. While Gardiner admitted that it is not at all clear from the grammar whether the scribe Amenḥotpe is to be viewed as the subject or object of the clause, he concluded that we are dealing with "a loosely constructed relative clause referring to the piece of land of which the dimensions are about to be given."(95) Since the context of the Louvre Leather Fragments suggests that the plot rather than Amenḥotpe is the object of the clause, it is likely that Gardiner was correct in his interpretation of the grammatical construction in these five unusual entries.

On the assumption that both the Louvre Leather Fragments and the apportioning paragraphs of P. Wilbour should be interpreted as registers of rent owed to various institutions from fields cultivated by relatively independent smallholders, Gardiner translated the verb *ỉnỉ* in both texts as "acquired." This translation of the verb proceeds from the connotation of *ỉnỉ* as "to buy" or "to purchase." Such a non-committal rendering of the verb is certainly well-suited to the context of a lease. If Gardiner's understanding is correct, the entries of the Louvre Leather Fragments may well be analogous to the apportioning entries of Text A of P. Wilbour where the verb *pš* which occurs in many paragraph headings is easily comprehensible in the context of a lease.

The *ỉnỉ* clauses of the land-cubit measured plots of the P. Wilbour apportioning entries are interpreted by Menu as evidence of the freedom enjoyed by private smallholders over the disposition--including actual sale--of the holdings they occupied.(97) Thus, she interprets the verb *ỉnỉ* in its connotation "to buy" or "to purchase," identifying the smallholder whose name and occupation begin the entry as the vendor of the plot. The single aroura measured plot of A37,42 with its marginal notation  she views as an exceptional but significant case "qui marque peut-être la première étape de l'évolution qui conduit souvent la tenure, au cours de ses différentes manifestations dans l'histoire, vers un régime de propriété plus ou moins libre."(98) While this speculation is certainly to be given some serious consideration, this aroura measured entry gives rise to some misgivings. If the marginal notation for this entry does indeed refer to a sale of property, it does seem strange that no second party is mentioned. It is unclear, therefore, whether the stablemaster Psiūr was the vendor or vendee of the transaction.

If Menu's assessment of the verb *ỉnỉ* in P. Wilbour is correct, it might, but would not necessarily affect the interpretation of the *ỉnỉ* headings in the Louvre Leather Fragments. The fact that the date of the Louvre Leather Fragments to the third month of *šmw*, year 2 of Ramesses II or Merenptaḥ would have just about coincided with the time of year (April to early May) when crops were most easily assessed could be used as support for the hypothesis that the entries of the Louvre Leather Fragments reflect the assessment of the ripened crops of various smallholders on an apportioning domain of the House of Amūn.(99) Rents could be said to have been "acquired" by the land-owning institution at a time when the crops were ready for harvesting.

Another possible interpretation of the Louvre Leather Fragments would be to view the verb *ỉnỉ* in its most basic meaning of "to bring"; hence line a,5 might be rendered: "Brought...15Ø sacks." The occurrence of a total of grain measured in sacks at the end of each *ỉnỉ* heading suggests that the focal point of these headings was neither the number of arouras assessed nor the rate applicable, but rather the actual amount of grain expected as revenue by the land-owning institution. The fact that the sums given in the headings fail to tally correctly with the data of the subsequent entries may simply reflect the character of the Louvre Leather Fragments as "informal jottings" of incomplete data.(100)

(8) Texts in Complaint of Excess Tax or Rent

(a) P. Valençay I

One of the most important contemporary documents of immediate relevance to P. Wilbour is the letter known as P. Valençay I.(101) P. Valençay I is an indignant letter of complaint written by the mayor of Elephantine Merōn to the chief taxing-master Menmaʿrenakhte. The occurrence of Menmaʿrenakhte dates the letter no earlier than the reign of Ramesses XI.(102)

The body of the letter begins with Merōn's description of the visit to Elephantine of the scribe Patjēwenteamūn of the House of the (Divine) Adoratress of Amūn, and his demand for 100 sacks of grain (i͗t) allegedly owed by the mayor on a holding (3ḥt) of khato-land in the gezīrah of Ombi. According to Patjēwenteamūn, the grain in contention had been "fixed" (?) or "settled" (?) (tks WB. V 335, 17-18) sometime previously for the House of the (Divine) Adoratress of Amūn.

An understanding of the letter clearly turns upon the interpretation of both the relationship between Merōn and the House of the (Divine) Adoratress and the technical use of the verb tks which establishes the relationship between the two parties. The role of Menmaʿrenakhte in these proceedings is also of crucial importance, since it needs to be ascertained in what capacity he exercised his authority. Presumably, the chief taxing-master not only had prior knowledge concerning the situation at hand, but also had the authority to adjudicate and expedite matters.

Merōn appears to have been the official held responsible for the administration of khato-land of Pharaoh in the gezīrah of Ombi and the payment of that portion of the harvest assessed as owing to the State (Stuchevsky's 30% of the "standard average grain harvest"). Merōn's involvement in these proceedings is consistent with the jurisdiction of mayors of provincial towns over cultivated fields in the surrounding rural areas (ḳʿḥt).(103) Mayors were entrusted with the collection and transportation of tax revenue in grain and other products within the area of their jurisdiction. Thus, Merōn may represent the civil administration of the nome in which khato-land of Pharaoh was located.

Text A of P. Wilbour establishes the fact that mayors were frequently charged with the administration of both khato-land and minĕ-land of Pharaoh. The compound preposition r-ḫt in the headings of these paragraphs denotes a level of responsibility above the cultivation and day-to-day administration of these plots. Only prophets occur as frequently as mayors as the administrators of these lands. In Section III of Text A, the unidentified chief taxing-master occurs twice. He occurs once as the administrator of khato-land (§201) and once as the administrator of minĕ-land (§200) in the company of both mayors and prophets as fellow administrators of these lands.

We know from Text B of P. Wilbour which is concerned exclusively with khato-land that the Royal scribe and steward (of Amūn) Usimaʿrenakhte was the principal administrator of khato-lands of Pharaoh, the extent of the holdings for which he was responsible (r-ḫt) exceeding that of any other administrator several times over. In Text A, the title Steward of Amūn occurs in several domain headings as the administrator (r-ḫt) of various domains of the House of Amun-Rēʿ, King of the Gods (§§52, 117, 152, 208).(104) This official is never identified by name in these headings. Two references to a "steward Usimaʿrenakhte," likely to be the same person, occur in apportioning paragraphs. One reference occurs in a herbage paragraph of the House of Amun-Rēʿ, King of the Gods (A65,11) and the other in a herbage paragraph of the House of Re-Ḥarakhte (A67,23). Both plots are indicated as cultivated "by the hand of" (m-ḏrt) a surrogate cultivator. In one paragraph pertaining to khato-land in Section III (§201), an unidentified chief taxing-master is named as chief administrator (r-ḫt) of plots of khato-land which occur again in B3,24.26 under the charge of (r-ḫt) the Royal scribe and steward Usimaʿrenakhte. Since the data of Text B by and large agree with those of Text A to which Text B is a later addition, it is likely that some khato-lands were simultaneously under the jurisdiction of the same person holding both the office of Royal Scribe and Steward of Amūn and that of Chief Taxing-Master. It is not inconceivable, therefore, that Menmaʿrenakhte inherited the responsibilities of such a predecessor in the office of Chief Taxing-Master as Usimaʿrenakhte, and was therefore responsible for a considerable number of plots of khato-land--including khato-land situated (B3,8) "on fie[lds of the House of the Ador]atress [of the God] in the House of Amūn..." In light of the responsibilities of the chief taxing-master, it is altogether fitting and appropriate that Merōn should appeal to Menmaʿrenakhte for redress of the allegedly false claims of Patjēwenteamūn. Merōn does not explain the role of the House of the (Divine) Adoratress of Amūn in his letter, but it is likely that a situation in which a scribe of a Theban institution undertakes a lengthy and no doubt arduous journey to personally confront a delinquent party concerning revenue alleged to be in arrears, suggests that the House of the (Divine) Adoratress had a vested interest in the revenue to be collected.

The House of the (Divine) Adoratress is not frequently documented during the Ramesside Period.(105) This estate of the principal Theban priestess is much better known from the Late Period, since the Divine Adoratress of the God (God's Wife of Amūn) achieved high political prominence only beginning with the Twenty-first Dynasty and continuing throughout the Late Period. Several officials and employees of the staff of the House of the (Divine) Adoratress, however, are known from the royal tomb-robberies papyri of the Late Ramesside Period.(106) The estate is far less well-known from the Griffith Fragments (col. II, 5) where one of its domains occurs in a paragraph heading belonging to column II. Unfortunately, no entries are enumerated to indicate the variety or extent of the estate's landholdings in these records of the Antaeopolite nome of Upper Egypt. The only occurrence of the House of the (Divine) Adoratress in P. Wilbour is the occurrence in Text B (B3,8). The 60 arouras of khato-land recorded in this line are the only indication we have of the land wealth of this Theban institution. There is no mention of the House of the (Divine) Adoratress in Text A in any role whatsoever.

Gardiner interpreted P. Valençay I as a letter of complaint from an administrator of khato-land addressed to the chief taxing-master as "the highest fiscal authority in the land."(107) He tentatively identified the House of the (Divine) Adoratress of Amūn as an intermediary designated to collect taxes (in grain) owed to the government. Accordingly, he viewed Patjēwenteamūn as a "tax-collector" of sorts, assigned the unenviable task of pursuing delinquent officials in order to secure the revenue for which they were held responsible. Gardiner further suggested that the House of the (Divine) Adoratress may have received a subsidy from the temple of Amun-Rēᶜ in return for the services of an official attached to it on the condition that this official collect the revenue from a specified tax-payer.(108)

The role of intermediary in the collection of tax revenue which Gardiner proposed for the House of the (Divine) Adoratress is unfortunately unparalleled. It is unlikely that we are to equate the activities of the scribe Patjēwenteamūn with those of the scribe of the Necropolis Ḏḥutmosĕ. The activities of Ḏḥutmosĕ in collecting grain revenues from khato-land of Pharaoh may reflect a situation of relative urgency resulting in serious shortages of grain intended for the payment of the workmen's rations. In any case, Ḏḥutmosĕ's activities according to the Turin Taxation Papyrus were undertaken specifically on behalf of the community of Necropolis workmen of which he was an important official. Ḏḥutmosĕ therefore had a self-interest in the successful execution of these proceedings. We do not know enough about the circumstances under which the scribe Penroy operated in P. Louvre 3171 to be able to compare his role with that of Patjēwenteamūn. If it were known to what institution Penroy was attached, we might be able to make some judgment on this point.

The 100 sacks of grain demanded by Patjēwenteamūn of Merōn on khato-land of Pharaoh allegedly in the latter's charge is indicated as having been tks r the House of the (Divine) Adoratress. If Gardiner was correct in viewing Patjēwenteamūn as a "tax-collector," empowered by the chief taxing-master to collect revenue on behalf of the government, the verb tks could be understood as expressing that authority, the grain "fixed" (?) or "settled" (?) for the House of the (Divine) Adoratress to collect on behalf of the government. The sum of 100 sacks may have included such a subsidy as Gardiner conjectured the House of the (Divine) Adoratress may have been allowed for collecting the revenue. It does not seem likely that the scribe of an estate located so far to the north would have embarked upon such a journey without sharing in some way in the fruits of that considerable expenditure of time and effort.

The Coptic verb ⲦⲰⲔⲤ (L.Eg. tks) has a connotation which makes sense in this context. Crum ascribed to the Coptic verb the meaning "to be fixed" or "to be settled" derived from the basic meaning "to pierce," "to penetrate," or "to pain" cited by Černý.(109) Westendorf gives the meanings "stecken," "anheften," and "befestigen" which might justify Gardiner's translation "fixed." (110) Gardiner made passing note of the relevance of the Coptic verb to the Late Egyptian tks, but did not pursue the point. He also noted a text which is relatively close in date to P. Valençay I where the verb tks has a connotation which may be relevant to the context of P. Valençay I. The verb tks occurs in a Twenty-first Dynasty papyrus in the Cairo Museum in a context in which several individuals are "singled out" or "stigmatized" by the god: "The list of the people whom the god stigmatized (tks) as having acted impurely..."(111) With the exception of the negative connotation, the usage of the verb tks in this context is not that far removed from what may have been the intended meaning of the verb in P. Valençay I. The 100 sacks of grain could be said to have been "singled out," "marked," or even "earmarked" for the House of the (Divine) Adoratress to collect. Although there is no indication that the verb tks also pertains to the second item of income (vs. 4-11) of 40 sacks of barley successfully collected by Patjēwenteamūn from Merōn on a holding of khato-land in the region of Edfu, such is likely to have been the case.

It was Gardiner's hypothesis on the basis of P. Valençay I that khato-lands of Pharaoh consisted of fields which remained "unlet" or otherwise uncultivated by an institution and were consequently cultivated by various officials on behalf of the Crown.(112) He also suggested that Merōn's claim that the khato-land in question was not his responsibility, but that of nmḥw who paid gold to the Treasury of Pharaoh, leads to the conclusion that "tenanted land ipso facto ceased to be under the jurisdiction of the controller of Khato-land, and paid its own taxes directly to the Treasury, or to whatever other institution the Treasury might direct." This speculation is not inconsistent with the evidence of Text B of P. Wilbour to the effect that certain plots of khato-land had been "formerly apportioned for" (wnw pš n) such smallholders as occur in the Text A apportioning entries. The condition of Text B with its numerous notations and corrections certainly suggests the fluid legal status of many of the plots located in this area of Middle Egypt. If Gardiner's interpretation of P. Valençay I was correct at least in essence, the fluidity in the status of plots of khato-land would suggest an atmosphere of cooperation and mutual assistance in which the staff of the various institutions collaborated with State officials to maximize productivity and ensure the continuous stability of the agricultural economy. Although the details of the system of administration of such properties differ from those envisaged by Stuchevsky, the end result is essentially the same.

The ascription of the holding of khato-land in the gezīrah of Ombi to "private persons," as Gardiner translates the word nmḥy in P. Valençay I (vs. 2-3), is no doubt the key to the understanding of this letter and its relevance to P. Wilbour. Merōn ascribes the khato-land in question to nmḥw "who pay gold to the Treasury of Pharaoh" (f3 nbw r pr-ḥd n Pr-ˁ3). To understand this statement we must examine some contemporary and near-contemporary occurrences of the term nmḥ.

Closest in date to both P. Valençay I and P. Wilbour is the Will of Naunakhte, a legal document dating to year 3 of Ramesses V which deals with the property of the lady (ʿnḫt n niwt) Naunakhte.(113) Document I is the official transcription of an oral deposition made by the lady Naunakhte in the presence of fourteen witnesses, probably constituting a court. At the beginning of this document, Naunakhte declares herself to be a nmḥ (ir ink, ink nmḥ) of the land of Pharaoh (I,2,1) which, from the context, appears to mean that she was free to dispose of her property as she saw fit. This property probably consisted in part of land, since in 4,10, she refers to the property (swt) of her first husband which is clearly not to be inherited by four of her children from her second marriage to the workman Khaʿemnūn.(114)

As early as the Middle Kingdom, the word nmḥ (WB. II 268, 4.5.6) was used to refer to "freemen" as opposed to "slaves" (b3k), i.e., men of relatively low social status and inferior financial condition who were nevertheless free to own land and cultivate it on their own behalf. The nmḥ was clearly a smallholder of land rather than a great land-owner.(115) The Will of Eueret, an important legal document dating to the late Twenty-third Dynasty concerning property given to an endowment, describes the property as 3ḫ nmḥw nʿ purchased from nmḥw p3 t3.(116) The context suggests that nmḥw were smallholders whose lands were independent of temple lands. In a similar vein is the evidence of the Twenty-second Dynasty Dakhleh Stela which establishes the independent rights of nmḥw over wells in the Oasis (mw-nmḥy) which are juxtaposed with wells of Pharaoh (mw-Pr-ʿ3).(117) From the Saite Period come three demotic land leases which record the sale of khato-land. All three of these documents treat the properties as private property, although nominally situated on temple domain.(118)

In 1909, Griffith asserted that nmḥw in the demotic papyri were best described as "serfs" or "pensioners" as "...these (i.e., the nmḥw) would not have the freehold; they would at least pay dues to the temple or some other over-lord."(119) This view, however, reflects an understanding of nmḥ prior to Spiegelberg's equating of the term nmḥ with the Coptic ⲣⲙϩⲉ in 1917.(120) Spiegelberg defined 3ḫt nmḥw as "Ländereien, die zwar Eigentum der Krone (Staatsland), aber dabei doch in Privatbesitz waren." Such a definition appears to correspond to the ἰδιόκτητος γῆ of Ptolemaic Greek papyri.

It was Gardiner's conjecture that the status of the individuals described as nmḥy in P. Valençay I may have corresponded to that of the smallholders of the P. Wilbour apportioning entries "whose position either was, or else closely resembled, that of private owners."(121) Gardiner's equating of 3ḫt nmḥw with the plots enumerated in the Text A apportioning paragraphs is derived from his interpretation of the terms 3ḫ nmḥw nʿ and 3ḫ št3 tni which are juxtaposed in the Will of Eueret. 3ḫ nmḥw nʿ he translates as "clean (lit. 'smooth') tenanted land" as opposed to 3ḫ št3 tni which he translates as "fields with scrub and tired land." Gardiner's interpretation of these terms led him to equate 3ḫ nmḥw nʿ with k3yt-land and 3ḫ št3 tni with tni-land. Although neither term occurs in Text A of P. Wilbour as a designation of a variety or quality of land, k3yt-land probably underlies the rate 5 mc.

(sacks) per aroura which occurs in the majority of non-apportioning entries of Text A. Tnỉ-land, on the other hand, probably underlies the rate $7\frac{2}{4}$ mc. (sacks) that occurs in some non-apportioning entries. Since much of the land which occurs in Text B is ḳ3yt-land, and since some of this land is indicated as having been "formerly apportioned for" (wnw pš n) various smallholders, Gardiner inferred that the 3ḥt nmḥy of P. Valençay I may have corresponded to the plots of the various smallholders of the Text A apportioning entries.(122)

Baer voiced objection to Gardiner's translation of 3ḥ nmḥw nʿ as "clean (lit. 'smooth') tenanted land" and his identification of 3ḥ nmḥw nʿ with ḳ3yt-land and 3ḥ št3 tnỉ with tnỉ-land such as occur in Text B of P. Wilbour. Instead, he offered the translation "free and clear" for nmḥw nʿ citing the evidence of Thompson and, ironically, that of Gardiner himself marshalled in the latter's several discussions of the subject.(123) Baer's conclusion after reviewing the evidence is that nmḥw nʿ is correctly understood as "privately owned." It should be recognized, however, that the small payments which the smallholders of the apportioning entries were evidently obligated to pay from the harvest of their plots could as easily be termed "rent" as "taxes." The organization of Text A along institutional lines certainly suggests that the former is as valid a definition as the latter. The type of economy operant in Ramesside Egypt, which we have sketched upon the basis of a variety of contemporary and near-contemporary documents, leaves room for nmḥw making payments which could be termed either rent or taxes. Documents of the period suggest, moreover, that such a distinction was simply immaterial. The smallholders of Text A can be identified as nmḥw regardless of whether we choose to label the payments they made as "rent" or "taxes." Regardless of the terminology, they remain "freeholders" or "private persons" cultivating plots to which they did not necessarily have full ownership rights. That they were at least "virtual owners" is certainly indicated by the small quantities of grain they were assessed as well as the right to inherit the land. Stuchevsky avoids the problem altogether by denying the existence of any private property whatsoever and defining nmḥw as "private possessors" of land which ultimately belonged to the State.(124)

According to vs. 2-4 of P. Valençay I, the nmḥw in question paid "gold" (i.e., "gold (in grain)") to the Treasury of Pharaoh.(125) The grammatical construction with the verb swḏ in vs. 3-4 (ỉw.w ʿḥʿ <ḥr> swḏ p3y.f nbw) indicates that the payments were made on a regular basis.(126) Stuchevsky notes that it is the direct payment of their taxes in grain which distinguished the relatively independent nmḥw from the ỉḥwtyw labouring on khato-land who simply delivered their harvest to the State.

The Treasury of Pharaoh occurs only in Text A of P. Wilbour in both apportioning and non-apportioning paragraphs. Lines A46,46-49 are Pōsh B entries occurring in an apportioning paragraph of a domain of the funerary temple of Ramesses V wherein two plots of 9 arouras each are indicated as having been cultivated on behalf of the Treasury of Pharaoh. The corresponding Pōsh A entries belong to two non-apportioning paragraphs (§§196, 197) of the Treasury of Pharaoh. According to Stuchevsky's interpretation of the corresponding Pōsh A and B entries, the funerary temple of Ramesses V cultivated and administered two plots ascribed to the Treasury of Pharaoh and was duly compensated for this "service" in the amount of 7.5% of the expected yield ("standard average grain harvest"). The total number of arouras ascribed to the Treasury of Pharaoh in these two paragraphs is 60 arouras. There is also a white goat paragraph (§192) ascribed to the Treasury of Pharaoh. The 17 plots enumerated in this paragraph account for an additional 83 arouras. The only other reference to the Treasury of Pharaoh in P. Wilbour is in an apportioning entry of the funerary temple of Ramesses V (A47,3) in which the smallholder is identified as a treasury-scribe of the Treasury of Pharaoh.

The Treasury of Pharaoh is much better known from the Miscellanies where the context is that of the administration of khato-land. P. Sallier I 4,5-5,4 (pp. 80-82, LEM) is a model letter written by the scribe Pentwēre to his superior, the chief of the record-keepers of the Treasury of Pharaoh, Amenemōnĕ. The letter in part concerns the šmw (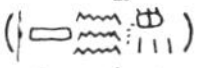) of khato-land of Pharaoh and the administration of this property, but contributes little or nothing by way of new understanding. The Treasury of Pharaoh is also encountered further on in P. Sallier I in lines 9,1-9,9 (pp. 87-88, LEM) which comprise what appears to be another model letter between the same two correspondents. This letter concerns the apparent misappropriation of 30 arouras of land intended to provide fodder for the horse-team of Pharaoh under the administration of the stablemaster Amenemuia of the Great Stable of Ramesses-meriamūn of the Residence by the steward Nodjme of the funerary temple of Ramesses II.

It is learned from the latter of these two letters that the authority of the chief of the record-keepers of the Treasury of Pharaoh extended to such varied properties as khato-land, minĕ-land, šmw-land, and rmnyt-land, and affected the smallholders of at least two institutions, the Great Stable of Ramesses-meriamūn of the Residence and the funerary temple of Ramesses II. Only the latter of the two institutions occurs in P. Wilbour in the headings of both non-apportioning and apportioning paragraphs. The role of the stablemaster brings to mind the stablemasters of the "3ḥt n ḥtrỉ" entries of the Text A apportioning paragraphs which record various plots of land set aside to provide food for the horse-teams (of Pharaoh) along with the names of the individual stablemasters responsible for them.

The discussion in P. Sallier I 9,1-9,9 seems to revolve around the allotment of State land to individual smallholders. The 30 arouras of field apparently incorrectly allocated to the steward Nodjme may have been Crown-land which was previously "unlet," i.e., "untenanted" for which a new tenant (the stablemaster Amenemuia) was presently available, following Gardiner's interpretation of Crown-land based upon P. Valençay I. The letter ends with the instructions to Pentwēre to demarcate for Amenemuia what appear to have been additional fields from the various categories of Crown-land "so long as they are (presently) untended (?) (ỉw.w nḥ3)."(127) The use of nḥ3 (WB. II, 290) here is unique and may convey the idea that the land was "wild" in the sense of being uncultivated as Caminos' translation "untended" implies. If such was the case, there were evidently some lands among those administered by State officials which were in need of a cultivator's attention. The negative connotation of the word nḥ3 in all of its usages ("wild," "schrecklich," "gefährlich") suggests that the fields were in poor condition, whether because they had never been cultivated, or had too long remained fallow or dry from lack of irrigation, we cannot say. Following Stuchevsky's interpretation of Crown-land (including khato-land) as a type of State land either cultivated collectively by ỉḥwtyw under the direction of a temple or other institution, or by such smallholders as occur in the P. Wilbour apportioning paragraphs ("private possessors"), the plot of 30 arouras may have been in the process of reassignment from one system of exploitation to the other. The connotation of the word nḥ3 becomes very important in this regard. The word seems to imply that some of the so-called Royal lands were either uncultivated or undercultivated. If so, the system of land exploitation envisioned by Stuchevsky as operant during the Ramesside Period did not always maximize the productivity of the cultivable land available.

P. Valençay I ends with Merōn's explanation of "the matter of another (vs. 5) holding in the region of Edfu which had not been flooded (irrigated) (tḫb)."(128) Only 4 arouras of this land apparently received irrigation and were subsequently cultivated by one man and one yoke of oxen. Merōn claims that 40 sacks of barley apparently representing the total yield of the plot was handed over to Patjēwenteamūn. A yield of 40 sacks from a plot of 4 arouras implies a productivity rate of 10 sacks per aroura--the rate of expected yield of nḫb-land in both the non-apportioning paragraphs of Text A and Text B of P. Wilbour according to Stuchevsky. The land in the area of Edfu for which Merōn was responsible, therefore, may have been nḫb-land, the expected yield of which was 10 sacks per aroura. If the rate of 10 sacks per aroura also applies to the land in the gezīrah of Ombi concerning which Merōn denies responsibility, the amount of land which might be expected to produce 100 sacks could have been 10 arouras or even less if the actual yield exceeded the expected yield of 10 sacks per aroura. We would expect the plot in Ombi to have been no larger than 20 arouras assuming it was ḳ3yt-land with an expected yield of 5 sacks per aroura. Since the yield of 5 sacks per aroura was the most common of the three rates occurring in the P. Wilbour non-apportioning paragraphs and is the only rate applicable to khato-land in Text A, a minimum yield of 5 sacks per aroura is to be expected--unless unusual circumstances prevailed. The size of the plot in the gezīrah of Ombi is thus likely to have been no greater than 20 arouras. Another clue to the size of the plot in Ombi is Merōn's description of the 4 aroura plot in the region of Edfu as  nkt (WB. II, 347, 10). This depreciatory use of nkt implies that 4 arouras was considered a small area of land. The likelihood of this is supported by evidence of the plots of khato-land in the non-apportioning paragraphs of P. Wilbour. There, the mean size of plot is 16.8 arouras. The modal size of plot (most frequently occurring) is 10 arouras with frequencies of 18 of the 57 plots or 31.6%.

The land which Merōn admits to having had cultivated in the region of Edfu warrants a consideration of the geographical extent of khato-lands administered by mayors in the Ramesside Period. That a mayor of Elephantine should have been responsible for fields as far distant as Edfu is not at all surprising in light of P. Wilbour where several mayors occur as senior administrators of khato-land.

Khato-land paragraphs in Text A are found only in Sections I, II, and III, since Section IV breaks off in a harem paragraph in the course of which the text has been erased. In Section I, both khato-land and minĕ-land enumerated under the administration of the mayors of Mi-wēr (§§42, 45) and Southern She (§§43, 46) were situated in measurement areas consistent with the location of both towns in zone 1. In the case of Section III, khato-land enumerated under the administration of the mayor of Spermeru (§202), a town tentatively situated near the northern extremity of zone 3 near the Baḥr Yūsuf, was mostly situated in measurement areas limited to zone 3 with some fields situated in Sōshen, a measurement area common to both zones 2 and 3. In the case of khato-land enumerated in Section II under the administration of the mayor of Ḥardai (Cynopolis) (§115), a town situated at the border between zones 3 and 4, the measurement areas of plot location are limited to zone 2. Thus, although there is some tendency for khato-land to have been situated within the same geographical zone in which the administrative seat of the mayor was located, or in a zone contiguous to that zone, there is evidence that khato-land was sometimes situated some distance from the administrative seat of the mayor responsible for the land.

In the case of Text B, it is difficult to generalize about the geographic location of plots of khato-land vis-à-vis the seat of administration of the same, since many measurement areas occur only in Text B and are virtually, if not entirely, unknown. The khato-land administered by the mayor of Spermeru, was located in measurement areas common to both Sections II and III, as well as in measurement areas known only from Text B. In view of the location of Spermeru in the proximity of the border between zones 2 and 3, it is not surprising that khato-land under the administration of Spermeru's mayor would have been located in both zones without these holdings necessarily having been very far distant from each other or from Spermeru itself.

The occurrence of the Village of Neḥseroy (?) in Text B as a location of khato-land administered under the authority of the mayor of Spermeru in §15 (B17,1?) and the mayor of Mi-wēr in §12 (B15,19) certainly complicates matters. Unless these locations are homonyms, it would appear that the mayors of two towns relatively distant from each other both administered khato-land in the same location. Moreover, the third occurrence of the Village of Neḥseroy in Text B (B14,12) is in a paragraph (§10) enumerating khato-land under the authority of the overseer of fields of the Southern Province. Thus, three administrators of khato-land appear to have governed the administration of separate fields of khato-land in very close proximity to each other.

As regards the khato-land under the administration of the mayor of Ḥarsperu (Ḥardai) in Text B (§16), a relatively large geographical area appears indicated. Khato-land administered by this mayor was situated in measurement areas common to both zones 3 and 4 of Text A as would accord with the location of Ḥarsperu (Ḥardai) at the border between zones 3 and 4. Khato-land was also located in Mi-ēḥu, a measurement area which occurs in Text A only in association with zone 2. Additional plots of khato-land were located in Iy-idḥu, a measurement area which occurs in both zones 2 and 3 of Text A, and thus may have been located at or near the border between these two zones. Thus, it seems that the authority and responsibility of the mayor of Ḥarsperu (Ḥardai) may have included khato-land at some distance from his administrative seat.

Since P. Wilbour is concerned only with fields located within a limited stretch of the Nile Valley in Middle Egypt, we have no way of knowing whether the mayors who occur as administrators of khato-land in P. Wilbour administered landholdings beyond the limits of this geographic area. The possibility that some or all of these mayors may have been responsible for properties at a greater distance from their respective administrative seats therefore cannot be precluded. It remains a very real possibility that khato-land in the area of Edfu was administered by the mayor of Elephantine. The attribution to Merōn of the administration of fields in Ombi is even less difficult to imagine, Kōm Ombo being less than half the distance from Elephantine to Edfu.

(b) P. Bologna 1094, 5,8-7,1

P. Bologna 1094, 5,8-7,1 is one of the model letters of the Miscellanies (pp. 5-6, LEM) which voices a complaint against what may be interpreted as excessive taxation. In this letter, a prophet of the House of Seth at Punodjem, Praʿemḥab writes to the steward Sety concerning what he considered to be "excessive money" (p3 ḥd ʿš3t) levied on both the khato-land of Pharaoh under his administration and the landholdings belonging to his own temple, the House of Seth. He bemoans the injustice of the situation, telling his correspondent in no uncertain terms that "it is not my due tax (ḥtr) at all." The demand for these revenues was made by a retainer (šmsw) whose role appears to have been that of go-between with apparently no decision-making authority. Praʿemḥab requests his correspondent to report (smi) the situation to the vizier who as Chief Justice would have had the authority to adjudicate the matter. At the end of the letter, he refers to the alleged injustice as "the excessive ṯs (literally 'appointment') placed upon me." The term ṯs here is evidently an abbreviation for ṯs prt "sowing order" encountered above in P. Bologna 1086, 20-28 as consisting of 700 sacks ascribed to three men and a youth.

The vizier is very seldom mentioned in contemporary literature in a context which illuminates this model letter. Neferronpě, who was vizier over the reigns of Ramesses IV, Ramesses V, and Ramesses VI, occurs in Text A of P. Wilbour in two Pōsh C entries (A76,13 and 90,13) which place him in the same category as the deities whose sanctuaries were granted aroura measured plots. The produce of these plots was evidently intended for their use.(129) The same applies to the Pōsh C entry (A36,41) in which an unidentified dispatch-writer of Pharaoh is named as recipient.

Whether we understand these entries as signifying that a plot was apportioned for a sanctuary or a high-ranking official (Gardiner), or merely the grain anticipated as harvest from such a plot cultivated by a smallholder (Stuchevsky), these entries clearly represent unusual circumstances. The vizier Neferronpě also occurs in Text A in an apportioning entry (A92,27) which describes the plot as cultivated "by the hand of" (m-drt) a iḥwty. The apportionees of other such entries include such high-ranking officials as the high priest of Heliopolis, the high priest of Amūn, the steward of Amūn, the overseer of the Treasury, and the chief of thr-warriors.

There is one other vizier whose name occurs in P. Wilbour. The name of Raʿḥotpe, the well-known vizier of Ramesses II, occurs in the title of a foundation called "The Foundation (m3wd) of the Vizier Raʿḥotpe, who is dead" (§10), the remains of which were found at Sedment just northwest of Heracleopolis.(130) The occurrence of this non-apportioning paragraph in P. Wilbour is additional evidence of the exalted status of holders of the office of vizier during the Ramesside Period. The minimum of 140 arouras of field attributed to this foundation in §10 is comparable to the holdings of many of the smaller institutions enumerated in the non-apportioning paragraphs of Text A. The poor state of preservation of P. Wilbour at the beginning of Text A unfortunately precludes an exact computation of the number of arouras enumerated for this institution. This figure of 140 arouras could possibly be very much underestimated, if there was an entry in one of the missing lines on the order of A9,20 where a single holding of 60 arouras is recorded.

While the foregoing data from P. Wilbour are indicative of the significantly high status and prestige of the vizier in Ramesside times, they give no indication whatsoever of any role for him in the collection, registration, or disposition of grain revenues. It is striking, moreover, that the vizier does not occur in connection with either khato-land or minĕ-land. Nor does he occur in connection with the supervision of domains of any of the various temples and secular institutions. Fortunately, there are three letters in the collection of Late Ramesside Letters which serve to augment the information derived from P. Bologna 1094, 5,8-7,1.

In P. Bibliothèque Nationale 198, III (No. 47 LRL), an unidentified vizier occurs in connection with grain provisions intended for the workmen of the Theban Necropolis. In this context, the vizier was undoubtedly acting in his capacity as the chief administrator of the Royal Necropolis and superior of the scribes of the Necropolis. It is known from the Turin Strike Papyrus, which dates to years 29 and 30 (?) of Ramesses III, that the vizier To was involved in the difficulties resulting from the strikes of the Necropolis workmen. We also learn that he intervened eventually to put an end to the disturbances which had arisen in part because of ineptitude on the part of various officials in providing the required rations.(131)

Both P. Bibliothèque Nationale 199, III (No. 48 LRL) and P. Geneva D 191 (No. 37 LRL) provide some detail concerning the role of the vizier in the collection of grain revenue. P. Bibliothèque

Nationale 199, III, a letter where both author and addressee are unknown, concerns the registration (sp̲ẖr) of both the grain and the ḥmy (?) with which the vizier was directly involved.(132) Some damage (bt3) had evidently occurred to the grain to which the author refers. The remainder appears to have been set aside or stored (?) (w3ḥ). The author indicates that a report shall be made to the vizier concerning this matter. This is the only contemporary reference which suggests a role for the vizier in the registration of grain. It should, of course, be viewed in the context of the vizier's role as the chief administrator of the Theban Necropolis. In P. Geneva D 191 (No. 37 LRL), a letter dating to year 2 of the Wḥm Mswt, the chantress of Amūn Ḥenttowĕ writes to the scribe of the Necropolis Nesamenopĕ (her husband) concerning oipĕ-measures for weighing grain at the granary (of the House of Amūn). The vizier was evidently involved in the weighing of the grain as he is said to have dispatched a "measurer" (ḫ3y) with an oipĕ-measure larger by one hin than that of the granary of the House of Amūn.

The key to the understanding of these passages perhaps may be found in a consideration of the inscriptions from the tomb of Rekhmirēˁ, the vizier of Upper Egypt under Tuthmosis III. This valuable treatise concerning the duties of the vizier, which is well-preserved in Rekhmirēˁ's tomb at Thebes, evidently had its origins in the late Middle Kingdom. Nevertheless, much of the content of these inscriptions appears to have been valid to a considerable degree in the early New Kingdom as well.(133)

The inscriptions from the tomb-chapel indicate that the primary function of the vizierate was to govern Egypt and direct her internal affairs in accordance with the wishes of the king with whom the vizier met daily. The vizier coordinated the various departments of the central government, acting as "the coordinator and mainspring of the pharaoh's government" in the words of Hayes.(134) The vizier was responsible for the appointment of numerous government officials including judges and priests; presided over the Great Court (k̲nbt) in the capacity of Chief Justice; made judgments in important civil law cases referred to him by local courts; saw to the construction and maintenance of canals and public buildings; and attended to the conservation of monuments. He also presided over the General Staff of the Army, levying and inspecting troops; received foreign tribute for government use; maintained government archives; and communicated to the king all matters of importance to the well-being and economic stability of the Egyptian State. Although tax revenues in gold, silver, cattle, and textiles seem to have been handled directly by the vizier, as in the late Middle Kingdom, payments in grain were collected by mayors aided by functionaries of the central bureau of granaries. Since the vizier met daily with the overseer of the Treasury, he was kept informed to the last minute of financial matters great and small of importance to the efficient administration of the Egyptian State.(135)

During the Nineteenth Dynasty, the vizierate was usually vested in the person of a single official, breaking the earlier tradition of a dual vizierate established in the Eighteenth Dynasty and continued into the early Nineteenth Dynasty. The role of the vizier in the adjudication of disputes concerning landholdings is exemplified in the Inscription of Mose which describes at some length the proceedings of a court case during the reign of Ramesses II concerning ownership rights to a parcel of land near Memphis. The presiding vizier studied the case, heard testimony, and made a judgment. The rights to property were thus determined in the last resort by the vizier. In view of the evidence of the Inscription of Mose, it is not surprising to find the prophet of the House of Seth in P. Bologna 1094, 5,8-7,1 appealing to the vizier for the redress of injustices real or imaginary.

P. Bologna 1094, 5,8-7,1 provides additional data the feasibility of which may be tested against data of both Text A and Text B of P. Wilbour. The prophet Praʿemḥab describes himself as both a prophet of the House of Seth (of Punodjem) and an administrator of the House of Nephthys perhaps also situated at the otherwise unknown locality of Punodjem. The letter indicates that Praʿemḥab's responsibilities also included the administration of khato-land of Pharaoh.

Three temples of Seth occur in Text A of P. Wilbour: the House of Seth, Lord of Spermeru (§92); the House of Seth, Lord of Pi-Wayna (§99); and the House of Seth, Lord of Wealth and Might (§167). The last of these institutions is to be identified with the House of Seth, Powerful-is-His-Mighty-Arm (A45,11) and appears to have been a shrine or chapel within the domain of the House of Seth, Lord of Spermeru. In the case of the House of Seth, Lord of Spermeru, there was evidently a small dependency called the "House of Nephthys of Ramesses-meriamūn (in the House of Seth)" (§§94, 168). In Section I §28, there is another occurrence of a "House of Nephthys of Ramesses-meriamūn which is in the House of Seth" which may possibly be the very same institution as occurs in §§94 and 168, although the position of the paragraph of the House of Nephthys in Section I seems to indicate that it pertains to a different House of Seth from that located at Spermeru in Section II (§92).

Gardiner suggested that §28 and subsequent §29 pertaining to the "Sunshade of Re-Ḥarakhte which is in this House" refer to Su, a town which occurs in P. Harris I, 61b,15 in a position just preceding Amūn-in-the-Backland. There, Seth may have had Nephthys as his consort. Since §30 in Text A pertains to the House of Amūn, Lord of Thrones of the Two Lands in the Backland, this identification has an element of credibility. Gardiner readily admitted that the very existence of a Nephthys of Su is only conjectural, and further, that it would be quite a coincidence to encounter two separate chapels of Nephthys both established by Ramesses II and both followed in P. Wilbour by sunshades of Re-Ḥarakhte (§29 and §169). Nevertheless, he favoured the Su hypothesis because of the near certain reading of the name "Su" in the Text A measurement line A16,39 (§29) and the reference in Text B (§52) to a prophet of the House of Seth, Lord of Su who was an administrator of khato-land of Pharaoh.(136)

Prophets of both the House of Seth, Lord of Spermeru (Ḥuy in §205) and the House of Nephthys of Ramesses-meriamūn (Merybarsĕ in §§116 and 206) occur as administrators of khato-land of Pharaoh in Text A of P. Wilbour. In Text B §30, a prophet Penpmer of the

House of Nephthys occurs as an administrator of khato-land of Pharaoh described as situated "(on) fields of this House"; whereas in Text B §23, the prophet Ḥuy of the House of Seth, Lord of Spermeru occurs once again in charge of khato-land of Pharaoh also described as situated "(on) fields of this House." What cannot be established from the evidence of P. Wilbour is the authority of any particular prophet of the House of Seth over the House of Nephthys, since the Text A paragraphs devoted to the House of Nephthys do not specify the chief administrative officer. In Text A §92, the prophet Ḥuy is identified as the chief administrator of the House of Seth, Lord of Spermeru. He is undoubtedly the same individual who occurs in both Text A (§205) and Text B (§23) as an administrator of khato-land of Pharaoh. It is possible that Ḥuy was the very administrator whose name is deleted in §§94 and 168 pertaining to the House of Nephthys, such deletions of the names of chief administrators of smaller temples being the rule in Text A. Although Ḥuy may have been the chief administrator of the House of Nephthys as well as his own temple, he was most certainly not in charge of the administration of the khato-land of Pharaoh situated (on) fields of the House of Nephthys, such fields being the responsibility of two prophets of Nephthys, Merybarsě in Text A and Penpmer in Text B. This information does not actually contradict the evidence of P. Bologna 1094, 5,8-7,1, however, since the prophet Praʿemḥab never identifies the khato-land for which he was responsible as having anything to do with the House of Nephthys. It could just as well have been khato-land situated on fields of the House of Seth to which he was referring.

An interesting question to arise out of the P. Wilbour data in reference to these two temples is why two prophets of the House of Nephthys were required to administer khato-land of Pharaoh situated presumably on fields of the House of Nephthys, while only one prophet (Ḥuy) was required for the administration of the more extensive holdings of khato-land of Pharaoh situated on fields of the House of Seth. Since the prophet Ḥuy of the House of Seth, Lord of Spermeru was in charge of khato-land of Pharaoh in both Text A and Text B, and since the landholdings of the House of Seth, Lord of Spermeru appear to have been far more extensive than those of the House of Nephthys, it is possible that the occurrence of the prophet of Nephthys, Penpmer in Text B reflects either the death of Merybarsě or his replacement by a new administrator. This conclusion certainly appears well-justified, since it can be established without question that Text B postdates Text A.

(9) Texts Relating to the Acquisition and Allocation of Landholdings

(a) The Inscription of Mose

The Inscription of Mose, a Memphite tomb-chapel inscription from the reign of Ramesses II, is the colourful story of the litigation concerning a land grant awarded to the ship-master (i͗my-r ʿḥʿw) Neshi by ʿAḥmose I following the war against the Hyksos.(137) The inscription provides much valuable insight into the way in which land grants to private smallholders were handed down over the course of the Eighteenth and Nineteenth Dynasties. It is certain proof that landed property awarded to individuals for unusual bravery, loyalty, outstanding service, etc., to king and country continued to be honoured for many generations, and that disputes concerning the administration of such properties were routinely appealed to the Great Court (ḳnbt) under the aegis of the vizier himself as Chief Justice. Although the actual size of plot has not been preserved, it is evident from line N19 that the plot was no less than 13 arouras in size. The Memphite estate was handed down from generation to generation apparently without dispute until the reign of Ḥaremḥab when three rival branches of the family each claimed sole rights of trusteeship over the course of five lawsuits heard in the Great Court and presided over by the vizier. Although the text is incomplete, it appears that the case was finally resolved in favour of the plaintiff Mose, in the reign of Ramesses II. Scenes of jubilation in the tomb-chapel at Saḳḳara, together with the very prominence of the inscription, leave no doubt as to the outcome of the proceedings.

Several interesting points emerge from the narrative. First, the descent of trusteeship over four generations to the defendant Khay suggests that it may have been customary in the New Kingdom to administer estates by means of an hereditary trusteeship on behalf of the co-heirs.(138) This trusteeship was apparently subject to review, however, and could be transferred to another heir upon appeal to the Great Court. In this manner, the lady Wernero appealed and won the first and third lawsuits. Second, the division of an estate among the co-heirs may have been an unusual procedure, since the outcome of the second lawsuit in which the lady Takharu obtained the division of the property among the six co-heirs in the reign of Ḥaremḥab was hotly contested by the father of Mose in a subsequent court battle.(139) Third, some title-deeds and related documents were kept at the capital of Pi-Ramesses in the Delta where offices of the Treasury of Pharaoh and the Granary of Pharaoh were both located.(140) The records of both of the offices were apparently quite separate and independent, in addition to being probably of more or less equal weight in such litigation. Moreover, as the text reveals, these records were not altogether inviolable. It was possible to falsify documents by bribing the officials in charge as did Khay in order to win the fourth lawsuit in year 18 of Ramesses II.

The involvement of the Treasury of Pharaoh in these proceedings could be interpreted as support for the interpretation of the 3ḥt nmḥy of P. Valençay I as private landholdings in light of the clear attestation by Meron that the nmḥw regularly made their payments (ỉw.w ʿḥʿ <ḥr> swḏ p3y.f nbw) directly to the Treasury of Pharaoh. In the case of the disputed estate in the Inscription of Mose, however, payment to both the Treasury of Pharaoh and the Granary of Pharaoh is implied rather than actually stated. Use of what appear to have been two independent land registers as documentary proof of legal claim to trusteeship, together with testimony by Mose's witnesses to his father's regular cultivation of the property, implies that both government offices regularly exacted payments from private smallholders which could be described as tax or rent owing to the State. Such certainly was the opinion of Gardiner who maintained that land granted by royal gift as a reward for meritorious service was definitely not tax exempt in either grain due to the office of the Granary of Pharaoh or in other products due to the Treasury of Pharaoh. (141)

(b) P. British Museum 10412

P. British Museum 10412 (No. 36 LRL), a letter from the scribe of the Necropolis Nesamenopĕ to the chantress of Amūn Mutenopĕ, concerns the application for and allocation of agricultural land. The scribe Nesamenopĕ writes to say that Essobek, deputy (ỉdnw) of the Temple of Medīnet Habu, had written to the prophet of Mont, Lord of Armant to say that he desires a field of one aroura in Peniufneri (AEO I, 12*) next to the house of the god's father of Mont Ahauaa so that fruit (dḳrw) might be cultivated (ỉrỉ). (142) The prophet of Mont agrees to give the land and asks that someone be sent to receive it. Nesamenopĕ tells Mutenopĕ to send an agent to the prophet of Mont to receive the land, presumably on behalf of the deputy Essobek, and to give 10 hin of fruit so that fruit might be grown there. The details of the transaction are not provided, however, such that it is not at all certain whether the transaction was a matter of simple purchase, interinstitutional exchange, or outright gift.

The size of the plot is extremely small, more reminiscent of the plots enumerated in the Louvre Leather Fragments than the assessed aroura measured plots recorded in the Text A apportioning paragraphs of P. Wilbour. In P. Wilbour, four plots of one aroura occur as the smallest size of aroura measured plots of Variety I. There is a stronger correspondence between the two texts, however, in the fact that at least six deputies occur as smallholders in P. Wilbour, all unfortunately without institutional affiliation. The plots allocated to these deputies are both aroura and land-cubit measured. They range in size from 50 land-cubits (A16,19 [.10.]40) to 20⌟5 arouras (A28,4). The plots come under the headings of a great variety of religious institutions including the royal funerary establishments of Ramesses II, Ramesses III, and Ramesses V. In the case of A68,38, a deputy occurs as the cultivator of a 5 aroura plot apportioned for the steward Usimaʿrenakhte. It is possible, however, that Essobek's plot is comparable to the land-cubit measured plots which may have been planted with crops of fruits and vegetables as well as flax, as is suggested by several of the apportioning entries analyzed by means of variable 17 Special Entry.

The location of the newly allocated plot of the deputy Essobek next to a plot of a god's father (ỉt-nṯr) has a parallel in Text A of P. Wilbour. The plots of both the god's father Pbēs (A87,23) and the god's father Nakhtḥikhopshef (A87,24) are modest in size (.2.98 land-cubits), situated in the immediate vicinity of two equal size land-cubit measured plots (1.99 and .100 wsf) cultivated by a deputy (A87,6-7). Immediately following these plots is a significantly larger plot in a Pōsh B entry (A87,8-9) cultivated under the authority of (r-ḥt) the same deputy on behalf of the funerary temple of Ramesses V. Thus, the situation described in P. British Museum 10412 is quite feasible in light of data of P. Wilbour.

(c) P. Berlin 3047

P. Berlin 3047, a valuable but unfortunately poorly preserved legal document dating to year 46 of Ramesses II, is the record of a lawsuit concerning a disputed share in a parcel of agricultural land.(143) The plaintiff, the scribe of the Royal Offering Table Neferʿabĕ, claimed a share in an estate administered by the chief of the Storehouse of the House of Amūn, Niay as trustee of the unidentified co-heirs. The court, which included the prophet Wenennefer of the House of Mūt, heard the case and decided in favour of the plaintiff, requiring Niay to recognize the claim of Neferʿabĕ. It was further decided that Neferʿabĕ should hand over (swḏ, possibly with the connotation "to lease") the property to which he was entitled to the prophet Wenennefer, possibly as part of an earlier agreement between the two parties as Baer has suggested.(144) The inventory of the property follows as well as the terms of the agreement decided upon by both parties.

There are numerous points of interest which this text shares with the apportioning paragraphs of Text A of P. Wilbour. In deciding that the property should be handed over to the prophet Wenennefer, the court may have been giving official approval to a contract between a land-owner (lessor) and a tenant (lessee) with the terms of the lease actually stipulated in the body of the court decision. The agreement may reflect contemporary custom in which private individuals entered into term contracts with lessees just as institutions entered into such contracts with lessees (smallholders) according to the evidence of the Text A apportioning paragraphs. In the apportioning paragraphs, contracts between and among the smallholders themselves are suggested by those entries in which one party cultivates the plot on behalf of another party, the preposition m-ḏrt introducing the name of the "surrogate cultivator" who may have been a sub-lessee. In Text A, there are 94 instances in which a plot is apportioned for one party and indicated as having been "(cultivated) by the hand of" a second party. In 28 of these instances, the plot is recorded as cultivated "by the hand of his(her) children (m-ḏrt msw.f(s))." The situation may have been one in which responsibility for the cultivation of a plot, as well as financial liability, devolved upon the children of a smallholder as the heirs to the property. In the case of 20 of the 28 cases, the smallholder is indicated as being deceased (nty mt). In these cases, it is possible that the smallholder had died within the year to which the document dates, the event of his death and subsequent transfer of the rights and responsibilities with respect to the property explaining the enumeration of the plot in P. Wilbour.

In another 9 of the 94 cases, a plot is described as cultivated "by his hand (m-ḏrt.f)" with the probable nuance "by his (own) hand." These entries may be instances of the revocation of a prior agreement between the apportionee and his surrogate cultivator and the return of full responsibility for the actual cultivation of the plot to the apportionee. In the case of A23,4: "The First Prophet, (cultivated) by his hand...," Gardiner was quite possibly correct in supposing that the antecedent is the servant Nesamūn of A23,2. It is unlikely that such a high status individual as the First Prophet of Amūn would have cultivated the plot with his own hand. It is not so obvious, however, that we should "take our cue from this case, however difficult some of the examples quoted (e.g. 28,29) may appear" as Gardiner suggested.(145) Only in one other case (A45,12), where the apportionee is identified as His Majesty's charioteer, is the individual of sufficiently high status to suggest that the suffix f in m-ḏrt.f refers to the previous smallholder as antecedent. As for the two cases where the name of a woman smallholder is followed by the phrase m-ḏrt.f rather than the expected m-ḏrt.s (A65,27; 86,38), it is possible that the suffix f is a simple error on the part of a scribe accustomed to writing the masculine suffix. Menu, however, holds that the suffix refers back to a male smallholder as antecedent.(146) Menu interprets the masculine suffix of the two cases (A32,5; 35,33), where the name of a female apportionee is followed by the phrase ḥnʿ snw.f "together with his brothers (or brethren)," as referring to the woman's uncles (brothers of her deceased father).

Those entries in the Text A apportioning paragraphs where the name of a smallholder is followed by the phrase (ḥr) tp.f "on his (own) behalf" appear to refer to the smallholder's cultivation of a plot for his own personal benefit. Whereas two of these entries (A17,21; 86,20) follow entries where the same smallholder is identified as the agent or surrogate cultivator of another individual's plot (the preposition m-ḏrt), the other two entries (A56,4; 86,47) follow Pōsh B entries. The prepositional phrase (ḥr) tp.f is not to be confused with the prepositional phrase m-ḏrt.f. In the case of (ḥr) tp.f, the emphasis is on the identification of a particular plot as the holding--the personal holding--of a particular smallholder who also cultivates a plot on behalf of another party. In the case of m-ḏrt.f, the emphasis is upon the status of a particular smallholder as his own agent, probably in the event of the abrogation or revocation of a prior agreement in which some other individual cultivated his plot.

In the remaining cases of delegated responsibilities, fifteen apportionees are charioteers, while twelve are scribes. Among the apportionees are also persons of relatively high professional rank including the high priest of Heliopolis, the high priest of Amūn, the steward of Amūn, the overseer of the Treasury, and the chief of thr-warriors. Of these individuals, only the chief of thr-warriors occurs after the preposition m-ḏrt as the cultivator of a plot apportioned for another party identified as a scribe of the Granary. In most cases, the surrogate cultivators are iḥwtyw, but Sherden occur in seven cases and scribes in five cases. There are no instances in the P. Wilbour apportioning entries, however, where a prophet of any temple occurs after the preposition m-ḏrt. The evidence of P. Wilbour is therefore unfortunately inconclusive as a check upon the verisimilitude of the evidence of P. Berlin 3047.

It would appear that the contested property in the case of P. Berlin 3047 was administered by a single member of the family as trustee (rwḏw) on behalf of the co-heirs as was also the case with the estate of Neshi in the Inscription of Mose. In lines 7-8 of P. Berlin 3047, it is learned that the scribe of the Royal Offering Table Nefer'abě sued Niay, the chief of the Storehouse of Amūn as the trustee of his brothers in an attempt to establish his claim to the property by right of inheritance. He claims that he inherited "...arouras of field together with (his) brothers." This phrase immediately brings to mind the occasional mention in the P. Wilbour apportioning paragraphs of plots described as having been "(cultivated) together with his(her) brothers (ḥnʿ snw.f(s))" of which there are only 31 cases. The majority of the plots are 5 or 10 arouras in size. Whereas nearly two-thirds of the plots are Variety I plots, one-third of the plots are Sub-variety IA plots. In light of the fact that Sub-variety IA entries probably denote plots which were substantively different from plots of Variety I in one or more respects, the relatively high frequency of Sub-variety IA entries suggests that the qualification ḥnʿ snw.f(s) had legal standing. Only one plot (A97,23) is indisputably land-cubit measured (Variety II "10.40"). Twelve of the smallholders are priests, seven are women smallholders, and four are retainers. The remaining apportionees are of such varied occupations as Medjay, herdsman, and stablemaster. The evidence of P. Wilbour suggests that plots available for cultivation by smallholders as private parties were seldom cultivated jointly by two or more heads of households. The "brothers" referred to in these relatively unusual entries probably included younger brothers who had not yet married and started families of their own as well as younger cousins in the same situation.

NOTES

1Gardiner, RAD, pp. xiii-xiv, 35-44; idem, "Ramesside Texts Relating to the Taxation and Transport of Corn," JEA 27 (1941), pp. 22-37; W. Pleyte and F. Rossi, Papyrus de Turin, 2 vols. (Leiden, 1869-76), p. 1 = pl. 65,c; p. 2 = pl. 100; p. 3 = pl. 155 (in part 101); p. 4 = pl. 156; p. 5 = pl. 157 (in part 97); vs. p. 1 = pl. 96. See too Wilhelm Spiegelberg, Rechnungen aus der Zeit Setis I (Strassburg, 1896), p. 34.

2Gardiner's restoration of rt. 1,3-1,5 in the Turin Taxation Papyrus, JEA 27, p. 23.

3I.A. Stuchevsky abstracted by Jac. J. Janssen in "Agrarian Administration in Egypt During the Twentieth Dynasty," review and summary of I.A. Stuchevsky, Zemledel'tsy gosudarstvennogo khozyaistva drevnego Egipta epokhi Ramessidov (The Cultivators of the State Economy in Ancient Egypt During the Ramesside Period) (Moscow, 1982) forthcoming in BiOr.

4Gardiner, Commentary, p. 6.

5Ibid., pp. 169-70, Nos. 4, 16, and 21. These references are too complex to cite merely the Text B entry. Nos. 16 and 21 are considered doubtful.

[6] Edward F. Wente, "The Suppression of the High Priest Amenhotep," JNES 25 (1966), pp. 73-87, figs. 1-3.

[7] Černý, CAH vol. II, pt. 2, p. 628.

[8] Černý, LRL; see too below n. 16.

[9] Gardiner, JEA 27, p. 26. So too Jaroslav Černý, A Community of Workmen at Thebes in the Ramesside Period, Institut français d'archéologie orientale du Caire [Bibliothèque d'étude 50] (Cairo, 1973), p. 214.

[10] T. Eric Peet, The Great Tomb-robberies of the Twentieth Egyptian Dynasty, 2 vols. (Oxford, 1930).

[11] As Černý remarked, P. Bibliothèque Nationale 199, II (No. 33 LRL) is not really a letter. It is included among the Late Ramesside Letters because it may be related to No. 32 (P. Bibliothèque Nationale 199, I) which makes reference to the chief taxing-master and dates to year 6 of the Wḥm Mswt or later. See Edward F. Wente, Late Ramesside Letters [SAOC 33] (Chicago, 1967), p. 15.

[12] For 3ʿʿ see T. Eric Peet, "The Supposed Revolution of the High-Priest Amenḥotpe under Ramesses IX," JEA 12 (1926), pp. 257-58; idem, "The Chronological Problems of the Twentieth Dynasty," JEA 14 (1928), pp. 67-68; Alan H. Gardiner, "The Egyptian Word for 'Dragoman,'" PSBA 37 (1915), pp. 117-25; Lanny David Bell, "Interpreters and Egyptianized Nubians in Ancient Egyptian Foreign Policy," (Ph.D. Dissertation, University of Pennsylvania (Philadelphia, 1976)), pp. 88-89 (§96).

[13] Gardiner, JEA 27, pp. 31-32.

[14] P. British Museum 10053, verso in Peet, The Great Tomb-robberies of the Twentieth Egyptian Dynasty, vol. 1, pp. 112-22; vol. 2, pls. 19-21; Wente, LRL, p. 2, n. 4; p. 4, n. 16 for date of P. British Museum 10068, vs. 2-8; idem, JNES 25, pp. 85-86 with n. 52.

[15] Wente, JNES 25, p. 85.

[16] Of the letters published in Černý, LRL, Nos. 1-13, according to Černý, were written by Dḥutmosĕ and Nos. 14-27A were addressed to Dḥutmosĕ (see List of Papyri, etc., in Černý, LRL, p. xxv). See also Wente, LRL, pp. 16-17 for table of letters translated. Janssen, however, disagrees with Wente's dating of P. Bibliothèque Nationale 198, II to year 12 of Ramesses XI, stating that the span between the earliest and latest letters in the Dḥutmosĕ-Butehamūn correspondence cannot be more than ten years (private correspondence, August, 1984).

17Janssen also restores the name Nesamenopě. He notes that he has located another letter written by Nesamenopě in London (private correspondence, August 1984).

18Černý, LRL, 69,16-70,3. See translation of Gardiner in JEA 27, p. 23 and John A. Wilson, The Burden of Egypt: An Interpretation of Ancient Egyptian Culture (Chicago, 1951), p. 279; Wente, LRL, p. 82.

19Janssen disagrees with Wente's conclusion that P. Bibliothèque Nationale 198, III probably was written at Ombos because of the occurrence of the name "the Ombite" (Seth) in the salutation. He remarks that in an unpublished letter of this correspondence, Seth of Ombos occurs together with Thoth of Hermopolis and Ḥeryshef which suggests a trip fairly far north (private correspondence, August 1984).

20Wente, LRL, pp. 1-2.

21Ibid., p. 6. Wente arranges the letters, supposedly written while Dḥutmosě was on a trip north of Thebes, in a chronological sequence beginning with No. 1 to which he considers No. 14 the probable reply, followed by No. 44 and No. 5. Letters Nos. 5 and 44 appear to be related, No. 44 possibly being the letter to which No. 5 was the reply. He identifies the general of No. 14 with Paiankh and therefore dates the letter no earlier than year 6 or 7 of the Wḥm Mswt when Paiankh took over the function of general from Ḥeriḥor. He also cites the case of the chief workman Amennakhte in No. 1 who was chief workman at least as early as year 3 of Ramesses X, and uses this evidence to date these related letters to the earlier part of Paiankh's tenure of office (see too his nn. 22-24, p. 7).

22Ibid., pp. 12-13. Černý, however, dated this "year 10" to the reign of "an early Tanite king of XXI Dynasty" in A Community of Workmen at Thebes in the Ramesside Period, p. 363.

23Wente, LRL, p. 6, n. 21.

24Ibid., p. 19, note j to 2,3.

25Ibid., p. 47, note b to 28,3 ḥty (Coptic ϩⲟⲧⲉ) "danger"; note c to 28,3 stn or sḫn (?) translated by Wente as "⌜removed⌝."

26Černý, CAH vol. II, pt. 2, p. 620; Jac. J. Janssen, Commodity Prices From the Ramessid Period: An Economic Study of the Village of Necropolis Workmen at Thebes (Leiden, 1975), pp. 460-63.

27Janssen, Commodity Prices From the Ramessid Period, p. 464, Table A.

28The 3ʿʿw named in the Turin Taxation Papyrus, and also in documents relating to the royal tomb-robberies, are probably to be identified with the troops of Penḥasi. The 3ʿʿw who occur in the

Turin document paying out grain to Ḍhutmosĕ may reflect the age-old custom of rewarding the military with grants of land upon which they could settle and farm. See too Henry Fischer, "The Nubian Mercenaries of Gebelein During the First Intermediate Period," Kush 9 (1961), pp. 40-80.

[29]Gardiner, LEM, pp. XIX, 121-24; idem, Translation, pp. 134-35; idem, JEA 27, p. 20, n. 4; idem, RAD, pp. xxiv, 82-83.

[30]Gardiner, Translation, p. 134.

[31]Caminos, LEM, p. 449.

[32]The words in brackets are Gardiner's restoration.

[33]For a recent article about a scribe of this office from Deir el-Medīna see Jac. J. Janssen, "The Mission of the Scribe Pesiūr (O. Berlin 12654)," in Gleanings from Deir el-Medîna, R.J. Demarée and Jac. J. Janssen, eds. [Egyptologische Uitgaven I] (Leiden, 1982), pp. 133-47.

[34]Jac. J. Janssen, "The Role of the Temple in the Egyptian Economy During the New Kingdom," in State and Temple Economy in the Ancient Near East II, Edward Lipiński, ed. [Orientalia Lovaniensia Analecta 6] (Leuven, 1979), p. 509.

[35]Gardiner, RAD, pp. vi-vii, 1-13; idem, JEA 27, pp. 37-56, pl. 7.

[36]Jaroslav Černý, "Datum des Todes Ramses' III. und der Thronbesteigung Ramses' IV.," ZÄS 72 (1936), p. 109; Jean Capart, Alan H. Gardiner, and B. van de Walle, "New Light on the Ramesside Tomb-Robberies," JEA 22 (1936), p. 177; P.W. Pestman, "The 'Last Will of Naunakhte' and the Accession Date of Ramesses V," in Gleanings from Deir el-Medîna, R.J. Demarée and Jac. J. Janssen, eds. [Egyptologische Uitgaven I] (Leiden, 1982), pp. 173-81; Jac. J. Janssen, "Year 8 of Ramesses VI Attested," Göttinger Miszellen 29 (1978), p. 46.

[37]The three major breaks occur between lines 2,11 and 3,1 where there are twelve or more lines missing as also between lines 3,15 and 4,1; and 4,12 and 5,1.

[38]The possible exception is the "House of Ramesses-meriamūn in the House of Amūn of Ḥe-e-pwoid" (rt. 5,5). Since the place name follows the phrase "in the House of Amūn," it is possible, however, that the phrase "of Ḥe-e-pwoid" describes the location of its fields in rt. 5,5 as Gardiner suggests in JEA 27, p. 44. In any event, Ḥe-e-pwoid may be associated with Tjebu, capital of the Xth nome of Upper Egypt, and probably located at modern-day Ḳāw el-Kebīr. See also Michel Malinine, Review of Alan H. Gardiner, Ramesside Administrative Documents (Oxford, 1948) in BiOr 16, no. 5/6 (Sept.-Nov., 1959), pp. 217-18.

[39]Gardiner, JEA 27, pp. 40-41; idem, RAD, pp. 6-7, lines 4,5.10 and 5,3.4.

[40]Gardiner, RAD, p. 7a, n. 10a (Peet); idem, JEA 27, p. 40, n. 8.

[41]Gardiner, JEA 27, p. 46.

[42]Bernadette Menu, Le régime juridique des terres et du personnel attaché à la terre dans le Papyrus Wilbour (Lille, 1970), pp. 141-42.

[43]I.A. Stuchevsky in Janssen, review and summary, forthcoming in BiOr.

[44]William C. Hayes, CAH vol. II, pt. 1, p. 357, nn. 2 and 3; p. 384, n. 9; David O'Connor, "The Geography of Settlement in Ancient Egypt," in Man, Settlement and Urbanism, Peter J. Ucko, Ruth Tringham, and G.W. Dimbleby, eds. (London, 1972), pp. 690-92.

[45]Gardiner, JEA 27, p. 42.

[46]Ibid., p. 48. See too Malinine, BiOr 16, p. 217.

[47]Gardiner, JEA 27, p. 41. See too pp. 64-70.

[48]Menu, Le régime juridique, pp. 14, 49, 52 and n. 90, 53, 55, 68, 114, 136, 139, 143.

[49]Ibid., p. 52.

[50]I.A. Stuchevsky in Janssen, review and summary, forthcoming in BiOr.

[51]Gardiner, JEA 27, pp. 62-64; idem, LEM, pp. 93-96; C.W. Goodwin, "Notes on the Calendar-question," ZÄS 5 (1867), pp. 57-60; Étienne de Rougé, "Lettre à M. Lepsius sur les fragments écrits au verso du Papyrus Sallier No. 4," ZÄS 6 (1868), pp. 129-34.

[52]Gardiner, RAD, pp. xxii-xxiv, 73-82; idem, JEA 27, pp. 60-62; Pleyte and Rossi, Papyrus de Turin, pls. 51-60; T. Eric Peet, "A Historical Document of Ramesside Age," JEA 10 (1924), pp. 116-27; Wilhelm Spiegelberg, "Ein Papyrus aus der Zeit Ramses' V," ZÄS 29 (1891), pp. 73-84; Serge Sauneron, "Trois personnages du scandale d'Éléphantine," RdE 7 (1950), pp. 53-62.

[53]Is this deity's name "Khnūm" or "Amūn"? See RAD, p. 78a, n. 9b-c. We might expect "Amūn" on the basis of rt. 2,8, but neither name looks probable.

[54]In P. Harris I, barges are said to transport the products of Punt (T3 Nṯr) (29,1 and 48,6) and b3kw of Phoenicia (Ḏ3hy) (48,6).

[55]Ships which may have belonged to the House of Ptaḥ are mentioned in P. Leyden 348, verso 9,1-9,2. See Gardiner, LEM, p. 135;

Caminos, *LEM*, p. 492.

[56]Gardiner, *JEA* 27, p. 61; idem, *RAD*, p. 79a, n. 6a-b.

[57]Gardiner, *JEA* 27, pp. 56-58. See too Spiegelberg, *Rechnungen aus der Zeit Setis I*, pp. 29-30; 74-76; pl. 18.

[58]Baer, *JARCE* 1, pp. 30-31 with n. 43.

[59]These calculations are based upon Stuchevsky's assumption that the rate 5 sacks per aroura which occurs in non-apportioning entries in Text A is the expected (standard) rate of yield of *ḳ3yt*-land. See too Gardiner, *Commentary*, pp. 71-72 with nn. 2-5 on p. 71. See too Menu, *Le régime juridique*, pp. 78-81.

[60]P. Turin 1882, verso (P. Turin A) 2,2-2,9 in Gardiner, *LEM*, pp. 122-23. See too Caminos, *LEM*, pp. 452-54.

[61]Walther Wolf, "Papyrus Bologna 1086: Ein Beitrag zur Kulturgeschichte des Neuen Reiches," *ZÄS* 65 (1930), pp. 89-97. See too Gardiner, *Commentary*, p. 115.

[62]Spiegelberg, *Rechnungen aus der Zeit Setis I*, p. 77; S.R.K. Glanville, "Book-keeping for a Cult of Ramses II," *JRAS* (Jan. 1929), pp. 19-26 and pl. 1; Gardiner, *RAD*, pp. xviii, 59; idem, *JEA* 27, pp. 58-60.

[63]Hayes, *CAH* vol. II, pt. 1, pp. 354-55.

[64]Ibid., pp. 358-59.

[65]Ibid., p. 359.

[66]The terms *šnwt* (rt. 3,11), *šmyt* (rt. 2,5 and passim), and *šꜥyt* (rt. 5,4). See Gardiner, *JEA* 27, p. 24, n. 2; 62, n. 1.

[67]Some signs of the text, especially , are most similar to forms typical of the latter years of the Twentieth Dynasty at the very earliest. The royal nomen Ramesses-meri[amūn], however, does not belong to any of the last three kings of that dynasty. So Gardiner, *JEA* 27, p. 65. See too Gardiner, *RAD*, p. xxi where he dates the text to the middle of the Twentieth Dynasty. An isolated date "...Year 6, ...month [of the...season]" affords little help. There are additional (unpublished) fragments said to be in Paris and "seen" by Malinine, according to Janssen, who remarks that the scribal hand certainly postdates the Twentieth Dynasty (private correspondence, August 1984).

[68]Gardiner, *JEA* 27, pp. 66-67.

[69]Malinine, *BiOr* 16, p. 220.

[70]Baer, *JARCE* 1, pp. 32-33.

[71]Janssen agrees that the title "Chief Taxing-Master" is probably better translated "Chief Assessing-Master" (private correspondence, August 1984).

[72]Gardiner, *JEA* 27, pp. 66 and 69.

[73]Hermann Kees, "Die Kopenhagener Schenkungsstele aus der Zeit des Apries," *ZÄS* 72 (1936), pp. 46-49.

[74]Gardiner, *JEA* 27, p. 70.

[75]Janssen hopes to publish this papyrus sometime in the near future.

[76]See too Janssen, *State and Temple Economy*, p. 509.

[77]Two prime examples are P. Sallier I 9,1-9,9 and P. Turin A vs. 2,10-5,11.

[78]Gardiner, *RAD*, pp. viii-xiii, 14-35, idem, *Commentary*, pp. 206-7. Note differences between these two renderings of Fragment M.

[79]The word *ms* ( in 2,3; 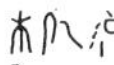 in 3,6, probably also 2,7 and 3,9), from the verb *msỉ* "to bear," "to be born," is possibly to be understood as "interest" after the Coptic S ⲙⲏⲥⲉ B ⲙⲏⲥⲓ (*WB*. II, 142, 2). See too *WB*. II, 142, 1, a word of similar appearance meaning "produce" found in Graeco-Roman texts. Gardiner, *Commentary*, pp. 206-7 with n. 10, p. 206 translates *ỉt n ms* in 2,3 as "interest in corn?", a translation which interprets the preposition *n* as *m*. Janssen suggests as a possible translation "interest-corn" (literally "corn of the *ms*." See too "*ms*-corn" in 3,6) which would be grammatically correct (private correspondence, March 1986).

[80]The compound preposition *ḥr-s3* "later" (Gardiner, *Egyptian Grammar* §178) applies to the payment of an unidentified woman (*ʿnḫ(t) n nỉwt*) and a *ỉḥwty* in *RAD*, p. 33, 11-12 (lines 9 and 10).

[81]Gardiner, *Commentary*, p. 44 with nn. 2 and 3.

[82]Ibid., p. 45 with n. 3.

[83]Gardiner, *RAD*, pp. xix-xx, 60-63; idem, *Commentary*, pp. 208-9; idem, *JEA* 27, pp. 70-71.

[84]Gardiner, *JEA* 27, p. 71; idem, *RAD*, pp. xix-xx.

[85]Gardiner, *RAD*, p. 60a, n. 10a-b.

[86]Ibid., p. 60; idem, *Commentary*, p. 209. See too *JEA* 27, p. 71 where Gardiner originally transcribed the rate in a,5 as 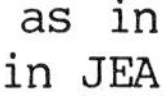 "at (?) 12 sacks" rather than "at (the rate of) 2 sacks" as in *RAD*, p. 60. Note too the different numbering of the lines in *JEA* 27, p. 71 and *RAD*, p. 60.

[87]Malinine, *BiOr* 16, p. 219; Gardiner, *Commentary*, pp. 208-9.

[88]I.A. Stuchevsky in Janssen, review and summary, forthcoming in *BiOr*. Moreover, Stuchevsky uses these poorly preserved lines as support for his contention that State cultivators paid 30% of their harvest to the State. According to Stuchevsky, the *ỉḥwty* Khonsu paid 20 sacks or 20% of his harvest of 100 sacks on 10 arouras. He equates this percentage with the 22.5% of the harvest he maintains that *ỉḥwtyw* had to turn over to the owner-temple according to Text A of P. Wilbour (the additional 7.5% of the 30% general assessment rate paid over to the local administration as an administrative fee).

[89]As in P. Harris I 65b,11 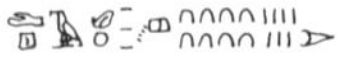 "Fruit, 87$\frac{1}{2}$ *oipĕ*."

[90]Gardiner, *Commentary*, p. 63.

[91]Černý quoted in Gardiner, *Commentary*, pp. 63-64.

[92]Gardiner, *JEA* 27, p. 71; idem, *Commentary*, pp. 208-9; Malinine, *BiOr* 16, p. 219; Baer, *JARCE* 1, p. 32.

[93]I.A. Stuchevsky agrees, according to Janssen, review and summary, forthcoming in *BiOr*.

[94]Gardiner, *Commentary*, p. 209.

[95]Ibid., p. 77.

[96]T. Eric Peet, "The Egyptian Words for 'Money', 'Buy', and 'Sell,'" in *Studies Presented to F. Ll. Griffith*, Egypt Exploration Society (Oxford, 1932), pp. 122-27.

[97]Menu, *Le régime juridique*, pp. 127-28, 138. See also her *Recherches sur l'histoire juridique, économique et sociale de l'ancienne Égypte* (Versailles, 1982), pp. 27-28.

[98]Menu, *Recherches*, p. 24.

[99]The loss of the day in the date of the text (Fragment A: "Regnal year 2, third month of *šmw* . . .") means that the reign could be that of either Ramesses II or Merenptaḥ. Janssen notes that the time of year would have been late March to early April in the case of Merenptaḥ, but April to May in the case of Ramesses II. He notes that if the missing day was over 20, year 2 of Merenptaḥ would be quite possible; whereas if the day was a low number, year 2 of Ramesses II would be equally possible (private correspondence, March 1986).

[100]Gardiner, *RAD*, pp. xix-xx.

[101]Alan H. Gardiner, "A Protest Against Unjustified Tax-Demands," *RdE* 6 (1951), pp. 115-33; idem, *RAD*, pp. xxii, 72-73; idem, *Commentary*, pp. 205-6.

[102] Gardiner, RdE 6, p. 123 with n. 1.

[103] See above n. 44.

[104] §117 pertains to a "Domain of the House of Ramesses-meriamūn in the House of Amūn" probably to be identified with the Karnak temple of which the Hall of Columns is the most well-known component.

[105] Erhart Graefe, Untersuchungen zur Verwaltung und Geschichte der Institution der Gottesgemahlin des Amun vom Beginn des Neuen Reiches bis zur Spätzeit [Ägyptologische Abhandlungen 37] 2 vols. (Wiesbaden, 1981).

[106] Gardiner, JEA 27, p. 69.

[107] Gardiner, RdE 6, p. 123.

[108] Gardiner, Commentary, p. 206.

[109] W.E. Crum, A Coptic Dictionary (Oxford, 1962), pp. 406-7; Jaroslav Černý, Coptic Etymological Dictionary (Cambridge, 1976), p. 185.

[110] W. Westendorf, Koptische Handwörterbuch (Heidelberg, 1965-77), p. 228.

[111] Gardiner, RdE 6, p. 119 (g).

[112] Ibid., pp. 123-24.

[113] Jaroslav Černý, "The Will of Naunakhte and the Related Documents," JEA 31 (1945), pp. 29-53, pls. 8-12.

[114] Janssen translates swt as "immovables," understanding the word swt as referring mainly to buildings, but also to the ground upon which they stood (private correspondence, March 1986).

[115] Herbert Thompson, "Two Demotic Self-Dedications," JEA 26 (1941), p. 74.

[116] Georges Legrain, "The Will of Eueret," ZÄS 35 (1897), p. 13; Thompson, JEA 26, pp. 74-75 and n. 1 to p. 75.

[117] Alan H. Gardiner, "The Dakhleh Stela," JEA 19 (1933), p. 19; Thompson, JEA 26, p. 75.

[118] F. Ll. Griffith, Catalogue of the Demotic Papyri in the John Rylands Library, Manchester, vol. III (Manchester, 1909), p. 17, no. 6; ibid., p. 18, no. 9; N.J. Reich, ed., Papyri juristischen Inhalts in hieratischen und demotischen Schrift aus dem British Museum [Denkschriften des kaiserlichen Akademie der Wissenschaften in Wien 55] (Vienna, 1914), pp. 9-25.

[119]F. Ll. Griffith, Rylands Papyri III, p. 52, n. 7 and Menu, Recherches, p. 30 with n. 115.

[120]Wilhelm Spiegelberg, "Demotische Miszellen: 1 [hieroglyphs] nmḥw = ⲣⲙϩⲉ 'frei,'" ZÄS 53 (1917), p. 116.

[121]Gardiner, Commentary, p. 75.

[122]Ibid., p. 29 with n. 1. The relative values of 3ḥ nmḥw nʿ and 3ḥ št3 tnỉ in the Will of Eueret prompted Gardiner to say that "the rates of assessment in Text A would appear to be in inverse proportion to the purchase prices of the three types of land" (i.e., k3yt, tnỉ, and nḫb). See too p. 29, n. 2 and Commentary, p. 206.

[123]Baer, JARCE 1, p. 26, n. 10 cites Gardiner, JEA 19, p. 21; idem, RdE 6, pp. 117, 121 note n; Thompson, JEA 26, pp. 74-75. See too Gardiner, Commentary, pp. 29, n. 1; 206.

[124]Gardiner, Commentary, p. 206; I.A. Stuchevsky in Janssen, review and summary, forthcoming in BiOr.

[125]The situation of nmḥw paying "gold" means essentially that they made a payment in goods of some value. Nbw like ḥḏ probably simply meant "money," i.e., "valuable goods." Janssen suggests that we understand here "gold (in grain)" to be compared with ḥḏ m 3ḫt nb (private correspondence, August 1984).

[126]For ʿḥʿ <ḥr> swḏ see Gardiner, RdE 6, p. 121 note p. See too Jean-Marie Kruchten, Études de syntaxe néo-égyptien, Institut de philologie et d'histoire orientales et slaves [Annuaire, Supplément I] (Brussels, 1982), p. 54.

[127]For nḫ3 see Caminos, LEM, p. 326 and p. 328, note to 9,7.

[128]Gardiner, RdE 6, p. 121 note r; see too Černý, LRL, 56,1.

[129]Full references to minor cults of Amūn, Ḥatḥōr, Sobek, Seth, and Tawēret are given by Gardiner in Commentary, p. 90.

[130]W.M.F. Petrie and Guy Brunton, Sedment II (London, 1924), pp. 28-31.

[131]Gardiner, RAD, pp. xiv-xvii, 45-58; facsimile in Pleyte and Rossi, Papyrus de Turin, pls. 35-48 and analysis by Pleyte, pp. 50-65; William F. Edgerton, "The Strikes in Ramses III's Twenty-ninth Year," JNES 10 (1951), pp. 137-45; R.O. Faulkner, CAH vol. II, pt. 2, p. 246.

[132]For hmy see Wente, LRL, p. 82, note a to 70,10.

[133]Hayes, CAH vol. II, pt. 1, p. 355. A thesis on this document by Mr. G. van den Boorn (Leiden) is in preparation.

[134]Ibid., p. 354.

[135]Ibid., see pp. 355-57; 384-85 for complete references.

[136]Gardiner, Commentary, §28, pp. 127-28.

[137]Alan H. Gardiner, The Inscription of Mes: A Contribution to the Study of Egyptian Judicial Procedure [Untersuchungen zur Geschichte und Altertumskunde Aegyptens IV, 3] (Leipzig, 1905) and G.A. Gaballa, The Memphite Tomb-Chapel of Mose (Warminster, 1977). See too Menu, Recherches, pp. 23-24.

[138]Gardiner, The Inscription of Mes, p. 13, n. 13 and Gaballa, The Memphite Tomb-Chapel of Mose, p. 26, n. 4 where references to trusteeship are given.

[139]Menu, Recherches, p. 23. Note that the second lawsuit is dated to "year 59" of Ḥaremḥab. This highly inflated regnal year undoubtedly includes the reigns of the Amarna pharaohs. See Gardiner, The Inscription of Mes, p. 22 [108], n. 72.

[140]N14-N15. See Gardiner, The Inscription of Mes, p. 39. See too P. Sallier I 9,9 where the transference of land from one person to another is "...recorded in writing (9,9) in the office of the Granary of Pharaoh (L.P.H.)" in Gardiner, LEM, pp. 87-88. It cannot be established, however, whether all title-deeds and related legal documents were filed together at a central location, or whether the situation described in the Inscription of Mose was relevant only to land granted to individuals by royal gift.

[141]Gardiner, The Inscription of Mes, p. 39. We do not know whether Gardiner's conclusions in this very early work of his changed as a result of his subsequent studies of P. Wilbour and the documents included in RAD.

[142]For ỉrỉ with the meaning "to farm" or "to cultivate" see Wente, LRL, p. 70, note b to 55,11.

[143]Adolf Erman, "Beiträge zur Kenntniss des ägyptischen Gerichtsverfahrens," ZÄS 17 (1879), pp. 71-76 and pl. I; Wolfgang Helck, Materialien zur Wirtschaftsgeschichte des Neuen Reiches II, Akademie der Wissenschaften und der Literatur in Mainz [Abhandlungen der Geistes-und Sozialwissenschaftlichen Klasse Nr. 11] Jahrgang 1960, pp. 263-64; 271-73; Baer, JARCE 1, pp. 36-39; Wolfgang Helck, "Der Papyrus Berlin P. 3047," JARCE 2 (1963) pp. 65-73, pls. 9-12.

[144]Baer, JARCE 1, p. 36.

[145]Gardiner, Commentary, p. 214.

[146]Menu, Le régime juridique, p. 130.

8 Major Findings and Research Agenda

The aim of the present study has been to establish a methodology by which and a framework within which the socio-economic data both explicit and implicit in the P. Wilbour apportioning paragraphs may be retrieved, analyzed, and evaluated. Emphasis has necessarily been placed upon the rigorous definition of the variables and their categories and the methodological and consistent classification of the data according to these categories. As the limitations of time and space preclude the exhaustive analysis of the data, it has been necessary to restrict attention to such preliminary undertakings as the detailed description of the apportioning data by means of SPSS subprograms CONDESCRIPTIVE and FREQUENCIES, and the two-way crosstabulation of variables and their evaluation by means of subprogram CROSSTABS.

In this final chapter, we shall review six areas in which the findings have been especially noteworthy and conclude with the delineation of future avenues of research and the suggestion of appropriate analytical methodology for these areas of research.

The comment should be made at this juncture that the conclusions reached in the present study may undergo modification as the result of more detailed analysis of the present tables or the application of supplementary types of analysis. This is the nature of statistical analysis in an area of study where so much is unknown. Thus, the statistical analysis of such data as are provided in P. Wilbour can be said to be an evolving process in which preliminary conclusions lead to the testing of new hypotheses. We can expect our preliminary results to undergo some modification as the massive data of P. Wilbour are more thoroughly evaluated and more knowledge is generated.

(1) Sub-variety IA Entries: An Evaluation of Menu's Interpretation

The aroura measured apportioning entries referred to by Gardiner as Sub-variety IA are interpreted by Menu as examples of scribal shorthand ("cette méthode de calcul rapide") in which the identical data of two or more consecutive Variety I entries enumerated in the same measurement area are consolidated into a single line.(1) Menu interprets the sign ┘ (∠ or L), the presence of which distinguishes these entries from Variety I entries, as signifying the size of plot of each of the plots the data of which are allegedly consolidated into a single line. Her interpretation of these entries is derived from the fact, belatedly recognized by Gardiner in his study of P. Wilbour, that the numerals "1" (sometimes), "2," "3," and "4" (always), which occur as the size of plot in Variety I entries where the full writing of the word "aroura" does not occur, are distinguished by a sort of "hook" at the top left extremity.(2) This hook is never attached to numerals where the unit of measure is the land-cubit. In his translation of Text A, Gardiner denotes the presence of the hook by the abbreviation "ar."

Menu rejects the one suggestion made by Gardiner which is not invalidated by the discovery of the aroura-signifying hook, i.e., that the sign ┘ may be related to the similar sign ┘ in Greek papyri used to signify subtraction.(3) Amending the 6 cases of the Sub-variety IA group "5┘5" (A60,11; 66,20; 81,30; 89,16; 91,42.43) to "5┘1" in accord with Gardiner's suggestion to this effect,(4) she notes that the ┘ figure in each Sub-variety IA entry is in every case smaller than the preceding black figure (variable 9 Arouras) and that the initial black aroura figure is nearly always evenly divisable by the ┘ figure (except for A32,21 and A49,5). She contends that Sub-variety IA groups such as 10┘5 should be equated with the black aroura figure of the Variety I entries which certainly should be interpreted as the size of the plot. Since Menu understands the numeral following the sign ┘ as the size of each of the plots in the alleged multiple plot entry, she compares the values of this datum with those of the black aroura figure in the Variety I entries and notes that the sizes of plots of Sub-variety IA entries "sont du même ordre de grandeur que ceux écrits en noir dans la variété I."(5) This correspondence between the black aroura figure of Variety I entries and the black ┘ figure of Sub-variety IA entries leads her apparently to conclude that there is no intrinsic difference between Variety I and Sub-variety IA entries.

The interpretation of Sub-variety IA entries as scribal shorthand has a significant impact not only upon the quantitative analysis of plot size and assessment, but also upon the size of the data file ("sample"), as the number of cases in the file would exceed the absolute number of apportioning entries recorded in Text A. The same can be said of the frequencies of each of the categories of the socio-economic variables which may be identified in each alleged multiple plot entry. It is important, therefore, to determine as far as possible the validity of such an interpretation of the Sub-variety IA entries. There are several flaws in Menu's admittedly ingenious interpretation which have come to light in the course of the present investigation which will be set out point by point with suggestions for alternate interpretations wherever possible.

The most cursory glance at P. Wilbour reveals the fact that the scribes responsible for the version of the document we have today did not by any means exploit fully the potential for abbreviation afforded by the apportioning entries. The scribes of P. Wilbour frequently used the "ditto" dot (.) to recall the preceding land measure (aroura and land-cubit alike) as well as the horizontal slash (___) to repeat both the various explanations for the lack of assessment in Sub-variety IIA entries and the filiation (X son of Y) of two consecutive entries (2 cases, A45,6 and A57,21). On the other hand, the Wilbour scribes passed up the golden opportunity to eliminate, or at least abbreviate, the one datum constant to each and every entry of Variety I and Sub-variety IA, i.e., the invariable rate of assessment $\underline{1\frac{2}{4}}$ mc. (per aroura). This datum could conceivably have been further abbreviated, if not eliminated altogether, without jeopardizing the clarity of the entries to those who were intended to make use of the data. It could be argued that the simple notation of the rate of assessment in the first Variety I or Sub-variety IA entry at the beginning of a new column, or even paragraph, should have been ample reminder of the rate of assessment. Notwithstanding, the Wilbour scribes chose to repeat this datum in each and every entry of Variety I and Sub-variety IA. Scribes who monotonously and mechanically repeat a fixed datum in at least 1440 entries, where they could just as easily have omitted it in the vast majority of cases without jeopardizing clarity, seem unlikely to have invented so curious a form of bookkeeping shorthand as that suggested by Menu as the explanation of the Sub-variety IA entries.

The likelihood of such a technique of shorthand seems remote from the point of view of an accountant, since it rearranges the internal order of the quantitative data so as to run the risk of error in subsequent use of the data. It is a well-known principle of accounting to provide each individual ledger item with a separate ledger line to preclude the possibility of an item being missed in subsequent use of the data. Combining the data of two or more identical entries requires the reader to shift his eye from the first datum in the case of Variety I entries to the second datum in the case of Sub-variety IA entries in order to identify the actual size of plot. A shift in gaze on the part of the reader runs the risk of failure to return to the correct subsequent item. Thus, a subsequent entry could easily be accidentally deleted. There is also a notable risk of error in the calculation of the total revenue forthcoming from the individual plot. Such an entry as (A35,35) ".2Ø⅃ 5.$\underline{\frac{1}{2}}$, mc.$\underline{1\frac{2}{4}}$" runs the risk of being mistaken as 5 plots of 4 arouras rather than 4 plots of 5 arouras each assessed as $\underline{\frac{1}{2}}$ aroura at the invariable rate of $\underline{1\frac{2}{4}}$ mc. per aroura. Had the scribe wanted to efficiently abbreviate the data of identical consecutive Variety I entries, it would have made more sense and been much more useful for him to have summed the abbreviated data to read ".2Ø⅃ 5.$\underline{2}$" rather than ".2Ø⅃ 5.$\underline{\frac{1}{2}}$" ($\underline{\frac{1}{2}}$ ar. x 4 plots), thus providing the actual amount of land subject to assessment at the rate $\underline{1\frac{2}{4}}$ mc. per aroura. If Sub-variety IA entries do constitute a form of shorthand, the method is singularly awkward and leaves far too much room for simple arithmetic error.

Gardiner created a series of tables (i-v) pertaining to the 232 Sub-variety IA entries with complete quantitative data in order to display the frequencies of the various aroura values both individually and in combination.(6) Table v usefully consolidates the data of tables i-iv such that the first three items of each Sub-variety IA entry are given together with the frequency for each combination, so 10⅃5.$\frac{1}{4}$ 29. Referring to table v (which Menu reproduces), it is soon evident that 109 entries or 47.0% of the 232 Sub-variety IA entries are such that would have saved the scribe the repetition of only a single line, so: 10⅃5.$\frac{1}{4}$ (29 cases); 10⅃5.$\frac{1}{2}$ (39 cases); 10⅃5.1 (31 cases); 20⅃10.1 (3 cases); etc. Another 51 entries or 22.0% of all Sub-variety IA entries would have saved the scribe the repetition of only three additional lines, e.g., 20⅃5.$\frac{1}{4}$ (14 cases); 20⅃5.$\frac{1}{2}$ (16 cases); and 20⅃5.1 (15 cases) according to Menu's interpretation of the Sub-variety IA entries. Adding the 11 entries or 4.7% wherein the repetition of just two additional lines would have been saved, there are 171 entries or 73.7% of the 232 Sub-variety IA entries where the net savings accomplished by abbreviating identical consecutive Variety I entries seems too small to have warranted a method of abbreviation with so high a potential for error. The combinations 20⅃1.$\frac{1}{4}$ (1 case); 60⅃1.$\frac{1}{4}$ (2 cases); 60⅃5.$\frac{1}{4}$ (1 case); 60⅃5.1 (1 case); 80⅃5.2 (1 case); and 100⅃5.2 (1 case) are really the only instances in which this method of abbreviation seems at all warranted, as the repetition of more than 10 lines would have been saved per entry.

There is some internal evidence in the Text A apportioning entries which argues against Menu's interpretation of the Sub-variety IA entries. In A46,43.44, for example, there is a Sub-variety IA entry which immediately follows a Variety I entry with precisely the same data the Sub-variety IA entry allegedly condenses:

A46,43	The stablemaster Raʿmosĕ .5.1, mc. 1$\frac{2}{4}$
A46,44	Another measurement (made) for him .10⅃5.1, mc. 1$\frac{2}{4}$

There is no discernible reason why the data of A46,43 could not have been included in the Sub-variety IA entry A46,44, especially as doing so would have saved yet another line. The data of the two lines could just as well have been written 15⅃5.1, mc. 1$\frac{2}{4}$. Not only would one more line have been eliminated, but the words "Another measurement (made) for him" (k(y) ḫ3y n.f) in A46,44 would also have been eliminated. The only explanation of the separate line entries of identical data which makes sense in Menu's understanding is that the two plots of A46,44 were contiguous with each other but not with the plot in A46,43. The two plots of A46,44 were merely the next plots to be enumerated in the same measurement area. The occurrence of the words k(y) ḫ3y n.f argues strongly against these lines being interpreted as an example of inconsistency on the part of the scribe in applying a method of shorthand.

Another case in point is A70,27.28 where two identical entries each read: "The soldier Setkhaʿ .3 ar..$\frac{1}{4}$, mc. 1$\frac{2}{4}$." No new measurement area intervenes nor is there any filiation appended to either name to indicate that there were two Setkhaʿ's who both happen to have been soldiers to whom plots with identical quantitative data were ascribed. To all appearances, the Wilbour scribe could have condensed the two lines into a single line to read: ".6⌋3.$\underline{\frac{1}{4}}$, mc. $\underline{1\frac{2}{4}}$." Admittedly, this example could be a case of simple inconsistency on the part of the scribe. There is also the possibility that the two plots were not contiguous even though no other plot intervenes.

A third notable case in point occurs just a few lines later in A70,32.33 where the herdsman Iotnaʿy is ascribed a plot the data of which read: ".5.$\underline{\frac{1}{2}}$, mc. $\underline{1\frac{2}{4}}$" followed by two (?) plots in a Sub-variety IA entry which reads: "Another measurement (made) for him 10⌋5.$\underline{\frac{1}{2}}$, mc. $\underline{1\frac{2}{4}}$." These lines are a parallel example to A46,43.44 and could conceivably be similarly explained. And yet it can be argued that were brevity such a prime consideration in this document, these examples from col. 70, written in the hand of the first (and more reliable) scribe, would seem unsettling exceptions.

We now turn to two entries, A95,44.45, the first of which is a Pōsh C entry. The second of these entries is possibly, although not necessarily, also a Pōsh C entry:

A95,44 Apportioned for Khaʿsebprēʿ arouras (?) 60⌋1 $\underline{\frac{1}{4}}$, mc. $\underline{1\frac{2}{4}}$
A95,45 Another measurement (made) for him arouras (?) 10⌋?1 $\underline{\frac{1}{4}}$, mc. $\underline{1\frac{2}{4}}$

Although the initial black aroura figures of the two entries differ, the ⌋ figure (1) is the same in both entries as is also the red aroura figure ($\frac{1}{4}$) which provides the assessment value. Both plots, located in the same measurement area, appear to have been apportioned for "Khaʿsebprēʿ" and could theoretically have been written: "70⌋1 $\underline{\frac{1}{4}}$, mc. $\underline{1\frac{2}{4}}$."(7) The only conceivable reason why these entries were not combined would be if the second entry (A95,45) which commences with the words "Another measurement (made) for him" was not intended to be understood as a Pōsh C entry. The other Pōsh C entries afford little help: in only one case (A84,4) is a Pōsh C entry connected with an adjacent line. The two consecutive lines which follow the Pōsh C entry of A84,4 and commence with the words k(y) ḫ3y n.f (i.e., Amūn of the Canal) refer to plots which are land-cubit measured and therefore unlikely to be Pōsh C entries. Those Pōsh C plots in Text A, which are not clear examples of Variety I or Sub-variety IA, belong to aroura measured Variety I/II.

Another point of interest which comes to mind from an internal examination of the figures of the Sub-variety IA entries requires a brief consideration in this context. This point of interest is the use of red and black ink in Text A. In Variety I entries, the assessment value in arouras (variable 14 Assessed Arouras) and the invariable assessment rate $\underline{1\frac{2}{4}}$ mc. per aroura are always written in red; whereas the aroura figure signifying the size of the plot is always written in black. In the non-apportioning entries, the size of plot, the rate applicable, and the amount of grain expected as yield from the plot are all written in red. The data of Variety II land-cubit measured plots, on the other hand, are always written in black. The absence of any rate figure in these land-cubit measured entries may mean that these plots did not produce any revenue for the State, or at least any revenue of the type with which P. Wilbour is concerned. Indeed, Menu views these very small plots as rent-free compensation to individuals who cultivated aroura measured plots directly on behalf of the various land-owning institutions.(8) This leaves plots of Variety I and Sub-variety IA as the only plots of smallholders assessed at a given rate to permit a calculation of the revenue which appears to have been owed by the smallholders directly to the institution as a kind of rent or tax ultimately delivered to State granaries.

The data written in red in entries of Variety I and Sub-variety IA are without exception necessary to a calculation of the revenue expected from each plot. We do not actually need the size of the plot in entries of Variety I to determine the expected revenue, since the red aroura figure provides the assessed value of the plot to be multiplied by the invariable rate $1\frac{2}{4}$ mc. per aroura in order to obtain the expected revenue. Not surprisingly, the size of plot is written in black. When we examine entries of Sub-variety IA, we find that once again the only figures written in red are the assessment value (in arouras) and the rate $1\frac{2}{4}$ mc. per aroura. If the use of red and black ink in the figures of the Text A entries reflects what is almost certainly the highlighting of essential data as Gardiner conjectured,(9) does not the total absence of red ink in Sub-variety IA entries beyond the red aroura figure and the rate of assessment suggest that the red aroura figure was intended to be understood exactly as is, without subsequent arithmetic manipulation as would be required if more than one plot was condensed in the Sub-variety IA entry? In other words, in an entry such as "10 ⌋ 5.$\frac{1}{2}$, $1\frac{2}{4}$ mc.," the assessed arouras value $\frac{1}{2}$ aroura just might be the total amount of land assessed in the entry. Here again, we come back to the inescapable thought that had the scribe intended the entry to represent two or more identical plots, he would have been best advised to sum the assessed arouras on each plot and give that sum as the red aroura figure. This sum could then have been multiplied directly by $1\frac{2}{4}$ mc. to provide the total revenue forthcoming in parallel with the Variety I entries. While the use of red and black ink in the entries of Text A is not by any means a conclusive argument against Menu's interpretation of the Sub-variety IA entries, it is something that should be kept in mind while examining all the evidence.

It is possible to assess Menu's understanding of the Sub-variety IA entries with the aid of statistical analysis and establish on statistical grounds the likelihood of that understanding. It has already been established that the distribution of the percentage of assessment in Sub-variety IA entries where the aroura figure following the sign ⌋ is interpreted as the size of plot is significantly different from that of Variety I entries where the black aroura figure is obviously the size of plot. This finding has warranted a further examination of Variety I entries and Sub-variety IA entries in order to determine whether or not there are any other substantive differences between the two data formats which would cast doubt upon Menu's interpretation of the Sub-variety IA entries. If the Sub-variety IA entries reflect nothing more than the condensation in one line of two or more identical consecutive Variety I entries, we would not expect to find substantive differences between the two data formats. In order to determine whether or not there are any substantive differences between Sub-variety IA and Variety I entries, we set up a series of crosstabulations in which the new variable (45) Type of Aroura Measured Entry (Variety I or Sub-variety IA) is crosstabulated with various socio-economic variables such as geographic location, land-owning institution, occupation or title of smallholder, type of land, etc. If the tables generated are indicative of relationships which are both statistically significant (chi-square) and substantively important (Cramer's V), Menu's interpretation of the Sub-variety IA entries is likely to be an inadequate explanation of these entries. The correct interpretation of the Sub-variety IA entries would therefore likely entail a substantive difference or set of differences between Variety I and Sub-variety IA entries which would account for their very different ways of recording the data of size of plot.

Using crosstabulation analysis, it has been ascertained that Sub-variety IA plots do indeed differ from Variety I plots in several important respects, the most significant of which is their geographic distribution (see chapter 6 (2)(j)). While there is relatively little difference between Variety I and Sub-variety IA entries in their location over the four sections (zones) of Text A (Cramer's V value of only 0.17728), there is a great difference between these two categories of plots as they are distributed over the 185 measurement areas of the Text A apportioning paragraphs (variable 31 Geographic Location). The relatively high Cramer's V value of 0.59368 indicates that the relationship between these two categories of aroura measured entries and the geographic locations of the plots they enumerate is both statistically significant and substantively important.

We also find that there is a substantive difference in the occupations of the smallholders of Variety I and Sub-variety IA plots. The Cramer's V value of 0.42994 for the relationship between variable 45 Type of Aroura Measured Entry and variable 7 Occupation or Title of Smallholder indicates that occupation or title of smallholder constitutes a substantive difference between Variety I and Sub-variety IA entries (see chapter 6 (2)(ee)). Analysis of the data of this crosstabulation suggests that the relationship between the variables is not likely to be a direct causal relationship, but rather the result of one or more "linking factors" which has an effect upon the observed relationship.

A third difference of substance between entries of Variety I and Sub-variety IA is reflected in the crosstabulation of variable 45 Type of Aroura Measured Entry and variable 17 Special Entry (ḥnk, 3ḥt n ḥtrỉ, mḥt, w3ḏ) which is characterized by a high phi value of 0.74866 (see chapter 6 (2)(k)). Entries of plots cultivated in flax and "vegetables" or "herbs" drop out of the table altogether as they are without exception land-cubit measured. We find that 76.7% of the ḥnk entries in the table are Sub-variety IA entries; whereas only 23.3% are Variety I entries. On the other hand, 95.5% of the 3ḥt n ḥtrỉ entries are Variety I entries; whereas only 4.5% are Sub-variety IA entries. Thus, the ratio of Variety I 3ḥt n ḥtrỉ entries to Sub-variety IA 3ḥt n ḥtrỉ entries is far greater than the ratio of Variety I to Sub-variety

IA entries for the apportioning entries as a whole (just greater than 5 to 1). In the case of the ḥnk entries, on the other hand, the correlation with Sub-variety IA is extremely high. The frequencies of these categories of special entry are not what would be expected were Menu's hypothesis for the interpretation of Sub-variety IA entries correct. The data of the crosstabulation suggest that the Sub-variety IA entry is indicative of something more substantive than the mere condensation of identical data.

Three other crosstabulations are also worthy of consideration in this context as they too are indicative of substantive differences between Variety I and Sub-variety IA entries despite the fact that these relationships have lower Cramer's V values than the relationships described above. The crosstabulations of variable 45 Type of Aroura Measured Entry by variable 4 Land-owning Institution and variable 5 Deity or King are both indicative of systematic relationships (Cramer's V values of Ø.32546 and Ø.3Ø158 respectively) between the variables. Although the relationships reflected in these two tables do not indicate a strong degree of association between the variables, they do indicate that the factors of land-owning institution and cult of deity worshipped played some significant role in determining whether a plot was recorded in the format of a Variety I or a Sub-variety IA entry. Another substantive difference between Variety I and Sub-variety IA entries occurs with respect to variable 21 Type of Apportioning Paragraph. While this statistically significant relationship has a relatively low Cramer's V value of Ø.21412, it bears mention in the present context because it reveals some peculiar findings. The category šmw pš which tallies entries occurring in paragraphs commencing with the words šmw pš, thought by Gardiner to pertain to small to medium size temples, has a distribution which is not what would be expected were there no substantive difference between Variety I and Sub-variety IA entries. The 68 assessed aroura measured plots which occur in this table under the paragraph heading šmw pš are found to be evenly distributed between Variety I and Sub-variety IA formats. This is curious in view of the fact that the ratio of Variety I to Sub-variety IA entries among the apportioning entries as a whole is just greater than 5 to 1. While these data may reflect "sampling error" which must be taken into account wherever the data do not constitute a truly random sample, the possibility is nevertheless very real that we have here a significant and substantive difference between Variety I and Sub-variety IA entries.

The above observations derived from crosstabulation analysis indicate that there are some substantive differences between Variety I entries and Sub-variety IA entries apart from the substantive difference in the distributions of percentage of assessment in these two types of aroura measured apportioning entries where an assessment value has been assigned to the plot and the size of the plot identified in accordance with Menu's interpretation of the Sub-variety IA entries. The evidence clearly suggests that we seek another explanation for the curious Sub-variety IA entries which does not conflict with the statistical evidence at hand.

On present evidence, it appears incontestable that the value following the sign ⌋ in the Sub-variety IA entries is an amount of land measured in arouras. It is not so certain, however, that this figure is the size of two or more identical consecutive Variety I plots consolidated into a single entry as a type of shorthand. One possible interpretation of the black ⌋ figure would be that it signifies a portion of a single plot the total size of which is provided in the initial black aroura figure. This amount of land may have played some role in determining the assessed value of the plot. Such a view calls to mind Gardiner's observation that the sign ⌋ in the Sub-variety IA entries resembles the Greek sign ⌋ for subtraction. There is, however, no apparent relationship between the aroura figure following the sign ⌋ and the red aroura figure which substantiates this interpretation. Another possible interpretation, tentatively suggested by Janssen, views the black ⌋ figure as the size of a single aroura measured plot belonging to a larger block or parcel of plots, the total area of which is given as the initial black aroura figure.(1Ø) An entry such as (A35,35) ".20⌋5.½, mc. $1\frac{2}{4}$," according to Janssen's interpretation, enumerates a single plot of 5 arouras assessed as ½ aroura (x $1\frac{2}{4}$ mc. per aroura) belonging to a larger parcel of 20 arouras. The initial black aroura figure would thus serve to identify the parcel or block to which the single plot specified after the sign ⌋ belongs so as to provide a reference to earlier assessment records. Along the same lines is Vleeming's suggestion that P. Wilbour records only those plots which had recently been placed into a new category--perhaps because of a change in tenant.(11) Thus, the group 20⌋5 could refer to a plot of 5 arouras belonging to a family or otherwise jointly held parcel henceforth split off from the larger parcel to become the full responsibility of a single family (or other group) member--perhaps a son and his household. There is undoubtedly merit in these suggestions especially as they go so well hand in hand. One reservation which comes immediately to mind, however, is the fact that such a notation as 20⌋5 is a singularly imprecise and inconvenient means of crossreferencing documents, as it necessitates the careful scrutiny of all entries for a given measurement area of the same parcel size. If previous assessment records were organized along the lines of P. Wilbour, the individual measurement area might be expected to occur in many places throughout the document. Going back to previous records also entails the possibility that the identity of the smallholder of such a (family or other group) parcel might differ from one register to another as heads of households died or were otherwise replaced by another member. Considering the fact that, according to Fairman's calculations, the data of Text A comprise no more than 2.5% of the cultivable land in the area of Middle Egypt to which P. Wilbour pertains, the task of locating the desired parcel in earlier records where the list of plots would undoubtedly not have been the same, or if a complete listing, would have been monstrously long, is likely to have been a formidable undertaking.

There is another possible interpretation of the Sub-variety IA entries which, while certainly plagued with uncertainties, does perhaps better fit the results of crosstabulation analysis than the interpretations put forward thus far. This interpretation is a variation upon those of Menu and Janssen and views the Sub-variety IA entry as the record of the actual physical consolidation of two or more plots such as are recorded in the ordinary Variety I entries. According to this hypothesis, the black aroura figure which follows the sign ⌋ is interpreted as the size of each of the component plots which comprise the new plot represented by the initial black aroura figure. This interpretation is not at all inconsistent with our understanding of the ḥnk entries, for example, wherein donations of landholdings comprised of two or more equal size equally assessed plots would be quite conceivable. The distribution of ḥnk entries between Variety I and Sub-variety IA data formats is, moreover, one of the clearest indications that Menu's interpretation of the Sub-variety IA entries is unlikely to be correct. The difficulty with the interpretation of the Sub-variety IA entries as instances of the consolidation of two or more individual plots of the same size and assessment located in the same measurement area arises with respect to the red aroura figure. Does this figure represent the assessment value of each of the component plots or of the parcel newly consolidated? If the latter is the case, as the use of red and black ink suggests, the considerable difference in the proportion the assessment value constitutes of the size of plot in Variety I entries as compared with Sub-variety IA entries requires some explanation. The great advantage of this interpretation of the Sub-variety IA entries, despite the questions it provokes, is that it envisions the Sub-variety IA entry as signifying a change in the assessment records which is at once the reason for the entry's inclusion in Text A, and the explanation for the substantive differences between Variety I and Sub-variety IA entries indicated by crosstabulation analysis.

One thing is certain from these analyses, however: we would undoubtedly be correct in asserting with Janssen that P. Wilbour was no "final document" ready for use in State granaries. Quite to the contrary, it was probably one in a regular series of documents leading to a final product which summarized precisely and efficiently the net income accruing to the State from the estates of various religious and secular institutions (Stuchevsky's "State authorities") after the ỉḥwtyw of all three types had been allocated their share of the harvest, and interinstitutional income transfers had been taken into account.

(2) Zones of Plot Location and Institutional Groups

Two-way crosstabulation analysis of variable 3 Institutional Group by variable 1 Section of Text (Geographic Zone) has proved especially valuable in establishing that the locations of the major cult centres of Thebes and Heliopolis with which temples of the Theban and Heliopolitan groups were affiliated do not appear to have determined the geographic distribution of their land-holdings such that large numbers of plots cluster around these centres with decreasing numbers of plots occurring as we move farther and farther away from them. With the distribution of plots ascribed to the temples of the Theban Group, for example, such that the Theban Group accounts for a decreasing number and percentage of plots in each zone as we go southward from zone 2 to zone 4 (zone 1 data omitted because of the incomplete condition of Section I), preconceived notions about the logical distribution of plots zone by zone based upon the factor of relative distance from the major cult centres are brought into question.

The data of the crosstabulation of variable 3 Institutional Group and variable 1 Section of Text reveal that 71.1% of the plots in zone 2 are ascribed to temples of the Theban Group; whereas 47.7% of the plots in zone 3 are ascribed to Theban temples. Temples of the Theban Group account for 39.5% of the plots in zone 4. When we consider the areal extent of Theban landholdings in these zones, the data of the crosstabulation are overwhelmingly supported: Theban landholdings in zone 2 amount to a total of 2,623.8 arouras as compared with 2,085.3 arouras in zone 3, and 1,433.1 arouras in zone 4. There is, therefore, a steady marked decrease in not only the number of landholdings ascribed to Theban temples as we go southward from zone 2 to zone 4, but also in the total area of these landholdings. It is noteworthy that 30 of the Theban plots in zone 2 are lacking data of size of plot, meaning that the areal extent of Theban plots in zone 2 was actually greater than the 2,623.8 arouras calculated from the extant data. Three Theban plots in zone 3 and 5 plots in zone 4 are also lacking in data of size of plot. These missing data would increase the areal extent of Theban landholdings in zones 3 and 4, but are unlikely to have any significant impact upon the pattern observed.

The zone by zone distribution of landholdings of temples of the Heliopolitan Group follows the reverse pattern of that of the Theban landholdings: the absolute number and corresponding percentage of landholdings ascribed to temples of the Heliopolitan Group increase as we progress southward from zone 2 to zone 4 (or alternately, decrease as we progress northward from zone 4 to zone 2). Although temples of the Heliopolitan Group tend to be located in or near the cult centre of Heliopolis, one temple, the Mansion of Ramesses-meriamūn, Beloved Like Rēᶜ (§237), was situated far enough south of Heliopolis (in the vicinity of Kōm Medīnet Ghurāb near the entrance to the Fayyūm) to be located within zone 1, the northernmost zone of Text A.(12) We find that 3.1% of the plots in zone 2 are ascribed to temples of the Heliopolitan Group; whereas 18.1% of the plots in zone 3 are ascribed to this group. Temples of the Heliopolitan Group account for 30.4% of the plots in zone 4. When we consider the areal extent of landholdings in these zones, the results of the crosstabulation are confirmed, despite the fact that the increase in total area is less marked from zone 3 to zone 4 than is the corresponding decrease in the total area over these two zones in the case of temples of the Theban Group (see Table 1 below). The increase in the areal extent of the Heliopolitan landholdings from 199.0 arouras in zone 2 to 779.7 arouras in zone 3 is considerably more marked (392%) than is the case with the decrease in total area over these same two zones in the case of the Theban Group (79.5%). The relatively small increase of 14.2% in the areal extent of Heliopolitan landholdings over zones 3 and 4 (779.7 arouras to 890.7 arouras) is to a considerable extent the result of a large number of these plots

TABLE 1

LANDHOLDINGS OF THE THEBAN, HELIOPOLITAN, AND MEMPHITE GROUPS
ACCORDING TO SECTION OF TEXT (GEOGRAPHIC ZONE)
(APPORTIONING PARAGRAPHS ONLY)

	LANDHOLDINGS IN AROURAS
SECTION I (ZONE 1)	
THEBAN GROUP	706.80
HELIOPOLITAN GROUP	15.00
MEMPHITE GROUP	122.00
SUBTOTAL	843.80
SECTION II (ZONE 2)	
THEBAN GROUP	2623.80
HELIOPOLITAN GROUP	199.00
MEMPHITE GROUP	169.00
SUBTOTAL	2991.80
SECTION III (ZONE 3)	
THEBAN GROUP	2085.28
HELIOPOLITAN GROUP	779.74
MEMPHITE GROUP	617.00
SUBTOTAL	3482.02
SECTION IV (ZONE 4)	
THEBAN GROUP	1433.10
HELIOPOLITAN GROUP	890.69
MEMPHITE GROUP	147.42
SUBTOTAL	2471.21
SECTIONS I–IV	
THEBAN GROUP	6848.98
HELIOPOLITAN GROUP	1884.43
MEMPHITE GROUP	1055.42
GRAND TOTAL	9788.83

being land-cubit rather than aroura measured. Only one Heliopolitan plot in zone 2 and one in zone 4 are lacking data of size of plot.

Memphite landholdings, however, exhibit no discernible pattern in their distribution over zones 2, 3, and 4, either in the absolute number and corresponding percentage of the plots in these zones, or in the areal extent of these landholdings. The 1Ø4 plots of the Memphite Group located in zone 3 total 617.Ø arouras as compared with 169 arouras in zone 2 and 147.4 arouras in zone 4. These 617.Ø arouras comprise 58.5% of the total area of Memphite landholdings in the Text A apportioning paragraphs. Although there is no particular pattern in the zone by zone distribution of the Memphite Group landholdings, the high degree of association between temples of this group and zone 3 indicates that the location of the cult centre at Memphis, where many of the Memphite Group temples were to be found, did not dictate the geographic distribution of their plots such that a greater number of plots were located in zones nearer to Memphis.

Given these results, it would be indeed worthwhile to consider the locations of plots granted to temples by royal gift in order to ascertain whether or not there is any textual evidence for the existence of a government policy or guideline in awarding land grants based upon relative distance from the major cult centre. Certainly, if all temples and secular institutions were in fact equal (or theoretically equal) in importance as "State authorities" in determining State policy, and there was a lack of strong centralized authority over and against these entities, we would not expect such patterns to emerge from the data. Given the probability that the data of P. Wilbour represent plots the specifics of which had changed since the previous record, such that the document was one in a regular series of similar documents, the data of P. Wilbour may be closer to the ideal of a random sample than might be otherwise imagined. If so, we ought to take the pattern which emerges in the crosstabulation described above as worthy of serious consideration.

An additional point of interest related to the above is the finding that in the case of 117 of the 185 measurement areas of the Text A apportioning paragraphs (63.2%), all plots are ascribed to institutions of only one institutional group. When the 26 single occurrence measurement areas are excluded, we are left with 91 measurement areas or 49.2% of the 185 measurement areas where plots are ascribed to institutions of a single institutional group. Just less than half of the 185 measurement areas, therefore, are examples of localities where institutions of more than one of the five institutional groups were ascribed neighbouring plots such that more than one cult centre may have determined the fiscal policies and priorities of individual measurement areas and the settlement(s) they would have encompassed.

(3) The Unit of Land Measure and the Classification of Unassessed Plots

In this study, it has been possible to provide statistical

evidence of the likelihood that Gardiner was essentially correct in his hypothesis concerning entries which resemble unassessed land-cubit measured Sub-variety IIA entries in the format of their data, but probably should be interpreted as aroura measured. To test this hypothesis, unassessed entries of uncertain land measure were assigned to a separate category, "Variety I/II," so named because of affinities to both aroura measured entries (Gardiner's Variety I and Sub-variety IA) and land-cubit measured entries (Gardiner's Sub-variety IIA). The data of size of plot in the case of the new Variety I/II entries were analyzed under the heading of quantitative variable 10 Arouras Special Case; whereas the data of size of plot of the land-cubit measured Sub-variety IIA entries were analyzed under the heading of quantitative variable 13 Land-cubits Single Figure.

It is evident from cases of the value "3" preceded by the hook, which elsewhere in Text A signifies a plot measured in arouras, that some entries incorporating the explanations m šwt, wšr (??), wsf, and bw ptrỉ.f (?) (e.g., A75,45-47) should certainly be understood as aroura measured. Two-way crosstabulation analysis has confirmed Gardiner's suggestion that the values "5" and "10" which occur in previously supposed Sub-variety IIA entries, in close proximity to the hooked hieratic "3's," should perhaps also be interpreted as aroura measured. He refrained, however, from so identifying them in his Translation. His suggestion that isolated cases of unassessed entries with the values "5" and multiples of 5 short of 100 may also be aroura measured is also validated. These 277 aroura measured entries stand in contrast to the 210 entries which can be more or less unequivocably categorized as land-cubit measured (Sub-variety IIA).

The statistical confirmation of the probable validity of Gardiner's hypothesis was undertaken by the creation of two additional variables computed from data of variable 2 Format of Entry (Variety I, Sub-variety IA, Variety I/II, Variety II, Sub-variety IIA) and the assignment of unassessed plots which may be aroura measured to a separate category of format, Variety I/II. Variable 43 Land Measure I Arouras or Land-cubits and variable 44 Land Measure II Arouras or Land-cubits were created in order to crosstabulate data of format of entry with various qualitative variables by distinguishing individual entries according to their unit of land measure, aroura or land-cubit. Since variable 43 Land Measure I excludes data of all unassessed plots in order that the inferences drawn from the table have the highest potential of being correct, it has the character of a "control variable" in contrast to variable 44 Land Measure II which includes data of the less securely classified entries of Variety I/II and Sub-variety IIA and serves therefore as a "test variable."

If the system of classification adopted for the present study is correct, pairs of crosstabulations involving these two computed variables of land measure ought to have very similar Cramer's V values indicative of the degree of association present in each relationship. A series of crosstabulations involving these two variables does indeed reveal pairs of Cramer's V values which are in statistical terms sufficiently close to verify the present system of classification derived from Gardiner's observations. The table below (Table 2) provides the Cramer's V values for each pair of crosstabulations in the series of crosstabulations executed. It will be noted that pairs of statistically significant relationships of relatively high substantive importance as well as those of relatively low substantive importance have Cramer's V values which are very close indeed.

It is important, moreover, to note that this analysis also serves to identify relationships which are indicative of substantive differences between aroura and land-cubit measured plots, and thus provides direction in the search for the explanation of land use in the area of the P. Wilbour assessment. We learn, for example, that the geographic location of a plot and, to a lesser extent, the zone of plot location were significant factors in determining whether land was to be allocated for the production of grain (barley or emmer wheat) on relatively large aroura measured plots, or for the production of such horticultural crops as flax (mḥt) and "vegetables" (w3ḏ) which we know from data of Text A to have been cultivated on relatively small land-cubit measured plots. Other important factors in determining land use appear to have been the land-owning institution and, to a slightly lesser extent, the deity or king of the temples or funerary foundations. The occupation or title of smallholder has also been identified as a significant factor. Not surprisingly, the same can be said of the type of land (pꜥt, ỉdb, or Neither). The correlation between unit of land measure and type of special entry (ḥnk, 3ḥt n ḥtrỉ, mḥt, w3ḏ) in crosstabulations with both variable 43 Land Measure I and variable 44 Land Measure II is found to be perfect (Cramer's V value of 1.00000), since no category of Special Entry occurs in association with both aroura measured and land-cubit measured entries. It is possible, therefore, to be absolutely correct in predicting the category of the one variable with prior knowledge of the category of the other variable. The relatively small number of cases of special entry among the 2245 apportioning entries in the present data file, however, serves as a caution to too heavy reliance upon the results of crosstabulation analysis with this variable. The relatively low Cramer's V values of the crosstabulations of variable 43 Land Measure I and variable 44 Land Measure II by variable 20 Type of Pōsh Entry (Pōsh B, Pōsh C, Neither) are also subject to some cautious reservations in light of the relatively small frequencies of Pōsh B and Pōsh C entries occurring in the table as compared with non-Pōsh entries.

As for the interpretation of those pairs of crosstabulations for which the Cramer's V values are especially high, we can conclude in the simplest terms that there was a tendency for plots differentiated on the basis of unit of land measure to be situated in different measurement areas, to be owned by different institutions, to be cultivated by individuals of different occupations, and to consist of different types of land (pꜥt, ỉdb, or Neither). Furthermore, it can be said that the inclusion of data of the unassessed plots differentiated on the basis of land measure according to Gardiner's hypothesis actually raises slightly the Cramer's V values of most of these relationships. The slightly higher Cramer's V values could, in fact, be interpreted

TABLE 2

CRAMER'S V VALUES OF CROSSTABULATIONS
with
Variable 43 Land Measure I (Variety I, Sub-variety IA, Variety II)
and
Variable 44 Land Measure II (Variety I, Sub-variety IA, Variety I/II, Variety II, Sub-variety IIA)

V43 by V1 Section of Text	Cramer's V = 0.47242
V44 by V1 Section of Text	Cramer's V = 0.43137
V43 by V3 Institutional Group	Cramer's V = 0.31594
V44 by V3 Institutional Group	Cramer's V = 0.35141
V43 by V4 Land-owning Institution	Cramer's V = 0.57338
V44 by V4 Land-owning Institution	Cramer's V = 0.58227
V43 by V5 Deity or King	Cramer's V = 0.52105
V44 by V5 Deity or King	Cramer's V = 0.51788
V43 by V7 Occupation or Title of Smallholder	Cramer's V = 0.43375
V44 by V7 Occupation or Title of Smallholder	Cramer's V = 0.48655
V43 by V15 Type of Land	Cramer's V = 0.39505
V44 by V15 Type of Land	Cramer's V = 0.44896
V43 by V16 Occupational Group	Cramer's V = 0.36105
V44 by V16 Occupational Group	Cramer's V = 0.41224
V43 by V17 Special Entry	Cramer's V = 1.00000
V44 by V17 Special Entry	Cramer's V = 1.00000
V43 by V20 Type of *Pōsh* Entry	Cramer's V = 0.12559
V44 by V20 Type of *Pōsh* Entry	Cramer's V = 0.14400
V43 by V21 Type of Apportioning Paragraph	Cramer's V = 0.41275
V44 by V21 Type of Apportioning Paragraph	Cramer's V = 0.40520
V43 by V31 Geographic Location	Cramer's V = 0.75261
V44 by V31 Geographic Location	Cramer's V = 0.77519
V43 by V39 Dyn. of Founding of Institution	Cramer's V = 0.26466
V44 by V39 Dyn. of Founding of Institution	Cramer's V = 0.28832

as further evidence of the validity of Gardiner's belated but astute observations concerning the unassessed plots of the Text A apportioning entries.

(4) The Headings of the Apportioning Paragraphs: A Preliminary Appraisal

A series of nine crosstabulations involving variable 21 Type of Apportioning Paragraph reveal a number of statistically significant and substantively important differences between two or more of the five categories of this variable (Herbage, rmnyt pš, šmw pš, White Goat, None of These) which, while not in themselves resolving all the problems they entail, provide a sound basis for further investigation.

The crosstabulation of variable 21 Type of Apportioning Paragraph by variable 4 Land-owning Institution has a relatively high Cramer's V value of 0.64992 indicative of a relatively high degree of association between the variables. It serves to statistically verify the conclusion suggested by Gardiner that the terms rmnyt pš and šmw pš are mutually exclusive vis-à-vis the individual institutions of the apportioning paragraph headings: no institution is ascribed both a rmnyt pš paragraph and a šmw pš paragraph.(13) Gardiner noted that whereas rmnyt pš paragraphs tend to be ascribed to the larger and more distant temples, šmw pš paragraphs tend to be ascribed to the smaller temples. Neither rmnyt pš nor šmw pš paragraphs are ascribed to secular institutions. It is not unusual, however, for institutions with rmnyt pš paragraphs to also have an herbage paragraph or a white goat paragraph ascribed to them. All eleven temples with rmnyt pš paragraphs are also ascribed herbage paragraphs, although the ratio of rmnyt pš entries to herbage entries is very uneven and varies widely from institution to institution. Of these eleven institutions, only two are ascribed paragraphs with no heading other than the name of the institution--a point which could be said to support the view that institutions with rmnyt pš paragraphs were "relatively large." The validity of all discussion of "relatively large" and "small to medium size" institutions rests, of course, upon the assumption that the evidence we have to date concerning the relative wealth and standing of the various institutions is indeed representative of the economic and political reality of the day. Needless to say, we ought not place too much reliance upon the validity of this assumption until the evidence of P. Wilbour is thoroughly evaluated.

The crosstabulation of variable 21 Type of Apportioning Paragraph by variable 3 Institutional Group has a somewhat lower Cramer's V value (0.54086) than that of the previous crosstabulation, but reflects essentially the same moderately high degree of association between the variables. Not surprisingly, 99.0% of the šmw pš entries are ascribed to temples of the group Other Religious. Rmnyt pš entries, on the other hand, belong predominantly to Theban temples, the Theban cases constituting 70.7% of the rmnyt pš cases in the apportioning paragraphs. Heliopolitan rmnyt pš entries and Memphite rmnyt pš entries constitute 22.4% and 6.3% respectively of the rmnyt pš entries. It is not surprising that temples of the group Other Religious account for only 0.5% of the rmnyt pš entries. There are no rmnyt pš entries ascribed to institutions of the Secular Group. This crosstabulation also reveals that 54.4% of the white goat entries are ascribed to Theban temples, a finding which suggests that land set aside for the production of food for herds of white goats reflects a specialized agricultural use in which Theban temples played the leading role. A similar conclusion may be reached regarding Theban temples and herbage entries as 54.6% of the herbage entries are ascribed to Theban temples. Heliopolitan and Memphite temples account for much lower frequencies of herbage entries: 24.7% in the case of the Heliopolitan temples and 11.3% in the case of the Memphite temples. Temples of the group Other Religious account for 9.4% of the herbage entries, while secular institutions have no association whatever with this specialized agricultural use.

The crosstabulation of variable 21 Type of Apportioning Paragraph by variable 18 Institutional Class (Religious or Secular) reflects a moderately high degree of association between the variables (Cramer's V value of 0.63764) explained by the fact that herbage entries, šmw pš entries, and rmnyt pš entries are limited exclusively to temples. The white goat entries are distributed such that 75.9% occur in association with temples and only 24.1% occur in association with secular institutions. This distribution is especially noteworthy in view of the fact that only 8.2% of the plots in the apportioning paragraphs are ascribed to secular institutions. Secular institutions, to which no herbage entries, šmw pš entries, or rmnyt pš entries whatever are ascribed, are therefore likely to have had a special association with the specialized agricultural use denoted by white goat paragraph headings shared by the Theban temples which themselves account for 54.4% of these entries. The nearly even distribution of the entries which occur in paragraphs with no special heading (None of These) between temples and secular institutions is also noteworthy. This distribution suggests an affinity between secular institutions and some temples (mostly those of the group Other Religious) in the way in which revenues accruing from plots cultivated by smallholders were ultimately disbursed.

The lower Cramer's V value (0.44327) for the relationship between variable 21 Type of Apportioning Paragraph and variable 19 Type of Religious Institution (Funerary or Cult) indicates that while the relationship between these variables is both statistically significant and substantively important, the association is not as strong as in the previous table. It is certainly noteworthy, however, that rmnyt pš entries are nearly evenly distributed between funerary and ordinary cult temples: 606 rmnyt pš entries or 53.7% are ascribed to funerary temples, while 522 rmnyt pš entries or 46.3% are ascribed to ordinary cult temples. Funerary temples account for only 35.3% of the 2245 apportioning entries in Text A; whereas ordinary cult temples account for 56.6% of these entries. It is not surprising, however, that šmw pš entries are almost perfectly correlated (99.0%) with ordinary cult temples. Funerary temples, with the exception of that of Ramesses IV, are ascribed rmnyt pš paragraphs in Text A.

No other funerary temple is ascribed a šmw pš paragraph.(14) Two other important tables which provide evidence of differences among entries of the various types of apportioning paragraphs are the crosstabulations of variable 21 with variable 43 Land Measure I Arouras or Land-cubits and variable 44 Land Measure II Arouras or Land-cubits. The crosstabulation of variable 21 Type of Apportioning Paragraph by variable 43 Land Measure I Arouras or Land-cubits, which is characterized by a moderate degree of association (Cramer's V value of Ø.41275), is concerned only with plots which have actually been assessed. The crosstabulation is therefore limited to data of aroura measured Variety I and Sub-variety IA and land-cubit measured Variety II. In this crosstabulation, it is the distribution of rmnyt pš and šmw pš entries between aroura measured and land-cubit measured categories which is the most revealing and intriguing finding. Unlike rmnyt pš entries which are predominantly aroura measured (89.3%), only 44.2% of the šmw pš entries are aroura measured, while 55.8% are land-cubit measured. The sharp contrast in the distribution of rmnyt pš and šmw pš entries according to the unit of land measure casts some doubt upon Gardiner's hypothesis that rmnyt pš paragraphs perform for the so-called "larger" more distant institutions the same function that šmw pš paragraphs perform for the so-called "smaller" often local institutions which he based upon the mutual exclusivity of these headings vis-à-vis the individual institutions. The crosstabulation of variable 21 Type of Apportioning Paragraph by variable 44 Land Measure II Arouras or Land-cubits, which includes unassessed plots of aroura measured Variety I/II and land-cubit measured Sub-variety IIA, also reflects a moderate degree of association between the variables (Cramer's V value of Ø.4Ø52Ø) and confirms the frequencies observed in the previous crosstabulation in the distribution of rmnyt pš and šmw pš entries between aroura measured and land-cubit measured categories. While there is a slightly higher ratio of land-cubit measured šmw pš entries to aroura measured šmw pš entries evident in the second crosstabulation, the two tables are sufficiently similar in the way in which rmnyt pš and šmw pš entries are distributed between the two categories of land measure to cast doubt upon the validity of Gardiner's hypothesis. In seeking an alternative understanding of these entries, note should be taken of the possibility, however tentative, that land-cubit measured plots may have been cultivated with horticultural crops as suggested by the occurrences of the words mḥt and w3ḏ in the land-cubit measured entries in contrast to the aroura measured plots of Variety I and Sub-variety IA which were evidently cultivated exclusively with grain (𓏏). The possibility that land-cubit measured plots were cultivated with different crops from those of aroura measured plots certainly heightens the impression that rmnyt pš and šmw pš paragraphs should not be axiomatically viewed as being on the same footing vis-à-vis "relatively large" and "small to medium size" institutions. Needless to say, the very different way in which land-cubit measured plots were assessed (for whatever purpose) as suggested by the format of their data, together with the fact that no amount of the harvest is identified as revenue forthcoming from these plots, further diminishes

Gardiner's hypothesis of equivalence of rmnyt pš and šmw pš paragraphs.

The crosstabulation of variable 21 Type of Apportioning Paragraph by variable 39 Dynasty of Founding of Land-owning Institution is also an important table in bringing out differences between and among the various types of apportioning paragraphs. This relationship is found to be statistically significant with a moderate degree of association indicated by the Cramer's V value of 0.43497. We find that there is a very high percentage of herbage entries (61.2%) and white goat entries (48.1%) in association with temples of the Nineteenth Dynasty, a finding which suggests that herbage domains and domains intended for the cultivation of food for white goats were created as and when the need arose. The older institutions, therefore, might be expected to account for a larger proportion of these entries than more recently established institutions. It is also possible, however, that herbage and white goat plots were of lower agricultural value than plots enumerated in the rmnyt pš and šmw pš paragraphs such that later kings did not bother to appropriate them for their own funerary estates.

Another noteworthy finding concerns the distribution of rmnyt pš entries between Nineteenth and Twentieth Dynasty institutions. Fully 51.5% of the rmnyt pš entries occur in paragraphs ascribed to Twentieth Dynasty institutions; whereas only 29.2% occur in paragraphs ascribed to Nineteenth Dynasty institutions. These percentages reflect, at least in part, the appropriation of plots belonging to older institutions by the funerary estates of Twentieth Dynasty kings, most notably Ramesses III and Ramesses V. Lands belonging to the funerary estate of the Nineteenth Dynasty pharaoh Ramesses II are very likely to have been appropriated by later kings because of the much lower frequency of apportioning entries ascribed to the great monarch's estate than might be expected in comparison with the frequencies of the funerary estate of Ramesses III and especially that of the undistinguished Ramesses V. Evidence of P. Harris I (11,7; 10,3) certainly invites the conjecture that Ramesses III appropriated for himself land and personnel belonging to the Ramesseum. It is unlikely, however, that either Ramesses III or Ramesses V restricted himself to the appropriation of lands belonging to the Ramesseum. Most of the predecessors of Ramesses III and Ramesses V are not represented in P. Wilbour by so much as a single paragraph; those few kings whose temples are mentioned are ascribed relatively few landholdings--facts which certainly pique our curiosity. Earlier kings whose temples have relatively low frequencies of apportioning entries include Tuthmosis II (or Amenophis II?), Ḥaremḥab, Sety I, and Merenptaḥ. The deified king Sesostris III (Khaʿkhaurēʿ) occurs in the name of a temple in Text A, but in a non-apportioning paragraph heading (§36) rather than an apportioning paragraph heading. Considering the fact that institutions located as far to the north of the P. Wilbour area as Tell el-Yahūdiyāh (§77 "Those of the Mansion of Ramesses-ḥeḳ-Ōn in the House of Rēʿ north of Ōn") and as far to the south as Hermonthis (§249 "The House of Mont, Lord of Hermonthis") are represented as land-owning institutions in Text A, the lack of representation of the vast majority of New Kingdom pharaohs in P. Wilbour cannot be satisfactorily explained in terms of their temples being too far distant from this area of Middle Egypt. Moreover, if the data of P. Wilbour represent plots concerning which some change in status or specification had taken place since the previous enumeration, as very probably they must in light of the very negligible percentage of the cultivable area of Middle Egypt they represent, we might expect a wider range of royal affiliation than is the case. This finding confirms the likelihood that lands ascribed to either funerary temples of earlier kings or ordinary cult temples founded by and named after them were not uncommonly reduced in size and wealth over time (often apparently a relatively short time) by later kings eager to expand their own agricultural domains at the expense of those of their predecessors.

The crosstabulation of variable 21 Type of Apportioning Paragraph by variable 31 Geographic Location provides evidence of yet another systematic relationship (Cramer's V value of Ø.67193) and thus contributes to a better understanding of the data of P. Wilbour. In sum, we see that there is a strong tendency for plots enumerated under each of the five types of paragraph headings to occur in association with particular measurement areas, many measurement areas occurring in association with only one type of paragraph heading. Since such paragraph headings as Herbage and White Goat appear to identify separate and distinct domains of various institutions which may have had prescribed service functions, it would appear that the tendency was for the local economies to be dominated by the policies and priorities of a single type of domain. Thus, it may be valid to subclassify measurement areas as to the purpose for which the assessed portion of their harvest was intended.

Relatively large measurement areas such as Sakō, Spermeru, Ḥuiniuti, Sharopě, and Menʿonkh are found to be largely comprised of rmnyt pš plots in combination with herbage plots, white goat plots, or plots enumerated in paragraphs with no special heading. In contrast, just over half of the 49 measurement areas in which šmw pš plots occur are comprised solely of šmw pš plots. We also learn that despite the fact that there are more than three times as many rmnyt pš entries as šmw pš entries in Text A (113Ø as compared with 312), rmnyt pš plots occur in proportionately fewer measurement areas than do šmw pš plots (95 as compared with 49). This is even more evident when single occurrence measurement areas are excluded from the calculations. This suggests that the landholdings of the relatively large institutions, which include funerary as well as ordinary cult temples, tended to cluster within a limited number of localities where the environmental conditions (soil quality, potential for irrigation, etc.) may have been superior. As a result perhaps, these localities, which include Sakō, Spermeru, Ḥuiniuti, Sharopě, and Menʿonkh, may have become relatively large population centres in Middle Egypt as was unequivocably the case with Spermeru.(15)

(5) ỉdb and pʿt: Location and Unit of Measure

The topographical terms ỉdb and pʿt which occur frequently in Text A (more than 80 examples of ỉdb-land pertaining to 184 apportioning entries and nearly 40 examples of pʿt-land pertaining to 58 apportioning entries) have been understood by Gardiner as probably antithetical to each other on the basis of both their usage in P. Wilbour and their occurrence in the Golénischeff Onomasticon (I,12) where they occur side by side following the terms šʿy "sand" and m3wt "new land," the latter of which also occurs in P. Wilbour. Gardiner concluded that both terms evidently had to do with irrigation in some technical sense (exact sense unknown), ỉdb-land likely to be understood as "riparian land" (so WB. I, 153, I "Ufer," "Uferland"). The common expression ỉdbwy Ḥr, "the two river-banks of Horus," frequently employed as a synonym for "Egypt," is rather convincing evidence in favour of the general meaning of ỉdb as riparian land. It does not, however, exclude the possibility that ỉdb might have had a more restrictive, precise usage in an agricultural context possibly, though not necessarily, in contrast to the term pʿt. The mathematical use of ỉdb in one problem of the Moscow Mathematical Papyrus suggested to Gardiner that plots described as ỉdb-land most probably had the shape and proportions of the sign which is a determinative of the term. Thus, he reasoned, plots of ỉdb-land may have been long narrow strips of land abutting upon the river or a canal, and as such, may have been considerably more valuable than plots with no direct access to water. The occurrence of ỉdb in the text of a donation stela of King Tefnakhte in which ỉdb is determined by the water sign is also supportive of this understanding (see chapter 5 (2)(m)).

The term pʿt-land (WB. I, 504, 2 "Ufer") is more difficult to grasp as there are considerably fewer textual references to this variety of land. There is a reference to pʿt-land in P. Amiens (4,10) as well as examples from Philae, Aniba (the tomb of Penne), and Edfu, the last of which suggested to Gardiner that pʿt-land may refer to "an island or the like, with sandy shores descending to the blue water."(16) He also suggested that the older form may have been p3ʿt (Pyr. 1183.1205) which, despite the translation "ein Gewässer am Himmel" in WB. I, 497, 19 (on the basis of the determinative with variants , must refer to land "flooded with water" as the second example of Pyr. 1205 suggests ("the p3ʿt is opened, the p3ʿt becomes full of water").(17) The suggestion of Gardiner that pʿt was the word at the root of such words as ỉry pʿt "hereditary prince" and pʿt "patricians," "mankind" with the meaning "tilth" or "fertile land" is another idea which may be evaluated in the following discussion.(18)

The crosstabulation of variable 15 Type of Land by variable 31 Geographic Location has a relatively high Cramer's V value of 0.72785 and provides evidence of the geographic distribution of plots identified as consisting of ỉdb-land, on the one hand, and plots identified as consisting of pʿt-land, on the other hand. One ỉdb plot drops out in this table which analyzes a total of 2157 entries because the measurement area for the entry A7,40 is lacking. Since only 183 plots of a total of 2157 plots reflected in the table or 8.5% are identified as consisting of ỉdb-land and only 58 plots or 2.7% are identified as consisting of pʿt-land, it is probable that both of these terms had a very limited application in the area of Middle Egypt to which P. Wilbour pertains. The term pʿt in particular probably had an especially limited application to account for so minuscule a percentage of the plots detailed in the Text A apportioning paragraphs. The table indicates that plots identified as either ỉdb-land or pʿt-land tended to occur in relatively few measurement areas: 31 measurement areas in the case of ỉdb-land and 11 measurement areas in the case of pʿt-land of a total of 185 measurement areas identified in the measurement lines of the apportioning paragraphs. Plots of both ỉdb-land and pʿt-land occur in only four measurement areas, two of which (the New Land of ... and the Tomb of Pernūte) occur in the only partially preserved Section I of Text A. Even the most tentative conclusions, therefore, must be based upon the limited evidence of only two measurement areas, the Village of Djasasati in Section II (zone 2) and Sharopĕ in Section III (zone 3). The table indicates that whereas 17 plots of a total of 36 plots (47.2%) are identified as pʿt-land in the Village of Djasasati, only one is identified as ỉdb-land--a finding which suggests that the geographic locations which provide the frame of reference for fixing the locations of the plots detailed in Text A tended to be sufficiently limited in their areal extent to encompass only a single variety of land, possibly but not necessarily defined by the appropriate method of irrigation. In the zone 3 measurement area Sharopĕ, which has a relatively high frequency of 76 plots, there are only 4 cases of plots identified as ỉdb-land and only one case of a plot identified as pʿt-land. Thus, neither variety of land appears to have been characteristic of this "relatively large" measurement area, although both do occur. If the terms ỉdb and pʿt do identify land characterized by immediate access to irrigation, either by their location on the actual river-bank or on a major canal, measurement areas where these plots constitute but a small fraction of the plots enumerated probably extended just over the periphery of such tracts.

The distribution of plots of ỉdb-land and pʿt-land over the 42 measurement areas where they are attested strengthens the impression that the two varieties of land are fundamentally different not only from the vast majority of plots enumerated in the apportioning paragraphs, but also from each other. It must be emphasized, however, that "fundamentally different from" does not necessarily mean "antithetical to." Plots of pʿt-land are distributed over the 11 measurement areas in which they occur such that 77.6% occur over as few as 4 measurement areas (2 in zone 1 and 2 in zone 2). Plots of ỉdb-land are distributed over the 31 measurement areas in which they occur such that 25.1% occur in a single measurement area (Menʿonkh) in which no plots of pʿt-land occur whatever. A noteworthy difference between the two types of land is the fact that plots of ỉdb-land are much more evenly distributed over the 31 measurement areas in which they are attested, despite the fact that 25.1% occur in Menʿonkh (zone 4). Thus, plots of pʿt-land probably were very distinct from plots of ỉdb-land in both their absolute and relative frequencies and in their geographic location, tending to be restricted to relatively few measurement areas where specific topographical features or environmental conditions prevailed. These features or conditions distinguished them from the overwhelming majority of measurement areas of the Text A apportioning paragraphs. The type of irrigation available may be the factor which distinguished these two types of land both from each other and from the plots detailed in the vast majority of apportioning entries.

The crosstabulations of variable 15 Type of Land by both variable 43 Land Measure I Arouras or Land-cubits and variable 44 Land Measure II Arouras or Land-cubits provide another indication of a substantive difference between plots of ỉdb-land and plots of pꜥt-land vis-à-vis the plots which are not so identified as they are distributed between the two categories of land measure. These tables have Cramer's V values of 0.39505 and 0.44896 respectively, values indicative of a moderately high degree of correlation between the variables. The curious discovery in the first table (variable 43 Land Measure I where only plots of Variety I, Sub-variety IA, and Variety II are analyzed) is the fact that plots identified as consisting of ỉdb-land and plots identified as consisting of pꜥt-land stand in marked contrast to the vast majority of plots which are not so identified in their distribution between the two categories of land measure. Plots which did not consist of either ỉdb or pꜥt-land are 90.7% aroura measured; whereas plots identified as consisting of either ỉdb-land or pꜥt-land are predominantly land-cubit measured. In the case of ỉdb-land, 54.5% of the plots are land-cubit measured; whereas in the case of pꜥt-land, a substantial 72.4% of the plots are land-cubit measured. The distribution of ỉdb and pꜥt plots in the case of the second table (variable 44 Land Measure II), which includes data of Variety I/II and Sub-variety IIA plots, is even more skewed--suggesting that the trend we encounter in the first and more conservative table may be even stronger than indicated. These figures suggest that there was something about ỉdb-land and pꜥt-land which made them especially suitable for cultivation as relatively small land-cubit measured plots. Indications in the apportioning paragraphs that land-cubit measured plots may have been cultivated with horticultural crops such as fruits and vegetables (w3ḏ A6,x+15; 40,10; 44,33) as well as flax (mḥt A6, x+17; 7,43.48; 8,4), together with the fact that the produce of assessed aroura measured plots (Variety I and Sub-variety IA) is always indicated as measured by the grain measure abbreviated ,
suggests that a major difference between aroura and land-cubit plots may have been the crop cultivated. Pꜥt-land, therefore, may have been especially well-suited for cultivation as relatively small land-cubit measured plots utilized for garden or flax cultivation. ʾIdb-land, on the other hand, may have been just about equally well-suited for cultivation as both grain producing aroura measured plots and horticultural land-cubit measured plots. We do know that the environmental requirements of garden (including orchard) crops as well as flax include plenty of moisture and a temperate climate. Flax in particular requires an abundance of potassium and phosphorus in the soil which would be available in good supply were plots to be situated on the river-bank or to abut directly upon a major canal. Flax, moreover, is a crop which is

well-suited to small parcels of land as it is sown densely to prevent branching and gathered before maturity. The nearly equal distribution of plots of ỉdb-land between aroura and land-cubit measures probably was the result of a complex combination of socio-economic factors which determined the agricultural use and might be expected to change over time. If such was the case, the presence of at least some of these plots in the P. Wilbour enumeration might perhaps indicate a change in the crop cultivated since the previous assessment.

The specification of only four land-cubit measured plots as cultivated in flax (mḥt) in the apportioning paragraphs does not necessarily detract from the validity of such a hypothesis, as three of the occurrences of the term mḥt (A7,43.48; 8,4) are abnormal entries not merely in the fact that they specify a particular crop, but also because they differ in format from most apportioning entries. These entries commence with the words "Flax of the House of [Ḥeryshef?]"; "Flax ..."; and "[Flax] of Ḥerysh[ef]"instead of the name and occupation of the smallholder. The point of emphasis may be that these particular entries denote plots cultivated in flax exclusively for the benefit of the cult of Ḥeryshef, on a parallel perhaps with the much more frequent aroura measured ḥnk entries (plots cultivated on behalf of "the god(s) of Pharaoh"), in contrast to the "ordinary" apportioning entries in which a plot is cultivated by a smallholder on his own behalf. The fourth occurrence of the word mḥt (A6,x+17) belongs to a series of 10 land-cubit measured plots unique in Text A as they are ascribed to a single individual, the overseer of cattle ʿAshaemḥab(sed?). One of these plots is indicated as cultivated m w3ḏ (A6,x+15), four more were possibly cultivated with flax, while another four were evidently fallow (wsf).

Last of all, we ought to reflect upon Gardiner's idea that the term pʿt may have been at the root of such familiar words as ỉry pʿt "hereditary prince" and pʿt "patricians," "mankind" such that it meant "fertile land" or "tilth." While the evidence gathered thus far from the data of P. Wilbour does not either prove or disprove this conjecture, it does strongly suggest that by the Ramesside Period, the term pʿt had acquired a rather restrictive application. The same conclusion also appears to apply to the term ỉdb translated by Gardiner as "riparian land." The only real alternative to this conclusion is to assume that the use of the terms ỉdb and pʿt in Text A is more or less random and, therefore, without rational plan or forethought. In view of the fact that by and large Text A has been recorded with considerable consistency of format and detail, and is relatively free of error, despite the occasional lapses of the second scribe with respect to the unit of measure, it seems unlikely that we should look in that direction for our explanation of the occurrences of the terms ỉdb and pʿt and the plots to which they apply. We should be open to the very real possibility that both these terms over centuries came to have a much more precise and limited application in the context of land assessment than is conveyed by the earlier dating occurrences of these terms and related words which evidently had broader applications.

(6) Two Significant Determinants of Size of Plot and Assessment Value

(a) The Variables of Size of Plot

A series of four tables in which variables of size of plot are crosstabulated with variable 31 Geographic Location indicates that the variables of size of plot are relatively highly correlated with the geographic location of the plot (i.e., measurement area). Although we cannot say which variable determines the values of the other variable, we can state that the size of both aroura measured and land-cubit measured plots and the geographic location of these plots are relatively highly correlated, i.e., reveal a systematic relationship such that prior knowledge of the value of the one variable enables us to predict the corresponding value of the other variable with a relatively high degree of confidence in the results. It should be noted at the outset that some reduction in the number of values of each quantitative variable has taken place in each crosstabulation in order to reduce the tables to a manageable size. The elimination of low frequency values serves to reduce the distortion caused by the occurrence of zero and low frequency cells in the table which may affect the Cramer's V value.

Variable 9 Arouras, which pertains to 1344 assessed aroura measured plots of Variety I and Sub-variety IA, has a much lower degree of correlation (Cramer's V value of Ø.49777) than is the case with variable 1Ø Arouras Special Case, which pertains to unassessed aroura measured plots (Cramer's V value of Ø.754Ø4). The difference in the degree of correlation expressed in the Cramer's V values of the two crosstabulations could be interpreted to mean that the particular conditions or circumstances which resulted in the lack of assessment of the 241 Variety I/II plots analyzed in the table were highly localized phenomena.

In the case of the crosstabulation of variable 9 Arouras by variable 31 Geographic Location, the high frequency sizes of plots (5, 3, 1Ø, and 2Ø arouras) each tend to occur in association with a particular group of measurement areas where they are found to be the predominant size of plot. Measurement areas with plots of 5, 3, and 1Ø arouras were located primarily in zone 3, the zone with the highest frequency of apportioning entries. Measurement areas to which the lower frequency sizes of plots, 2 and 2Ø arouras, are ascribed tend to be located in zone 4. When measurement areas with frequencies of fewer than 1Ø cases are excluded from the analysis, the remaining measurement areas are not uncommonly found to be characterized by three or four sizes of plots, one of which is usually predominant. It would be useful to consider the 151 measurement areas which occur in the crosstabulation with variable 9 Arouras with an eye to classifying them according to the various sizes of aroura measured plots ascribed to them. This analysis would enable us to distinguish various patterns in the distribution of sizes of assessed aroura measured plots which would provide some insight into the system of land allocation operative in individual measurement areas over the four zones of Text A.

There is one additional remark which should be appended to the above comments. First, it would be most valuable to rerun the above crosstabulation distinguishing between Variety I entries in which the size of plot is clearly the initial black aroura figure and Sub-variety IA entries in which the value of the black ⅃ figure may be the actual size of plot. The resulting two tables could then be compared, both with each other, and with the present table in which the initial black aroura figure is understood as the size of both Variety I and Sub-variety IA plots.

In the case of the crosstabulation of variable 31 Geographic Location by variable 10 Arouras Special Case, the high frequency sizes of plots (5, 10, 3, and 20 arouras) tend to occur in association with measurement areas which have relatively low frequencies of assessed aroura measured plots of Variety I or Sub-variety IA, or with different measurement areas altogether which are highly concentrated in zone 4. When low frequency measurement areas are excluded from the analysis, the number of measurement areas is greatly reduced. The remaining measurement areas include the high frequency measurement areas Sakō and Menʿonkh in zone 4 which also have relatively high frequencies of Variety I and Sub-variety IA plots. Other high frequency measurement areas such as Sharopĕ and Spermeru in zone 3, however, are ascribed relatively few unassessed aroura measured plots. High frequency (large?) measurement areas, therefore, do not necessarily attest relatively high frequencies of both assessed and unassessed aroura measured plots. Most relatively high frequency measurement areas which occur in the table are characterized by two or even three sizes of plots, one of which is usually found to be predominant. These data suggest that the location of a plot, as indicated by the measurement area, may have been to some considerable extent the explanation for the lack of assessment on the plot: plots in certain predictable measurement areas being subject to conditions or circumstances which prevented their assessment in the current fiscal year.

The Cramer's V values of the crosstabulations in which variable 28 Land-cubits Subtotal 11 and 12 and variable 13 Land-cubits Single Figure are each crosstabulated with variable 31 Geographic Location indicate a very similar degree of moderately high association: 0.63283 in the case of variable 28 (Variety II entries) and 0.58682 in the case of variable 13 (Sub-variety IIA entries). This suggests that land-cubit measured plots were nearly equally restricted in their geographic location regardless of whether or not they were assessed. Relatively few measurement areas occur in the two crosstabulations: 49 measurement areas (of a total of 185) in the case of the crosstabulation with variable 28 Land-cubits Subtotal 11 and 12, and 45 measurement areas in the case of the crosstabulation with variable 13 Land-cubits Single Figure. These figures may be compared with the 151 measurement areas which occur in the crosstabulation with variable 9 Arouras (Variety I and Sub-variety IA entries) and the 47 measurement areas which occur in the crosstabulation with variable 10 Arouras Special Case (Variety I/II entries). In contrast to the data of the two crosstabulations where the unit of measure is the aroura, those measurement areas which have relatively high frequencies of assessed land-cubit measured plots (variable 28) also tend to have relatively high frequencies of unassessed land-cubit measured plots (variable 13), although there are measurement areas where assessed and unassessed land-cubit measured plots occur very disproportionately. We also find that the relatively few measurement areas to which land-cubit measured plots are ascribed are generally characterized by two to four sizes of plots when the low frequency measurement areas (fewer than 5 entries) are excluded from the analysis. The predominance of a single size of land-cubit measured plot among the relatively high frequency measurement areas is not as evident as it is in the case of aroura measured plots distributed among measurement areas of relatively high frequency.

The divergencies we observe between the two pairs of crosstabulations are directly reflected in their Cramer's V values. The Cramer's V values of the relationships between assessed and unassessed aroura measured plots and geographic location are quite different, the latter crosstabulation having a much higher degree of correlation than the former. The Cramer's V values of the relationships between assessed and unassessed land-cubit measured plots and geographic location, on the other hand, are very close indeed. These differences in the degree of correlation of the two pairs of crosstabulations as reflected in their Cramer's V values could be interpreted as one more indication of substantive differences between aroura measured and land-cubit measured plots as explored in section 3 of this chapter by means of the two variables of land measure, variable 43 Land Measure I Arouras or Land-cubits and variable 44 Land Measure II Arouras or Land-cubits. Substantive differences between plots measured in arouras and plots measured in land-cubits have also been suggested in the discussions of the crosstabulations of variable 21 Type of Apportioning Paragraph and variable 15 Type of Land by variable 31 Geographic Location (sections 4 and 5 above) where a difference in crop(s) cultivated may be the essential difference. This possibility is one which also should be taken into consideration in assessing the two pairs of crosstabulations described above.

Another statistically significant and substantively important variable in determining the size of a plot in the apportioning entries is variable 7 Occupation or Title of Smallholder. The Cramer's V values of three of the four crosstabulations in which high frequency sizes of plots are crosstabulated with variable 7 Occupation or Title of Smallholder are very close. The Cramer's V value of the crosstabulation of variable 10 Arouras Special Case and variable 7 Occupation or Title of Smallholder, however, is considerably higher. Therefore, while all four crosstabulations are both statistically significant and substantively important, that in which values of variable 10 Arouras Special Case are analyzed with respect to the various occupations of smallholders is particularly noteworthy.

Looking at the 25 occupations to which unassessed aroura measured plots (Variety I/II) are ascribed, and comparing them with the data of the crosstabulation of variable 7 Occupation or Title of Smallholder by variable 9 Arouras, we note that the frequencies of the occupations ʿnḫ(t) n nỉwt and priest differ considerably in the two tables. Both of these occupations account for a greater proportion of unassessed Variety I/II entries than they do of assessed Variety I and Sub-variety IA entries with respect to at least one size of plot. The modal size of plot in distributions of both variable 9 Arouras and variable 10 Arouras Special Case is 5 arouras. This size of plot is most illustrative of the differences between the two tables. The occupation ʿnḫ(t) n nỉwt accounts for 84 plots or 11.4% of the 734 plots of 5 arouras which belong to the distribution of variable 9 Arouras (Variety I and Sub-variety IA plots). In the crosstabulation of variable 7 Occupation or Title of Smallholder by variable 10 Arouras Special Case, however, women smallholders account for 33 of the 143 plots of 5 arouras or 23.1%. A similar increase in the proportion of unassessed aroura measured plots ascribed to women smallholders occurs with plots of 3 and 10 arouras. Priests also account for a greater proportion of unassessed aroura measured plots of 5 arouras than they do of assessed aroura measured plots of Variety I and Sub-variety IA which are 5 arouras in size. Priests are ascribed 56 assessed aroura measured plots of 5 arouras or 7.6% as compared with 19 unassessed aroura measured plots of 5 arouras or 13.3%. Priests also account for a greater proportion of unassessed aroura measured plots of 10 arouras (21.7%) than they do of assessed aroura measured plots of 10 arouras (11.4%). It is also interesting to note that the occupation soldier, which is most highly correlated with plots of 3 arouras, accounts for a larger proportion of unassessed aroura measured plots of 3 arouras than it does of assessed aroura measured plots of this size (24 plots of a total of 37 plots or 64.9% as compared with 195 plots of a total of 333 plots or 58.6%). In the case of the occupation ʿnḫ(t) n nỉwt, we are perhaps observing instances of the transfer of aroura measured plots to widows or other female heirs, a situation in which plots were either not assessed that year or possibly not cultivated at all. In the case of the occupation soldier, on the other hand, it is tempting to conclude that the lack of assessment on aroura measured plots of 3 arouras was the consequence of absence resulting from compulsory military service. The data of other occupations are also of interest and well worth examining.

It seems evident from the crosstabulation of variable 9 Arouras with variable 7 Occupation or Title of Smallholder (Cramer's V value of 0.47453) that we would be correct in asserting with Menu that there was probably some sort of policy of land allocation in effect during the Ramesside Period which determined the size of plot allocated to individual smallholders differentiated on the basis of occupation.(19) Many low frequency occupations, of course, cannot be said to follow any discernible pattern. High frequency occupations such as stablemaster, soldier, and herdsman, however, have a tendency toward very high correlation with a single size of plot. We can also say that as plots increase in size, their distribution among the occupations with which they occur becomes more and more even.

Crosstabulations effected between the two land-cubit measured variables 28 and 13 and variable 7 Occupation or Title of Smallholder reveal an almost identical degree of correlation with

Cramer's V values of 0.49474 and 0.48651 respectively. Thus, regardless of whether or not land-cubit measured plots of various sizes were assessed, the degree of correlation with variable 7 is virtually the same. The crosstabulation of variable 7 by variable 28 Land-cubits Subtotal 11 and 12 indicates that land-cubit measured plots of Variety II tend to be highly correlated with the occupations *ỉḥwty*, priest, scribe, and stablemaster (in declining order of frequency). Of these four occupations, only *ỉḥwty* and stablemaster tend to occur predominantly in association with one size of plot (24 land-cubits in the case of *ỉḥwty* and 12 land-cubits in the case of stablemaster). In the case of unassessed plots of Sub-variety IIA (variable 13 Land-cubits Single Figure), we see by and large a high correspondence between the occupations which occur in this table and those of the previous crosstabulation with variable 28, despite the fact that the occupation prophet has a higher frequency than stablemaster. There is a notable difference between the two tables, however, in the modal size of plot. The modal size of plot in the case of variable 28 is 24 land-cubits (58 cases, 29.6%). The high frequency occupation *ỉḥwty* has by far the highest frequency of plots 24 land-cubits in size (26 cases, 44.8%). In the case of variable 13, on the other hand, the modal size of plot is 12 land-cubits (63 cases, 36.2%). As in the previous table, it is the occupation *ỉḥwty* which has the highest frequency of plots of the modal size (18 cases, 28.6%) followed closely by priest (16 cases, 25.4%). There is, moreover, a relatively high correspondence among the distributions of high frequency occupations in the two tables over the three largest sizes of plots, 50, 100, and 200 land-cubits. Thus, it is also possible to say that the data of the two crosstabulations show sufficient correspondence to suggest that unassessed plots classified as land-cubit measured Sub-variety IIA are very likely correctly classified.

(b) Assessment Value (Variable 14 Assessed Arouras)

The quantitative variable 14 Assessed Arouras, created to analyze the data of the red aroura figure in entries of Variety I and Sub-variety IA, has been crosstabulated with both variable 7 Occupation or Title of Smallholder and variable 31 Geographic Location to reveal relationships which are both statistically significant and substantively important. The crosstabulation of variable 14 with variable 7 Occupation or Title of Smallholder has a Cramer's V value of 0.36271 which, while not especially high, is still worthy of our consideration (see chapter 6 (2)(t)). As was the case with the variables of size of plot, values of variable 14 with low frequencies (here less than 20 cases) were eliminated from the analysis in order to reduce the number of zero and low frequency cells which tend to distort the Cramer's V value. The analysis has been limited to the five highest frequency values of variable 14: *¼*, *½*, *1*, *2½*, and *5* arouras.

The crosstabulation suggests that the occupation or title of smallholder was a socio-economic factor of some importance in determining the value of the red aroura figure in entries of Variety I and Sub-variety IA. The lower Cramer's V value of this crosstabulation in comparison with that of the crosstabulation of variable 7 Occupation or Title of Smallholder by variable 9 Arouras (0.47453), however, suggests that the occupation or title of smallholder is likely to have been a more important determinant of the size of a plot of Variety I or Sub-variety IA, as specified in the initial black aroura figure, than it was of the assessment value placed upon the plot.

The table indicates that while the lower assessment values ¼ and ½ aroura occur in association with the majority of the 48 occupations of smallholders with which there is joint association, both assessment values occur predominantly in association with the occupations soldier and stablemaster. The occupations herdsman and ꜥnḫ(t) n nỉwt also have relatively high frequencies of the two lower assessment values. The remaining 44 occupations have relatively low frequencies of both assessment values. The distribution of the assessment value 1 aroura among the various occupations is quite different, however. While the number of occurrences of this mid-range assessment value is highest with the occupation stablemaster, the occupation soldier has a relatively low frequency. The occupations priest, ꜥnḫ(t) n nỉwt, and herdsman, however, have relatively high frequencies of this assessment value. The two highest assessment values in the table, 2½ and 5 arouras, have substantially lower frequencies among the data of variable 14 and are most highly correlated with the occupation ỉḥwty. It should be kept in mind, however, that the table takes into account the 128 Pōsh B entries that are very highly correlated with such ỉḥwtyw as may have constituted a separate category of ỉḥwtyw (Stuchevsky's "agents of the fisc") to be distinguished from the ỉḥwtyw of the ordinary aroura measured apportioning entries. The high correlation of the occupation ỉḥwty with the higher assessment values 2½ and 5 arouras therefore reflects, to a large degree, the generally higher assessments of the Pōsh B plots. The same can be said of the occupation priest which is also very highly correlated with Pōsh B entries. Occupations such as stablemaster, ꜥnḫ(t) n nỉwt, and soldier, which have relatively high correlations with the lower assessment values, each account for only 1 or 2 occurrences of the assessment value 2½ arouras. Of these occupations, only that of soldier occurs in association with the assessment value 5 arouras. Thus, we would probably be correct in concluding that the higher assessment values reflect a very special circumstance within a system of land assessment wherein the occupation or title of the smallholder played some significant role in determining the assessment value.

The relatively low Cramer's V value of 0.36271 for this table suggests that there were one or more determinants of the assessment value of aroura measured plots which may have been more significant than the occupation or title of the smallholder. On the basis of the evidence of the numerous tables considered in the present preliminary study, which suggests that many of the variables identified thus far are highly interrelated, it is likely that the variable(s) we seek has both a higher correlation with variable 14 Assessed Arouras than variable 7 Occupation or Title of Smallholder and a relatively high correlation with variable 7 Occupation or Title of Smallholder. Further crosstabulation analysis with variable 14 Assessed Arouras indicates that the variable we seek is likely to be variable 31 Geographic Location, the relationship of which to variable 14 is both statistically significant and substantively important at a much higher Cramer's V value (Ø.64682) than was the case with variable 7 Occupation or Title of Smallholder. Although the relationship of variable 31 to variable 7 Occupation or Title of Smallholder has a considerably lower Cramer's V value of Ø.4Ø665, it is also statistically significant and substantively important. Thus, it appears that Geographic Location may be the variable that is both highly correlated with Occupation or Title of Smallholder and more highly correlated with the variable Assessed Arouras than is Occupation or Title of Smallholder. It is possible, therefore, that Geographic Location was the primary determinant of the assessment value placed upon aroura measured plots of Variety I and Sub-variety IA.

A noteworthy finding in the crosstabulation of variable 14 Assessed Arouras and variable 31 Geographic Location is that of the 148 measurement areas that occur as the geographic reference points of plots of Variety I and Sub-variety IA where the red aroura figure has been preserved, 64 or 43.2% occur in association with only one assessment value. Thirty of these measurement areas have frequencies of one plot only. Of the remaining 34 measurement areas, 9 occur only in association with the assessment value ¼ aroura, 19 occur only in association with the assessment value ½ aroura, while 5 occur only in association with the assessment value 1 aroura. One measurement area (Opě in zone 2) occurs only in association with the assessment value 2½ arouras. We also discover that there is a tendency for the high frequency assessment values ½ and 1 aroura to occur in association with measurement areas of zone 3. The value ¼ aroura, on the other hand, occurs predominantly in association with measurement areas of zone 4. The lower frequency assessment values 2½ and 5 arouras are more evenly distributed over the four zones of Text A. Overall, there appears to have been a degree of homogeneity of assessment value among plots distinguished on the basis of geographic location consistent with and even greater than the homogeneity of assessment value among plots distinguished on the basis of occupation or title of smallholder.

These findings suggest that there existed during the Ramesside Period a highly developed system of land assessment according to which the assessment value of a plot was determined primarily by the location of the plot, but also to some extent by the occupation or title of smallholder. Since the occupation or title of smallholder was moderately highly correlated with the geographic location of the plot, it is clear that we are looking at variables that are highly interrelated and possibly interdependent. Moreover, since the geographic location of plots of Variety I and Sub-variety IA appears to have been a highly significant determinant of the assessment value of the plot, it is quite possible that the individual assessment values reflect the relative irrigability of such plots in the numerous measurement areas within this area of Middle Egypt. Such irrigability is to be considered in conjunction with the expected (standard) yield of the various plots (Stuchevsky's "standard average grain harvest") which we know from the totals of Text B to have been calculated as 5 mc. per aroura for ḳ3yt-land, 10 mc. per aroura for nḫb-land, and $7\frac{2}{4}$ mc. per aroura for tnỉ-land--the very same rates found in the non-apportioning paragraphs of Text A and relevant certainly to the Pōsh B apportioning entries at the very least.

(7) Directions of Future Research

(a) Detailed Analysis of the Crosstabulations

The crosstabulation tables briefly described in the present study require further detailed examination in order to describe and adequately assess the vast quantity of data which have been generated. A detailed analysis of these tables will enable us to draw conclusions based upon patterns which are not immediately discernible in a preliminary study. The very long tables, such as those in which variable 4 Land-owning Institution, variable 5 Deity or King, and variable 7 Occupation or Title of Smallholder are crosstabulated with variable 31 Geographic Location, should be considered a source of reference for those who are interested in particular institutions, cults, occupations, and measurement areas as they relate to each of the socio-economic factors with which crosstabulation has been effected.

It would also be useful to reduce the number of categories of variable 31 Geographic Location (185), variable 4 Land-owning Institution (50), variable 5 Deity or King (26), and variable 7 Occupation or Title of Smallholder (54) in order to determine both the direction and degree of distortion resulting from the occurrence of a relatively large number of zero and low frequency cells in the crosstabulations effected with these variables. This can be done by eliminating single and low frequency categories which, although valuable to the Egyptologist, are considered "trivial" by the statistician. In the case of variable 31 Geographic Location, for example, it is possible to reduce the number of measurement areas from 185 to 73 by eliminating the 112 measurement areas with frequencies of fewer than 10 cases or 0.5% of the total entries. The 73 measurement areas can be further reduced to 28 by eliminating all measurement areas with frequencies of less than 1.0% (22 cases). This is probably the lower limit of the reduction in the number of measurement areas below which so much data would be eliminated as to jeopardize the meaningfulness of the crosstabulation. This lower limit is prescribed by our familiarity with the subject matter and consequent judgment of how much data we are willing to eliminate from the analysis for the sake of increasing the precision in the Cramer's V value. Reducing the number of categories of variable 31 Geographic Location to 28 does not, however, completely eliminate the problem of distortion. Limiting the analysis to the 10 measurement areas with the highest frequencies (1.7% or more) would achieve this goal, but would entail the loss of much of the data of geographic location. Reduction in the number of categories of variable 31 from 185 to 28 appears to be the optimal solution to the problem of distortion. Similar reductions in the number of variable categories can be applied to the data of variable 4 Land-owning Institution, variable 5 Deity or King, and variable 7 Occupation or Title of Smallholder in order to increase the precision of the Cramer's V values of crosstabulations effected with these variables.

Crosstabulations with Cramer's V values of between 0.30000 and 0.40000 which have not already been examined could also be considered at this juncture, since the Cramer's V value of 0.40000 is, after all, a rather arbitrary cut-off point for substantive importance in crosstabulation analysis. There are numerous tables with Cramer's V values within the range 0.30000 to 0.40000 which are worthy of consideration, even though they reflect only minor trends among the P. Wilbour data. While the Cramer's V value is an extremely useful index of the relationship between the various socio-economic factors we have identified among the apportioning data, we must supplement this indicator with the special knowledge of our discipline in selecting for discussion tables where the frequencies of some cells provide new or unexpected information despite the fact that the table as a whole may not reflect a particularly high degree of association.

(b) Crosstabulation Analysis of the Percentage of Assessment Variables

The crosstabulation analysis of variable 33 Percentage of Assessment 1 and variable 37 Percentage of Assessment 2 by various qualitative variables could not be completed for inclusion in the present study because of technical problems that could not be resolved in the short-term. Crosstabulation analysis with these variables is especially important as the variables express the relationship between the size of a plot and the assessment value placed upon the plot in Variety I and Sub-variety IA entries.

(c) Analysis of the Abbreviated Expressions in the Sub-variety IIA Entries

Of the four abbreviated expressions evidently intended to explain why the Sub-variety IIA entries consist of only a single land-cubit figure rather than two often very unequal figures as is the case with Variety II entries, only m šwt (Gardiner's "being dry") can be considered beyond dispute in its interpretation.(20) The term wsf, which Gardiner renders "resting," "idle," or "fallow," is also likely to be in essence correctly understood, although in contemporary Ramesside usage, the stem wsf does not apply to fields. The correct understanding of the term wšr (??) is quite uncertain, since the orthography varies greatly over Text A. Gardiner noted the form with the prefixed |J (A3,x+11?; 14,46) and another unique variant which he tentatively read as m bw-wšr (??) in A2,x+7. He rejected bw ḏw, an abstract of the type bw nfr, however, as it seems unlikely in this period. He also rejected the possibility that the bw could be the negative word because of the lack of suffix. His suggestion that ἄβροχος "unwatered" may be a Greek parallel would place wšr (??) close in meaning to m šwt, both terms possibly having to do with a lack of adequate irrigation. If correctly understood, the fourth expression bw ptrỉ.f (?) "it was not seen?" could denote any of a host of circumstances not necessarily having anything to do with the physical condition of the land.

Thus, the terms m šwt, wsf, and possibly wšr (??) all likely pertain to the actual physical condition of the plot cultivated. It is possible, therefore, to execute crosstabulations which analyze the Sub-variety IIA entries in order to determine whether or not there are substantively important differences between entries in which these terms occur as the explanation for the lack of assessment and entries in which the plot is described as bw ptrỉ.f (?). Such an analysis is effected by the creation of a new variable from the data of variable 2 Format of Entry in which Sub-variety IIA entries in which the terms m šwt, wsf, and wšr (??) occur are assigned to one category and Sub-variety IIA entries in which the term bw ptrỉ.f (?) occurs are assigned to a second category. The bivariate statistics chi-square and Cramer's V computed from the crosstabulations of the new variable with specified variables in the variable list provide a means of judging whether or not there are any intrinsic differences between the two categories of Sub-variety IIA explanation which lead to a better understanding of what these terms signify.

It is also possible to create a new variable from the data of variable 2 Format of Entry which assigns Sub-variety IIA entries in which the term m šwt occurs to one category of a dichotomous variable, and relegates entries in which the term wšr (??) occurs to a second category. Sub-variety IIA entries in which the terms wsf and bw ptrỉ.f (?) occur would be excluded from the analysis. Such an analysis is analogous to that in which Variety I entries were assigned to one category of the new variable 45 Type of Aroura Measured Entry and Sub-variety IA entries were assigned to a second category preliminary to the execution of crosstabulations which identify substantively important differences between the two aroura measured formats. Similarly, another series of crosstabulations could be executed by creating a variable which assigns Sub-variety IIA entries in which the terms m šwt and wšr (??) occur to one category, and relegates Sub-variety IIA entries in which the terms wsf and bw ptrỉ.f occur to a second category. The crosstabulations effected with this new variable would assist in determining whether or not it is correct to interpret the terms m šwt and wšr (??) as denoting a similar condition of plot, as distinguished from the terms wsf and bw ptrỉ.f which appear to denote different circumstances entirely.

It should be noted that the same crosstabulations may be executed to the same ends with data of unassessed aroura measured Variety I/II. The results of these crosstabulations may be compared with those executed upon data of unassessed land-cubit measured Sub-variety IIA entries, both as a check upon the validity of the classification of Variety I/II plots as aroura measured, and as a means of identifying any substantive differences between aroura and land-cubit measured plots.

(d) Variable 40 Individual Smallholder

Variable 40 Individual Smallholder has been created from the combined data of variable 7 Occupation or Title of Smallholder, variable 16 Occupational Group, and variable 8 Name of Smallholder. The variable has been further refined by means of a FORTRAN print-out of all such "identities" together with the zone and measurement area of each entry in which they occur. This table makes it possible to readily distinguish between occurrences of these "identities" which may pertain to the same individual and occurrences which for geographic reasons are unlikely to pertain to the same individual. A "short file" containing a listing of these "refined identities," together with data of variables of special interest, can be created as a means of reducing the otherwise unmanageable size of the data file. This short file can then be sorted on the basis of such variables as Format of Entry, Land-owning Institution, Type of Land, Type of Apportioning Paragraph, etc., in order to provide a composite picture of landholding from the perspective of individual smallholders.

It should be emphasized that the variable Individual Smallholder provides only one possible gauge of the population of smallholders for the measurement areas of the Text A apportioning paragraphs in the current data file, and is by no means intended to represent absolute numbers. Nor does it claim to be the most accurate gauge of such a population, for there are certainly other ways of approaching the data with the population of smallholders in mind. The numbers generated represent only a proportion (at present unknown) of the actual population over the four zones of the Text A apportioning paragraphs, and are valuable only when viewed in this light. The variable is perhaps most valuable when taken in conjunction with data of the quantitative variables which compute total land cultivated (in arouras, land-cubits, or both summed and expressed in arouras) in order to compare the relationship between the amount of land cultivated and the number of smallholders with respect to individual measurement areas, institutions, cults, types of land, etc.

(e) Three-way Crosstabulation Analysis

After the results of two-way crosstabulation have been considered, and a relationship between variables has been determined to be both statistically significant and substantively important as indicated by the chi-square and Cramer's V values, the relationship may be subjected to further statistical analysis which controls for "hidden factors" that may influence the relationship.

This further step in crosstabulation analysis is valuable because the observed relationship between two variables summarized in a two-way crosstabulation table may not be the result of a direct causal relationship between the variables. The relationship we observe may be the result of the effect of a third factor, or combination of factors, upon this relationship. The effect of suspicious extraneous factors may be eliminated by controlling for them in a series of three-way or greater crosstabulations. By constructing three-way or greater tables, it is possible to determine whether or not the observed relationship holds true when the effects of hidden factors are removed.

Thus, the relationship between occupation or title of smallholder and land-owning institution, for example, could be further evaluated by controlling for the effect of geographic location, a factor which is highly correlated with both occupation or title of smallholder and land-owning institution.

(f) Subprogram BREAKDOWN

SPSS subprogram BREAKDOWN provides a particularly valuable type of analysis for evaluating the data of P. Wilbour. Subprogram BREAKDOWN provides sums, means, and standard deviations of various quantitative variables with respect to categories of such qualitative variables as Land-owning Institution, Deity or King, Occupation or Title of Smallholder, Type of Land, Type of Apportioning Paragraph, etc. These descriptive statistics may be calculated, for example, for aroura measured plots of Variety I in order to compare data of size of plot of the various occupations, land-owning institutions, measurement areas, types of land, etc. The descriptive statistics generated by this subprogram could also be used to compare the percentage of assessment among the various institutions, cults, occupations of smallholders, types of land, etc. The descriptive statistics available in subprogram BREAKDOWN could be supplemented by modes, medians, and minimum and maximum values computed by means of a FORTRAN sort program.

Subprogram BREAKDOWN also allows the computation of the valuable statistic eta-squared which is a measure of the proportion of variance in the quantitative variable that is explained by the qualitative variable. This means that we may determine, for example, to what extent the variation in the distribution of values of percentage of assessment was due to each of the factors identified in the variable list: geographic location (measurement area), land-owning institution, occupation or title of smallholder, type of land, etc. The value of eta-squared may be expressed conveniently as a percentage.

Another particularly valuable aspect of subprogram BREAKDOWN is that it makes possible the rank ordering of categories of the qualitative variables on the basis of sum total land cultivated. Such rank ordering could be used in conjunction with the results of the FORTRAN program described above in (d) which provides a gauge of the population of smallholders ("heads of households") among the measurement areas of the Text A apportioning paragraphs. Although we do not know exactly what proportion of the total agricultural land in this area of Middle Egypt the data of Text A represent, or precisely why these particular landholdings were enumerated, the relationship between land wealth and population is still very much worth pursuing.

(g) Analysis of the Non-Apportioning Paragraphs; Analysis of Text B

It is possible to study both the non-apportioning paragraphs of Text A of P. Wilbour and the paragraphs of Text B by following a very similar methodology to that employed in the present study in the analysis of the apportioning paragraphs of Text A. Variables need to be identified and their respective categories defined as precisely as possible. The data must then be prepared for computer input and subjected to appropriate types of statistical analysis.

(h) A Study of Proper Names in P. Wilbour

It is evident that the names of the smallholders in P. Wilbour provide a worthwhile and extremely interesting topic which would necessitate a study in itself. With the present analysis at hand and the framework intact for expanding upon the present data file, the accomplishment of such a study is very much facilitated. The names of the measurement areas, as well as the names of smallholders and other individuals who occur in the document, will provide fertile ground for further study. Both the names of smallholders in the apportioning entries and the names of measurement areas which occur in the measurement lines of the apportioning paragraphs of Text A already exist in the data file as variable 8 Name of Smallholder and variable 6 Geographic Location respectively. The analysis could be easily expanded to include proper names from both the non-apportioning and harem paragraphs of Text A as well as the 65 paragraphs of Text B.

NOTES

[1]Bernadette Menu, Le régime juridique des terres et du personnel attaché à la terre dans le Papyrus Wilbour (Lille, 1970), pp. 103-7.

[2]Gardiner, Commentary, pp. 211-12, 214-15.

[3]Ibid., pp. 92, 214.

[4]Ibid., p. 214.

[5]Menu, Le régime juridique, p. 105.

[6]Gardiner, Commentary, pp. 92-93 (i-v).

[7]Ibid., p. 90. The proper name "Khaʿsebprēʿ" (A95,44; 96,29) is convincing neither as the name of a god nor a person.

[8]Menu, Le régime juridique, p. 103.

[9]Gardiner, Commentary, p. 106.

[10]Jac. J. Janssen (private correspondence, March 1983).

[11]S.P. Vleeming as cited by Jac. J. Janssen (private correspondence, March 1983).

[12]Gardiner, Commentary, p. 12. The House of the Nile-god Ḥaʿpy (§238) was located at Atar en-Naby, on the east bank, 2 kilometers south of Old Cairo. The temple referred to as "Those of the Mansion of Ramesses-ḥeḳ-Ōn in the House of Rēʿ north of Ōn (non-apportioning paragraph 77) was undoubtedly located at Tell el-Yahūdīyah, 19 kilometers north of Heliopolis. Both of these temples, however, were located considerably nearer to Heliopolis than the Mansion of Ramesses-meriamūn, Beloved Like Rēʿ (§237).

[13]Ibid., pp. 24-25.

[14]One point which needs to be addressed is whether the unknown temples of Ramesses II, described as ḥwt rather than pr, were also funerary temples. These temples have such descriptions as "in the House of Amūn," "Beloved Like Rēʿ," and "in the House of Ptaḥ." It would be interesting to reclassify these temples as funerary temples and execute crosstabulation analysis upon the newly reclassified data.

[15]David O'Connor, "The Geography of Settlement in Ancient Egypt," in Man, Settlement and Urbanism, Peter J. Ucko, Ruth Tringham, and G.W. Dimbleby, eds. (London, 1972), pp. 691-92.

[16]Gardiner, Commentary, p. 27, n. 1.

[17]Gardiner, AEO, p. 13*.

[18]Raymond O. Faulkner, A Concise Dictionary of Middle Egyptian (Oxford, 1962), p. 88.

[19]Menu, Le régime juridique, pp. 107-15.

[20]Gardiner, Commentary, pp. 94-95.

Bibliography

Alexander Badawy, A History of Egyptian Architecture: The Empire, or the New Kingdom (Berkeley and Los Angeles, 1968).

Klaus Baer, "An Eleventh Dynasty Farmer's Letters to his Family," JAOS 83 (1963), pp. 1-19.

-----, "The Low Price of Land in Ancient Egypt," JARCE 1 (1962), pp. 25-45.

A.M. Bakir, Slavery in Pharaonic Egypt [Supplément aux ASAE Cahier 18] (Cairo, 1952).

Lanny David Bell, "Interpreters and Egyptianized Nubians in Ancient Egyptian Foreign Policy," Ph.D. Dissertation, University of Pennsylvania (Philadelphia, 1976).

S. Berger, "A Note on Some Scenes of Land-Measurement," JEA 20 (1934), pp. 54-56.

Hubert M. Blalock, Jr., Causal Inference in Non-experimental Research (Chapel Hill, 1964).

-----, Social Statistics (New York, 1960).

James Henry Breasted, Ancient Records of Egypt: Historical Documents, 5 vols. (Chicago, 1906-7).

Henri Brugsch, Dictionnaire géographique de l'ancienne Égypte (Leipzig, 1877-80).

Bernard Bruyère, Rapport(s) sur les fouilles de Deir el Médineh (1922-1951) [FIFAO 1-8, 10, 14-16, 20, 21, 26] (Cairo, 1924-53).

Ricardo A. Caminos, Late-Egyptian Miscellanies [Brown Egyptological Studies I] (London, 1954).

-----, "Papyrus Berlin 10463," JEA 49 (1963), pp. 29-37.

Jean Capart, Recueil de monuments égyptiens, 2 vols. (Brussels, 1902-5).

Jean Capart, Alan H. Gardiner, and B. van de Walle, "New Light on the Ramesside Tomb-Robberies," JEA 22 (1936), pp. 169-93.

Jaroslav Černý, Catalogue des ostraca hiératiques non littéraires de Deir el Médineh, vols. 1-5, 7 [DFIFAO 3-7, 14] (Cairo, 1935-70).

-----, A Community of Workmen at Thebes in the Ramesside Period, Institut français d'archéologie orientale du Caire, [Bibliothèque d'étude 50] (Cairo, 1973).

-----, "The Contribution of the Study of Unofficial and Private Documents to the History of Pharaonic Egypt," in Le fonti indirette della storia egiziana, S. Donadoni, ed. [Studi semitici 7] (Rome, 1963), pp. 31-57.

-----, Coptic Etymological Dictionary (Cambridge, 1976).

-----, "Datum des Todes Ramses' III. und der Thronbesteigung Ramses' IV.," ZÄS 72 (1936), pp. 109-18.

-----, "Egypt: From the Death of Ramesses III to the End of the Twenty-first Dynasty," in The Cambridge Ancient History, I.E.S. Edwards, C.J. Gadd, and N.G.L. Hammond, eds. 3rd ed. (Cambridge, 1970-75), vol. II, pt. 2, pp. 606-57.

-----, "Une famille de scribes de la nécropole Royale de Thèbes," CdE 22 (July 1936), pp. 247-50.

-----, "Fluctuations in Grain Prices during the Twentieth Egyptian Dynasty," Archiv Orientální 6 (1933), pp. 173-78.

-----, Late Ramesside Letters [Bibliotheca Aegyptiaca IX] (Brussels, 1939).

-----, Ostraca hiératiques [CCG, nos. 25501-832] 2 vols., (Cairo, 1930-35).

-----, "Prices and Wages in Egypt in the Ramesside Period," Cahiers d'histoire mondiale I (1954), pp. 903-21.

-----, "The Will of Naunakhte and the Related Documents," JEA 31 (1945), pp. 29-53, pls. 8-12.

Jaroslav Černý and Alan H. Gardiner, Hieratic Ostraca, I, The Griffith Institute (Oxford, 1957).

Lincoln L. Chao, Statistics: Methods and Analyses, 2nd ed. (New York, 1974).

L. Christophe, "L'organisation de l'armée égyptienne à l'époque ramesside," Revue du Caire 39 (1957), pp. 387-405.

-----, "Quatre enquêtes ramessides," Bulletin de l'Institut d'Égypte 37 (1956), pp. 5-37.

-----, "Ramsès IV et le musée du Caire," Cahiers d'histoire égyptienne, series III, fasc. I (Cairo, 1950), pp. 47-67.

W.E. Crum, A Coptic Dictionary (Oxford, 1962).

S. Dairaines, L'Égypte économique sous la 18e dynastie pharaonique (Paris, 1934).

N. de G. Davies, The Tomb of Rekh-mi-Rēʿ at Thebes [The Metropolitan Museum of Art Egyptian Expedition Publications, XI] 2 vols. (New York, 1943).

Étienne Drioton and Jacques Vandier, L'Égypte [Clio. Introduction aux études historiques -1, Les peuples de l'Orient méditerranéen, -2 L'Égypte] 4th ed., (Paris, 1962).

G. Dykmans, Histoire économique et sociale de l'ancienne Égypte, 3 vols. (Paris, 1936-37).

William F. Edgerton, "The Nauri Decree of Seti I. A Translation and Analysis of the Legal Portion," JNES 6 (1947), pp. 219-30.

-----, Review of Alan H. Gardiner, The Wilbour Papyrus, 3 vols. (Oxford, 1941-48) in JAOS 70 (1950), pp. 299-304.

-----, "The Strikes in Ramses III's Twenty-ninth Year," JNES 10 (1951), pp. 137-45.

W. Erichsen, Papyrus Harris I: Hieroglyphische Transkription [Bibliotheca Aegyptiaca V] (Brussels, 1933).

Adolf Erman, "Beiträge zur Kenntniss des ägyptischen Gerichtsverfahrens," ZÄS 17 (1879), pp. 71-83.

-----, Neuägyptische Grammatik (Hildesheim, 1968).

Adolf Erman and Hermann Grapow, Wörterbuch der aegyptischen Sprache, 5 vols., Belegstellen, 5 vols. in 6 vols. (Berlin, 1971).

Adolf Erman and Hermann Ranke, Aegypten und aegyptisches Leben im Altertum (Tübingen, 1923).

H.W. Fairman, Review of Alan H. Gardiner, The Wilbour Papyrus, 3 vols. (Oxford, 1941-48) in JEA 39 (1953), pp. 118-23.

Raymond O. Faulkner, A Concise Dictionary of Middle Egyptian (Oxford, 1962).

-----, "Egypt: From the Inception of the Nineteenth Dynasty to the Death of Ramesses III," in The Cambridge Ancient History, I.E.S. Edwards, C.J. Gadd, and N.G.L. Hammond, eds. 3rd ed. (Cambridge, 1970-75), vol. II, pt. 2, pp. 217-51.

-----, "Egyptian Military Organisation," JEA 39 (1953), pp. 32-47.

-----, "Egyptian Seagoing Ships," JEA 26 (1940), pp. 3-9.

Henry Fischer, "Nubian Mercenaries of Gebelein During the First Intermediate Period," Kush 9 (1961), pp. 40-80.

R.J. Forbes, Studies in Ancient Technology, vol. 2, 2nd ed. rev. (Leiden, 1965).

G.A. Gaballa, The Memphite Tomb-Chapel of Mose (Warminster, 1977).

Alan H. Gardiner, Ancient Egyptian Onomastica, 3 vols. (Oxford, 1947).

-----, The Chester Beatty Papyrus No. I, Description of a Hieratic Papyrus with a Mythological Story, Love-songs, and Other Miscellaneous Texts (London, 1931).

-----, "The Dakhleh Stela," JEA 19 (1933), pp. 19-30.

-----, Egypt of the Pharaohs (Oxford, 1961).

-----, Egyptian Grammar: Being an Introduction to the Study of Hieroglyphs, 3rd ed. (Oxford, 1957).

-----, Egyptian Hieratic Texts Series I, Part 1 The Papyrus Anastasi I and the Papyrus Koller (Leipzig, 1911).

-----, "The Egyptian Word for 'Dragoman,'" PSBA 37 (1915), pp. 117-25.

-----, "The Harem at Miwēr," JNES 12 (1953), pp. 145-49.

-----, Hieratic Papyri in the British Museum, vol. I, Third Series (London, 1935).

-----, The Inscription of Mes: A Contribution to the Study of Egyptian Judicial Procedure [Untersuchungen zur Geschichte und Altertumskunde Aegyptens IV, 3] (Leipzig, 1905).

-----, Late-Egyptian Miscellanies [Bibliotheca Aegyptiaca VII] (Brussels, 1937).

-----, "A Protest Against Unjustified Tax-Demands," RdE 6 (1951), pp. 115-33.

-----, Ramesside Administrative Documents (Oxford, 1948).

-----, "Ramesside Texts Relating to the Taxation and Transport of Corn," JEA 27 (1941), pp. 19-73.

-----, "Some Reflections on the Nauri Decree," JEA 38 (1952), pp. 24-33.

-----, "The Stela of Bilgai," ZÄS 50 (1912), pp. 49-57.

-----, The Wilbour Papyrus, 3 vols. (Oxford, 1941-48), vol. IV Index by Raymond O. Faulkner (Oxford, 1952).

Alan H. Gardiner, George A. Wainwright, and W.M.F. Petrie, Tarkhan I and Memphis V [Egypt Research Account] (London, 1913).

Henri Gauthier, Dictionnaire des noms géographiques contenus dans les textes hiéroglyphiques, 7 vols. (Cairo, 1925-31).

S.R.K. Glanville, "Book-keeping for a Cult of Ramses II," JRAS (Jan. 1929), pp. 19-26 and pl. 1.

C.W. Goodwin, "Notes on the Calendar-question," ZÄS 5 (1867), pp. 57-60.

Erhart Graefe, Untersuchungen zur Verwaltung und Geschichte der Institution der Gottesgemahlin des Amun vom Beginn des Neuen Reiches bis zur Spätzeit [Ägyptologische Abhandlungen 37] 2 vols. (Wiesbaden, 1981).

Hermann Grapow, "Aegyptische Personenbezeichnungen der Angabe der Herkunft aus einem Ort," ZÄS 73 (1937), pp. 44-53.

F. Ll. Griffith, "The Abydos Decree of Seti I at Nauri," JEA 13 (1927), pp. 193-208, pls. 37-43.

-----, Catalogue of the Demotic Papyri in the John Rylands Library, Manchester, 3 vols. (Manchester, 1909).

-----, "Notes on Weights and Measures: II Measures of Area," PSBA 14 (1891-92), pp. 410-20.

Battiscombe Gunn and T. Eric Peet, "Four Geometrical Problems from the Moscow Mathematical Papyrus," JEA 15 (1929), pp. 167-85.

J.R. Harris, ed., The Legacy of Egypt, 2nd ed. (Oxford, 1971).

William C. Hayes, "Egypt: Internal Affairs from Tuthmosis I to the Death of Amenophis III," in The Cambridge Ancient History, I.E.S. Edwards, C.J. Gadd, and N.G.L. Hammond, eds. 3rd ed. (Cambridge, 1970-75) vol. II, pt. 1, pp. 313-416.

-----, The Scepter of Egypt: A Background for the Study of the

Egyptian Antiquities in The Metropolitan Museum of Art Part II: The Hyksos Period and the New Kingdom (1675-1080 B.C.) (Cambridge, Mass., 1959).

F.M. Heichelheim, An Ancient Economic History from the Palaeolithic Age to the Migration of Germanic, Slavic and Arabic Nations, vol. 1, 2nd ed. rev. (Leiden, 1958).

Wolfgang Helck, "Das Dekret des Königs Haremheb," ZÄS 80 (1955), pp. 109-36.

-----, Materialien zur Wirtschaftsgeschichte des Neuen Reiches, parts I and II, Akademie der Wissenschaften und der Literatur in Mainz [Abhandlungen der Geistes-und Socialwissenschaftlichen Klasse Jahrgang 1960, Nr. 10, 11] (Mainz, 1961).

-----, "Der Papyrus Berlin P. 3047," JARCE 2 (1963), pp. 65-73, pls. 9-12.

-----, Zur Verwaltung des Mittleren und Neuen Reiches [Probleme der Ägyptologie ed. Hermann Kees, III] (Leiden-Cologne, 1958).

Melville J. Herskovits, Economic Anthropology (New York, 1952).

Uvo Hölscher, Excavations at Ancient Thebes 1930-1 [Oriental Institute Communication 15] (Chicago, 1932).

J. Hornell, "On the Carrying Capacity of Ramesside Grain-ships," Brief Communication, JEA 29 (1943), pp. 76-78.

George R. Hughes, Saite Demotic Land Leases [SAOC 28] (Chicago, 1952).

Jac. J. Janssen, "Agrarian Administration in Egypt During the Twentieth Dynasty," review and summary of I.A. Stuchevsky, Zemledel'tsy gosudarstvennogo khozyaistva drevnego Egipta epokhi Ramessidov (The Cultivators of the State Economy in Ancient Egypt During the Ramesside Period) forthcoming in BiOr.

-----, Commodity Prices from the Ramessid Period: An Economic Study of the Village of Necropolis Workmen at Thebes (Leiden, 1975).

-----, "The Mission of the Scribe Pesiūr (O. Berlin 12654)," in Gleanings from Deir el-Medîna, R.J. Demarée and Jac. J. Janssen, eds. [Egyptologische Uitgaven I] (Leiden, 1982), pp. 133-47.

-----, "The Role of the Temple in the Egyptian Economy During the New Kingdom," in State and Temple Economy in the Ancient Near East II, Edward Lipiński, ed. [Orientalia Lovaniensia Analecta 6] (Leuven, 1979), pp. 505-15.

-----, "Die Struktur der pharaonischen Wirtschaft," Göttinger Miszellen 48 (1981), pp. 59-77.

----, Two Ancient Egyptian Ship's Logs, Rijksmuseum van Oudheden [Oudheidkundige Medelelingen 42] (Leiden, 1961).

-----, "Year 8 of Ramesses VI Attested," Göttinger Miszellen 29 (1978), pp. 45-46.

E. Jelínková-Reymond, "Recherches sur le rôle des 'Gardiens des Portes' (ỉry-ʿ3) dans l'administration générale des temples égyptiens," CdE 28 (1953), pp. 39-59.

Hermann Kees, Ancient Egypt: A Cultural Topography (London, 1961).

-----, "Die Kopenhagener Schenkungsstele aus der Zeit des Apries," ZÄS 72 (1936), pp. 40-52.

-----, Das Priestertum im ägyptischen Staat vom Neuen Reich bis zur Spätzeit [Probleme der Ägyptologie I] 2 vols. (Leiden-Cologne, 1953, 1958).

Barry J. Kemp, "Temple and Town in Ancient Egypt," in Man, Settlement and Urbanism, Peter J. Ucko, Ruth Tringham, and G.W. Dimbleby, eds. (London, 1972), pp. 657-80.

Kenneth A. Kitchen, The Third Intermediate Period in Egypt (1100-650 B.C.) (Warminster, 1973).

Jean-Marie Kruchten, Études de syntaxe néo-égyptienne, Institut de philologie et d'histoire orientales et slaves [Annuaire, Supplément I] (Brussels, 1982).

A. Lansing, "The Egyptian Expedition 1915-1916," Bull. MMA 12 (1917), Supplement, pp. 7-26.

Gustave Lefèbvre, Histoire des grands prêtres d'Amon de Karnak jusqu'à la XXIe dynastie (Paris, 1929).

-----, Inscriptions concernant les grands prêtres d'Amon Romê-Roÿ et Amenhotep (Paris, 1929).

Georges Legrain and Adolf Erman, "The Will of Eueret," ZÄS 35 (1897), pp. 13-16, 19-24.

Richard Lepsius, Denkmäler aus Ägypten und Äthiopien, Text, 5 vols. (Leipzig, 1897-1913).

Jean-Philippe Lévy, The Economic Life of the Ancient World (Chicago, 1964).

Miriam Lichtheim, Ancient Egyptian Literature: A Book of Readings, vol. 1: The Old and Middle Kingdoms (Los Angeles, 1973).

Michel Malinine, Choix de textes juridiques en hiératique 'anormal' et en démotique [Bibliothèque d'étude de l'École des hautes études, fasc. 300] (Paris, 1953).

-----, Review of Alan H. Gardiner, Ramesside Administrative Documents (Oxford, 1948) in BiOr 16 no. 5/6 (Sept.-Nov., 1959), pp. 216-21.

-----, Review of Alan H. Gardiner, The Wilbour Papyrus, 3 vols. (Oxford, 1941-48) in BiOr 8 no. 2/3 (March-May, 1951), pp. 64-72.

Michel Malinine and Richard A. Parker, "Papyrus Reinhardt (Étude paléographique, philologique et historique)," Akten des 24. Internationalen Orientalisten-Kongresses (1957), pp. 78-80.

William Mendenhall and Lyman Ott, Understanding Statistics (Belmont, 1972).

Bernadette Menu, Recherches sur l'histoire juridique, économique et sociale de l'ancienne Égypte (Versailles, 1982).

-----, Le régime juridique des terres et du personnel attaché à la terre dans le Papyrus Wilbour (Lille, 1970).

Georg Möller, Hieratische Lesestücke, 3 vols. (Leipzig, 1909-10).

-----, Hieratische Paläographie, 3 vols. (Leipzig, 1909-12).

Pierre Montet, Everyday Life in Egypt in the Days of Ramesses the Great (London, 1958).

Michael J. Moroney, Facts from Figures (Baltimore, 1951).

John H. Mueller, Karl F. Schuessler, and Herbert L. Costner, Statistical Reasoning in Sociology, 2nd ed. (Boston, 1970).

Percival E. Newberry, "Notes on Seagoing Ships," JEA 28 (1942), pp. 64-66.

N.H. Nie, C.H. Hull, J.G. Jenkins, K. Steinbrenner, and D.H. Brent, SPSS: Statistical Package for the Social Sciences, 2nd ed. (New York, 1975).

Charles F. Nims, Thebes of the Pharaohs: Pattern for Every City (New York, 1965).

David O'Connor, "The Geography of Settlement in Ancient Egypt," in Man, Settlement and Urbanism, Peter J. Ucko, Ruth Tringham, and G.W. Dimbleby, eds. (London, 1972), pp. 681-98.

-----, "A Regional Population in Egypt to circa 600 B.C.," in Population Growth: Anthropological Implications, Brian Spooner, ed. (Cambridge, Mass. and London, 1972), pp. 78-100.

Eberhard Otto, Aegypten, der Weg des Pharaonenreiches (Stuttgart, 1953).

-----, Topographie des thebanischen Gaues [Untersuchungen zur

Geschichte und Altertumskunde Aegyptens 16] (Berlin, 1952).

T. Eric Peet, "The Chronological Problems of the Twentieth Dynasty," JEA 14 (1928), pp. 52-73.

-----, "The Egyptian Words for 'Money', 'Buy', and 'Sell'," in Studies Presented to F. Ll. Griffith (London, 1932), pp. 122-27, pls. 10 and 11.

-----, The Great Tomb-robberies of the Twentieth Egyptian Dynasty, 2 vols. (Oxford, 1930).

-----, "A Historical Document of Ramesside Age," JEA 10 (1924), pp. 116-27.

-----, The Mayer Papyri A and B, Nos. M. 11162 and 11186 of the Free Public Museums, Liverpool, The Egypt Exploration Society, (London, 1920).

-----, "The Supposed Revolution of the High-priest Amenḥotpe under Ramesses IX," JEA 12 (1926), pp. 254-59.

P.W. Pestman, "The 'Last Will of Naunakhte' and the Accession Date of Ramesses V," in Gleanings from Deir el-Medîna, R.J. Demarée and Jac. J. Janssen, eds. [Egyptologische Uitgaven I] (Leiden, 1982), pp. 173-81.

Kurt Pflüger, "The Edict of King Haremhab," JNES 5 (1946), pp. 260-76, pls. I-VI.

W.M.F. Petrie and Guy Brunton, Sedment II (London, 1924).

W. Pleyte and F. Rossi, Papyrus de Turin, 2 vols. (Leiden, 1869-76).

Bertha Porter and Rosalind L.B. Moss, Topographical Bibliography of Ancient Egyptian Hieroglyphic Texts, Reliefs and Paintings, vols. I and II, 2nd ed. (Oxford, 1960-72).

Georges Posener, Catalogue des ostraca hiératiques littéraires de Deir el Médineh [DFIFAO 1 and 18] 2 vols. (Cairo, 1934-72).

N.J. Reich, Papyri juristischen Inhalts in hieratischen und demotischen Schrift aus dem British Museum [Denkschriften des kaiserlichen Akademie der Wissenschaften in Wien 55] (Vienna, 1914).

C. Robichon and A. Varille, "Fouilles des temples funéraires thébains (1937)," RdE 3 (1938), pp. 99-102.

Étienne le Vte. de Rougé, "Lettre à M. Lepsius sur les fragments écrits au verso du Papyrus Sallier No. 4," ZÄS 6 (1868), pp. 129-34.

George A. Reisner, "The Viceroys of Ethiopia," *JEA* 6 (1920), pp. 28-55, 73-88.

Serge Sauneron, *Catalogue des ostraca hiératiques non littéraires de Deir el Médineh*, vol. 6 [*DFIFAO* 13] (Cairo, 1959).

-----, "Trois personnages du scandale d'Éléphantine," *RdE* 7 (1950), pp. 53-62.

Herbert D. Schädel, *Die Listen des grossen Papyrus Harris: Ihre wirtschaftliche und politische Ausdeutung* [*Leipziger Ägyptologische Studien* 6] (Glückstadt-Hamburg-New York, 1936).

Alan R. Schulman, *Military Rank, Title, and Organization in the Egyptian New Kingdom* [*MÄS* 6] (Berlin, 1964).

Kurt Sethe, "Die angebliche Rebellion des Hohenpriesters Amenḥotep unter Ramses IX," *ZÄS* 59 (1924), pp. 60-61.

-----, *Die Einsetzung des Veziers unter der 18. Dynastie. Inschrift im Grabe des Rekh-mi-rēꜥ zu Schech Abd el Gurna* [*Untersuchungen zur Geschichte und Altertumskunde Aegyptens* V, 2] (Leipzig, 1909).

-----, *Untersuchungen zur Geschichte und Altertumskunde Aegyptens*, 7 vols. (Leipzig, 1896-1915).

Kurt Sethe et al., *Urkunden des ägyptischen Altertums* (Leipzig, 1906-).

William Stevenson Smith, *The Art and Architecture of Ancient Egypt* (Harmondsworth, 1958).

Wilhelm Spiegelberg, "Briefe der 21. Dynastie aus El-Hibe," *ZÄS* 53 (1917), pp. 1-30.

-----, "Demotische Miszellen: 1  *nmḥw* = ⲣⲙ̄ϩⲉ '(frei)'," *ZÄS* 53 (1917), pp. 116-17.

-----, *Die demotischen Papyri Loeb* (Munich, 1931).

-----, "Ein Papyrus aus der Zeit Ramses' V," *ZÄS* 29 (1891), pp. 73-84.

-----, *Rechnungen aus der Zeit Setis I*, 2 vols. (Strassburg, 1896).

-----, "Die Tefnachthosstele des Museums von Athen," *Rec. trav.* 25 (1903), pp. 190-98.

I.A. Stuchevsky, "Data from the Wilbour Papyrus and Other Administrative Documents Relating to the Taxes Levied on the State ('Royal') Land-Cultivators in Egypt of the Ramesside Era," English summary, *Vestnik Drevnei Historii* (1974), pp. 20-21.

Herbert Thompson, "Two Demotic Self-Dedications," JEA 26 (1941), pp. 68-78.

P. Turaev, Papyrus Prachov [Zapiski Vostočnogo Otdeleniya Russkogo Arkheologičeskogo Obščestva 12] (Leningrad, 1927).

B. van de Walle, Review of Alan H. Gardiner, The Wilbour Papyrus, 3 vols. (Oxford, 1941-48) in CdE 25, no. 49 (Janvier 1950), pp. 60-68.

Raymond Weill, Review of Alan H. Gardiner, The Wilbour Papyrus, 3 vols. (Oxford, 1941-48) in RdE 7 (1950), pp. 154-66.

Edward F. Wente, Late Ramesside Letters [SAOC 33] (Chicago, 1967).

----, "The Suppression of the High Priest Amenhotep," JNES 25 (1966), pp. 73-87, figs. 1-3.

W. Westendorf, Koptische Handwörterbuch (Heidelberg, 1965-77).

John A. Wilson, The Burden of Egypt: An Interpretation of Ancient Egyptian Culture (Chicago, 1951).

Walther Wolf, "Papyrus Bologna 1086: Ein Beitrag zur Kulturgeschichte des Neuen Reiches," ZÄS 65 (1930), pp. 89-97.

APPENDIX A

LABELS FOR VARIABLE 4 LAND-OWNING INSTITUTION

(1) H AMUN-RE, KG	The House of Amun-Rēʿ, King of the Gods
(2) H MUT, LADY ISHRU	The House of Mūt, the Great, Lady of Ishru (or Ashru)
(3) H TIO	The House of Tiʿo in the House of Amūn
(4) M USIMARE-SKHEPERENRE	The Mansion of Millions of Years of the King of Upper and Lower Egypt Usimaʿrēʿ-skheperenrēʿ in the House of Amūn (The Mansion of Millions of Years of Ramesses-Amenḥikhopshef-meriamūn and the Mansion of Pharaoh)
(5) M HEKMARE-SETPENAMUN	The Mansion of the King of Upper and Lower Egypt Ḥeḳmaʿrēʿ-setpenamūn in the House of Amūn
(6) M USIMARE-MERIAMUN	The Mansion of the King of Upper and Lower Egypt Usimaʿrēʿ-meriamūn in the House of Amūn
(7) M USIMARE-SETPENRE	The Mansion of the King of Upper and Lower Egypt Usimaʿrēʿ-setpenrēʿ in the House of Amūn
(8) H HAREMHAB	The House of Ḥaremḥab in the House of Amūn
(9) M KING AKHEPERENRE	The Mansion of King ʿAkheperen(?)rēʿ in the House of Amūn
(10) H RM H AMUN	The House of Ramesses-meriamūn in the House of Amūn
(11) M RAMESSES-MERIAMUN	The Mansion of Ramesses-meriamūn in the House of Rēʿ
(12) H RE-HARAKHTE	The House of Re-Ḥarakhte
(13) M RM BELOVED RE	The Mansion of Ramesses-meriamūn, Beloved Like Rēʿ
(14) H HAPY FATHER GODS	The House of Ḥaʿpy, Father of the Gods

(15) H PTAH L ANKHTOWE	The House of Ptaḥ, the Great, South of His Wall, Lord of ʿAnkhtowĕ
(16) GREAT SEAT RM	The Great Seat of Ramesses-meriamūn in the House of Ptaḥ
(17) M RM BELOVED PTAH	The Mansion of Ramesses-meriamūn, Beloved Like Ptaḥ
(18) H RM REPEATER SED	The House of Ramesses-meriamūn, Repeater of Sed-festivals in the House of Rēʿ (sic)
(19) M RM H PTAH	The Mansion of Ramesses-meriamūn in the House of Ptaḥ
(20) LP PHAR HARDAI	The Landing-Place of Pharaoh in Ḥardai
(21) LP PHAR KEEP ONAYNA	The Landing-Place of Pharaoh in the Keep of ʿOnayna
(22) FIELDS PHARAOH	Fields of Pharaoh
(23) H HERYSHEF K TWO LANDS	The House of Ḥeryshef, King of the Two Lands
(24) H SOBEK SHEDTITE	The House of Sobek the Shedtite, [Horus in the midst of To (?)-She]
(25) H SOBEK LORD...	The House of Sobek, Lord of ...
(26) SUNSHADE RH SHE	The Sunshade of Re-Ḥarakhte which is in She
(27) H OSIRIS LORD ABYDUS	The House of Osiris, Lord of Abydus, the Great God, Ruler of Eternity
(28) M KING MENMARE ABYDUS	The Mansion of King Menmaʿrēʿ in Abydus (The Mansion the Heart of King Menmaʿrēʿ is Pleased in Abydus)
(29) H THOTH NAY-USIMARE-M	The House of Thoth, Taking Pleasure in Truth, in Na-Usimaʿrēʿ-meriamūn
(30) H THOTH P-WADJOI	The House of Thoth of P-Wadjoi
(31) H BATA LORD SAKO	The House of Bata, Lord of Sakō
(32) H SETH LORD SPERMERU	The House of Seth, Lord of Spermeru
(33) H NEPHTHYS OF RM	The House of Nephthys of Ramesses-

	meriamūn which is in the House of Seth
(34) H SETH PI-WAYNA	The House of Seth, Lord of Pi-Wayna
(35) H AMUN BEAU FORE MEMPHIS	The House of Amūn of the Beautiful Foreland in Memphis
(36) H HARMIN ISIS	The House of Ḥar-Min and Isis
(37) H SOBEK-RE LORD ANASHA	The House of Sobek-Rēʿ, Lord of Anasha
(38) H AMUN FORE VIC SAKO	The House of Amūn, Foreteller of Victory, which is in Sakō
(39) SUNSHADE RH SAKO	The Sunshade of Re-Ḥarakhte which is in Sakō
(40) H AMUN TJAYEF	The House of Amūn Tjayef which is in the Village of Tjayef
(41) H AMUN LORD SHAROPE	The House of Amūn, Lord of Sharopě
(42) H MONT LORD HERMONTHIS	The House of Mont, Lord of Hermonthis
(43) H THOTH LORD HERMOP	The House of Thoth, Lord of Hermopolis
(44) H ANTI U ANTI	The House of ʿAnti in U-ʿAnti
(45) H HATHOR U ANTI	The House of Ḥathōr, Lady of the Two Lands, in U-ʿAnti
(46) H ONURIS LORD THIS	The House of Onūris, Lord of This
(47) H K WIFE H T	The House of the King's (Great) Wife (Ḥenwʿōte or Twertenro)
(48) TREASURY PHAR	The Treasury of Pharaoh
(49) H OSIRIS KHANT ARU	The House of Osiris Khant-ʿAru
(50) H PTAH MERENPTAH RA	The House of Ptaḥ of Merenptaḥ and Ramesses-meriamūn

APPENDIX B

LABELS FOR VARIABLE 22 DUAL GEOGRAPHIC LOCATION A

(1)	IAN-MUT	Ian-Mūt
(2)	OPE	Opĕ
(3)	VWEBKHE	The Village of Webkhe
(4)	CIOT	The Castle of Iōt
(5)	SPERMERU	Spermeru
(6)	MKAROTI	Mound of Karoti
(7)	VKASHA	The Village of Kasha
(8)	MIEHU	Mi-ēḥu
(9)	PKMEBUO	P-kme-Buʿo
(10)	TSUCHUS	The Temple of Sobek

LABELS FOR VARIABLE 23 DUAL GEOGRAPHIC LOCATION B

(1)	MPHANA	The Mound of P-hana
(2)	MAIRE-WOODE	Maire-woodĕ
(3)	TMY	T-my
(4)	MOUNDTOM	The Mound of the Tomb
(5)	PENWEDHU	Pen-Wedḥu
(6)	PBUHU	P-buḥu
(7)	NAWE	N-ʿawĕ
(8)	VSINUHE	The Village of Sinūhe
(9)	MPIWON	The Mound of Pi-Wōn
(10)	MHEDJRI	The Mound of Ḥedjri
(11)	MERGASTULUM	The Mound of the Ergastulum Workers

APPENDIX C

LABELS FOR VARIABLE 31 GEOGRAPHIC LOCATION

(1) -NUKHESH	...nukhesh
(2) PHBAALIT	The Pond of the House of Baʿalit
(3) PIKHASE	Pi-Khasě
(4) KAMI	Kami...
(5) MKAE	Mound of Kaě
(6) STABLE	The Stable
(7) HPAUNA	The House of P-auna...
(8) HPTAHMOS	The House of Ptaḥmosĕ
(9) MENHEH	Mound of (En)ḥeḥ
(10) TIRKAK	The Tomb(s) of İrkak
(11) NINSU	Ninsu
(12) NL-	The New Land of...
(13) TMIEHITJ	T(?)-miē-ḥi-tjayef
(14) -ERSHATI	...ershati
(15) HOSIRIS	The House of Osiris
(16) HALR	The House of Amūn, Lord of Returning
(17) PIOKER	Pi-Ōḳer
(18) HSLD	The House of Sobek, Lord of Djedu
(19) LB	The Lake's Beginning
(20) TPERNUTE	The Tomb of Pernūte/Pond of the Tomb of Pernūte
(21) LANBU	The Lake of ʿAnbu
(22) GERG	Gerg
(23) PMISOBK	P-mi-Sobk
(24) GREABYRE	The Great Byre
(25) SWAMLAKE	The Swampy Lake
(26) PMY	P-My (?)
(27) LAKEGOLD	The Lake of Gold
(28) BARNA	Barna
(29) NLBUNERO	The New Land of Bunero
(30) SASA	Sasa
(31) PIIATOMB	The Pond of Iia's Tomb
(32) VINROYSH	The Village of Inroyshes
(33) IAOHB	The Island of Amūn Overrunning-<His>-Boundary
(34) IAMBD	The Island of Amūn Manifold-of-Brave-Deeds
(35) OPE	Opĕ
(36) PIHENWOT	Pi-Ḥenwōtey
(37) TENTHEMY	Tent-ḥemy
(38) PIMEDJWE	Pi-Medjwe
(39) VDJASASA	The Village of Djasasati
(40) SMAA	Smaʿa
(41) HSAHNE	Ḥ-saḥne
(42) CMERYSET	The Castle of Merysēt
(43) SEKHENWA	Sekh-(en-)-Wʿab-yeb
(44) PIWAYNA	Pi-Wayna
(45) MDOH	Mound of Dōḥ
(46) MRE	The Mound of Rēʿ

(47)	CMERYRE	The Castle of Meryrēʿ
(48)	IANMUT	Ian-Mūt
(49)	HSAHTO	Ḥ-saḥto
(50)	KEB	Ḳeb
(51)	BHORUS	The Byre of Horus
(52)	M-NUFE	The Mound of...-[nūf?]e
(53)	-THOTH	...-Thoth
(54)	PIPMA	Pi-p-ma
(55)	IAUHE	The Island of Amūn Uniting-Himself-with-Eternity
(56)	MIEHU	Mi-ēḥu
(57)	PIKHAFT	Pi-Khaft
(58)	VWEBKHE	The Village of Webkhe
(59)	BSON	The Byre of Sŏn (?)
(60)	PMIMEKI	P-mi-meki
(61)	PIDJASA	Pi-Djasa
(62)	KWADJMOS	The Keep of Wadjmosĕ
(63)	LAMUN	The Lake of Amūn
(64)	NLTKAHA	The New Land of (T-)Ḳaha
(65)	LHESMENY	The Lake of Ḥesmen-yeb
(66)	VRURU	The Village of Ruru
(67)	PMA	P-ma
(68)	VSOLDIER	The Village of the Soldiers
(69)	RAPID-	The Rapid of...(possibly identical to no. 71)
(70)	VWEBEN	The Village of Weben
(71)	-RAPID	...of the Rapid
(72)	PCHOTPE	The Pond of the Castle of Ḥotpe
(73)	AN	ʿAn
(74)	KTENTNE	The Keep of Tent-nē
(75)	MTJEME	The Mound of Tjēme
(76)	SOSHEN	Sōshen
(77)	IYIDHU	Iy-idḥu
(78)	TSETH	The Temple of Seth
(79)	OPEISY	Opĕ-isy
(80)	MYEBES	The Mound of Yēbes
(81)	MHU-	The Mound of Ḥu...
(82)	YAYA	Yaya
(83)	PENKENRO	Pen-Kenroy (possibly identical to no. 143)
(84)	DSPERMER	The Dyke of Spermeru
(85)	PTSETH	The Pylons of the Temple of Seth
(86)	PENSHOS	Pen-Shōs
(87)	PENITY	Pen-Ity
(88)	HUINIUTI	Ḥuiniuti
(89)	CIOT	The Castle of Iōt
(90)	MNAHIHU	The Mound of Naḥiḥu
(91)	ENTORE	Entōre
(92)	PENNNHAS	Pen-n-Nḥasy
(93)	SAPA	Sapa
(94)	SHAROPE	Sharopĕ
(95)	NAYROTI	Nayroti
(96)	GRANREED	The Granary of Reeds
(97)	PENROHU	Pen-Roḥu

(98)	PENRONYE	Pen-Ro-en-yeb
(99)	SPERMERU	Spermeru
(100)	GRANITEF	The Granary of Itefto
(101)	PENON	Pen-Ōn
(102)	AARUIA	ʿAaruia
(103)	SHENOPD	Shen-ōpd
(104)	CAMUN	The Copse of Amūn
(105)	PWERKHAF	The Village of P-wēr-khaft
(106)	PIWON	Pi-Wōn
(107)	HKHAEMOP	The House of Khaʿemopĕ
(108)	PENHAYMA	Pen-Ḥaymasha
(109)	MANIUMER	Maniu-Merōn
(110)	PENMEDJA	Pen-Medja(ry?)
(111)	HPSIUR	The House of Psiūr
(112)	HREKHPAH	The House of Rekhpaḥtef
(113)	HYEB	The House of Yeb
(114)	LDIME	The Lake of Dīme
(115)	PDEBEN	P-Deben
(116)	HTJAWATI	The House formerly of Tjawati
(117)	BYEB	The Byre of Yeb
(118)	PENSONBE	Pen-Sonbe
(119)	CONEWERE	The Cutting (?) of Ōnĕ-wērĕ
(120)	PKMEBUO	P-kme-Buʿo
(121)	HMERYRE	The House of Meryrēʿ
(122)	GABU	Gabu (Gawĕ)
(123)	VIRKAK	The Village of Irkak
(124)	CPIOT	The Castle of Piōt
(125)	PENTUTU	Pen-Tutu
(126)	AAB	ʿAʿab
(127)	LAKEPHAR	The Lake of Pharaoh
(128)	PMEDJAY	P-Medjay
(129)	HWOSER	The House of Wōser
(130)	TAYHAROW	Tay-harowĕ
(131)	GTKAIAY	The Granary of T-kaiay
(132)	HHUNERO	The House of Ḥunero
(133)	MIEMSAH	Mi-emsaḥ
(134)	HERENUFE	The House of Erenūfe
(135)	TPDEBEN	The Tract of P-Deben
(136)	GKAROIA	The Granary of Karoia
(137)	PENIKARY	Pen-Iḳarya
(138)	HHKAMOSE	The House of the Herdsman Kamosĕ
(139)	PIKHAY	Pi-Khay
(140)	MDJADJAB	(The) Mound of Djaʿdjaʿbu
(141)	PIKASHA	Pi-Kasha
(142)	HGROOMS	The Houses of the Grooms
(143)	PENPKENR	Pen-p-Kenroy
(144)	SHAHURUS	Shaḥurusharu
(145)	VKASHA	The Village of Kasha
(146)	HARKHAAE	Ḥarkhaʿaʿef
(147)	TAYANKHE	Tay-ʿankhe
(148)	IMYTAYMT	Imy-tay-m-t-nē
(149)	SAKO	Sakō
(150)	NAAMUN	Na-Amūn
(151)	SSAKO	The Shelter of Sakō

(152)	VNURU	The Village of Nuru
(153)	MHEKSET	The Mansion of Ḥeḳmaʿrēʿ-setpenamūn
(154)	SIRKAK	The Sycomores of Irkak
(155)	MENONKH	Menʿonkh
(156)	UANTI	U-ʿAnti
(157)	HIRKAK	The Houses of Irkak
(158)	MROMA	The Mounds of Roma
(159)	TSUCHUS	The Temple of Sobek
(160)	PENNEHTO	Pen-ne-ḥtōre-mḥīt
(161)	MOKA	The Mound of the Overseer of the King's Apartments
(162)	PENHEDJ	Pen-Ḥedj
(163)	PITJEU	Pi-tjeu (?)
(164)	IYMARYAF	Iy-maryaf (Iy-merwōtef)
(165)	KAHIAHWE	Ḳaʿḥ-iaḥwe
(166)	TENTMERI	Tent-mer-iteḥu
(167)	VSINUHE	The Village of Sinūhe
(168)	NLNEBY	The New Land of Neby
(169)	PSASA	P-sasa (probably identical to no. 173)
(170)	PENSHETE	Pen-Shete
(171)	VMEREK	The Village of Merek
(172)	NNUHENSH	N-<n>ūhe-n-she
(173)	PSASARIR	P-sasa-rir
(174)	AWENGROV	The ʿawen-grove
(175)	AKHSU	Akh-su
(176)	TSEKERAN	T-seker-(m-U-)ʿAnti
(177)	KHERSHA	Khersha
(178)	MGRANARY	(The) Mound of the Granary
(179)	DPIOHE	The Dyke of Pi-ōhe
(180)	MDJEDSU	(The) Mound of Djed-su
(181)	TWEBDE	T-webde
(182)	IRKAK	Irkak
(183)	PKHARURU	P-Kharuru
(184)	TUTA	Tuta
(185)	MINENA	The Mound of Inena

Note: Names of measurement areas follow Gardiner as listed in R.O. Faulkner's Index (vol. IV to Alan H. Gardiner, The Wilbour Papyrus, 3 vols. (Oxford, 1941-48)) published in 1952 (Oxford).

APPENDIX D

List of Occupations and Occupational Groups

	OCCUPATION	OCCUPATIONAL GROUP
(1)	Alabaster Worker (?) šsy	Crafts (Skilled Labour)
(2)	Brander (of Cattle?) ṯ3y 3bw	Animal Husbandry
(3)	Bearer of Divine Offerings (?) f3y (ḥtpw?) nṯr	Religious
(4)	Beekeeper bỉty	Animal Husbandry
(5)	Builder (or Potter) ỉḳd	Crafts (Skilled Labour)
(6)	Carpenter ḥmww	Crafts (Skilled Labour)
(7)	Charioteer kṯ	Military
(8)	Controller rwḏw	Administration
(9)	Coppersmith ḥmty	Crafts (Skilled Labour)
(10)	His Majesty's Captain of Retainers ḥry šmsw n ḥm.f	Military
(11)	Captain of the Shieldbearers of Pharaoh ḥry ḳn Pr-ʿ3	Military
(12)	Cultivator ỉḥwty	Agriculture
(13)	Deputy ỉdnw	Other
(14)	Embalmer wtw	Crafts (Skilled Labour)
(15)	Fattener of Cattle wš3 ỉḥw	Animal Husbandry
(16)	Fisherman wḥʿ	Other
(17)	God's Father ỉt-nṯr	Religious
(18)	Greatest of Seers wr m3w	Religious
(19)	Head of the Cow Stable ḥry mḏwt	Animal Husbandry
(20)	Herdsman mnỉw	Animal Husbandry
(21)	King's Son s3 nsw	Other
(22)	Lady (Citizeness) ʿnḫ(t) n nỉwt	Other
(23)	Adjutant of Chariotry ỉdnw n tnt-ḥtr	Military
(24)	Medjay Mḏ3y	Military (paramilitary)
(25)	Member of a Ship's Crew ỉst mnšw	Military
(26)	Overseer of Cattle ỉmy-r ỉḥw	Animal Husbandry (or Administration)
(27)	Overseer of the Treasury ỉmy-r pr-ḥḏ	Administration
(28)	Oxherd mnỉw ỉḥw	Animal Husbandry
(29)	Physician swnw	Other
(30)	Prophet ḥm-nṯr	Religious
(31)	Priest wʿb	Religious
(32)	Quartermaster (?) 3tw	Military
(33)	Retainer šmsw (but Retainer of the Sherden is Military)	Other (or Military)
(34)	Standardbearer ṯ3y sryt	Military
(35)	Scribe sš	Administration
(36)	Servant sḏmw	Domestic
(37)	Sherden Šrdn	Military
(38)	Skt-Officer	Military
(39)	Slave ḥm	Domestic

(40) Stablemaster ḥry iḥ	Animal Husbandry
(41) Soldier wʿw	Military
(42) Shepherd mniw siw	Animal Husbandry
(43) Shieldbearer kn (krʿ)	Military
(44) Steward (of Amūn) imy-r pr (ʾImn)	Religious (or Administration)
(45) Scout ḥp	Military
(46) Swordbearer (?) ḥpšy	Military
(47) Tender of Crocodiles (?) sprw msḥ (?)	Animal Husbandry
(48) Tjuk Ṯk	Military
(49) Chief of Thr-Warriors ʿ3 thr	Military
(50) Vizier ṯ3ty	Administration
(51) Weaver sḫty	Crafts (Skilled Labour)
(52) Goatherd mniw ʿnḫ	Animal Husbandry
(53) Groom mri	Animal Husbandry
(54) First Prophet of Amūn ḥm-nṯr tpy ʾImn	Religious

*As several occupations among this group are difficult to classify, it would be valuable to rerun crosstabulations involving variable 16 using alternate classifications (chiefly retainer and stablemaster as Military). Other occupations which lend themselves to alternate classifications as, for example, ist mnšw as Other (if not Military) and steward of Amūn as Administration (if not Religious) fortunately have very low frequencies. It is certainly also valuable to put pastoral occupations into a separate category from that of Animal Husbandry and rerun the relevant crosstabulations.

APPENDIX E

Data of Subprogram CONDESCRIPTIVE*

VARIABLE V9 AROURAS--VARIETY I AND SUB-VARIETY IA

MEAN	7.232	STD ERROR	0.222	STD DEV	8.438
VARIANCE	71.199	KURTOSIS	47.536	SKEWNESS	5.751
RANGE	109.000	MINIMUM	1.000	MAXIMUM	110.000
SUM	10493.000				

VALID OBSERVATIONS: 1451 MISSING OBSERVATIONS: 794

VARIABLE V9 AROURAS--VARIETY I ONLY

MEAN	5.636	STD ERROR	0.158	STD DEV	5.457
VARIANCE	29.780	KURTOSIS	126.337	SKEWNESS	8.575
RANGE	109.000	MINIMUM	1.000	MAXIMUM	110.000
SUM	6724.000				

VALID OBSERVATIONS: 1193 MISSING OBSERVATIONS: 0

VARIABLE V9 AROURAS--SUB-VARIETY IA ONLY

MEAN	14.135	STD ERROR	0.854	STD DEV	13.370
VARIANCE	178.765	KURTOSIS	17.175	SKEWNESS	3.683
RANGE	98.000	MINIMUM	2.000	MAXIMUM	100.000
SUM	3463.000				

VALID OBSERVATIONS: 245 MISSING OBSERVATIONS: 2

VARIABLE V10 AROURAS SPECIAL CASE

MEAN	9.069	STD ERROR	0.890	STD DEV	14.760
VARIANCE	217.860	KURTOSIS	104.681	SKEWNESS	8.859
RANGE	197.000	MINIMUM	3.000	MAXIMUM	200.000
SUM	2494.000				

VALID OBSERVATIONS: 275 MISSING OBSERVATIONS: 1970

VARIABLE V14 ASSESSED AROURAS

MEAN	0.772	STD ERROR	0.030	STD DEV	1.157
VARIANCE	1.339	KURTOSIS	86.388	SKEWNESS	7.248
RANGE	20.500	MINIMUM	0.250	MAXIMUM	20.750
SUM	1115.250				

VALID OBSERVATIONS: 1445 MISSING OBSERVATIONS: 800

VARIABLE V11 LAND-CUBITS FIRST FIGURE

MEAN	7.042	STD ERROR	0.514	STD DEV	7.558
VARIANCE	57.119	KURTOSIS	21.058	SKEWNESS	3.666
RANGE	59.000	MINIMUM	1.000	MAXIMUM	60.000
SUM	1521.000				

VALID OBSERVATIONS: 216 MISSING OBSERVATIONS: 2029

VARIABLE V12 LAND-CUBITS SECOND FIGURE

MEAN	42.907	STD ERROR	2.530	STD DEV	37.189
VARIANCE	1382.996	KURTOSIS	2.680	SKEWNESS	1.530
RANGE	191.000	MINIMUM	4.000	MAXIMUM	195.000
SUM	9268.000				

VALID OBSERVATIONS: 216 MISSING OBSERVATIONS: 2029

VARIABLE V13 LAND-CUBITS SINGLE FIGURE

MEAN	58.256	STD ERROR	5.217	STD DEV	73.601
VARIANCE	5417.121	KURTOSIS	18.100	SKEWNESS	3.637
RANGE	496.000	MINIMUM	4.000	MAXIMUM	500.000
SUM	11593.000				

VALID OBSERVATIONS: 199 MISSING OBSERVATIONS: 2046

VARIABLE V28 LAND-CUBITS SUBTOTAL 11 AND 12

MEAN	49.949	STD ERROR	2.834	STD DEV	41.646
VARIANCE	1734.430	KURTOSIS	2.626	SKEWNESS	1.527
RANGE	194.000	MINIMUM	6.000	MAXIMUM	200.000
SUM	10789.000				

VALID OBSERVATIONS: 216 MISSING OBSERVATIONS: 2029

VARIABLE V27 GRAND TOTAL AROURAS 9 AND 10

MEAN	7.524	STD ERROR	0.234	STD DEV	9.742
VARIANCE	94.906	KURTOSIS	112.175	SKEWNESS	8.122
RANGE	199.000	MINIMUM	1.000	MAXIMUM	200.000
SUM	12987.000				

VALID OBSERVATIONS: 1726 MISSING OBSERVATIONS: 519

VARIABLE V29 GRAND TOTAL LAND-CUBITS 11, 12, AND 13

MEAN	53.933	STD ERROR	2.908	STD DEV	59.235
VARIANCE	3508.793	KURTOSIS	22.350	SKEWNESS	3.705
RANGE	496.000	MINIMUM	4.000	MAXIMUM	500.000
SUM	22382.000				

VALID OBSERVATIONS: 415 MISSING OBSERVATIONS: 1830

VARIABLE V38 GRAND TOTAL LAND 27 AND 29/100

MEAN	6.170	STD ERROR	0.198	STD DEV	9.176
VARIANCE	84.196	KURTOSIS	119.660	SKEWNESS	8.192
RANGE	199.960	MINIMUM	0.040	MAXIMUM	200.000
SUM	13210.820				

VALID OBSERVATIONS: 2141 MISSING OBSERVATIONS: 104

* The descriptive statistics for variable 46 ⌋ Figure were computed by hand and therefore do not occur in the computer print-out.

APPENDIX F

Tables of Subprogram FREQUENCIES

V1 SECTION OF TEXT (GEOGRAPHIC ZONE)

CATEGORY LABEL	ABSOLUTE FREQ	RELATIVE FREQ (%)	ADJUSTED FREQ (%)	CUM FREQ (%)
SECTION (ZONE) I	269	12.0	12.0	12.0
SECTION (ZONE) II	575	25.6	25.6	37.6
SECTION (ZONE) III	780	34.7	34.7	72.3
SECTION (ZONE) IV	621	27.7	27.7	100.0
TOTAL	2245	100.0	100.0	

VALID CASES: 2245 MISSING CASES: 0

V2 FORMAT OF ENTRY

CATEGORY LABEL	ABSOLUTE FREQ	RELATIVE FREQ (%)	ADJUSTED FREQ (%)	CUM FREQ (%)
VARIETY I	1193	53.1	55.6	55.6
SUB-VARIETY IA	247	11.0	11.5	67.2
VARIETY II	217	9.7	10.1	77.3
VARIETY I/II	277	12.3	12.9	90.2
SUB-VARIETY IIA	210	9.4	9.8	100.0
MISSING	101	4.5	MISSING	100.0
TOTAL	2245	100.0	100.0	

VALID CASES: 2144 MISSING CASES: 101

V3 INSTITUTIONAL GROUP

CATEGORY LABEL	ABSOLUTE FREQ	RELATIVE FREQ (%)	ADJUSTED FREQ (%)	CUM FREQ (%)
THEBAN	1085	48.3	48.3	48.3
HELIOPOLITAN	352	15.7	15.7	64.0
MEMPHITE	168	7.5	7.5	71.5
OTHER RELIGIOUS	457	20.4	20.4	91.8
SECULAR	183	8.2	8.2	100.0
TOTAL	2245	100.0	100.0	

VALID CASES: 2245 MISSING CASES: 0

V4   LAND-OWNING INSTITUTION

CATEGORY LABEL	ABSOLUTE FREQ	RELATIVE FREQ (%)	ADJUSTED FREQ (%)	CUM FREQ (%)
H AMUN-RE, KG	255	11.4	11.4	11.4
H MUT, LADY ISHRU	3	0.1	0.1	11.5
H TIO	4	0.2	0.2	11.7
M USIMARE-SKHEPERNRE	359	16.0	16.0	27.7
M HEKMARE-SETPENAMUN	3	0.1	0.1	27.8
M USIMARE-MERIAMUN	266	11.8	11.8	39.6
M USIMARE-SETPENRE	152	6.8	6.8	46.4
H HAREMHAB	29	1.3	1.3	47.7
M KING AKHEPERENRE	12	0.5	0.5	48.2
H RM H AMUN	2	0.1	0.1	48.3
M RAMESSES-MERIAMUN	240	10.7	10.7	59.0
H RE-HARAKHTE	30	1.3	1.3	60.4
M RM BELOVED RE	78	3.5	3.5	63.8
H HAPY FATHER GODS	4	0.2	0.2	64.0
H PTAH L ANKHTOWE	24	1.1	1.1	65.1
GREAT SEAT RM	69	3.1	3.1	68.2
M RM BELOVED PTAH	1	0.0	0.0	68.2
H RM REPEATER SED	8	0.4	0.4	68.6
M RM H PTAH	63	2.8	2.8	71.4
LP PHAR HARDAI	85	3.8	3.8	75.1
LP PHAR KEEP ONAYNA	14	0.6	0.6	75.8
FIELDS PHARAOH	48	2.1	2.1	77.9
H HERYSHEF K TWO LAN	111	4.9	4.9	82.9
H SOBEK SHEDTITE	48	2.1	2.1	85.0
H SOBEK LORD...	2	0.1	0.1	85.1
SUNSHADE RH SHE	15	0.7	0.7	85.7
H OSIRIS LORD ABYDUS	6	0.3	0.3	86.0
M KING MENMARE ABYDU	39	1.7	1.7	87.8
H THOTH NAY-USIMARE-	10	0.4	0.4	88.2
H THOTH P-WADJOI	21	0.9	0.9	89.1
H BATA LORD SAKO	8	0.4	0.4	89.5
H SETH LORD SPERMERU	11	0.5	0.5	90.0
H NEPHTHYS OF RM	1	0.0	0.0	90.0
H SETH PI-WAYNA	16	0.7	0.7	90.7
H AMUN BEAU FORE MEM	8	0.4	0.4	91.1
H HARMIN ISIS	1	0.0	0.0	91.1
H SOBEK-RE LORD ANAS	111	4.9	4.9	96.1
H AMUN FORE VIC SAKO	6	0.3	0.3	96.3
SUNSHADE RH SAKO	6	0.3	0.3	96.6
H AMUN TJAYEF	1	0.0	0.0	96.7
H AMUN LORD SHAROPE	2	0.1	0.1	96.7
H MONT LORD HERMONTH	2	0.1	0.1	96.8
H THOTH LORD HERMOP	6	0.3	0.3	97.1
H ANTI U ANTI	5	0.2	0.2	97.3
H HATHOR U ANTI	1	0.0	0.0	97.4
H ONURIS LORD THIS	9	0.4	0.4	97.8
H K WIFE H T	19	0.8	0.8	98.6

TREASURY PHARAOH	17	Ø.8	Ø.8	99.4
H OSIRIS KHANT ARU	11	Ø.5	Ø.5	99.9
H PTAH MERENPTAH R	3	Ø.1	Ø.1	1ØØ.Ø
TOTAL	2245	1ØØ.Ø	1ØØ.Ø	

VALID CASES: 2245 MISSING CASES: Ø

V5 DEITY OR KING

CATEGORY LABEL	ABSOLUTE FREQ	RELATIVE FREQ (%)	ADJUSTED FREQ (%)	CUM FREQ (%)
AMUN-RE	255	11.4	12.4	12.4
AMUN	52	2.3	2.5	14.9
HEKMARE-SETPENAMUN	3	Ø.1	Ø.1	15.Ø
USIMARE-MERIAMUN	266	11.8	12.9	27.9
USIMARE-SKHEPERENRE	359	16.Ø	17.4	45.3
USIMARE-SETPENRE	152	6.8	7.4	52.7
AKHEPERENRE	12	Ø.5	Ø.6	53.3
OSIRIS SETY	39	1.7	1.9	55.2
OSIRIS	17	Ø.8	Ø.8	56.Ø
BATA	8	Ø.4	Ø.4	56.4
HATHOR	1	Ø.Ø	Ø.Ø	56.5
MONT	2	Ø.1	Ø.1	56.5
HERYSHEF	111	4.9	5.4	61.9
HAR-MIN ISIS	1	Ø.Ø	Ø.Ø	62.Ø
MUT	3	Ø.1	Ø.1	62.1
NEPHTHYS	1	Ø.Ø	Ø.Ø	62.2
ONURIS	9	Ø.4	Ø.4	62.6
RE	318	14.2	15.4	78.Ø
RE-HARAKHTE	51	2.3	2.5	8Ø.5
PTAH	168	7.5	8.1	88.7
HAPY	4	Ø.2	Ø.2	88.8
SETH	27	1.2	1.3	9Ø.2
SOBEK-RE	111	4.9	5.4	95.5
SOBEK	5Ø	2.2	2.4	98.Ø
THOTH	37	1.6	1.8	99.8
ANTI	5	Ø.2	Ø.2	1ØØ.Ø
EXCLUDED	183	8.2	MISSING	1ØØ.Ø
TOTAL	2245	1ØØ.Ø	1ØØ.Ø	

VALID CASES: 2Ø62 MISSING CASES: 183

V7 OCCUPATION OR TITLE OF SMALLHOLDER

CATEGORY LABEL	ABSOLUTE FREQ	RELATIVE FREQ (%)	ADJUSTED FREQ (%)	CUM FREQ (%)
ALABASTER WORKER	1	Ø.Ø	Ø.Ø	Ø.Ø
BRANDER OF CATTLE	1	Ø.Ø	Ø.Ø	Ø.1

BEARER OF DIVINE OFFS	1	0.0	0.0	0.1
BEEKEEPER	22	1.0	1.0	1.2
BUILDER	1	0.0	0.0	1.2
CARPENTER	1	0.0	0.0	1.3
CHARIOTEER	47	2.1	2.2	3.5
CONTROLLER	28	1.2	1.3	4.8
COPPERSMITH	1	0.0	0.0	4.9
CAPT RETAINERS	4	0.2	0.2	5.1
CAPT SHIELDBEARERS	1	0.0	0.0	5.1
IḤWTY	204	9.1	9.7	14.8
DEPUTY	22	1.0	1.0	15.8
EMBALMER	3	0.1	0.1	16.0
FATTENER CATTLE	1	0.0	0.0	16.0
FISHERMAN	1	0.0	0.0	16.1
GOD'S FATHER	7	0.3	0.3	16.4
GREATEST OF SEERS	4	0.2	0.2	16.6
HEAD COW STABLE	1	0.0	0.0	16.6
HERDSMAN	148	6.6	7.0	23.6
KING'S SON	1	0.0	0.0	23.7
ʿNḪ(T) N NIWT	228	10.2	10.8	34.5
ADJUTANT OF CHARIOTRY	2	0.1	0.1	34.6
MEDJAY	2	0.1	0.1	34.7
MEMBER SHIP CREW	3	0.1	0.1	34.8
OVERSEER CATTLE	19	0.8	0.9	35.7
OVERSEER TREASURY	16	0.7	0.8	36.5
OXHERD	3	0.1	0.1	36.6
PHYSICIAN	1	0.0	0.0	36.7
PROPHET	51	2.3	2.4	39.1
PRIEST	249	11.1	11.8	50.9
QUARTERMASTER	5	0.2	0.2	51.1
RETAINER	40	1.8	1.9	53.0
STANDARDBEARER	24	1.1	1.1	54.2
SCRIBE	108	4.8	5.1	59.3
SERVANT	9	0.4	0.4	59.7
SHERDEN	59	2.6	2.8	62.5
SKT OFFICER	2	0.1	0.1	62.6
SLAVE	9	0.4	0.4	63.0
STABLEMASTER	471	21.0	22.3	85.4
SOLDIER	253	11.3	12.0	97.3
SHEPHERD	1	0.0	0.0	97.4
SHIELDBEARER	7	0.3	0.3	97.7
STEWARD	6	0.3	0.3	98.0
SCOUT	2	0.1	0.1	98.1
SWORDBEARER	4	0.2	0.2	98.3
TENDER CATTLE	4	0.2	0.2	98.5
TJUK	6	0.3	0.3	98.8
CHIEF THR WARRIORS	5	0.2	0.2	99.0
VIZIER	1	0.0	0.0	99.1
WEAVER	1	0.0	0.0	99.1
GOATHERD	3	0.1	0.1	99.2
GROOM	12	0.5	0.6	99.8

HIGH PRIEST AMUN	4	0.2	0.2	100.0
MISSING	135	6.0	MISSING	100.0
TOTAL	2245	100.0	100.0	

VALID CASES: 2110 MISSING CASES: 135

V15 TYPE OF LAND

CATEGORY LABEL	ABSOLUTE FREQ	RELATIVE FREQ (%)	ADJUSTED FREQ (%)	CUM FREQ (%)
P‘T	58	2.6	2.6	2.6
IDB	184	8.2	8.2	10.8
NEITHER	2003	89.2	89.2	100.0
TOTAL	2245	100.0	100.0	

VALID CASES: 2245 MISSING CASES: 0

V16 OCCUPATIONAL GROUP

CATEGORY LABEL	ABSOLUTE FREQ	RELATIVE FREQ (%)	ADJUSTED FREQ (%)	CUM FREQ (%)
CRAFTS (SKILLED LABOUR)	8	0.4	0.4	0.4
MILITARY	451	20.1	21.4	21.8
ADMINISTRATION	123	5.5	5.8	27.6
RELIGIOUS	345	15.4	16.4	44.0
DOMESTIC	18	0.8	0.9	44.9
ANIMAL HUSBANDRY	691	30.8	32.7	77.6
AGRICULTURE	205	9.1	9.7	87.3
OTHER	269	12.0	12.7	100.0
MISSING	135	6.0	MISSING	100.0
TOTAL	2245	100.0	100.0	

VALID CASES: 2110 MISSING CASES: 135

V17 SPECIAL ENTRY

CATEGORY LABEL	ABSOLUTE FREQ	RELATIVE FREQ (%)	ADJUSTED FREQ (%)	CUM FREQ (%)
ḤNK	37	1.6	39.8	39.8
3ḤT N ḤTRI	49	2.2	52.7	92.5
MḤT	4	0.2	4.3	96.8

W3D	3	Ø.1	3.2	1ØØ.Ø
EXCLUDED	2152	95.9	MISSING	1ØØ.Ø
TOTAL	2245	1ØØ.Ø	1ØØ.Ø	

VALID CASES: 93 MISSING CASES: 2152

V18 INSTITUTIONAL CLASS

CATEGORY LABEL	ABSOLUTE FREQ	RELATIVE FREQ (%)	ADJUSTED FREQ (%)	CUM FREQ (%)
RELIGIOUS	2Ø62	91.8	91.8	91.8
SECULAR	183	8.2	8.2	1ØØ.Ø
TOTAL	2245	1ØØ.Ø	1ØØ.Ø	

VALID CASES: 2245 MISSING CASES: Ø

V19 TYPE OF RELIGIOUS INSTITUTION

CATEGORY LABEL	ABSOLUTE FREQ	RELATIVE FREQ (%)	ADJUSTED FREQ (%)	CUM FREQ (%)
FUNERARY	792	35.3	38.4	38.4
ORDINARY CULT	127Ø	56.6	61.6	1ØØ.Ø
EXCLUDED	183	8.2	MISSING	1ØØ.Ø
TOTAL	2245	1ØØ.Ø	1ØØ.Ø	

VALID CASES: 2Ø62 MISSING CASES: 183

V2Ø TYPE OF PŌSH ENTRY

CATEGORY LABEL	ABSOLUTE FREQ	RELATIVE FREQ (%)	ADJUSTED FREQ (%)	CUM FREQ (%)
PŌSH B	128	5.7	5.7	5.7
PŌSH C	37	1.6	1.6	7.3
NEITHER	2Ø8Ø	92.7	92.7	1ØØ.Ø
TOTAL	2245	1ØØ.Ø	1ØØ.Ø	

VALID CASES: 2245 MISSING CASES: Ø

V21 TYPE OF APPORTIONING PARAGRAPH

CATEGORY LABEL	ABSOLUTE FREQ	RELATIVE FREQ (%)	ADJUSTED FREQ (%)	CUM FREQ (%)
HERBAGE	381	17.0	17.0	17.0
WHITE GOAT	79	3.5	3.5	20.5
ŠMW PŠ	312	13.9	13.9	34.4
RMNYT PŠ	1130	50.3	50.3	84.7
NONE OF THESE	343	15.3	15.3	100.0
TOTAL	2245	100.0	100.0	

VALID CASES: 2245 MISSING CASES: 0

V22 DUAL GEOGRAPHIC LOCATION A

CATEGORY LABEL	ABSOLUTE FREQ	RELATIVE FREQ (%)	ADJUSTED FREQ (%)	CUM FREQ (%)
IAN-MUT	3	0.1	5.0	5.0
OPE	2	0.1	3.3	8.3
VWEBKHE	12	0.5	20.0	28.3
CIOT	8	0.4	13.3	41.7
SPERMERU	6	0.3	10.0	51.7
MKAROTI	21	0.9	35.0	86.7
VKASHA	1	0.0	1.7	88.3
MIEHU	5	0.2	8.3	96.7
PKMEBUO	1	0.0	1.7	98.3
TSUCHUS	1	0.0	1.7	100.0
EXCLUDED/MISSING	2185	97.3	MISSING	100.0
TOTAL	2245	100.0	100.0	

VALID CASES: 60 MISSING CASES: 2185

V23 DUAL GEOGRAPHIC LOCATION B

CATEGORY LABEL	ABSOLUTE FREQ	RELATIVE FREQ (%)	ADJUSTED FREQ (%)	CUM FREQ (%)
MPHANA	3	0.1	5.0	5.0
MAIRE-WOODE	2	0.1	3.3	8.3
TMY	12	0.5	20.0	28.3
MOUNDTOM	5	0.2	8.3	36.7
PENWEDHU	6	0.3	10.0	46.7
PBUHU	3	0.1	5.0	51.7
NAWE	21	0.9	35.0	86.7
VSINUHE	1	0.0	1.7	88.3
MPIWON	5	0.2	8.3	96.7
MHEDJRI	1	0.0	1.7	98.3

MERGASTULUM	1	Ø.Ø	1.7	1ØØ.Ø
EXCLUDED/MISSING	2185	97.3	MISSING	1ØØ.Ø
TOTAL	2245	1ØØ.Ø	1ØØ.Ø	

VALID CASES: 6Ø MISSING CASES: 2185

V31 GEOGRAPHIC LOCATION

CATEGORY LABEL	CODE	ABSOLUTE FREQ	RELATIVE FREQ (%)	ADJUSTED FREQ (%)	CUM FREQ (%)
-NUKHESH	1.	12	Ø.5	Ø.6	Ø.6
PHBAALIT	2.	16	Ø.7	Ø.7	1.3
PIKHASE	3.	4	Ø.2	Ø.2	1.5
KAMI	4.	1	Ø.Ø	Ø.Ø	1.5
MKAE	5.	1	Ø.Ø	Ø.Ø	1.6
STABLE	6.	3	Ø.1	Ø.1	1.7
HPAUNA	7.	1	Ø.Ø	Ø.Ø	1.8
HPTAHMOS	8.	1Ø	Ø.4	Ø.5	2.2
MENHEH	9.	1	Ø.Ø	Ø.Ø	2.3
TIRKAK	1Ø.	1	Ø.Ø	Ø.Ø	2.3
NINSU	11.	13	Ø.6	Ø.6	2.9
NL-	12.	39	1.7	1.8	4.7
TMIEHITJ	13.	29	1.3	1.3	6.1
-ERSHATI	14.	8	Ø.4	Ø.4	6.4
HOSIRIS	15.	6	Ø.3	Ø.3	6.7
HALR	16.	1Ø	Ø.4	Ø.5	7.2
PIOKER	17.	12	Ø.5	Ø.6	7.7
HSLD	18.	6	Ø.3	Ø.3	8.Ø
LB	19.	3	Ø.1	Ø.1	8.1
TPERNUTE	2Ø.	17	Ø.8	Ø.8	8.9
LANBU	21.	5	Ø.2	Ø.2	9.2
GERG	22.	8	Ø.4	Ø.4	9.5
PMISOBK	23.	2	Ø.1	Ø.1	9.6
GREABYRE	24.	32	1.4	1.5	11.1
SWAMLAKE	25.	1	Ø.Ø	Ø.Ø	11.2
PMY	26.	4	Ø.2	Ø.2	11.3
LAKEGOLD	27.	4	Ø.2	Ø.2	11.5
BARNA	28.	1	Ø.Ø	Ø.Ø	11.6
NLBUNERO	29.	13	Ø.6	Ø.6	12.2
SASA	3Ø.	4	Ø.2	Ø.2	12.4
PIIATOMB	31.	1	Ø.Ø	Ø.Ø	12.4
VINROYSH	32.	57	2.5	2.6	15.Ø
IAOHB	33.	16	Ø.7	Ø.7	15.8
IAMBD	34.	18	Ø.8	Ø.8	16.6
OPE	35.	11	Ø.5	Ø.5	17.1
PIHENWOT	36.	16	Ø.7	Ø.7	17.9
TENTHEMY	37.	21	Ø.9	1.Ø	18.8
PIMEDJWE	38.	13	Ø.6	Ø.6	19.4
VDJASASA	39.	36	1.6	1.7	21.1
SMAA	4Ø.	28	1.2	1.3	22.4
HSAHNE	41.	4	Ø.2	Ø.2	22.6

CMERYSET	42.	6	0.3	0.3	22.9
SEKHENWA	43.	26	1.2	1.3	24.1
PIWAYNA	44.	31	1.4	1.4	25.5
MDOH	45.	5	0.2	0.2	25.7
MRE	46.	1	0.0	0.0	25.8
CMERYRE	47.	2	0.1	0.1	25.9
IANMUT	48.	7	0.3	0.3	26.2
HSAHTO	49.	15	0.7	0.7	26.9
KEB	50.	3	0.1	0.1	27.0
BHORUS	51.	15	0.7	0.7	27.7
M-NUFE	52.	8	0.4	0.4	28.1
-THOTH	53.	5	0.2	0.2	28.3
PIPMA	54.	11	0.5	0.5	28.8
IAUHE	55.	4	0.2	0.2	29.0
MIEHU	56.	52	2.3	2.4	31.4
PIKHAFT	57.	1	0.0	0.0	31.5
VWEBKHE	58.	8	0.4	0.4	31.8
BSON	59.	18	0.8	0.8	32.7
PMIMEKI	60.	1	0.0	0.0	32.7
PIDJASA	61.	1	0.0	0.0	32.8
KWADJMOS	62.	7	0.3	0.3	33.1
LAMUN	63.	4	0.2	0.2	33.3
NLTKAHA	64.	1	0.0	0.0	33.3
LHESMENY	65.	3	0.1	0.1	33.5
VRURU	66.	1	0.0	0.0	33.5
PMA	67.	11	0.5	0.5	34.0
VSOLDIER	68.	7	0.3	0.3	34.3
RAPID-	69.	1	0.0	0.0	34.4
VWEBEN	70.	2	0.1	0.1	34.5
-RAPID	71.	1	0.0	0.0	34.5
PCHOTPE	72.	2	0.1	0.1	34.6
AN	73.	4	0.2	0.2	34.8
KTENTNE	74.	2	0.1	0.1	34.9
MTJEME	75.	2	0.1	0.1	35.0
SOSHEN	76.	8	0.4	0.4	35.4
IYIDHU	77.	4	0.2	0.2	35.5
TSETH	78.	3	0.1	0.1	35.7
OPEISY	79.	2	0.1	0.1	35.8
MYEBES	80.	15	0.7	0.7	36.5
MHU-	81.	1	0.0	0.0	36.5
YAYA	82.	30	1.3	1.4	37.9
PENKENRO	83.	17	0.8	0.8	38.7
DSPERMER	84.	3	0.1	0.1	38.8
PTSETH	85.	6	0.3	0.3	39.1
PENSHOS	86.	17	0.8	0.8	39.9
PENITY	87.	10	0.4	0.5	40.4
HUINIUTI	88.	59	2.6	2.7	43.1
CIOT	89.	33	1.5	1.5	44.6
MNAHIHU	90.	11	0.5	0.5	45.1
ENTORE	91.	12	0.5	0.6	45.7
PENNNHAS	92.	18	0.8	0.8	46.5
SAPA	93.	8	0.4	0.4	46.9
SHAROPE	94.	76	3.4	3.5	50.4
NAYROTI	95.	18	0.8	0.8	51.2

GRANREED	96.	46	2.Ø	2.1	53.4
PENROHU	97.	35	1.6	1.6	55.Ø
PENRONYE	98.	18	Ø.8	Ø.8	55.8
SPERMERU	99.	35	1.6	1.6	57.4
GRANITEF	1ØØ.	3	Ø.1	Ø.1	57.6
PENON	1Ø1.	14	Ø.6	Ø.6	58.2
AARUIA	1Ø2.	5	Ø.2	Ø.2	58.4
SHENOPD	1Ø3.	1	Ø.Ø	Ø.Ø	58.5
CAMUN	1Ø4.	2	Ø.1	Ø.1	58.6
PWERKHAF	1Ø5.	11	Ø.5	Ø.5	59.1
PIWON	1Ø6.	2	Ø.1	Ø.1	59.2
HKHAEMOP	1Ø7.	2	Ø.1	Ø.1	59.3
PENHAYMA	1Ø8.	4	Ø.2	Ø.2	59.5
MANIUMER	1Ø9.	4	Ø.2	Ø.2	59.6
PENMEDJA	11Ø.	3	Ø.1	Ø.1	59.8
HPSIUR	111.	18	Ø.8	Ø.8	6Ø.6
HREKHPAH	112.	3	Ø.1	Ø.1	6Ø.8
HYEB	113.	5	Ø.2	Ø.2	61.Ø
LDIME	114.	9	Ø.4	Ø.4	61.4
PDEBEN	115.	7	Ø.3	Ø.3	61.7
HTJAWATI	116.	4	Ø.2	Ø.2	61.9
BYEB	117.	8	Ø.4	Ø.4	62.3
PENSONBE	118.	6	Ø.3	Ø.3	62.6
CONEWERE	119.	5	Ø.2	Ø.2	62.8
PKMEBUO	12Ø.	6	Ø.3	Ø.3	63.1
HMERYRE	121.	5	Ø.2	Ø.2	63.3
GABU	122.	4	Ø.2	Ø.2	63.5
VIRKAK	123.	21	Ø.9	1.Ø	64.5
CPIOT	124.	8	Ø.4	Ø.4	64.8
PENTUTU	125.	1	Ø.Ø	Ø.Ø	64.9
AAB	126.	2	Ø.1	Ø.1	65.Ø
LAKEPHAR	127.	1	Ø.Ø	Ø.Ø	65.Ø
PMEDJAY	128.	5	Ø.2	Ø.2	65.2
HWOSER	129.	7	Ø.3	Ø.3	65.6
TAYHAROW	13Ø.	3	Ø.1	Ø.1	65.7
GTKAIAY	131.	4	Ø.2	Ø.2	65.9
HHUNERO	132.	2	Ø.1	Ø.1	66.Ø
MIEMSAH	133.	12	Ø.5	Ø.6	66.5
HERENUFE	134.	1	Ø.Ø	Ø.Ø	66.6
TPDEBEN	135.	8	Ø.4	Ø.4	67.Ø
GKAROIA	136.	3	Ø.1	Ø.1	67.1
PENIKARY	137.	21	Ø.9	1.Ø	68.1
HHKAMOSE	138.	6	Ø.3	Ø.3	68.3
PIKHAY	139.	2	Ø.1	Ø.1	68.4
MDJADJAB	14Ø.	15	Ø.7	Ø.7	69.1
PIKASHA	141.	15	Ø.7	Ø.7	69.8
HGROOMS	142.	14	Ø.6	Ø.6	7Ø.5
PENPKENR	143.	13	Ø.6	Ø.6	71.1
SHAHURUS	144.	3	Ø.1	Ø.1	71.2
VKASHA	145.	17	Ø.8	Ø.8	72.Ø
HARKHAAE	146.	8	Ø.4	Ø.4	72.4
TAYANKHE	147.	13	Ø.6	Ø.6	73.Ø
IMYTAYMT	148.	13	Ø.6	Ø.6	73.6
SAKO	149.	91	4.1	4.2	77.8

NAAMUN	150.	29	1.3	1.3	79.1
SSAKO	151.	16	0.7	0.7	79.9
VNURU	152.	7	0.3	0.3	80.2
MHEKSET	153.	17	0.8	0.8	81.0
SIRKAK	154.	29	1.3	1.3	82.3
MENONKH	155.	83	3.7	3.8	86.2
UANTI	156.	17	0.8	0.8	87.0
HIRKAK	157.	15	0.7	0.7	87.6
MROMA	158.	18	0.8	0.8	88.5
TSUCHUS	159.	25	1.1	1.2	89.6
PENNEHTO	160.	4	0.2	0.2	89.8
MOKA	161.	2	0.1	0.1	89.9
PENHEDJ	162.	6	0.3	0.3	90.2
PITJEU	163.	9	0.4	0.4	90.6
IYMARYAF	164.	8	0.4	0.4	91.0
KAHIAHWE	165.	2	0.1	0.1	91.1
TENTMERI	166.	22	1.0	1.0	92.1
VSINUHE	167.	2	0.1	0.1	92.2
NLNEBY	168.	14	0.6	0.6	92.8
PSASA	169.	4	0.2	0.2	93.0
PENSHETE	170.	2	0.1	0.1	93.1
VMEREK	171.	1	0.0	0.0	93.2
NNUHENSH	172.	1	0.0	0.0	93.2
PSASARIR	173.	1	0.0	0.0	93.2
AWENGROV	174.	24	1.1	1.1	94.4
AKHSU	175.	1	0.0	0.0	94.4
TSEKERAN	176.	4	0.2	0.2	94.6
KHERSHA	177.	19	0.8	0.9	95.5
MGRANARY	178.	6	0.3	0.3	95.7
DPIOHE	179.	3	0.1	0.1	95.9
MDJEDSU	180.	4	0.2	0.2	96.1
TWEBDE	181.	2	0.1	0.1	96.2
IRKAK	182.	50	2.2	2.3	98.5
PKHARURU	183.	1	0.0	0.0	98.5
TUTA	184.	8	0.4	0.4	98.9
MINENA	185.	24	1.1	1.1	100.0
MISSING	0.	84	3.7	MISSING	100.0
TOTAL		2245	100.0	100.0	

VALID CASES: 2161 MISSING CASES: 84

V34 SEX OF CULTIVATOR

CATEGORY LABEL	ABSOLUTE FREQ	RELATIVE FREQ (%)	ADJUSTED FREQ (%)	CUM FREQ (%)
MALE	1882	83.8	89.2	89.2
FEMALE	228	10.2	10.8	100.0
MISSING	135	6.0	MISSING	100.0
TOTAL	2245	100.0	100.0	

VALID CASES: 2110 MISSING CASES: 135

V39 DYNASTY OF FOUNDING OF LAND-OWNING INSTITUTION

CATEGORY LABEL	ABSOLUTE FREQ	RELATIVE FREQ (%)	ADJUSTED FREQ (%)	CUM FREQ (%)
EIGHTEENTH DYNASTY	48	2.1	2.1	2.1
NINETEENTH DYNASTY	656	29.2	29.2	31.4
TWENTIETH DYNASTY	647	28.8	28.8	60.2
UNDATED	894	39.8	39.8	100.0
TOTAL	2245	100.0	100.0	

VALID CASES: 2245 MISSING CASES: 0

V43 LAND MEASURE I

CATEGORY LABEL	ABSOLUTE FREQ	RELATIVE FREQ (%)	ADJUSTED FREQ (%)	CUM FREQ (%)
AROURAS-I, IA	1440	64.1	86.9	86.9
LAND-CUBITS-II	217	9.7	13.1	100.0
EXCLUDED	588	26.2	MISSING	100.0
TOTAL	2245	100.0	100.0	

VALID CASES: 1657 MISSING CASES: 588

V44 LAND MEASURE II

CATEGORY LABEL	ABSOLUTE FREQ	RELATIVE FREQ (%)	ADJUSTED FREQ (%)	CUM FREQ (%)
AROURAS-I,IA,I/II	1717	76.5	80.1	80.1
LAND-CUBITS-II,IIA	427	19.0	19.9	100.0
EXCLUDED	101	4.5	MISSING	100.0
TOTAL	2245	100.0	100.0	

VALID CASES: 2144 MISSING CASES: 101

V45 TYPE OF AROURA MEASURED ENTRY

CATEGORY LABEL	ABSOLUTE FREQ	RELATIVE FREQ (%)	ADJUSTED FREQ (%)	CUM FREQ (%)
VARIETY I	1193	53.1	82.8	82.8
SUB-VARIETY IA	247	11.0	17.2	100.0
EXCLUDED	805	35.9	MISSING	100.0
TOTAL	2245	100.0	100.0	

VALID CASES: 1440 MISSING CASES: 805

V9 AROURAS--VARIETY I AND SUB-VARIETY IA

AROURAS	ABSOLUTE FREQ	RELATIVE FREQ (%)	ADJUSTED FREQ (%)	CUM FREQ (%)
1	4	0.2	0.3	0.3
2	23	1.0	1.6	1.9
3	339	15.1	23.4	25.2
5	752	33.5	51.8	77.1
6	4	0.2	0.3	77.3
7	4	0.2	0.3	77.6
8	3	0.1	0.2	77.8
9	3	0.1	0.2	78.0
10	175	7.8	12.1	90.1
12	2	0.1	0.1	90.2
14	1	0.0	0.1	90.3
15	4	0.2	0.3	90.6
17	1	0.0	0.1	90.6
18	1	0.0	0.1	90.7
20	100	4.5	6.9	97.6
25	4	0.2	0.3	97.9
30	8	0.4	0.6	98.4
40	6	0.3	0.4	98.8
50	7	0.3	0.5	99.3
60	6	0.3	0.4	99.7
80	1	0.0	0.1	99.8
100	2	0.1	0.1	99.9
110	1	0.0	0.1	100.0
EX/MISS*	794	35.4	MISSING	100.0
TOTAL	2245	100.0	100.0	

MEDIAN: 5 MODE: 5
VALID CASES: 1451** MISSING CASES: 794

* EXCLUDED OR MISSING DATA

**Note that the 1451 valid cases in this table include 13 values of variable 9 where insufficient data are preserved to enable us to assign these values to either Variety I or Sub-variety IA. Thus, the 1193 Variety I entries and 245 Sub-variety IA entries in the following two frequencies tables total 1438 entries.

V9 AROURAS--VARIETY I ONLY

AROURAS	ABSOLUTE FREQ	RELATIVE FREQ (%)	ADJUSTED FREQ (%)	CUM FREQ (%)
1	4	0.3	0.3	0.3
2	21	1.8	1.8	2.1
3	325	27.2	27.2	29.3
5	711	59.6	59.6	88.9
6	4	0.3	0.3	89.3
7	4	0.3	0.3	89.6
8	2	0.2	0.2	89.8
9	3	0.3	0.3	90.0
10	55	4.6	4.6	94.6
12	2	0.2	0.2	94.8
14	1	0.1	0.1	94.9
15	4	0.3	0.3	95.2
17	1	0.1	0.1	95.3
18	1	0.1	0.1	95.4
20	40	3.4	3.4	98.7
25	4	0.3	0.3	99.1
30	6	0.5	0.5	99.6
40	3	0.3	0.3	99.8
60	1	0.1	0.1	99.9
110	1	0.1	0.1	100.0
TOTAL	1193	100.0	100.0	

MEDIAN: 5 MODE: 5
VALID CASES: 1193 MISSING CASES: 0

V9 AROURAS--SUB-VARIETY IA ONLY

AROURAS	ABSOLUTE FREQ	RELATIVE FREQ (%)	ADJUSTED FREQ (%)	CUM FREQ (%)
2	1	0.4	0.4	0.4
3	11	4.5	4.5	4.9
5	40	16.2	16.3	21.2
8	1	0.4	0.4	21.6
10	118	47.8	48.2	69.8
20	60	24.3	24.5	94.3
40	3	1.2	1.2	95.5
50	4	1.6	1.6	97.1
60	4	1.6	1.6	98.8
80	1	0.4	0.4	99.2
100	2	0.8	0.8	100.0
EX/MISS	2	0.8	MISSING	100.0
TOTAL	247	100.0	100.0	

MEDIAN: 10 MODE: 10
VALID CASES: 245 MISSING CASES: 2

V1Ø AROURAS SPECIAL CASE

AROURAS	ABSOLUTE FREQ	RELATIVE FREQ (%)	ADJUSTED FREQ (%)	CUM FREQ (%)
3	43	1.9	15.6	15.6
5	149	6.6	54.2	69.8
1Ø	5Ø	2.2	18.2	88.Ø
2Ø	22	1.Ø	8.Ø	96.Ø
4Ø	5	Ø.2	1.8	97.8
5Ø	4	Ø.2	1.5	99.3
8Ø	1	Ø.Ø	Ø.4	99.6
2ØØ	1	Ø.Ø	Ø.4	1ØØ.Ø
EX/MISS	197Ø	87.8	MISSING	1ØØ.Ø
TOTAL	2245	1ØØ.Ø	1ØØ.Ø	

MEDIAN: 5 MODE: 5
VALID CASES: 275 MISSING CASES: 197Ø

V14 ASSESSED AROURAS

AROURAS	ABSOLUTE FREQ	RELATIVE FREQ (%)	ADJUSTED FREQ (%)	CUM FREQ (%)
Ø.25	499	22.2	34.5	34.5
Ø.5Ø	536	23.9	37.1	71.6
Ø.75	4	Ø.2	Ø.3	71.9
1.ØØ	276	12.3	19.1	91.Ø
1.25	18	Ø.8	1.2	92.2
1.5Ø	7	Ø.3	Ø.5	92.7
1.75	4	Ø.2	Ø.3	93.Ø
2.ØØ	11	Ø.5	Ø.8	93.8
2.25	3	Ø.1	Ø.2	94.Ø
2.5Ø	38	1.7	2.6	96.6
3.ØØ	3	Ø.1	Ø.2	96.8
3.75	4	Ø.2	Ø.3	97.1
4.25	1	Ø.Ø	Ø.1	97.2
4.5Ø	1	Ø.Ø	Ø.1	97.2
5.ØØ	28	1.2	1.9	99.2
6.25	5	Ø.2	Ø.3	99.5
7.5Ø	4	Ø.2	Ø.3	99.8
1Ø.ØØ	1	Ø.Ø	Ø.1	99.9
15.ØØ	1	Ø.Ø	Ø.1	99.9
2Ø.75	1	Ø.Ø	Ø.1	1ØØ.Ø
EX/MISS	8ØØ	35.6	MISSING	1ØØ.Ø
TOTAL	2245	1ØØ.Ø	1ØØ.Ø	

MEDIAN: Ø.5Ø MODE Ø.5Ø
VALID CASES: 1445 MISSING CASES: 8ØØ

V11 LAND-CUBITS FIRST FIGURE

LAND-CUBITS	ABSOLUTE FREQ	RELATIVE FREQ (%)	ADJUSTED FREQ (%)	CUM FREQ (%)
1.	14	0.6	6.5	6.5
2.	50	2.2	23.1	29.6
3.	2	0.1	0.9	30.6
4.	49	2.2	22.7	53.2
5.	27	1.2	12.5	65.7
10.	49	2.2	22.7	88.4
20.	23	1.0	10.6	99.1
60.	2	0.1	0.9	100.0
EX/MISS	2029	90.4	MISSING	100.0
TOTAL	2245	100.0	100.0	

MEDIAN: 4 MODE: 2
VALID CASES: 216 MISSING CASES: 2029

V12 LAND-CUBITS SECOND FIGURE

LAND-CUBITS	ABSOLUTE FREQ	RELATIVE FREQ (%)	ADJUSTED FREQ (%)	CUM FREQ (%)
4.	1	0.0	0.5	0.5
8.	20	0.9	9.3	9.7
10.	20	0.9	9.3	19.0
11.	6	0.3	2.8	21.8
14.	8	0.4	3.7	25.5
19.	2	0.1	0.9	26.4
20.	33	1.5	15.3	41.7
22.	14	0.6	6.5	48.1
23.	3	0.1	1.4	49.5
26.	1	0.0	0.5	50.0
34.	1	0.0	0.5	50.5
40.	30	1.3	13.9	64.4
45.	15	0.7	6.9	71.3
48.	6	0.3	2.8	74.1
49.	1	0.0	0.5	74.5
73.	1	0.0	0.5	75.0
80.	21	0.9	9.7	84.7
90.	8	0.4	3.7	88.4
95.	9	0.4	4.2	92.6
98.	5	0.2	2.3	94.9
99.	4	0.2	1.9	96.8
140.	3	0.1	1.4	98.1
180.	2	0.1	0.9	99.1
190.	1	0.0	0.5	99.5

195.	1	0.0	0.5	100.0
EX/MISS	2029	90.4	MISSING	100.0
	2245	100.0	100.0	

MEDIAN: 30 MODE: 20
VALID CASES: 216 MISSING CASES: 2029

V28 LAND-CUBITS SUBTOTAL 11 AND 12

LAND-CUBITS	ABSOLUTE FREQ	RELATIVE FREQ (%)	ADJUSTED FREQ (%)	CUM FREQ (%)
6.	1	0.0	0.5	0.5
10.	2	0.1	0.9	1.4
11.	2	0.1	0.9	2.3
12.	42	1.9	19.4	21.8
24.	60	2.7	27.8	49.5
36.	2	0.1	0.9	50.5
50.	52	2.3	24.1	74.5
75.	1	0.0	0.5	75.0
100.	47	2.1	21.8	96.8
150.	1	0.0	0.5	97.2
200.	6	0.3	2.8	100.0
EX/MISS	2029	90.4	MISSING	100.0
TOTAL	2245	100.0	100.0	

MEDIAN: 36 MODE: 24
VALID CASES: 216 MISSING CASES: 2029

V13 LAND-CUBITS SINGLE FIGURE

LAND-CUBITS	ABSOLUTE FREQ	RELATIVE FREQ (%)	ADJUSTED FREQ (%)	CUM FREQ (%)
4.	1	0.0	0.5	0.5
6.	7	0.3	3.5	4.0
12.	66	2.9	33.2	37.2
18.	1	0.0	0.5	37.7
24.	21	0.9	10.6	48.2
36.	3	0.1	1.5	49.7
50.	42	1.9	21.1	70.9
75.	3	0.1	1.5	72.4
100.	41	1.8	20.6	93.0
200.	11	0.5	5.5	98.5
500.	3	0.1	1.5	100.0
EX/MISS	2046	91.1	MISSING	100.0
TOTAL	2245	100.0	100.0	

MEDIAN: 50 MODE: 12
VALID CASES: 199 MISSING CASES: 2046

APPENDIX G

EXAMPLES OF TABLES OF SUBPROGRAM CROSSTABS:
CROSSTABULATION OF V43 LAND MEASURE I BY V15 TYPE OF LAND

V43	COUNT / ROW % / COL % / TOTAL %	V15: PʿT	IDB	NEITHER	ROW TOTAL
AROURAS-I,IA		8	45	1387	1440
		0.6	3.1	96.3	86.9
		27.6	45.5	90.7	
		0.5	2.7	83.7	
LAND-CUBITS-II		21	54	142	217
		9.7	24.9	65.4	13.1
		72.4	54.5	9.3	
		1.3	3.3	8.6	
COLUMN TOTAL		29	99	1529	1657
		1.8	6.0	92.3	100.0

CHI-SQUARE = 258.59888 WITH 2 DEGREES OF FREEDOM
SIGNIFICANCE = 0.0000 CRAMER'S V = 0.39505
NUMBER OF MISSING OBSERVATIONS = 588

CROSSTABULATION OF V44 LAND MEASURE II BY V15 TYPE OF LAND

V44	COUNT / ROW % / COL % / TOTAL %	V15: PʿT	IDB	NEITHER	ROW TOTAL
AROURAS-I,IA,I/II		8	54	1655	1717
		0.5	3.1	96.4	80.1
		16.0	31.2	86.2	
		0.4	2.5	77.2	
LAND-CUBITS-II,IIA		42	119	266	427
		9.8	27.9	62.3	19.9
		84.0	68.8	13.8	
		2.0	5.6	12.4	
COLUMN TOTAL		50	173	1921	2144
		2.3	8.1	89.6	100.0

CHI-SQUARE = 432.15546 WITH 2 DEGREES OF FREEDOM
SIGNIFICANCE = 0.0000 CRAMER'S V = 0.44896
NUMBER OF MISSING OBSERVATIONS = 101

CROSSTABULATION OF V43 LAND MEASURE I BY V21 TYPE OF APPORTIONING PARAGRAPH

V43 (COUNT / ROW % / COL % / TOTAL %)	HERBAGE	WHITE GOAT	ŠMW PŠ	NONE OF THESE	RMNYT PŠ	ROW TOTAL
AROURAS-I,IA	271 18.8 92.8 16.4	75 5.2 100.0 4.5	68 4.7 44.2 4.1	257 17.8 93.5 15.5	769 53.4 89.3 46.4	1440 86.9
LAND-CUBITS-II	21 9.7 7.2 1.3	0 0.0 0.0 0.0	86 39.6 55.8 5.2	18 8.3 6.5 1.1	92 42.4 10.7 5.6	217 13.1
COLUMN TOTAL	292 17.6	75 4.5	154 9.3	275 16.6	861 52.0	1657 100.0

CHI-SQUARE = 282.28514 WITH 4 DEGREES OF FREEDOM
CRAMER'S V = 0.41275 SIGNIFICANCE = 0.0000
NUMBER OF MISSING OBSERVATIONS = 588

CROSSTABULATION OF V44 LAND MEASURE II BY V21 TYPE OF APPORTIONING PARAGRAPH

V44 (COUNT / ROW % / COL % / TOTAL %)	HERBAGE	WHITE GOAT	ŠMW PŠ	NONE OF THESE	RMNYT PŠ	ROW TOTAL
AROURAS-I, IA, I/II	343 20.0 90.7 16.0	78 4.5 100.0 3.6	112 6.5 39.9 5.2	289 16.8 88.9 13.5	895 52.1 82.7 41.7	1717 80.1
LAND-CUBITS-II, IIA	35 8.2 9.3 1.6	0 0.0 0.0 0.0	169 39.6 60.1 7.9	36 8.4 11.1 1.7	187 43.8 17.3 8.7	427 19.9
COLUMN TOTAL	378 17.6	78 3.6	281 13.1	325 15.2	1082 50.5	2144 100.0

CHI-SQUARE = 352.02449 WITH 4 DEGREES OF FREEDOM
CRAMER'S V = 0.40520 SIGNIFICANCE = 0.0000
NUMBER OF MISSING OBSERVATIONS = 101

CROSSTABULATION OF V1 SECTION OF TEXT BY V3 INSTITUTIONAL GROUP

COUNT / ROW % / COL % / TOT %	V3: THEBAN	HELIO-POLITAN	MEMPHITE	OTHER RELIGIOUS	SECULAR	ROW TOTAL
(ZONE) 1	59	4	19	187	0	269
	21.9	1.5	7.1	69.5	0.0	12.0
	5.4	1.1	11.3	40.9	0.0	
	2.6	0.2	0.8	8.3	0.0	
(ZONE) 2	409	18	20	59	69	575
	71.1	3.1	3.5	10.3	12.0	25.6
	37.7	5.1	11.9	12.9	37.7	
	18.2	0.8	0.9	2.6	3.1	
(ZONE) 3	372	141	104	88	75	780
	47.7	18.1	13.3	11.3	9.6	34.7
	34.3	40.1	61.9	19.3	41.0	
	16.6	6.3	4.6	3.9	3.3	
(ZONE) 4	245	189	25	123	39	621
	39.5	30.4	4.0	19.8	6.3	27.7
	22.6	53.7	14.9	26.9	21.3	
	10.9	8.4	1.1	5.5	1.7	
COLUMN TOTAL	1085	352	168	457	183	2245
	48.3	15.7	7.5	20.4	8.2	100.0

CHI-SQUARE = 767.09253 SIGNIFICANCE = 0.0000
DEGREES OF FREEDOM = 12
CRAMER'S V = 0.33749 NUMBER OF MISSING OBSERVATIONS = 0

Index of Egyptian Words and Phrases in P. Wilbour

3ḥ(t) n ḥtrỉ, 73, 114, 117-19, 119-21, 213, 242, 249; 3ḥt n ḥtrỉ ḏd.n ḥry ỉḥ PN, 74, 118
3ḥw(t) Pr-ʿ3, 4
3tw, 16
ỉpt (oipě), 12, 203-4; oipě-measure, 218
ỉmy-r pr ʾImn, 6
ỉnỉ, 202, 204-6
ỉḥwty(w), 11, 16-17, 22, 71-72, 75, 134-37, 139-42, 142-43, 145, 147-48, 149, 166-67, 170, 173-74, 186, 189-91, 192, 193-95, 198-99, 200-1, 202, 212, 214, 217, 224, 232 n. 88, 245, 263, 264; ỉḥt, 17, 18, 202
ỉḳd, 16, 72; ḳd, 174
ỉsbt, 78
ỉt-nṯr, 5, 16, 222
ỉdb-land, 30, 59, 73, 150-51, 151-53, 249, 254-58
ỉdnw, 6, 26 n. 20, 71, 141, 143, 145, 190, 222; ỉdnw n mšʿ, 6, 190; ỉdnw n tnt-ḥtr, 16
ʿ3 n št, 197
ʿ3 thr, 141, 143, 217, 224
ʿnḫ(t) n nỉwt, 16, 71-72, 133-35, 139-42, 143, 145, 149, 166, 187, 191, 200, 211, 262, 264
w3ḏ (m w3ḏ), 73, 75, 110, 113, 117-18, 119-20, 242, 249, 252, 257-58
wʿw, 6, 16, 38, 70, 202, 204
wʿb, 5, 16, 70
wnw pš n, 171, 210, 212
wnmt, 86 n. 25
wr m3w, 5, 16, 64
wḥʿ, 72
wsf, 13-14, 50, 54, 177, 205, 222, 248, 258, 267-68
wš3 ỉḥw, 16, 72
wšr (??), 13, 50, 54, 108, 248, 267-68
wtw, 16
bw ptrỉ.f, 13, 50, 54, 248, 268
pʿt-land, 30, 59, 72-73, 150-51, 151-53, 249, 254-58
pr, 3, 4, 5, 11, 26 n. 8, 64, 272 n. 14; pr ʾImn, 3
pr ḫnr, 4
pš, 8, 11, 18, 20, 205-6; pš n, 22-23, 75
Pōsh A and B entries, 17, 18-22, 24 n.1, 74, 116, 143, 147-48, 170, 187-90, 199, 204, 212-13
Pōsh B entries, 79-80, 83, 118, 142-43, 145, 147-48, 188, 200, 222, 264, 266
Pōsh A, B, and C entries, 18, 75
Pōsh C entries, 22, 75, 142, 216, 240
Pōsh B and C entries, 75, 142, 249
f3y (ḥtpw?) nṯr, 72
mỉnt (minĕ)-land, 4, 8, 17, 23, 60, 171, 200, 207-8, 213, 215, 217
mnỉw(t) Pr-ʿ3, 4
mnỉw, 16
mnỉw sỉw, 16, 72
mḥt, 73-75, 110, 113, 117, 119-20, 242, 249, 252, 257-58

mḥ-t3, 1, 13-15
mk ı͗b ḥḏ, 7, 75-76
nḥb-land, 21, 85 n. 15, 196, 199, 203, 214, 234 n. 122, 266
nty mt, 6, 223
rwḏw, 6, 16, 141, 142, 145, 189-90, 194, 199, 200, 224
rmnyt, 2, 4, 5, 8, 18, 184, 191; rmnyt ı͗b ḥḏ, 76; rmnyt mt(t?), 191; rmnyt-land, 213
rmnyt pš, 8, 11, 75, 77, 121, 123-28, 128-29, 130-31, 132-33, 147, 205, 250-54
ḥwt, 3, 64, 272 n. 14
ḥm, 146
ḥm-nṯr, 5, 16, 94, 183; ḥm-nṯr tpy, 17
ḥmww, 16, 72, 147
ḥmty, 16, 72, 202
ḥnꜥ snw.f(s), 16, 224-25
ḥnk, 51, 73-74, 113-14, 117-19, 119-21, 242-43, 245, 249, 258; m ḥnk, 74
ḥry ı͗ḥ, 16, 70, 118, 144
ḥry mḏwt, 16, 72
ḥry s3w sšw, 6
ḥry ḳn Pr-ꜥ3, 72
ḫ3-t3 (khato)-land, 4, 6, 8, 17, 21, 23, 60, 76, 94, 169-74, 188-89, 194, 196, 199, 200-1, 207-16, 217, 219-20
ḫpšy, 16
r-ḫt (r-)ḫt, 4-8, 17, 74, 94, 119, 176, 184, 189, 191, 207-8, 222
ẖ3r (khar), 12, 21, 196, 202-4
n ẖny, 16
s3 nsw, 17, 72, 145
swnw, 16, 72
smw, 7, 75-76
srw, 6, 7, 26 n. 20
sḫty, 16, 72
sš, 16; sš šꜥt n Pr-ꜥ3, 6, 22
sšm-ḫw, 4, 17, 74
sṯ3t, 1, 12, 15
sdf, 74
sḏmw, 141, 143, 146
m šwt, 13-14, 50, 54, 108, 248, 267-68
šwt-Rꜥ-Ḥr-3ḫty, 4, 17
šmw, 8, 18, 75, 173, 182-83, 193, 200, 213; šmw-land, 213; ı͗t šmw, 169
šmw pš, 8, 11, 75-76, 118, 121-28, 128-30, 130-31, 132-33, 243, 250-54
šmsw, 71, 118, 140, 216; šmsw n mšꜥ, 187
šrdn, 16
šsy, 16, 72
ḳ3yt-land, 21-22, 24, 73, 85 n. 15, 193, 196, 199, 211-12, 214, 230 n. 59, 234 n. 122, 266
kꜥḥ(t), 198, 207
ḳrꜥ (ḳn), 16
k(y) ḫ3y n.f, 239-40
(ḥr) tp.f, 224
tnı͗-land, 21, 85 n. 15, 212, 234 n. 122, 266
ṯ3y 3bw, 72, 174
ṯ3ty, 17, 72
dnı͗t, 78
m-ḏrt, 5, 17, 22, 23, 75, 142, 181-82, 189, 191-92, 195, 200, 208, 217, 223-24; m-ḏrt msw.f(s), 16, 223
m3wḏ, 217

Index of Measurement Areas in P. Wilbour

ʿawen-grove, 101, 106, 113, 153
The Byre of Horus, 160
The Castle of Iōt, 118, 159-60
The Castle of Merysēt, 156
The Dyke of Spermeru, 78
Gerg, 156
The Granary of Reeds, 77, 101, 118, 144, 147, 153, 159, 187
The Great Byre, 107, 131, 161-62
Ḥ-saḥto, 103, 156
The House of Erenūfe, 145
The House of Psiūr, 131, 158
The House of Ptaḥmosĕ, 10, 91, 154
The Houses of the Grooms, 162
The Houses of Irkak, 131, 160
Ḥuiniuti, 77, 101, 103-4, 107, 118, 130, 144, 146, 148, 153-54, 159-60, 254
Imy-tay-m-t-nē, 113, 131, 146
Irkak, 77, 100, 107, 112, 144, 146-47, 154, 158, 161-63, 163-64, 187
The Island of Amūn Manifold-of-Brave-Deeds, 145, 162
The Island of Amūn Overrunning-<His>-Boundary, 146
The Island of Amūn Uniting-Himself-with-Eternity, 162
Iy-idḥu, 91, 216
The Keep of Wadjmosĕ, 113
The Lake of ʿAnbu, 156
The Lake of Dīme, 103
Maire-woodĕ, 77
Menʿonkh, 77, 107, 112, 130, 145-47, 152, 154, 156-57, 161-62, 163-64, 254, 256, 260; as location of Sunshade, 4
Mi-ēḥu, 77, 107, 130, 144, 146, 153-54, 159, 187, 216
Mi-emsaḥ, 91, 131
The Mound of Naḥiḥu, 10, 118
The Mound of Yēbes, 131, 158
The Mounds of Roma, 156
Na-Amūn, 144, 156
The New Land of..., 77-78, 112, 117-18, 145, 152, 163-64, 256
The New Land of Bunero, 152, 162
The New Land of Swo, 9
Ninsu (Heracleopolis), 17, 102, 118, 162; Ḥeryshef, tutelary god of, 97; as location of Sunshade, 4; prophet at, 5
Opĕ, 10, 77, 91, 160, 265
P-ma, 131
P-Kharuru, 146
P-mi-Sobk, 106
Pen-Iḳarya, 153
Pen-Ity, 158
Pen-Kenroy, 130
Pen-Ḥedj, 113
Pen-n-Nḥasy, 160
Pen-Roḥu, 113, 144, 153-54, 159
Pen-Shete, 104
Pen-Shōs, 103, 118, 153; Ḥatḥōr of (Pen-)Shōs, 23
Pi-Kasha, 160
Pi-Medjwe, 101
Pi-p-ma, 146, 164
Pi-Wayna, 93, 103, 145, 156; as location of the House of Seth, Lord of Pi-Wayna, 92-94, 118,

120, 123, 219
The Pond of the House of Baʿalit, 156-57
The Pond of Iia's Tomb, 17
Sakō, 77-78, 101, 103-4, 107, 130, 144-47, 153, 156, 158-59, 254, 260; as location of several temples, 93-94; as location of Sunshade, 4; prophet at, 5
Sapa, 130
Sekh-(en)-Wʿab-yeb, 130
Sharopĕ, 77, 85 n. 13, 101, 103, 107, 117-18, 130, 144, 146-48, 152, 153-54, 158-60, 254, 256, 260; as location of the House of Amūn, Lord of Sharopĕ, 94
The Shelter of Sakō, 78, 104, 153
Smaʿa, 107, 156
Sōshen, 91, 215
Spermeru, 78, 93, 101, 118, 130, 144, 153-55, 160, 254, 260; as location of the House of Seth, Lord of Spermeru, 5, 94, 123, 219-20; as location of Sunshade, 4; mayor of, 215; prophet at, 5
The Stable, 91
The Sycomores of Irkak, 107, 153, 158
Tayʿankhe, 107
Temĕ, 93
The Temple of Seth, 118
The Temple of Sobek, 106, 113, 154-55, 158
Tent-ḥemy, 101, 107, 152
Tent-mer-iteḥu, 145, 162, 163
T(?)-miē-ḥi-tjayef, 107, 145, 162, 164
Tmy, 187
The Tomb of Pernūte, 145, 152, 162, 256
U-ʿAnti, 146
The Village of Djasasati, 78, 107, 152, 156, 162, 163, 256
The Village of Inroyshes, 77, 103, 107, 130, 144-45, 153, 156, 158, 187
The Village of Kasha, 162
The Village of Neḥseroy (?), 215
The Village of Webkhe, 187
Yaya, 153-54
...ershati, 162
...nukhesh, 145, 152, 163
The Mound of Karoti, 77
N-ʿawĕ, 77

Index of Persons in P. Wilbour

ʿAkheperenrēʿ, (Tuthmosis II or Amenophis II with name emended), 3, 26 n. 7, 64, 69, 124, 128, 253

Dḥutmosĕ, mayor, 74

Ḥaremḥab, 3, 26 n. 8, 64, 221, 253

Merenptaḥ, 3, 6, 24, 26 n. 11, 28 n. 53, 65, 200, 201, 206, 232 n. 99, 253

Neferʿabĕ, mayor of Ḥardai, 6

Neferronpĕ, vizier, 216-17

Pēl, steward of Amūn, 6

Raʿḥotpe, vizier, 217

Ramessenakhte, high priest of Amūn, 5; steward of Amūn, 184

Ramesses II (Usimaʿrēʿ-setpenrēʿ), 3, 8, 25 n. 4, 64-65, 67, 67-68, 69, 91-95, 99, 104-5, 116, 117, 119-21, 122, 127-28, 128-29, 181, 188, 194, 200, 201, 206, 213, 217, 219, 220-221, 222, 223, 232 n. 99, 253, 272 n. 14

Ramesses III (Usimaʿrēʿ-meriamūn), 3, 6-7, 25 n. 4, 66-67, 67-68, 69, 74, 76, 86 n. 25, 92-95, 99, 104-5, 115, 117, 119-21, 122-23, 126-28, 128, 174, 184-86, 188, 192, 217, 222, 253

Ramesses IV (Ḥeḳmaʿrēʿ-setpenamūn), 3, 5-6, 8, 66-67, 68, 69, 76, 93, 97, 99, 123, 126-27, 128, 181, 184, 216

Ramesses V (Usimaʿrēʿ-skheperenrēʿ), 1, 3, 6, 24 n. 1, 25 n. 3, 64, 66-67, 67-68, 69, 74, 92-95, 99, 104-5, 115, 117, 119-21, 122-23, 127-28, 128, 171, 184, 192, 199, 211, 212-13, 216, 222, 253

Sesostris III (Khaʿkhaurēʿ), 4, 253

Sety I (Menmaʿrēʿ), 70, 92-93, 98, 120, 122, 125, 127, 129, 186, 253

Tiʿo, consort of Amenophis II, 3, 64, 66, 124

Usimaʿrenakhte, Royal scribe and steward of Amūn, 6, 171-72, 199, 208; chief taxing-master, 171-72, 199, 208

Additions

p. 140. Add to line 2 following sentence:"...common assessment value.": The 82 occurrences of the assessment value ½ aroura constitute 38.5% of the 213 occurrences of the occupation soldier in this table.

p. 145. Add to paragraph 3 following the last sentence:
The 201 plots ascribed to occupations of the group Agriculture are distributed among 69 measurement areas. While 11 measurement areas have perfect correlations with the group Agriculture, 7 of these measurement areas are single occurrence measurement areas. Menʿonkh in zone 4 has the highest frequency of plots ascribed to this group. Twenty-one of the 81 plots ascribed to Menʿonkh in this table (25.9%) were cultivated by individuals of this occupational group, all of whom were ỉḥwtyw. They constitute 10.5% of the 201 plots ascribed to the group Agriculture in this table. The remaining 180 plots are, for the most part, evenly distributed among the 68 measurement areas, the highest frequencies occurring in measurement areas of zone 2. Five of these 68 measurement areas have frequencies of more than 5 plots (2.5% of the 201 plots). The Village of Djasasati (10 plots), the Village of Inroyshes (8 plots), the Island of Amūn Overrunning-<His>-Boundary (6 plots), and Smaʿa (8 plots) are located in zone 2. The New Land of Neby in zone 4 accounts for 7 of these plots, while the New Land of... in zone 1 accounts for 11 of these plots. The remaining 62 measurement areas have frequencies of 5 such plots or fewer. Sharopĕ in zone 3 is the measurement area in reference to which the single scribe of the granary of Pharaoh is ascribed a plot. Menʿonkh's relatively high frequency of 21 plots (25.9%) ascribed to ỉḥwtyw is due in part to its relatively high frequency of 81 plots analyzed in the table. It is noteworthy, however, that the great majority of high frequency measurement areas have substantially lower frequencies of plots ascribed to the group Agriculture--or none at all.